THE COMPLETE
JACK THE
RIPPER
A TO Z

THE COMPLETE
JACK THE RIPPER
A TO Z

Paul Begg, Martin Fido
and Keith Skinner

JOHN BLAKE

Published by John Blake Publishing Ltd,
3 Bramber Court, 2 Bramber Road,
London W14 9PB, England

www.johnblakepublishing.co.uk

First published in hardback in 2010

ISBN: 978-1-84454-797-5

British Library Cataloguing-in-Publication Data:

A catalogue record for this book is available from the British Library.

Design by www.envydesign.co.uk

Printed in Great Britain by CPI William Clowes, Beccles, NR34 7TL

1 3 5 7 9 10 8 6 4 2

Papers used by John Blake Publishing are natural, recyclable
products made from wood grown in sustainable forests.
The manufacturing processes conform to the environmental
regulations of the country of origin.

Every attempt has been made to contact the relevant copyright-holders,
but some were unobtainable. We would be grateful if the
appropriate people could contact us.

In memory of
Jeremy Beadle, MBE
1948–2008

CONTENTS

ACKNOWLEDGEMENTS

We are extremely grateful to our literary agent Robert Smith and for their assistance, advice and knowledge to: Andy Aliffe, Debra Arif, Coral Atkins, John Barber, Phill Barnes-Warden, Judy Begg. Sioban Begg, John Bennett, George Bird, Enid Blake, Peter Bower, Bernard Brown, Howard Brown, Prof. D. Bryce-Smith, John Carey, Joe Chetcuti, Robert Clack, Ken Cobb, Nicholas Connell, Dr. Andrew Cook, Doreen Cooper, Jane Coram, Patricia Cornwell, Mike Covell, Dr. Christopher Davies, Paul Dew, Melanie Dolman, Ivor Edwards, Stewart Evans, Bertil Falk, Shani Feldman, Karen Fido, Professor Ian Findlay, Suzanne Foster and Winchester College, Michael Fountain, the late Jean Overton Fuller, Saul Gallagher, Anna Gardiner, Christopher T. George, the late D.S. Goffee, Douglas Gordon, Alan Hayday, Stawell Heard, Rob House, Philip Hutchinson, Christopher Jones, Richard Jones, Philip Hutchinson, Susan E. King (National Police Library, Bramshill), Loretta Lay, Jeff Leahy, Birgitta Leufstadius, Jaakko Luukanen, Robert Linford, Bill Locke, John Pope De Locksley, Delia Lorenson, Peter McClelland, Alan McCormick, David McKie, Robert McLaughlin, David and Elizabeth Meynell, Frogg Moody, Adrian Morris, Caroline Morris, Christopher J. Morley, Alan Moss, Simon Newcombe, Iris Niall, Dan Norder, Robin Odell, Simon Ovens, Andy and Sue Parlour, Neil R. Paterson, Jennifer Pegg, Eleanor Perkins, Alex Pinhorn, John Piper, Commander Ian Pirnie, RN, David Powell, Gordon Prebble, Timothy Riordan, Bruce Robinson, Julia E. Robinson, Donald Rumbelow, Stephen P. Ryder, John Sager, David Savory, Chris Scott, Alan Sharp, Neil Shelden, Edna Sickert, Lindsay Siviter, Don Souden, Revd. Andy Spallek, Wendy Spratling, Barbara Stanners, Barbara Street, Philip Sugden, Nevill Swanson, M.J. Trow, Helen Vanderburg, Nick Warren, Susan Wates, John Wilding, Gareth Williams, Colin Wilson, A.P. Wolf, Sheila Wolfe, Adam Wood, Julie Yeo and Eduardo Zinna.

PAUL BEGG, MARTIN FIDO AND KEITH SKINNER

Along with almost everyone who has in recent years written anything about the history of the Metropolitan Police, we are extremely grateful for the indefatigable help and support given by Maggie Bird, curator of the Metropolitan Police Historical Collection, who tragically died as this book was being compiled and who is, and always will be, missed by the authors.

INTRODUCTION

It has been well over a decade since the last update of *The Jack the Ripper A to Z* and during that time there have been vast strides in Ripper studies.

The biggest impact has been the growth of the Internet. Digitalisation of newspapers and genealogical records has made important information available to researchers who would previously not have had easy access to it – made it available, moreover, at the click of a mouse without hours of searching paper records. This has thrown up details which might never have been found otherwise.

Unfortunately much of the information in learned journals or official archives is still only readily available to those with access through universities or institutional library facilities, and some local newspaper material is still only available in regional libraries. Fortunately, gems of discovery are shared on internet sites and message boards, and a large number of sites devoted to, or connected with the Ripper have sprung up over the years. The magisterial Casebook Jack the Ripper, founded by Stephen P. Ryder and John Piper, deserves special mention, offering, as it does, a great deal of information, reviews, dissertations, and an active and sometimes vituperative message board.

From the researcher's point of view perhaps the most invaluable thing about the Casebook is its transcription of newspaper reports. The Casebook Press Project, as this truly invaluable resource is called, was the brainchild of the late Adrian M. Phypers, who took on the daunting responsibility of transcribing and painstakingly checking the transcriptions of the press reports, soon heading a small team of volunteers who, since Mr Phypers' unexpected death on 17 April 2003, have continued the work (see his obituary in *Ripperologist*, 51, January 2004). As the Casebook's founder, Stephen Ryder, observed: 'It's not an exaggeration to say that without him the Casebook wouldn't be half the site it is today.' At the time of writing, well over 5,000 fully transcribed contemporary articles are available from 289 different newspapers from around the world.

There are several journals available, notably *Ripperana*, the venerable first Ripper publication which commenced in July 1992, *Ripperologist* (which ceased to be printed and is now a monthly e-journal), and the *Whitechapel Journal*, and *Ripper Notes* and the wonderfully named but short-lived Australian publication *Ripperoo* which are no longer with us. Readers will realise just how important these journals have become when they see how many articles have been cited by the authors as being necessary reading.

In addition, the number of new books about Jack the Ripper has grown tremendously. The last edition of the *A to Z*, published in 1996, listed 53 non-fiction books entirely devoted to the Ripper. There are now over 160 and we are aware of several others due to be published or being submitted for publication. This publishing boom has in part been a response to the ever-growing interest in the subject and the knowledge that Ripper books sell. The upside of this is that we have seen a plethora of worthwhile publications, specialist titles, and reprints of old and long out-of-print books. The Ripperological Preservation Society here merits special note for the number of titles that it has discovered and made available over the years. Sadly, there is a downside. Some publishers have picked up titles which have little merit and self-publication has seen quite a few badly written and poorly argued books, which would never have seen the light of day with a commercial publisher, nor left the world of Ripperology a sadder place by their non-appearance.

All of this has had a tremendous impact on the *A to* Z. There was once a time when it was possible to give everyone who had written on the subject their own biographical entry. It simply isn't possible to do so anymore and we reluctantly decided to include biographical entries only for the dead. It has been depressing to note how many Ripperologists have been taken from us: Jeremy Beadle, Tom Cullen, Donald Bell, Daniel Farson, Paul Feldman, D.S. Goffee, Wilf Gregg, Jean Overton Fuller, Melvin Harris, Donald McCormick, Des McKenna, John Morrison, Adrian Phypers, Julian Rosenthal, Joseph Sickert, Christopher S. Smith, Frank Spiering, Jim Tully and Stephen Wright.

All this research has had an impact on what is known about the Jack the Ripper case – and all those who have achieved a sort of immortality because of it. Most of the characters involved, from police constables patrolling their lonely night-time beats to the ordinary folk going about the routine of their daily lives, would have been forgotten; just names in some genealogical index. Now they may be researched almost as thoroughly as politicians. We may never know much about them beyond the names of their family, and perhaps a single-line pen-portrait of their physical appearance, but it is wonderful to have even that little bit of flesh added to the bare bones of their name. Here, one must acknowledge the remarkable work of Chris Scott, whose exhaustive on-line trawls through the birth/marriage/death indexes, census returns and digitised newspapers has been invaluable.

As for the more prominent players caught up in the drama of the Whitechapel murders, research into the lives of the victims has been extraordinary. In May 2002, a *Family History* magazine featured an article –'Was your ancestor a Ripper victim?' – by an amateur genealogist, detailing her research into the five canonical victims. But perhaps one of the most exciting and perhaps most revealing discoveries to have been made by the gifted and enterprising researcher and author Neal Shelden was the photograph of Annie Chapman in life. So far as is known, this is the only image that we possess of a victim of Jack the Ripper which is not a mortuary photograph, and while we are all aware that the victims were real people, whose tragic lives were cut short by the Ripper, the photograph of Annie in former days, in a fine dress with her husband and an unsuspected future ahead of her, makes the tragedy of the lives and deaths of the victims all the more real, all the more horrible.

Suspects, witnesses and investigators, too, have had a fair share of discoveries. Photographs of Michael Ostrog, Frances Tumblety and the mad butcher Joseph Isenschmid have all been discovered; there is a new photograph of witness Joseph Lawende, and several new photos of policemen, notably Sgt. Thick in old age, with his daughters (who were memorably described by American author Jack London). And, of course, quite a lot of information has been uncovered about these people.

The upshot of all this is that the subject is now vast and hardly a day goes by without some new titbit being unearthed, leading to facts which need to be checked, entries revised and new ones penned. Updating the *A to Z* should be a full-time job, but sadly, that would be impossible and so we are grateful to everyone who shares their discoveries, but only too well aware that we are but human, so mistakes and omissions will occur. Like everyone else, we do our best to strive for perfection, but if you do spot an error or something else that we need to take note of for future editions, please let us know.

Note: Emboldening indicates the existence of an entry for this subject. MEPO and HO when used in relation to files mean Metropolitan Police and Home Office respectively. MEPO and HO files are held in the National Archives.

Paul Begg, Kent
Martin Fido, Cape Cod
Keith Skinner, London

A

AARONS, JOSEPH

Treasurer of the Whitechapel **Vigilance Committee**.

Landlord (1882–89) of The Crown at 74 Mile End Road, at the junction with Jubilee Street (the pub no longer exists), and The Horns (1891–99, when the pub was taken over by Solomon Aarons) at 53 Middlesex Street.

From about 11 September 1888, when the Whitechapel Vigilance Committee was formed, nightly meetings were held in an upstairs room in The Crown. Aarons was one of the men approached by **George Lusk**, following his receipt of the kidney and who accompanied Lusk to the offices of the *Evening News* (*Evening News*, 19 October 1888) to show journalists the kidney before taking it to the police.

ABBERLINE, INSPECTOR FREDERICK GEORGE (1843–1929)

Metropolitan Police Inspector in charge of detectives on the ground in the Whitechapel murders investigation.

No certain photograph of Inspector Abberline has been discovered, although there are a number of pen-and-ink portraits. **Walter Dew**, who served under Abberline in the early part of his career, described him in his autobiography as 'portly and gentle speak-ing. The type of police officer – and there have been many – who might easily have been mistaken for the manager of a bank or a solicitor.'

Born in Blandford, Dorset, the fourth and youngest child of Edward Abberline, and Hannah (née Chinn). Frederick was apprenticed to a clock and watchmaker, and served 35 days in the militia before joining the Metropolitan Police in 1863 (warrant no. 43519) and being posted to N Division (Islington). In August 1865, he was promoted to sergeant and then transferred to Y Division (Highgate) in October. He spent the whole of 1867 in plain clothes investigating Fenian activities. On 18 March he married labourer Tobias Mack-ness's 25-year-old daughter Martha, but she died of consumption in May 1868 at Elton, Northam-ptonshire. The 1871 Census lists him as resident at Kentish Town Road Police Station with 11 other officers, all widowers.

In 1873, he was promoted to inspector and transferred to **H Division** (Whitechapel), where he remained for the next 14 years. Married Emma Beament, daughter of merchant Henry Beament, in 1876. Two years later, promoted to local inspector (head of Divisional CID). The 1881 Census shows Frederick and Emma resident at Commercial Road Police Station. Inspector Henry Bugby and his wife Mary also lived there.

In 1885, Abberline was extremely active in the case against Fenian dynamitards Burton and Cunningham, who intended to explode a bomb at the Tower of London. At that point death threats were made against him.

In 1887, he transferred first to A Division (Whitehall: the Division originally stationed at the back of the Commissioner's Office in Whitehall Place, facing out onto Scotland Yard), and then to CO Division (Commissioner's Office, Whitehall Place, by now colloquially known as 'Scotland Yard' since entrance was normally through the A Division premises at the back of the building). This effectively moved him onto the 'general staff' of the Metropolitan Police and out of field work. Promoted inspector first class in 1888 and chief inspector in 1890 (Career information and militia service from Register of A Division Inspectors).

On 7 June 1890, the Police Orders reported the Commissioner had received a letter from the Director of Public Prosecutions commending Abberline and the police for 'tact caution and judgement displayed by them throughout the lengthy proceedings and investigations that have taken place during the last nine months in connection with the **Cleveland-street** case.' Much of his time as local inspector in Whitechapel was taken up with gambling dens, dog-stealing, and disorderly drunkenness. After transfer to Scotland Yard, he worked on more renowned cases (the Ripper, the Cleveland Street male brothel, the Netherby Hall burglars who murdered a policeman), as well as a good deal of fraud and some pornography suppression.

He and Emma lodged in a household headed by Miss Anne Polsford in Mayflower Road, Clapham in 1891. Retired on full pension in 1892 and worked as a private enquiry agent, including three seasons at Monte Carlo. He accepted the European agency of Allen Pinkerton's famous detective agency in 1898. Then, in 1901 he and Emma headed a household in Clapham Road with a servant and two lodgers (census data). One of the lodgers, John Philip Collins, was a journalist on the *Pall Mall Gazette*, which may be of interest in connection with the important interviews Abberline gave to that journal, two years later.

1904, retired to Methuen Road, Bournemouth, moving in 1911 to nearby Holdenhurst Road, where he died in 1929. A plaque in his memory was placed on

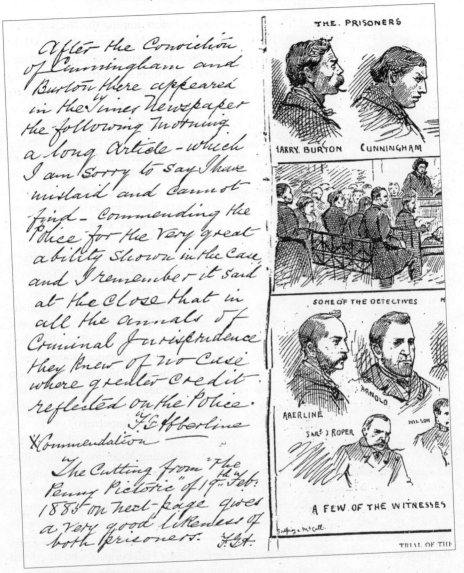

the building at the 2004 Ripper conference. Buried in an unmarked grave (no. Z259N) in Wimborne Road Cemetery, Bournemouth. His death was registered by Bella Huslling [spelled thus on the death certificate]. His wife, Emma, died in 1930. A headstone was erected for both in 2007 as a result of the dedicated efforts of retired Metropolitan Police officer, Arthur Robin Stanners, who died in 2008.

Theorists have sometimes argued for a suspicious significance in Abberline's retirement aged only 49, especially as he investigated both the Ripper and the Cleveland Street Scandal. However, the 1890 Police Bill (*see* **Henry Matthews** and **James Monro**) provided for early retirement with improved pension opportunities and, although only intended for officers injured or debilitated by

Reminiscences of a Detective Chief Inspector F.G. Abberline C.I.D. Scotland Yard.

Three Successive Seasons, or Twelve months behind the Scenes at Monte Carlo.

Monte Carlo in appearance is Simply a paradise, and one can understand the many thousands of wealthy people flocking there every winter.

The Season proper lasts only about 4 or 5 months although the Casino is open all the year round.

Many of the hotels close from May until Nov. or Dec.

The best and richest in Society can be seen there also the lowest that can find money to get there.

The English thieves have the credit there – whether they deserve it or not – of being the Smartest and the English Visitors frequenting the Casino were being robbed by a their duties, it created a lucrative opportunity to enjoy well-paid leisure and the freedom to earn additional money. Abber-line was one of many to seize the opportunity.

Very little is known about Abberline. How-ever, towards the end of his life he compiled a press-cutting book for a friend, Walter Green, with brief handwritten annotations. He observed that at the time of his retirement he had received 84 commendations and awards, something which he felt was near to a record. Also, at that time the authorities objected to officers writing their memoirs – which, he agreed, tended to reveal police methods to the criminal classes. Nevertheless, he did start writing 'Reminiscences', of which there are 28 handwritten pages concerning a 'missing person' case and a further 12 recounting his recollections of Monte Carlo. In neither the press-cutting book nor the 'Reminiscences' does he allude to what are today regarded as his most important cases.

All accounts agree that he was able and efficient, and possessed more intimate knowledge of the East End and its underworld than any police contemporary. Walter Dew stressed in his autobiography that Abberline's 'strong suit was his knowledge of crime and criminals in the East End… No question at all of Inspector Abberline's abilities as a criminal hunter.'

Because of the importance of his role in the investigation, Abberline's thoughts on the Ripper case deserve detailed consideration. The *Star* and the *Daily Telegraph* (15 September 1888) reported that 'Mr Phillips personally has hitherto withheld information from reporters upon conscientious grounds, and Inspector Abberline himself says that the surgeon has not told him what portions of the body were missing.' Martin Fido deduces from this that Inspector Abberline was under-informed. *Cassells Saturday Journal,* 22 May 1892, quoted him as saying, 'Theories!… we were lost almost in theories: there were so many of them.' But the paper then commented, 'Nevertheless, he has one which is new. He believes from the evidence of his own eyesight that the Miller's Court atrocity was the last of the real series, the others having been imitations, and that in Miller's Court the murderer reached the culminating point of gratification of his morbid ideas.'

In 1903 Abberline gave two extremely important interviews to the *Pall Mall Gazette* (24 and 31 March). These were in response to press suggestions that the Ripper was **Severin Klosowski**, who had recently been convicted of murder under the name of **George Chapman**. The journalist reportedly found Abberline 'surrounded with a sheaf of documents and newspaper cuttings' dealing with the Whitechapel murders and in the process of writing to **Sir Melville Macnaghten** about 'how strongly [he] was impressed with the opinion' that Chapman was the Ripper. The article continued:

'I have been so struck with the remarkable coincidences in the two series of murders,' he continued, 'that I have not been able to think of anything else for several days past-not, in fact, since the Attorney-General made his opening statement at the recent trial, and traced the antecedents of Chapman before he came to this country in 1888. Since then the idea has taken full possession of me, and everything fits in and dovetails so well that I cannot help feeling that this is the man we struggled so hard to capture fifteen years ago.

'My interest in the Ripper cases was especially deep. I had for fourteen years previously been an inspector of police in Whitechapel, but when the murders began I was at the Central Office at Scotland Yard. On the application of Superintendent Arnold I went back to the East End just before Annie Chapman was found mutilated, and as chief of the detective corps I gave myself up to the study of the cases. Many a time, even after we had carried our inquiries as far as we could – and we made out no fewer than 1,600 sets of papers respecting our investigations – instead of going home when I was off duty, I used to patrol the district until four or five o'clock in the morning, and, while keeping my eyes wide open for clues of any kind, have many and many a time given those wretched, homeless women, who were Jack the Ripper's special prey, fourpence or sixpence for a shelter to get them away from the streets and out of harm's way.

'As I say,' he went on, 'there are a score of things which make one believe that Chapman is the man; and you must understand that we have never believed all those stories about Jack the Ripper being dead, or that he was a lunatic, or anything of that kind. For instance, the date of the arrival in England coincides with the beginning of the series of murders in Whitechapel; there is a coincidence also in the fact that the murders ceased in London when "Chapman" went to America, while similar murders began to be perpetrated in America after he landed there. The fact that he studied medicine and surgery in Russia before he came here is well established, and it is curious to note that the first series of murders was the work of an expert surgeon, while the recent poisoning cases were proved to be done by a man with more than an elementary knowledge of medicine. The story told by "Chapman's" wife of the attempt to murder her with a long knife while in America is not to be ignored, but something else with regard to America is still more remarkable.

'While the coroner was investigating one of the Whitechapel murders he told the jury a very queer story. You will remember that Dr Phillips, the divisional surgeon who made the post-mortem examination, not only spoke of the skilfulness with which the knife had been used, but stated that there was overwhelming evidence to show that the criminal had so mutilated the body that he could possess himself of one of the organs. The coroner, in commenting on this, said that he had been told by the sub-curator of the pathological museum connected with one of the great medical schools that some few months before an American had called upon him and asked him to procure a number of specimens. He stated his willingness to give £20 for each. Although the strange visitor was told that his wish was impossible of fulfilment, he still urged his request. It was known that the request was repeated at another institution of a similar character in London. The coroner at the time said: 'Is it not possible that a knowledge of this demand may have inspired some abandoned wretch to possess himself of the specimens? It seems beyond belief that such inhuman wickedness could enter into the mind of any man; but, unfortunately, our criminal annals prove that every crime is possible!

'It is a remarkable thing,' Abberline pointed out, 'that after the Whitechapel horrors America should have been the place where a similar kind of murder began, as though the miscreant had not fully supplied the demand of the American agent.

'There are many other things extremely remarkable. The fact that Klosowski, when he came to reside in this country, occupied a lodging in George Yard, Whitechapel Road, where the first murder was committed, is very curious, and the height of the man and the peaked cap he is said to have worn quite tallies with the descriptions I got of him. All agree, too, that he was a foreign-looking man – but that, of course, helped us little in a district so full of foreigners as Whitechapel. One discrepancy only have I noted, and this is that the people who alleged that they saw Jack the Ripper at one time or another, state that he was a man about thirty-five or forty years of age. They, however, state that they only saw his back, and it is easy to misjudge age from a back view.'

Pall Mall Gazette, 24 March 1903

For further consideration of 'Chapman's wife,' *see* references to Lucy Baderski under Klosowski. For the coroner's theory of the American doctor, *see* **Wynne Baxter**. For the witnesses with a rear view, *see* **Mrs Darrell**, but *cf.* **Joseph Lawende** and **Israel Schwartz**.

The interview was immediately challenged by some commentators, notably **George R. Sims** in the *Referee* (29 March 1903), who wrote, 'It is perfectly well known at Scotland Yard who "Jack" was, and the reasons for the police conclusions were given in the report to the Home Office, which was considered by the authorities to be final and conclusive' – which spurred the *Pall Mall Gazette* into interviewing Abberline again:

Since the *Pall Mall Gazette* a few days ago gave a series of coincidences supporting the theory that Klosowski, or Chapman, as he was for some time called, was the perpetrator of the 'Jack the Ripper' murders in Whitechapel fifteen years ago, it has been interesting to note how many amateur criminologists have come forward with statements to the effect that it is useless to attempt to link Chapman with the Whitechapel atrocities. This cannot possibly be the same man, it is said, because, first of all, Chapman is not the miscreant who could have done the previous deeds, and, secondly, it is contended that the Whitechapel Murderer has long been known to be beyond the reach of earthly justice.

In order, if possible, to clear the ground with respect to the latter statement particularly, a representative of the *Pall Mall Gazette* again called on Mr F. G.

Abberline, formerly Chief Detective Inspector of Scotland Yard, yesterday, and elicited the following statement from him:

'You can state most emphatically,' said Mr Abberline, 'that Scotland Yard is really no wiser on the subject than it was fifteen years ago. It is simple nonsense to talk of the police having proof that the man is dead. I am, and always have been, in the closest touch with Scotland Yard, and it would have been next to impossible for me not to have known all about it. Besides, the authorities would have been only too glad to make an end of such a mystery, if only for their own credit.'

To convince those who have any doubts on the point, Mr Abberline produced recent documentary evidence which put the ignorance of Scotland Yard as to the perpetrator beyond the shadow of a doubt.

'I know,' continued the well-known detective, 'that it has been stated in several quarters that "Jack the Ripper" was a man who died in a lunatic asylum a few years ago, but there is nothing at all of a tangible nature to support such a theory.

Our representative called Mr Abberline's attention to a statement made in a well-known Sunday paper, in which it was made out that the author was a young medical student, who was found drowned in the Thames.

'Yes,' said Mr Abberline, 'I know all about that story. But what does it amount to? Simply this. Soon after the last murder in Whitechapel the body of a young doctor was found in the Thames, but there is absolutely nothing beyond the fact that he was found at that time to incriminate him. A report was made to the Home Office about the matter, but that it was "considered final and conclusive" is going altogether beyond the truth. Seeing that the same kind of murders began in America afterwards, there is much more reason to think the man emigrated. Then again, the fact that several months after December, 1888, when the student's body was found, the detectives were told still to hold themselves in readiness for further investigations seems to point to the conclusion that Scotland Yard did not in any way consider the evidence as final.'

But what about Dr **Neill Cream**? A circumstantial story is told of how he confessed on the scaffold – at least, he is said to have got as far as 'I am Jack' – when the jerk of the rope cut short his remarks.

'That is also another idle story,' replied Mr Abberline. 'Neill Cream was not even in this country when the Whitechapel murders took place. No, the identity of the diabolical individual has yet to be established, notwithstanding the people who have produced these rumors and who pretend to know the state of the official mind.

'As to the question of the dissimilarity of character in the crimes which one hears so much about,' continued the expert, 'I cannot see why one man should not have done both, provided he had the professional knowledge, and this is admitted in Chapman's case. A man who could watch his wives being slowly tortured to death by poison, as he did, was capable of anything; and

8

the fact that he should have attempted, in such a cold-blooded manner, to murder his first wife with a knife in New Jersey makes one more inclined to believe in the theory that he was mixed up in the two series of crimes. What, indeed, is more likely than that a man to some extent skilled in medicine and surgery should discontinue the use of a knife when his commission – and I still believe Chapman had a commission from America – came to an end, and then for the remainder of his ghastly deeds put into practice his knowledge of poisons? Indeed, if the theory be accepted that a man who takes life on a whole-sale scale never ceases his accursed habit until he is either arrested or dies, there is much to be said for Chapman's consistency. You see, incentive changes; but the fiendishness is not eradicated. The victims, too, you will notice, continue to be women; but they are of different classes, and obviously call for different methods of despatch.'

Pall Mall Gazette 31 March 1903

For the man who died in an asylum, *cf.* **David Cohen**, **Aaron Kosminski, J.W. Sanders**. For the young medical student found drowned, *cf.* **M.J. Druitt**, **Michael Ostrog**, **Basil Home Thomson**. Abberline's certainty that Scotland Yard did not know the identity of the Ripper is, or seems to be in direct conflict with contrary statements by Sir **Robert Anderson**, Chief Inspector **Donald Swanson** and, to some extent, Sir Melville Macnaghten. Nevertheless, Abberline's comments should not be overlooked.

It is not known what documentary evidence Abberline produced to prove Scotland Yard was still ignorant of the murderer's identity. It is evident that he knew nothing of the information incriminating Druitt that Macnaghten subsequently claimed to have seen, although one should observe his comments in the *Cassells* interview, where his view of the murderer's state of mind is not quite consistent with that he expressed in the *Pall Mall Gazette* interviews.

Finally, **H.L. Adam** wrote in his introduction to *The Trial of George Chapman* (London: William Hodge, 1930).

Chief Inspector Abberline, who had charge of the investigation into the East End murders, thought that Chapman and Jack the Ripper were one and the same person.

Abberline never wavered in his firm conviction that Chapman and Jack the Ripper were one and the same person. When Godley arrested Chapman, Abberline said to his confrere, 'You've got Jack the Ripper at last.'

Abberline had retired by the time Godley arrested Chapman in October 1902, so it is hard to suppose when he might have said this, especially as he admitted in the *Pall Mall Gazette* interview that his suspicions were roused following the Attorney-General's opening statement at the trial, but H.L. Adam acknowledges the assistance of George Godley in the writing of the book, so there is probably some basis for this statement.

Many crime historians have questioned Abberline's conclusions, noting that, apart from the killing of vagrant **Carrie Brown**, there were no Ripper-like murders in either New York or New Jersey during Klosowski's residence there in the early 1890s. R. Michael Gordon demurs and identifies four murders he believes were committed by Klosowski in America (Brown, **Mary Anderson**, **Hannah Robinson** and **Elizabeth Senior**. *See The American Murders of Jack the Ripper*). Philip Sugden (*The Complete History of Jack the Ripper*) gives serious weight to Abberline's suspicion of Chapman, noting this view was supported by ex-Superintendent **Arthur Neil**. He does not, however, endorse the claim that Abberline suspected Chapman in 1888 (*See* **Dr Dutton**).

Nigel Morland (1905–86, founder-editor of *Criminologist Magazine*) was reported in the *Evening News* of 28 June 1976 as saying that Abberline, towards the end of his life, told him, 'You'd have to look for him [the Ripper] not at the bottom of society, but a long way up.'

Joseph Gorman Sickert's final version of the alleged Freemasons' conspiracy behind the Ripper crimes rested on cryptic entries in the **Abberline Diaries**.

ABBERLINE DIARIES
See The Ripper and the Royals.

ABBERLINE'S WALKING STICK
A 3ft ebony stick, carved to resemble blackthorn, with a small but ornate silver plate, inscribed, 'PRESENTED TO INSP. ABBERLINE as a mark of esteem by 7 officers engaged with him in the Whitechapel murders of 1888'. The handle is carved into the representation of a man's head encased in a shallow hood and stained brown. It has been suggested by Donald Rumbelow in **The Complete Jack the Ripper** that this might be a monk's cowl and the figure could represent 'Brother Martin', a mad monk who allegedly murdered a nun in 1530 at the Mitre Square priory according to a sensational booklet written in 1888 by John Brewer. N.P. Warren speculated in *Criminologist* (vol. 19, no. 4, winter 1995) that it might represent a caul: the membrane which covers a foetus *in utero,* and is sometimes delivered clinging to the baby's head. Since an old tradition alleged that a caul preserves the owner from drowning,

Warren proposes the hypothesis that the carving wryly exonerates the drowned suspect M.J. Druitt. The authors note the hood frames the face rather in the manner of a shroud, but the very masculine image looks distinctly alive.

Abberline's walking stick is exhibited in a case at the National Police Library in Bramshill, Hampshire. The case carries the inscription:

THE WHITECHAPEL MURDERS
  THE WHITECHAPEL MURDERS IN 1888, COMMONLY
KNOWN AS THE 'JACK THE RIPPER' MURDERS, TOOK PLACE
IN LONDON BETWEEN AUGUST 31ST AND NOVEMBER 9TH.
  THE OFFICER IN CHARGE OF THE INVESTIGATION WAS
INSPECTOR (LATER CHIEF INSPECTOR) FREDERICK G.
ABBERLINE AND THIS STICK APPEARS TO HAVE BEEN
PRESENTED TO HIM BY HIS TEAM OF SEVEN DETECTIVES AT
THE CONCLUSION OF THE ENQUIRY.
  WHILST THE MURDERER WAS NEVER IDENTIFIED, IT
IS KNOWN THAT INSPECTOR ABBERLINE FAVOURED
THE THEORY THAT THE RIPPER WAS A DR. ALEXANDER
PEDACHENKO OR OSTROG, AN ALLEGED RUSSIAN
ANARCHIST LIVING IN THE LONDON AREA AT THE TIME,
AND THE HEAD OF THE STICK MAY WELL BE BASED ON HIS
FEATURES.
  THE STICK WAS FOUND AMONGST THE POSSESSIONS OF
EX-CHIEF INSPECTOR HUGH PIRNIE (DORSET AND
BOURNEMOUTH) BY HIS SON, COMMANDER IAN PIRNIE,
R.M. [sic: sc. RN] AND PRESENTED BY HIM TO THE COLLEGE.
  CHIEF INSPECTOR PIRNIE SERVED ON THE DIRECTING
STAFF FROM MARCH 1950 TO DECEMBER 1953.

The inscription appears to draw its information from **Donald McCormick**'s ***The Identity of Jack The Ripper***, accepting the belief that Abberline endorsed the **Pedachenko** theory.

Chief Inspector Pirnie joined the Hampshire Constabulary in 1927, was awarded the King's Police Medal for gallantry when he was 28, and was seconded to the staff of the newly founded Police Staff College at Ryton-on-Dunsmore in 1950, before returning as acting superintendent to Bournemouth County Borough Police in 1954.

Commander (later Rear Admiral) Pirnie remembers the stick being banished to a closet in his family home – his mother thought it was hideous. He does not know how it came into his father's possession. Although the Chief Inspector's house was in a street close to the Bournemouth street where Abberline retired, Commander Pirnie does not believe his father ever met Abberline or his widow.

In February 1974, Commander Pirnie presented the stick to Bramshill in memory of his father, (*see Police Review*, 17 May 1974) and in October 2006 was

11

invited by the College to draft a revised annotation to replace the original inscription. The stick was exhibited at the Jack the Ripper Conference in Bournemouth, 2001.

ABERCONWAY, CHRISTABEL MARY MACLAREN, 2ND BARONESS (1890–1974)

Younger daughter of Sir **Melville Macnaghten**. Married (1910) Henry Duncan MacLaren, suc. Baron Aberconway, 1911. Transcribed copy of Macnaghten memoranda from original manuscript which had passed from her mother to her elder sister, Mrs Julia Donner. (*See also* **Gerald Melville Donner**.)

In 1959, Lady Aberconway showed these notes to **Daniel Farson**, thereby initiating serious post-war study of the Whitechapel murders. In a letter to the *New Statesman* dated 7 November that year, she denied the likelihood of her father burning any Ripper documents (but *see also* **Melville Macnaghten**). Until 1965, she insisted the names of suspects in the memoranda not be published. In 1966, she published her own memoirs under the quizzical title, *A Wiser Woman?* (London: Hutchinson).

In the *Sunday Express,* 24 May 1992, Michael Thornton recalled her saying mischievously in 1972 that the memoranda gave 'the official line' and the truth could 'cause the Throne to totter'. On the other hand, in the *Daily Mail,* 2 December 2006, he reported her as merely saying her father was convinced the Ripper was Druitt.

ABRAHAMS, ISAAC
See **Isaac Kosminski**.

ABRAHAMS, WOOLFE (1861–1944)
Brother-in-law of **Aaron Kosminski**. Born in Russia and a master tailor. He married Aaron's sister Betsy and they had seven children. On 12 July 1890, Aaron Kosminski was admitted to the Mile End Old Town Workhouse Infirmary from 3 Sion Square, the residence of Woolfe. (*Cf.* **Morris Lubnowski**.)

ABRAHAMSEN, DAVID (1903–2002)
Author of *Murder and Madness: The Secret Life of Jack the Ripper*.

Born on 23 June 1903, in Trondheim, Norway; received medical training at the Royal Frederick University in Oslo, graduated in 1929 and, after a short stay in Copenhagen, went to London, where he worked for the Tavistock Clinic and the London School of Economics. Went to the United States in 1940. He studied criminal psychopathology, taught at several major hospitals, worked in prisons in New York and Illinois, and at the New York State Psychiatric Institute of Columbia University's College of Physicians and Surgeons. Also, a research associate in psychiatry at the College of Physicians and Surgeons. Expert witness in the investigations of Leopold and Loeb, Lee Harvey Oswald and David Berkowitz ('Son of Sam'). Author of several books, notably *The Psychology of Crime* (New

York: Columbia University Press, 1960), *Nixon vs. Nixon: An Emotional Tragedy* (New York: Farrar, Straus & Giroux, 1977) and *Confessions of Son of Sam* (New York: Columbia University Press, 1985). Obituary published in *The New York Times*, 22 May 2002.

ACCOMPLICES OF THE RIPPER (HANSARD)
Inferentially alleged by **Henry Matthews** to exist. Home Secretary Matthews observed, when answering a Parliamentary question on the offer of a pardon for any indirectly involved accomplice (23 November 1888): 'In the case of [Mary Jane] Kelly there were certain circumstances which were wanting in the earlier cases, and which make it more probable that there were other persons who, at any rate after the crime, assisted the murderer.' These circumstances are unknown.

ADAM, HARGRAVE LEE (1867–1946)
True-crime writer. Publications include *Police Work from Within* (London: Holden & Hardingham, 1914), *The Police Encyclopaedia*, with Introduction by Sir **Robert Anderson** (London: Waverley Book Co., 1920), *The Trial of George Chapman* (ed. London: Wm Hodge, 1930) and *C.I.D.: Behind the Scenes at Scotland Yard* (London: Sampson Low & Marston, 1931).

Acquaintance of Dr Robert Anderson, Sir **Charles Warren** and Sir **Melville Macnaghten**, Adam has left important descriptions of each. He also remarked in the introduction to *The Trial of George Chapman* that, 'Several prominent officials have from time to time asserted that they had established his [the Ripper's] identity. The late Sir Melville Macnaghten, the late Sir Robert Anderson, Sir **Henry Smith**, and many others of less importance have assured us regarding this' (but *cf.* Smith's apparently categorical denial in *From Constable to Commissioner*).

Macnaghten wrote his memoirs, **Days of My Years,** at Adam's instigation.

In Volume VI of the *Police Encyclopaedia*, Adam observed most prostitute murders were by men who imagined themselves to have been venereally infected by their victims and said it was 'generally believed' that this was the motive in the Whitechapel case. This may reflect the belief of all, or any of the policemen above.

'ALASKA'
Name ascribed in 1888 to the suspect Malay sea-cook by an English seaman named George M. Dodge (*New York Tribune*, 5 October 1888), who claimed that he had disembarked in London on 13 August and had gone to the Queen's Music Hall in Poplar High Street. There, he met a Malay cook called Alaska, who had been paid two years' wages, amounting to more than $500, and had bought clothes and a gold watch, but said that he had been robbed by a woman in Whitechapel of what remained. He threatened to murder and mutilate every Whitechapel woman he met until he found the woman who robbed him and recovered his property. The *Chicago Tribune* (6 October 1888) reported that detectives had visited the East End Home for Asiatics and received from the

manager, Mr Freeman, the eminently sensible suggestion that 'Alaska' was garbling of 'a lascar' (an East Indian seaman).

Wolf Vanderlinden: *From the Newspaper Morgue, Ripper Notes*, 27, April 2007.

ALBERICCI, FREDERICO

Alleged Ripper co-conspirator. Identified 1991 by Melvyn Fairclough in *The Ripper and the Royals* as an Italian-American footman employed at 74 Brook Street, the West End residence of Sir **William Gull** in the early 1880s. Subsequently declined to a life of crime in the East End, where he was known as 'American Freddy' or 'Fingers Freddy'. It is suggested he was employed to assist Gull and **Lord Randolph Churchill** in 1888, when they initiated and executed the alleged Freemasons' conspiracy to preserve the secret of Prince **Albert Victor**'s illegal marriage.

ALBERT EDWARD, PRINCE OF WALES (1841–1910)

King Edward VII, 1901–10. Alleged in oral tradition (heard by one of the authors *c*. 1989) to have been Jack the Ripper, or a leading suspect. There may be confusion with his son Prince **Albert Victor**, whose family nickname was 'Eddie'. (Albert Edward's was 'Bertie'.)

See also **Jack the Ripper Revealed**.

ALBERT VICTOR CHRISTIAN EDWARD, PRINCE (1864–92)

From 1891 Duke of Clarence and Avondale.

Ripper suspect proposed by Dr **Thomas Stowell**: orally from the 1950s; in print in 1972.

Grandson of Queen Victoria and Heir Presumptive to the throne. Trinity College, Cambridge, 1883. Hon. LLD, 1888. Aide-de-camp to Queen Victoria, 1889. Duke of Clarence and Avondale and Earl of Athlone, 1891. Engaged to Princess May of Teck (subsequently Queen Mary), December 1891, but died in January 1892 of pneumonia complicating influenza contracted in epidemic.

The allegation that he was the Ripper was first published by Philippe Jullian in *Edouard VII* (Paris: Librairie Hachette, 1962): Jullian claimed the Prince and 'the Duke of Bedford' were severally rumoured to be responsible for the murders. It was also given widest currency by Dr Thomas Stowell in a 1970 article in *Criminologist* magazine. Stewart Evans has demonstrated the probability that Jullian received the story from Stowell via Colin Wilson and Harold Nicolson (*Ripper Notes*, October 2002).

Stowell did not name his suspect, but called him 'S', then said he was 'the heir to power and wealth' and proceeded to give sufficient details to make identification with Prince Albert Victor certain. He believed 'S' contracted syphilis on a cruise as a midshipman.

Stowell believed 'S' was arrested within an hour or two of the murder of **Eddowes**, was certified insane and placed under restraint in a private mental home in the Home Counties, but that he escaped and murdered **Mary Jane Kelly** before

15

being apprehended again. According to Stowell, 'S', 'was, throughout, under the care of the great physician, **Sir William Gull**', under whom he regained sufficient strength to undertake some official duties in 1889–90. Stowell, however, notes that while 'S' made several public speeches, each one contained little more than 100 words, from which he deduced 'S''s health was declining.

Stowell says the authorities laid many false trails to mislead the police and mollify the press, but curiously states that as a scapegoat, the rumourmongers picked on Sir William Gull, writing: 'It is said that on more than one occasion Sir William Gull was seen in the neighbourhood of Whitechapel on the night of a murder.' The authors do not know to what Stowell was referring because there is no known association between Gull and the Ripper prior to Stowell's own article. Stowell suggested Gull was in the East End to certify the murderer insane.

Stowell tells the story of the medium **Robert James Lees**, who took the police to the imposing mansion of a famous physician whose wife described his uncommon behaviour and absences at the time of the Ripper crimes. He wondered if the story was, 'a variation of one told me by Sir William Gull's daughter, Caroline.' Caroline Acland was the wife of Theodore Dyke Acland, at one time Stowell's superior and intimate friend, whom Stowell visited many times over the years. Caroline Acland told him that at 'the time of the Ripper murders, her mother, Lady Gull, was greatly annoyed one night by an unappointed visit from a police officer, accompanied by a man who called himself a "medium" and she was irritated by their impudence in asking her a number of questions which seemed to her impertinent. She answered the questions with non-committal replies, such as "I do not know," "I cannot tell you that," "I am afraid I cannot answer that question." Later Sir William himself came down and in answer to the questions said he occasionally suffered from "lapses of memory since he had had a slight stroke in 1887"; he said that once he had discovered blood on his shirt. This is not surprising, if he had medically examined the Ripper after one of the murders.'

Stowell went on to say that Caroline Acland told him that she had seen 'in her father's diary an entry, "informed Blank that his son was dying from syphilis of the brain". The date of the entry was November 1889, after "S" had returned from his recuperative voyage.' The Prince contracted syphilis on his long cruise as a midshipman in 1880–82, surmised Stowell.

Stowell claimed to have been told of an 1889 entry in the diary of royal physician Sir Theodore Dyke Acland, saying he had told someone's father – (the prince's, it was insinuated) – that his son was dying of 'syphilis of the brain'. This illness supposedly led Albert Victor to commit the murders and a successful cover-up by the authorities concealed this from the public.

Frank Spiering, in *Prince Jack* (1975), made an unsubstantiated claim to have seen the Acland journal in the New York Academy of Medicine Library: otherwise there is no evidence whatsoever to support Stowell's story or to suggest that the prince suffered from syphilis, though one prescription drawn up for him by Dr Alfred Fripp might possibly have been intended to treat a gonorrhoeal infection.

Prince Albert Victor was central to several scandals, although the only one to become public was the **Cleveland Street** scandal. In 1889 his name was linked with a homosexual brothel frequented by several young aristocrats, but a cover-up kept his name out of the British newspapers. (See H. Montgomery Hyde, *The Cleveland Street Scandal*. London: W.H. Allen, 1976 and Colin Simpson, Lewis Chester and David Leitch, *The Cleveland Street Affair*, London: Weidenfeld and Nicolson, 1977; Theo Aronson, *Prince Eddy And The Homosexual Underground*, New York: Barnes & Noble, 1995. Also, *The Ripper Legacy, Epiphany of the Whitechapel Murders* and *Jack the Ripper: The Satanic Team*. In the 1930s, Mrs Henry Haddon and later her son Clarence Haddon claimed Clarence had been conceived in a liaison between Prince Albert Victor and Mrs Haddon following a ball in India, in 1889. The release of Special Branch papers in 2005 revealed both palace and police had been at some pains to pay off and send them abroad and there seems every possibility that the Haddon's claim was true. And a note written by the Duke of Clarence in 1891 to his solicitor, George Lewis, discussed paying £200 (almost £12,000 in today's money) for the return of letters written to a Miss Richardson and another woman, thought by modern commentators to have been prostitutes, who were blackmailing the Prince following the announcement of his engagement to Princess May of Teck. The note was auctioned by Bonhams in 2002 and bought by Patricia Cornwell. An effort to rehabilitate the Prince was made in 2006 (*see* Andrew Cook, *Prince Eddy: The King Britain Never Had*, Tempus Publishing Ltd, 2006).

A chronology of the whereabouts of Prince Albert Victor during the period of the murders, compiled from Court Circulars, diaries, and journals, is as follows:

29 August–7 September 1888: The Prince was staying with Viscount Downe at Danby Lodge, Grosmont, Yorkshire. (Court Circulars, vol. IX, p.60. Nichols murdered, 31 August.)

7–10 September 1888: The Prince was at the Cavalry Barracks in York. (Court Circulars, vol. IX, p.60. Queen Victoria's Journal, 10 September 1888, *ff.* Chapman, murdered 8 September.)

27–30 September: The Prince was at Abergeldie, Scotland, where Queen Victoria recorded in her journal that he lunched with her on 30 September. (Court Circulars, vol. IX, pp.65, 66. Queen Alexandra's Engagement Diary. Stride and Eddowes murdered between 1.00 and 2.00am, 30 September.)

1 November: Arrived in London from York.

2–12 November: The Prince was at Sandringham. (Prince of Wales' Engagement Diary; Princess of Wales' Engagement Diary. Kelly murdered 9 November.)

Prince Albert Victor also plays a major role in the story concerning Jack the Ripper originally told by **Joseph Sickert** to the BBC and presented to the public as fact by the late Stephen Knight. This claims that Prince Albert Victor secretly and illegally married Mr Sickert's grandmother, **Annie Elizabeth Crook** – a potential scandal which the authorities sought to suppress by incarcerating Annie in a lunatic asylum. No historical evidence to support this narrative has ever been found, although there is some evidence that elements of the story were circulating prior to 1950. (See *The Ripper and the Royals*, *Sickert and the Ripper Crimes*, **Florence Pash**.)

Claims that the Prince secretly survived the pneumonia of 1892 and lived incarcerated in Glamis Castle until the 1930s are made in *The Ripper and the Royals*. There was also a rumour, mentioned by Michael Harrison, that the Prince's death was clandestinely hastened 'to make way for one better suited to be King and Emperor.'

(*See also* **Death of a Prince** and **Prince Ripper and the Royal Family**.)

ALBROOK or ALLBROOK, LIZZIE (*b.* 1868?)

Friend of **Mary Jane Kelly**. Mentioned in a few newspapers and by **Walter Dew** in *I Caught Crippen*. Her name is variously spelled (as above) and her age is given as 20 in the *St James's Gazette* (12 November 1888), but exhaustive searches of the birth registrations and census records have failed to identify her. It has even been suggested that she might have been **Maria Harvey**.

According to her statements she lived in Miller's Court and worked at a lodging-house in Dorset Street. She visited Kelly on the night of her murder and was there when **Joseph Barnett** called on Kelly between 7.30 and 7.45pm. Speaking of Kelly, Albrook said, 'About the last thing she said was, "Whatever you do, don't you do wrong and turn out as I have." She had often spoken to me in this way and warned me against going on the streets as she had done. She told me, too, that she was heartily sick of the life she was leading and wished she had money enough to go back to Ireland, where her people lived. I do not believe she would have gone out as she did, if she had not been obliged to do so to keep herself from starvation.'

Walter Dew wrote that Lizzie Albrook found Kelly in tears and remained in Kelly's room for two hours. *Cf.* **Elizabeth Foster**.

ALIAS JACK THE RIPPER: BEYOND THE USUAL SUSPECTS

Book by R. Michael Gordon (Jefferson NC: McFarland, 2001).

Presents a detailed case against **Severin Klosowski** (**George Chapman**) and includes very full biographical details on Klosowski and his victims.

(*The American Murders of Jack the Ripper*; *The Thames Torso Murders* and *The Poison Murders of Jack the Ripper*).

ALLEN, ELIZABETH

Told a reporter for the *Echo* (14 September 1888) who visited 35 Dorset Street that Annie Chapman would sometimes sleep there three or four nights a week, insisting on a an eightpenny bed which carried greater privilages than cheaper ones. Saw Chapman in the house on the afternoon of the murder, Chapman saying , "Betty, I'm sick of this. I've no money, and shan't come in here tonight. If someone would give me a pair of boots I should go off hopping at once...Goodbye, Betty. Be good."

It was reported that as a result of information given by Allen and **Eliza Cooper** 'certain of the authorities have had cause to suspect a man actually living not far from Buck's Row.' (*Echo*, 20 September 1888); see **Buck's Row Suspect**.

ALLEN, PC JOSEPH, 423H (b. 1853)
On beat where **Alice McKenzie**'s body was found.

Served in Plymouth police for over three years before joining the Metropolitan Police in 1880. warrant no. 64896. Retired in 1905.

Allen had eaten a light supper under the lamp-post where **Walter Andrews** found McKenzie's body 20 minutes later. On leaving Old Castle Street, he spoke to Andrews in Wentworth Street and was subsequently summoned by **Sergeant Badham** from Commercial Street and despatched to the police station.

ALLEN, OSWALD
Journalist on the staff of the *Pall Mall Gazette* who gave an account of the discovery of **Annie Chapman**'s body to **William Stewart,** who recounts it in chapter four of his book. The account includes a quote from a report Allen submitted for editing and which he says 'was the substance of an article which appeared in a special edition' of the *Pall Mall Gazette*. At the conclusion of his report Allen wrote: 'A curious feature of this crime is the murderer had pulled off some brass rings which the victim had been wearing and these, together with some trumpery articles which had been taken from her pockets, were placed carefully at the victim's feet.'

AMERICAN MURDERS OF JACK THE RIPPER, THE:
Book by R. Michael Gordon (Westport, Connecticut: Praeger, 2003).

R. Michael Gordon's third book on the Whitechapel murders, each reflecting the author's conviction that **Severin Klosowski (George Chapman)** was Jack the Ripper. This one focuses on four murders in New York and New Jersey between 1891 and 1892: *see* **Carrie Brown, Hannah Robinson, Elizabeth Senior** and **Herta Mary Anderson**. (*cf. Alias Jack the Ripper, The Thames Torso Murders* and *The Poison Murders of Jack the Ripper*.)

ANDERSON, HERTA MARY (d. 1894)
Victim, proposed by R. Michael Gordon in 2005.

Teen-aged New Jersey hotel maid, found shot and stabbed near Perth Amboy. Suggested as Ripper victim because hers is the unsolved murder of a woman in the New York/New Jersey area in the period when **Severin Klosowski** was somewhere around there, and **Abberline** asserted that Ripper-like murders took place.

ANDERSON, JOHN (d. 1895)
Suspect named by seaman James Brame in 1896.

According to *Lloyds Weekly Newspaper*, 18 October 1896, Brame described Anderson as a former shipmate aboard the *Annie Speer,* sailing to Iquique, Chile. There, Anderson was taken mortally ill and confessed to Brame that he had been the Ripper. He claimed to have been robbed by a woman of the streets and decided to avenge himself on the whole class. To this end, he left sailing and took

19

lodgings in a farm-like house near Bromley, Kent, from which he would travel to Whitechapel in the evenings. He had an accomplice who stood by with a clean smock to cover his bloodstained clothes. Anderson found the murders frightening and suffered delirious visions of them two days before he died. He was buried in Iquique.

Since Anderson was described as red-haired, with a prominent moustache and small beard, and a pock-marked face, he has been suggested as similar to the blotchy-faced man described by **Mary Ann Cox**. But *cf.* **John Sanderson**; also the **Malay sea cook**.

ANDERSON, DR (LATER SIR) ROBERT (1841–1918)

Assistant Commissioner, Metropolitan Police CID. Named as a suspect in *Jack the Ripper: The Final Solution* and as a co-conspirator in *The Ripper and the Royals*.

Born in Mountjoy Square, Dublin, Ireland, on 29 May 1841, the son of Crown Solicitor Matthew Anderson. Educated privately in Dublin, Boulogne and Paris. Spent 18 months working for a Dublin brewer, then entered Trinity College, Dublin, where he took his BA in 1862, being called to the bar at King's Inn, Dublin, in 1863. Called to the Irish bar, he went on the North-West Circuit.

In 1860 Anderson was converted to extreme evangelical Christianity by Dr John Hall and became a millenniarist believer in the imminent second coming of Christ.

In 1865, Matthew Anderson, the Crown Solicitor, deputed to his eldest son, Samuel Lee Anderson, his responsibilities in preparing the case against several Fenians, and in turn Samuel Lee invited his brother Robert Anderson to work with him. In 1867 Anderson came to London as deputy head of a short-lived anti-Fenian intelligence branch. Remained as Home Office Advisor on Political Crime, and spymaster controlling *(inter alia)* **Thomas Miller Beach**. Called to the London bar in 1870.

In 1873, he married Lady Agnes Moore (1848–1925), sister of the ninth Earl of Drogheda, and had three sons: Arthur and Alan (who became missionaries) and Graham, a surgeon in the Royal Navy, who was killed in World War I when his ship, H.M.S. *Clan Macnaghton*, was lost with all hands in the North Sea; and one daughter, Augusta.

He received an Ll.D in 1875 and in 1882 was made Home Office liaison and recipient of information from the newly formed Dublin covert political branch under former Cyprus police chief Colonel Henry Brackenbury, but Brackenbury was almost immediately replaced by Edward Jenkinson, private secretary to the Liberal viceroy, Lord Spencer. In 1883, Anderson was made Home Office liaison and recipient of information from the newly formed Irish Bureau under **Superintendent Williamson** at Scotland Yard. Jenkinson told Liberal Home Secretary Sir William Harcourt that Anderson was 'a second-class detective' and Williamson was the only man worth anything at Scotland Yard. Anderson was then cut out from the chain of information, but Beach refused to report to anyone else, believing only Anderson was sufficiently discreet to safeguard his life as a spy. Anderson was downgraded to secretary to the Prison Commissioners with a reduction in salary, although £2,000 compensation was granted him in 1886, the year in which he was formally relieved of political duties by Liberal Home Secretary Hugh Childers. Jenkinson was dismissed in January 1887 and **James Monro**, who since 1884 had been assistant commissioner CID, combined Jenkinson's duties with Scotland Yard's Special Irish Department. Monro appointed Anderson as his Home Office 'assistant in secret work' with a greatly increased salary.

In May 1887, Anderson contributed three articles to *The Times* entitled 'Parnellism and Crime: Behind the Scenes in America'. An earlier series, 'Parnellism and Crime', written chiefly by journalist Woulfe Flanagan and unknowingly based on forged letters attributed to Charles Stewart Parnell, had sought to link Parnell to Fenian atrocities, especially the murder of Lord Frederick Cavendish and his secretary in Phoenix Park, Dublin, in 1882. These articles would become notorious. Anderson's articles did not accuse Parnell of fomenting or endorsing the Phoenix Park atrocity, but leaked information about British-based Nationalists' connections with American Fenians. In 1910, a mistake led to his apparent admission in his serialised memoirs in *Blackwood's Magazine* that he had authored the first series of articles and outraged Liberals and Irish Nationalists, who in reality were shooting at higher political game, accused him of abusing his official position and there were calls to revoke Anderson's pension. Anderson – who claimed the articles thwarted a plot to assassinate Queen Victoria during her Jubilee celebrations in Westminster Abbey – denied having used any material derived through official sources, but somewhat hair-splittingly to have used personal papers in his possession and belonging to Henri Le Caron. A further and more difficult political problem was caused when James Monro wrote to **Charles Edward Troup** denying Anderson's claim that he had sanctioned the articles (HO144/926). This caused a dilemma for Political and Civil Service heads, who did not want their involvement in *The Times*'s campaign against Parnell looked into too closely; which Winston Churchill, Liberal Home Secretary, met by wittily dismissing Anderson's memoirs as being 'written in a style of gross boastfulness – they are written, if I may say so, in the style of "How Bill Adams won the Battle of Waterloo". The writer seems anxious to show how invariably he was right, and how much more he could tell if only his mouth was not, what he pleased to call, closed.' Anderson reportedly enjoyed the hub-bub he caused, or at least claimed he did, telling a journalist: 'It has made me feel ten years younger,' (*New York Tribune*, 10 April 1910).

James Monro resigned as assistant commissioner C.I.D. and, on 1 September

PARNELLISM AND CRIME.

BEHIND THE SCENES IN AMERICA.

REPRINTED FROM

The Times.

PRICE ONE PENNY.

LONDON:

PRINTED AND PUBLISHED BY GEORGE EDWARD WRIGHT, AT
THE TIMES OFFICE, PRINTING-HOUSE SQUARE.

1887.

1888, Anderson was appointed his replacement, but had been prescribed sick leave due to overwork by Dr **Gilbart-Smith** and in a letter dated 28 August, **Sir Charles Warren** – who was himself on holiday – recommended Anderson take his sick leave a couple of days after his anticipated return to London on 7 September (letter in private collection: quoted in *The Ultimate Jack the Ripper Sourcebook*). Anderson accordingly left for Switzerland on 8 September, the day after **Mary Ann Nichols** was murdered, for which he would in due course be criticised in the press (*Pall Mall Gazette*, 8 October 1888). After the double murders, he was recalled.

Following the resignation of Sir Charles Warren in November 1888, Monro became commissioner, but he would resign in 1890 and the close friendship with Anderson came to an abrupt end for reasons unknown. For the next decade Anderson was seen as a very successful assistant commissioner, but his standing was completely overshadowed by his successor, Sir Edward Henry. In 1901, Anderson retired from the Metropolitan Police and received a knighthood. *Police Review* (14 June 1901) claimed his deep religious convictions and lack of 'the requisite kind of knowledge of the world and men' had made him an ill choice for the position of Assistant Commissioner CID. Other assessments did not agree (see *Pall Mall Gazette*, 29 April 1901).

Anderson devoted himself to writing articles and letters, penning numerous abstruse theological works and lecturing a great deal about penology, on which he was considered an authority. His final years were spent feeling isolated by his deafness, which cut him off from many of his interests, and the death of so many friends. On 15 November 1918, after an evening spent writing and reading his Bible, Anderson died in his bed from sudden heart failure following influenza.

In his memoirs, *The Lighter Side of My Official Life*, Anderson referred to the Ripper murders, stating that he spent the day of his return reviewing the available facts and the following day had a conference with Sir Charles Warren and the Home Secretary, **Henry Matthews**. The latter charged him with the responsibility of finding the murderer, to which Anderson retorted that he would hold himself responsible for taking 'all legitimate means to find him.'

Most controversially, he claimed that during his absence abroad the police had made a house-to-house search, investigating every man in the district who lived alone and who would therefore have been able to get rid of bloodstains unobserved. Anderson does not say or suggest the house-to-house search produced any suspects, but implies that all men living alone were exonerated, the police theorising as a consequence that the murderer must be living with people who observed him washing away his bloodstains and must have entertained suspicions which they self-evidently were not conveying to the police. This in turn led to the suggestion that the murderer was a low-class Jew (i.e. one of the recent immigrants who came to Britain in huge numbers in the 1880s to escape the pogroms in Eastern Europe) because, he said, 'it is a remarkable fact that people of that class in the East End will not give up one of their number to Gentile justice.' The result, said Anderson, proved the theory correct on every point.

It is generally accepted that the house-to-house investigation referred to was the one begun on 3 October 1888 and completed on 18 October, and therefore took place *after* Anderson returned from abroad and not, as he claimed, while he was away, but it appears to have been conceived and organised during his absence, the now-famous 'Police Notice – To the Occupier' handbill prepared for the house-to-house investigation and left at every house visited by the police, is dated 30 September 1888 and does not refer to the Double Event.

No mention of this theory has been found in surviving documents and Anderson acknowledged in a memo to the Home Office dated 23 October 1888 that the investigation lacked direction: 'That a crime of this kind should have been committed without any clue being supplied by the criminal, is unusual, but that five successive murders should have been committed without our having the slightest clue of any kind is extraordinary, if not unique, in the annals of crime' (HO144/221/A49301C, ff116–118). In August 1889, Anderson remarked to the American journalist R. Harding Davis: 'After a stranger has gone over [Whitechapel], he takes a much more lenient view of our failure to find Jack the Ripper, as they call him, than they did before' (*Pall Mall Gazette*, 4 November 1889) (*see* **David Cohen** for implications). However, within a few years of the Whitechapel murders he alluded in assorted interviews, articles and books to the identity of Jack the Ripper being known and to his having been insane.

In 1892, in *Cassell's Saturday Journal*, Anderson (in response to an interviewer who appears to have asked him about Ripper theories) produced photographs of the victims and said, 'There, there is my answer to people who come with fads and theories about these murders. It is impossible to believe they were acts of a sane man – they were those of a maniac revelling in blood' (*Cassell's Saturday Journal*, 11 June 1892).

In 1895 **Alfred Aylmer** ('The Detective In Real Life,' *The Windsor Magazine*, vol. 1 no. 5, May 1895) recorded that 'Much dissatisfaction was vented upon Mr. Anderson at the utterly abortive efforts to discover the perpetrator of the Whitechapel murders. He has himself a perfectly plausible theory that Jack the Ripper was a homicidal maniac, temporarily at large, whose hideous career was cut short by committal to an asylum.'

In 1901 Anderson wrote in a short article on penology: 'Or, again, take a notorious case of a different kind, "the Whitechapel murders" of the autumn of 1888. At that time the sensation-mongers of the newspaper press fostered the belief that life in London was no longer safe, and that no woman ought to venture abroad in the streets after nightfall And one enterprising journalist went so far as to impersonate the cause of all this terror as "Jack the Ripper," a name by which he will probably go down to history. But all such silly hysterics could not alter the fact that these crimes were a cause of danger only to a particular section of a small and definite class of women, in a limited district of the East End; and that the inhabitants of the metropolis generally were just as secure during the weeks the fiend was on the prowl as they were before the mania seized him, or after he had been safely caged in an asylum.' ('Punishing Crime', *The Nineteenth Century*, February 1901.)

In 1904, in a lecture at the London Institute, he reportedly said, 'The Whitechapel Murderer, known as "Jack the Ripper" was, said Sir Robert, undoubtedly insane, and was ultimately confined within an asylum.' (*Otago Witness*, 18 December 1904.)

In *Criminals and Crime* (London: Nisbet, 1907), he repeated verbatim what he had said in the penological article of 1901.

In an interview (*Daily* Chronicle, 1 September 1908) about the contamination of crime scenes and destruction of evidence prompted by the 1908 Luard murder case, Anderson said:

> Something of the same kind happened in the Ripper crimes. In two cases of that terrible series there were distinct clues destroyed – wiped out absolutely – clues that might very easily have secured for us proof of the identity of the assassin.
>
> In one case it was a clay pipe. Before we could get to the scene of the murder the doctor had taken it up, thrown it into the fire-place and smashed it beyond recognition.
>
> In another case there was writing in chalk on the wall – a most valuable clue; recognised as belonging to a certain indivual. But before we could secure a copy, or get it protected, it had been entirely obliterated...

Anderson went on to say that the police had no authority to enter private property to investigate a crime or to otherwise secure evidence, and concluded:

> I told Sir William Harcourt, who was the Home Secretary, that I could not accept responsibility for the none-detection of the author of the Ripper crimes, for the reasons, among others, I have given you.

This discussion was possibly the one he described in *The Lighter Side of My Official Life* as taking place on his return from abroad in September 1888: both accounts wrongly state that the Home Secretary was Harcourt when it was Henry Matthews, both accounts conclude with Anderson's refusal to accept responsibility for the non-detection of Jack the Ripper, and both concern the legitimacy of police action.

Writing in 1947 Arthur Posonby Moore Anderson refers to the destruction of these clues in *The Life of Sir Robert Anderson* (*Sir Robert and Lady Anderson*):

'The police reached the conclusion that he and his people were aliens of a certain low type, that the latter knew of the crimes but would not give him up. Two clues which might have led to an arrest were destroyed before the C.I.D. had a chance of seeing them, one a clay pipe, the other some writing with chalk on a wall. Scotland Yard, however, had no doubt that the criminal was eventually found. The only person who ever had a good view of the murderer identified the suspect without hesitation the instant he was confronted with him; but he refused to give evidence. Sir Robert states as a fact that the man was an alien from Eastern Europe, and believed that he died in an asylum.'

Then, in 1910 he repeated his explicit statement that the Ripper had been identified when his memoirs, *The Lighter Side of My Official Life,* were published, first in serialised form in *Blackwood's Magazine,* and subsequently as a book, in which certain changes were made. In *Blackwood's* he wrote:

One did not need to be a Sherlock Holmes to discover that the criminal was a sexual maniac of a virulent type; that he was living in the immediate vicinity of the scenes of the murders; and that, if he was not living absolutely alone, his people knew of his guilt, and refused to give him up to justice. During my absence abroad the Police had made a house to house search for him, investigating the case of every man in the district whose circumstances were such that he could go and come and get rid of his blood-stains in secret. And the conclusion we came to was that he and his people were low-class Jews, for it is a remarkable fact that people of that class in the East End will not give up one of their number to Gentile Justice.
    And the result proved that our diagnosis was right on every point. For I may say at once that 'undiscovered murders' are rare in London, and the "Jack-the-Ripper" crimes are not in that category. And if the police here had powers such as the French police possess, the murderer would have been brought to justice. I will only add here that the "Jack the Ripper" letter which is preserved in the Police Museum in Scotland Yard is the creation of an enterprising London journalist.

In a footnote he added: 'Having regard to the interest attaching to this case, I should almost be tempted to disclose the identity of the murderer and of the pressman who wrote the letter above referred to, provided that the publishers would accept all responsibility in view of a possible libel action. But no public benefit would result from such a course, and the traditions of my old department would suffer. I will only add that when the individual whom we suspected was caged in an asylum, the only person who had ever had a good view of the murderer at once identified him, but when he learned that the suspect was a fellow-Jew he declined to swear to him.'

A further footnote was: 'I am here assuming that the murder of Alice M'Kenzie on 17th July 1889 was by another hand. I was absent from London when it occurred, but the Chief Commissioner investigated the case on the spot. It was an ordinary murder, and not the work of a sexual maniac.'

In the book edition of these memoirs, Anderson made certain changes:

One did not need to be a Sherlock Holmes to discover that the criminal was a sexual maniac of a virulent type; that he was living in the immediate vicinity of the scenes of the murders; and that, if he was not living absolutely alone, his people knew of his guilt, and refused to give him up to justice. During my absence abroad the Police had made a house to house search for him, investigating the case of every man in the district whose circumstances were such that he could go and come and get rid of his bloodstains in secret. And the conclusion we came to was that he and his people were certain lowclass Polish Jews; for it is a remarkable fact that people of that class in the East End will not give up one of their number to Gentile justice.

And the result proved that our diagnosis was right on every point. For I may say at once that "undiscovered murders" are rare in London, and the "Jack-the-Ripper" crimes are not within that category. And if the Police here had powers such as the French Police possess, the murderer would have been brought to justice. Scotland Yard can boast that not even the subordinate officers of the department will tell tales out of school, and it would ill become me to violate the unwritten rule of the service. So I will only add here that the "Jack-the-Ripper" letter which is preserved in the Police Museum at New Scotland Yard is the creation of an enterprising London journalist.

Having regard to the interest attaching to this case, I am almost tempted to disclose the identity of the murderer and of the pressman who wrote the letter above referred to. But no public benefit would result from such a course, and the traditions of my old department would suffer. I will merely add that the only person who had ever had a good view of the murderer unhesitatingly identified the suspect the instant he was confronted with him; but he refused to give evidence against him.

In saying that he was a Polish Jew I am merely stating a definitely ascertained fact. And my words are meant to specify race, not religion. For it would outrage all religious sentiment to talk of the religion of a loathsome creature whose utterly unmentionable vices reduced him to a lower level than that of the brute.

He included the footnote in Blackwoods concerning **Alice McKenzie** and added: 'And the Poplar case of December, 1888, was a death from natural causes, and but for the "Jack the Ripper" scare, no one would have thought of suggesting that it was a homicide.' (*cf.* **Rose Mylett.**)

The principle changes Anderson made were to add 'certain' before 'low–class' and 'Polish' before 'Jews' and he changed 'declined to swear to him' to 'refused to give evidence'. He made three deletions: (a) the comment about his publisher accepting the costs of libel action if he named the author of the Jack the Ripper letters, (b) the reference to the suspect being caged in an asylum when he was identified (*see* **David Cohen** for implication), and (c) the reference to the witness also being a Jew and refusing to give evidence against the suspect when he learned that he was also a Jew. Anderson also added the new paragraph in which he stated, 'In saying that he was a Polish Jew, I am merely stating a definitely ascertained fact.'

The serial publication of the memoirs brought Anderson unwelcome notoriety. Irish MP Jeremiah MacVeagh asked Winston Churchill, the Home Secretary, whether his attention had been called to Anderson's Ripper revelations and whether he had been sanctioned to write what he had. Winston Churchill replied: 'Sir Robert Anderson neither asked for nor received any sanction to the publication, but the matter appears to me of minor importance in comparison with others that arise in connexion with the same series of articles' (*The Times*, 20 April 1910).

In the *Jewish Chronicle* the editor (Leopold Jacob Greenberg, 1861–1931), writing under the pseudonym 'Mentor', vehemently objected to Anderson, saying the suspect's family shielded him that the witness refused to give evidence *because* he was a Jew and accused Anderson of having no proof that the suspect *was* a Jew (*Jewish Chronicle*, 4–11 March 1910). In reply, Anderson – most of whose changes in the volume edition of his memoirs appear to be in response to 'Mentor's' criticisms – said, 'When I stated that the murderer was a Jew, I was stating a simple matter of fact. It is not a matter of theory. In stating what I do about the Whitechapel Murderer, I am not speaking as an expert in crime, but as a man who investigated the facts' (*The Globe*, 7 March 1910).

Two years after Anderson's death, his last statement about the Ripper was printed in an introduction to H.L. Adam's *Police Encyclopaedia* (London: Waverley Book Co., 1911): 'So again with the "Whitechapel Murders" of 1888. Despite the lucubrations of many an amateur "Sherlock Holmes", there was no doubt whatever as to the identity of the criminal, and if our London "detectives" possessed the powers, and might have recourse to the methods, of Foreign police forces, he would have been brought to justice. But the guilty sometimes escape.'

It is perhaps also worth noting that in volume IV of the *Police Encyclopaedia*, **H. L. Adam** wrote: 'A great deal of mystery still hangs about these horrible Ripper outrages, although in a letter which I have just received from Sir Robert Anderson, he intimates that the police knew well enough at the time who the miscreant was, although unfortunately, they had not sufficient legal evidence to warrant them laying hands upon him.'

In an article in *The People* (9 June 1912), Adam wrote: 'Sir Robt. Anderson has assured the writer that the assassin was well known to the police, but unfortunately, in the absence of sufficient legal evidence to justify an arrest, they were unable to take him. It was a case of moral versus legal proof. The only chance the police had, apparently, was to take the miscreant red-handed.'

It is important to note that with the possible exception of the **Swanson marginalia**, Anderson's claim that the Ripper was a Polish Jew has no firm corroboration from any other police source, is implicitly rejected by some (**Abberline, Littlechild, Godley**, etc.) and specifically rejected by others (**Reid, Major Smith**).

It has been argued that Anderson's story was geriatric wishful thinking, but this forces the additional postulation that **Donald Swanson** suffered similar geriatric self-deception and stumbles at the possibility that Swanson might have reached his conclusion by 1895 (*see* **The Complete History of Jack the Ripper**). A similar theme, citing H.L. Adam's anecdote about an occasion when Anderson confused cases and Adam's conclusion that Anderson's memory had begun to fail him, argues Anderson similarly confused the identification of the Polish Jew with the identification of Gentile sailor **Thomas Sadler**, and suggests that 'the Seaside Home' referred to by Swanson as the place where the identification took place was confusion with the Sailor's Home, where Sadler allegedly bought a knife (*see* **Jack the Ripper: Scotland Yard Investigates**). It has been noted, however, that Anderson prefaced his comments to H.L. Adam by writing, '"I am too tired to-night to recall it…", which leaves the fairness of Adam's conclusion open to question. It is questionable whether mixing up the details of murders that took place decades earlier is comparable with thinking the most famous unsolved murder case in recent memory was solved; also uncertain that Anderson would have persisted with his geriatric self-deception in the face of criticism from the likes of 'Mentor'.

It has also been suggested Anderson's story was an out-and-out lie, it being claimed that Anderson was sufficiently flighty with the truth often enough for it to be commented on and citing in support a Parliamentary quip by Jeremiah Macveagh (1870–1932), the Nationalist MP for South Down, that Anderson's claim to have had James Monro's sanction to write 'Parnellism and Crime: Behind the Scenes in America' was 'another edition of Anderson's Fairy Tales,' an allusion to Hans Christian Andersen's *Fairy Tales* which was greeted with much hilarity (*The Ripper File* – **Melvin Harris**). However, Macveagh was distinguished for his wit and was dubbed the 'licensed jester to the House of Commons', and it is debatable whether his allusion to Hans Christian Andersen's *Fairy Tales* allows Harris's construal.

Anderson acknowledged that the police engaged in 'utterly unlawful things' (memorandum initialled by Anderson, 13 December 1898, HO/451025/X36450, sub.77), which were probably fairly innocuous by today's standards, such as searching premises without a warrant (Bernard Porter in *Plots and Paranoia*, London: Unwin Hyman, 1989), but which may have been far more serious if we accept accusations by William Henry Joyce that Anderson used *agents provocateur* to plant bombs on suspected Fenians to justify their arrest. (Joyce is quoted by Leon O'Broin, *The Prime Informer*, London: Sidgwick and Jackson, 1971). One assessment of Anderson's character is that lying to achieve a greater good, such as securing the conviction of terrorists and murderers, was compatible with Anderson's religious beliefs which would otherwise have prohibited lying in self-interest or to benefit his department's reputation (*see* **The Crimes Detection and Death of Jack the Ripper**).

Anderson's papers are held at the National Archives, HO 144/1537 and 1538. Obituary published in *The Times*, 18 November 1918. A.P. Moore-Anderson: *Sir Robert Anderson; A Tribute And Memoir* (A signed copy was sent to Donald Swanson from A.P. Moore-Anderson, [either *For* or *Mr*] *Donald S. Swanson with the sincere regards of AP Moore-Anderson Nov. 1919*. Expanded and republished as *The Life of Robert Anderson: London: Marshall, Morgan and Scott, 1947*. Also see Paul Begg, 'Sir Robert Anderson: A Source Analysis', **Ripperologist**, 100, February 2009.)

ANDREWS, PC WALTER 272H (*b.* 1857)

Discovered the body of **Alice McKenzie**. Born Heveningham, Suffolk. Joined Metropolitan Police, 1880. Retd. 1906. Warrant no. 64735.

On beat duty between Old Castle Street and Goulston Street, he found the body at the top of the alley and summoned assistance with his whistle, calling back **Sgt. Edward Badham**, who had inspected him a few minutes earlier at the bottom of the alley. He restrained passer-by **Isaac Lewis Jacobs** from leaving the alley to collect his supper, and after Badham's arrival, remained in charge of the body until the medical officer arrived.

Andrews also reported having seen PC **Joseph Allen** in Wentworth Street shortly after Allen had eaten a snack under the lamp-post where McKenzie was murdered, 20 minutes later.

ANDREWS, INSPECTOR WALTER SIMON (1847–99)

Transferred from Scotland Yard to assist with enquiries in Whitechapel. May have made enquiries in New York respecting Dr **Francis Tumblety** in December, 1888.

Born Boulge, Suffolk. Married Jane Carr, 1867. Joined Metropolitan Police, 1869. warrant no. 52192. Det. Sgt., 1875; Inspector, 1878. Retired through ill health in October 1889; his fellow officers presented him with a clock, vases and an address on vellum (*Birmingham Daily Post*, 4 November 1889). For eight years he was a private inquiry agent in London, but retired from that job in 1897 because of deteriorating health and moved to Farnham. Committed suicide by hanging when very depressed in 1899 (*Hants and Sussex News*, 30 August 1899).

Walter Dew, who describes Andrews as 'a jovial, gentlemanly man, with a fine personality and a sound knowledge of his job', lists him along with **Chief Inspector Moore** and **Inspector Abberline** as having been seconded to Whitechapel from Scotland Yard to take charge of the Ripper investigation. However, his name is not mentioned in extant Scotland Yard papers on the case, leading Stewart Evans and Paul Gainey to argue in *The Lodger* that Tumblety was his exclusive responsibility and mention of him would be in the missing Tumblety dossier.

On 13 September 1888, Andrews arrested a notorious criminal, Roland Gideon Israel Barnett, on charges of fraud in Toronto and he was remanded for a week. In December 1888, Andrews escorted Barnett from London to Toronto, where he arrived on 11 December and deposited Barnett, who would in due course be sentenced to seven years' imprisonment. For over a week he stayed in Toronto, then went to Montreal, where he arrived on 20 December. He visited Chief of Police Hughes, but ran into a journalist to whom he reputedly said 'there were 23 detectives, 2 clerks and 1 inspector employed on the Whitechapel murder cases and that the police were without a jot of evidence upon which to arrest anybody.

"How many men have you working in America?"

"Half a dozen," he replied; then hesitating, continued: "American detective agencies have offered to find the murderer on salaries and payment of expenses. But we can do that ourselves, you know."

"Are you one of the half dozen?"

"No. Don't say anything about that. I meant detective agencies."

"But what are you here for?"

"I had rather not say just at present."'

The newspaper went on to state that it was announced at police headquarters that Andrews and two other Scotland Yard men were seeking The Ripper in America, a man suspected of knowing a great deal about the crimes having left England for America, some three weeks earlier (*St Louis Republican*, 22 December 1888). According to the *New York Herald* (23 December 1888), just before departing Montreal Andrews admitted that he had been seeking National League informers, but had been unsuccessful. Nevertheless, he said the British had detectives undercover inside the nationalist organisations and this force was commanded by Fred Jarvis and Chief Inspector Shore, with whom Andrews had a meeting at Niagara.

Irish MPs thought Andrews had gone to America in connection with the Parnell Commission and on 21 March 1889 the Irish MP Timothy Healy (1855–1931) asked Home Secretary **Henry Matthews** in the House of Commons whether this was the case and specifically whether Andrews had seen **Henri Le Caron** and whether it was Andrews who had persuaded Le Caron to break cover to testify on behalf of *The Times*. Matthews replied that Andrews' 'business was not connected with the charges and allegations made before the Royal Commisssion', but said that he did not know whether Andrews had seen Le Caron (*Freeman's Journal and Daily Commercial* Advertiser, 21 March 1889; *Birmingham Daily Post*, 22 March 1889).

It was reported that Andrews left Montreal for New York, but no reports have so far been found that he actually went there.

ANNIE CHAPMAN, JACK THE RIPPER VICTIM: A SHORT BIOGRAPHY

Booklet by Neal Shelden (pseudonym of Neil Stubbings), (Hornchurch, Essex: Neal Shelden, 2001). The first of Shelden's specialised accounts of individual victims (cf. **Jack the Ripper and His Victims, Catherine Eddowes: Jack the Ripper Victim**).

ARNOLD, JOHN aka JOHN or STEPHEN CLEARY, DENIS LYNCH (fl. 1889)

Unsubstantiated witness. News vendor, who informed the London office of the *New York Herald* at 1.15am, on Sunday, 8 September 1889, that he had been told by a soldier he met in Fleet Street that there had been another horrible murder in Backchurch Lane. Arnold gave his name as Kemp because he did not want his estranged wife to discover his whereabouts and the newspaper misreported this as John Cleary. On seeing the report of the Pinchin Street murder in the press two days later, Arnold also told ex-Inspector Lansdowne in Charing Cross. While his original story appeared to be a false report (and may have been based on the finding of an unconscious woman in Whitechapel High Street at midnight, on 7 September), the discovery of the **Pinchin Street torso** led to a frenzied search for the 'John Cleary' who apparently had advance information about the murder. On learning of this, Arnold came forward and identified himself to Sergeant Froest (*New York Herald*, No. 122, London edn., 11 September 1889; MEPO 3/140 ff. 162-4).

ARNOLD, SUPERINTENDENT THOMAS (1835–1906)

Head of **H Division** (Whitechapel) at the time of the murders. Absent on leave prior to the double murders (*see* **Acting Superintendent West**). Worked as a grocer before joining the Metropolitan Police in 1855, but subsequently resigned, volunteering for the Crimean War. Returned to England in 1856 and rejoined the police. Warrant no. 35059. Served his entire career in the East End, except for a brief posting to B Division. He was involved in many of the district's most celebrated criminal cases, including the **Lipski** murder.

On 30 September 1888, it was Arnold, as the man responsible for preserving the peace in Whitechapel and Spitalfields, who was most anxious to have the **Goulston Street graffito** erased. He had sent an inspector with a wet sponge to await orders to wipe it out when **Sir Charles Warren** visited the site at dawn and concurred it should be removed.

In an interview given to the *Eastern Post* on his retirement in February 1893, he made a number of comments on the Ripper case and related topics: 'I have now had a continuous association with H Division as Chief Inspector and Superintendent for eighteen years. To take [the Whitechapel murders] first, I still

hold what you may consider some curious opinions on the subject. For instance, for reasons which I am sure you would consider sufficiently convincing, but which are too long to detail now, I still hold to the opinion that not more than four of these murders were committed by the same hand. They were the murders of **Annie Chapman** in Hanbury Street, Mrs. Nicholls [*sic.* **Nichols**] in Buck's Row, **Elizabeth Stride** in Berner Street, and **Mary Kelly** in Mitre Square [*sic*]. We police came in for a very large share of blame at the hands of the public at that time for not acting as some people considered we ought to have acted in the matter, but I can assure you that no stone was left unturned by the police in endeavouring to detect the criminal. We were told, for instance, that we ought to have used bloodhounds. I can tell you now that we had two of the finest bloodhounds in England soon after the perpetration of the earliest of the murders; but what was the use of them after some hundreds of people had passed over the spot where the murderer would have escaped? Our detective department was very considerably augmented at that time, and so was our general force. We had some of the finest men from all parts of London, but all their efforts were useless.

'And now for hard, matter-of-fact details. The East End is better protected today than it has ever been – and, indeed, I may say it is better protected than a good many other parts of the metropolis I could name. It is now, and recollect I am speaking simply of the one and a half square miles covered by H Division – under the care of one superintendent of police, 29 inspectors, 45 sergeants, and 560 police constables. It has some of the smartest men attached to its criminal investigation department. I need only mention the names of Detectives **Thick**[e] and Read [*sic.* **Reid**]. The condition of the East End itself has very materially improved since when I knew it first. I can go back to the time when the drinking-houses and dancing-saloons were open all night, when certain public-houses in the Ratcliff Highway were the resorts of the biggest ruffians that the world contained, and when fatal fights were of almost daily occurrence. Now all that has changed. The criminal community has changed, too. You can still see your Fagins and your Nancys, but Bill Sykes, instead of resorting to a common lodging-house in Whitechapel or a thieves kitchen, now lives in a luxurious country house, speaks two languages, and plays tennis. The clever thieves have gone from the East End.'

Arnold's retirement in 1893 was marked by unusual recognition of his excellent service. H Division officers gave him a massive silver-mounted claret jug and biscuit holder, and Chief Constable Captain Dean came down from Scotland Yard to give him the good wishes of the top brass (*The Times,* 16 March 1893). On this occasion Arnold stated, to cheers and 'hear hear's, that he had stayed in the service a few years longer in the hope of solving the Whitechapel mystery. This had been a terrible time when a great cloud hung over Whitechapel, and without the support of the people of the district he did not think he could have stood it (*Police Review,* 5 June 1893).

He passed his retirement in Leytonstone, taking a keen interest in politics as a member of the Conservative Salisbury Club. At the end of 1907, he died of heart failure and his obituary in *The Eastern Mercury* (8 January 1907) included the remarkable observation that Jack the Ripper's 'identity to this day is a matter of dispute, although it is freely stated that the man is actually a farmer in one of our most prosperous colonies.'

ARTHUR, SIR GEORGE COMPTON ARCHIBALD, 3rd Bt. (1860–1946)

Distinguished biographer and military historian. Briefly suspected. A captain in the Royal Horse Guards and man-about-town, in November 1888 Arthur went 'slumming' on his own in Whitechapel, wearing an old shooting coat and a slouch hat. To the intense amusement of fellow-clubmen he was arrested by two policemen, who thought he answered the popular description of Jack the Ripper (*New York World, San Francisco Chronicle*, 18 November 1888).

(see Andy Aliffe, 'Slumming in the East End – Another Royal Connection?', *Ripperana*, no 15, January 1996)

AUSTEN or AUSTIN, DICK

Suspect, accused 1888 by James Oliver, an old soldier of the 5th Lancers, resident in Rotherham. According to Oliver, Austin had been in the Lancers, where he was very violent, expressed constant hatred of women and a wish to 'kill every whore and cut her insides out'. Oliver believed Austin had endured a violent and possibly criminal life before joining the Army and thought he had gone to London after his discharge. He volunteered this information to the Rotherham Police and claimed the **Dear Boss letter** resembled Austin's hand-writing. The Rotherham police informed Scotland Yard, but apparently desultory efforts to trace Austin were unsuccessful.

(Information taken from MEPO files now missing, but accessed independently by Donald Rumbelow and Stephen Knight in the 1970s, and transcribed by BBC producer Paul Bonner.)

AUSTIN, MARY ANN (*b.c.* 1873–1901)

Murder victim, 1901.

28-year-old prostitute. 5ft 4in, medium build, dark complexion, black hair, blue/grey eyes. Wife of sometime stoker and navvy William Austin, married eight years; two children: Elizabeth, aged 4, and Frances, aged 3. Alcoholic, quarrelsome when drunk. Lived at 37 Dorset Street (run by Anne McCarthy, 32-year-old daughter of **William Crossingham** and widow of Daniel McCarthy, brother of **John McCarthy**).

In May 1901 she took a stranger to 35 Dorset Street, during the night was violently stabbed and, following an examination by a local doctor was taken to London Hospital, where she was not examined for 12 hours and died soon after the full extent of her injuries was discovered. The police were then called. Staff and residents at the lodging-house were uncommunicative and uncooperative, even to the extent of misidentifying the cubicle in which Austin was attacked, and the actions of Daniel Sullivan (William Crossingham's brother-in-law) appeared particularly suspicious. In due course Marie Moore, wife of the deputy, identified William Austin, the victim's estranged husband, as her companion. There was no evidence against him and he was released.

In August, the Cardiff police contacted Scotland Yard with information about **George Neating**, a violent wife-beater suspected of being a murderer, who they thought matched the description of the man seen with Austin. It was alleged Neating was a member of the Metropolitan Police at the time of the Whitechapel murders.

In the event no one was convicted of Austin's murder.

(Case file MEPO 3/162 held at the National Archives. See Derek Osborne, 'Line of Enquiry', *Ripperana* 42, October 2002. Robert Clack, 'Murder, Death And The Lodging-House: The Strange Case Of Mary Ann Austin', *Ripper Notes*, 24 October 2005.)

AUTUMN OF TERROR: JACK THE RIPPER HIS CRIMES AND TIMES

Book by **Tom Cullen** (London: Bodley Head, 1965). Published in the US as *When London Walked in Terror* (Boston: Houghton Mifflin, 1965). UK paperback published as *Autumn of Terror: The Crimes and Times of Jack the Ripper* (London: Fontana, 1966). US paperback (New York: Avon, 1968). Issued in UK paperback as *The Crimes and Times of Jack the Ripper* (London: Fontana, 1973).

This was the first publication to use the **Macnaghten memoranda** and make known **Montague John Druitt**'s full name. Cullen accepted Macnaghten's identification of Druitt as the Ripper. He established some biographical details about Druitt's schooldays and also postulated a social motivation, drawing attention to Toynbee Hall and the University Settlements movement (*cf.* **Samuel Barnett**), with the suggestion that Druitt might have intended to call public notice to the squalid conditions prevailing in the East End.

Autumn of Terror is generally considered the first post-war book on Jack the Ripper to make a serious and responsible effort to establish a full and, as far as possible, accurate account of the murders. It has been identified as having used material which **Daniel Farson** believed was purloined from his files at the Associated-Rediffusion Television offices (*see Jack the Ripper*, 1972). The loss of the files meant that Farson could not prove the existence of some material, such as the Knowles letter (*see* under **The East End Murderer – I knew Him**) existed, but Cullen's use of the material, which was removed from the second edition of his book (*The Crimes and Times of Jack the Ripper*, 1973), confirms the existence of the files.

AYLMER, ALFRED

Writer. Contributed articles to the *Windsor Magazine*, notably 'The Detective in Real Life', May 1895, 'Buried Treasure: A Strange True Story of Lloyd's, October 1895, and 'Detective Day at Holloway', June 1897.

In 'The Detective In Real Life' he wrote:

'Much dissatisfaction was vented upon Mr. Anderson at the utterly abortive efforts to discover the perpetrator of the Whitechapel murders. He has himself a perfectly plausible theory that Jack the Ripper was a homicidal maniac, temporarily at large, whose hideous career was cut short by committal to an asylum.'

('Alfred Aylmer' has been identified as a pseudonym of **Major Arthur Griffiths** (see **The Man Who Hunted Jack the Ripper,** 1999), but contrast Aylmer above with Griffiths' statement the following year in *Cassell's Family Magazine* (see under Griffiths). It has also been noted that the September 1895 and October 1895 issues of *The Windsor Magazine* carried articles by Griffiths and Aylmer respectively.)

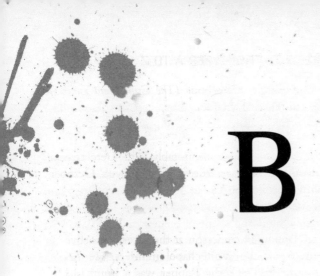

B

BACHERT, WILLIAM ALBERT (*b.* 1860)

Name variously spelt Backert, Baskert, Baskett, Bechart, Beckett.

Frequently in the press over Jack the Ripper, self-publicist, member and latter chairman of a Whitechapel Vigilance Society, agitator on behalf of the unemployed.

Born in London, the eldest of three children of John, a tailor from Mecklenburg, and his wife, Georgina. Lived at 13 Newnham Street. Worked for engraver named Dix in Porridge Court (Fleet Street).

His first known appearance in the press was in August 1887 when he complained to Franklin Lushington, magistrate at the Thames Police Court, that he had heard that the police were conspiring to bring unfounded charges against him following an altercation in which a female acquaintance had been ill-treated by two constables, who had mistaken her for a prostitute, and he had been struck by them when he intervened. Lushington said he would remember Bachert's complaint, should a case come before him (*The Eastern Post and City Chronicle*, 20 August 1887).

The following month he appeared in a state of distress at the Thames Police Court, asking that publicity be given to the disappearance of his father, who a week earlier had gone into the City with £400 and a quantity of jewellery, including a large diamond ring, on his person and not been seen since (*The Times*, 20 September 1887). He was evidently safe as he appears in the census for both 1891 and 1901.

In January 1888 he appeared in court to give testimony concerning the Trafalgar Square riots of the previous year (*The Times*, 18 January 1888). Then, in September 1888, he wrote to the *Evening News* 'on behalf of a number of tradesmen and shopkeepers in Whitechapel' expressing horror at the murders (*Evening News*, 6 September 1888) and on 30 September, the night of the Double Event, he reportedly talked with a dark man wearing a morning coat and a black hat and carrying a shiny black bag in The Three Tuns (or The Three Nuns, accounts differ) in Aldgate. The man furtively asked questions about streetwalkers. Bachert and the man left the pub at closing time (12 o'clock) and parted company outside Aldgate Railway Station (*The* Times, 1 October).

In subsequent reports Bachert said that the conversation had been sparked by an elderly and very shabbily dressed match-woman asking him to buy some matches. The man remarked that those persons were a nuisance and proceeded to ask about the local prostitutes, asking Bachert if he thought one of them would go with him down Northumberland Alley, off Fenchurch Street. He then went outside and spoke to the match-seller and gave her something. Following this, he returned to the pub and Bachert bid him goodnight (*The Times*, 2 October).

On 20 October, Bachert received an alleged Ripper postcard, written in red ink and addressed to Mr Toby Baskett of 13 Newman Street, Whitechapel, which read:

> Dear Old Baskett
> Yer only tried ter get yer name
> in the papers when yer thought you
> had me in the Three Tuns Hotel
> I'd like to punch yer bleeding nose
> Jack the Ripper

On 19 November Bachert was woken by an unnamed police constable, who told him there was chalk graffito written on the outside of his home at 13 Newnham Street. The message read: 'DEAR BOSS − I am still about. Look out − Yours, "JACK THE RIPPER."' The words were afterwards partly obliterated to avoid attracting a crowd (*Irish Times*, 20 November 1888; *The Walthamstow and Leyton Guardian*, 24 November 1888).

Bachert was subpoenaed by Charles Bradlaugh, MP, to testify on his behalf in the case of Bradlaugh v Peters, which Bradlaugh subsequently lost and was ordered to pay damages and costs, but Bachert claimed he did not receive recompense. Bradlaugh produced evidence showing that Bachert had been paid what was due him (*The Times*, 6, 12 October 1888).

In March 1889, according to *The Identity of Jack the Ripper*, Bachert was confidentially told by police that the murderer had died by drowning at the end of 1888. This has not been traced beyond that book. It was reported in July 1889 that Bachert, who it was claimed had taken a leading part in the Vigilance proceedings the previous year, had along with the police received letters from the murderer claiming he would recommence his work that month. The letter was supposed to have come from the 'Eastern Hotel, Pop.' and police apparently made enquiries and established there was an Eastern Hotel in the East India Dock Road, Poplar, frequented by sailors and giving rise to speculation that the murderer had been at sea since the murder of **Mary Jane Kelly** (*Alderley and Wilmslow Advertiser*, 19 July 1889; *Newcastle Weekly Courant*, 20 July 1889).

On 22 July 1889, the *New York Herald* published an interview with him. In September, in a letter to the press he described himself as 'chairman of the last-formed Whitechapel Vigilance Committee' and said that he and his committee had been very active until interest in the murders diminished at the time of the dock labourers' strike (August 1889), when some of his supporters relaxed their efforts (*East London Advertiser*, 14 September 1889), and that he also tipped off the press that the police were investigating a suggestion that the murderer was 'a tall, strong woman [who] has for some time been working at different slaughter-houses, attired as a man' (*Eastern Post and City Chronicle* and *The Police Chronicle and Guardian, 21 September*). In October he claimed to have received another letter from the murder (*East London Advertiser*, 19 October 1889).

An Albert Backert, described as an engraver – and his age given as 21, so he may not be the same man – was charged with several other men, including Albert Stanley (alias Waple) and John Smith (alias Huddy), for passing counterfeit florins at two pubs and with stealing a pewter pot from another. Backert and another man, Henry Norman, were acquitted, it being Smith's *modus operandi* to befriend young men and inveigle them into passing the counterfeit coins. Smith received 8 months hard labour. (*Ipswich Journal*, 7 December 1889).

In 1890 Bachert provided an early version of a 'Lodger' story (*cf.* **The East End Murderer – I Knew Him, The Lodger**) (*The People*, 12 October 1890).

Writing on 14 February 1891, Bachert claimed he and a friend saw **Frances Coles** at 12.15am outside Leman Street Railway Station talking with a man. At 1.05am he arrived home, which he described as a few yards from the scene of the murder, and he saw her talking to a man opposite his house. He overheard the man ask the woman to come home with him and then say, 'If you don't, you will never go home with another man.' The couple then walked off towards the arches, where Coles would be found murdered. Bachert said that he had been called to serve on the jury and reform the Vigilance Committee if he thought Coles had been murdered by Jack the Ripper (*Birmingham Daily Post*, 16 February 1891). At the inquest Bachert was rejected by **Wynne Baxter** as a substitute juror, Baxter refusing to give a reason and Bachert protesting: 'You decline simply because I happen to be chairman of the Vigilance Committee, and you think I shall fully investigate this matter. I have a right to be on the jury' (*The Times*, 16 February 1891).

At the beginning of July 1891, Bachert received a threatening letter from Jack the Ripper, which gave his initials as G.W.B. and address as George Yard (*Lloyd's Weekly Newspaper*, 5 July 1891).

Bachert (who was called Alfred Backert in the report) appeared before the magistrate Montagu Williams at Thames Police Court charged with disorderly conduct and causing a crowd to assemble outside a butcher's shop at 4 Whitechapel High Street on 29 June, when he had shoved a butcher, Tomas Davis, who had struck Bachert in retaliation. Bachert was ejected from the shop four times before being arrested by PC 325H. Davis said Bachert often came into his shop when drunk and that he was very often drunk, especially on Mondays and Tuesdays. In return, Bachert said he had been struck by Davis and asked PC 325H to arrest him, but Davis had arrested Bachert instead. Bachert received 5s or five days (*Lloyd's Weekly Newspaper*, 5 July 1889). On Saturday, 25 July 1891, Bachert, who was described as 'of "Catch Jack the Ripper" notoriety' appeared at the Thames Police Court and applied for warrants against two H Division officers, whom he believed guilty of perjury. He was advised to appeal to Montagu Williams, the magistrate on the bench when the case was originally heard (*Reynolds's Newspaper*, 26 July 1891).

In November 1891, described as 'the chairman of the so-called Whitechapel Murder Vigilance Committee', Bachert was charged with being drunk and disorderly, but claimed it was a false charge and produced numerous witnesses to say that he was pushed by a policeman (*Birmingham Daily Post*, 17 November 1891).

On 18 November 1891, an Albert Edward Backert – described as an engraver of Aldgate – appeared as a witness at the inquest into the death of a 14-year-old boy, Arthur Charles Puleston, who was killed when struck by a cast-iron roof ornament (*The Times*, 19 November 1891).

In January 1892 he appeared in the magistrates court saying that, in consequence of a letter allegedly from Jack the Ripper threatening to start work again, he had gone with some friends to patrol the streets and saw people sleeping rough and now sought advice as to whether he could arrange for them to be removed to a workhouse or shelter (*Reynolds's Newspaper*, 3 January 1891).

Then, in March 1892 he again appeared at the Thames Police Court claiming to have received a paper signed A.F.P. with a coffin and cross-bones drawn on it. Bachert claimed that he thought he knew the author of all the Jack the Ripper letters – which the magistrate dismissed as 'nonsense' – and wanted to know if he could arrest him. He was told to leave the man alone and go to the police (*Aberdeen Weekly Journal*, 2 March 1892).

In September 1892 he was charged with stealing clothing and a bag containing £350 from his father (*The Illustrated Police News*, 3 September 1892). *Reynolds's Newspaper* (11 December 1892) reported that Bachert was discharged.

By November 1892 Bachert was beginning to get attention in the press as an anti-Socialist labour leader and agitator, arranging to hold a meeting in Trafalgar Square one hour after the Social Democratic Federation (*Reynolds's Newspaper*, 6 November 1892), delivering a 'violent harangue' at Tower Hill (*The Times*, 14 December 1892). He became a member of the Tower Hamlets Unemployed Investigation and Relief Committee, a society instituted for the purpose of distributing food and other articles among the destitute poor (*The Times*, 22 December 1892; 8 March 1893).

On 4 February, Bachert went to the shop of a Mrs Pascoe and presented an order for bread and flour without the authority to do so. Later that month, he went to live in Bristol, where he wrote a letter to the local newspaper stating his intention to rally the unemployed. A warrant was issued for his arrest by H Division and, as Bachert's letter contained his address, the Bristol police had no difficulty arresting him on 9 January. He appeared before the Thames Police Court magistrates on the 10th, where he pleaded innocent, but it was shown that he gave the goods to a widow who kept a beershop and he was found guilty and sentenced to three months' hard labour (*The Bristol Mercury and Daily Post,* 9 and 10 February 1893; *Daily News,* 11 February 1893; *The Times,* 8 March 1893). In June 1893, having completed his three-month sentence, he complained at the Thames Police Court of being wrongly convicted and would have appealed against the sentence, had there been the means to do so as he had been asked to stand for Parliament and for a set on the County Council, the conviction having destroyed opportunity for either. The magistrate said there was nothing he could do. Bachert added that a fund had been opened for the purpose of sending him abroad and that he intended to go (*Lloyd's Weekly Newspaper,* 8 June 1893). It is not currently known whether he did so.

BADHAM, SERGEANT EDWARD, 31H (*b.* 1862)

Variously called Baddam, Bedham, Betham, Baugham, Barry and Berry in the press.

Former coachman. Joined the Metropolitan Police 1880 (warrant no. 65001); resigned 1905.

Took **Annie Chapman**'s body from Hanbury Street to the mortuary, where he took down a description furnished by **Sergeant Thick**. At the inquest, on 13 September 1888, he was asked by the coroner whether he was certain he'd taken away every portion of the body, to which he replied 'Yes'.

Apparently accompanied **Inspector Walter Beck** to the scene of the **Kelly** murder (*Manchester Guardian,* 10 November 1888). Also took down **George Hutchinson**'s statement.

On 17 July 1889, Badham was on duty inspecting beat constables and spoke briefly to Police Constable **Walter Andrews** in Castle Alley, but on proceeding to the next constable's beat was recalled by Andrews' whistle on discovery of **Alice McKenzie**'s body. He later conveyed the body to the Whitechapel mortuary.

BALFOUR, ARTHUR JAMES (1848–1930)

Chief Secretary for Ireland, 1887–91; Prime Minister 1902–06.

The late Douglas G. Browne wrote in *The Rise of Scotland Yard* (London: Harrap, 1956), 'A third head of the CID, **Sir Melville Macnaghten**, appears to identify the Ripper with the leader of a plot to assassinate Mr Balfour at the Irish Office.' This extraordinary claim, unsupported by any extant writing of Macnaghten's, cannot be casually dismissed. Browne had access to the Scotland Yard and Home Office files on the Ripper at least 20 years before they were opened to the public and presumably saw documents which have since gone missing. There *were* Fenians aspiring to assassinate Balfour, so Macnaghten may have heard and recorded suspicion of a Fenian as the Ripper prior to hearing the information that convinced him the Ripper was **Montague John Druitt**.

Queen Victoria noted in her journal that 'the Government had had notice from America of a plot to kill Mr. Balfour' (ed. George Earle Buckle, *The Letters of Queen Victoria,* Vol. I, London: John Murray, 1930) and suggestive details emerge in the private manuscript memoir written by **James Monro** in 1903 and secret files deposited in the Home Office archives by **Sir Robert Anderson**. According to Monro, the Fenians determined on a campaign of assassinations in 1888, aimed especially at killing Balfour. The prominent Fenian and double agent General Millen travelled to France to control the operation, and there he was confronted by a Scotland Yard man and decided not to enter England. His Irish subordinate, Roger McKenna, was also seen in Paris and given to understand that his movements were watched. Through him, the leading perpetrator in England – a man called Walsh – was uncovered. But the plot came to nothing. Sir Robert Anderson's filed notes state that **Superintendent Williamson** went to France and frightened off the organiser of the Jubilee Bomb Plot. Monro's manuscript reminiscence, written 15 years later, ascribes that journey to Inspector Melville and states that the following year, Williamson scared off General Millen.

(*See* Martin Fido, 'Anderson, Monro and jsfmboe', *Ripperologist,* 80, June 2007.)

BARKER, EMILY (*d.* 1888)
Briefly thought to be the **Pinchin Street torso**.

A young woman from Northampton, whose parents thought she was the Pinchin Street torso, but the police and her father concluded otherwise when she did not match the physical description. (Various newspapers between 30 September to 6 October 1889, but *see Lloyds Weekly Newspaper,* 6 October 1889; *see* **Lydia Hart**, **Rosina Lydia Smith**.)

BARLAS, JOHN (1860–1914)
Suspect, unnamed, but described in *The New York Times,* 24 October 1897 and identified as Barlas by David A. Green ('In Hours of Red Desire: John Barlas and the Scottish Lunatic Suspect', *Ripper Notes*, 26, September 2006).

Socialist poet, educated Merchant Taylors' and New College, Oxford. Friend of Oscar Wilde. Wealthy with private means, but in 1888 believed to be living in squalor with a prostitute at Hercules Buildings, Lambeth Road. He had periods of insanity following a blow from a policeman's truncheon at a socialist demonstration in 1886.

The New York Times claimed on the word of a 'perfectly trustworthy authority' that the Whitechapel Murderer was an unnamed lunatic confined to a Scottish asylum. It described him as an Oxford graduate who, *c.* 1887, won a reputation as a minor poet. His name was distinguished and famous in Scottish history 'in connection with a young woman who saved a King's life in a heroic way'. He was also married to a descendant of a famous English Admiral.

David A. Green says the case against him is that he was a potentially violent lunatic, incarcerated in asylums from 1892, and at the time of the Ripper murders was known to take night walks in London and believed to associate with prostitutes.

BARNARDO, DR THOMAS JOHN (1845–1905)

Alleged suspect.

Born in Dublin, 4 July 1845, the son of a furrier, he converted to Evangelical Christianity in 1862, preached in the slums of Dublin and conceived an ambition to be a medical missionary in China, moving to London for medical studies at the London Hospital in Whitechapel, where he discovered the plight of homeless children. By 1868, he was able to open his first home for destitute children.

It was reported (*East London Advertiser*, 13 October 1888) that Dr Barnardo visited 32 Flower and Dean Street. There, he discussed the murders with women who included **Elizabeth Stride**. Barnardo also wrote letters (*see The Times*, 9 October 1888) and conducted meetings at which reference was made to the attention the murders had drawn to the condition of children and common lodging-houses.

Dame Gillian Wagner wrote in her biography (*Barnardo*, London: Weidenfeld & Nicolson, 1979), 'it is hardly surprising that Barnardo's name should have been included among [the suspects]. He was known to frequent the streets and courts where the murders had taken place, and was well known to both the police and in the common lodging-houses.' Gillian Wagner's source is given in the notes as 'private information'. The *Evening Standard* (12 June 1995) claimed that he was rumoured to have kept a diary in which dates of the Ripper murders were left blank.

So far as the authors have been able to establish, Dr Barnardo was first advanced as a suspect in the 1962 edition of *The Identity of Jack the Ripper*, but this did not say when or by whom he had been accused.

A fuller argument for Barnardo as the Ripper is made in *Revelations of the True Ripper* (2006),

BARNES, PC JAMES JOSIAH (*b.* 1861)

Left in charge of **Annie Chapman**'s body at the mortuary by **Inspector Chandler**.

A former railway porter. Joined the Metropolitan Police in 1886 (warrant no. 72174). Retired 1911.

BARNETT, DANIEL (*b.* 1851)

Brother of **Joseph Barnett**.

Maurice Lewis's claim to have seen **Mary Jane Kelly** drinking with **'Julia'** and 'Danny' on the night of her murder has been variously interpreted as meaning that Joe was sometimes known as Danny, that Lewis confused the two brothers or that actually, Mary Jane was drinking with Daniel Barnett.

(*See* Bruce Paley, *Jack the Ripper: The Simple Truth*; Mark Madden, *Ripperana*, 6, 1993, and Neal Shelden, *Jack the Ripper and His Victims*. Also Paul Harrison, *Jack the Ripper: The Mystery Solved*.

BARNETT, MRS HENRIETTA née ROWLAND (1851–1936)

Social reformer who drafted a petition to Queen Victoria in response to the Ripper murders urging men to abandon the immorality that led to prostitution and requesting the closure of common lodging-houses.

Born into a wealthy family, she was introduced by the pioneer feminist Octavia Hill to Revd. **Samuel Barnett** when he was a curate in Bryanston Square. Married Barnett in 1873 and accompanied him to Whitechapel, where she supported his many philanthropic ventures. After the night of the double murder she drafted her petition, which was signed by several thousand East End women. Micky Watkins gives an account of her life at this period in *Henrietta Barnett in Whitechapel: Her First Fifty Years* (London: Hampstead Garden Suburb Archive Trust, 2005).

J BARNETT
THE FRIEND OF THE
' DECEASED

BARNETT, JOSEPH (1858–1926)

Suspect investigated and cleared by police 1888. Revived as suspect by Bruce Paley ('A New Theory on the Jack the Ripper Murders', True Crime, April 1982; *see **Jack the Ripper: The Simple Truth***). Lover of **Mary Jane Kelly**, with whom he lived until two weeks before her death.

Fourth of the five children of a fish porter, who died when Joseph was aged 6. Joseph's mother seems to have deserted the family shortly afterwards, leaving him to be brought up by his older brothers, Denis and Daniel, and his sister Catherine. With his younger brother, John, attended school until age 13. Effective orphaning apparently gave him the speech defect echolalia – compulsively repeating the last few words of anything said to him.

All four Barnett brothers were licensed as Billingsgate Market fish porters in 1878, Joseph's licence describing him as 5ft 7in tall and fair-haired with blue eyes.

Met Kelly in Commercial Street on Good Friday, 8 April 1887. They met again the following day, and thereafter lived together at various East End addresses, culminating in 13 Miller's Court. Lost his job at Billingsgate around July 1888; Bruce Paley deduces he was dismissed for theft. Licence not restored until 1906. After a dispute with Kelly on 30 October 1888, apparently over their room being shared by another prostitute (or prostitutes), he left and took lodgings at Mr

Buller's boarding-house, Bishopsgate. After the separation, Barnett visited Kelly almost daily and gave her money. On Thursday, 8 November he called at Miller's Court between 7.30pm and 8.00, finding her with 'a female who lived in the same court', whose name he apparently did not know (*see* **Lizzie Albrook**, **Elizabeth Foster**, **Maria Harvey**). He left her room about 8.00pm and returned to Buller's for the remainder of the evening. **Maurice Lewis**, however, claimed to have seen the man who had lived with Kelly up to a few weeks previously drinking with Kelly and **'Julia'** in The Horn of Plenty, though Lewis called the man 'Danny'. After the murder, Barnett moved by his own account to live with his sister at 21 Portpool Lane, Gray's Inn, an address given by his brother Daniel as his own in 1891 (*see* Mark Madden, 'Jack the Ripper?' *Ripperana*, 6, 1993).

The *Wheeling Register* (19 November 1888), an American newspaper, reported that: 'Last week I saw the man, Joe Barnett, who lived with the woman Kelly up to a short time before she was butchered. He then begged for money to bury his poor dear, and wanted it understood that he had a heart as well as men with black coats on. He was furiously drunk at the inquest and is living with a certain notorious Whitechapel character, who testified at the inquest and became enamored of the drunken brute because, as she said, of the romantic interest attaching to him, which illustrates life in London's slums.'

After the murders, Barnett was questioned by police for four hours and his clothes held and examined for bloodstains. He emerged from this investigation cleared of suspicion to the police's satisfaction and lived an uneventful life thereafter, residing in Shadwell for at least the last seven years of his life with his common-law wife, Louisa.

See also **Jack the Ripper: The Mystery Solved** (which erroneously describes as Kelly's lover another Joe Barnett, who lived from 1860–1927) and *Catch Me When You Can*.

BARNETT, REVD. SAMUEL AUGUSTUS (1844–1913)

Suspect, named 2006 by J. Michael Straczynski.

Educated Wadham, Oxon, 1862–65. Curate of St Mary's, Bryanston Square, London, 1867–73. Co-founder of the Charity Organisation Society, 1869. Married Henrietta Rowland in 1873 and became vicar of St Jude's, Whitechapel, the same year. Founded Toynbee Hall (University settlement in Whitechapel), 1884. Resigned St Jude's 1893 to become canon of Bristol Cathedral, but continued association with Whitechapel for the rest of his life. Canon and sub-dean of Westminster, 1905–13.

A noted philanthropist, with his wife he

started the university settlement movement, which encouraged undergraduates to reside with the poor and share educational and cultural opportunities with them. In his lifetime was connected with almost every philanthropic venture aiding the urban poor.

During the Ripper scare, Barnett wrote four letters to *The Times* (published 19 and 29 September, 11 October and 16 November 1888). The first spelled out the desirable reforms which 'at last' (Barnett's phrase stressed by his own quotation marks) might be introduced in Whitechapel. These comprised: 1 efficient police supervision to prevent fighting and theft on the streets; 2 adequate street lighting and cleaning; 3 removal of slaughterhouses; and 4 control of tenement houses by responsible landlords. The last point constituted Barnett's most successful campaign in the wake of the Ripper scare. He called the district north of Toynbee Hall in Commercial Street 'the wicked quarter-mile' (it included Flower and Dean Street, and Dorset Street) and urged slum clearance there.

Barnett was named as a suspect by noted television script-writer Michael Straczynski in *Babylon 5: The Scripts of J. Michael Straczynski, Vol. 4* (Los Angeles: Synthetic Worlds Publishing, 2006), who wrote, 'that the Reverend Samuel Barnett was the Ripper is something I believe almost to a certainty.' His reasons for this belief are that a man thought by some to be the Ripper said to **Catherine Eddowes** [*sic: sc.* **Elizabeth Stride**], 'you would say anything except your prayers,' which to Straczynski suggests he was a man of the cloth; that Barnett suffered a nervous breakdown shortly before the murders; that his social work led to his moving unsuspected through the streets at night; that he was the last person known to have seen two of the victims before their murders; that his wife wrote a letter to *The Times* effectively exonerating the Ripper; that Joseph Barnett was directly related to Samuel and that just as the murders ended, Samuel was reassigned outside England, possibly to America, where more Ripper-type murders occurred.

The case for dismissing this suspicion is that Barnett was not relocated abroad and retained his connection with Whitechapel all his life; that his wife wrote no letter to *The Times*, nor did her letter to Queen Victoria exonerate the Ripper (*see* **Henrietta Barnett**); that there is no evidence Augustus was even remotely related to Joseph Barnett; that to the best of the authors' knowledge, Barnett suffered no nervous breakdown at any time – before, during or after the murders – and he is not known to have been the last person to have seen any of the victims alive.

Cassell's Saturday Journal for 5 April 1899 includes an interview with him on his experience of Whitechapel over 25 years. His wife's work *Canon Barnett: His Life, Work and Friends,* (London: John Murray, 1918) includes a chapter in the second volume that deals with social conditions in Whitechapel and mentions the Ripper scare.

BARRETT, PC THOMAS 226H, (*b.* 1856)

Joined **H Division**, Metropolitan Police, 1883 (warrant no. 67481). Retired, 1908.

Saw a soldier he said was a Grenadier Guardsman, aged 22–26, 5ft 9in tall, of fair complexion, dark hair, with a small brown moustache turned up at the ends, loitering in Wentworth Street at 2.00am on 7 August 1888. The soldier told Barrett he was, 'waiting for a chum who had gone with a girl.' Barrett averred that he would recognise the soldier, if he saw him again (*see* **Martha Tabram**). Barrett was summoned to the scene of **Martha Tabram**'s murder by **John Saunders Reeves** and despatched another constable for **Dr Killeen**.

In an identity parade at the Tower of London, on 15 August 1888, Barrett picked two men, who were both able to establish they were not in or near Wentworth Street on 7 August. (MEPO 3/140 ff.43–48.)

BATCHELOR, J.H.

According to the press, private detective assisting **Le Grand**'s investigations after **Elizabeth Stride**'s murder. **Sgt. Stephen White** reported the two had taken **Matthew Packer** to the mortuary on 4 October 1888, and later in the day took him in a hansom cab to Scotland Yard to see **Sir Charles Warren** (MEPO 3/140/221/A49301Cff212-214). But Le Grand was a confidence trickster who was deceiving the *Evening News* for reasons of his own.

It has been suggested that Batchelor may have been the Woolwich Polytechnic College clerk James Hall, who testified at Le Grand's trial in 1891 that he had worked for him as a clerk, from 1888–89 in the private enquiry agent business run by Le Grand in the Strand. It has similarly been suggested that he was the same man as James Batchelor listed in 1899 as proprietor of the Lion Public House at 309 the Strand, eight doors away from Le Grand's former enquiry agency.

(Gerry Nixon, 'Le Grand of the Strand', *Ripperologist*, 18, August 1998. Repr. *Ripperologist*, 42, August 2002; Tom Wescott, 'Jack and the Grapestalk' *Ripper Notes*, 25, January 2006.)

BATES, THOMAS

Witness at **Elizabeth Stride**'s inquest. Watchman at 32 Flower and Dean Street. Testified that he knew Stride as 'Long Liz' and she tried to make her living charring. He repeated her story about losing her family in the *Princess Alice* riverboat collision disaster; said she left the lodging-house about 7.30pm, seeming cheerful. He further apologised for her prostitution with the words, 'Lor' bless you, when she could get no work she had to do the best she could for her living, but a neater and a cleaner woman never lived' (the *Star*, 1 October 1888).

BATTY STREET LODGER, THE

A simple story made complex by conflicting and often piecemeal news reports about a bloodstained shirt left with a laundress at 22 Batty Street. *The Lodger* argues that the lodger was Francis Tumblety, but this is dismissed in *Prince of Quacks*.

This incident appears to have occurred on the morning of 30 September, following the murders of **Elizabeth Stride** and **Catherine Eddowes** (*Pall Mall Gazette*, 17 October 1888). It was first reported that a lodger awoke his landlady, **Mrs Kuer**, by moving around during the early morning. He claimed that he was going away for a few days, which was not an uncommon thing for him to do, and left with her a shirt for washing. Later in the morning, the landlady, on examining the shirt, found the wristbands and sleeves to be saturated with blood. She gave the shirt to the police, who then maintained surveillance on the house.

It was reported that a man was arrested on suspicion of being the lodger and was released (*Evening News*, 17 October 1888), and following an interview with Mrs Kuer, it was later reported that the man was not one of her lodgers but someone who used her services as a laundress and had brought her a bundle of four shirts for washing. He was a foreigner and a ladies' tailor, who worked in the West End; he had been arrested and released by the police. The blood, she said, was that of one of her lodgers, who had had an accident (*Evening News, Daily News*, 18 October 1888). Further clarification was given by a lodger in the house, Carl Noun, a baker who had been working in Margate for the summer and had just returned, and a man named Joseph, who worked for the Norwegian Lager Beer Company (*Evening News*, 18 October 1888).

(*See* Gavin Bromley, 'Mrs Kuer's Lodger', *Ripperologist*, 81, July 2007.)

BAXTER, WYNNE EDWIN (1844–1920)

Coroner presiding over inquests on **Mary Ann Nichols, Annie Chapman**, **Elizabeth Stride**, **Rose Mylett**, **Alice McKenzie** and **Frances Coles**. Born and resident in Lewes, where his family published the local newspaper. Became a solicitor instead of entering the family firm; nonetheless retained a strong interest in Sussex newspaper publishing. Junior headborough of Lewes, 1868. The same year married Kate Bliss Parker and set up house in her native borough of Stoke Newington. Opened a second solicitor's practice in London, 1875. Under-sheriff of London and Middlesex, 1876–79 and 1885–86; junior constable 1878; junior high constable of Lewes, 1878; senior high constable 1880 and 1881; and first mayor (1881).

A large portrait of Baxter hangs in Lewes Town Hall: it was prsented by the Worshipful Company of Gold and Silver Wyredrawers, of which he was an active and energetic member, as he was also an active Freemason. His publications include the standard work on *Judicature Acts and Rules* (3rd edn., London: Butterworths, 1879), though he narrowly won a lawsuit charging him with breach of copyright.

So firmly associated with the duties of coroner that by the end of his life he was using the telegraphic address 'Inquest, London'. Coroner for Sussex in 1880; deputy coroner for the City of London and Borough of Southwark in 1885. He won the hotly contested election of 1886 to replace recently deceased Sir John Humphreys as coroner for East Middlesex (*see* Dr **Roderick MacDonald**).

A year later, the division was subdivided. Baxter became coroner for Whitechapel and Spitalfields, while Dr Roderick MacDonald became coroner for Hoxton and Hackney.

According to press reportage of the Ripper inquests, Baxter was a flamboyant and dressy coroner.

At Mary Ann Nichols' inquest, held in the Whitechapel Working Lads' Institute (next to the present Whitechapel Underground station) on 1 September (reconvened 3, 17, 23 September), he seemed critical of the police. He criticised them for failing to observe the abdominal mutilations before taking the body to the mortuary, and for not having ordered the washing of the body under their own observation. **Inspector Helson**'s claim that the mortuary had acted without regard to police instructions was rebutted by pauper **James Hatfield**, who laid the body out. When a juror pointed out that Hatfield's memory was so poor that he had denied the body wore stays, although he had personally shown them to the jury when they visited the mortuary, Baxter snappishly defended Hatfield.

Annie Chapman's inquest in the Working Lads' Institute (12, 13, 14, 19, 26 September) saw the zenith of Baxter's public standing in the Ripper affair. In summing up, he suggested the motive was the extraction of the missing uterus for sale, since an American doctor's offer of £20 each for specimens to enclose with subscription copies of a monograph he was writing indicated a possible market. He was praised in the press for drawing attention to this abuse and contrasted favourably with Scotland Yard, but the *British Medical Journal* corrected Baxter, who did not repeat the theory at Elizabeth Stride's inquest (1, 2, 3, 5, 23 October in the Vestry Hall, Cable Street).

Hostile elements in the press too suggested it had always been a foolish idea. Moreover, Baxter's summation was of dubious legality, since it amounted to his putting himself before the jury as an unsworn witness. Nevertheless, according to a Press Association interview with Dr **George Bagster Phillips** (*Freeman's Journal 27 September 1888*), the police surgeon took the American doctor story very seriously indeed, and it was in order not to alert any interested doctor or supplier that he tried to suppress evidence of the posthumous injuries to Annie Chapman at the inquest.

Baxter conducted Rose Mylett's inquest (21 December 1888; 3, 9 January 1889, in Poplar Coroner's Court) and at Frances Coles' inquest, on 15 February 1891, Baxter refused to let **Albert Bachert** appear as a reserve juror.

In *Jack the Ripper: The Final Solution*, Stephen Knight claimed that Baxter's protracted inquests brought him into conflict with the Freemasons, who did not want the murders investigated. Baxter was himself a Freemason. A very thorough account of Baxter's career (Adam Wood, 'Inquest, London', *Ripperologist, 61*, September 2005), concludes that he was an active, conscientious and highly responsible coroner, who made great improvements in the system.

Robert Lindford, John Savage and David O'Flaherty, who, in *Ripperologist 64*, March 2006, give the best account of the East Middlesex coroner's election, followed it in 69 (July 2006) with an exhaustive survey of the possible whereabouts of coroners' papers. Baxter's inquest papers on the Ripper victims have long been among the most highly desired missing documents, but none have ever been found. Lindford, Savage and O'Flaherty discovered Victorian coroners usually retained their papers as they could charge those who wanted copies of testimony. On their deaths, the local authorities made efforts to recover them. Baxter, it transpired, had carefully preserved 840 foolscap volumes of inquest notes and transcripts (an estimated two tons of paperwork). After his death, his son offered them to the London County Council, which was already short of storage space, and proposed keeping them in County Hall. Though there is no record of the handover, it seems likely the Council did accept and subsequently destroyed them in a salvage drive.

BAYLEY, JOSEPH and THOMAS
Packing-case makers operating from 23a Hanbury Street (the yard of The Black Swan public house). A piece of crumpled paper, saturated in blood, was found in their yard on 11 September and believed to prove that the murderer had followed the route indicated by Laura Sickings' supposed blood-stain in no. 25. But police asserted the paper had not been there on the day of the murder. *See also* **James Green, James Kent**.

BAYNE, THOMAS VERE (1829–1908)
Suspect, proposed in 1996.

Educated Radley and Christ Church, Oxford. Fellow and tutor of Christ Church, where he became senior censor and archivist. Colleague of **Charles Lutwidge Dodgson** (**Lewis Carroll**), who had been a friend from childhood.

Claimed in *Jack the Ripper: 'Light-Hearted Friend'* to have been implicated with Carroll in the Ripper murders and possibly to have written the **'Dear Boss' letter**, 'proving' this with anagrams of passages from Carroll's journals and writings.

BEACH, THOMAS MILLER (MAJOR HENRI LE CARON), (1841–94)
Informant. Spy, controlled by Dr **Robert Anderson**. Infiltrated Fenian movement in America. Published *Twenty-five Years in the Secret Service* (Henri Le Caron,

London: Heinemann, 1892), which highly praises Anderson. For unknown reasons, some sources give his middle name as Millis or Billis.

BEADMOORE, BEADMORE, BEATMORE, BEEDMORE, BEETMORE, or PEATMORE, JANE, aka JANE SAVAGE (1861–88)

Murder victim, briefly suspected of having fallen prey to the Ripper. *See Alias Jack the Ripper*, **William Waddle**.

BECK, INSPECTOR WALTER (1852–1927)

Probably first policeman at the site of Mary Jane Kelly's murder.

A former gardener, joined Metropolitan Police in 1871 (warrant no. 53559). Resigned in 1896.

On duty as station inspector, Commercial Road Police Station, 9 November 1888, Beck deposed at the inquest: 'I was the first police officer called to 13 Miller's Court by McCarthy...[I]t was shortly after 11 o'clock when I was called.' **Abberline** noted Beck went to the scene with constables on duty. No mention is made in contemporary police reports of the presence of **Walter Dew**, **Sergeant Godley** or **Sergeant Badham**, who were all at one time or another described by themselves or others as first at the scene.

BEDFORD, DUKE OF

Alleged suspect. *See* **Francis Russell**, **George Russell**.

BEDHAM, SERGEANT

See **Sergeant Badham**.

BELL TOWER, THE: THE MYSTERY OF JACK THE RIPPER FINALLY SOLVED... IN AMERICA

Work by Robert Graysmith. (Washington DC: Regnery Publishing: 1999). The book argues that **Revd. John George Gibson** was Jack the Ripper.

An account of the rivalry between William Randolph Hearst and sensational newspaper publishers, the De Young brothers, leads to re-examination of San Francisco's most famous sexual killings and concludes pastor of Emmanuel Baptist Church, John Gibson, was the accomplice of a militiaman who gave evidence against Theodore Durrant, who was executed for the crimes – wrongly, Graysmith concludes. Noting the pastor's career had spaces at the times of the Ripper and **Carrie Brown** murders, Graysmith focuses on the idea of Gibson as Jack the Ripper. The book is written in a dramatising style with individuals' thoughts and conversations being given when they could not have been known. One prominent journalist described in the account is admitted to be a fictional character and it is ultimately impossible to know where fact ends and imagination takes over.

BELLORD, EDMUND JOSEPH (1857–1927)

A founder and leading committee member of Providence Row Night Refuge. Solicitor and, according to *Jack the Ripper: The Final Solution*, partner in Perkins and Bellord, estate agents of Cleveland Street. Admitted to the Roll, 1881; practised in Queen Victoria Street, 1881–93. *Jack the Ripper: The Final Solution* claims that when the tobacconist at 22 Cleveland Street needed an assistant, **Walter Sickert** approached 'a lawyer who ran an East End refuge for poor working women', who brought **Mary Jane Kelly** to Cleveland Street. This is apparently a reference to Bellord.

BELLOSELSKI, PRINCE SERGE (1867–1951)

Informant. Russian exile. Allegedly showed **Donald McCormick** (*see* **The Identity of Jack the Ripper**) copy of the *Ochrana Gazette* for January 1909 containing request for return of files on **Vassily Konovalov**.

If, as described, this item did give **Alexei Pedachenko** as Konovalov's alias, it supplies the only known link between Konovalov and Pedachenko (otherwise known to us from **William Le Queux**).

BENCH AND THE DOCK, THE

Book by Charles Kingston (London: Stanley Paul, 1925).

Contains a chapter about **Adolphus Williamson** and another on **James Monro**, the latter containing a brief account of the Ripper, in which mention is made of a 'dark and dour' alley where a murder was committed, despite it being watched day and night by the police. States that a well-known West End doctor was among those denounced, but investigation proved that he had been in Italy when the murders were committed. Refers to another suspect as a young medical student at St. Bartholomew's who had suddenly gone mad.

BENELIUS, NIKANER A. (b. c. 1861)

Suspected and cleared 1888. Swedish traveller, arrested by **PC Imhoff** on 17 November 1888, after unlawfully entering Harriet Rowe's house in Buxton Street and grinning at her without speaking. Previously he had written two letters to 'The City Mayor of London' (which were forwarded to **Major Henry Smith** of the City Police). The first, dated 4 October 1888, asked the mayor to ensure that 'the young Miss Wilkinson' or 'another lady' should be in the city on 5 October to meet with Benelius at 'the same cathedral'. The second, dated 18 October and acknowledging reply from the Mayor, asked him to introduce Benelius into his family circle and help him if he (the Mayor) knew that Benelius had lost something.

It transpired Benelius was behaving strangely and preaching in the streets. **Walter Dew** testified Benelius had previously been questioned about **Elizabeth Stride**'s murder and **Inspector Reid** told the press Benelius had been fully investigated and cleared of all connection with the murders (*The Times*, and the *Star*, 19 November 1888). The Charity Organization Society offered to try and arrange for him to emigrate to America (the *Star*, 23 November 1888). It is suggested he suffered from paranoid delusions.

(Jan Bondeson, 'More About the Suspect Benelius', *Ripperologist,* 57, January 2005.)

BERRY, JAMES (1852–1913)
Public hangman.

According to Newmarket journalist **Ernest A. Parr**, writing on 28 March 1908 to the Secretary of State for Scotland, James Berry – who hanged **William Henry Bury** at Dundee Prison in April 1889 – explicitly told him that Bury was known to have been Jack the Ripper. Parr acknowledged he had come across the statement in a paper which claimed that Bury had confessed in writing to having committed the murders and this confession was passed to the Secretary of State for Scotland so Berry may only have been repeating this story, but having executed Bury, he might have been privy to some private information.

In *Thomson's Weekly News* (12 February 1927), using a complilation of notes and diaries which had recently been discovered, Berry was recalled as saying that two detectives from Scotland Yard had approached him after the execution for his opinion on whether Bury was Jack the Ripper. 'I think it is him right enough,' Berry replied. 'And we agree with you,' replied one of the detectives. 'We know all about his movements in the past, and we are quite satisfied that you have hanged "Jack the Ripper" – there will be no more Whitechapel crimes.'

Berry wrote an autobiography, *My Experiences as an Executioner* (London: Lund & Co, 1892), which mentions neither Bury nor Jack the Ripper; and he has been the subject of a book by Stewart P. Evans, *Executioner: The Chronicles of James Berry, Victorian Hangman* (Stroud, Gloucestershir, The History Press, 2005). Evans remarks that Berry perhaps tried a little too hard to prove that Bury was Jack the Ripper.

BEST, –
Journalist. Alleged author of **'Jack the Ripper' letters**.

Nigel Morland, in *Crime and Detection* (Oxford: Tallis Press, June 1966), described meeting, in 1931, a 'very spry and clear-minded' 70-year-old ex-journalist named Best, who spoke of his days as a freelance penny-a-liner on the *Star* newspaper. He claimed to have covered the Whitechapel murders from the discovery of **Tabram** and 'claimed that he, and a provincial colleague, were responsible for *all* the "Ripper" letters, to "keep the business alive…" Best did not mind me having these facts so many years later and said a close reading of the *Star* of the time might be informative, and that an experienced graphologist with an open mind would be able to find in the original letters "numerous earmarks" of an experienced journalist at work; the pen used was called a "Waverly Nib" and was deliberately battered to achieve the impression of semi-literacy and "National School" training! Best scoffed at the notion that the "Ripper" had written a single word about his crimes.'

We may note Best was probably unaware of the full total of 'Ripper' letters sent to the police and held on file, but his confidence suggests he claimed responsibility for the most widely reported missives, including the **'Dear Boss' letter**, although this does not fit the description of having been written with a battered nib, which better described the Lusk Letter.

BEST, J.
Witness at **Elizabeth Stride**'s inquest. Labourer, residing 82 Lower Chapman Street. With **John Gardner**, saw a woman he later identified as Stride leave The Bricklayers' Arms in Settles Street with a man shortly before 11pm on 29 September 1888. The couple were sheltering from a rainstorm when Best and Gardiner started 'chipping' them, saying, 'That's "**Leather Apron**" getting round you'. The man they saw was about 5ft 5in tall, with a black moustache and weak, sandy eyelashes; he wore a morning suit and billycock hat. He was definitely English (*Evening News*, 1 October 1888). *Cf.* **William Marshal**.

BEST, FREDERICK (*b. c.*1858)
Journalist working for the *Star*.

Alleged in *Jack the Ripper* (Andrew Cook, 2009) to have been sent to Whitechapel with a colleague named Michael O'Brien to obtain human interest stories about the Whitechapel murders, that he originated the '**Leather Apron**' story and when that story petered out, following the exoneration and release of **John Pizer**, wrote the **'Dear Boss' letter**. Graphologist Elaine Quigley compared Best's handwriting with that of the 'Dear Boss' letter and concluded: 'I am as sure as I can be. I really do not think that it's anyone other than Best that wrote the "Dear Boss" letter.'

Support for this contention is a letter dated 7 July 1890 from John Brunner, a principle shareholder of the Star, in which he wrote: 'I have submitted on a number of occasions that Mr O'Connor's former use of compatriots such as Messrs. Best and O'Brien have not only been responsible for several potential legal actions against the *Star*, but in the unfortunate case of Mr. Parke, a somewhat more serious consequence in January last.

'Furthermore, Mr Best's attempt to mislead Central News during the Whitechapel Murders should have led to an earlier termination of his association with the newspaper.'

It has been noted the letter's signature line was typed 'John J Brunner' whereas Brunner's initial was 'T' (Tomlinson).

Cook does not connect Frederick Best with the journalist **Best**. In a letter to the authors (September 2009), he explained that while he was aware of Best's confession, he omitted it for fear it would 'interrupt the flow of his narrative'. Cook appears to have been unaware of **Harry Dam**, an American journalist employed by the *Star*, and claims Frederick Best was the only journalist working for that newspaper who had American connections, having just returned from a sojourn in America.

BETTLES, PC WILLIE, 190H (1867–1938)
Warrant no: 72919.

Left by **PC Long** to guard the **Goulston Street graffito** for about two hours, while Long went to summon assistance (not, as has sometimes been suggested, William Henry Bate). Labourer before joining **H Division** in November 1887. Transferred to C Division 1890 and retired as Station Sergeant (V Division) in April 1913. Died in Richmond, Surrey.

At the inquest PC Long stated that following his discovery of the Goulston Street graffito, he left the site in charge of PC 190 H, whose name he did not know. A report at the time of his retirement recalled: 'Ex-Sergeant Bettles has many memories, not all pleasant, for while at the Commercial-road Station the "Jack the Ripper" crimes horrified all London, and in four of them he was so closely connected that his evidence was necessary at the inquests' (*Richmond And Twickenham Times*, 10 May 1913).

BIERMAN, ROSE
Witness. Described the assault on **Ada Wilson** (*Eastern Post,* 31 March 1888).

BIRRELL (or BURRELL), EMILY
Vagrant, friend of **Catherine Eddowes**.

Emily Birrell, with her man, met Catherine Eddowes and **John Kelly** on their return from hop-picking in Kent, September 1888. Emily gave Eddowes a London pawnbroker's ticket for a man's shirt, since she and her man were going to Cheltenham. The ticket in her name was subsequently found in the mustard tin beside Eddowes' body, and on reading press reports of the name 'Birrell', Kelly came forward and identified Eddowes (the *Star* 1, 2 October 1888; *The Times*, 2, 3 October 1888).

BLACKWELL, DR FREDERICK WILLIAM (1851–1900)

Doctor called to pronounce **Elizabeth Stride** dead.

LRCP, LRCS (Edin.), 1882. Resided at 100 Commercial Road, where he shared offices with a **Dr Kay**.

PC Collins went directly to the office (Dr Kay being familiar to the police as having worked on the Lipski case), where Blackwell was asleep. The doctors' assistant, Edward Johnston, woke him and he dressed and proceeded to Berner Street. Blackwell arrived at the murder scene at 1.16am precisely and determined Stride had been dead no more than 20 minutes. Blackwell believed she had been killed standing up, her head dragged back by the silk handkerchief around her neck and her throat cut. He described her right hand as open and empty; her left was clasping cachous wrapped in tissue, which he spilled as he removed them. He did not see any grapestalks and did not hear anybody refer to them.

He was robbed of a watch stolen in Whitechapel High Street by John Cook in 1892 (*Lloyd's Weekly News*, 1 May 1892) and in 1896 he vaccinated a child, Florence Sweeny, who died. An inquest, held by **Dr Houchin,** eventually concluded that death was not caused by the vaccination.(*Reynolds's Newspaper*, 12 April 1896)

BLAVATSKY, HELENA PETROVNA (1831–91)

Misunderstood to be suspect. Comparative religion pioneer; co-founder of the Theosophical Society. **Aleister Crowley**, in an unpublished essay considering occultist suspicions relating to Jack the Ripper, remarked: 'It is hardly one's first, or even one's hundredth guess that the Victorian worthy in the case of Jack the Ripper was no less a person than Helena Petrovna Blavatsky.' By this, he meant Mme Blavatsky was obviously *not* the Ripper, but a few readers misconstrued him as saying that she was.

BLENKINGSOP or BLENKINSOP, JAMES

Informant. Nightwatchman, overseeing roadworks in St James's Place (adjacent to, and accessible from Mitre Square). Told the *Star* (1 October 1888) that at about 1.30am, on 30 September 1888, a respectably dressed man approached him and asked, 'Have you seen a man and a woman go through here?' Blenkingsop replied that he had seen some people pass, but had not taken any notice. It seems inconceivable this story was not fully investigated by the City Police. Blenkingsop was not called to the inquest. *The Complete History of Jack the Ripper* suggests he may have been 10 minutes or more out in his estimate of the time and the man who questioned him could have been a plain-clothes police detective. (*Cf.* **unidentified witnesses at Mitre Square**.)

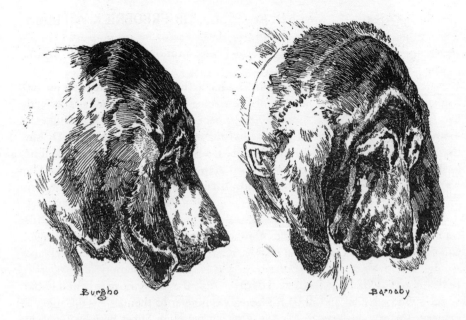

Burgho   Barnaby

BLOODHOUNDS

That bloodhounds be used in hunting the murderer appears to have been first suggested by 'A Whitechapel Workman' (*Lloyd's Weekly Newspaper*, 9 September 1888) and was much discussed in Whitechapel. At the inquest on **Annie Chapman** (19 September), in reply to the jury, **George Bagster Phillips** said that in his opinion bloodhounds would probably scent the blood of the murdered woman (*The Times*, 20 September 1888). On 2 October 1888, a bloodhound breeder named Percy Lindley wrote to *The Times* saying they would be useless unless put on the scent as soon as the body was discovered. Various newspapers reported on 6 October an official statement that **Sir Charles Warren** had made inquiries and had ascertained that dogs accustomed to work in a town were available.

Letters about the effectiveness of bloodhounds were widely published in newspapers and journals, including the *Field*, and the *Pall Mall Gazette* (9 October 1888) even published 'A Ballad of Bloodhounds', which began:

> Shall Jack the Ripper's arts avail
> To battle Scotland-yard forsooth?
> Quick – on the flying murderer's trail
> Unleash the bloodhound, Truth!

Edwin Brough, a breeder of Scarborough who wrote a letter to *The Times* on 8 October, was invited to bring two dogs, Burgho and champion Barnaby, to London. Police trials in Regent's Park on 9 October were very successful; in Hyde Park the following day, less so. **Sir Charles Warren** sportingly offered himself as 'fox' for the second trial, for which he was ridiculed, though it is not true that the dogs bit him. (This legend appears to have been started by an innuendo in *Police Review* for 29 October 1897.)

On 19 October a canard appeared in the press to the effect that Barnaby and Burgho had been taken on training in Tooting and were lost. In fact, Burgho was in the care of Mr Edward Taunton, being trained at Hemel Hempstead. Barnaby had been returned to Mr Brough. Experiment had shown the dogs could not follow trails through crowded city streets and the police decided against buying them. Nevertheless, this decision was so far from being made known to the CID in Whitechapel that **Abberline**, **Reid** and **Arnold** delayed entering **Mary Jane Kelly**'s room for two hours in case Scotland Yard should want the dogs to be first on the murder scene.

(The National Achives have a Home Office file, HO 144/221/A49301E concerning bloodhounds. Nick Connell, 'The Bloodhound Experiment', *Criminologist*, Vol. 22, No. 4, 1998.)

BOGAN, PC WILLIAM (*b. c.* 1860)

Witness who testified to some of **Thomas Sadler**'s movements on the night of **Frances Coles**' murder.

Born County Cork. Worked as a clerk before joining Metropolitan Police (**H Division**; warrant no. 66142) in December 1881.

At 1.15am, on 13 February 1891, Bogan found Sadler lying drunk outside the main gate to London Docks. Sadler asked Bogan to let him in, but Bogan said he was too drunk and apparently permitted an altercation, which Sadler started with two dock workers, to develop into a fight in which Sadler took a relatively severe beating. At 2.00am, when Sadler was complaining to **Sgt. Wesley Edwards** and **PC Hyde**, Bogan joined them, and Sadler left. The altercation led to a question in Parliament, on 26 February 1891, as to whether Sadler should not have been given police protection in his drunken state. **Henry Matthews** defended Bogan's action,

P. C. Bogan on duty at the London Docks.

saying the Police Commissioner reported Sadler's claim to have suffered severe bruising was unsupported and Bogan reckoned him insufficiently intoxicated to warrant arrest. Bogan was transferred to L Division on 9 March 1891. The transfer may have been a mild disciplinary action for having acted in such a way as to cause a question in Parliament. Bogan was dismissed on 20 November for refusing to pay for fried fish he had obtained when drunk and assaulting the shopkeeper who asked for payment.

BOND, DR THOMAS (1841–1901)

Police surgeon to A Division (Whitehall). Submitted reports on **Mary Jane Kelly**, **Alice McKenzie** and **Rose Mylett**; also a general report on the Ripper murders for **Robert Anderson**'s benefit. Educated at King's College and King's College Hospital. MRCS, 1864; MB, 1865; FRCS, 1866. Served with Prussian Army, 1866. Surgeon to A Division, Metropolitan Police, 1867. Assistant surgeon, Westminster Hospital, 1873; surgeon, 1897, where he was also a lecturer on forensic medicine, a post he had held since at least 1872, and contemporary sources refer to him as an 'acknowledged expert' an 'expert witness'. He was probably *the* expert of his day, esteemed by his colleagues, often brought in when other medical evidence was in dispute. No criticism of him has been found in contemporary legal and medical sources. Committed suicide, throwing himself from bedroom window, after a long period of insomnia and depression followed by a painful illness.

Bond's first Ripper-related action was a post-mortem report on the Whitehall Mystery torso, which he presented to the inquest on 8 October 1888. This, he found to be the torso of a well-nourished, plump, tall (*c.* 5ft. 8in) woman with a fair complexion and dark hair, suffering pleurisy in one lung. Bond was unable to determine the cause of death, but believed from the bloodless heart that it was not drowning or suffocation. He found that the arm recovered from the Thames at Pimlico was from the same woman, likewise a leg found lightly buried and heavily decomposed in the same New Scotland Yard building site vault as the torso. The limbs had been skilfully disarticulated, the torso very efficiently tied and bundled. When examining the site where the leg was found, Bond also determined the torso had been in the vault far longer than police evidence claimed, as decomposition fluid had seeped into the place where it previously lay, showing it had been there for some weeks.

On 16 October, he examined a dangerous lunatic brought to King Street Police Station, who made rambling remarks about the Whitechapel murders and threatened to cut the sergeant's head off.

Then, on 25 October, Robert Anderson asked Bond to assist in the Ripper investigation. He studied the inquest testimony on the first four canonical murders and, having seen Mary Jane Kelly's body, submitted the following report on 10 November:

I beg to report that I have read the notes of the four
Whitechapel Murders, viz:
1. Buck's Row
2. Hanbury Street

3. Berner's [sic] Street
4. Mitre Square.

I have also made a Post Mortem Examination of the mutilated remains of a woman found yesterday in a small room in Dorset Street:

1. All five murders were no doubt committed by the same hand. In the first four the throats appear to have been cut from left to right. In the last case owing to the extensive mutilation it is impossible to say in what direction the fatal cut was made, but arterial blood was found on the wall in splashes close to where the woman's head must have been lying.
2. All the circumstances surrounding the murders lead me to form the opinion that the women must have been lying down when murdered and in every case the throat was first cut.
3. In the four murders of which I have seen the notes only, I cannot form a very definite opinion as to the time that had elapsed between the murder and the discovering of the body. In one case, that of Berner's [sic] Street, the discovery appears to have been made immediately after the deed – in Buck's Row, Hanbury Street, and Mitre Square three or four hours only could have elapsed. In the Dorset Street Case the body was lying on the bed at the time of my visit, two o'clock, quite naked and mutilated as in the annexed report – Rigor Mortis had set in, but increased during the progress of the examination. From this it is difficult to say with any degree of certainty the exact time that had elapsed since death as the period varies from 6 to 12 hours before rigidity sets in. The body was comparatively cold at 2 o'clock and the remains of a recently taken meal were found in the stomach and scattered about over the intestines. It is, therefore, pretty certain that the woman must have been dead about twelve hours and the partly digested food would indicate that death took place about 3 or 4 hours after the food was taken, so 1 or 2 o'clock in the morning would be the probable time of the murder.
4. In all the cases there appears to be no evidence of struggling and the attacks were probably so sudden and made in such a position that the women could neither resist nor cry out. In the Dorset Street case the corner of the sheet to the right of the woman's head was much cut and saturated with blood, indicating that the face may have been covered with the sheet at the time of the attack.
5. In the four first cases the murderer must have attacked from the right side of the victim. In the Dorset Street case, he must have attacked in front or from the left, as there would be no room for him between the wall and the part of the bed on which the woman was lying. Again, the blood had flowed down on the right side of the woman and spurted on to the wall.
6. The murderer would not necessarily be splashed or deluged with blood,

60

but his hands and arms must have been covered and parts of his clothing must certainly have been smeared with blood.

7. The mutilations in each case excepting the Berner's [sic] Street one were all of the same character and showed clearly that in all the murders the object was mutilation.

8. In each case the mutilation was inflicted by a person who had no scientific nor anatomical knowledge. In my opinion he does not even possess the technical knowledge of a butcher or horse slaughterer or any person accustomed to cut up dead animals.

9. The instrument must have been a strong knife at least six inches long, very sharp, pointed at the top and about an inch in width. It may have been a clasp knife, a butcher's knife or a surgeon's knife. I think it was no doubt a straight knife.

10. The murderer must have been a man of physical strength and of great coolness and daring. There is no evidence that he had an accomplice. He must in my opinion be a man subject to periodical attacks of Homicidal and erotic mania. The character of the mutilations indicates that the man may be in a condition sexually, that may be called satyriasis. It is of course possible that the Homicidal impulse may have developed from a revengeful or brooding condition of the mind, or that Religious Mania may have been the original disease, but I do not think either hypothesis is likely. The murderer in external appearance is quite likely to be a quiet inoffensive looking man probably middle-aged and neatly and respectably dressed. I think he must be in the habit of wearing a cloak or overcoat or he could hardly have escaped notice in the streets if the blood on his hands or clothes were visible.

11. Assuming the murderer to be such a person as I have just described he would probably be solitary and eccentric in his habits, also he is most likely to be a man without regular occupation, but with some small income or pension. He is possibly living among respectable persons who have some knowledge of his character and habits and who may have grounds for suspicion that he is not quite right in his mind at times. Such persons would probably be unwilling to communicate suspicions to the Police for fear of trouble or notoriety, whereas if there were a prospect of reward it might overcome their scruples.

This report is identified by Prof. David Canter in *Criminal Shadows* (London: Harper Collins, 1994), as an early example of criminal profiling. Scotia J. Hicks and Bruce D. Sales in *Criminal Profiling* (Washington DC: American Psychological Association, 2006) call it the first-ever genuine criminal profile, preceded only by the fictional profiles drawn up in the short stories of Edgar Allen Poe and the novels of Wilkie Collins.

Bond's deductions are of limited intrinsic value, since he argues for instantaneous and silent killing in every case, despite the defence wounds on Mary

Jane Kelly's hands which he had observed. He accepts circumstantially impossible times of death for the cases on which he had read notes, but he sets up immediate conflict with **Dr Phillips**, who argued the five murders were *not* by the same hand and that skill *was* shown in **Chapman**'s, **Stride**'s and Kelly's cases, though not, apparently, in that of Eddowes.

His report on Mary Jane Kelly, recovered by Scotland Yard in 1987, follows:

Position of body
The body was lying naked in the middle of the bed, the shoulders flat, but the axis of the body inclined to the left side of the bed. The head was turned on the left cheek. The left arm was close to the body with the forearm flexed at a right angle & lying across the abdomen. The right arm was slightly abducted from the body & rested on the mattress, the elbow bent & the forearm supine with the fingers clenched. The legs were wide apart, the left thigh at right angles to the trunk & the right forming an obtuse angle with the pubes.

The whole of the surface of the abdomen & thighs was removed & the abdominal Cavity emptied of its viscera. The breasts were cut off, the arms mutilated by several jagged wounds & the face hacked beyond recognition of the features. The tissues of the neck were severed all round down to the bone.

The viscera were found in various parts viz: the uterus & Kidneys with one breast under the head, the other breast by the Rt foot, the Liver between the feet, the intestines by the right side & the spleen by the left side of the body. The flaps removed from the abdomen and thighs were on a table.

The bed clothing at the right corner was saturated with blood, & on the floor beneath was a pool of blood covering about 2 feet square. The wall by the right side of the bed & in a line with the neck was marked by blood which had struck it in a number of separate splashes.

Postmortem examination
The face was gashed in all directions, the nose, cheeks, eyebrows and ears being partly removed. The lips were blanched & cut by several incisions running obliquely down to the chin. There were also numerous cuts extending irregularly across all the features.

The neck was cut through the skin & other tissues right down to the vertebrae the 5th & 6th being deeply notched. The skin cuts in the front of the neck showed distinct ecchymosis.

The air passage was cut at the lower part of the larynx through the cricoid cartilage.

Both breasts were removed by more or less circular incisions, the muscles down to the ribs being attached to the breasts. The intercostals between the 4th, 5th & 6th ribs were cut through & the contents of the thorax visible through the openings.

The skin & tissues of the abdomen from the costal arch to the pubes were removed in three large flaps. The right thigh was denuded in front to the bone, the flap of skin, including the external organs of generation & part of the right buttock. The left thigh was stripped of skin, fascia & muscles as far as the knee.

The left calf showed a long gash through skin & tissues to the deep muscles & reaching from the knee to 5 ins above the ankle. Both arms & forearms had extensive & jagged wounds.

The right thumb showed a small superficial incision about 1in long, with extravasation of blood in the skin & there were several abrasions on the back of the hand moreover showing the same condition.

On opening the thorax it was found that the right lung was minimally adherent by old firm adhesions. The lower part of the lung was broken & torn away.

The left lung was intact: it was adherent at the apex & there were a few adhesions over the side. In the substances of the lung were several nodules of consolidation.

The Pericardium was open below & the Heart absent.

In the abdominal cavity was some partly digested food of fish & potatoes & similar food was found in the remains of the stomach attached to the intestines.

In two detailed articles in *The Criminologist* (vol. 21, no. 1, spring 1997 and *The New Criminologist,* 23 April 2006, and a supporting article in **Ripperana,** 56, April 2006, Stephen Gouriet Ryan argues this report, lacking Bond's signature and the date, and omitting information supplied by Bond's assistant **Dr Hebbert** for inclusion in an American book on medicine and the law, must be missing its last page (or pages). These would have shown clearly that Bond's cryptic phrase 'heart absent' definitely meant the heart was removed from the room; not merely that it was extracted from the thorax. And he notes the omission of any reference in the report to numerous organs known to have been extracted allows the possibility that **Inspector Moore** and the contemporary press were, in fact, perfectly correct in suggesting parts of the body had been draped over nails in the wall.

We may note that Bond makes the error of describing the body as naked, though it actually wore the remains of a chemise. The extraction of the heart through the severed diaphragm suggests to some researchers a degree of medical skill. Abberline was apparently unaware of, or had forgotten the discovery of the uterus when he told the *Pall Mall Gazette* that the murderer was harvesting wombs for sale to an American doctor.

In Mylett's case, Bond at first confirmed the opinion of previous doctors that she had been strangled with a piece of string, but after a second visit opined she had choked to death, having compressed her larynx against the neck of her jacket, concluding the mark on the neck – which other doctors thought had been made with a cord – had been made by the collar of the jacket, possibly after death.

In Alice McKenzie's case he again disputed George Bagster Phillips' findings: 'I see in this murder evidence of similar design to the former Whitechapel Murders viz: sudden onslaught on the prostrate woman, the throat skilfully & resolutely cut with subsequent mutilation, each mutilation indicating sexual thoughts & a desire to mutilate the abdomen & sexual organs.

'I am of opinion that the murder was performed by the same person who committed the former series of Whitechapel Murders.'

This time, his conclusions were not accepted.

BOOTH, 'GENERAL' WILLIAM (1829–1912)

Erroneously alleged theorist. Evangelist; founder of Christian Mission in Whitechapel, 1865 (renamed Salvation Army, 1878). Confused by Colin Wilson, when working from memory, with **Commissioner David Lamb** of the Salvation Army, who did suggest a suspect. Booth is not known to have held any views on the identity of the Ripper.

In January 1890, Booth was brought before the magistrates charged with keeping an unregistered lodging-house, which he had opened as a night shelter for streetwalkers endangered by the Ripper.

BOSWELL, SERGEANT FRANCIS WILLIAM (*b.*1852)

Joined Metropolitan Police in 1873 (warrant no. 56813); resigned 1899. W Division (Clapham). Officer who took charge of 1891–93 investigation of **James Thomas Sadler**, following complaints from his wife that he assaulted and threatened to murder her. Mrs Sadler and an elderly lodger, James Moffatt, confirmed Sadler was an extremely violent man, who persistently used startlingly vile language. The desultory investigation dragged on until Sadler left his wife in March 1893 (MEPO 3/140 ff.92–97, 109–111).

BOULTBEE, WALTER ERNEST (1853–97)

Marital connection of the Druitt family. Private secretary to **Sir Charles Warren**, **James Monro** and **Sir Edward Bradford** successively. Married 1885, Ellen Baker, niece of Alfred Mayo, a lasting friend and distant relative of Thomas Druitt (*d.* 1891). In fact, the interrelated Druitt, Mayo and Elton families, all with members who emigrated to Australia, have retained links to the present day and long shared mutual genealogical interests. It is, at the very least, food for thought that a connection of this clan should have been ensconced in Scotland Yard when **Melville Macnaghten** picked up 'private information' about the family's suspicions of **Montague John Druitt**.

BOUSFIELD, JAMES WILLIAM (c. 1880–1960)

Informant.

Son of **Mary Bousfield**, who, shortly before his death, gave **Tom Cullen** an interview and showed him a key chain from **Martha Tabram**'s stock as a hawker, which he retained as a souvenir.

BOUSFIELD, MRS MARY (alias Luckhurst)

Witness at **Martha Tabram**'s inquest.

Formerly Martha's landlady at 4 Star Place, where she lived with her husband, wood chopper William Bousfield. Martha left, her rent unpaid, about three weeks before her death. According to Mrs Bousfield, she sold matches for a living. MEPO Files 3/140/4 and the press give her name as Bousfield; MEPO file 3/140/3 gives it as Luckhurst.

BOWYER, THOMAS, 'INDIAN HARRY'

Discoverer of **Mary Jane Kelly**'s body. A 'somewhat sharp featured man with a coal begrimed visage' (*Sunday Times,* 11 November 1888). **Walter Dew** recollected a young man, describing him variously in *I Caught Crippen* as 'a young fellow' and 'the youth'.

Bowyer was an Indian army pensioner, residing at 37 Dorset Street. He worked for **John McCarthy** and was sent to collect Kelly's arrears of rent at 10.45am, on 9 November 1888. Unable to get an answer or to open the spring-locked door, he pulled back the coat and curtain hanging behind the broken window pane and saw the mutilated body on the bed.

Attempts to identify Bowyer from the census records have been unsuccessful. *See also* unidentified man seen by **Thomas Bowyer**.

BRADFORD, COL. SIR EDWARD RIDLEY COLBORNE, Bt (1836–1911)

Metropolitan Police Commisioner during the last part of the public Ripper scare.

Educated Marlborough. Madras Cavalry, 1853; served Persia, 1856–57, and through latter part of Indian Mutiny. 1860, Col. i/c 1st Indian Horse and Political Assistant in West Malwa. In 1863, he lost his left arm to a tigress in a shooting incident. 1874–78, general supervisor of operations against thugee (Kali-worshipping highwaymen murderers) and *dacoiti* (bandits). 1878, Gov-General's Agent, Rajputana, and Chief Commissioner, Ajmir. KCSI, 1885. 1887, Secretary to Secret and Political Dept, India Office, London. 1889–90, conducted **Prince Albert Victor** on tour around India. 1890–1903, Metropolitan Police Commissioner. Bt, 1902.

An easy man to get on with, and a very successful commissioner after the short, unhappy terms of **Warren** and **Monro**. Not known to have expressed any opinions on the Ripper's identity.

(*See* Constance Bradford, *Truly A Great Victorian: A Quiet Man Before Whom Rogues Trembled*. Privately published, 2004.)

BREMEN, HOMOSEXUAL HAIRDRESSER OF
Suspect. *See* **Mary**.

BRICE, ARTHUR
Alleged victim of indecent assault by **Dr Tumblety** on 31 August, 1888. (PRO CRIM 4/1037, 21927.)

BRILL, NATHAN (*b.* 1874)
Hairdresser.

Born in Russia and married to Esther (née Kockanski), he moved to England and at the time of the 1901 Census was living at 1 Hanbury Street with his wife and children, Harry, Mark, Leah and Hannah, and his mother-in-law, Zoe. In 1895 **Amelia Richardson** moved out of 29 Hanbury Street and her shop was taken over by Morris Modlin, who traded as a hairdresser until 1905, at which time it was taken over by Nathan Brill, who was there until 1950, when Maurice Stanton took over – although the latter never changed the name-board and it remained so until the building was demolished in 1970.

Colin Wilson recalled in 'A Lifetime in Ripperology' (see *The Mammoth Book of Jack the Ripper*) how he visited the shop when writing a series of articles for the *Evening Standard* ('My Search For Jack the Ripper', 8–12 August 1960) and was told by Mrs Brill how a friend was using the outside lavatory when Mrs Brill remarked that Jack the Ripper's second victim had been found in the yard. The lady visitor immediately leaped to her feet and ran indoors, forgetting to pull up her knickers. He told a less risqué version of the story in the *Evening Standard* (10 August 1960) and attributed the tale to Mrs Kathleen Manning, who was then living in the house. The article is accompanied by a photograph of her with Wilson. A different photograph appears in Colin Wilson's autobiography, *Dreaming to Some Purpose* (London: Century, 2004).

BRITISH MEDICAL JOURNAL, THE
Professional organ for doctors; less radical than *The Lancet* in the nine-teenth century.

In an important report on 6 October 1888, it discredited **Wynne Baxter**'s theory that an American doctor was offering money for specimen uteri, saying:

It is true that enquiries were made at one or two medical schools [contemporary press reports indicate these were University College Hospital and the Middlesex Hospital] early last year by a foreign physician, who was spending some time in London, as to the possibility of securing certain parts of the body for the purpose of scientific investigation. No large sum, however, was offered. The person in question was a physician of the highest reputability and exceedingly well accredited to this country by the best authorities in his own, and he left London fully eighteen months ago. There was never any real foundation for the hypothesis, and the information communicated, which was not at all of the nature the public has been led to believe, was due to the erroneous interpretation by a minor official of a question which he had overheard and to which a negative reply was given. This theory may be dismissed, and is, we believe, no longer entertained by its author.

Despite this quite conclusive refutation, which silenced Mr Baxter on the subject, **Abberline** still believed the theory, some 15 years later.

BRITTAIN, CHARLES
Slaughterman. Joined **Tomkins** and **Mumford** to look at **Mary Ann Nichols**' body.

BROADMOOR PATIENT
See **Taylor**.

BRODIE, WILLIAM WALLACE (b. c. 1856)
Confessed to being Jack the Ripper and to having murdered **Alice McKenzie**.

In May 1877, William Wallace Brodie was convicted of larceny in a dwelling house and sentenced to 14 years imprisonment. He was discharged on licence in August 1888 after serving 11 years (*The Times*, 7 August 1889). On 6 September 1888, he sailed on S.S. *Athenian* from Southampton to Kimberley, South Africa, where he spent about 10 months at the Sultfontein Mine. In June 1889 he went to Capetown 'for a spree' and afterwards confessed to the police there that he had committed the Whitechapel murders. He appeared to be suffering delirum and on being brought before the Magistrate was duly discharged and advised to give up drinking (*Kimberley Advertiser*, 29 June 1889). On 15 July 1889, he returned to England aboard S.S. *Trojan*, working his passage as a fireman, and a few days later turned up at Leman Street Police Station, where he confessed to the Ripper murders and in particular to the recent murder of Alice McKenzie.

Brodie was charged on his own confession, but the police quickly established that he had been discharged from prison on 23 August 1888 and immediately went to South Africa. It was further established that a Mr Salvage of 2 Harveys Buildings, Strand, stated that Brodie was 'very drunk by 11pm on the night McKenzie was murdered and had been put to bed at that time, not leaving until about 10.20 next morning' (*The Times*, 2 August 1889). Brodie was examined by doctors and declared sane, but at the time of the confession to have been suffering acute alcoholism that caused hallucinations. Brodie was discharged, but immediately rearrested for defrauding a jeweller named Peter Rigley Pratt on a watch. He was found guilty and ordered to serve the remaining term of the sentence given for the 1877 crime, with an additional six months' hard labour for the fraud.

BROUGH, EDWIN (1844–1929)

Provided bloodhounds for police trials during the Ripper scare. Breeder and trainer of bloodhounds in Scarborough.

Wrote to *The Times*, 8 October 1888, praising English bloodhounds, though expressed some reservations as to their effectiveness in city streets. He must already have been engaged to send Burgho and champion Barnaby down to London for police trials.

After the trials in the parks, Brough was indignant to learn from Mr Edward Taunton, who had care of the dogs, that the police had taken one of them to the scene of a burglary to see whether he could track the criminal. The dog proved incapable of following scent through the city streets, but Mr Brough feared vengeful villains might try to injure his valuable and uninsured animal. He demanded its immediate return: hence the widely reported absence of the animals when they were wanted and supposed to have been lost on Tooting Bec.

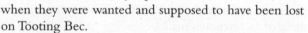

In *The Bloodhound and Its Use in Tracking Criminals* (1904), Brough wrote, 'It is a very significant fact that at the time of the "Jack the Ripper" outrages in the East End there were no murders committed for the two months during which Sir Charles Warren had arranged for a couple of Bloodhounds to be kept in London, but directly it was announced that the hounds had been sent back, another of this series of horrible murders was perpetrated.'

(*See* 'The Hounds of Jack the Ripper', ***Ripperana***, 51, January 2005.)

BROWN, AMELIA (b. c.1868)

The daughter of a Stepney licensee, she described being used by the police as a decoy to catch Jack the Ripper, being provided with a whistle and being shadowed by two detectives named Gill and Payne.

> Never shall I forget that evening just before the last Ripper murder was committed. I met them at midnight. We decided to walk round the block where the London Hospital then stood. I had my police whistle in my hand, and the two detectives were close behind me. As I reached the back wall of the hospital a rope was dropped from the top. It just missed my shoulders, and I blew my whistle for all I was worth.
>
> Gill and Payne arrived within seconds. But there was no sign of the person

who had dropped the rope. I still think Jack the Ripper was a doctor – and he was after me that night.

Sunday Chronicle, 6 February 1949

BROWN, CARRIE 'OLD SHAKESPEARE' (*d.* 1894)

Alleged victim: the primary case offered for suspicion **of Severin Klosowski** in New York. Tentatively proposed by various writers, culminating in R. Michael Gordon's full examination in **The American Murders of Jack the Ripper**.

Elderly prostitute, whose nickname derived from her habit of quoting Shakespeare when drunk. Found dead of multiple stab-wounds in Manhattan waterfront hotel in April 1894. Mortuary photographs show severe injuries to lower abdomen and around anus.

Amir Ben Ali, fellow hotel resident, was arrested and convicted on shaky evidence of bloody footmarks between the rooms (possibly created by investigating police officers). Pardoned 11 years later, leaving her murder a mystery. Police chief **Thomas Byrnes** is often accused of over-zealous and dishonest pursuit of a conviction, though he claimed to have been instrumental in securing Ali's pardon.

The case for suspecting Klosowski rests largely on his moustaches matching those of an unknown man seen with old Shakespeare shortly before her death.

Cf. **Mary Anderson, Arbie La Bruckman, Hannah Robinson, Elizabeth Senior**.

BROWN, DR FREDERICK GORDON (1843–1928)

City Police surgeon responsible for report on **Catherine Eddowes**. Also accompanied **Dr Phillips** to inspect **Alice McKenzie**'s body in situ and joined **Dr Hebbert** in attending Dr Phillips' autopsy of the Pinchin Street torso.

Born in the City of London, son of Dr Thomas Brown and educated at Merchant Taylors, St Thomas's Hospital and Paris. Married Emily Appleford, 21 January 1869. City police surgeon, 1886–1914. A very prominent Freemason, at one time grand officer of the Grand Lodge of England.

His post-mortem report is preserved at the London Metropolitan Archives. It is imperfectly punctuated, as it is in the form of notes taken verbatim by Coroner **Langham**. For convenience, we have added correct punctuation. We have not inserted the coroner's questions, which (particularly towards the end) determine the brief comments and repetitions.

The body was on its back, the head turned to left shoulder. The arms by the side of the body as if they had fallen there. Both palms upwards, the fingers slightly bent. Left leg extended in a line with the body. The abdomen was exposed. Right leg bent at the thigh and knee.

The throat cut across.

The intestines were drawn out to a large extent and placed over the right shoulder – they were smeared over with some feculent matter. A piece of about two feet was quite detached from the body and placed between the body and the left arm, apparently by design. The lobe and auricle of the right ear was cut obliquely through.

There was a quantity of clotted blood on the pavement on the left side of the neck round the shoulder and upper part of arm, and fluid blood-coloured serum which had flowed under the neck to the right shoulder, the pavement sloping in that direction.

Body was quite warm. No death stiffening had taken place. She must have been dead most likely within the half hour. We looked for superficial bruises and saw none. No blood on the skin of the abdomen or secretion of any kind on the thighs. No spurting of blood on the bricks or pavement around. No marks of blood below the middle of the body. Several buttons were found in the clotted blood after the body was removed. There was no blood on the front of the clothes. There were no traces of recent connection.

When the body arrived at Golden Lane [mortuary] some of the blood was dispersed through the removal of the body to the mortuary. The clothes were taken off carefully from the body. A piece of deceased's ear dropped from the clothing.

I made a post mortem examination at half past two on Sunday afternoon. Rigor mortis was well marked; body not quite cold. Green discoloration over the abdomen.

After washing the left hand carefully, a bruise the size of a sixpence, recent and red, was discovered on the back of the left hand between the thumb and first finger. A few small bruises on right shin of older date. The hands and arms were bronzed. No bruises on the scalp, the back of the body or the elbows.

The face was very much mutilated. There was a cut about a quarter of an inch through the lower left eyelid, dividing the structures completely through the upper eyelid on that side, there was a scratch through the skin on the left upper eyelid – near to the angle of the nose the right eyelid was cut through to about half an inch. There was a deep cut over the bridge of the nose, extending from the left border of the nasal bone down near to the angle of the jaw on the right side of the cheek, across the cheek – this cut went into the bone and divided all the structures of the cheek except the mucous membrane of the mouth.

The tip of the nose was quite detached from the nose by an oblique cut from the bottom of the nasal bone to where the wings of the nose join on to the face. A cut from this divided the upper lip and extended through the substance of the gum over the right upper lateral incisor tooth. About half an inch from the top of the nose was another oblique cut. There was a cut on the right angle of the mouth as if the cut of a point of a knife. The cut extended an inch and a half, parallel with lower lip.

There was on each side of cheek a cut which peeled up the skin, forming a triangular flap about an inch and a half.

On the left cheek there were two abrasions of the epithelium. There was a little mud on the left cheek – 2 slight abrasions of the epithelium under the left ear.

The throat was cut across to the extent of about six or seven inches. A superficial cut commenced about an inch and a half below the lobe below (and about two and a half inches below and behind) the left ear, and extended across the throat to about three inches below the lobe of right ear. The big muscle across the throat was divided through on the left side. The large vessels on the left side of the neck were severed. The larynx was severed below the vocal chord. All the deep structures were severed to the bone, the knife marking intervertebral cartilages. The sheath of the vessels on the right side was just opened. The carotid artery had a fine hole opening. The internal jugular vein was opened an inch and a half – not divided.

The blood vessels contained clot. All these injuries were performed by a sharp instrument like a knife, and pointed.

The cause of death was haemorrhage from the left common carotid artery. The death was immediate and the mutilations were inflicted after death.

We examined the abdomen. The front walls were laid open from the breast bone to the pubes. The cut commenced opposite the enciform cartilage. The incision went upwards, not penetrating the skin that was over the sternum. It then divided the enciform cartilage. The knife must have cut obliquely at the expense of the front surface of that cartilage.

Behind this, the liver was stabbed as if by the point of a sharp instrument. Below this was another incision into the liver of about two and a half inches, and below this the left lobe of the liver was slit through by a vertical cut. Two cuts were shewn by a jagging of the skin on the left side.

The abdominal walls were divided in the middle line to within a quarter of an inch of the navel. The cut then took a horizontal course for two inches and a half towards the right side. It then divided round the navel on the left side, and made a parallel incision to the former horizontal incision, leaving the navel on a tongue of skin. Attached to the navel was two and a half inches of the lower part of the rectus muscle on the left side of the abdomen. The incision then took an oblique direction to the right and was shelving. The incision went down the right side of the vagina and rectum for half an inch behind the rectum.

There was a stab of about an inch on the left groin. This was done by a pointed instrument. Below this was a cut of three inches going through all tissues making a wound of the peritoneum [sc. perineum] about the same extent.

An inch below the crease of the thigh was a cut extending from the anterior spine of the ilium obliquely down the inner side of the left thigh and separating the left labium, forming a flap of skin up to the groin. The left rectus muscle was not detached.

There was a flap of skin formed from the right thigh, attaching the right labium, and extending up to the spine of the ilium. The muscles on the right side inserted into the frontal ligaments were cut through.

The skin was retracted through the whole of the cut in the abdomen, but the vessels were not clotted. Nor had there been any appreciable bleeding from the vessels. I draw the conclusion that the cut was made after death, and there would not be much blood on the murderer. The cut was made by someone on [the] right side of [the] body, kneeling below the middle of the body.

I removed the content of the stomach and placed it in a jar for further examination. There seemed very little in it in the way of food or fluid, but from the cut end partly digested farinaceous food escaped.

The intestines had been detached to a large extent from the mesentery. About two feet of the colon was cut away. The sigmoid flexure was invaginated into the rectum very tightly.

Right kidney pale, bloodless, with slight congestion of the base of the pyramids.

There was a cut from the upper part of the slit on the undersurface of the liver to the left side, and another cut at right angles to this, which were about an inch and a half deep and two and a half inches long. Liver itself was healthy.

The gall bladder contained bile. The pancreas was cut, but not through, on the left side of the spinal column. Three and a half inches of the lower border of the spleen by half an inch was attached only to the peritoneum.

The peritoneal lining was cut through on the left side and the left kidney carefully taken out and removed. The left renal artery was cut through. I should say that someone who knew the position of the kidney must have done [it].

The lining membrane over the uterus was cut through. The womb was cut through horizontally, leaving a stump of three quarters of an inch. The rest of the womb had been taken away with some of the ligaments. The vagina and cervix of the womb was uninjured.

The bladder was healthy and uninjured, and contained three or four ounces of water. There was a tongue-like cut through the anterior wall of the abdominal aorta. The other organs were healthy.

There were no indications of connexion.

I believe the wound in the throat was first inflicted. I believe she must have been lying on the ground.

The wounds on the face and abdomen prove that they were inificted by a sharp pointed knife, and that in the abdomen by one six inches long.

I believe the perpetrator of the act must have had considerable knowledge of the positions of the organs in the abdominal cavity and the way of removing them. The parts removed would be of no use for any professional purpose. It required a great deal of medical knowledge to have removed the kidney and to know where it was placed. Such a knowledge might be possessed by someone in the habit of cutting up animals.

I think the perpetrator of this act had sufficient time, or he would not have nicked the lower eyelids. It would take at least five minutes.

I cannot assign any reason for the parts being taken away. I feel sure there was no struggle. I believe it was the act of one person.

The throat had been so instantly severed that no noise could have been emitted. I should not expect much blood to have been found on the person who had inflicted these wounds. The wounds could not have been self-inflicted.

My attention was called to the apron. It was the corner of the apron, with a string attached. The blood spots were of recent origin. I have seen the portion of an apron produced by Dr Phillips and stated to have been found in Goulston Street. It is impossible to say it is human blood. I fitted the piece of apron which had a new piece of material on it which had evidently been sewn on to the piece I have, the seams of the borders of the two actually corresponding. Some blood and, apparently, faecal matter was found on the portion found in Goulston Street. I believe the wounds on the face to have been done to disfigure the corpse.

This is one of the most important yet contentious of all documents in the history of Jack the Ripper. The postmortem was observed by Drs **Sequeira**, **Sedgwick Saunders** and **George Bagster Phillips**. The two former gave evidence at the inquest suggesting that they did not think much expertise was evinced by the murderer, and stated that in this they agreed with Dr **Brown**. Phillips did not contradict Coroner **Wynne Baxter**, who described the Mitre Square murderer as an unskilled imitator. Brown responded to the coroner's repeated questions as to whether the murderer had surgical *skill* with the reply that he had *anatomical knowledge,* enabling him to identify and remove the kidney. He did not at any time volunteer information on this subject.

The kidney remains another point of controversy. Richard Whittington-Egan, the only crime historian with medical training and experience of dissecting cadavers, concluded that the murderer was unskilled and the kidney extracted by chance. He consulted leading renal authorities before publishing this conclusion. But N. P. Warren, the only practising surgeon to have made a substantial contribution to the history of the Ripper, demurs. He believes, from experience, that the kidney is so difficult to expose from the front of the body that the murderer must have had some anatomical experience, and he draws attention to Brown's remark that the kidney had been 'carefully' extracted.

The authors are not medically trained, and cannot say conclusively whether the medical evidence suggests that the Ripper was skilled or not, as doctors disagree today as they did at the time. There is no dispute, however, that N. P. Warren is correct in saying this report does show clear signs of Bright's disease in the right kidney. [*See* **Major Smith**, **Lusk kidney**, for relevance.)

Other points of interest are the sexual focus, indicated by ripping the victim upward, from the pubes to the breastbone, and then concentrating on some very detailed cutting in the genital area which extracted the womb and almost detached one side of the external genitalia.

It is interesting that Brown reports no trace of sexual connection and refers to the absence of secretion of any kind on the thighs, pointing to his possible expectation that premature ejaculation or masturbation over the body might have occurred. This, like **Bond**'s report and **Anderson**'s remarks, points to a surprisingly confident and accurate recognition of the practices of sadistic serial murderers; a sophisticated knowledge not possessed by the press or the junior police of the period.

The portion of the ear which fell off in the mortuary does not indicate any attempt to remove the ears, as promised in the **'Dear Boss' letter**.

The throat was cut as deeply as **Annie Chapman**'s and **Mary Ann Nichols**' – like theirs, too, it had been cut across twice. Abrasions on the cheek below the left ear are reminiscent of the bruising on Nichols and Chapman. The small bruise to the back of the hand suggests an intercepted attempt at defence blocked by a hand or fist rather than the knife. (*See* **Elizabeth Stride**, **Mary Jane Kelly** for relevance.)

In 1905 Brown and two detectives guided a small group whose number included **Sir Arthur Conan Doyle**, **Ingleby Oddie**, and **John Churton Collins**, round Whitechapel and Spitalfields, and Brown gave the opinion (as he had at the Medico-Legal Society, two years previously) that the Ripper had some knowledge of human anatomy, but used cuts suggestive of a butcher.

(see obituary *British Medical Journal*, 21 January 1928. *The Times* 20 and 21 January 1928. Also see Neil Bell and Robert Clack, 'City Beat: Dr Frederick Gordon Brown, L.S.A., M.R.C.S., L.M.' **Ripperologist**, 112, March 2010)

BROWN, JAMES

Witness at **Elizabeth Stride**'s inquest. Testified that at 12.45am he was passing along Fairclough Street on his way home to no. 35, and saw Stride with her back to the wall of the Board School, talking to a stoutish man, about 5ft 7in tall, wearing a long coat which almost reached his heels. He had his arm against the wall, as if to stop her from leaving, and she was saying, 'No, not tonight. Maybe some other night.'

Brown did not see the man's face or notice his cap. He did not observe the flower on Stride's dress. About 15 minutes later, before he had finished his supper, he heard cries of 'Murder!' as members of the International Workingmen's Educational Club went to find the police.

His reported sighting coincides exactly with the time at which Israel Schwartz said he saw Stride being thrown to the pavement outside Dutfield's Yard. If both men correctly identified Stride, one of them was wrong about the time.

The *Evening News* learned that a courting couple was in a road crossing Berner Street at the time, and it has been suggested Brown might have mistaken them for Stride and a man. Brown was self-confessedly not very observant.

BROWN, GENERAL SAM (*fl.* 1888)
Suspected and cleared, 1888.

General Brown was accused in a misdirected letter from a gentleman to his son that had either been received by a Miss Jane Bromley or contained a letter from her, included by mistake. Apparently the first few lines said that the General operated on horses for racing (presumably gelding them) and this so horrified the lady (or the gentleman) that the writer inevitably suspected the General. A file of seven letters and memoranda indicates the police and Home Office embarrassment at having to investigate the General (HO144/221/AQ4930/C, f103).

Army lists of the time show two General Samuel Browns, one of whom invented the shoulder-strapped belt. The authors have been unable to determine which was the suspected General.

BROWNE, DOUGLAS G. (1884–1963)
See The Rise of Scotland Yard.

BROWNFIELD, DR MATTHEW (1832–1908)
Registered (Edinburgh) 1859.

K Division Metropolitan Police Surgeon. Conducted postmortem on **Rose Mylett** and concluded, in consequence of a mark on her neck suggestive of strangulation with a piece of cord, that she had been murdered. He did not convey his conclusion to the police, who believed Mylett had died from natural causes before the inquest and thereby he inadvertently caused a sequence of events in which it appeared that a series of doctors were sent by the police to re-examine the body, leading some modern commentators to suggest the police were attempting to influence the conclusion of the inquest. He voiced a personal theory in a controversial interview in *The Star* that Rose Mylett was a victim of Jack the Ripper, suggesting that the Ripper's victims had first been strangled with a cord and then had their throats cut along the line of the mark (*Star*, 24 December 1888).

BRUCE, ALEXANDER CARMICHAEL (1850–1926) *pictured p.76*
Assistant Commissioner, Metropolitan Police, 1884–1914.

The fourth son of Canon David Bruce of Ferry Hill, Durham. Educated at Rossall School and Brasenose, Oxon. Graduated in 1873. Called to the bar, Lincoln's Inn, 1875, practising on the North-Eastern Circuit. Appointed assistant commissioner, Metropolian Police, 1884. Retired 1914, knighted

1908. Married Helen Fletcher in 1876 – she predeceased him.

Adopted **Robert Anderson**'s duties during his absence on sick leave. Visited Buck's Row and Hanbury Street murder sites, and made notes on the interrogation of **Matthew Packer**. Liaised between Scotland Yard, Home Office and Sir Samuel Montagu MP over the question of a reward (HO144/220/A49301B ff 184–5).

BUCHAN, EDWARD (1859–88)

Suspect suggested 1990. Marine store dealer (said in one newspaper report to have been a shoemaker) of Robin Hood Lane, Poplar, who committed suicide on 19 November 1888. Advanced as suspect by Roger Barber ('Did Jack the Ripper Commit Suicide?', *Criminologist,* autumn 1990) on the basis that the sudden cessation of the crimes following the murder of Kelly is most likely explained by the suicide of the killer.

BUCK'S ROW SUSPECT

On 20 September 1888 the *Echo* reported that suspicion had fallen on a man shortly after the murder of **Martha Tabram** and that **Reid, Enright** and Goadby [**Godley**] had followed up a clue given them by **Mary Ann Connelly** ('Pearly Poll') which had not been thought of much at the time. However, coupling that clue with statements by **Elizabeth Allen** and **Eliza Cooper** at the time of the inquiries into the murder of Annie Chapman 'certain of the authorities have had cause to suspect a man actually living not far from Buck's Row. At present, however, there is only suspicion against him.' It is not known who this man was, although *The Crimes Detection and Death of Jack the Ripper* argues that it 'was obviously **Leather Apron**' and sees the article as proof that the police were still interested in this suspect 20 days after the release of **John Pizer**.

BUKI, MRS

Former landlady of **Mary Jane Kelly**. According to the *Star* of 12 November 1888, Mrs Buki was the 'lady' living in one of the roads off St George's Street (the western end of The Highway) with whom, according to **Mrs Carthy**, Kelly lodged on first coming to the East End. Mrs Buki accompanied Kelly to Knightsbridge, where they recovered a number of Kelly's clothes from another lady's house.

A single newspaper report gives us no guarantee that the name was correctly heard and spelled.

BULLING, THOMAS JOHN (1847–1934)

Journalist, employed by the Central News Agency in 1888. Identified in the **Littlechild letter** (with his surname mis-spelled Bullen) as the man Scotland Yard believed to be the 'originator' of the **'Jack the Ripper' letters**.

The **'Dear Boss' letter** and **'Saucy Jacky'** postcard were sent to Scotland Yard from the Central News Agency. On 5 October 1888, Bulling sent Scotland Yard a transcript of a third letter signed 'Jack the Ripper', claimed by Bulling to be in the same hand as the others. In July 1892 Bulling and John Moore (*cf.* **Charles Moore**) visited the Black Museum at Scotland Yard, together giving the Central News Agency offices at New Bridge Street as their address.

Bulling apeared at Marlborough Street Court on a charge of being drunk and disorderly (*The Times,* 10 June 1895) and he was said by Littlechild to have been fired from the Central News Agency (by Moore) when he sent a crude telegram reporting Bismarck's death (1898).

In *The Lodger* it is suggested that Bulling could be the journalist described by R. Thurston Collins in *Life and Death at the Old Bailey* (London: Herbert Jenkins, 1935), who lost his job after a breakdown and thereafter behaved eccentrically and evinced an obsession with the Ripper. Thomas Wescott (*Ripperologist*, 34/5, April/July 2001) argues this suspicion of Bulling may be misplaced.

BURNS, ELIZABETH

Prostitute well known to the police, married according to *The Star* (2 October 1888) living at 55 Flower and Dean Street (*Echo*, 2 October 1888 – this was Cooney's lodging house where **Catherine Eddowes** lived). According to the Press Association, she was 18 years old and had one arm, so she may well have been **'One-Armed Liz'** who also lived in Flower and Dean Street.

On 18 September 1888 she took **Charles Ludwig** under a railway arch off the Minories, where he threatened her with a knife, bringing PC **John Johnson** to her aid..

BURROWS, EDWIN

Suspected and cleared, 1888. A vagrant, who sometimes resided at Victoria Lodging House, Whitechapel. Burrows was arrested on 8 December 1888 because he wore a peaked cap similar to that described by **Israel Schwartz**. He was released when his brother in Sutton confirmed by telegram that he made him an allowance (MEPO files, now missing, but transcribed severally by Paul Bonner, Stephen Knight and Donald Rumbelow). It is of interest that Schwartz's description was still seen as important in December.

BURY, ELLEN (*d.* 1889)

Alleged victim. If **William Henry Bury** was Jack the Ripper, it follows inevitably that the wife he strangled and mutilated was the last of the Ripper's victims.

BURY, WILLIAM HENRY (1859–89)

Suspect, suggested 1889.

From October 1887 Bury had been resident in Bow, where he worked selling sawdust on behalf of a general dealer called James Martin. Martin claimed to have employed Ellen Elliot as a maid, but confessed under questioning by **Inspector Abberline** that he had known her to be a prostitute working out of his house. Bury married Elliot in April 1888; Martin sacked Bury for stealing in March 1888. Although working as a prostitute, Elliot owned shares worth about £20,000 at today's values and Bury persuaded her to cash about two-thirds of them and hand most of the money over to him.

Bury bought a horse and cart and sold sawdust on his own account. He also began to drink heavily and threatened his wife with a knife to obtain more money from her. In May he contracted a venereal disease and passed it on to Ellen. Then, in December, he sold the horse and cart and prepared to move to Dundee, telling his landlord that he was going to Australia.

Bury and Ellen had come to Dundee in January 1889. On 10 February 1889, Bury went to the Central Police Office in Dundee and 'said he was "Jack the Ripper," or "A Jack the Ripper," or something to that effect' (*Aberdeen Weekly Journal*, 12 February 1889), and explained that on 4 February he and Ellen had gone to bed after a night of heavy drinking and that on waking he found her lying on the floor with a rope around her neck. He had panicked, stabbed the corpse with a knife and forced it into a trunk, breaking one leg in so doing.

The police visited Bury's flat and discovered the body, which had deep abdominal mutilations reminiscent of **Mary Ann Nichols**' injuries, only more severe. Chalked on a door were the words, 'Jack Ripper is at the back of this door'. On the stairway wall leading to the basement was chalked, 'Jack Ripper is in this sellar'. The police did not believe Ellen could have strangled herself with the rope and despite some medical testimony supporting the possibility of Bury's story, he was convicted and hanged in Dundee for the murder of his wife in April 1889.

There were early comparisons with the Whitechapel murders in the press, it being described as 'a case of murder and mutilation equalling in atrocity any of the late Whitechapel outrages' (*Aberdeen Weekly Journal*, 12 February 1889). It was also reported that 'Inspector Abberline and other detectives who were engaged in investigating the recent Whitechapel murders have been instituting enquiries among the relatives of the woman Bury, who was murdered in

Dundee' (*Birmingham Daily Post*, 12 February 1889). An Irish newspaper even reported Bury 'was well known in Whitechapel. Some of the officers who had charge of the Whitechapel investigation have gone to Dundee' (*Freeman's Journal and Daily Commercial Advertiser*, 12 February 1889). In the US, several newspapers were more explicit: 'THINK THEY HAVE HIM. IS THE DUNDEE MURDERER "JACK THE RIPPER"?' was one such headline, the attendant article claiming, 'Bury was a resident of Whitechapel, London, and his antecedents, which have been traced suggest that he is probably "Jack the Ripper" and that he is subject to unconscious fits of murder mania' and continuing, 'The theory of the police officials is that Bury's wife knew of facts connecting him with the East End atrocities, and that she took him to Dundee in the hope of preventing a recurrence of the crimes' (*Boston Daily Advertiser*, 12 February 1889).

See **James Berry** for his claim that two Metropolitan police officers vsited Bury in Dundee and assured Berry that they were satisfied that he'd hanged Jack the Ripper, and **Ernest A Parr** who claimed that Bury had confessed in writing to the murders and that this confession was passed to the Secretary of State for Scotland. Abberline appears to have concluded Bury was a drunken domestic murderer unconnected with the Whitechapel killings. A letter from Eleanor Lynch of Dundee claimed that her great-grandfather, David Robb, served on the jury which found Bury guilty and was of the opinion that the murder was committed through alcoholism (*Dundee Courier and Advertiser*, 2 December 1977).

(*See* National Archives of Scotland HH/16/69. William Beadle, *Jack the Ripper: Anatomy of a Myth* and *Jack the Ripper Unmasked*; Euan Macpherson, *The Trial of Jack the Ripper: The Case of William Bury (1859–1889)*).

BUSWELL, HARRIET (1843–72)

Suggested suspect. Similarities between her death and Ripper crimes were noted in 2005 on **Casebook: Jack the Ripper** by A.P. Wolf. Advanced as Ripper victim by Trevor Marriott in *The Evil Within: The World's Worst Serial Killers* (2008) (*see also* **Emma Jackson**). Murdered, 1872.

Prostitute, found strangled in her lodgings at Great Coram Street on Christmas Day, 1872. Descriptions of a man she had been seen with the previous night led to the suggestion that he might be the engineer of a German emigrant ship bound for South America, which was docked for repairs at Ramsgate. When witnesses were taken to the vessel to make the identification, five out of seven identified

the ship's chaplain, who had insisted on being placed in the identification parade because he believed in the engineer's innocence and mistrusted British police methods.

The police insisted on charging him despite testimony from the staff of the German Hotel in America Square (close to the Tower of London) that the chaplain had spent the whole Christmas holiday there with his wife, bed-ridden with a severe feverish chill, and the hotel's possession of his clothes and boots meant he could not possibly have left the building on Christmas Eve. The case was thrown out of court by the magistrate and the Foreign Office had to apologise to the Prussian government for the unwarranted harassment of a German national.

Sixteen years later, a few months before the Ripper murders, the case was still the outstanding unsolved London mystery and referred to as such by Jerome K. Jerome in chapter 5 of *Three Men in a Boat* (1889). By the time his book appeared, the Great Coram Street murder had been eclipsed by the Whitechapel murders.

(*See* **Jack the Ripper: A 21st Century Investigation**. There is a file on the Great Coram Street murders at the National Archives: MEPO 3/109-115)

BUTLER, DETECTIVE CHIEF SUPERINTENDENT ARTHUR HENRY (1917–1992)

Theorist.

Joined the Metropolitan Police in 1938; retired 1968. In August 1972, Butler contributed articles to the *Sun*, which embellished **William Stewart**'s suggestion (in *Jack the Ripper: A New Theory*) of a midwife-abortionist 'Jill the Ripper'. Butler said she lived near Brick Lane and mutilated bodies to disguise failed abortions; was blackmailed by **Emma Elizabeth Smith** and an accomplice named **'Fingers Freddy'**, and wheeled bodies to their dumping-spots in a perambulator.

Butler claimed his source was oral tradition from people whose uncles and aunts personally remembered the details.

BY EAR AND EYES: THE WHITECHAPEL MURDERS, JACK THE RIPPER AND THE MURDER OF MARY JANE KELLY

Book by Karyo Magellan (pseudonym) (Derby: Longshot Publishing, 2005).

A serious re-examination of the case based on medical and inquest reports, and concluding **Mary Jane Kelly** may not have been a Ripper victim, while **Alice McKenzie** and **Frances Coles** might have been.

BYFIELD, SERGEANT JAMES GEORGE (*b. c.*1848–1927)

Joined City of London Police 1868; City Warrant no. 4171; retired 1895. Station sergeant at Bishopsgate Police Station, on duty at 8.45pm, 29 September 1888, when a very drunk **Catherine Eddowes** was brought into the station. Byfield put her in a cell until she sobered up. At 1.00am she gave Police Constable **George Hutt** her name as Mary Ann Kelly and her address as Fashion Street before being released.

BYRNES, CHIEF INSPECTOR THOMAS (1842–1910)

Chief of New York Municipal Police Detective Bureau in 1888.

After leaving school, worked as a gas fitter and joined volunteer fire company. In 1861, he joined the Union Army and fought at the Battle of Bull Run. Mustered out (1863) and joined NY Metropolitan Police. Patrolman, 15th Precinct (1863–68). In 1868, promoted to roundsman; sergeant in 1869. In 1870, NY Metropolitan Police was replaced by NY Municipal Police (the outcome of political rivalry between City and State government) and Byrnes was promoted to captain. From 1870–78, he commanded various precincts and the Broadway squad. By putting pressure on the watchman (1879), he solved the great Metropolitan Bank robbery case and had several major gang members convicted. In a decade when the police notoriously failed to solve major crimes, this made his name and in 1880 he was promoted to inspector and placed in charge of the Detective Bureau.

When **Dr Tumblety** was under observation in New York, Byrnes told the press that although he might be wanted in England, he could not be arrested in America. Nevertheless, he was keeping an eye on him. In 1889, he challenged Jack the Ripper to come across the Atlantic to New York – a foolish move as his Bureau didn't have a very good reputation for solving murders. His own proposed method would have been to place women on the streets as decoys, ruthlessly observing that if one were killed, it wouldn't matter so long as he got the murderer.

In the **Carrie Brown** case, Byrnes secured the conviction of Amir ben Ali, but he was widely believed to have been the wrong man and it has been argued that Byrnes was recklessly determined to see someone hang for the crime (*see The American Murders of Jack the Ripper*). James Lardner and Thomas Repetto (*NYPD: A City and its Police*, New York: Henry Holt, 2000) state Byrnes was instrumental in securing ben Ali's pardon several years later, though it has been argued this was because Byrnes by then believed the murderer to have been ben Ali's cousin, Arbie La Bruckman.

In 1896, Byrnes was forced to resign because Police Commissioner Theodore Roosevelt (i.e. political overlord of the Police Department) refused to work with him. Roosevelt was one of many who suspected Byrnes might be corrupt.

C

CADOCHE, CADOSCH or CADOSH, ALBERT (*b.* Paris, *c.* 1860)

Witness at **Annie Chapman**'s inquest. Young carpenter, resident at 27 Hanbury Street, next door to murder site. Testified that at 5.30am, on 8 September, he went into the yard of his house and heard from the yard of no. 29 a voice say, 'No!' A few minutes later, he heard what he believed to be something falling against the wooden fence dividing the yards. He heard nothing more and his suspicions were not aroused. Following this, he went to work, passing Spitalfields Church at 5.32, and saw no one in Hanbury Street as he left his house.

Coroner **Wynne Baxter**, summing up nine days later, said that Cadoche had mistakenly reported hearing the cry at 5.15 – 15 minutes before **Mrs Darrell** saw Annie Chapman alive on the street. In fact, if *The Times* reports are accurate, it was Mr Baxter who had confused the witnesses' times.

CAIRNS, HECTOR

Alleged informant.

According to a short article by Jasper Sayer (*Glasgow Evening News*, 27 November 1947), Cairns, described as an octogenarian criminologist of Tangier, a native of Edinburgh and former Greenock business man, possessed a collection of crime relics which included a document reputed to have been written by **Rasputin** which identified **Dr Alexander Pedachenko** as Jack the Ripper. This story was received by the newspaper from a correspondent named 'G.D.K. M'Cormick' – **George Donald King McCormick**. **Donald McCormick** cites this article cautiously (wrongly attributing its authorship to Cairns) in support of his belief that Pedachenko was the Ripper, without noting that he supplied the paper with the information in the first place.

Nothing further is known about Cairns, but he has been tentatively identified as Hector Macdonald Cairns, resident in Glasgow 1939–47.

CALLAGHAN, MARY

Witness. Talking with **Ellen Marks** and the cokeman **Frank Ruffle** on 21 November 1888, when the man accused of trying to cut **Annie Farmer**'s throat ran out of 19 George Street. She heard his profane remark and later told the press that Annie was respectably connected and had fallen through drink to being an habituée of the railed yard round Spitalfields Church ('Itchy Park' of the vagrants).

'CALOR'

Possibly nickname or garbling of 'Carl Nielson' (real name **Emil Totterman** – *Bluefield Daily Telegraph*, 22 December 1903).

CAMERON, PROFESSOR JAMES MALCOLM (1930–2003)

Pathologist at the Department of Forensic Medicine at the London Hospital.

Reported in *The Complete Jack the Ripper* to have concluded that the Ripper throttled victims from behind, as they prepared for anal intercourse (*see* **Dr Matthew Brownfield**, who believed the victims were strangled), before using the knife and that the London Hospital drawings and photographs of **Catherine Eddowes** indicate a right-handed murderer from the drag to the right of the abdominal incision.

CAMPBELL, DUNCAN (*fl.* 1891)

Seaman. Witness who testified that **James Thomas Sadler** had sold him a clasp knife at the Sailors' Home in Well Street on the morning after **Frances Coles** was murdered. Sadler denied this, and produced a reliable witness – **Edward Gerard Delaforce** (or Edward Delaforce Gray) – to testify he was in the Tower Shipping office collecting wages due to him at the time. Nevertheless, the police appear to have taken Campbell's evidence very seriously and had him attend an identification parade at the police station. Suggested in *Jack the Ripper: Scotland Yard Investigates* that this incident may lie behind the **Swanson marginalia**'s reference to 'the Seaside Home' as the place where the identification of **Anderson**'s suspect occurred.

CAMPS, FRANCIS (1905–72)

Pathologist. Publications include: *The Investigation of Murder* (with Richard Barber, London: Michael Joseph, 1966), in which he pointed out that Victorian pathologists all assumed the Ripper killed his victims quickly and cleanly with a knife. But modern experience shows that sadistic sexual murderers most frequently strangle their victims. Throat-cutting would not have been quick, clean and quiet compared with strangulation. Camps was thus probably the first person in the twentieth century to point towards one of today's impressions of the Ripper's MO: throttling the victim until she passed out and cutting her throat as she lay on the ground.

Camps wrote 'More About Jack the Ripper' for the *London Hospital Gazette* to accompany drawings and diagrams supplied to Mr **Langham** for **Catherine**

Eddowes' inquest, which Camps' assistant Sam Hardy discovered in the basement of the London Hospital.

CANONICAL FIVE

Generic term coined by Martin Fido in 1987 to describe five of the murdered women – **Mary Ann Nichols**, **Annie Chapman**, **Elizabeth Stride**, **Catherine Eddowes** and **Mary Jane Kelly**, who the police, in 1888, believed to be part of the same series (*Pall Mall Gazette*, 31 December 1888).

(Stewart Evans, 'The Canonical Five', *Ripperana*, 9, July 1994)

CAUSBY, INSPECTOR WILLIAM (*b.* 1852)

Joined the Metropolitan Police 1870 , Warrant no. 52772. Resigned 1895.

With **Sergeant Thick**, organised the parade at which **Emmanuel Violenia** identified **John Pizer** as the man he had heard threaten a woman on the night of the murder.

CARROLL, LEWIS (1832–98)

Suspect, proposed 1996.

Nom de plume of the Revd. **Charles Lutwidge Dodgson** and used by him for authorship of his children's books: *Alice's Adventures in Wonderland, Through the Looking-Glass and What Alice Found There, Sylvie and Bruno,* and *Sylvie and Bruno Concluded.*

Educated at Rugby and Christ Church, Oxford. Fellow and mathematics tutor of Christ Church 1855–81, and retained rooms in college until his death.

Carroll's many friendships with pre-pubescent girls and pioneering artistic nude photographs of them at one period of his life led to the post-Freudian belief that he was a more or less repressed paedophile. This caused psychotherapeutic social worker **Richard Wallace** to accuse Carroll and his friend and colleague Thomas Vere Bayne of having perpetrated the Ripper murders. (*See* **Jack the Ripper: 'Light-hearted Friend'**), claiming this was proved by anagrams in Carroll's writings, and the ways in which the ages of the Ripper's victims hovered around the number 42, shown in Carroll's works to be a number he occasionally enjoyed using for the logical and arithmetical word and language games that delighted him.

It has been pointed out that for certain of the murder dates neither Carroll nor Wallace were within reach of London and that anagrams taken from *Sylvie and Bruno* could not possibly refer to the Ripper murders since the work existed in manuscript form in 1887.

Carroll, however, made one reference to the murders in his journals. *See* **Dr G.H.R. Dabbs**.

CARTHY, or CARTY, MRS

Informant. Landlady, from Breezer's Hill, Ratcliff Highway. Told press that **Mary Jane Kelly** had lodged with her after a period lodging with a woman in St George's Street (the western end of the Ratcliff Highway) when she left the West

End. Claimed the St George's Street landlady had accompanied Kelly to a French 'lady's' residence in Knightsbridge to reclaim her box and expensive dresses. This is the only known corroboration for Kelly's reported claim to have worked in a 'gay house' with French connections in the West End.

Mrs Carthy said that Kelly left Breezer's Hill in late 1886 and went to live with a man connected with the building trade (possibly **Joseph Fleming**). **Joseph Barnett** called Mrs Carthy's 'a bad house'.

See also **Mrs Phoenix**, **Mrs Buki**.

CARTWRIGHT, PC

Several newspapers reported the inquest testimony of **Inspector Spratling** that, 'Between five and six o'clock the same morning he directed Police Constable Cartwright to examine the neighbourhood where the deceased was found, including the walls, the yards, and the adjoining railway' (*Daily News*, 4 September 1888; *East London Observer, Eastern Argus & Borough of Hackney Times*, 8 September 1888). Other newspapers report Spratling giving these instructions to **PC Thain** (*Echo*, the *Star*, 3 September 1888; the *Bristol Mercury and Daily Post*, 4 September 1888; *Woodford Times*, 7 September 1888).

No PC Cartwright has ever been identified.

(*See also* Bernard Brown, 'Cartwrights To Ponder Over', *Ripperologist*, April 2002.)

CASEBOOK: JACK THE RIPPER (www.casebook.org)

Created in January 1996 by webmaster Stephen P. Ryder (*b.* 1978) and technical consultant John Piper ('Johnno'), Australian musician and photographer with his own website at www.xenedis.net.

The first and largest of the websites dedicated to Ripper material and an outstanding resource for anyone interested in the case, offering information about suspects, victims and policemen, along with original documents and other source material. Transcripts of contemporary newspaper reports, the brainchild of Adrian Phypers, are particularly valuable. There is also an active message board. Archived material from the early years of the Casebook is available on CD-ROM.

CASEBOOK ON JACK THE RIPPER, A

Book by Richard Whittington-Egan (London: Wildy & Sons, 1975).

Whittington-Egan (*b.* 1924) is a medically trained former journalist writing for *Weekend* magazine and on the board of *Contemporary Review*. He is an authority on crime, ghosts, and fin-de-siècle literature.

Devoted almost entirely to dispassionately discussing the theories as they were at the time of publication and divided into two parts. Part One discusses the literature and suspects down to 1972 and consists of three articles originally written for *Contemporary Review* in November and December 1972 and January 1973, and subsequently reprinted and published in an edition limited to 100 copies. Part Two reviews the literature and suspects from 1973 until 1975. The author offers no solution of his own, but many corrections of legendary accretions.

CATCH ME WHEN YOU CAN
Book by Leanne Perry (Perry Publishing, 2007).

Summarises case for **Joseph Barnett** being Jack the Ripper and advances some new observations and ideas.

CATHERINE EDDOWES: JACK THE RIPPER VICTIM
Booklet by Neal Shelden (Hornchurch, Essex: Neal Shelden, 2003).

Third publication about Jack the Ripper's victims (*see* **Jack the Ripper and His Victims** (1999) and **Annie Chapman: Jack the Ripper Victim. A Short Biography** (2001)), looking at their lives, families and descendants.

CAUNTER, SERGEANT ELI (*b.* 1852)
pictured

Joined the Metropolitan Police in 1872 (warrant no. 55750). Involved in the investigation of **Martha Tabram**'s murder and traced 'Pearly Poll' (*see* **Mary Ann Connolly**), who had gone into hiding with her cousin. **F.P. Wensley** described him as a valued colleague in **H Division**, nicknamed 'Tommy Roundhead'.

CHANDLER, INSPECTOR JOSEPH LUNNISS (1850–1923)
First senior policeman to handle the finding of **Annie Chapman**'s body. Joined the Metropolitan Police in 1873 (warrant no. 56638). Demoted to sergeant for drunkenness on duty in 1892; retired, 1898.

Chandler was on duty at Commercial Street Police Station at 6.02am, on 8 September 1888, when he saw men running up Hanbury Street. Told of the murder, he went to the site, sent for **Dr Phillips**, sent to the station for an ambulance and notified Scotland Yard. He cleared the passage in 29 Hanbury Street of people and covered the body with sacking.

On 12 September he was reported in the *Star* as saying 'with a laugh' that the alleged bloodstains on the fence of 25 Hanbury Street seen by **Laura Sickings** were sprinkles of urine.

Chandler's investigation of the envelope found by Chapman's body established, through a visit to the Surrey Regiment camp at Farnborough, that the envelope had been posted from Messrs Summer and Thirkettle, who supplied this officially stamped stationery to the canteen where the men could purchase it, and nearly all did. Chandler found that none of the men acknowledged correspondence with anyone in Spitalfields or anyone whose address began with 2; that none of their signatures in the paybook matched the initials on the envelope and similar stationery could be purchased direct from Summers and Thirkettle by anyone, regardless of whether or not they were attached to the regiment (MEPO 3/140 ff16–17).

CHAPMAN, ANNIE (1841–88)

Second Ripper victim.

Born Eliza Anne Smith in Paddington. Father, George Smith, a lifeguardsman, married her mother, Ruth Chapman, in 1842. The family moved to Windsor in 1856. She married John Chapman at All Saints Church, Knightsbridge (1869). Lived in West London until 1881, when she moved back to Windsor. Two daughters (one died 1882), one (crippled) son. Shortly before her daughter Emily's death, Annie abandoned her family and returned to London, receiving sporadic allowances from Chapman until his death in 1886.

Allegedly her alcoholism and immorality broke up the marriage, but acquaintances described her as only occasionally drunk (*cf.* John Chapman's death). Thereafter lived variously by hawking her own crochet work, selling matches or flowers, living off men friends, and occasionally prostituting herself. She may be the same as the Annie Chapman (aged 45) who is recorded in the Thames Police

Court Register on 10 October 1885 as being convicted of stealing a hammer, being fined *20/- or 14 days*.

During 1886, she lived at 30 Dorset Street with a sievemaker named (or nicknamed) Jack Sivvey.

From about May 1888, she lived mainly at Crossingham's Lodging House, 35 Dorset Street.

She stood 5ft tall and was stout, with dark wavy brown hair, blue eyes and a thick nose. Police and press said front teeth were missing from her lower jaw, though **Dr George Bagster Phillips** stated her front teeth were perfect. Phillips also reported that at the time of her death she was undernourished, with chronic diseases of the lungs and brain membranes, which would before long have killed her.

During the first week of September she fought with **Eliza Cooper**. According to Annie's friends, the dispute arose because Annie told **'Harry the Hawker'** that she had seen Eliza steal a florin (2-shilling piece, value 10p) from him, replacing it with a halfpenny. According to Eliza, the provoking halfpenny had been thrown at her by Annie in lieu of the return of her soap, which had been borrowed for the use of **Ted Stanley**. Both accounts agree that a halfpenny and a man who appeared to be sharing the ladies' favours lay behind the fight, which was variously described as taking place on 28 or 30 August, or 1, 2, 4, 5 or 6 September, and in The Britannia, in the kitchen at Crossingham's, or starting in one and resuming in the other.

Annie suffered a black eye and bruising about the chest from this fight and complained to **Amelia Palmer** that she would have to go to the infirmary. No woman matching her description was admitted to Whitechapel or Spitalfields Workhouse Infirmaries at this time, but she may have collected some medication.

At 11.30pm, on 7 September **Timothy Donovan** – deputy of Crossingham's – let her into the kitchen. **William Stevens** saw her there at 12.12am, slightly the worse for drink. She took a box of pills from her pocket and when the box broke, put the pills in a torn piece of envelope taken from the floor. It bore the crest of the Sussex Regiment, the letter 'M' in a man's handwriting and a postmark: 'London, 28 August, 1888'. She probably left the lodging-house then and went for a drink shortly afterwards (*see* **Frederick Stevens**). By 1.35am she had returned. Donovan said he found her drunk and eating a baked potato in the kitchen. He asked for her doss money, to which she replied, 'I haven't got it. I am weak and ill, and have been in the infirmary.' She left, saying, 'Don't let the bed. I'll be back soon.'

Watchman **John Evans** reported that she had just returned to Crossingham's and had told him that she had been to see one of her sisters in Vauxhall and had just slipped out for a pint of beer. She also said to him, 'I won't be long, Brummy. See that Tim keeps the bed for me.' Evans saw her go into Paternoster Row in the direction of Brushfield Street.

It is probable Donovan, Stevens and Evans all mistook Chapman's general ill-health for intoxication (*see* **Dr Phillips**).

She was reportedly seen in The Ten Bells, opposite Spitalfields Market soon after it opened at 5.00am, but this was a mistake in identity (*see* **Edward McKenna**). Around 5.30, **Elizabeth Darrell** saw a woman whom she identified as Chapman on the pavement outside 29 Hanbury Street, talking to an apparently foreign man, a little taller than herself, who said to her, 'Will you?' to which Chapman replied, 'Yes.' Very shortly afterwards, **Albert Cadoche** possibly overheard the murderous assault in the back yard of no. 29.

Shortly before 6.00am **John Davis** went into the back yard of 29 Hanbury Street, where he found Chapman's body lying on her back parallel to the fence (which was on her left), with her head close to the back-door steps of the house.

Her dress was pulled above her knees, exposing her striped stockings, and her intestines lay across her left shoulder. (*See* Dr George Bagster Phillips for detailed injuries.)

A small crowd gathered in the passage running from the Hanbury Street door of no. 29 to the back door (*see* **Henry Holland**, **James Green**, **James Kent** and **Mrs Hardyman**) and **Inspector Chandler** took charge shortly after 6.00am. The immediate police search discovered the piece of torn envelope and two pills in a screw of paper. There was also a folded and saturated leather apron about two feet away from the standpipe in the yard. (*See* **'Leather Apron'** for significance.)

Dr George Bagster Phillips arrived at about 6.30. After examining the body, he ordered it to be taken to Whitechapel Workhouse Infirmary Mortuary in Eagle Street, off Old Montague Street. He then discovered the contents of Annie Chapman's pocket (which had been cut open) lying in a surprisingly neat or deliberate pile: a piece of coarse muslin, two combs and almost certainly two farthings, which may have been brightly polished (*see* **Inspector Reid**, **Major Henry Smith**). The coins were described in press reports the same day, but were not mentioned in reports of the inquest. However, according to some authorities they reappeared in newspaper reports (so far unconfirmed by the authors) two weeks later, accompanied by or incorporating an alleged 'pile' of Annie Chapman's rings.

Chapman had been wearing two brass rings when she left Crossingham's and they were missing from her body. Abrasions on her ring finger showed where one had been torn off, probably by her murderer. The rings were never traced, despite widely publicised police enquiries.

The body was washed and laid out by **Mary Simonds** and **Frances Wright**, to the annoyance of George Bagster Phillips when he came to carry out the postmortem. At 11.30am, Annie was identified by **Amelia Palmer**. On Monday, 10 September, **Emmanuel Violenia** was shown the body in the mortuary.

On Friday, 14 September Annie Chapman was secretly buried at Manor Park. Members of her family attended the funeral.

CHAPMAN, FREDERICK RICHARD (1851–88)

Alleged suspect.

MB and CM, 1874 (Glasgow). MO, Brixton District. Former MO, Fever and Smallpox Hospital, Hull and surgeon, Hull and Sculcoates Dispensary. Born in Poona, India; son of an army NCO. Came to London from provincial practice, 1886. Wrote pamphlets on medical subjects and letters to the professional press. Died of septic tubercular abscess, conspicuously poor, probably because of long illness.

Suggested real name of **'Dr Merchant'**, pseudonymously identified by B.E. Reilly ('Jack the Ripper – The Mystery Solved?', *City: The Magazine of the City of London Police*, February 1972) as the only Brixton doctor whose death coincided with the ending of the murders and therefore probably Police Constable Robert Spicer's suspect. It was discussed by N.P. Warren ('"Dr Merchant"' Was Not Jack the Ripper' *Criminologist*, Spring 1992). Christopher J. Morley (*Jack the Ripper: Eliminating the Suspects*) notes that apart from the coincidental time of his death, there is nothing whatsoever to link Dr Chapman with the murders.

CHAPMAN, GEORGE (1865–1903)

Abberline's suspect following his arrest for wife-murder in 1903. *See* **Severin Klosowski**.

CHAPMAN, JOHN (1843–86)

Husband of **Annie Chapman**. Domestic head coachman. A relative of her mother, Ruth Chapman, he married Annie on 1 May 1869.

In 1870, the couple lived in Bayswater, London. Then, in 1873, in a mews off Berkeley Square. **Timothy Donovan** alleged Mrs Pearcer of Hackney, a friend of Annie's, told him that Chapman lost his post as valet to a gentleman in Bond Street because of Annie's dishonesty.

By 1881 he was working for Josiah or Joseph Weeks at St Leonard's Mill Farm Cottage, Windsor. In 1882 the marriage broke down. According to the police this was because of Annie's 'drunken and immoral ways'. He paid her 10/- (50p) a week, though not, apparently, absolutely regularly until his death at Grove Road, Windsor, on Christmas Day, 1886. He died of cirrhosis of the liver and dropsy, which throws a question over *Annie's* supposed alcoholism as causing the marital breakdown.

Amelia Palmer alleged, incorrectly, that he was a veterinary surgeon.

CHAPPELL, MARY

Friend of **Mrs Fiddymont** who, like her, saw a strange man with a bloodstained hand in the Prince Albert Tavern. Chappell left the pub by a different door and pointed the man out to **Joseph Taylor**.

CHARLIE THE RIPPER

Suspect, psychically proposed in *Reveille* (12 March 1976) by Mrs Carmen Rogers, a medium, who said that she believed the Ripper was an impotent, nondescript, pasty-faced 35- to 40-year-old fish gutter, whom she called 'Charlie'.

CHARRINGTON, FREDERICK NICHOLAS (1850–1936)

Spoof suspect, proposed 1999.

Eccentric philanthropist and temperance reformer Frederick Charrington was heir to a huge East End brewery, from which he derived his income yet he was a teetotal extremist who picketed pubs and music halls. On one occasion he seized the mace from the House of Commons in protest against the bars in the Palace of Westminster. He conducted tent meeting crusades in the East End and built a huge mission hall, where he distributed free teas to the poor. In 1887 he started a campaign against prostitution, noting down the identities of clients visiting brothels and threatening to reveal their names.

In the **Mammoth Book of Jack the Ripper** M.J. Trow presented a case for Charrington as the Ripper, omitting only the sinister fact that during the autumn and early winter of 1888, Charrington temporarily terminated his public activities following an encounter with a brothel bully. Trow concluded his piece by observing that Charrington was 'a good man doing a difficult job at a difficult time and no more Jack the Ripper than I am.' The whole exercise was intended as a valuable demonstration of the ease with which an innocent man might be slipped into the frame as Jack the Ripper.

CHEEKS, MARGARET 'MOG'

Prostitute fellow-lodger of **Alice McKenzie**, who was missed from her lodgings on the night of McKenzie's murder, 17 July 1889. Estranged wife of Charlie Cheeks. Mog was missing for two days after the discovery of McKenzie's body, leading to a short-lived fear that she, too, had been murdered. In fact, she had been staying with her sister.

'CHERINTON, NELIS'

Suggested witness. Prostitute said by **Tomas Romero** to have dined with him and his suspect one night, and so to be capable of visually identifying the man. Since Romero spoke little or no English, she may well have been called something like 'Nelly Charrington' (HO144/221/ A49301D, ff 83–96).

CHISHOLM, SUPERINTENDENT COLIN (*b. c.* 1841)

Born in Inverness, Colin Chisholm joined the Metropolitan Police in 1868 (warrant no. 49855). He resigned in 1899.

As chief inspector, in 1891 he joined **Inspector Race** and **Sergeant McCarthy** in tracing **Thomas Hayne Cutbush**'s criminal record (Macnaghten memoranda).

CHRONICLE OF CRIME, THE

Three handwritten books of notes and observations on the major crimes of *c.* 1870 to *c.* 1930, compiled by **Dr Thomas Dutton**; given by him to Miss Hermione Dudley and not seen since. **Donald McCormick** claimed to have seen the books in 1932 and uses them extensively in *The Identity of Jack the Ripper*, but the late **Melvin Harris** pointed out (*Jack the Ripper: The Bloody Truth*) that Dr Dutton's description of the murderer as given by Miss Dudley in a newspaper interview (*Sunday Chronicle*, 17 November 1935) was at serious variance with McCormick's account.

CHURCHILL, GEORGE CHARLES SPENCER, MARQUIS OF BLANDFORD, subsequently 8TH DUKE OF MARLBOROUGH (1844–92)

Alleged suspect. Listed in *The Ripper and the Royals* as co-conspirator with his brother, **Lord Randolph Churchill**.

CHURCHILL, LORD RANDOLPH HENRY SPENCER (1849–94)

Suspect, first alleged 1991.

Conservative statesman. Son of Sixth Duke of Marlborough and father of Sir Winston Churchill. Secretary of State for India, 1885–86. Chancellor of the Exchequer, 1886, but resigned office the same year, effectively terminating his political career.

The Ripper and the Royals argues that in 1888 Lord Randolph was the very highest Freemason in the land and was responsible for organising the conspiracy of Freemasons in which **Sir William Gull**, assisted by **John Netley**, **Frederico Albericci** and, possibly, **J.K. Stephen**, protected **Prince Albert Victor**'s good name and the position of the crown by murdering the East End prostitutes centring on **Mary Jane Kelly**, who were allegedly attempting to use their knowledge of his supposed secret marriage to **Annie Elizabeth Crook** for blackmailing purposes.

See *Jack the Ripper: The Final Solution* and **Joseph Gorman Sickert**. Also, N.P. Warren, 'Lord Randolph Churchill', **Ripperana**, 14, October 1995.

CITY OF DREADFUL DELIGHT: NARRATIVES OF SEXUAL DANGER IN LATE VICTORIAN LONDON

Book by Judith R. Walkowitz (Chicago: University of Chicago Press, 1992).

Walkowitz (*b.* 1945) is Professor of Modern European Social History at Johns Hopkins University and a leading feminist academic commentator on Jack the Ripper and women's role in Victorian society.

The book expands her 1982 essay, 'Jack the Ripper and the Myth of Male Violence' (*Feminist Studies*, Vol. 8, No. 3 autumn, 1982), and places it as the climactic centrepiece in a survey of changing social habits and attitudes in the late nineteenth century, which determined English culture's opinions about and treatment of women up to the rise of late twentieth-century feminism. Walkowitz maintains the apparent threat that the Ripper posed to unprotected women empowered men to unnecessarily assume the role of being their guardians in a way that restricted an area of women's independence.

See Also: *Prostitution and Victorian Society: Women, Class and the State* (New York: Cambridge University Press, 1980); 'Myths and Murderers,' (review of books on Jack the Ripper), *Women's Review of Books*, 5 March 1988, 'Jack the Ripper and the Myth of Male Violence,' *Feminist Studies* 8, no. 3 (fall 1982): 543–74.

CITY OF LONDON POLICE

Founded 1839, following the success of Robert Peel's Metropolitan Police Force, which the City of London had refused to accept in replacement of its tried and tested constables. Responsible to the Corporation of the City of London, its jurisdiction covers the administrative area of the City (roughly the square mile lying north of London Bridge). **Catherine Eddowes** was the only Ripper victim murdered in the City. The force was expected to liaise with the Metropolitan Police once involved in the Whitechapel murders investigation. According to **Walter Dew**, cooperation between the two forces was very good throughout the case, but *see* **Henry Matthews, James McWilliam**.

In 1888–89 the City Commissioner was **Sir James Fraser**; his deputy was **Major Henry Smith** and **James McWilliam** was head of the CID.

CITY POLICE SUSPECT

Term used to describe Detective Constable **Sagar**'s suspect, usually assumed to be conflated with **Inspector Harry Cox**'s suspect. So the man was an East Ender, about 5ft 6in tall, with short black curly hair. A misogynist, who had once been wronged by a woman, it was this rather than sheer madness that accounted for his murderous rage. He was of the same abysmally low class as the prostitutes he killed. Also, given to late night walks, 'occupied' several shops in the East End and was once seen visiting a shop near Leman Street, where several criminals lived. Occasionally insane, he had to go to a Surrey asylum for treatment from time to time (Cox). He worked in Butcher's Row, Aldgate; was undoubtedly insane and ultimately removed to a private asylum by his relatives, after which the murders stopped (Sagar).

It has been suggested that this suspect might be **Hyam Hyams**.

In *The Man Who Hunted Jack the Ripper* (p.141) it is suggested that the City Police suspect is 'referred to by **Swanson** in his marginalia'. Since Swanson states that his 'suspect was **Kosminski**', this introduces the positive note that Kosminski was indeed interned by his relatives, who appear to have taken some financial responsibility for him, though he was never placed in a private asylum. Nor was he ever in an asylum in Surrey. It is not known whether Aaron might at one time have worked in Butcher's Row.

The authors note the possibility that the City Police kept observation on more than one suspect, and these accounts might be describing to one, two or three people.

CLAPP, GEORGE THOMAS (*b.* 1863)
Witness at **Catherine Eddowes**' inquest. A clerk and also caretaker at no. 5 Mitre Street, whose bedroom overlooked Mitre Square. His wife was evidently ill or disabled, as a Mrs Tew — a nurse attending her — was also sleeping in the house. None of the occupants heard anything of the murder (Inquest testimony at London Metropolitan Archives)

CLARENCE, DUKE OF
See **Albert Victor, Prince**.

CLARENCE: THE LIFE OF HRH THE DUKE OF CLARENCE AND AVONDALE (1864–1892)
Book by Michael Harrison (London: W.H. Allen, 1972; published in the US as *Clarence: Was He Jack the Ripper?* New York: Drake Publishing, 1974).

Advances theory that **James Kenneth Stephen** was Jack the Ripper, believing that Stephen killed prostitutes when they used a triggerword 'dear'. Appearing on BBC2's *Late Night Line-Up*, Harrison explained he did not accept that the Ripper was Prince Albert Victor, '…but I couldn't leave the reader high and dry, so what I did was find somebody who I thought was a likely candidate.' *Daniel Farson*, who appeared on the programme with Harrison and Colin Wilson, observed about the triggerword 'dear', 'And this set him off because he had been deer-stalking with Clarence, years before. Well, you can make out a better case for Queen Victoria' ('Relatively Ripping', *The Listener*, 17 August 1972).

CLARK, DR PERCY JOHN (1865–1942)
Newly-qualified assistant to Dr **George Bagster Phillips**.

Registered (Edinburgh) 1887. Lic.Soc.Apoth, Lond, 1887. MRCS, 1888. Metropolitan Police Surgeon, Spitalfields, 1888–1925. Retired, 1925.

Attended postmortems on **Alice McKenzie** and the **Pinchin Street torso**. He wrote his own report on the latter and recorded the opinion that the body had been dead about 24 hours (MEPO 3/140 ff 170–3, 259–62). His inquest testimony was reported thus in *Eastern Post and City Chronicle,* 28 September 1889:

Mr. Percy John Clark, assistant to Dr. Phillips, surgeon to the H Division of police said: Shortly before six o'clock on the morning of September 10th I was called by the police to Pinchin Street. Under the railway arch there, about 8ft. from the road, and about a foot from the right wall of the arch, I saw the trunk of a woman, minus the head and legs. The arms were not severed from the body. There was no pool of blood, nor were there any signs of a struggle having taken place there; but on moving the body I found that there was a little blood underneath where the neck had been. This blood had apparently oozed out from the cut surface of the neck. On the remains were the remnants of what had been a chemise of common make. It had been torn down the front and cut from the front of the arm holes on each side. There was no distinguishing mark on the garment. The body was taken to the mortuary, and an examination there showed it to be that of a woman of stoutish build, of dark complexion, about 5ft 3ins in height, and between 30 and 40 years old. I should think the body must have been dead about 24 hours. Besides the wounds caused by the severance of the head and legs, there was a wound 15 ins. long through the external coats of the abdomen. The body was not blood-stained, except where the chemise had rested upon it. The body seemed to have been recently washed. On the back there were four bruises, all caused before death. One was under the spine, on a level with the lower part of the shoulder blade. An inch lower down was a similar bruise. About the middle of the back also, over the spine, was a bruise about the size of half a crown. On a level with the top of the hip bone, and 3 ins. to the left of the spine, was a bruise 2? ins in diameter, such as might be caused by a fall or a kick. None of the bruises were of old standing. On the right arm there were eight distinct bruises, and seven on the left, all caused before death and of recent date. The backs of both forearms and hands were much bruised. On the other side of the left forearm, about 3 ins. above the wrist, was a cut about 2 ins. in length, and ? in lower down was another cut, both caused after death. The bruises on the right arm were such as would have been caused by the arm having been tightly grasped. There was an old injury on the index finger of the right hand over the last joint. Two vaccination marks were on the left arm. The arms were well formed. Both elbows were hardened and discoloured, as if they had been leant upon. The hands and nails were pallid, and the former were not indicative of any particular kind of work. There was no sign of maternity about the body.

Interviewed by the *East London Observer*, 14 May 1910, Clark denied a medical student or doctor had committed the murders, claiming, 'There was nothing of a professional character about these wounds. The bodies were simply slashed about from head to foot.' He also expressed doubt that the murders were committed by the same man, saying, 'I think perhaps one man was responsible for three of them,' and on the subject of the murderer's identity claimed, 'there was never the slightest clue to anybody…' His statements were used in ***Jack the Ripper*** (Cook, 2009) to bolster the claim that a single murderer was a journalistic invention.

Following his retirement in 1925, he went to live in San Francisco with his wife and daughter, but later returned to England. In 1941, he attended the funeral of George George Bagster Phillips' 101-year-old widow. He died in Chertsey, in 1942 – see obituary in the *Surrey Comet*, 10 January 1942.

CLARKE, GEORGE

Builder's merchant, who kept materials in the yard between 106 and 108 Poplar High Street, where **Rose Mylett**'s body was found.

CLARKSON, WILLY (1861–1934)

Theatrical wig-maker, who believed he had sold a disguise to the Ripper. In an article in *The People* (27 March 1932), Clarkson said that shortly after the double murder a policeman came into his shop with a 'light brown wig of ample curly hair'. He said it had been found near **Catherine Eddowes**' body and after he had left, Clarkson recalled selling such a wig to a wiry, medium-sized man with a sallow complexion, greying hair and full lips. He was obviously of the professional classes and his eyes were cold, resolute and magnetic.

Clarkson also believed he had sold a wig to the murdering burglar Charlie Peace and had pictures of murderers Dr Crippen, Herbert Bennett and Ronald True added to his article, suggesting he had helped them with disguises they are not known to have used.

CLEARY, JOHN

Name ascribed by the *New York Herald* (London edition) to **John Arnold**.

CLEVELAND STREET SCANDAL

Discovery and closure of a male brothel staffed by telegraph boys in Cleveland Street, London. The proprietor fled abroad, but his assistant was prosecuted and convicted. Important to the Ripper case because notes on one 'P.A.V' in the National Archives support the insinuation in the *North London Press* (16 November 1889) that efforts had been made to conceal the fact that it had been visited by **Prince Albert Victor** and because **Inspector Abberline** was prominent in the proceedings. *Epiphany of the Whitechapel Murders* argues **Mary Kelly** worked there and that the Ripper murders were committed to prevent her from making public the visits of the Prince.

See also **Ernest Parke, Lord Euston, Lord Arthur Somerset, Donald Swanson**.

CLIPPINGS BOOK

Victorian ledger into which have been pasted original newspaper reports about the Whitechapel murders, purchased by Patricia Cornwell from an antiquarian bookshop in London. The book was originally acquired at auction in 2001, but its provenance has not yet been disclosed.

The cuttings, running from approximately August 1888 to October 1889, have been marked up and annotated in contemporary handwriting and the comments suggest they were written by a well informed person. Among the most extensive annotations are those against the reports of 16 September 1888 on the inquest into the death of **Annie Chapman**: 'Was also called "dark Annie"/Is this [**Amelia Farmer**] the woman who was nearly murdered?/ What

Regiment did Grant belong to? Try War Office'. Other annotations, against other reports, include comments such as: 'Find this man/Are any of the "Suspected" left-handed?/Saw him in Veteran – just before latter appeared/Lady in Veteran saw him & remarked as well/Short 5.3 – stoutish, dark whiskers & hair dark eyes – 40/Ask informant about this man His evidence is "unsatisfactory"/Important. Find the woman/ Jewes – Juees – Jews – Jeues – Jewes/ Who is Mrs Hilt?'

CLOAK AND DAGGER CLUB
See **Whitechapel 1888 Society**.

COHEN, AARON DAVIS aka DAVID COHEN (1865–89)
Proposed in 1987 by Martin Fido as Anderson's suspect and probably Jack the Ripper. 'A young foreign Jew with dark brown hair, beard and eyes' (Colney Hatch case notes) brought before Thames Magistrates Court, 7 December 1888, by Police Constable **J. Patrick** 91H, as a lunatic wandering at large. Named as Aaron Davis Cohen. Committed by court to Workhouse Infirmary for observation. His hearing minuted with those of Gertrude Smith, Mary Jones and Ellen Hickey. Delivered to Whitechapel Workhouse Infirmary by PC Patrick at 5.00pm the same day under the name of David Cohen.

The Workhouse Infirmary Records read:

3983: Cohen, David; Age 23; Admitted from Thames Police Court, PC 91H; Single; Tailor; Insane; Hebrew;

Admitted by order of Medical officer at 5.30 pm December 7 1888; Sent to BG Ward; Discharged 21/12/88 To Colney Hatch Asylum.

The Asylum Casebook records read:

Admission No. 10,523; David Cohen; Admitted Dec 21 1888; Age 23; Parish Whitechapel; [Overwritten insert] Ill 28 Dec. 88; Single; Tailor; Hebrew; If first attack Yes; Previous care and treatment Nowhere; Duration of Existing Attack 2 weeks; Supposed cause Unknown; Subject to epilepsy No; Suicidal Yes; Dangerous to Others Yes; Nearest relative Unknown.

Fact indicating insanity observed by Medical Officer:
Patient was brought in by police, who found him wandering at large and unable to take care of himself. Is supposed to have tried to commit suicide. Has been very violent since admission.

Threatened other patients. Refused his food for some days, but takes it now. very noisy at night & very difficult to manage.

Other facts indicating Insanity communicated to him by others:
By Attendant Henry Williams – States he spits about the ward & is very violent. Tore down the leaden pipe in the ward & also the wire guard of the window. Shouts and dances about the ward when he is free.
Signed HERBERT LARDER
Whitechapel Infirmary

OBSERVATIONS
FORM OF DISORDER Mania

A young foreign Jew with dark brown hair, beard and eyes, who is brought to the asylum in restraint, and in a state of great excitement; the first thing he did on admission was to throw himself on the ground with considerable violence, he is exceedingly restless and refuses all nourishment; he is pale and exceedingly thin.

To be fed by tube when necessary.

1888 Dec 24 Been restless since admission. Refused food 2nd day after admission and was fed through oesophagal tube twice. Takes his food now with some persuasion. Asks for liquid food and after filling his mouth will spit it out again. Dressed in strong dress and kept under constant watch.

26th Takes food better now, but still only in liquid form.

28th Kept apart from other patients as patient is restless and agitated. Incoherent and rambling. Chiefly speaks in German.

30th Not so restless. Sleeps better at night. No violence recorded.

1889 Feb 5. Since last note has had several small boils on his arms near wrists which are now cured. Continues in an excited state, but not to such a degree as before. Requires constant supervision. Destructive to clothing. Manner flighty and uncertain. Ordered 2 eggs extra each day. Speech is incoherent. Gesticulates frequently. Habits dirty occasionally. Takes food well.

April 8th Restless and excited: frequently kicks passers-by; habits uncleanly and destructive, he is gaining strength.

July 7th Mischievous. Takes food well. Destructive to clothing. Requires constant attention. health fair.

Oct 15th Removed to C5 lately. Becoming feebler lately and unable to walk without help. Examined him. Found him to be excited but incoherent as before. Temperature 108.2 evening. Left infra axillary region dull on percussion also infra mammary and infra scapular left side. Tubular breathing. Friction sound heard interiorly and moist sounds above. Does not speak. Expectorates a mucous, purulent fluid. Confined to bed. Ordered liquid diet. poultices not retained. Stimulating expectorant mixture ordered. [notes by Drs Seward and Swanton]

Oct 20 Died.

The formal letter, dated 21 October, from Dr Seward to the coroner states, 'The cause of death was Exhaustion of Mania and Pulmonary Pthisis, and the duration of illness was over 10 months' (Middlesex County Lunatic Asylum, Colney Hatch. Register of Admissions. Males. Vol3, folio 2).

The case for David Cohen being Jack the Ripper is based on the belief that he was, or was confused with **Robert Anderson**'s Polish Jew suspect: of three asylum occupants (*cf.* **Aaron Kosminski**, **Hyam Hyams**), who loosely match the mutually contradictory comments of Anderson, **Swanson** and **Macnaghten**; he is the only one whose incarceration coincided with the cessation of the murders and his death (uniquely among Jewish patients) was soon after committal, as Swanson asserted. Seeming admissions by Anderson that the Ripper had not been caught, as appears to be the case in his interview with **Richard Harding Davis** in August 1889, are discounted because they took place before Cohen died, and the theory is that the eye-witness identification probably took place after the suspect had been committed, as Anderson stated in the serialisation of his memoirs (omitted from the volume edition), which would therefore place the identification after the Davis interview.

Dr Luigi Cancrini, professor of psychology at the University of Bologna, who gave a paper on the psychopathology of Jack the Ripper in Cattolica in 1988, concluded the increasing violence of the murders indicated growing internalised rage that must ultimately have turned against the self and led the killer to commit suicide. When shown the case notes of Cohen, of whom he had no previous knowledge, he expressed to Martin Fido that Cohen fitted his reading, since the frustration of heavy policing obviating Cohen's ability to relieve his tension by murder could have induced such extravagant mania that his immediate incarceration inevitably followed.

However, Dr P.T. d'Orban, consultant psychiatrist at the Royal Free Hospital, on being shown the case notes of Cohen and Aaron Kosminski the following year, appears not to have entertained the idea of Cohen's sudden deterioration into uncontrollable mania and wrote to Martin Fido that he did not think either likely to have been the Ripper, but of the two thought Kosminski 'the more likely' because he felt that Cohen's extreme mania would have undermined the self-control required to murder and escape successfully (letter in the authors' possession).

World-renowned FBI profiler John Douglas, who on the 1988 TV programme, *The True Identity of Jack the Ripper*, had endorsed **Aaron Kosminski**, embraced David Cohen when he learned of him, writing, 'I'm now prepared to say that Jack the Ripper was either the man known to the police as David Cohen... or someone very much like him.' (John Douglas and Mark Olshaker, *The Cases That Haunt Us*, New York: Scribner, 2000).

The case against Cohen being Anderson's suspect is that Macnaghten identifies a Polish Jew suspect as Kosminski and Swanson names Kosminski as Anderson's suspect. Anderson's continued vigorous investigation of further Ripper alarms after Cohen's incarceration and death has suggested to some commentators that he continued to believe the Ripper was at large.

COHEN, JACOB

Lay witness for certification of **Aaron Kosminski**. Resided at 51 Carter Lane, EC. Said Kosminski refused food from others and went about the streets, picking up bread from the gutters and drinking from standpipes. Refused to be washed and had not worked for years. Took up a knife and threatened his sister's life.

COHEN, MORRIS
See **Morris Lubnowski**.

COHEN, N.
Should have appeared to charge **Ellen Hickey** with assault before Thames Magistrates Court at the same time and under the same Minute of Attendance as **Aaron Davis Cohen**. Hickey was discharged as N. Cohen did not appear.

COHN, DR (or Koch)
Suspect in, or about 1888; named by Inspector Keaton in 1969. *See* **Keaton** for details.

COINS AND RINGS, pile of
See **Annie Chapman**, **Oswald Allen**.

FRANCES COLES

COLES, FRANCES (1865–91)
Aka 'Carrotty Nell', Frances Hawkins, Frances Coleman.

Final alleged Ripper victim. Good-looking daughter of a respectable former bootmaker, whom she frequently visited in Bermondsey Workhouse. Employed as wholesale chemist's packer until *c.* 1884, when she went on the streets.

At 2.20 am, 13 February 1891, Police Constable **Ernest Thompson** 240H approached Swallow Gardens, a narrow alley running under the railway arches between Chambers Street and Rosemary Lane (today's Royal Mint Street), when he heard the receding footsteps of someone walking at an ordinary rate away from him in the direction of Mansell Street. Turning into Swallow Gardens, he discovered Frances Coles. Her throat had just been cut and was bleeding profusely, but her eyes were open and she was still alive, though would die on the stretcher produced to take her to hospital.

The threat of a revived 'Ripper' scare in the newspapers brought **Superintendent Arnold**, **Inspector Reid**, Chief Constable **Melville Macnaghten** and Assistant Commissioner **Robert Anderson** to the scene of the crime the following morning, and the site of crime was very carefully examined. Blood was taken for analysis and 2/- (10p), presumed to be the woman's earnings (*cf.* 'Rosy'), found hidden behind a lamp-post or gutterpipe at the end of the alley. Enquiries in the docks revealed Coles had spent most of the previous two days with **James Thomas Sadler** until they quarrelled. Sadler was subsequently arrested.

Coles' inquest was conducted by Coroner **Wynne Baxter** at the Working Lads' Institute, Whitechapel, on 15, 16, 20, 23 and 27 February. Sadler was exonerated and the jury found 'Murder by a person or persons unknown' and he was discharged.

COLLARD, INSPECTOR EDWARD (1846–92)

Witness at **Catherine Eddowes**' inquest. Joined City of London Police, 1868. Warrant no. 4157. Died 1892, as chief inspector, Bishopsgate Division. Station inspector on duty in Bishopsgate, 30 September 1888. Collard was called to Mitre Square to see the body and timed his arrival as 2.03am. He organised an immediate search of the district and house-to-house interviews the following day.

COLLIER, GEORGE (c. 1821–94)

Born in Calcutta, India. Barrister.

Deputy coroner for the South Eastern Division of Middlesex; conducted inquest on **Martha Tabram**.

COLLINS, RESERVE PC ALBERT, 12HR (b. 1847)

Joined the Metropolitan Police in 1873 (warrant no. 56929). Subsequently transferred to Reserve.

At 5.30am on 30 September 1888 Collins washed away all traces of blood from Dutfield's Yard.

COLLINS, JOHN CHURTON (1848–1908)

Author, journalist, essayist, literary critic.

Born at Burton-on-the-Water, Gloucestershire, and educated at King Edward's School, Birmingham, and Baliol College, Oxford. Became English Literature professor at Birmingham University (1904). In 1908, in poor health and apparently suffering from acute depression, he went to stay with an old friend, Dr Daniel, at his home in Oulton Broad, near Lowestoft. On 25 September he walked to a rural spot he was fond of and took a sleeping draught. It seems likely that he awoke later that night and stumbled into a water-filled ditch, where he drowned, the inquest recording the verdict of accidental death.

His papers record a visit on Wednesday, 19 April 1905, to the scenes of the Whitechapel murders in the company of **Sir Arthur Conan Doyle**, **Ingleby Oddie**, and others. They were escorted by two detectives and their guide was **Dr Gordon Brown** who Collins said told him that 'he was inclined to think that he (the murderer) was or had been a medical student, as he undoubtedly had a knowledge of human anatomy, but that he was also a butcher, as the mutilations, slashing the nose, etc., were butchers' cuts.' Brown dismissed the drowned doctor theory (see **Montague John Druitt**) because 'the last murder, possibly the last two murders, were committed after the body was found' Brown being 'strongly of opinion that the last two were Ripper murders'. Brown also dismissed the idea that the murderer was ever seen by anyone and 'was absolutely of opinion that they [the murders] still remain an unsolved mystery.'

According to Collins, Brown thought the **Goulston Street Graffito** was probably genuine and also that the Pinchin Street torso (for some reason called 'the trunk found in Finbury St.' by Collins) bore 'the same incision as was characteristic of the Ripper murders, but it may have been an imitation'.

(see *The Life and Memoirs of John Churton Collins*. Laurence Churton Collins. London: The Bodley Head, 1912)

COLOCOTT, JOHN EDWIN (*b. c.* 1864)

Variously called in the press John, Edward and Edwin; his surname rendered Colocott, Colicott, Colocitt and Calcutt.

John E. Colocott lived at 43 Aldebert Terrace, Lambeth, London with his parents, John Thomas Colocott, a wealthy jeweller, and his wife Hannah. The 1891 Census noted he had a 'Weak Intellect'.

According to *Lloyd's Weekly News* (19 April 1891) during late 1890 and early 1891, police stations in Brixton, Clapham, Stockwell and Kennington were inundated with reports of young women being stabbed in the back by a young man who afterwards ran off. An American newspaper (*Centralia Enterprise and Tribune*, 14 March 1891) reported that upwards of 60 women, most plump young girls aged between 14 and 18, were stabbed, but no reports of these incidents in the press have been so far been found.

On 20 January, a man named Charles Myers claimed to have seen Colocott strike a woman on the back. She walked away, but Myers caught hold of Colocott, who was arrested by PC 67 W. On being charged, Colocott said, 'Not this time. I never touched them, I had no knife.' On 21 January 1891, he appeared at Lambeth Police Court charged with having stabbed Victoria Charter, Christina Grey, Laura Horsley, Anne Elizabeth Lewis and Maud Merton. From the outset of the proceedings his defence counsel argued this was a case of mistaken identity, adding no knife had been found nor had any proof been offered that the prisoner was in the habit of carrying one. Dr Gilbert, who had examined Colocott in prison, testified he considered him harmless and inoffensive. Colocott was nevertheless found guilty, but on the arrest of **Thomas Cutbush** on similar charges he was discharged.

Sir **Melville Macnaghten** obviousy considered Colocott guilty because he expressed the opinion in the Macnaghten memoranda that Thomas Hayne Cutbush was imitating Colocott.

(Also see Nick Connell, 'Colocitt', *Ripperana*, no 19, January 1997)

COLONIAL FARMER (UNNAMED)
Suspect. *See* **Thomas Arnold**, whose obituary describes this suspect.

COLWELL, MRS SARAH
Informant. Resident of Brady Street (at eastern end of Buck's Row), who claimed to have been awakened during the small hours of 31 August by the noise of a running woman, screaming. It appeared to Mrs Colwell that the woman was being struck as she ran, but there was no sound of pursuing footsteps. The following morning, Mrs Colwell and certain journalists believed they saw spots of blood in Brady Street and some newspapers speculated that **Mary Ann Nichols** might have been killed there and removed to Buck's Row. The police discounted this entirely and doubted the presence of the blood spots. No other witness heard anything untoward in Brady Street.

COMPLETE HISTORY OF JACK THE RIPPER, THE
Book by Philip Sugden (London: Constable Robinson, 1994; New York: Carroll and Graf, 1994; paperback London: Robinson 1995; paperback New York: Carroll and Graf, 1995. 'New edition' with a new introduction London: Robinson, 2000).

Documented account of the murders from **'Fairy Fay'** to **Frances Coles**, based as far as possible on a return to, and new recension of primary sources. Attentive use of the *Daily Telegraph* reports provided many of the new details and corrections of minutiae. The last five chapters comprise discussions of some of the problems involved in trying to identify the Ripper, with detailed consideration of the suspects **M.J. Druitt**, **Aaron Kosminski**, **Michael Ostrog** and **Severin Klosowski**.

Many of Sugden's views and opinions were directed to redressing what he saw as imbalances in previous work on the Ripper. Thus he argued against giving serious weight to the opinions of senior Scotland Yard staff (**Anderson**, **Swanson**, Macnaghten), attempted to reinstate **Major Smith**'s reputation for veracity and, in reverting to placing great faith in **Abberline**, concluded Severin Klosowski was the 'best suspect', although Sugden admitted there was nothing concrete to suggest he was the Ripper.

For subsequent detailed work and arguments in suspect and other fields since 1995, the reader should now be referred to *Jack the Ripper: The Facts*, *Jack the Ripper: Scotland Yard Investigates*, **Casebook**, and **jtrforums.com**.

COMPLETE JACK THE RIPPER, THE

Book by Donald Rumbelow (*b.* 1941). (London: W.H. Allen, 1975; hardback Boston, Mass: New York Graphic Society, 1975; paperback New York: Signet, 1975; paperback Star Books, 1976; Paperback London: Star Books, 1981; published as *Jack the Ripper: The Complete Casebook*, Chicago: Contemporary Books, 1988; revised hardback London: W.H. Allen, 1987; revised paperback with addendum London: Penguin, 1988; fully revised London: Penguin, 2004).

A former City of London police sergeant, Rumbelow is author of books on police history, Victorian London and crime history, and is also a Blue Badge London guide.

The first attempt to present an overview of the whole case in its historical context, together with a survey of theories put forward as to the Ripper's identity and the use made of the figure of the Ripper in the Arts and popular culture. For 30 years, probably the most popular introduction to the case.

CONDER, Col. CLAUDE REGNIER (1848–1910)

Suspect, first proposed by Tom Slemen and Keith Andrews in 2003.

Officer in the Royal Engineers, where he met **Charles Warren**. Like Warren, distinguished as an archaeologist. Retired to Cheltenham, where he died of a stroke and was survived by his wife.

Allegedly protected by the police as a friend of Warren and acquaintance of Inspector Abberline (who at one time lived next door to a cousin of Conder's). Conder is said by Slemen and Andrews to have become a devil worshipper, who collected human organs for Satanic rituals. The markings on **Catherine Eddowes'** face are claimed as Moabite writing, delivering the cryptic message 'twos' to Warren. **Annie Chapman** is alleged to have worked as a cleaner for Conder and to have stolen Masonic items, which she used in attempts to blackmail him and sold on to **Louis Diemschütz**. Conder intended to kill Diemschütz and his wife for this, but mistook **Elizabeth Stride** for Mrs Diemschütz. He was further said to have known **Mrs Buki**, who introduced him to **Mary Jane Kelly** as **Morganstone**, but he realised that he would have to kill Kelly because she had recognised him as Jack the Ripper.

If there is evidence for any of this story it has yet to be produced by Slemen and Andrews.

(See Des McKenna, 'Jack the Ripper: The French Connection', *Ripperologist*, August 2001.)

CONFERENCES

Annual events alternating between the UK and USA, where Ripperologists get together to hear papers and socialise. The inaugural conference was held in April 1996.

CONNELL, JAMES (b. c. 1856)
Suspected and cleared, 1888.

A draper and clothier of New Cross Road, Connell spoke to Mrs Martha Spencer near Marble Arch, walked with her in Hyde Park, but frightened her with conversation about Jack the Ripper, so that she appealed for help to PC Fountain (271A), who arrested Connell and took him to Hyde Park Police Station. A telegram to Greenwich Police Station produced confirmation of Connell's identityand he was released. (Missing MEPO files transcribed severally by Paul Bonner, Stephen Knight and Donald Rumbelow, and reproduced in *The Ultimate Jack the Ripper Sourcebook*.)

CONNELLY, or CONNOLLY, MARY ANN (b. 1838)
Aka 'Pearly Poll'. 'Mog' Witness at Martha Tabram's inquest.

Unmarried prostitute; a big, masculine woman with low, husky voice and a drink-reddened face, she had for two months resided at Crossingham's Lodging House in Dorset Street and had known **Tabram** (as Emma Turner) for four to five months.

A Mary A. Connelly appears several times in the records of the Whitechapel Infirmary, where her age is given as 35 and her address as 19 George Street (where Tabram also lived):

Admitted: 27/04/88 Mary A Connelly, 35, 19 George St Single Hawker (Laryngitis) Discharged: 12/05/88
Admitted: 18/06/88 Mary A Connelly, 35, 19 George Street Single Charing (Bronchitis) Discharged: 30/06/88
Admitted: 20/07/88 Mary A Connelly, 35, 19 George Street Single Prostitute (Myalgia) Discharged: 04/08/88

Connelly would have been discharged only two days before the murder of Tabram.

Testified that she and Tabram were together in the company of a guardsman and a corporal from c. 10.00 pm, 6 August. Drank together in several pubs until c. 11.45pm, when Connelly took the corporal up Angel Alley, while Martha Tabram took the guardsman up George Yard (today's Gunthorpe Street). Connelly left the corporal at the corner of George Yard, c. 12.15am.

After initial police questioning, Connolly disappeared and was only traced by **Sergeant Caunter** to her cousin's (Mrs Shean of 4 Fuller's Court, Drury Lane) some days later. Following this, she was taken to an identity parade of Scots Guards at the Tower of London, but failed to recognise the men she and Martha had been with. She now claimed the soldiers had white cap bands, which the police said indicated the Coldstream Guards, so she was taken by police to Wellington Barracks, Birdcage Walk, where she picked out Guardsmen **George** and **Skipper** from a parade of Coldstreams. Both established firm alibis and police concluded Connolly did not intend to help.

Researchers have since questioned the veracity of Connolly's statement, pointing out that **Mary Ann Morris** saw Tabram standing outside the White Swan alone, that nobody appears to have seen Tabram, Connolly and the two soldiers in any of the pubs they visited, that Connolly misidentified the men with whom she had spent the evening (http://www.jtrforums.com).

The *Echo* (20 September 1888) reported there were detectives working on, 'a slight clue given them by Pearly Poll', which 'was not thought much of at the time' but, now supported by **Eliza Cooper** and **Elizabeth Allen**, seemed to point suspicion at 'a man actually living not far from Buck's Row'. It is not known what the clue was.

CONWAY, THOMAS

Husband, probably common-law, of **Catherine Eddowes**.

Former private in the 18th Royal Irish Foot, from which he drew a pension under the name of Thomas Quinn. Cohabited with Eddowes from *c.* 1864 in Wolverhampton. She bore him three children, had his initials tattooed on her arm and claimed they were legally married. According to Wolverhampton press, the couple lived by selling chap-books written by Conway – chapbooks were inexpensive books sold on the streets by peddlers and were political or religious tracts, histories, nursery rhymes, or accounts of current events.

The marriage broke down *c.* 1880. Eddowes' daughter **Annie Phillips** blamed her drinking and frequent absconding, while her sister, **Elizabeth Fisher**, blamed Conway's drinking and wife-beating. By the time of her murder they had not seen each other for some years.

COONEY'S LODGING HOUSE

A common lodging house at 55 Flower and Dean Street, originally known as Smith's Lodging House (after its former owners). **Catherine Eddows** lived here with **John Kelly** from about 1881. Other residents were **Eliza Gold** and **Elizabeth Burns** (also see, **Frederick Wilkinson)**.

Taken over in 1884 by John Cooney and his wife Elizabeth (the sister of Jimmy Smith), who lived next door at 54 Flower and Dean Street. 55 Flower and Dean Street was demolished in 1891during redevelopments.Cooney also owned other lodging houses in the area, including nos 16-17 Thrawl Street, which was possibly where **Mary Jane Kelly** was living when she met **Joseph Barnett** (no lodging huse owner named Cooley having been found in the records; Cooley's was possibly a mishearing for Cooney's). He was also landlord of the Sugar Loaf pub in Hanbury Street. Arthur Harding recalled 'Johnny Cooney' as a prominent East End figure at the turn of the century in *East End Underworld* (London: Routledge and Keegan Paul, 1981) and that behind the bar were signed photos of music hall stars Marie Lloyd and Harry Champion.

COOPER, ELIZA

Described herself as a hawker. Had known Annie Chapman for about fifteen months. Lived at 35 Dorset Street for five months. Said she had quarreled with

Chapman over some soap in the lodging house and that this led to blows being exchanged later in the Britannia (the Ringers) public house. Others claimed that Cooper had struck Chapman when the latter saw her palm a companion's florin and replace it with a penny. Testified at Chapman's inquest that at that time Chapman had been wearing three brass rings which she had earlier bought 'from a black man'.

It was reported that as a result of information given by Cooper and **Elizabeth Allen** that 'certain of the authorities have had cause to suspect a man actually living not far from Buck's Row.' (*Echo*, 20 September 1888); see **Buck's Row Suspect**.

An Eliza Cooper, aged 39, a vendor of stationery, living at 35 Dorset Street, was charged on 15 October 1888 at the Clerkenwell Police Court, with assaulting a Thomas Wilne, at Clerkenwell Road on the 13th. She was fined £5 and bound over to keep the peace for six months (*Islington Gazette*, 17 October 1888).

COPSEY, MR AND MRS

Residents in 29 Hanbury Street (**Annie Chapman**'s murder site). Cigar-makers, occupying the second-floor back room. In one press report described as 'The Misses Huxley'.

CORAM, THOMAS (born c. 1870)

Witness at **Elizabeth Stride**'s inquest. Labourer in coconut-fibre factory. Resident of Plumber's Row. Returning home from Bath Gardens, off Brady Street, at 12.30am on 1 October 1888, he found a dagger-shaped knife with a 9 to 10in blade, its handle wrapped in a bloodstained handkerchief, on the doorstep of Mr Christmas's laundry at 252 Whitechapel Road (north side). He summoned **PC Drage** and went with him to Leman Street Police Station.

CORNISH, PHILIP GAD (b. c. 1865)

Schoolmaster of Ratling Hope School, Pontesbury, near Shrewsbury, who persuaded a local blacksmith to accompany him to London, where he said he had been appointed to come up and catch Jack the Ripper, for which he would be paid a large sum. The blacksmith observed his demeanour to change on the journey and Cornish's erratic behaviour caused him to be arrested in Praed Street as a lunatic at large. Sympathetically, the magistrate sent him by cab to the workhouse. The case was heard on the same day as John Avery, John Brinckley, John Newman and George Sweeney appeared in different magistrates' courts for drunken and disorderly behaviour, including claims to be or to be interested in arresting the Ripper, perhaps marking the zenith of the Ripper scare (*Daily News*, 14 November 1888).

CORONER, MARIA (*b.* 1867)

Hoaxer.

Canadian-born employee of Bradford mantle-maker said to be respectable. Charged 21 October 1888 with causing a breach of the peace by sending letters signed 'Jack the Ripper' to the Chief Constable and a local paper, declaring the murderer's intention of coming to Bradford to 'do a little business'. (*Cf.* **Charlotte Higgins**, **Miriam Howells**, **Walter Sickert**.)

COSTELLO, PC THOMAS (*b.* 1841)

Accompanied Sergeant **Robert Golding** at the finding of **Rose Mylett**'s body.

Name given in press reports as Costella (*see The Times*, 22 December 1888, for example). Born Ireland. Joined K Division (Stepney) in 1863. Warrant no. 44294. Resigned to pension (1889). He had gone on duty at 10.00pm on 19 December 1888, passed Clarke's Yard, Poplar at least six times during the course of his duty without seeing anything to arouse his suspicions and was in the company of Sgt. Golding when he discovered the body of Mylett. Costello was left in charge of the body while Sgt. Golding fetched the doctor.

COTTRELL, MRS OR 'MOTHER' (*d.* 1927)

The Sunday News (10 April 1927) reported that 'Mother' Cottrell, who had recently died, aged 86 years, at her home in Krondall Street, Hoxton [sic – Crondall Street], had been a member of the Salvation Army in the East End. The article claimed she was taking a prostitute through Middlesex Street to a Salvation Army home when the girl disappeared to see a friend. 'Mother' Cottrell waited, then went to look for the girl and saw her mutilated body in an alley doorway. Moments later, a policeman arrived on the scene. The newspaper report gave no further details.

COURTENAY, JOHN (*d.* 1936)

Alleged suspect, named in *The Ripper and the Royals* (1991).

According to **Joseph Gorman Sickert**, some sort of 'manservant' to one of the conspirators. No evidence corroborating his existence has been found.

COW, DOUGLAS (*b. c.* 1853)

Suspected and immediately cleared, 1888.

On 31 October 1888, Mrs Fanny Drake of the Clerkenwell Green Conservative Club reported to Rochester Row Police Station that she was sure a man who had just passed her on Westminster Bridge was the murderer as he answered to the description and, 'gave her such a grin as she should always remember.' Inspector Walsh followed the man she described to the Army and Navy Stores, while the suspect accompanied Walsh to the station to confront Mrs Drake. His papers proved him to be Douglas Cow of the Cow Rubber Company, whereupon Mrs Drake apologised to him and he was free to leave. (Missing MEPO files formerly accessed severally by Paul Bonner, Stephen Knight and Donald Rumbelow.)

COWDRY, SAMUEL and SARAH (*b.* 1827 and 1828 respectively)

Clerk of Works in the Police Department and his wife. Employers of **Mary Ann Nichols**, who worked for these devout teetotallers at Ingleside, Rose Hill Road, Wandsworth in May and July 1888, describing them to her father as 'very nice people'. She then absconded, stealing clothing valued at £3.10s.0d. (*See* Mary Ann Nichols for her full description.)

COX, INSPECTOR HARRY (HENRY) (*fl.* 1859–1918)

City police detective. Joined City Police in 1881 (warrant no. 5465). Ten years after his retirement in 1896, he began to write a series of articles for *Thompson's Weekly News* (published between 8 September 1906 and the end of the year). Some appeared on the front page. One printed inside the newspaper was 'The Truth About the Whitechapel Murder' (*Thomson's Weekly News,* 1 December 1906), in which he recalled maintaining surveillance on a suspect in a predominantly Jewish area (*cf.* **Kosminski, City Police suspect**) and claiming the local Jewish population only assisted them and talked freely about the Jack the Ripper murders because they pretended to be factory inspectors looking for sweatshops to close down.

COX, MARY ANN (*b. c.* 1857)

Witness at **Mary Kelly**'s inquest.

'A widow and an unfortunate', in her own words, residing at 5 Miller's Court. Described as 'a wretched looking specimen of East-end womanhood' (*Star,* 12 November 1888). She gave important evidence about Kelly's return home drunk around midnight in the company of a blotchy-faced man with a carrotty moustache, her singing and footsteps leaving Miller's Court at dawn. Mrs Cox accepted the footsteps might be those of the beat policeman.

A report of Mrs Cox's recollections which differs from her testimony at the time was given by her niece to **Daniel Farson**:

The night of the murder of Mary Kelly my aunt was standing at her door. She saw Mary coming through the iron gate with this gentleman, a real toff. This night as they got under the lamp in the court they stopped. Mary's words was,

'All right, love. Don't pull me along.' My aunt said he was a fine looking man, wore an overcoat with a cape, high hat, not a silk one, and Gladstone bag.

This story is a fascinating piece of oral history, showing the hold of the top-hatted toff Ripper image, though the niece's reservation that the hat was 'not a silk one' might indicate a homburg rather than top hat, as shown in *Illustrated Police Gazette* drawings of **George Hutchinson**'s suspect.

Mrs Cox appeared in Thames Magistrates Court August 1887 and January 1888 on assault charges. For the first, which may have been an assault on the arresting Police Constable Batten, she was sentenced to a month's imprisonment. For the second, an assault on Eliza Smith, she was fined five shillings after two remands. We take her estimated age from the court records.

COX, SARAH
Resident of 29 Hanbury Street, **Annie Chapman**'s murder site. An old woman, allowed to stay in a third floor room as a charity by **Mrs Richardson**.

CRAWFORD, ERNEST (*b c.*1866)
Correspondent of **G.R. Sims**, who cited the theories of 'Mr S'.

A portrait and landscape photographer who wrote a six-page letter to G.R. Sims dated 24 September 1907 and sent from 2 Rosehill Terrace, Larkhill, Bath, partially quoted in *The True Face of Jack the Ripper*:

Mr S as I will call him, told me that he believed that the outrages were performed by the Jesuits who had reasons for getting foreign detectives into the London service (you remember that the importation of foreign detectives was talked of at the time), the miscreant never passed through the cordon of police because in the centre of the district was a Jesuit college in which he took refuge after his deeds. The Jesuits according to Mr S left the sign of the cross on all their

work and sure enough lines drawn from the points on your map make a fairly regular cross. I am afraid Mr S's theory must be regarded as a wild speculation but it is curious nevertheless. I am not aware that there is any Jesuit religious house in that particular locality. Another theory by the same gentleman is more plausible; you remember that the cut in the throat of the victims gave the impression that the murderer was left handed. Mr S thought the Ripper had induced the women to allow connection from behind, a very convenient position for concealing his purpose and using the knife effectively.

CRAWFORD, HENRY HOMEWOOD (1850–1936) *pictured*

City of London solicitor, acting for police at **Catherine Eddowes**' inquest. Educated at Thanet College. Admitted solicitor, 1872; practised in partnership with Samuel Chester at 90 Cannon Street, EC until 1935. Freemason and amateur actor. At Eddowes' inquest, he requested the withholding of **Joseph Lawende**'s description of the man outside Church Passage with Eddowes, saying, 'I have special reason for not giving details as to the appearance of this man.'

CREAM, DR THOMAS NEILL (1850–92)

Alleged suspect.

Murdered Daniel Stott of Garden Prairie, east of Chicago, Illinois, in February 1881 and was sentenced to life imprisonment in the Illinois State Penitentiary at Joliet. Granted clemency and released in 1891, he returned to London where, between 1891–92, he poisoned four prostitutes, for which he was hanged at Newgate on 15 November 1892. Hangman James Billington claimed that he heard Cream say, 'I am Jack the…' as the trap opened beneath his feet. It has been suggested Cream might have bribed his way out of Joliet Prison or escaped in 1888 and committed the Whitechapel murders (Donald Bell, 'Jack the Ripper – The Final Solution' in the *Criminologist*, summer 1974, and an article in the *Toronto Star*, 17 and 18 February 1979) and that Cream's writing matches that of two Ripper letters (Derek Davies, 'Jack the Ripper – The Handwriting Analysis', *Criminologist*, 1974). Evidence of affadavits from Cream's relatives and other facts, however, show that Cream was incarcerated at the time of the murders (*see* **The Complete Jack the Ripper**).

CREMERS, BARONESS VITTORIA (*d.* 1939)

Informant about 'Dr D'Onston'.

Born in Pisa, Italy, the daughter of Manrico Vittorio Cassini and Agnes Elizabeth Rutherford. Married Baron Louis Cremers, a Russian, in New York on 26 November 1886; separated 1887. An admirer of the writings of Mabel Collins, she became a theosophist, met Helena Petrovna Blavatsky in London in 1888 and in the early 1890s came to know Mabel's lover Dr D'Onston – **Robert Donston Stephenson**. Went into business with Collins and Stephenson, founding Pompadour Cosmetique Company in Baker Street. The venture was doomed and Collins had to declare bankruptcy in 1892. Subsequently came to believe, with Mabel, that D'Onston had been Jack the Ripper – a belief she felt was confirmed when she found a number of possibly blood-stained pre-formed bow cravats in a tin box with papers of D'Onston's. Her story was garbled by **Betty May** in 1925 and known to **Aleister Crowley** in 1929. She reported it to **Bernard O'Donnell** during the 1930s and he purported to record her verbatim in his typescript (now available on **jtrforums.com**).

CRIMES AND TIMES OF JACK THE RIPPER
*See **Autumn of Terror**.*

CRIMES, DETECTION AND DEATH OF JACK THE RIPPER, THE
Book by Martin Fido (*b.* 1939) (London: Weidenfeld and Nicolson, 1987; paperback with revised final chapter, London: Weidenfeld, 1989; with new introduction New York: Barnes and Noble, 1993).

Fido was freelance writer and broadcaster at the time of publication; previously, and now again, university teacher.

Identified David (Aaron Davis) **Cohen** and made the case for his being the Ripper. Also identified **Aaron Kosminski**, **Nathan Kaminsky**, **Ada Wilson** and **Rose Mylett** (previously only known as Emily Davis and unidentified). Identified the **Macnaghten memoranda**'s Kosminski as being a reference to **Anderson**'s suspect. The first book to use more sources than editorials and reports in the press to assess the relative merits of contemporary police officers' memoirs, abilities and opinions, from which survey concluded **Sir Charles Warren** was habitually underestimated, **Major Smith** over-esteemed and Dr **Robert Anderson** the most reliable surviving contemporary source offering an identification of the Ripper.

CRIMES OF JACK THE RIPPER: AN INVESTIGATION INTO THE WORLD'S MOST INTRIGUING UNSOLVED CASE, THE
Book by Paul Roland (London: Arcturus, 2006).

Reasonably well-balanced overview which makes a good introduction to the case and benefiting from many illustrations. Roland suggests **Jacob Levy** as the Ripper.

CRIMINALS AND CRIME: SOME FACTS AND SUGGESTIONS
Book by Sir **Robert Anderson** (London: Nisbet, 1907).

His remarks on the Ripper case illustrate his conviction that the public habitually mistakes sensational crimes for important crimes. a) A signed copy of *Criminals and Crime* was sent to **Swanson** from Anderson, the inscription reading... 'for Donald S. Swanson with my good wishes R Anderson New Year's Day 1908.'

CROOK, ALICE MARGARET (1885–1950)
Alleged daughter of **Prince Albert Victor**. Father's name given as 'William Crook (deceased)' on marriage certificate to William Gorman.

According to **Joseph Sickert** and **Stephen Knight**, sole offspring of the liaison and illegal marriage between the prince and **Annie Elizabeth Crook**.

Allegedly two attempts were made to eliminate Alice in road accidents in 1888 and 1892. For the former, *see* **Lizzie Madewell**. The latter, according to **Jean Overton Fuller**, took place in the presence of **Florence Pash**.

Knight alleged Crook was brought up by **Walter Sickert** in Dieppe, leaving him when she was 18 – and subsequently marrying William Gorman – but returning to become Sickert's mistress for 12 years when Gorman proved impotent. In fact, Alice and William Gorman lived together until his death (1951), acknowledging four children between 1921 and 1927. Joseph Gorman (*b.* 1925) claimed in his BBC television insert that Walter Sickert had sired two sons by his mother, the first being 'Charles, who disappeared at the age of two about 1911.' No trace of this birth has ever been found. Joseph Gorman claimed to be the other son, the result of a renewed liaison between his mother and Sickert, which did not end her marital relations with William Gorman. All that can be substantiated of this story is that some parts of it were apparently known to Florence Pash prior to 1948.

See also **The Ripper and the Royals**.

CROOK, ANNIE ELIZABETH (1862–1920)

Alleged secret wife of **Prince Albert Victor**. Actual grandmother of **Joseph Sickert**, who claimed the Ripper murders were an establishment cover-up to preserve the secret. The marriage would have been illegal under the Royal Marriages Act (1772) as contracted without the Sovereign's permission.

Daughter of William Crook (*d.* 1891) and Sarah Ann Crook (1838–1916). In 1885, she gave birth to an illegitimate daughter, **Alice Margaret Crook** (father unknown), at St Marylebone Workhouse. She is described on her daughter's birth certificate as a 'confectionary assistant from Cleveland Street' and her address given as '6 Cleveland Street, Fitzroy Square'. The following year, the building was demolished. One of the flats thereafter erected on the site was occupied during 1888–93 by an Elizabeth Cook, who has sometimes been confused with her.

In January 1891, Annie Elizabeth was living at 9 Pitt Street, Tottenham Court Road. Various subsequent addresses are known and she spent much of her later life in workhouses. She died in the Lunacy Ward of Fulham Road Workhouse.

See also **The Ripper and the Royals**.

CROSS, CHARLES

Witness at **Mary Ann Nichols'** inquest and the person who discovered her body. Proposed as suspect, 2007.

Charles Cross's dates have been identified by researchers as 1849-1920. Born in St Anns, Soho, son of John Allen Lechmere and Maria Louisa (née Roulson); father died and mother married Thomas Cross, a policeman. Charles seems to have continuously used the name surname Lechmere, though for some reason gave his surname as Cross in connection with the Ripper.

A carman resident in Doveton Street, Cambridge Heath Road, Bethnal Green (MEPO 3/140 ff. 242–56), employed by Pickford's in Broad Street. At 3.45am saw the body lying opposite Essex Wharf, Buck's Row, and went to examine it, thinking at first that it was an abandoned tarpaulin. Joined by **Robert Paul**, Cross concluded the woman was dead and the two went on to Hanbury Street, where they found and informed Police Constable **Mizen**.

It has been suggested (Michael Connor, 'Charles Cross Was Jack the Ripper', **Ripperologist** 78, April 2007), that Cross might have been standing beside Nichols when Paul arrived because he had just killed her.

(*See* Derek Osborne, **Ripperana**,. 37, July 2001; John Carey, *Ripperana*. 40, April 2002); Michael Connor, *Ripperologist*, 72, October, 2006,)

CROSSINGHAM, WILLIAM CHARLES (1847–1907)

Lodging-house keeper.

Born in Romford, 1847, according to his gravestone. Two brothers, Albert and Herbert; one sister, Emma. Married widow Mary Robinson, 1866; daughter Ann Susannah Crossingham (*b.* 1867), married Daniel McCarthy, the brother of **John McCarthy**, 1890. William remarried following death of first wife, Margaret Sullivan, 1898. By 1901 he was living at 64 Western Road, Romford, but still owned several lodging-houses in Spitalfields. Died 28 February 1907, leaving nearly £7,000. Buried at Romford Cemetery, 7 March 1907. His wife Margaret died 25 June 1907. Owned several lodging-houses in Dorset Street, White's Row and Little Paternoster Row, Spitalfields. He was first registered as a lodging-house keeper in 1866 (*see* **Crossingham's Lodging House**).

In 1901, he was admonished by Wynne Baxter during the inquest into the murder of **Annie Austen**, who stated: 'I have, unfortunately, had to hold inquests on a number of people who have lodged in your houses.' Crossingham replied that sometimes people came to doss houses to die.

CROSSINGHAM'S LODGING HOUSE

The name given to several lodging-houses owned by **William Crossingham** in Dorset Street, Patrnoster Row and White's Row. In the Ripper case, it usually refers to 35 Dorset Street, Spitalfields. Managed by deputy **Timothy Donovan** and frequented by a very large number of people associated with the Ripper case. *See* **Elizabeth Allen**, **Annie Austin**, **Annie Chapman**, **Eliza Cooper**, **Mary Ann Connolly**, **'Leather Apron'**, **West**. It is often confused with another lodging-house owned by William Crossingham at 15–19 Dorset Street, opposite Miller's Court, outside of which **George Hutchinson** stood, and more properly known as Commercial Street Chambers (*see* **Caroline Maxwell**).

(*See* Derek F. Osborne 'A Place To Die: The Houses Of William Crossingham', *Ripperana*, 41, July 2002.)

CROW, ALFRED GEORGE (*b. c.* 1864)

Witness at **Martha Tabram**'s inquest. Drove cab no. 6,600 and resided at George Yard Buildings, where he saw a body, presumably Tabram's, on the first-floor landing at 3.30a on 7 August 1888 – but paid no attention, it being common to find people sleeping there.

CROWLEY, EDWARD ALEXANDER (ALEISTER) (1875–1947)

Alleged theorist.

Professional occultist. He made several claims to know the identity of Jack the Ripper. His recounting of **Vittoria Cremers**' story of the bloodstained ties erroneously reported them as being evening-dress white bowties – Cremers' version said that they were day-dress black cravat bows.

CROWLEY, JOHN (*fl.* 1888)

Alleged victim of indecent assault by **Dr Tumblety** on 14 October 1888 (PRO CRIM 4/1037, 21927).

CULLEN, GEORGE 'SQUIBBY' (*b. c.* 1863)

Briefly suspected in 1888. A notorious petty villain, wanted for street gambling, on Saturday, 1 September Cullen told PC Bates 166H that he would 'do for him' if he were interfered with again. Before running away, he threw a stone at the policeman, which missed him and hit a girl called Betsy Goldstein. On Saturday, 8 September, **Walter Dew** spotted Squibby and gave chase. A crowd quickly joined the pursuit of a fugitive they assumed to be the Ripper and Squibby was glad to give himself up to police custody in Flower and Dean Street, though it usually took four officers to restrain him. He received three months' hard labour for the assault on Betsy Goldstein (*Lloyds Weekly News*, 9 September 1888 – 'I Caught Crippen').

There is also a reference to Squibby by **Benjamin Leeson** (*Lost London*, London: Stanley Paul, 1934). In a discussion of Dorset Street, he referred to almost being hit by a knife thrown by a man he calls Billy Meers at 'Squibby, who Leeson described as "another well-known character in those parts, and had been charged more than once for using the knife, and had been at death's door himself as the result of being stabbed."'

(Also see 'Stephen Ryder nabs "Squibby"', *Ripperologist, no 57, January 2005*)

CULLEN, TOM ALDEN (1913–2001)

Born in Oklahoma City, the son of a hotelier, but moved to Long Beach, California as a child. Educated in San Pedro and at the University of California, where he studied economics and political science. Became a journalist on the *United Progressive News*, joined the Communist Party and campaigned for Upton Sinclair in his bid for governorship of California. After joining the Army as a journalist served in Europe and Africa during World War II. After the War, he worked for a trade magazine and attended the Sorbonne in Paris under GI Bill.

During the 1950s he was a freelance journalist in Europe and stayed on in Britain after his US passport was revoked because of his communist connections. Began writing books with ***Autumn of Terror***: *Jack the Ripper, His Crimes and Times* (1965), *The Empress Brown* (1969), *Maundy Gregory: Purveyor of Honours* (1974), *The Prostitutes' Padre* (1975) and *Crippen: The Mild Murderer* (1977).

Cullen is deeply esteemed by most writers on Jack the Ripper. It is a matter of regret that he did not retain the notes and sources used for his work in the 1960s.

CUMBERLAND, STUART (*b c.*1860–*d.*1922)

Journalist, author and 'thought-reader' who enjoyed considerable notoriety in the 1880s and 1890s. He had a vision of Jack the Ripper and experiences which parallel those attributed to **Robert James Lees**.

An Anglo-Australian, whose real name was Charles Gardner, he was able to detect almost imperceptible and involuntary muscle movements and from these could determine by asking specific questions whether someone was telling the truth or not. He travelled extensively, performed in theatres and at private events before many celebrated and distinguished people, and for two decades was rarely out of the press. Few understood what he did and his abilities were often referred to as telepathy or clairvoyance and his performances as séances. His abilities were investigated in 1881 and a report published in *Nature* (June 1881). A further investigation in 1882 partly led to the creation of the Society for Psychical Research.

Cumberland was consulted several times by journalists during the Whitechapel murder investigations and always replied that as he was not a clairvoyant, he could do nothing until confronted with a suspect (*Echo*, 5 October 1888). A long report of an interview with him on the subject appeared in the *Evening News* (10 November 1888), which he concluded by saying that he would be 'pleased to help the police all I could, if an opportunity offered. In fact, I am postponing my journey to Berlin for a week or so on the chance of my services being of any use.'

On 29 July 1889, in the *Illustrated Mirror* (a newspaper he edited), he published under the headline, 'MY VISION OF JACK THE RIPPER', an account of a dream in which he had seen the face of the murderer: 'The face was thinnish and oval in shape. The eyes were dark and prominent, showing plenty of white. The brow was narrow, and the chin somewhat pointed. The complexion was sallow – somewhere between that of a Maltese and a Parsee. The nose was somewhat Semitic in shape, and formed a prominent feature of the face. The formation of the mouth I could not very well see, it was shaded by a black moustache. Beyond the hair on the upper lip the face was bare. It was not a particularly disagreeable face, but there was a wild intensity about the dark full eyes that fascinated me as I gazed into them. They were the eyes of a mesmerist!'

Cumberland gave Scotland Yard a description of the man in his vision and claimed, 'Curious to say, the personal description published by the police of the "person wanted" seems to have been adopted from this dreamland-photograph.'

The following day he was returning from a visit to his solicitor, Theodore Lumley, in a hansom cab. In Regent Street, just above Piccadilly Circus, he passed another hansom cab and saw inside the man in his dream. He thought of turning and following the man, but at the time dismissed the idea as foolish. Afterwards he appeared to have regretted this, feeling that it foretold another murder within two weeks. Duly the torso was discovered in Pinchin Street. Cumberland gained access to the mortuary and viewed the remains, which he described and was reportedly 'now attempting to solve the mystery of the crime' (*Birmingham Daily Post*, 1 September 1889) and planned to spend a few nights in the East End in pursuit of the murderer. Some newspapers, noting Forbes Winslow promised to do the same, hoped they did not end up capturing each other (*Trewman's Exeter Flying Post or Plymouth and Cornish Advertiser*, 24 September 1889).

(Obituary in *The Times*, 3 March 1922.)

CUNNINGHAM, INSPECTOR JAMES HENRY (*b.* 1868)
Joined C Division in 1888 (warrant no. 73958) and was drafted to patrols in Whitechapel during the Ripper scare. Also frequently escorted **G.R. Sims** 'through some of the worst slums in London' (probably later in life), collecting material for articles.

CUSINS, MARY
Informant. Lodging-house keeper of Little Paternoster Row, Dorset Street. Reported that **Joseph Isaacs** stayed in her house for three or four days prior to Mary Kelly's murder. She had heard him pacing in his room at nights, and he left suddenly after the murder, leaving a violin bow in his room.

Police asked her to look out for him and report back. On 7 December, he returned for the bow and she followed him to Julius Levenson's pawnshop, hoping to find a policeman. None was about, and when Isaacs came running out of Levenson's she could do nothing but lay the information at a police station. Her description ensured his subsequent arrest.

CUTBUSH, SUPERINTENDENT CHARLES H. (1844–96)

Alleged uncle of **Thomas Cutbush** (the genealogical link yet to be established).

Born in Ashford, Kent, the son of Charles and Amelia Cutbush, he joined the Metropolitan Police in December 1867, A Division (warrant no. 49037). Promoted to sergeant in 1869, then inspector (1873), when he was transferred to C Division. Transferred to A Division in 1876, promoted to chief inspector (1879), then superintendent (1887). Retired in 1891, executive superintendent, Scotland Yard (in charge of supplies and pay).

Shot himself at his home at 3 Burnley Road, Stockwell, following years of headaches and insomnia, which he attributed to a blow he had received some years before. He had retired early from the police 'owing to an affection of the brain' (the *Ipswich Journal*, 14 March 1896) and had since suffered periodical bouts of depression. According to his doctor, he 'had a great antipathy to Roman Catholics, and was under the delusion they were the cause of his downfall.' The coroner's jury found he killed himself while temporarily insane. Described as: 'one of the best men who ever had charge of a case. An ideal detective, he was instrumental during his long career in bringing many notorious criminals to justice, while his conscientious vigilance in the discharge of his duties earned him the good opinion of the Commissioners and the respect of the men.'

He forwarded two of **Inspector Reid**'s reports on **Martha Tabram** to the assistant commissioner's office and so was loosely involved in the Ripper investigation at an early stage. In *Jack the Myth*, A.P. Wolf argues that Cutbush's paranoid schizophrenia might have led to his spending some time in the Seaside Home and this could somehow lie behind the puzzling declaration in the **Swanson marginalia** that **Kosminski** was taken there for identification.

Recent research as of yet unpublished strongly suggests Supt. Cutbush had entered into a bigamous marriage and was supporting two families.

(*See The Police Review and Parade Gossip*, 13 March 1896.)

CUTBUSH, THOMAS HAYNE (1865–1903)

Suspect at time of his committal to Broadmoor in 1891 and possibly earlier. Accused, though unnamed, in the *Sun* newspaper, 1894. Cleared in the **Macnaghten memoranda**, 1894; accusation revived in *Jack the Myth*.

The son of Thomas Taylor Cutbush and Kate Hayne, and according to **Sir Meville Macnaghten**, the nephew of **Supt. Charles Cutbush**, although the authors have so far been unable to establish the relationship as a fact. Shortly after his birth, his father went to New Zealand and Australia, where in 1885 he was still believed to be living (*The Times*, 15 June 1892). The *Sun* (17 February) claimed Cutbush's father treated his mother badly and bigamously remarried abroad. Macnaghten erroneously stated the father had died when Cutbush was young.

Kate moved in with her parents, John and Annie Hayne, at 14 Albert Street, Kennington. She and her sister Clara would remain in what was described as 'comfortable circumstances'.

In 1891, Thomas Cutbush was 5ft 9?in tall, of slight build with thin features, a dark complexion and 'very sharp' dark blue protuberant eyes. There was a tooth missing from his upper jaw. His hair was black and he had very short back whiskers. He was unmarried, belonged to the Church of England, but claimed to be agnostic. For some time he was employed as a clerk and a traveller at a tea merchant's near the Minories and subsequently canvassed the East End on behalf of the Directory. The *Sun* claimed Cutbush gained employment in the vicinity of the Minories on 24 July 1888. Following a bantering remark by an elderly official of the firm, Cutbush threw the man downstairs, remarking, 'Poor gentleman, he has fallen downstairs.' His victim was unconscious for several weeks and it was not until he regained consciousness that the truth was discovered and Cutbush fired.

He was taken ill in 1888, the nature of the illness being uncertain. Macnaghten says Cutbush contracted syphilis, but there is no mention in his Broadmoor medical papers. His aunt said he had a cold, while the *Sun* suggests the illness was imagined and that he was perfectly healthy. Cutbush himself claimed that in November 1888 (Broadmoor records), he sought treatment from a Dr Brooks of Westminster Bridge Road (Macnaghten). His aunt said he became very ill after taking the medicines prescribed by him and it is clear from the medical records that he developed the delusion that Brooks had tried to poison him.

He wanted to sue the doctor for £5,000 and Macnaghten says he threatened to shoot him. The *Sun* (15 February 1894) published a statement, apparently by Dr Brooks; also a letter from a shopkeeper, which shed a little insight into his dementia, and interviews with colleagues of Cutbush, who described his intention to shoot Dr Brooks. Cutbush also outlined his case to Lord Grimthorpe, who at the time was involved in a campaign to prohibit doctors dispensing their own medicines (chiefly an effort to bring homeopathic remedies under some sort of control). *Lloyds Weekly News* (16 April 1891) stated: 'Cutbush has for some time past been known to the authorities' and it was because of these letters.

He gave up any kind of work and instead studied medicine, apparently obsessively. According to his aunt, he was not accustomed to go out at night, except to post his letters and perhaps enjoy a short stroll. Macnaghten, on the other hand, said that Cutbush 'rambled about at night, returning frequently with his clothes covered with mud.'

Throughout the winter of 1890–91 considerable alarm was caused when a number of young women, all apparently plump, aged between 14 and 18 years, and living in the areas of Brixton, Clapham, Stockwell and Kennington, were stabbed in the back or bottom by a young man who quickly ran away. We know of the following cases:

8 January 1891: Anne Elizabeth Lewis, at about 11:00pm in South Lambeth Road. Christina Gray, no details known.

9 January 1891: Laura Horsley, at about 10:00pm in Clapham Road.

17 January 1891: Maud Merton or Kirton in Binfield Road.

21 January 1891: Charles Myers caught hold of Edwin Colocott, who he alleged had struck a woman on the back. He was identified by Maud Merton and others as the man who had stabbed them.

7 March 1891: IsabelAnderson stabbed.

8 March 1891: Grace Florence Johnson stabbed.

According to the *Sun* (17 February 1891), citing someone identified by the initials H.L., Cutbush had seized his mother or aunt by the throat and brandished a large knife, apparently with the intention of cutting her throat. She struggled and managed to escape, but became 'seriously afraid' of him and 'gave information' – presumably to the parochial authorities – but afterwards became sorry. This story appears to be slightly corroborated by the aunt's later claim that no fewer than five medical attendants came to take Cutbush to the workhouse and that she was afraid to remove a knife from his pocket until he had fallen asleep.

What is known beyond question is that early in March Cutbush's mother and aunt, concerned about his mental state, decided to have him examined by doctors at St Saviour's Infirmary and possibly certified, it being their intention to pay for him to receive treatment at a private asylum.

The workhouse authorities sent five men to the house at 7:00am, on 5 March 1891. According to an interview given by Cutbush's aunt to *Lloyd's Weekly News* and on which much of the details are drawn, Cutbush was in bed and alarmed by what was happening. He was taken to St. Saviour's Workhouse, but at midday the carelessness of an attendant gave him opportunity to escape. Dressed only in his nightshirt (or socks and undervests, according to his aunt), he scaled a 12ft-high wall and, taking advantage of the commotion caused by his escape, which brought neighbours to their doors and into the street, he entered a nearby house, stole clothes, boots and a hat, and calmly walked out through the front door to freedom.

According to his aunt, he went to Hyde Park Corner, where he saw his mother getting on a bus and later into a tramcar. Cutbush tried to attract her attention, but she did not recognise him. The time was about 8.20pm. At about 9:05pm, he spoke to Dr Clark, the sexton at City Temple; he also spoke to Mrs Clark, who gave him some water. He left just before 10:00pm and Mrs Clark saw him cross Fleet Street. Following this, he sought shelter at the Salvation Army barracks in Queen Victoria Street, but it was full and so he loitered around the Embankment until midnight, when he walked home.

He stayed there, bathing and changing his clothing. His aunt claimed that he possessed no knife and no money, but was given 10s by his mother so that he could go to Margate. He left at about 4:00 on the Friday morning.

That night he was in Camden Town and the *Sun* reported a strange, almost bizarre encounter with a man, whom the newspaper identified as 'W.K'. At about 10.30pm he got off a train with his young lady and was approached by a thin, tall young man in an excitable state: 'He made a long, rambling statement with great vehemence, saying he was wanted for a very serious charge: "You must know," said he, "that they say I am Jack the Ripper – but I am not, though all their insides are open and their bowels are all out. I am a medical man, you know, but not Jack the Ripper – you must not think I am. But they do, and they are after me, and the runners are after me, for they want the £500 which is offered for my capture, and I have only been cutting up girls and laying them out." The young man then said, "…show me the way to the fields – where I shall be safe!'"

The man went off and Mr W.K. followed him as far as Bayham Wharf.

This story is confirmed by the aunt's statement to *Lloyd's Weekly News* (19 November 1888), in which she stated neither mother nor aunt heard anything of Cutbush from his departure at 4am until 6pm, 'when we got a letter from a gentleman at Camden Town, saying he had met a gentlemanly young man who, he thought, was suffering from delusions, and who told him he was going to Hampstead Heath. He wanted the writer of the letter to hide him from men who were running after him, for they were going to murder him.' The *Sun* (15 February 1894) published what appears to be this letter:

Dear _____, I hope you will kindly pardon the liberty I take in writing these few lines, but I write to ask you if there is any truth in the statements of a young man I accidentally met last evening in Camden Town, about 10.30. He was so very excited and begged of me to let you know by post that I consider it my duty to thus address you and give you every information relating to his movements relying, as I do, on his own words. He told me he was wanted for some grave and serious charge – I understood him it was some hospital inquiry – and begged of me to hide him for a few days, as he was quite innocent, and that the whole of London was after him, and that the runners were tracking him down, and that £500 was offered for his apprehension, but he had managed to escape them but did not know where to go for safety.

He also informed me he had been placed in a hospital against his wish, and put with patients that were suffering from fever, but escaped. But if taken again the doctors would certify him mad and he would be placed in an asylum and there be murdered, and that _____ would never know his end. He then gave me an envelope with an address, and begged me to write _____, which I readily promised. I could not refuse his request, for he pleaded so earnestly for me to do so, and his excited manner and mental nervousness I consider justifies me making some inquiries, for I have reason now to believe that he suffers from delusions. Sincerely do I hope he is safe. For he was going to Hampstead, and wanted to get to the fields. He thought it would be safer for him. Poor fellow! I assure you, he has quite unnerved me, for he was quite the gentleman in manner and address, and if you will kindly grant me an interview this evening at 7.30 I will call and see you, and my young lady also, who can bear witness to my statements, she being with me at the time, and heard every word of this strange and startling incident.

Cutbush's movements are uncertain, but his aunt claimed that from 9pm until 10.15pm he was at Cotton's Wharf in Tooley Street, roughly where London Bridge Hospital now stands. In Cutbush's Broadmoor medical papers is reference to Cutbush himself saying: 'Man at Cotton's Wharf says he was there when the assault alleged was committed. A put up case.' This was the night when Isabel Anderson was stabbed. Cutbush's mother and aunt appear to have been confused about when the attacks took place, indeed Macnaghten said, 'little reliance could be placed on the statements made by his mother or his aunt, who both appear to have been of a very excitable disposition' and Cutbush himself said they were eccentric enough to merit care.

So, assuming there wasn't confusion with the man the previous night, it would appear Cutbush was seen in Southwark at roughly the time when Isabel Anderson was assaulted, at 10pm. It would be a major complaint by Cutbush's family and solicitor that the certification that he was unfit to plead denied them the opportunity to bring evidence and witnesses to prove his innocence.

Cutbush was home at 12.15am on Sunday, 8 March 1891, but left at 4am, returning at 1am for lunch, and staying indoors and taking a nap. His aunt had seen a knife in his pocket and took it while he was asleep. He left at 7pm and a short time later the police, who had been making enquiries on behalf of the workhouse authorities, called at the house and the mother and aunt admitted Cutbush had been staying there and the aunt subsequently gave them the knife. Apparently it was exactly the kind of knife that the police believed had been used in the stabbing cases and so it was that police attention focused on Cutbush for the crimes.

According to Macnaghten, the knife 'was bought in Houndsditch about a week before he was detained in the Infirmary.' However, *Lloyd's Weekly News* (16 April 1891) states Cutbush admitted to his aunt that he had bought it from a Mrs Dickinson in the Minories, who was in due course interviewed by a representative of the newspaper and reportedly seemed certain it was purchased on 7 March. The authors observe there could have been two knives, the large one with which Cutbush allegedly threatened his aunt, the act which almost unquestionably led to the decision to have him committed, and the knife which he bought in Minories on 7 March, presumably with the 10/- his mother gave him to go to Margate.

The knife was often reported in the press as being 'a toy', but as a newspaper pointed out, it was 'really a very formidable weapon, the sharp blade, tapering to a point, being nearly six inches in length, and also having a kind of strong sword hilt. The black handle is knotted, seven points on either side being tipped with pearl. It bears the name of a well known maker, and similar knives are exposed for sale at the East End. The point of the dagger has a stain upon it, believed to be blood.'

On Monday, 9 March 1891, at 7am, as Cutbush was trying to get back into his house, he was arrested by the police. According to **Inspector Race**, Cutbush asked: 'Is this for the Mile End job? I mean, the public house next to the Syndicate [Synagogue], where I just missed her that time. They took me to be of the Jewish persuasion, and I got away.' According to the *Sun*, it was discovered there was a public house next to a synagogue and at about the middle of September 1888, a prostitute declared in the public bar that a young man she had been talking to was Jack the Ripper. He immediately ran away. The incident was but briefly reported in the daily papers under the heading of 'ANOTHER JACK THE RIPPER SCARE', but a description of the man pointed out by the woman was given as that of a 'young man of 27 or 28 years, slight of build and of Jewish appearance, his face being thin and sallow' (according to *The Sun*, 17 February 1894).

When charged at the station, Cutbush – according to Inspector Race – denied the charge, saying, 'I could not commit the offence I am charged with. I read of a man in the newspapers stabbing girls at Clapham about five weeks back, and he is the man you want.' **Sergeant McCarthy** testified that he heard Cutbush tell his mother, 'I am all right – they can't do anything with me. The sheath was only found on me.' The aunt then said, 'Tom, we have given the knife to the police. Do tell us where you bought it.' He replied, 'Oh, you booby! They only found the sheath upon me.'

At his trial some drawings found on his person were produced. These were described as 'some torn pieces of thick paper or cardboard were found in one of his overcoat pockets, and, upon being pasted together, these were found to present diagrams of women. They were brought up by the police at the police court. One represented the trunk of a woman, with the walls of the stomach thrown open and the intestines exposed, and another was of a still more remarkable character, being partially drawn in red ink.' Macnaghten was dismissive, describing them as '2 *scribble* drawings of women in indecent postures were found torn up in Cutbush's room. The head and body of one of these had been cut from some fashion plate, and legs were added to shew a woman's naked thighs and pink stockings.'

On Monday, 23 March 1891, Thomas Cutbush appeared at the Lambeth Magistrate's Court before Mr Hopkins. A Mr Angus Lewis prosecuted and Mr George Kirk defended. Evidence was heard from several witnesses, including Isabel Fraser Anderson, who said that although she did not see the face of the man who stabbed her, his general appearance was like that of Cutbush and he was therefore remanded for trial (*The Times*, 24 March 1891). At the trial on 14 April it was decided on the evidence of Dr Gilbert, the medical officer at Holloway Prison where Cutbush was held, that he was insane.

On Thursday, 16 April 1891, Cutbush's solicitor, George Kirk, wrote to the *Daily Chronicle* complaining the newspaper had implied his client was guilty of the crimes with which he had been charged – which Kirk denied that he was – writing that he 'had a large number of witnesses present on defendant's behalf to establish his innocence, and I was advised by eminent counsel, whom I had instructed to defend him, that his acquittal was almost a matter of certainty.'

On 19 April 1891 *Lloyd's Weekly News* published a long article about the Cutbush case, in which it was argued the claims of those who believed him innocent should be rigorously investigated, especially in light of the case of **Colocott**. The newspaper remarked, 'For it is idle to deny that, in certain police circles, and among those who have had to inquire into the Brixton mystery, there is a growing feeling that it may in the end prove to be in some way connected with the darker and more tragic mysteries of the East End.' This seems to suggest very strongly that police and journalists thought Cutbush might have been Jack the Ripper. The conclusion perhaps gains some support from Macnaghten's statement that 'It was found impossible to ascertain his movements on the nights of the Whitechapel murders.'

Cutbush was committed to Broadmoor Criminal Lunatic Asylum, the medical records there revealing that he was obviously insane and dangerous:

On 24 April 1891 he was described as having a vacant expression and protruding eyes. He was restless and incoherent. He stated that the charges brought against him were absolutely false and that he had no recollection of doing anything to cause such charges to be brought against him. He said he had tuberculosis as a result of sulphur rising in his throat from a cavity in his left lung.

He also claimed to have been 'on a visit' to Peckham House Asylum for a few days but denied that there was any insanity in his family, although he regarded both his mother and aunt as eccentric enough to warrant care and admitted that he had fits of uncontrollable temper.

15 May 1891: he was refusing to accept letters

20 May 1891: At 8:20 a.m. without provocation and in front of an attendant he struck a patient named Gilbert Cooper in the face. Initially Cutbush said that Cooper had annoyed him, but later claimed that Cooper caught hold of him at the back of the neck, which the attendant denied had happened. Gilbert Cooper was presumably the curate who murdered William Farley, the vicar of Cretingham, on 2 October 1887 (a case which became a short-lived *cause célèbre*) and at trial on 15 November was deemed insane and to be held at Her Majesty's Pleasure.

At dinner time that same day Attendant Slater reported that Cutbush had declared that he would 'stick a knife in any one of us if he had a chance.'

23 May 1891: A Night Attendant named Bailey was listening outside Cutbush's window and heard him threatening to 'rip up the attendants or anyone else that upset him'.

16 March 1892: Was described as 'Violent & very destructive at times – is generally dull & apathetic & makes no attempt to answer when spoken to. Appears to be an imbecile.'

15 April 1893: 'Becoming more and more demented – scarcely ever speaks to anyone with the exception of the principal attendant. Refuses to see any of his relations when visited by them. Bodily health somewhat better – has been taking cod-liver oil for some time.'

Various notes over subsequent years show that he was 'dirty and degraded in his habits' (22 April 1894), 'dirty and destructive' (21 March 1895); his personal cleanliness improved, but his mental condition didn't, and from March 1898 his cleanliness declined so that by 1902 he was described as very dirty, giving much trouble and constantly noisy at night. He was demented and incoherent. On a visit from his mother and aunt, on 20 April 1903, Cutbush tried to bite his mother's face as she bent over to kiss him and then swore at them. Within months his health deteriorated so badly that the hospital contacted Mrs Cutbush with an urgent request that she visit her son. He died on 5 July 1903 from chronic kidney disease.

(*See* Broadmoor archive D/H14/D2/2/1/1523/1-43 at Berkshire Record Office. N.P. Warren, 'The Arrest of Thomas Cutbush', *Ripperana*, April 1993)

D

DA ROCHA, JOACHIM (*b. c.* 1866)
Suspect, proposed and discounted, 1889.

Portuguese seaman listed by **Edward Knight Larkin** as the possible murderer of **Alice McKenzie**.

DABBS, DR GEORGE HENRY ROQUÉ (1846–1913)
Theorist.

Educated at King's College, London (MRCS, LMS, 1867) and Aberdeen (MD, 1868). Started general practice in Shanklin, Isle of Wight (1870), where he remained until his death. **Lewis Carroll**, who took vacations on the Isle of Wight, recorded in his journal for 26 August 1891 that he had a talk with Dr Dabbs 'about his very ingenious theory about "Jack the Ripper"'. Unfortunately, neither Carroll nor Dabbs ever recorded what that theory was.

(Stephen Martin, 'Dr Dabbs Of Shanklin', *Ripperologist*, February 2002.)

DAM, HENRY JACKSON WELLS 'HARRY' (1856–1906)
Journalist in New York, San Francisco and London. Alleged to have worked up the 'Leather Apron' story, and to have written Jack the Ripper correspondence.

Born on 27 April 1856 in San Francisco, California, one of five children born to Alphonso Dam (1826–1902) and Lucy Ellen Dam (née Beck) (1827–1907), only two of whom – Harry and his brother, Cleveland Lincoln Dam (1864–1916) – survived.

Educated at the University of California, Berkeley, in 1875 he graduated with a Bachelor of Philosophy degree in Agriculture and entered journalism, working for several San Franscisco newspapers, including the *Chronicle* and the *Wasp* (alongside

Ambrose Bierce). He achieved a degree of early notoriety by grabbing a not-altogether successful interview with General Ulysses S. Grant.

Appointed executive secretary to California Governor George Stoneman (1822–94) in 1883, he held the post until Stoneman left office in January 1887. At the end of his term, Stoneman – a staunch believer in rehabilitating prisoners through parole – caused a furore by granting 260 pardons and commuting 146 prison sentences, several being to first- and second-degree murderers. Dam was accused of pardon brokering (accepting money in return for a pardon), an accusation he strenuously denied, that would dog him for the rest of his life.

In January 1887 Dam went to New York, where he worked for *The New York Times*. He also took his first tentative steps into the theatre, co-writing a comic opera called *Mizpah*, which bombed when it was staged in Chicago. Dam moved to London later in the year and found work with the *Star*, and as the London representative of other newspapers, including *The New York Times*, for which he was paid £4 a week, and afterwards for the London edition of the *New York Herald*.

In 1924, writing in his autobiography, *Some Piquant People*, the eminent journalist **Lincoln Sprinfield** wrote that following the pardon-brokering scandal,

'...Dam had arrived hastily and quietly from the States, had joined us on the *Star*, and had, like the rest of us, been put upon the job of solving the mystery of the Whitechapel murders. But Dam, a free-born American, was not, as were the rest of us, cowed by the English libel laws, and he created a sensation by developing a theory of the authorship of these grisly crimes. They were, he proceeded to demonstrate, the work of a miscreant known as 'Leather Apron,' and so known in consequence of the attire he wore at his everyday trade of tanning, or slipper-making, or whatever it was. Day after day, Dam gave the public all the thrills it wanted along these lines. But unfortunately there actually was in existence a man known to the nobility and gentry of the Mile End Road as 'Leather Apron,' and he was an honest, hard-working fellow, as innocent of the series of Whitechapel murders, or any one of them, as you or I.'

There were other, earlier possible references to Harry Dam. The *Echo* (5 September 1888) reported:

A very funny incident occurred in connection with the latest Whitechapel murder yesterday. An American journalist, anxious to distinguish himself in his paper, sent another scribe hailing from the other side of the Atlantic down into Whitechapel to interview the natives on the subject of the murder, and get their ideas. They gave him them, which were to the effect that they believed the murder had been committed by a "wild looking man, wearing a leather apron," who had been seen about in Whitechapel lately, and was believed to be an escaped lunatic.

Filled with this splendid idea, the young man made some "beautiful copy," which his chief telegraphed off to New York forthwith, only to learn, a very little while afterwards, that his assistant had been thoroughly well hoaxed, and that the real murderer is, if not actually known to the police, believed to be within very easy reach of a warrant – and quite sane.

In 1897, *Fun* (26 January 1897) commented that the birthday number of the *Star* acknowledged, 'that Mr H.J.W. Dam acted, through the medium of its columns, as "the historian of that shy but industrious person, Jack the Ripper."'

Then, in 1898 *Lippincott's Monthly Magazine* published an article in which the New York literary critic, novelist and poet Vance Thompson (1863–1925) referred to 'an idiot' employed on a newspaper edited by an Irish MP (a clear reference to **T.P. O'Connor** and the *Star*), who was sent to Whitechapel to write about the Whitechapel murders. Before going, he went into an inn and there he met the man who wrote the opera of *Billee Taylor* (Henry Pottinger Stephens, 1851–1903), who suggested the 'Leather Apron' idea.

The earliest known connection between Harry Dam and the authorship of the so-called 'Jack the Ripper' letters, is in an article by the Revd. Dr. Henry A. Monroe, the black pastor of St Mark's Methodist Episcopal Church, New York City ('A Pastor's Summer Abroad: Dr. Monroe Goes Slumming in the Modern Babylon', *New York Age*, 8 November 1890), in which he commented: 'Few people in London believe in the genuineness of the "Jack the Ripper" letters. They were simply the invention of some sensational fool or else a newspaper "fake". In fact, there is a strong suspicion that a *New York World* reporter might have been exercising his peculiar home talent, just to try its effect upon our British cousins.'

Harry Dam was the London correspondent of the *New York World*.

A factually inaccurate story in the *San Francisco Examiner* (2 December 1890), under the headline, 'DAM'S DEADLY WORK', implied Dam was responsible for the 'Dear Boss' letter. Refutation was swift, a story coming from Chicago:

AN IDLE STORY
That of Harry Dam Being the author of
The 'Jack the Ripper' Letters
Special to the Bulletin
CHICAGO, Dec. 4. – A special from San Francisco was published this morning saying that while Harry Dam, a New York and San Francisco journalist, was at work on the London *Star* he concocted the 'Jack the Ripper' letters which created such a sensation in London in connection with the Whitechapel murders. In reply to the inquiry as to the truth of the story, T.P. O'Connor, MP, who was editor of the *Star* at the time, says he never heard of the story before and doesn't believe a word of it. (*Daily Evening Bulletin* (San Francisco), 4 December 1890; *Los Angeles Times*, *Woodland Democrat*, 5 December 1890).

But the accusations refused to go away, and even at the time when his play *Diamond Deane* was staged some newspapers dug the dirt about Dam's past:
Harry Dam's 'Diamond Dean'
[Special to THE HERALD-Examiner Cable.]
London, March 19. – Harry Dam, who was private secretary of Governor Stoneman of California, and who was accused of selling pardons, is once more before the public. It will be recollected that while he was on T.P. O'Connor's *Star*, the first Jack the Ripper stories first saw the light. Harry was accused of 'faking' sensations to help increase the circulation of the newspaper. Now Dam comes to the front as a playwright...
(*Salt Lake Herald*, 20 March 1891.)

By 1890, Dam was working for the London edition of the *New York Herald* and beginning to make a name for himself as the author of articles with a scientific/technology angle. In 1890, he was almost killed in a ballooning accident and then, in 1891, he married actress Dorothy Dorr at All Saints Church, Gordon Square, S. Pancras. They went on to have two sons, Colby Dorr Dam (born on 7 August 1894) and Loring Dam (born 8 May 1896). By 1893, he was encountering severe financial difficulties and S.S. McClure (1857–1949), founder of *McClure's Magazine*, recalled a meeting with a tearful Dam, who was desperate for money.

In 1894, his most successful theatrical venture, *The Shop Girl*, opened at the Gaiety Theatre in London, the title role being taken by Ada Reeve (*see* **Take It For A Fact**).

Dam was one of a few journalists to interview Professor Wilhelm Roentgen (1845–1923) at his laboratory in Wurzburg, Bavaria, about the discovery of x-rays, writing 'The New Marvel In Photography' for *McClure's* (April 1896). He interviewed Gugliemo Marconi (1874–1937), his article, 'Telegraphing Without Wires: A Possibility of Electrical Science' appearing in *McClure's* and the *Strand* (March 1897), and in 1899 he covered the Dreyfus Affair for the *New York Herald*.

In September 1901, Dam sold an eight-page short story called 'The Transmogrification of Dan' for $85 to the literary magazine, *The Smart Set: A Magazine of Cleverness*, edited by George Jean Nathan and Henry Louis Mencken. But in 1906, he discovered the story had been turned into hugely popular play, *The Heir To The Hoorah*. Dam sued the producers, the Kirk La Shelle Theatrical Company, and in January 1910 the US Circuit Court of Appeals set a legal precedent by awarding all the profits of the play to Dam.
Over the years Dam v. La Shelle would be oft-cited in legal proceedings, most notably in the case of the movie, *Letty Lynton* (1930), which saw the ruling in Dam v. La Shelle overruled, but the film has not been shown since.

Dam never saw his legal case resolved. He died in Havana, Cuba, from stomach cancer in 1906. His funeral was held at the 'Little Church Around the Corner', the Church of the Transfiguration in New York, at 3pm on 10 May, the service conducted by the Revd. Dr Houghton. He was buried in Medford, Massachusetts, in the Dorr family plot. In the *Brooklyn Eagle*, the distinguished journalist Julius Chamber (1850–1920) noted that no members of the newspaper business turned up to say their farewells and pay their final respects – 'Tell me, please, what is the price of friendship?' he wrote.

Harry Dam's plays were: *Diamond Deane* (1891), *The Silver Shell* (1891), *Queen of the Brilliants* (1894), *The Shop Girl* (1894), *The White Silk Dress* (1896), *The Coquette* (1899), *A King of Fools* (1899), *La Madeleine* (1902), *Skipper and Co.*, *Wall Street* (1903), *The Red Mouse* (1903) and *The Elopers* (1906).

See also **Best, Frederick, *Jack the Ripper* (Cook)**.

(Paul Begg and Christopher George, 'Harry Jackson Wells Dam', **Ripperologist**, issues 106 and 107, September and October 2009.)

'DANNY'
Press reports on 10 November 1888 reported **Joseph Barnett** was also known as Danny, perhaps confusing him with his brother Daniel.
(Madden, Mark: 'Jack And The Ripper', **Ripperana**, October 1993.)

'DARKIE' *(fl. 1888)*
Witness. Mulatto watchman at 19 George Street, where **Annie Farmer** claimed a man tried to cut her throat on 21 November 1888. 'Darkie' said he admitted them at about 6a.m. and took little notice of them.

DARLING, CHARLES JOHN, MP (1849–1936)
MP for Deptford (1888–97). **Edward Knight Larkin**'s MP contacted the Home Office in January 1889, urging that attention be paid to his constituent's information. This provoked Dr **Robert Anderson**'s note characterising Larkin as 'a troublesome busybody.'

DARRELL or DURRELL, MRS
Alternative name of **Elizabeth Long**.

Described in the *Guardian,* 12 September 1888, and other papers of 13 September as having seen a man and a woman talking on the pavement outside 29 Hanbury Street at 5.30am on the morning of **Annie Chapman**'s murder. On 12 September, Mrs Darrell identified the body in the mortuary. Described as **Mrs Long** when testifying at the inquest. A note on police files calls her the woman 'Darrell or Long' (HO144/221/A49301C f.136).

DAVIES – (died c. 1882)
Alleged husband of **Mary Jane Kelly**, who told **Joseph Barnett** she had married Davies, a collier, *c.* 1879, and that he had died in a mine explosion two or three years later. No trace of this marriage has been found on the indexes nor has the mine accident been identified.

DAVIES, DR MORGAN (1854–1920)
Robert Donston Stephenson's alleged suspect, named to police in 1888.

Born in Whitechapel, according to 1881 and 1901 Censuses, but the 1891

Census places his birth in Llanwyrygan, Cardigan. Birth registers record a Morgan Davies born at Llandilofawr in the first quarter of 1854, and another in the fourth quarter at Llanfyl(illegible) – (refs 11a510 and 11b731). No Morgan Davies's birth was recorded in Whitechapel during 1854. It seems likely Davies, whose future wife was from Cardigan and who retired to Wales, was actually born in Wales, but taken to London while an infant or small child.

MB, MRCS, 1879 (London); LRCP, 1880 (London). House Phys., House Surg., and Resident Accoucheur, probably at London Hospital, 1881; FRCS, 1882. MD, 1884 (Aberdeen). Private residence and general practice, 10 Goring Street, Houndsditch 1888.

He was accused by Robert Donston Stephenson, who claimed that while under treatment in London Hospital he had witnessed Dr Davies (then visiting his sick friend Dr Evans, who was in the same ward as Stephenson) give a graphic performance of the way he believed the Ripper to have killed and sodomised his victims. Stephenson alleged this convinced him Davies was unbalanced, and when (as he claimed) he learned from **W.T. Stead** that medical reports indicated Mary Jane Kelly had been sodomised (something unsupported by surviving reports) he realised Davies must be the Ripper and started to spy on him.

Although papers now missing from Scotland Yard files referred to Stephenson, there was no reference in them to any questioning of Dr Davies.

In *Uncle Jack* it is claimed that Davies was a friend of **Sir John Williams** and the 'Morgan' addressed in the note supposedly saying that Williams would be in Whitechapel on 8 September 1888.

DAVIS, ELIZABETH or LIZZIE
See **Rose Mylett**.

DAVIS, JOHN (*b. c.*1832)
Witness at **Annie Chapman**'s inquest. Discovered her body.

Described as 'an elderly man with a decided stoop' (*East London Observer*, 15 September 1888) (he was actually only about 56 years old) and as an old and feeble man with a slightly humped back' (*Evening News*), he is variously described as being employed at Spitalfields Market or Leadenhall Market, and had been lodging with his wife, **Mary Davis**, and three sons, James, Benjamin and David, in the third-floor front room of 29 Hanbury Street for about two weeks. After a restless night, awake from 3 to 5am, then dozing for about half an hour, he got up at 5.45am (timed by Spitalfields Church clock bell, had a cup of tea and went into the yard where he discovered Chapman's body. He called **James Green** and **James Kent**, who went to look for police. Davis went to Commercial Street Police Station, then returned to 29 Hanbury Street.

DAVIS, MARY ANN (*b. c.*1838)
Wife of **John Davis** who discovered Annie Chapman's body. Told a journalist for the *Echo* "The bell was ringing for six o'clock, and that is how I know the time that my husband went downstairs. He then said to me, 'Old woman, I must now go down, for it is time I was on to my work.' He went down, but did not return, as he tells me that when he saw the deceased, and the shocking state in which she was, he at once ran off for the police. We never heard any screams, either in the night or this morning. I went down myself shortly after, and nearly fainted away at what I saw. The poor woman's throat was cut, and the inside of her body was lying beside her. Someone beside me then remarked that the murder was just like the one committed in Buck's-row. The other one could not have been such a dreadful sight as this, for the poor woman found this morning was quite ripped open. She was lying in the corner of the yard, on her back, with her legs drawn up. It was just in such a spot that no one could see from the outside, and thus, the dead creature might have been lying there for some time." (*Echo*, 8 September 1888)

DAVIS, WILLIAM DOMINIC (ACTING SUPERINTENDENT) (*b.*1848)
Joined Metropolitan Police, 1874 (Warrant No. 57863). Retired as Supt. CO 1903. As Acting Superintendent of J Division, on 7 September 1888, wrote a special report to the Assistant Commissioner C.I.D. (**Sir Alexander Carmichael Bruce,** who was covering **Robert Anderson** in that capacity during the latter's absence on sick leave) stating that the murder victim had been identified as **Mary Ann Nichols** and that a 'man named 'Pizer alias Leather Apron' has been in the habit of ill-using prostitutes in various parts of the Metropolis for some time past, and careful enquiries have been made to trace him, but without success. There is no evidence against him at present. Enquiries are being continued.' (MEPO 3/140 f.238)

DAYS OF MY YEARS
Book by **Sir Melville Macnaghten** (London: Longman, Green, 1914).

Memoirs of retired assistant commissioner, CID, written just one year after he told the press that he had no intention of writing his memoirs. The work recounts major cases and describes well-known colleagues, fully justifying his reputation for affability. It relies on memory and so contains various slips and errors. One chapter deals with Jack the Ripper. *See* Sir Melville Macnaghten and **Macnaghten memoranda** for discussion.

'DEAR BOSS' LETTER

The 'Dear Boss' letter was sent on to Scotland Yard on 29 September. It was written with red ink in a good educated copperplate hand and ran thus:

25 Sept. 1888.

Dear Boss, I keep on hearing the police have caught me but they wont fix me just yet. I have laughed when they look so clever and talk about being on the right track. That joke about Leather Apron gave me real fits. I am down on whores and I shant quit ripping them till I do get buckled. Grand work the last job was. I gave the lady no time to squeal. How can they catch me now. I love my work and want to start again. You will soon hear of me with my funny little games. I saved some of the proper <u>red</u> stuff in a ginger beer bottle over the last job to write with but it went thick like glue and I cant use it. Red ink is fit enough I hope <u>ha. ha.</u> The next job I do I shall clip the ladys ears off and send to the police officers just for jolly wouldnt you. Keep this letter back till I do a bit more work, then give it out straight. My knife's so nice and sharp I want to get to work right away if I get a chance. Good luck.

Yours truly
Jack the Ripper

Dont mind me giving the trade name

A second postscript, apparently in red crayon (although this conclusion, reached from visual inspection under a magnifying glass in 1988 has since been challenged), read:

wasnt good enough to post this before I got all the red ink off my hands curse it No luck yet. They say I'm a doctor now <u>ha ha</u>

See **Letters** for further discussion.

DEARDEN, DR HAROLD (1883–1962)

Narrator of brother-officer's theory. Author of 'Who was Jack the Ripper?' in A.J. Hale (ed.) *Great Unsolved Crimes* (London: Hutchinson, 1935).

On 9 November 1918, a companion in trenches on the Somme told Dearden this was the second time his birthday had been ruined, the other being the occasion of his tenth birthday. His father had been proprietor of a private lunatic asylum on the outskirts of London. At dinner time, a noisy and violent lunatic was brought in, disturbing the boy's birthday party. He was the son of one of his father's oldest friends and later, when calmed down, became a smiling and gently demented companion for the boy, with a great talent for drawing. By the time the boy was old enough to ask questions, his father was dead. 'But,' said Dearden's comrade, 'the last murder was on the night of November 8th, remember. Looks queer, doesn't it?' Searches in Dearden's regimental records have not as yet identified the brother officer.

DEATH OF A PRINCE: JACK THE RIPPER WITH OTHER SOULS

Book by Jeanette Han with Ann Ann (Milson's Pt, NSW: Arrow Books, 2001).

Scottish-born writer and tarot card reader Han, now resident in Australia, and prominent Australian psychic and spirit medium Ann tell of a coach tour taken through Great Britain in 1988 by Ann Ann and a group of her admirers. They sought spirit information about the *Titanic* disaster and the Ripper murders at the normal coach tourist stops in England, Scotland and Wales, and Ann Ann declared Ms Han had been an East End prostitute in a former life and another of their (female) companions had been **John Netley**.

Spirit information told them that the murders were perpetrated by Netley and other Freemason accomplices (including **Walter Sickert**) to conceal from the world **Prince Albert Victor**'s homosexual, transvestite and possibly hermaphrodite nature, and the birth of an illegitimate child to him and Princess Helene d'Orleans. They discovered from the spirit world and deliberately limited research that **Robert James Lees** was the executor of **Abberline**'s will; **Oscar Wilde** was a close friend of Prince Albert Victor, whom he portrayed as the eponymous hero of *The Picture of Dorian Gray*, and the spirits of Prince Albert Victor and **J.K. Stephen** haunted the chapel of Trinity College, Oxford, blissfully unaware (like Ms Han and Ms Ann) that their terrestrial association had been at Trinity College, Cambridge.

DEEMING, FREDERICK BAILEY (1853–92)

Suspect, suggested possibly by himself, in 1892. A plumber and fitter, as well as a confidence trickster. Murdered his wife and four children in Rainhill, Liverpool (1891); also murdered his second wife in Melbourne, Australia (1892), possibly other victims. After his conviction in Australia, Deeming was reported to have confessed to the 'last two' Ripper murders. His solicitor strenuously denied that he made any confession whatsoever. *See also* **The East End Murderer – I Knew Him.** Also Jeffrey Bloomfield, 'Deeming and the Privy Council: A Comedy of Terrors', *Ripperologist*, 51, Januarey 2004.

DE LA BOTT, CHARLES (fl. 1888)

Witness, whose statement to **Sir Charles Warren** on 3 November 1888 averred that up to 20 people were responsible for the Ripper murders, with official connivance. Warren described him as eccentric, but not actually lunatic. In 2004, Warren's note of the statement was discovered by Trevor Marriott (*see* **Jack the**

Ripper: The 21st Century Investigation), though he has not divulged its whereabouts to save the owner from harassment by Ripperologists.

DENNY, JOSEPH (*b.* 1868)
Suspect, accused and cleared at Old Street Police Station, 28 December 1888. Brought in by PC 177A Wraight and accused by Thomas and John Robert Hardy of suspiciously accosting women in Houndsditch and Finsbury Pavement. Since he had a slight moustache and wore an astrakhan-collared and cuffed overcoat (like **George Hutchinson**'s suspect), he seemed worth investigation. He was released when enquiries proved satisfactory (missing MEPO files seen separately by Paul Bonner, **Stephen Knight** and Donald Rumbelow).

DER TEUFEL VON WHITECHAPEL
Book by Graf Michael Alexander Soltikow (Nürnberg: Willmy Verlag 1944). Ripper chapter translated by Jesse Flowers and published with an introduction from Stephen Ryder by the Ripperological Preservation Society, 2002.

Michael Soltikow was born in 1902 and during World War II was a member of the Gestapo in Paris. *Der Teufel von Whitechapel*, a collection of essays ostensibly revealing a dark underbelly of English legal malpractice (but in fact an exercise in fanatically anti-Semitic propaganda), was written shortly before the collapse of the Reich. Thereafter, Soltikow would maintain he was working undercover in the Gestapo and write extremely pro-Semitic work. The chapter about Jack the Ripper – which is full of gross inaccuracies – twists many features familiar to Ripper researchers to claim the English government – 'most of [whom] were Jews themselves or the relatives of Jews' – covered up the crimes. Overall a nasty, albeit minor piece of Nazi anti-Semitic writing, but an interesting and curious use of Jack the Ripper murders in a wider (and in this case horrifying) historical context.

DESNOS, ROBERT (1900–1945)
Author of *Jack L'Eventreur* (originally published in 1927 as *La Liberté ou L'Amour Suivi de Deuil*).

Paris-born surrealist poet. After attending commercial college, he worked as a clerk before becoming literary columnist for the newspaper, *Paris-Soir*. His poems were first published in 1917 and 1919, and in 1922 he published his first book. In 1932, he began a career in broadcasting and in the war years was a member of the French Résistance until his arrest by the Gestapo in February 1944. He was sent successively to Auschwitz, Buchenwald, Flossenburg and finally Térézin, where shortly after the camp's liberation he died from typhoid (*see* Katharine Conley, *Robert Desnos, Surrealism, and the Marvelous in Everyday Life*. Nebraska: University of Nebraska Press, 2004).

Desnos' accounts of the Ripper crimes were factually-based, but sometimes described as fiction. He stated that he had met a man, known only by the initials 'W.W.', who claimed that he knew the Ripper. His father was a Scotsman, his mother was Welsh, and the family was well-off, though not of the nobility. Desnos acknowledged more than once that he could have been the victim of a hoax and it has been suggested he was the hoaxer himself (*see* Dr Keith Aspley, 'The Desnos Articles', *Ripperologist*, 34, April 2001).

DEW, CHIEF INSPECTOR WALTER (1863–1947)

Detective Constable, **H Division**, actively engaged on the Ripper case. Joined the Metropolitan Police in 1882 (warrant no. 66711). Posted to X Division (Paddington Green). Transferred to H Division (Whitechapel) CID, 1887. Nicknamed 'Blue Serge' from a suit he habitually wore. From 1889, enjoyed steady promotion until he was made chief inspector (1906). Resigned in 1910 and set up as 'confidential agent', resident in Wandsworth. His highly publicised pursuit and capture of Hawley Harvey Crippen made him the first Scotland Yard 'superstar' and he published his memoirs: *I Caught Crippen* (London: Blackie & Son, 1938). q.v. for a detailed account of his recollections of the Ripper case.

See Nicholas Connell, *Walter Dew: the Man Who Caught Crippen* (Stroud: Sutton, 2005; updated 2006).

DIARY OF JACK THE RIPPER, THE

Book by Shirley Harrison (London: Smith Gryphon Publishers, 1998). Published with three postscripts, an introduction by Robert Smith, a copy of the Rendell Report (*see* **Maybrick Journal**) and a Rebuttal by Robert Smith (New York: Hyperion, 1993; paperback London: Smith Gryphon, 1994. Kettering, Northants: Index, 1995. Rewritten London: John Blake, 1998. *See also* **Jack the Ripper: The American Connection**).

A descriptive account of James Maybrick's life with an account and facsimile reproduction of the Maybrick diary. The publisher's foreword and postscript argue strongly for the diary's being genuine, adducing the Maybrick Watch as evidence, and offer a rebuttal of Rendell's conclusions.

DICTIONARY OF NATIONAL BIOGRAPHY

Entry on Jack the Ripper by Richard Davenport-Hines (*b.* 1953. Sometime lecturer at the London School of Economics and author, co-author or editor of at least 17 books, several on business history).

Workmanlike survey of the history, compressed into a succinct 3,000 words. A few possibilities, e.g. the Ripper's education, anatomical skill and left-handedness, given as facts.

DID ALEISTER CROWLEY KNOW JACK THE RIPPER?
Book by Frater Achad Osher 583 (Berkley, California: Pangenetor Lodge Publications, 1993).

A small pamphlet discussing connections between **Aleister Crowley**, **Mabel Collins**, **Roslyn Donston Stephenson** and the Ripper murders. Includes the full text of *Jack the Ripper by Aleister Crowley*, another small pamphlet produced some years earlier.

DIEMSCHÜTZ, LOUIS (*b.* 1862)

Witness at **Elizabeth Stride**'s inquest. Discovered her body. Steward of International Workingmen's Educational Club. Street salesman of cheap jewellery. On Saturday, 29 August 1888, he was out all afternoon and evening, peddling his wares at Westow Hill Market, Sydenham. He returned to the club at approximately 1am (timed by tobacconist's clock in Commercial Road), driving his pony and cart, with the intention of leaving goods with his wife before stabling the pony in George Yard (Gunthorpe Street). When the pony turned in to Dutfield's Yard, it pulled to the left in the narrow entrance between the clubhouse and the cottages, and hesitated to go forward. Diemschütz felt something soft behind the gates with his long-handled whip, and descending, struck a match and found it was an unconscious woman. Believing her to be drunk, and momentarily suspecting she might be his wife, he went into the club. There, he told several members and went back to the gate with a group including **Morris Eagle** and **Isaacs Kozebrodsky**. When they found Stride's throat cut, Diemschütz and another member ran off unsuccessfully searching for a policeman, but met **Edward Spooner** at the corner of Fairclough Street and Christian Street. He returned with them to the club, where they examined the body for about five minutes before Police Constables **Lamb** and **Collins** arrived.

The general police and press impression was that Diemschütz's pony had disturbed the Ripper, who ran away before mutilating his victim (but *see* Elizabeth Stride for alternative suggestions). **Melville Macnaghten** seems to have confused Diemschütz with **Joseph Lawende**, **Joseph Hyam Levy** and **Harry Harris** (*see* **Macnaghten memoranda** for significance).

The following day, Diemschütz told *The Times* that Stride's body held a packet of cachous (some of which had spilled out) in the left hand and some grapestalks in the right hand. There was a flower pinned to her dress.

DIEMSCHÜTZ, MRS
Wife of Louis Diemschütz. Reported in *The Times* (2 October 1888) as saying, 'Just about 1.00 a.m. Sunday I was in the kitchen on the ground floor of the club and

close to the side entrance. I am positive I did not hear screams or sounds of any kind.' This was corroborated by a servant who said no sounds were heard from the yard between 12.40 and 1am.

DIMMOCK, 'PHYLLIS' (EMILY ELIZABETH) (1884–1907)

Murder victim, alleged by Patricia Cornwell to have been killed by Walter Sickert.

Emily Dimmock. a prostitute known locally as 'Phyllis', was the 23-year-old victim of the unsolved Camden Town murder in September 1907. **Walter Sickert**, who lived in another part of Camden Town, was fascinated by the murder and made a series of studies of a man sitting or standing near a bed bearing a nude woman. Some of the preparatory drawings are inscribed with precise reference to the murder of Emily Dimmock. They do not closely resemble accounts of the actual crime scene and the reason for Sickert's provision of alternative titles, such as *What Shall We Do About The Rent? Or The Camden Town Murder* is a matter of debate among Sickert scholars.

(John Barber, *The Camden Town Murder*. Oxford: Mandrake, 2007 contains a chapter that examines the suggestion that Dimmock was murdered by Jack the Ripper. A paperback containing two additional chapters was published in 2008.)

DIOSY, ARTHUR (1856–1923)

Born in London, the son of a famous Hungarian patriot named Martin Diosy, he was educated in London and Germany. Served with the Royal Naval Artillery Volunteers from 1875-1882: married in 1882 Florence Hill and the couple had one daughter. He wrote widely of Far Eastern affairs and was founder and vice-president of the Japan society. He died in Nice on 2 January 1923.

Diosy apparently claimed to have visited the police on 14 October 1888 and suggested a 'necromantic motive' for the Whitechapel murders and suggested that the crimes had an 'occult relation to magical strology' (*Pall Mall Gazette*, 3 December 1888 – Diosy had made these comments in response to an article in that newspaper by **Robert Donston Stephenson**). According to **Ingleby Oddie,** Diosy though the murders were committed by a practitioner of magic from the Far East who was making an *elixir vitae – Elixir of Life*, believed to give immortality - one of the ingredients of which, Diosy claimed, must come from a recently killed woman. Oddie said that Diosy became 'quite excited when he heard of the bright farthings and burnt matches were found at the murder scenes. According to a later commentator, Max Pemberton (*Sixty Years Ago and After*. London: Hutchinson, 1936), Diosy also claimed that goat's hair was found at most of the murder sites that the burned matches formed a pentagon of lights which conferred invisibility, so one murder was committed while policeman stood a few yards away. Oddie said Doisy put his theory to the police, 'but had been received without enthusiasm, as one can well understand.'

(Obituary in *The Times*, 3 January 1923. Also see Christopher T George, 'Diosy and Donston: Black Magic and Jack the Ripper', *Ripperologist*, 57, January 2005)

DIPLOCK, DR THOMAS BRAMAH (*b c.*1830–*d.*1892)

Coroner for West Middlesex and Western Division of the County of London. Conducted the inquest on **Montague John Druitt**.

Born Hastings, son of auctioneer and circulating library proprietor William Diplock, who died the following year. Apparently taken by his mother to live with her wealthy industrialist Bramah family. Educated at St Andrews and St George's Hospital. MD, 1856; MRCS, 1863. House surgeon at the Lock Hospital and surgeon to London Friendly Institution. Elected coroner, 1868, in a closely-fought election. Little is known about his political and social views, though he had powerful supporters in the election headed by Lord Ranelagh and appears to have insisted on the importance of coroners having medical, rather than legal, expertise.

(Obituary in the *Acton and Turnham Green Gazette*, 7 May 1892. *See* Robert Linford, John Savage and David O'Flaherty, 'The Green of the Peak – Pt.II' *Ripperologist*, 64. February 2006.)

DISCOVERING JACK THE RIPPER'S LONDON

Book by Richard Jones (London: New Holland Publishers, 2007).

Heavily illustrated with period and modern photographs, this overview of the crimes by one of the leading London walking-tour guides concentrates on the surviving geographical locations.

DIVALL, INSPECTOR TOM (1861–1943)

Informant.

Joined the Metropolitan Police in 1882 (warrant no. 67035). Local inspector, **H Division**, from 1900. *Scoundrels and Scallywags* (London: Ernest Benn, 1929) twice refers to the Jack the Ripper investigation with which he was not actively involved. Mentions first PC **Ernest Thomson** and later claims that 'the way the bodies were dissected showed a very skilfull knowledge of anatomy on the part of the murderer'; voiced his own opinion that the murderer was killing in a deluded attempt to stop the spread of venereal disease and concluded, 'We have never found any trace of this man, or of any connection of his, nor have we been able to ascertain definitely the end of him. The much lamented Assistant Commissioner of the C.I.D., **Sir Melville Macnaghten**, received some information that the murderer had gone to America and died there.'

Cf. **Francis Tumblety**, **Roslyn Donston Stephenson**, **Fogelma**.

DIXON, GEORGE

Witness. A blind boy, who went with **Alice McKenzie** to a public house near the Cambridge Music Hall shortly after 7pm on the night she was killed. Though he said he would recognise the voice of a man she spoke to there, **Inspector Moore** did not believe that he would be connected with her murder, some five hours later.

DODGE, GEORGE M.
Witness. Seaman who gave evidence in New York about the Malay sea cook suspect.

DODGSON, REVD. CHARLES LUTWIDGE (1832–98)
Suspect, proposed 1996. *See* **Lewis Carroll**.

DOLDEN, PC CHARLES (CID) (*b.* 1857)
Joined the Metropolitan Police in 1877 (warrant no. 61644). Resigned as sergeant (CID) in 1902.

Accompanied Sgt. **Stephen White** to interview **Matthew Packer** and his household.

DON, POLICE SERGEANT JOHN CARMICHAEL (b. 1858)
Born in Perth. A clerk before joining the Metropolitan police in 1879 (warrant no. 63176). Promoted to sergeant in August 1889; retired to pension in 1898.
Accompanied by P.C. **Gill**, arrested **James Thomas Sadler** in the Phoenix public house and turned him over to Chief Inspector **Donald Swanson** at Leman Street Police Station.

DONNER, GERALD MELVILLE (1907–68)
Grandson of **Sir Melville Macnaghten**.

Early in the 1950s, **Philip Loftus** saw a framed 'Jack the Ripper' letter on Donner's wall, which he took to be a facsimile. Donner assured him that it was an original and proceeded to show Loftus Sir Melville's notes on the case. *See* **Macnaghten memoranda** for details and discussion; also, **Lady Aberconway** for evidence that Donner's mother had owned the original version of the memoranda, of which Philip Loftus gave a description from memory.

Subsequently, Donner went to Madras, where he had three framed letters hanging on his wall. He returned to England in 1957–8, having expressed his intention of bringing his Ripper material with him. If he did so, it was assumed he would sell the documents. As they have never appeared in salerooms, the authors doubt whether this occurred. Donner died in India, leaving all his possessions to his wife (*d.* 1970). Searching enquiries strongly suggest she did not possess any Ripper material.

DONNER, MRS JULIA (1881–1938)
Elder daughter of **Sir Melville Macnaghten**. Inherited the version of Macnaghten memoranda from which **Lady Aberconway** transcribed her surviving copy. Present whereabouts of Mrs Donner's copy unknown, but it seems likely to have passed to her son **Gerald Melville Donner** and might just be the version that he showed to **Philip Loftus** in 1950.

DONOVAN, TIMOTHY

Witness at **Annie Chapman**'s inquest. The deputy (manager) of **Crossingham's Lodging House**, 35 Dorset Street.

Timothy Donovan was apparently born in Stratford, Essex in 1865. He married Margaret (née Dempsey, *b. c.* 1865) and had at least two children, Timothy (*b.* 1887) and John (*b.* 1891). The birth certificate for Timothy (son) gives the address as 35 Dorset Street.

'A thin, pale-faced, sullen-looking young man, with a plentiful lack of shirt collar and a closely twisted crimson scarf round his throat,' who in the course of giving evidence at the inquest was reprimanded by the coroner 'for his insolence of tone' (*Daily News*, 11 September 1888).

Donovan said he had known Chapman as a prostitute for about 16 months and as a lodger for 4 months. He had last seen her at 1.45am, on 8 September 1888, in the kitchen of the lodging-house, where she was eating a baked potato – and in his opinion was the worse for liquor. He asked her for her doss-money, which she had not got, and declined her request to let her stay on trust. She then left, saying she would be back soon, and asking him to save her bed. It has been noted Donovan's various statements to police, press and inquest steadily softened his severity with her, as if he recognised that it seemed unkind to have driven a homeless woman out on to the streets where she was murdered.

Donovan also told the press he knew '**Leather Apron**' well and about 12 months earlier had turned him out of the lodging-house after he had physically assaulted a woman whom he claimed had tried to rob him. Donovan disbelieved him and had since refused him entry to the house on several occasions (*Evening Standard*, 10 September 1888). Both Donovan and **West**, a resident at the lodging-house, described 'Leather Apron' as wearing a deerstalker hat, which matched a description provided by **Elizabeth Long** of a man she had seen with a woman she believed to have been Annie Chapman (*Echo*, 19 September 1888).

Donald Rumbelow (*The Complete Jack the Ripper*, 2004) has suggested that Donovan might have been Jack the Ripper because he knew not only Chapman, but possibly also **Catherine Eddowes** and **Mary Kelly**; that being known as the deputy of the lodging-house he would probably have been able to approach the victims without arousing suspicion, that the lodging-house would have provided a bolt hole where he could clean up after the crimes, and that Donovan's story and description of 'Leather Apron' may have been intended to divert attention away from himself.

Rumbelow identifies Donovan with 29-year-old Timothy Donovan of 7 Russell Court, St George's-in-the-East, who died on 1 November 1888 of cirrhosis of the liver, phthisis and exhaustion, and Rumbelow has pointed out that Donovan's deteriorating health could account for the absence of murders in October and would also mean that Mary Kelly was murdered by another hand. Recent research has shown that the lodging-house deputy Timothy Donovan was still alive in 1891.

A 27-year-old Timothy Donovan was brought before Thames Police Court on

9 November 1887, on a charge of being drunk, disorderly and using offensive language, by **W. Smith 452 H**.

D'ONSTON, DR ROSLYN
See **Robert Donston Stephenson**.

DOUGHTY, JOHN (*fl.* 1888)
Alleged victim of indecent assault by **Dr Tumblety** on 2 November 1888 (National Archives, CRIM 4/1037, 21927).

DOWSON, ERNEST CHRISTOPHER (1867–1900)
Suspect, identified 1999.

One of the finest poets of his generation; educated at Queen's College, Oxon, which he left without taking his degree in the spring of 1888. Moved to London, managing his father's declining boat-fitting business in Limehouse. Close friend of the librarian of Toynbee Hall; notorious for long nocturnal walks through back alleys and association with street prostitutes. Moved to Paris, where his addiction to absinthe ruined his health. Identified by Martin Fido (***Ripperana*** 29, July 1999) as Mr Moring – both were East End poets, both had a father with a prosperous East End business, both drank or drugged themselves to death, both were nocturnal perambulators and friends of prostitutes (*Cf*, however, **Francis Thompson** as an alternative proposal for Mr Moring).

DOYLE, SIR ARTHUR CONAN (1859–1930)
Theorist and occasional suspect.

Educated Edinburgh University (MD, 1885). Best known for being the creator of Sherlock Holmes. On 2 December 1892, in the company of his brother-in-law E.W. Hornung (creator of *Raffles*) and Jerome K. Jerome (author of *Three Men in a Boat*), he visited the Black museum in Scotland Yard, where he saw facsimiles of the **'Dear Boss'** letter and **'Saucy Jacky'** postcard. In 1894, he told an American journalist that he concluded they were written by an educated person who had visited America. He said that Holmes would have had the facsimiles published widely in the hope that the writing would be recognised (unaware this had already been done). The interview was reported in the *Portsmouth Evening News* (4 July 1894). Doyle also attended the Crimes Club tour of the murder sites guided by **Dr Frederick Gordon Brown** in 1905 (*see also* **Ingleby Oddie**).

Nigel Morland, former editor of *Criminologist,* claimed that when he was young Doyle had remarked to him that the Ripper was 'somewhere in the upper stratum' but he would never explain any further (Introduction to *Prince Jack*).

Doyle has long been described as proposing the theory that the Ripper might have been a midwife – as such, a woman could pass through the streets in bloodstained clothing without attracting attention. The authors have been unable to trace an original source claiming to have heard this firsthand from Doyle.

Australian psychic Ann Ann (*see* **Death of a Prince**) has initiated a good deal of interest in Doyle as a spirit informant on the Ripper, which has led to some (unfounded) suggestions that he was a black magician and the Ripper himself.

DRAGE, PC JOSEPH WILLIAM, 282H (*b.* 1847)

10 years' Army service with 48th Foot before joining the Metropolitan Police in 1879 (warrant no. 63548) and served on **H Division** (1879–89). A confidential letter in April 1886 to the Home Office from the Commissioner reported inquiries having been made into *a* PC Drage, with the result that doubts existed as to his suitability for the service and that it was necessary to keep him under observation. He resigned (with gratuity) in 1890.

12.30am on Monday, 1 October was on fixed-point duty at the junction of Great Garden Street and Whitechapel Road, when **Thomas Coram** pointed out to him the bloodstained blunted chandler's slicing knife on the doorstep opposite no. 253 Whitechapel Road.

Despite press and subsequent speculation, Dr **George George Bagster Phillips** gave the opinion that it was improbable that it was this knife that had wounded **Elizabeth Stride**.

Sixteen days later, Drage was officially cautioned for some minor disciplinary infringement.

Cf. **Jack the Ripper's Knife**.

DREW, THOMAS STUART (*b. c.* 1845)

Allegedly cohabited with **Mary Ann Nichols**, June 1883 to October 1887.

Blacksmith, with a shop in York Road, Walworth. He knew Mary Ann Nichols and was her sweetheart before she married **William Nichols**. When Mary Ann and William separated, she went to live with Drew but 'she made away with some of his goods for drink; then he abandoned her, and she went into the workhouse for food' (*Lloyd's Weekly News*, 2 September 1888). Twice-married: in 1866 to Matilda née Pond (who died in 1884), and in 1886, Elizabeth Baryan (or Beryan).

DRUITT, ANN (1830–90)

Mother of **Montague John Druitt**. Mentioned in letter or papers he left when contemplating suicide because he feared he was 'going to be like mother'. Suffered depression and paranoid delusions (that she was being electrocuted) following the death of her husband in 1885. Attempted suicide in 1888, and in July was sent to the Brooke Asylum, Clapton, where she was attended by Dr William Pavy and certified insane.

In September 1888, she was transferred on leave from asylum to Dr J.R. Gasquet's establishment in Brighton, where her certification lapsed by oversight and was renewed early in 1889, with formal transfer of her incarceration to Brighton, where she had remained uninterruptedly since the previous September. In May 1890, she was transferred to the care of the Tuke brothers at Manor House Asylum, Chiswick, where she died, six months later.

Diabetes seems to have been a hereditary condition, inducing melancholia and suicidal urges. Her mother committed suicide while insane, her sister also attempted it and spent a period in an asylum. Montague John's eldest sister killed herself in old age.

DRUITT, DR LIONEL (1853–1908)

First cousin of **Montague John Druitt** and alleged author of *The East End Murderer – I Knew Him*.

Educated at St David's, London and Edinburgh. MRCS, 1875; LRCP (Lond), MB, Mast. Surg. (Edin), 1877. MD (Edin), 1882. In 1879, listed in the Medical Register at 140 Minories, surgery of Dr Thyne. Also listed in the Medical Directory as assistant house surgeon, Craiglockhart Poorhouse, Edinburgh. It is not known in which order and for how many months he practised in each of these places. Subsequently at 122 Clapham Road; also frequently, but intermittently resident at his father's home in Strathmore Gardens. In 1886, he emigrated to Australia, living first with his uncle, Archdeacon Thomas Druitt, in Cooma, NSW. In 1888 he married Susan Murray in Wagga Wagga. From 1897–98, he lived in Dandenong Road, Melbourne and in 1903 was living in Drouin. He died in Mentone, Victoria.

Daniel Farson speculates his presence in The Minories in 1878 (or 1879) gave Montague John Druitt his introduction to the East End.

DRUITT, MONTAGUE JOHN (1857–88)

Suspect. Born Wimborne, Dorset.

Educated Winchester and New College, Oxford (BA, Lit.Hum., Class III, 1880). Successful debater and sportsman (fives and cricket) at school and college; unsuccessful amateur actor (poor performance as Sir Toby Belch in the school play). Steward of college junior common room. Employed as schoolmaster, Mr **George Valentine**'s school, Blackheath, 1880. Admitted Inner Temple (1882); called to the bar (1885), attached to Western Circuit. Joined Arthur

Jelf's chambers, 9 King's Bench Walk. Secretary Morden Cricket Club (1884); hon. sec. and treas., Blackheath Cricket, Football and Lawn Tennis Co. (1885). Special pleader, Western Circuit, 1887. Dismissed by Mr Valentine after being in 'serious trouble at the school', *c.* 30 November 1888. Last seen alive *c.* 3 December 1888, but see below.

His body was recovered from the Thames, off Thorneycroft's Torpedo Works, Chiswick, by waterman **Henry Winslade**, on 31 December and examined by PC **George Moulson**. Druitt's pockets contained: four large stones; £2. 17s.2d in cash, a cheque for £50 and another for £16, a silver watch on a gold chain with a spade guinea as seal, a pair of kid gloves, a white handkerchief and a second-half return from Hammersmith to Charing Cross, dated 1 December. There were said to be no papers or letters of any description, which suggests the cheques were the source from which his identity was established so that his family in Bournemouth could be notified. The body had been immersed for about a month.

He left a letter for Mr Valentine, alluding to suicide, and a paper addressed to his brother with words to the effect that, 'Since Friday I felt that I was going to be like mother [see Ann Druitt], and the best thing was for me to die' (*Acton, Chiswick and Turham Green Gazette*, 5 January 1889). The date proposed officially as that on which he was last seen alive, 31 November, appears to be an arithmetical deduction from **William Druitt**'s recollection that he heard on 11 December that Montague had not been seen in chambers for a week. The dating of the return half ticket suggests Druitt committed suicide in Hammersmith or Chiswick on 1 December 1888. On 2 January 1889, the inquest found 'suicide whilst of unsound mind', which permitted burial in consecrated ground at Wimborne cemetery.

He is named in the **Macnaghten memoranda** and described with only small differences between the two known versions: the Scotland Yard version adding that, 'He was sexually insane' and omitting the references to Druitt's age and the first-class half-season rail ticket from Blackheath to London found on his body.

It seems reasonably certain that **Macnaghten** drew upon Moulson's report, but less so that he was familiar with inquest testimony.

In *Days of My Years* Macnaghten wrote: 'Although, as I shall endeavour to show in this chapter, the Whitechapel Murderer, in all probability, put an end to himself soon after the Dorset Street affair in November 1888, certain facts pointing to this conclusion were not in possession of the police till some years after I became a detective officer.' Macnaghten took up his post at Scotland Yard in June 1889.

There was a family connection between the Macnaghtens and the Druitts. Macnaghten's father, the last chairman of the East India Company, appointed Montague's aunt's brother to the board in 1855 (**W. Boultbee**).

Donald McCormick claims **Albert Bachert** heard from the police in March 1889 that the Ripper had drowned in the Thames, but there is no independent corroboration of this story and it is seemingly unsupported by statements from Bachert that the Vigilance Committee remained very active until the dock strike, later that year.

In 1891, an unnamed West of England MP (*see* **Henry Richard Farquharson**) was attributed with alleging tthe Ripper was the son of a surgeon and committed suicide on the night of the last murder (*Bristol Times and Mirror,* 11 February 1891). This story is from Druitt's part of the country and roughly matches Macnaghten's account.

The only suggestion that other policemen shared his suspicions is a statement by **George R. Sims** that, 'the name of the man found drowned was bracketed with two others as a possible Jack, and the police were in search of him alive when they found him dead' (*The Referee*, 13 July 1902). Asked about the Thames' suicide suspect, the following year, **Inspector Abberline** said, "I know all about that story. But what does it amount to? Simply this. Soon after the last murder in Whitechapel the body of a young doctor was found in the Thames, but there is absolutely nothing beyond the fact that he was found at that time to incriminate him. A report was made to the Home Office about the matter..."' (*Pall Mall Gazette*, 31 March 1903).

Druitt came to notice in 1959, following the discovery of the **Aberconway** version of Sir Melville Macnaghten's memoranda. He was discussed without being named by **Daniel Farson** in his television series, *Farson's Guide to the British* (1959), given more prominence in *Autumn of Terror* (1965) and *Jack the Ripper* (1972), which included the results of research on Lionel Druitt (*see* ***The East End Murderer – I Knew Him***).

Donald McCormick incorporated Druitt into the 1972 revised edition of *The Identity of Jack the Ripper*, claiming oral information from an unidentified 'London doctor who knew [Walter] **Sickert** and whose father was at Oxford with Druitt'. The man apparently told McCormick that Druitt's mind gave way because a blackmailer had accused him of being the Ripper and that Walter Sickert believed that his suspect, the veterinary student, was called Druitt, Drewett or Hewitt. He also alleged Sickert had told his story to Macnaghten in the Garrick Club, and Macnaghten believed it must describe Montague John Druitt since, like the veterinary student, he had a mother in Bournemouth. None of McCormick's information has been substantiated.

Philip Loftus wrote privately to Lady Aberconway, giving a description of the version of the memoranda he had seen in **Gerald Melville Donner**'s possession. This described 'MICHAEL JOHN DRUITT, a DOCTOR of FORTY ONE years of age...' (Loftus's capitals and dots).

(*See also* ***Jack the Ripper Revealed*** for theory that Druitt and **J.K. Stephen** collaborated in committing the murders and supporting evidence of anagrams in the Goulston Street graffito and some of the Jack the Ripper letters. **Andrew J. Spallek**, 'Montague John Druitt: Still Our Best Suspect', *Ripper Notes*, 23, July 2005. Adrian

Morris, 'The Diminishing Case Of Mr Druit'
Journal of the Whitechapel Society, 13, April 2007)

DRUITT, WILLIAM HARVEY (1856–1909)

Suspect. **Montague John Druitt**'s elder
brother and witness at his inquest. Proposed by
Andrew Holloway ('Not Guilty', *The Cricketer*,
December 1990).

Educated at Clifton and Trinity (Oxon.).

A solicitor resident in Bournemouth, William
Druitt became concerned on learning that
Montague had not been seen in his chambers for
about a week preceding 11 December 1888.
Thereupon he went to London, learned of his
dismissal from **Mr Valentine**'s school on 30
November, and found suicide notes in his brother's
lodgings. At the inquest he reportedly described himself and his mother as
Montague's only relatives. (If he really said this, it was definitely untrue – five other
siblings were still living.)

Mr Holloway argues William murdered Montague to get control of the family
estates and gave police the bogus story that Montague was the Ripper to divert
suspicion. He further suggests Montague was drugged or poisoned, and his body
dumped in the Thames or dislodged from its hiding place when the river flooded.
No evidence is adduced to support this theory.

DUDMAN, SERGEANT AMOS (b. c. 1849)

City Police officer who, with **Inspector Izzard** and **Sergeant Phelps**, sought to
preserve public order after **Catherine Eddowes'** murder and was reported in the
Daily News, 1 October 1888, as having his attention drawn to a window-sill and
doorway in Mitre Street, which appeared to have recent blood stains.

Joined the City Police in 1870 (warrant no. 4347). Dismissed with forfeiture of
all pay, June 1889.

DUKES, DR WILLIAM PROFIT (b. c. 1838–95)

Police surgeon of **H Division**, resident 75 Brick Lane, and said by the
Carmarthen Journal to have been first medical man at the scene of **Mary Jane
Kelly**'s murder, although the *Daily News* (10 November 1888) has him joining
Dr Phillips, who apparently preceded him. Subsequently joined Drs **Bond**,
Phillips and **Gabe** at her postmortem.

In 1891, he was summoned to examine the body of **Charles Guiver**, a witness
in the **Frances Coles** case, who had been physically and mentally affected after
looking at Coles' body, soon after dying from a fit while in bed. After performing
an autopsy, Dr Dukes concluded Guiver had died from apoplexy accelerated by the
excitement and shock.

DUNDEE-BORN TEENAGE SUSPECT

Described to Robin Odell in 1962. A correspondent claimed his father, an East London apprentice in 1888, had committed the murders to avenge his employer, an engineer's wood pattern maker, who died of a venereal disease. The father was said to have been born in Dundee (1873) and a kindly and gentle man in adult life.

DURRELL, MRS

See **Mrs Darrell**.

DUTTON, DR THOMAS (1854–1935)

Theorist and Aldgate resident, suspected and immediately cleared, 1888.

Second of nine children born to George Dutton and his wife, Barbara. George Dutton was later manager of the London and Westminster Bank at 130 Whitechapel High Street (which still exists as a bank). Educated Bayswater Grammar School, Guy's Hospital, Edinburgh and Durham Universities. LM and LRCS, Edin. (1878); MB (1880); MD, Durham; MRCP, Edin. (1882). From 1881 to 1884, Admiralty surgeon and agent (Chichester Division) and MO, Mahood Division, Westhampnett Union, E. Member of Poor Law Medical Officers Association, Chichester and West Sussex Natural History and Microscopical Society, and the National League for Physical Education and Improvement. Hon. physician to Uxbridge Road Maternity and Child Welfare Clinic; hon. surgeon to the Royal Defence Corps and surgeon in the Mercantile Marine, serving on SS *Elysia* and RMS *Tongariro*. Fellow of the Hunterian Society, vice president of the Imperial Medical Reform Union; vice chairman of the Pure Food Society. Author of numerous, widely reviewed and apparently popular general medical books. From at least 1879–91 listed in directories as at 130 Aldgate High Street. Thus, he was in the locality at the time of the Whitechapel murders.

When Dr Dutton's sister, Miss B. Dutton (so far unidentified), called on her brother and was unable to gain access to his rooms at 290 Uxbridge Road, Shepherd's Bush, a sub-tenant named Willis entered and found Dr Dutton dead beside his bed. A postmortem revealed death was due to heart disease. It was claimed Dutton kept a diary for 50 years, that it referred to his friendship with the **Duke of Clarence** and that it made clear his interest in crimes (*Daily Express*, *Daily Sketch*, 12 November 1935; *Daily Express*, 13 November 1935).

A long article in the *Empire News* (17 November 1935) claimed Dr Dutton had been taken into protective custody a few days after the last Jack the Ripper murder when harassed by a mob because he was carrying a black bag. The article claimed he had taken a keen interest in the murders and had made enquiries of his women patients and was convinced the murderer possessed anatomical skills.

The longest and most Ripper-related article, published in the *Sunday Chronicle* (17 November 1935), was by a 'Special Correspondent' who reported he had been told by Miss Hermione Dudley, a friend and patient of Dr Dutton, that she had been given by him 'three volumes of handwritten comments on all the chief crimes of the past sixty years', which she called 'his *Chronicles of Crime*'. Dutton claimed Jack the Ripper was 'a middle-aged doctor, a man whose mind had been embittered by the death of his son. The latter had suffered cruelly at the hands of a woman of the streets, and the father believed this to be the cause of his brilliant son's death' (*see* **Dr Stanley**). Hermione Dudley had not been identified (Chris Scott, 'In Search of the Duttons and Miss Hermione Dudley' *Ripperologist*, 50, November 2003). This article was probably written by **Donald McCormick**, who recalled that when he was running the London and Provincial News Agency he had a story about Dr Dutton published in the *Sunday Chronicle* (letter dated 15 May 1995 to **Paul Feldman** in authors' possession).

In *The Identity of Jack the Ripper*, McCormick, who claimed to have read and taken notes from Dutton's diaries, said that Dr Dutton made micro-photographs of the handwriting of Ripper correspondence and the Goulston Street Graffito, but that **Sir Charles Warren** ordered the destruction of the prints of the latter. He also claims Dutton was a friend of, and advised **Inspector Abberline** – who, he says, suspected **Severin Klosowski** early in 1888 (but see Abberline's interviews with *Pall Mall Gazette* in 1903), and referred to **Pedachenko**.

Doubts are cast on McCormick's story in *Jack the Ripper: The Bloody Truth*, (*see also* **Melvin Harris**, 'The Maybrick Hoax: Donald McCormick's Legacy', **Casebook: Jack the Ripper.**

E

EAGLE, MORRIS

Witness at **Elizabeth Stride**'s inquest. Russian immigrant of 4 New Road, Commercial Road. Travelled in jewellery. On 29 September 1888, chaired discussion at the Workers' International Educational Club on the necessity for socialism among Jews. Left at 11.45pm to take his young lady home, returning 12.35am. Going through the passage at the gateway from Berner Street into Dutfield's Yard he saw nothing unusual, but, given the total darkness, could not swear the body was not there. Upstairs in the club he joined a friend in singing a Russian folk song. At about 12.55 a member called **Gilleman** came upstairs and said there was a dead woman in the passage. Eagle went out with Kozebrodsky (Isaacs) and saw the body.

MORRIS EAGLE

He proceeded to Commercial Street, where he found PC Lamb.

EAST END MURDERER – I KNEW HIM, THE

Alleged document supposedly written by Dr **Lionel Druitt** and privately published in Australia.

In a letter to **Daniel Farson**, early in 1959, Mr **A. Knowles** claimed to have seen a document called *The East End Murderer – I Knew Him*, written by a Lionel Druitt, Drewett or Drewery and 'printed privately by a **Mr Fell** of Dandenong in 1890.' The letter assumed importance when Farson found reference to Montague John Druitt in the Macnaghten memoranda and discovered his cousin Lionel had emigrated to Australia in 1887 (Farson never learned that the doctor actually lived in Dandenong Road, Melbourne, from 1897 to 1901). Unfortunately Farson's file containing Mr Knowles' letter had by this time been lost and Farson thought Mr Knowles was dead, believing him to be a Mr Arthur Knowles of Hackney, who died, aged 84, in June 1959.

Another letter to Farson was from Mr Maurice Gould of Bexleyheath, who said that between 1925 and 1930, he had independently been told by two men in Australia that Jack the Ripper was identified in papers they had seen, which were owned by a Mr W.G. Fell, an Englishman who he believed had died in 1935. Subsequent research by John Ruffels established that Mr Gould had known two Fells in Australia: a storekeeper called W.G. Fell from Lang Lang, and a journalist or printer from Melbourne (correspondence with Howells and Skinner, 1986–87).

In 1986, Martin Howells and Keith Skinner traced Maurice Gould, who said his conversation had originally concerned **Frederick Bailey Deeming**, and he described Fell's document as two or three sheets of handwritten paper, including the word 'Ripper' somewhere. Deeming was known to have used the alias 'Drewen' on coming to Australia and widely rumoured to have written a confession to 'the last two' Ripper murders. They concluded Mr Fell's document was Deeming's handwritten confession and had nothing to do with Lionel Druitt (*The Ripper Legacy*).

EAST END MURDERS FROM JACK THE RIPPER TO RONNIE KRAY
Book by Neil R. Storey (Stroud, Gloucestershire: The History Press, 2008).

Bulk of the book records the basic facts about the murders committed by Jack the Ripper and by **Israel Lipski**.

(*See also* **Grim Almanac of Jack the Ripper's London 1870–1900**.)

ECHOES OF THE RIPPER
Edited by B.A. Rogers (self-published, 2000).

With an informative introduction, reprints Ripper chapters from *Inquest* (1941) by S. Ingleby Oddie, *Murders and Murder Trials* (1932) by H.M. Walbrook, *Crime and the Supernatural* (1935) by Edwin Thomas Woodhall and *Great Thames Mysteries* (1929) by Elliott O'Donnell. *See also* **Shadows of the Ripper** and **Reflections on the Ripper**.

ECKERT, DR WILLIAM GAMM (1926–99)
Organiser of FBI Profile.

Born on 23 July 1926 in Union City, New Jersey. Educated at New York University, majoring in history; medical degree from Bellvue Medical School. Completed a residency at Tulane Medical School and worked at the public Health Hospital in New Orleans and the New Orleans Parish coroner's office. Was deputy coroner in Sedgwick County, Wichita, Kansas, and afterwards an independent consultant. Retired to Terrytown. Founded the Helpern Center for Forensic Sciences with his wife Haroldine Laugel Eckert. President, National Association of Medical Examiners, 1980-81. Founding editor, *American Journal of Forensic Pathology*.

It was at the recommendation of Eckert that the television production company Cosgrove-Meurer developed *The Secret Identity of Jack the Ripper* (1988), in which the FBI applied its newly-perfected psychological profiling (now known as criminal identification analysis) to the Ripper case. Eckert, who was a panellist on the programme, met with Donald Rumbelow and Martin Fido in London. On the programme, he demonstrated the murderer's possible MO of attacking from behind, as demonstrated by Rumbelow. According to Martin Fido, at the rehearsals he advocated **David Cohen** as the probable Ripper, but that the producers insisted that he name **Kosminski** on the programme because that was the only Polish Jew suspect they had advanced. Following the programme, Eckert wrote privately to Martin Fido that in his opinion Cohen remained the most likely of the so-far named candidates, but there was insufficient evidence to name anyone with certainty, admitting it could easily be someone entirely other.

He subsequently published 'The Ripper Project: Modern Science Solving Mysteries of History' (*The American Journal of Forensic Medicine and Pathology*, Vol. 10, 2, 1989; also, 'The Whitechapel Murders: The Case of Jack the Ripper' in the same journal).

See also **FBI Psychological Profile**, **Tom Sandrock**.

(Obituary in *The New York Times*, 24 September 1999; *Ripperologist*, April 2000, with a personal remembrance by Martin Fido.)

EDDOWES, CATHERINE (1842–88)

Fourth Ripper victim.

Born in Wolverhampton, the daughter of tinplate varnisher George Eddowes, who moved with his large family to Bermondsey before she was two. (The spelling 'Catherine' is taken from her birth certificate.)

Educated at St John's Charity School, Potter's Field, Tooley Street, until her mother, Catherine Eddowes, née Evans, died in 1855, when most of her siblings entered Bermondsey Workhouse and Industrial School. Thereafter her movements are uncertain. According to the *Wolverhampton Chronicle*, she returned to the care of her aunt in Biston Street, Wolverhampton and continued her education at Dowgate Charity School. Certainly, some time between 1861 and 1863 she left home with a pensioner named **Thomas Conway** (formerly enlisted in the 18th Royal Irish Regiment under the name Quinn and drawing a regimental pension under that name).

According to the newspapers, the couple lived by selling chapbooks (which Conway wrote) in Birmingham and the Midlands – chapbooks were inexpensive books sold on the streets by peddlers and were political or religious tracts, histories, nursery rhymes, or accounts of current events.

Catherine's friends said that she claimed she had legitimately married Conway and had his initials, TC, tattooed on her arm. No trace of this marriage has been found on the registers. They had three children: Annie (born *c.* 1865), George (*c.* 1868) and another son (*c.* 1873).

In 1880 the Conways separated, with Catherine taking custody of Annie and Conway looking after the boys. Annie said Catherine's habitual drinking and periodic absences caused the breakdown, while Catherine's sister, **Elizabeth Fisher**, attributed it to Conway's occasional drinking and violence.

Catherine joined an Irish porter (probably **John Kelly**, with whom she was still living, seven years later) in his lodgings in Flower and Dean Street in 1881. Annie married Louis Phillips, and she and her husband spent the next few years moving around Bermondsey and Southwark to avoid her mother's scrounging.

In September 1888, Catherine and Kelly went hop-picking in Kent. They failed to earn much and at the end of the month they returned on foot with another man and his common-law wife, **Emily Birrell**. It seems likely to have been early in their hopping trip, before their money ran out, that Kelly bought a pair of boots from **Arthur Pash** in Maidstone and Kelly purchased a jacket from Edmett's adjacent pawnshop (*The Times*, 4 October 1888, though this does not name Edmett's).

On 27 September, Catherine and Kelly reached London and spent the night in the casual ward at Shoe Lane. The following night, they separated. Catherine went to the casual ward at Mile End, while Kelly slept at no. 52 Flower and Dean Street

– he was not seen by the manager of the doss-house at Cooney's, 55 Flower and Dean Street (their usual lodging) until the following morning. At Shoe Lane, where she was well known, Catherine told the superintendent, 'I have come back to earn the reward offered for the apprehension of the Whitechapel Murderer. I think I know him.' He warned her to take care she was not murdered, to which she replied, 'Oh, no fear of that.' (One press report attributed this story to the superintendent of Mile End casual ward.)

At 8am, on 29 September, she arrived at Cooney's, having been turned out of Shoe Lane. She and Kelly agreed to pawn a pair of his boots and she took them to one Smith or Jones in Church Street, receiving 2/6d [12?p] and a ticket in the name of 'Jane Kelly'. The couple bought tea, sugar and food, and ate breakfast in the kitchen at Cooney's between 10.00 and 11.00.

By 2pm, they were again without money. (2/6d had a purchasing power of around £8, which suggests they bought liquor as well as breakfast.) They parted at 2pm in Houndsditch, with Catherine saying she was going to Bermondsey to borrow money from Annie and would be back by 4.00. Whatever she then did, she did not find Annie, and was not seen again until the evening. This found her causing a drunken disturbance outside 29 Aldgate High Street, where, according to **Tom Cullen**, she first attracted a small crowd by imitating a fire engine and then lay down on the pavement to sleep. With the help of PC **George Simmons**, PC **Louis Robinson** took her to Bishopsgate Police Station, where she gave her name as 'Nothing', and Station **Sergeant Byfl**eld locked her up in a cell.

At 8.50pm, Robinson looked in and found her asleep and smelling strongly of drink. Then, at 9.45pm, PC **George Hutt** came on duty and inspected the cells at regular intervals. At 12.15am Catherine was awake and singing softly to herself, while at 12.30, she called out to ask when she might be released. 'When you are capable of taking care of yourself,' Hutt told her. 'I can do that now,' she replied. At 1am, he released her and she asked the time. 'Too late for you to get any more drink,' he said.

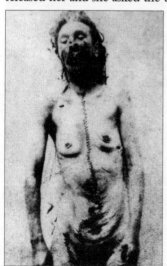

'I shall get a damn fine hiding when I get home,' she told him. 'And serve you right,' he responded. 'You have no right to get drunk.' She gave her name and address as Mary Ann Kelly of 6 Fashion Street. And Hutt said amiably, 'This way, missus', as he guided her through the passage and asked her to close the outer door after her. 'All right. Good night, old cock,' were Catherine's last recorded words.

At approximately 1.35am, **Joseph Lawende**, **Joseph Hyam Levy** and **Harry Harris** saw a woman later identified from her clothing as Eddowes standing in the Duke's Place entrance to Church Passage, a covered entry leading into Mitre Square, talking amicably with a man, her hand on his chest. Lawende and Levy identified her by her clothes: neither saw her face.

Very shortly after they left, at about 1.40am PC **James Harvey** came along Duke's Place and down Church Passage on his beat. He saw no one and heard nothing from the square, which he did not enter. At 1.45 (by his estimation) PC **Edward Watkins** came into the square from the opposite side and found Catherine Eddowes' body in the southwest corner. He immediately summoned **George Morris**, the night watchman at Kearley and Tonge's, to his assistance. Morris, running out into Aldgate, found PC **Harvey** and PC **Holland**. Subsequently, Holland went and fetched Dr **Sequeira** from Jewry Street: he, too, timed his arrival at 1.45am. Station Inspector **Edward Collard** at Bishopsgate Police Station was informed of the discovery at 1.55, and sent for police surgeon, **Frederick Gordon Brown**, before going to the square, which he reached at 2.03. Within a few minutes, Brown arrived, followed by Inspector **McWilliam** and Sergeant **Foster**. At some subsequent point, Major **Henry Smith** also arrived at Mitre Square.

Beside the body, Sergeant **Jones** found three boot buttons, a thimble and a mustard tin containing the pawn tickets for Emily Birrell's man's shirt and Kelly's boots. These ultimately established Eddowes' identity.

The body was transferred to Golden Lane Mortuary. (For Catherine Eddowes' appearance and injuries, *see* Frederick Gordon Brown.) The official police listing of her clothes and possessions, taken at the mortuary, was as follows (we omit phrases detailing cuts and bloodstains caused by the murder):

Black Straw Bonnet trimmed with green & black Velvet and black beads, black strings.
Black Cloth Jacket, imitation fur edging round collar, fur round sleeves…2 outside pockets, trimmed black silk braid & imitation fur.
Chintz Skirt, 3 flounces, brown button on waistband.
Brown Linsey Dress Bodice, black velvet collar, brown metal buttons down front.
Grey Stuff Petticoat, white waist band.
Very Old Green Alpaca Skirt.
Very Old ragged Blue Skirt, red flounce, light twill lining.
White Calico Chemise.
Mans White Vest, button to match down front, 2 outside pockets.
No Drawers or Stays.
Pair of Mens lace up Boots, mohair laces. Right boot has been repaired with red thread.
1 piece of red gauze Silk…found on neck.
1 large White Handkerchief.

2 Unbleached Calico Pockets.
1 Blue Stripe Bed ticking Pocket, waist band, and strings.
1 White Cotton Pocket Handkerchief, red and white birds eye border.
1 pr. Brown ribbed Stockings, feet mended with white.
12 pieces of white Rag, some slightly bloodstained.
1 piece of white Coarse Linen.
1 piece of Blue & White Shining (3 cornered).
2 Small Blue Bed ticking Bags.
2 Short Clay Pipes (black).
1 Tin Box containing Tea.
1 do do do Sugar.
1 Piece of Flannel & 6 pieces of soap.
1 Small Tooth Comb.
1 White Handle Table Knife & 1 metal Tea Spoon.
1 Red Leather Cigarette Case, white metal fittings.
1 Tin Match Box, empty.
1 piece of Red Flannel containing Pins & Needles.
1 Ball of Hemp.
1 piece of old White Apron.

Press reports add part of a pair of spectacles, one mitten and a printed card for cheesemonger 'Frank Cater, 305 Bethnal Green Road'. They describe the outer chintz dress as having a pattern of chrysanthemums or Michaelmas daisies and lilies. The white apron was so dirty that at first glance it seemed black (**Walter Dew** so described it).

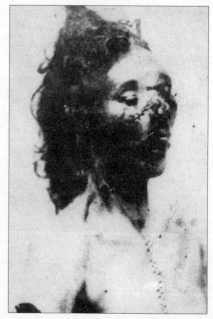

The other piece of the apron (approximately half) was picked up at 2.50am in the doorway of Wentworth Model Dwellings, underneath the Goulston Street graffito. Since there was no doubt whatsoever that the piece was from Catherine's apron (it crossed and matched a repair), this constituted the one physical clue ever left by the Ripper, demonstrating his escape route from Mitre Square was in the direction of northeast Whitechapel, Spitalfields or Mile End New Town.

The inquest on Catherine Eddowes was conducted by Coroner **Langham**. Although her daughter, Annie Phillips, testified to her scrounging to such an extent that her husband and children deliberately avoided her, others portrayed a more pleasant, if feckless, character. According to John Kelly, Elizabeth Fisher (another sister), **Eliza Gold** and the deputy at Cooney's (**Frederick William Wilkinson**), she was very good natured and cheerful, often singing and rarely drunk. None claimed to know that she prostituted herself and there is no direct evidence that she did so – only the suggestive facts that she apparently had no money at 2pm on 29 September, but had acquired enough to make a drunken scene six hours later and that shortly before she died, she was probably seen talking to a strange man at a dark corner in a direction leading away from the lodging-house where she was staying.

Catherine may not have known her precise age herself: her sister wrongly believed her to be only 43 when she died.

She was buried in an unmarked grave in Little Ilford on 8 October, the expenses for an elm coffin and a funeral cortège led by an open-glass hearse being met by the undertaker, **Mr Hawkes**. Crowds lined the streets for the funeral.

See Dr Frederick Gordon Brown for the postmortem report and discussion of her kidney.

EDDOWES' SHAWL
A rectangle of silk with a flowered print, long enough to make a wrap. Uncertainly dated by fabric experts as late nineteenth or early twentieth century. Property of descendants of PC **Amos Simpson**. In 1988, they cut out and framed two pieces which were displayed, first in a Thetford video shop and then in a Clacton antique dealer's. On the back of the frame is the inscription:

> Two silk samples taken from Catherine Eddowes' shawl at the time of the discovery of her body by Constable Amos Simpson in 1888 (end of September) victim of Jack the Ripper.
> Arabella Vincent (Fine Art)
> Hand-made Illustrated Mounts
> UK Studio, Tel Clacton –
> Surface printed silk
> Circa 1886.
> Framed 100 years to the day.
> Vincent

In September 1991, the main part of the shawl was donated to Scotland Yard's Crime Museum (the 'Black Museum') and reclaimed by the family in September 1997. Then, in June 2006, it was subjected to expert examination – in particular, for possible DNA evidence – for the Channel 5 documentary, *Jack the Ripper: The First Serial Killer*, with the conclusion that forensic science could offer no definite information. It was put up for auction by the family in March 2007 but failed to meet the reserve price. However, two weeks later, the person who had made the closing bid met with the family and the shawl was privately sold.

There is no suggestion of calculated deception on anyone's part: it is doubted that the shawl was really Eddowes' – for example, it is a costly item and therefore improbable that she might have possessed it and no such item is mentioned in descriptions of her, or her possessions and clothing.

Sue & Andy Parlour, 'Catharine Eddowes' Shawl' and 'The Eddowes' Shawl: The Auction', *The Journal of the Whitechapel Society*, 19, 2007.

EDE, THOMAS

Witness at the inquest on **Mary Ann Nichols**. Railway signalman. Despite queries as to the relevance, he was permitted by Coroner **Wynne Baxter** to give evidence on 17 September 1888 that he had seen a suspicious man in a two-peaked cap, with 4in of knife blade protruding from his pocket, outside the Foresters' Arms on 8 September. He returned to the inquest hearing of 22 September to confirm that he had now identified the harmless lunatic **Henry James** as the man he had seen.

EDWARDS, FRANK (*b. c.* 1853)

Suspect, named in 1959 by a cousin who had suspected him in 1888. Visited his 11-year-old cousin George's family in Chichester some hours after the double murders, wearing gold pince-nez and carrying a razor and a bloodstained shirt collar in his attaché case. George Edwards and another cousin, after reading about the sighting of **Leon Goldstein**, concluded Frank, who matched Goldstein's description, was the Ripper. George explained his long silence by saying that he feared that he might be 'done in, too.' *(Reynolds News*, 8 February 1959; *Worthing Gazette*, 11 February 1959)

EDWARDS, GEORGE HENRY (*c.* 1865–1950)

Clerk in the Commissioner's Office, 1886, rising to chief clerk. Awarded OBE, 1918. Secretary, Metropolitan Police (1925–27).

A copy of Major **Henry Smith**'s memoirs, *From Constable to Commissioner*, in the library at Scotland Yard contained the note: 'Presented from The Effects Of The Late George H Edwards OBE Secretary Metropolitan Police 1925–1927'. It contains a handwritten note on the title page: 'A good raconteur and a good fellow, but not strictly veracious: much of this book consists of after dinner stories outside his personal experience. In dealing with matters within his own knowledge he is often far from accurate as my own knowledge of the facts assure me. G.H.E.'

The book contains six marginal annotations and various underlinings. Only one concerns the Ripper. Concerning the Goulston Street graffito Major Smith wrote: '**Sir Charles Warren** was instantly apprised of this discovery, and, coming down himself, ordered the words to be wiped out, alleging as his reason for so doing that he feared a rising against the Jews. This was, I thought, a fatal mistake as **Superintendent MacWilliam** plainly told Sir Charles...' In the margin Edwards wrote, 'This was partly discussed in the Press at the time.'

ELIZABETH STRIDE AND JACK THE RIPPER: THE LIFE AND DEATH OF THE REPUTED THIRD VICTIM

Book by Dave Yost (Jefferson, North Carolina: McFarland, 2008).

In-depth account of the life and death of **Elizabeth Stride** with a detailed look at many of the questions surrounding her murder and explanation of why Yost does not believe Stride was murdered by Jack the Ripper.

ELLIOTT, P.C. GEORGE (*b.* 1859)

Joined the Metropolitan Police in 1881 (warrant no. 65447). Resigned, 1906.

One of the policemen coming to the assistance of PC **Ernest Thompson** when he discovered the body of **Frances Coles**.

ELLISDON, INSPECTOR ERNEST, J Division (1846–1901)

Joined the Metropolitan Police in 1868 (warrant no. 50657). Left and rejoined in 1872 (warrant no. 56308). Resigned, 1894. In January 1882, visited the Metropolitan and Police City Orphanage, where he recorded his satisfaction at the 'happy and contented appearance of the children.'

As divisional inspector, it would appear he played little part in the investigation, but was responsible for putting **Inspector Reid** in charge of the **Martha Tabram** inquiry.

ENRIGHT, DETECTIVE SERGEANT PATRICK, J Division (*b.* 1849)

Warrant no. 58207. Former tailor from Limerick. Served with the Royal Irish Constabulary before joining the Metropolitan Police in 1874. Resigned, 1890, suffering from tubercular infection of the lung. Given temporary charge of **Mary Ann Nichols**' body at the mortuary, he left strict instructions that it should not be touched. He was disregarded and the full extent of her injuries revealed before she had been properly medically examined. With **Abberline**, **Helson** and **Godley**, he observed Nichols' inquest on behalf of the CID.

With **Inspector Reid** and Sergeant Godley, he was named by the *Echo* (20 September 1888) as following up a clue given by 'Pearly Poll' (**Mary Ann Connolly**), which led the authorities 'to suspect a man actually living not far from Buck's Row'. (*See* **John Pizer, 'Leather Apron'**.) On 10 November 1888, he was gazetted in Police Printed Orders as receiving an award of 5/- [2Sp] at the same time as **Sergeant Thick** was awarded 7/-.

EPIPHANY OF THE WHITECHAPEL MURDERS

Book by Karen Trenouth (Bloomington, Indiana: AuthorHouse, 2006). *See also Jack the Ripper: The Satanic Team.*

Argues that at Queen Victoria's behest several young aristocratic patrons of Charles Hammond's homosexual brothel at 19 Cleveland Street set out to kill **Mary Kelly** to prevent her divulging that **Prince Albert Victor** was also a patron and they engaged surgeon **Alfred Pearson** to do the deed.

Ms Trenouth supposes (on no evidence whatsoever) that Kelly had worked for

Hammond when she arrived in London, was acquainted with what went on at 19 Cleveland Street and that she had informed Abberline.

EUSTON, EARL OF
See **Henry James Fitzroy**.

EVANS, JOHN
Witness at **Annie Chapman**'s inquest. Nightwatchman at **Crossingham's Lodging House**. An elderly man, nicknamed 'Brummy'. Testified to seeing Annie at Crossingham's, around 1.35am, 8 September 1888. Annie said she had just been out for a pint of beer; also that she had been to Vauxhall to see one of her sisters. She told Evans that she had not enough money for her bed, but would soon get it. Her last recorded words were to him: 'I won't be long, Brummy. See that Tim [**Donovan**] keeps the bed for me.' He saw her go up Little Paternoster Row in the direction of Brushfield Street. It was his impression that she was the worse for drink.

EYE TO THE FUTURE, AN
Book by Patricia Cory (Norwich: D&P Cory, 1994).

Argues **Prince Albert Victor** contracted syphilis through homosexual activities and various East End prostitutes refused to endorse the establishment cover story that he had acquired it in East End brothels. The murders are attributed to a plot by senior Freemasons, intending to silence the prostitutes' ringleaders and terrorise the rest, and using a procedure called 'An Eye to the Future' whereby, in effect, bogus clues are planted to deceive future generations.

Central to the thesis is an affidavit dated 22 March 1928, signed by James Avery of 1 Holland Hill, London, and witnessed by B. Lake, solicitor. Avery avows knowledge of the plot, but disclaims participation. No evidence or argument whatsoever is offered in support of the affidavit's authenticity.

F

'FAIRY FAY' (*d.* 1887)

Alleged murder victim.

First mentioned by Terence Robertson (*Reynolds News,* 29 October 1950) as the Ripper's first victim, who he claims was found murdered in backstreets behind Commercial Road on Boxing Night, 1887, having taken a shortcut home from a pub in Mitre Square. Robertson averred that **Inspector Reid** directed the enquiry, and after a few weeks informed Scotland Yard that for want of information the case had been shelved. The press paid scant attention.

With the possible exception of **Tom Cullen**, no subsequent researcher has found any other mention of this incident. There is no trace of Reid's report in the Scotland Yard files. The death registers show no 'Unknown Female' dying in the East End on Boxing Night 1887; the only such women to die in Whitechapel that month perished of starvation and exposure. Nor were Whitechapel women with interestingly similar names (Sarah Fayer, Alice Farber, Emma Fairy), who died in December 1887 and December 1886, murder victims.

'Fairy' was a term used in a letter sent to Sir Charles Warren from Edinburgh and dated 10 October 1888, which reads:

Dear Boss
You will be wondering why I have been so quiet.
Fact is I was nearly caught. over the last job Will
start again next week mean to be hard on the <u>Fairies.</u>
Jack the Ripper [Mepo 3/142 ff.378–9]

The name also appears in the second verse of the song, 'Polly Wolly Doodle', which originated in the US, *c.* 1880:

161

Fare thee well, fare thee well,
fare thee well, my fairy Fay
for I'm off to Lou'siana for to see my Susyanna
sing Polly wolly doodle all the day.

Several press reports after the start of the Ripper series refer back to a supposed murder the previous Christmas, without naming the victim or the investigating officers. Since they state that the victim was stabbed in the abdomen with a spike or rod-like implement, it seems most likely this was a misplaced recollection of **Emma Elizabeth Smith**, especially as articles that mention the Christmas victim (including Robertson's) omit Smith, and articles mentioning Smith do not refer to the Christmas victim. *Cf.* **Margaret Hames** for another possible confusion, however.

The name may have been suggested to Robertson by Tottie Fay, a well-known, garrulous and would-be ladylike drunk, whose appearances in the police courts were infamous and frequently reported in the press. According to the *Sun* (16 February 1894), she ended up suffering maniacal fits in Broadmoor.

FAMOUS CRIMES PAST AND PRESENT: JACK THE RIPPER
Book by Anonymous (Harold Furness/Caxton House, 1888. First volume reprinted by Dave Froggatt, 1999; all four volumes reprinted by Thomas Schachner, 2007, but limited to 50 copies).

Good and handsomely illustrated contemporary overview of the murders.

FARMER, AMELIA
See **Amelia Palmer**.

FARMER, ANNIE (born c. 1848)
Self-alleged Ripper victim.

Separated wife of a City Road tradesman, Annie Farmer picked up a shabby-genteel client at 7.30am, on 20 November 1888, and took him to Satchell's Lodging House, 19 George Street, Spitalfields, where he took a bed for the two of them.

At 9.30 Annie screamed, and the man, fully dressed, raced out of the doss-house, along George Street and into Thrawl Street, where he shouted to two women and a cokeman, 'What a – cow!' before disappearing into the crowd. Annie's throat was lightly cut and she claimed the man had attacked her. Police found it was a shallow wound, made with a blunt blade, quite unlike the Ripper's deep wounds which were inflicted with a sharp blade. They also

discovered she was hiding coins in her mouth, concluded she had tried to rob her client and devised the ingenious protection of injuring herself and accusing him of being Jack the Ripper. (*See also* **Mary Callaghan**, **'Darkie'**, **Ellen Marks**, **Frank Ruffle**.)

(Chris Roberts, 'A New Look at Annie Farmer'. *Ripperana*, no25, July 1998)

FARQUHARSON, Henry Richard (1857–95)

Born in Brighton, Sussex, the son of Henry James Farquharson and his wife, Fanny Marcia. Educated at Eton and at Jesus College, Cambridge. Married Constance Farquharson in 1878. Lived at Eastbury Park, Tarrant Gunville, Dorset. Elected Conservative MP for West Dorset in 1885, re-elected 1892. Sued for libel (1892) by Liberal opponent, C.T. Gatty, and lost, the case ruining his political future – although it was said that he was offered an East End seat. Died at sea, 17 April 1895, returning from his tea and cocoa plantations in Ceylon (now Sri Lanka).

The *Bristol Times and Mirror*, 11 February 1891, reported:

> I give a curious story for what it is worth. There is a West of England member who in private declares that he has solved the mystery of "Jack the Ripper". His theory – and he repeats it with so much emphasis that it might almost be called his doctrine – is that "Jack the Ripper" committed suicide on the night of his last murder. I can't give details, for fear of a libel action, but the story is so circumstantial that a good many people believe it. He states that a man with blood-stained clothes committed suicide on the night of the last murder, and he asserts that the man was the son of a surgeon, who suffered from homicidal mania. I do not know what the police think of the story, but I believe that before long a clean breast will be made, and that the accusation will be sifted thoroughly.

A year later, the *Western Mail* (26 February 1892) reported:

> Mr. Farquharson, MP for West Dorset, was credited, I believe, some time since with evolving a remarkable theory of his own on the matter. He believed that the author of the outrages destroyed himself.

See obituary *The Times*, 24 April 1895.

(*See* Andrew Spallek, 'West of England MP Identified', *Ripperologist,* Issue 88, February 2008.)

FARROW, PC JAMES, 106M (b. 1847)

Policeman accused of being Jack the Ripper.

Joined the Metropolitan Police in 1870 (warrant no. 53262). Resigned, 1893.

Was violently assaulted by the brother of a women that he allegedly frightened by leaping out from the shadows and kissing her in the early hours of Christmas Day, 1888. The woman later said she thought at first it was Jack the Ripper leaping out at her. Charges against Farrow, an officer bearing a hitherto exemplary character, were duly dismissed by the Magistrate.

(See *The Times*, 7 January 1889; *Southwark Recorder 5*, 12 January 1889; **Ripperana**, January 1996.)

FARSON, DANIEL NEGLEY (1927–97)

Theorist. Journalist, photographer, television presenter, author. BA (Cantab.). Journalist and staff photographer on *Picture Post*. Joined Associated Rediffusion Television, 1956, and became a pioneer of unsycophantic interviewing. Subsequently ran a pub, the Waterman's Arms, for one year in Narrow Street, Limehouse. A colourful and memorable character, who was the chronicler and almost the last survivor of the great Bohemian Soho populated by Francis Bacon, Lucian Freud and Geoffrey Bernard. His last years were spent in Barnstaple, Devon, where it was said in his obituaries that he had been barred from every pub but one in the town.

Two episodes of *Farson's Guide to the British* (5, 12 November 1959) are today recognised as the starting point for serious modern studies of the Ripper case. They reveal the initials of **Montague John Druitt**, whose name Farson had discovered in the Aberconway version of the **Macnaghten memoranda**. Research established the historical existence of Montague John Druitt (*see* **Jack the Ripper**, 1973; *see also* **The East End Murderer – I Knew Him**).

The autobiography, *Never A Normal Man* (London: HarperCollins, 1997), contains a brief account of Farson's research on Jack the Ripper. Obituary: *The Independent*, 1 December 1997.

FATHER OF G.W.B.

G.W.B., an Australian born *c.*1883, told **Daniel Farson** that in 1889 he was playing in the street when his mother called him to come in, or else Jack the Ripper would get him. His father (*b.* 1850) then patted him on the head and said he was the last person that the Ripper would injure. Years later, when G.W.B. remonstrated with his father for beating his mother, his father admitted he had been Jack the Ripper. He had always wanted a daughter and when his only female child was born imbecile, he took to drink and suffered mental problems, which led to his getting drunk and killing prostitutes. He said that he wore two pairs of trousers when killing and disposed of the bloodstained ones in manure, which he sold from a cart. The father urged G.W.B. to change his name, as he intended to confess before he died, but this confession never appeared in the press. No corroboration of G.W.B.'s statement has ever been found.

Coincidentally, in 1891 **Albert Bachert** received a threatening letter from someone purporting to be Jack the Ripper, which was signed G.W.B. (*Western Mail*, 27 June 1891).

FBI PSYCHOLOGICAL PROFILE OF THE RIPPER

Prepared, 1988, by John Douglas and Roy Hazlewood (respectively co-founder of psychological profiling and his successor as head of the FBI Criminal Identification Analysis section), on the suggestion of **William Eckert**, for Cosgrove Muerer TV Productions. Broadcast internationally in the programme, *The Secret Identity of Jack the Ripper*.

Salient features of the profile were: a male in his late twenties, locally resident. Employed, since murders were associated with weekends. Free from family accountability since the murders took place at night between the hours of midnight and 6am. Low-class, since murders evinced marked unfastidiousness. Not surgically or anatomically skilled. Likely to have been in some form of trouble with police prior to murders; likely to be seen by associates as a loner. Likely to have been abused as a child, especially by, or with concurrence from his mother. Given the suspects **Montague John Druitt**, **Prince Albert Victor**, **Sir William Gull**, **Roslyn Donston Stephenson** and **Aaron Kosminski** to assess, they concluded the Ripper was either Aaron Kosminski or someone very like him.

Both Douglas and Hazlewood made further comments on the profile and the Ripper case in books written after their retirement. In *The Cases That Haunt Us* (John Douglas and Mark Olshaker, New York: Scribner, 2000), Douglas examines new suspects omitted from the programme or who had arisen in the interim and dismisses **Dr Tumblety**, **Severin Klosowski**, **Neill Cream** and **James Maybrick**. He reveals, however, that at the time of the programme he had been given no information about **David Cohen**. Having now seen the case for him as the Ripper, he found it answered the misgivings he felt about Aaron Kosminski, and he now believed the Ripper to have been David Cohen, or someone very like him.

Hazlewood (in *Dark Dreams* with Stephen G. Michaud (New York: St Martin's Press, 2001) rehearses the original profile and its conclusions without researching further material.

FEIGENBAUM, KARL aka KARL ZAHN (*d.* 1896)

Spelling and other variations are Feigenbaum, Fiegenbaum and Carl Ferdinand Fiegenbaum; variations of his alleged real name are Anton Lahn, Carl Zahm.

Convicted murderer suspected of being the Ripper by his lawyer. Advanced as Jack the Ripper in the paperback edition of ***Jack the Ripper: The 21st Century Investigation***.

Mrs Juliana Hoffman, a 56-year-old widow, lived with her 16-year-old son in two rooms above a store at 544 East Sixth Street, New York, but to earn a little extra money, they had let out one of the rooms to Feigenbaum, who variously claimed to be a gardener or a florist, and who had formerly been a seaman aboard passenger ships.

Mrs Hoffman and Michael slept in the front room. On 31 August 1894, Michael Hoffman was awakened by a scream and on looking across to his mother's bed, he saw Feigenbaum standing over her, a large knife in his hand. Michael attacked

Feigenbaum, but when Feigenbaum turned his knife on the boy, he was forced to climb out of a window over the shop front and cry for help. Feigenbaum, meanwhile, cut Mrs Hoffman's throat and escaped the house, but was swiftly arrested. He maintained the murder had been committed by a friend, Jacob Weibel, who he secretly allowed to sleep in his room, but Michael Hoffman's testimony made it an open and shut case and Feigenbaum was quickly convicted and sentenced to death on 9 November 1894.

After various delays and appeals, he was executed on 27 April at New York's Sing Sing. It was the nineteenth execution at the prison, and according to the Warden and two attending clergymen, he protested his innocence up to the end (*The New York Times*, 28 April 1896).

After the execution his lawyer, William Sanford Lawton, claimed Feigenbaum had confessed his crimes to him, saying: 'I have for years suffered from a singular disease which induces an all-absorbing passion. This passion manifests itself in a desire to kill and mutilate every woman who falls in my way. I am unable to control myself.' Lawton thought of the Ripper case and, naming two of the murder dates, asked Feigenbaum if he had been in London on those days. Feigenbaum said, 'Yes,' and his lawyer subsequently asked if he had killed the women in Whitechapel. Feigenbaum replied that the Lord was responsible for his acts, and to him alone could he confess. Lawton took this to mean that Feigenbaum was the Ripper, and speculated he had most probably also killed Carrie Brown and some women in Wisconsin (various newspapers, including *Stevens Point Daily Journal,* Wisconsin, 28 April 1896; *Lloyd's Weekly Newspaper,* 10 May 1896).

The whole case that Feigenbaum was Jack the Ripper, or indeed, that he had murdered anyone else, depends on the claims made by William Sanford Lawton, who never made use of this in his defence of Feigenbaum or during the appeals, or even when he was trying to save him from execution by claiming he was insane. Moreover, his co-lawyer and one-time Baptist minister, Hugh Owen Pentecost, disassociated himself from Lawton's story.

On 13 February 1896, Lawton was found dead in Lincoln Park, Chicago. According to his business partner, Charles E. Foote, he had left New York with a considerable sum, which he was taking to settle an estate in San Francisco. He arrived at the City Hotel in Chicago on 3 February without any money, but he received sufficient cash to pay his $12 bill. On the Saturday, he sent a telegraph to New York and seemed greatly disappointed when he didn't receive a reply. An hour later, he shot himself in the park (*Denver Evening Post*, 15 February 1897).

(Wolf Vanderlinden, 'Carl Ferdinand Feignbaum – An Old Suspect Resurfaces', ***Ripper Notes***, 28, March 2008.)

FELDMAN, PAUL HOWARD (1953–2005)

Researcher and theorist. Executive producer and director of research for *The Diary of Jack the Ripper* (video). Author of ***Jack the Ripper: The Final Chapter***. A businessman who played a major role in bringing the movie *The Krays* (1990) to the screen. In 1992, he formed the ambition to produce a definitive Ripper documentary. His preliminary research encouraged him to see **Montague John Druitt** as the most likely suspect, and he first contacted Donald Rumbelow, then the authors. While discussing the project, he heard about the **Maybrick Diary** and made strenuous efforts to gain access to it. When he saw it and heard the work undertaken by Shirley Harrison and her research partner, Sally Evemy, he became convinced the diary was genuine and purchased the video rights. His vigorous investigations, lavishly financed from his own resources, evoked Anne Graham's claim that she had long known of the diary's existence and ultimately, her father Billy's confused suggestion that the Grahams might be descended from Florence Maybrick.

While Feldman's daring speculations often produced unconvincing hypotheses, his encouragement certainly produced new and valuable information about James Maybrick and his family (notably the residence of Maybrick's mistress in Whitechapel). At the same time, vociferous attempts to persuade all and sundry to share his beliefs stimulated strong opposition and the Maybrick Diary became central to some of the most vitriolic controversy in the history of Ripper studies.

After the production of the video, *The Diary of Jack the Ripper*, Feldman continued to assert Maybrick was definitely the Ripper and to make urgent efforts to find clinching proof to silence his many critics. After publication of *Jack the Ripper: The Final Chapter*, he claimed to be satisfied that he had completely vindicated his research and proved Maybrick's guilt. He died in 2005, shortly after his second marriage.

(An appreciation of Paul Feldman by Keith Skinner was published in *Ripperologist*, 60, July 2005. *See also* **Ripper Notes**, 23, July 2005.)

FENIANS AND FENIANISM

General term used to describe nineteenth-century Irish nationalists who accepted physical force as a means to achieve their goal. Of great importance to Ripper studies because counter-Fenianism brought **Robert Anderson** into association with **James Monro** and police work.

See also **Parnell Commission**, **Balfour**.

Martin Fido, 'Anderson, Monro and Jsfmboe', *Ripperologist*, 80, June 2007.

FENWICK, COLLINGWOOD HILTON (*b. c.* 1862)

Perpetrator of actual bodily harm, arrested by a civilian who thought he was Jack the Ripper. The son of a member of the firm of Liverpool solicitors, Aspinall and Fenwick, and of independent means, on 15 November 1888, Fenwick stabbed prostitute Ellen Worsfold in the abdomen with a small penknife. Jim Peters, a young man who rented the room next to hers in Waterloo Road, ran in to see what was happening, and in his bare feet joined Worsfold in chasing Fenwick to Tower Street, where he caught and held him, confiscated his knife and refused a bribe of a sovereign to let him go.

Plain clothes PC Bettle 95L made the formal arrest and Fenwick, a man of formerly good character who had been drinking, admitted at once to Bettle, 'I have made a great fool of myself.' He almost fainted when the doctor gave evidence in court of the half-inch wound to Worsfold's lower abdomen and her great loss of blood (*Daily News*, 16 November 1888). According to the newspapers, Fenwick was found guilty at the Old Bailey of unlawful wounding (*The Leeds Mercury*, 13 December 1888) but the Proceedings of the Old Baily (http://www.oldbaileyonline.org/) state that he was found not guilty.

FERRETT, INSPECTOR ARTHUR (b. 1844)
Joined the Metropolitan Police in 1865 (warrant no. 46631). Retired, 1891.

On 7 December 1888, Ferrett was the officer bringing charges against **Gertrude Smith** and **Mary Jones** for brothel-keeping, heard by Thames Magistrates Court under the same Minute of Adjudication (21451) as **Ellen Hickey** for assaulting N. Cohen, and producing **Aaron Davis Cohen** as a lunatic at large. (*See* Mary Jones, David Cohen, for importance.) He also arrested the transvestite, **Edward Hamblar**.

FIDDYMONT, MRS
Informant. Landlady of now-demolished Prince Albert, 21 Brushfield Street, Spitalfields (known locally as 'the Clean House'). Apparently the wife of Samuel Fiddymont (named as Samuel Piddymont in the 1891 Census and described as the servant and manager of the licensee Emma Mounteney; he was named Samuel Fiddymont when charged and convicted of adulterating the beer – see *Lloyd's Weekly Newspaper*, 27 October 1889).

Reported that a strange man entered the pub at 7am, on 8 September 1888, with spots of blood to the back of his right hand, dried blood between his fingers and a streak of blood below his right ear. After hurriedly drinking half a pint of beer, he left the pub and Mrs Fiddymont's customer, **Mary Chappell**, followed and pointed him out to **Joseph Taylor**.

An early press report claimed the police were not interested in Mrs Fiddymont's suspect. This cannot be reconciled with their use of Mrs Fiddymont to view an identification parade, including the suspect **Pigott**, another involving **John Pizer** and Inspector **Frederick Abberline**'s stated intention of having her see **Isenschmidt** in Bow Infirmary Asylum as soon as his condition permitted. Abberline also reported (19 September): 'Isenschmidt is identical with the man seen in the Prince Albert by Mrs Fiddymont.' Thereafter, the police rapidly lost interest in her.

On 12 November, however, another of her customers, Peter Maguire, became suspicious of a man at the bar, who left rapidly after talking earnestly with a young woman, who refused to accompany him. Maguire chased him to Spitalfield Market, where the man changed his gloves, and on to Shoreditch, where he boarded a bus. After Maguire persuaded a policeman to stop the bus, the man was taken to Commercial Street Police Station for enquiries – from which, it would seem, nothing ensued.

FILES

The Metropolitan Police and Home Office Files on the case have been open to researchers at the National Archives (formerly the Public Record Office) since 1976 and 1986 respectively, and were previously seen by a number of writers – notably Douglas Browne, Donald Rumbelow and **Stephen Knight.**

It is a misconception that the Metropolitan Police File on the Ripper case was closed officially in 1892. The original directive that it should not be opened until January 1992 was entered by civilian records staff when all Scotland Yard archives were transferred to the Public Record Office in the 1950s, at which time the closure period was academically determined by the date of the last active investigative paper on file.

Unfortunately, these papers were ruthlessly pillaged by souvenir-hunters until the PRO microfilmed them and denied researchers access to the originals under normal circumstances. Documents seen by living authors (such as the detailed report on Robert Donston Stephenson) are now missing. And the most important papers on suspects have never, as far as is known, been seen by living researchers. In fact, the 'Suspect File' (H0144/220/ 49301A) at the Home Office contains such insignificant information that it acknowledges on the binder that it holds 'mostly mad suggestions'.

The bulk of the Metropolitan Police and Home Office files on the case are transcribed with a commentary and supporting extracts from press reports in *The Ultimate Jack the Ripper Sourcebook*, while *Jack the Ripper: Scotland Yard Investigates* lists and describes the City Police files.

'FINGERS FREDDY'

According to a series of articles by ex-Detective Chief Superintendent **Arthur Butler** (*Sun*, 28 August-1 September 1972), he was a threadbare criminal street entertainer who performed conjuring tricks while accomplices picked the pockets of his audience. Butler heard that this man was also **Emma Elizabeth Smith**'s protector and associated with her in an attempt to blackmail Jill the Ripper (midwife) by threatening to denounce her as an illegal abortionist. Butler claims Freddy disappeared after Smith's murder. No one knew whether he himself had been murdered by a male accomplice of Jill the Ripper, or if he had fled, knowing his own life was in danger. Butler claimed to have heard this story so frequently that he overcame his initial disbelief.

The Ripper and the Royals suggests **Frederico Albericci** might also have been known by the nickname, 'Fingers Freddy'.

FIRST FIFTY YEARS OF JACK THE RIPPER VOL. I, THE

Edited by Stephen P. Ryder (Paramus, New Jersey: The Ripperological Preservation Society, 1997).

Includes the relevant chapters from **Sir Melville Macnaghten**'s *Days of My Years* (1914), **H.L. Adam**'s *The Police Encylopedia* (1920) and *The Trial of George Chapman* (1930), *The Life and Memoirs of John Churton Collins* (1912), **George R. Sims**' *Mysteries of Modern London* (1906) and *My Life: Sixty Years' Recollections* (1917) and **L. Forbes Winslow**'s *Recollections of Forty Years* (1910).

FIRST FIFTY YEARS OF JACK THE RIPPER VOL. II, THE

Edited by Stephen P. Ryder (Paramus, New Jersey: The Ripperological Preservation Society, 1997).

Contains the relevant pages from *More Studies in Murder* (1936) by Edmund Lester Pearson, *Later Leaves* (1891) byMontagu Williams, **Criminals and Crime** (1908) and ***The Lighter Side of My Official Life*** (1910) by **Robert Anderson**, *Forty Years At Scotland Yard* (1931; US Title *Detective* Days) by **Frederick Porter Wensley**, *Police Work From Within* (1914) by **H.L. Adam**, *Psychopathia Sexualis* by Richard Freiherr von Krafft-Ebing, **Mysteries of Police and Crime** (1898) by **Major Arthur Griffiths** and *From Constable to Commissioner* (1910) by **Major Henry Smith**.

FIRST JACK THE RIPPER PHOTOGRAPHS, THE

Book by Robert J. McLaughlin. (London: Zwerhaus Books, 2005).

One of the most important specialist Ripper books and also a vital contribution to the history of police photographers and scene-of-crime photography, the photograph of **Mary Kelly** being one of the earliest known examples. This well-written book looks in detail at the photographers who took the pictures of Jack the Ripper's victims, examines the photographs themselves and traces their publication history, from *De l'Éventration au point-de-vue medico-legal* by André Lamoureux in 1894, which is the earliest known publication of a photograph of Mary Kelly.

FISHER, ALBERT (*fl.* 1888)
Alleged victim of indecent assault by **Dr Tumblety** on 27 July 1888 (PRO CRIM 4/1037, 21927).

FISHER, ELIZABETH (*b. c.* 1838)
Sister of **Catherine Eddowes**. Married Charles Fisher and lived at 33 Hatcliffe Street, Greenwich. Told the *Wolverhampton Chronicle* that Eddowes had a good character and left **Thomas Conway** because he tended to get drunk and beat her whenever he drew his pension.

FISHER, L.E.
Unknown owner of undergarment in which the remains of a mutilated girl were wrapped, according to the *New York Herald*, no. 222, London edition, 11 September 1889. The *Herald* does not say when or where the remains and the undergarment ('marked in black ink, in a clear and clerkly hand with the name "L.E. Fisher"') were found. It makes the point that the case is not analogous with either the Pinchin Street torso, the Whitehall torso or the Ripper murders. It is not, as has sometimes been assumed, saying this mark was on the bloody chemise found with the Pinchin Street torso.

FISHER, LIZZIE
Spitalfields woman.

An unnamed source (probably the same woman as **'Margaret'**, who told the Press Association that **Mary Jane Kelly** had no money and intended to do away with herself at the time of her death) told *The New York Times* that she had seen Lizzie Fisher with a well-dressed man at 10.30pm, on 8 November 1888 and that Lizzie's little boy had spent the night at a neighbour's and was sent on an errand by the man, who was in his mother's second-floor lodging when he returned home in the morning.

Since much of the story is identical with 'Margaret's' and inapplicable to Kelly, it is probable that she too saw Lizzie Fisher and described her in error as Kelly. Though possible, it is highly unlikely she was **Catherine Eddowes'** sister, **Elizabeth Fisher**. It is probably coincidental that clothing wrapped around the remains of **Elizabeth Jackson** should carry a name tape inked L.E. Fisher.

'FITZGERALD, ANNIE'
Alleged to have been an alias used by **Elizabeth Stride** on her appearances in Thames Magistrates Court for drunk and disorderly conduct. She always denied being drunk and claimed she suffered from fits. (*The* Times, 1 October 1888). A 32-year-old Mary Ann Fitzgerald was fined 5/- [25p] on 10 June 1887 for drunk and disorderly behaviour and using obscene language.

FITZROY, HENRY JAMES, EARL OF EUSTON (1848–1912)
Alleged as co-conspirator in *The Ripper and the Royals* and *Epiphany of the Whitechapel Murders*.

Eldest son of Lt.-Col. Augustus Charles Lennox FitzRoy, 7th Duke of Grafton, but predeceased his father and never inherited the title. Educated at Harrow. Ensign with the Rifle Brigade, honorary colonel in 4th Battalion, Northamptonshire Regiment, Aide-de-Camp to King Edward VII (1901–902). Married Kate Walsh, 1871, no issue.

Accused of visiting a male brothel at 19 Cleveland Street by the *North London Press* and successfully sued for libel, claiming he had been misled into visiting the establishment in the belief that nude women were on display and immediately left when he learned the true meaning of what went on there. Chief Inspector **Donald Swanson**'s notebooks reveal that Euston subsequently attended a 'Buggers' Ball', where several known rent boys put in an appearance.

In *Jack the Ripper: the Final Solution*, **Stephen Knight** alleges that Euston was made grand master of the Mark Masons for his services to the crown in successfully suing the *North London Press*. *The Ripper and the Royals* added him to the list of co-conspirators led by **Lord Randolph Churchill** and *Epiphany of the Whitechapel Murders* as an organiser of the murders.

FLEMING, JOSEPH

Lover of **Mary Kelly** before she lived with **Joseph Barnett**.

Joseph Barnett said that prior to living with him, she had lived with a mason's plasterer, either in Pennington Street or was visited by him there and afterwards lived with him in Bethnal Green Road. Possibly to be identified with the 'Joe' referred to by **Julia Vanturney**.

Has been speculatively identified with Joseph Fleming or Flemming (1859–1920). The only son of Richard and Henrietta Fleming, he had an elder sister Jane and two younger sisters, Mary Ann and Jessie. The 1871 Census lists the family at 60 Wellington Street, Bethnal Green. In the 1881 Census, Joseph was living in lodgings in Crozier Terrace, Homerton, his occupation given as plasterer. It is probable that in 1891 he was in a lodging-house at 9 Victoria Park Square, Bethnal Green, but his name is spelt Joseph Flemming and his trade given as boot finisher. Identified with Joseph Fleming, otherwise James Evans, who died in Claybury Mental Hospital in August 1920.

Was admitted from 41 Commercial Street (The Victoria Home) to Whitechapel Workhouse Infirmary on 16 November 1889 with an injured leg, his occupation being given as dock labourer (admission record; also recorded as a dock labourer on death certificate, 1920). On 4 July 1892, police found him wandering the streets and he was sent to the City of London Union infirmary and thence to the City of London Lunatic Asylum at Stone, near Dartford, Kent, under the name of 'James Evans' (see **John Hewitt, Hyam Hyams, Oswald Puck[e]ridge**, suspects who were also sent to an asylum at Stone.). He was described as aged 37, a Dock labourer, single, 6ft 7in [sic] and weighed 11st 8lbs, and gave an address of Friends as Henrietta Fleming, 261 Nile Street. On 14 February 1895, he was transferred to the London County Asylum at Claybury (London Metropolitan Archives, City of London Lunatic Asylum). The death certificate records that Joseph Fleming was also known as James Evans (London Metropolitan Archives, CLA/001/B/02/010, Case Book, Males, No. 10, folios 63 and 97).

On 28 August 1920, he died at Claybury Mental Hospital. The records show: 'Joseph Fleming, otherwise James Evans. Male, 65 years. Of City of London Union Infirmary. Previous address unknown. Chargeable to Bethnal Green, a dock labourer. Cause of death, Pulmonary Tuberculosis, 6 months, 13 days P.M. Certified by F. Paine, acting Medical Superintendent, Claybury Mental Hospital, Ilford, 1 September 1920.'

(*Ripperana*, 13, July 1995; Mark King, 'Joseph Fleming – Part II'; *Ripperana*, 21, May 2008; Leanne Perry, 'Will You Lend Me Sixpence', ***Ripperologist*** 91, May 2008 suggests Fleming may also have used alias George Hutchinson. Christer Holmgren, 'An Affair of the Heart: The Case Against Joseph Fleming', *Ripperologist*, 97, November 2008.

FOGELMA, – (*d.* 1902)
Suspect. Norwegian sailor.

In the *Empire News* (23 October 1923), a correspondent described as a 'student of criminology' claimed, 'Every head of police knows that Jack the Ripper died in Morris Plains Lunatic Asylum in 1902.' The correspondent, who had worked in the asylum and known Fogelma, said that he had been sent to the asylum from Jersey City, in 1899, suffering maniac fits. In more lucid moments, however, he talked of things that clearly connected him with the crimes. Fogelma's sister, Elizabeth, later confided to the correspondent that her brother had press clippings about the crimes and in due course, Fogelma virtually confessed to them to Revd. J. Miosen, pastor of a Nestorian church in New York.

Research has shown that Morris Plains asylum (today called Greystone Park Psychiatric Hospital) has no record of a man named Fogelma and there is as yet no record of Rvd. J. Miosen. Similar searches have failed to identify his sister, Helen Fogelma, and an alleged former girlfriend, Olga Storsjan, who visited him in the asylum.

Cf. **Tom Divall**.

FOSTER, DETECTIVE SUPERINTENDENT ALFRED LAWRENCE (1826–97)
City Police (warrant no. 3636).

Born in Birmingham, but moved at an early age to Warwick, where he was educated. Worked for a local solicitor at the age of 13, and after five years went to London, where he joined the legal firm of Gregory, Faulkner, Gregory and Skirrow. Became deputy governor of Clerkenwell House of Detention and on 29 September 1864 was appointed superintendent in the City Police by Colonel Fraser. Rose to chief superintendent, but resigned in 1892. Married, with two daughters and five sons, one of whom became chief inspector at Cloak Lane Police Station. Died at his home in Kingston-on-Thames, Surrey, in December 1897 (*The Times*, 15 December 1897; *Police Review*, 7 January 1898). A lifelong abstainer and active in the Temperance Movement, Foster was noted for his integrity and extreme courtesy.

Present in Mitre Square soon after the discovery of **Catherine Eddowes**' body. Gave an interview in which he said that the firemen at the night fire station in St James's Place, adjacent to Mitre Square, had been questioned and had not noticed anyone around at the time of the murder (*Evening News*, 1 October 1888). Was reportedly one of the detectives into whose care **Joseph Lawende** was entrusted during his sequestration (*Evening News*, 9 October 1888). Interviewed at the time of his retirement, he said: 'But that Mitre Square murder fairly puzzled me. I have been interviewed by eminent spiritualists and others on the subject, and have had great hopes at different times of lighting upon some clue, but have completely failed. In fact, that crime is as great a mystery today as ever it was' (*Pall Mall Gazette*, 19 May 1892).

Foster refused the demonstrators in the **'Synagogue Parade'** of March 1889 their request to hold a meeting in Mitre Square and also refused them permission to hold a meeting within the jurisdiction of the City Police (*The Times*, 18 March 1889).

At the time of his retirement, a public subscription raised £500 for him and there was a presentation at which the highest regard was expressed (*The Times*, 20, 27 May; 30 July 1892).

(*See also* Bernard Brown, 'Someone To Watch Over Me', *Ripperologist*, 43, October 2002.)

FOSTER, ELIZABETH
Informant.

The *Yorkshire Post* (12 November 1888) reported:

A woman who, it is alleged, would be able to give evidence, has not yet been found. Her name is Elizabeth Foster, and it is said she was seen drinking with the deceased the night before the murder.

She was eventually found and gave a statement to the Press Association:

Elizabeth Foster, who lives in a lodging-house in Dorset street, and whose whereabouts were difficult to ascertain, made the following statement to a Press Association reporter:

"I have known **Mary Jane Kelly** for the last eighteen months, and we were always good friends. She used to tell me she came from Limerick. She was as nice a woman as one could find, and although she was an unfortunate, I don't think she went on the streets whilst she lived with Barnet. On Wednesday night I was in her lodgings with her, and the next evening I met her in the Ten Bells public house near Spitalfields Church. We were drinking together, and she went out about five minutes past seven o'clock. I never saw her after that"' (*Evening News*, 12 November 1888).

See **Maria Harvey** for how this impacts on her story.

The Thames Police Court records show that on 10 March 1888, an Elizabeth Foster, aged 48, received 14 days in prison for stealing a pair of boots worth 5/6d. It is not known if this is the same Elizabeth Foster.

FOSTER, FREDERICK WILLIAM (*b. c.* 1849)

City Surveyor. Witness at the **Catherine Eddowes'** inquest. The son of Detective Superintendent Alfred Lawrence Foster. Presented plans of Mitre Square, routes to Goulston Street and location of doorway containing Goulston Street graffito. Also, made sketches of Eddowes' injuries while the body was in the mortuary.

FOWLES, THOMAS (*fl.* 1891)

Wrongly identified as being in **Frances Coles'** company shortly before her murder. **William 'Jumbo' Friday** and two brothers called **Knapton** reported having seen Coles in Royal Mint Street with a foreign-looking man in a bowler hat at about 2am, on 13 February 1891. But Fowles, who knew Jumbo by sight, reported he was the man Jumbo had seen, and the woman was his friend **Kate McCarthy**, not Coles. He added he had commented at the time that Jumbo looked drunk (MEPO3/140ff.83–5).

FOX AND THE FLIES, THE: THE WORLD OF JOSEPH SILVER, RACKETEER AND PSYCHOPATH

Book by Charles Van Onselen (London: Jonathan Cape, 2007; US title *The Fox and the Flies: The Secret Life of a Grotesque Master Criminal*, New York: Walker and Company, 2007).

An look at the late Victorian underworld, as revealed by the life of racketeer, pimp, white slaver, burglar, gun-runner, rapist, police informant and psychopath **Joseph Lis** (aka **Joseph Silver**), concluding with a long chapter that argues that he was also Jack the Ripper. Van Onselen, South Africa's leading historian, was puzzled by Lis's attempts to conceal his presence in England, in 1888 (almost certainly in Whitechapel), until he noticed the Ripper murders had taken place – which made Lis, a pimp who might reasonably be suspected of causing the deaths of two other women, a plausible suspect.

FRANKLIN, MARGARET (*fl.* 1889)

Witness. Resident in Flower and Dean Street. Acquaintance of **Alice McKenzie's**, who had known her for 14 or 15 years simply as 'Alice' (who at one time lived with a blind man). She spoke to her in Brick Lane at about 11.40 on the night of her death.

FRASER, COL. SIR JAMES (1814–92)

Commissioner, City of London Police. Son of Colonel Robert Fraser and Sarah Forbes; entered the Army, rising to colonel of 54th Foot. In 1854, he resigned his commission and became chief constable of Berkshire. Hoped to become Metropolitan Commissioner, but took it with good grace when Sir Edward Henderson was appointed and instead accepted commissionership of the City Police in 1863. His relations with the Mayor and Corporation were always excellent.

By the time of the Whitechapel murders he was ready for retirement. He was on leave when **Catherine Eddowes'** murder in Mitre Square involved the City Force, but does not appear to have objected to **Major Henry Smith**'s continuing to vigorously pursue the case after his return. Fraser retired in 1890.

FRASER POSTCARD

London Metropolitan Archives (Police. Box 3.18, no. 224).

Card addressed to **James Fraser** purporting to have come from the murderer. Undated, and with postmark torn and illegible, but references to **Annie Chapman** suggest this was written between 9 and 30 September. The address reads:

James Fraser
City of London Police Office
26 Old Jewry
E.C.

The message is:

Fraser
You may trouble as long as you like for I mean doing my work I mean pollishing 10 more off before I stop the game. So I don't care a dam for you or any body else. I mean doing it. I aint a maniac as you say I am to dam clever for you
Written from who you would like to know

In place of a signature is a crude drawing of a curved knife labelled, 'my knife'.

Above the message are three drawings: a silhouette of a heart labelled 'hart', a face labelled 'poor annie' and two heavy circles labelled:

    rings
    I have those in
    my Possession
    good luck

Deborah K. Dobbin ('From Who You Would Like To Know' *Ripperologist* 78, April 2007) believes this to be in the same hand as the 'Dear Boss' letter and 'Saucy Jacky' postcard. She makes calligraphic comparison of individual characters in, and argues this is the first missive from the man who invented the sobriquet 'Jack the Ripper'.

FREINBERG, ALEXANDER
Coffee stall holder of 51 Leman Street, who anglicised his name to Alexander Finlay. Victim of threatened assault by **Charles Ludwig**.

FRIDAY, WILLIAM 'JUMBO' (*fl.* 1891)
A carman employed by the Great Northern Railway Company. Witness who claimed to have seen **Frances Coles** with a foreign-looking young man in a bowler hat in Royal Mint Street on the night of her death. According to press reports, Friday thought the man looked like a ship's fireman and was quite sure the woman was definitely not, as he had at first supposed, a young woman known to him, called Kate McCarthy (Inquest testimony, *The Times*, 28 February 1891). This evidence, supposedly incriminating **James Thomas Sadler**, was conclusively disproved by **Thomas Fowles** and **Kate McCarthy**, who had seen him pass them carrying a whip and in Fowles' opinion,. looking drunk.

(William Friday gave a long interview to *Lloyds Weekly Newspaper*, 15 February 1891.)

FROEST, DET. SGT. FRANK CASTLE (1858–1930)
Born Clifton, Gloucestershire. Joined the Metropolitan Police in 1879 (warrant no. 63456). Promoted to first-class sgt. CID in 1884 (but see below). Transferred to CO (CID, Special Branch) in 1887; promoted to chief inspector (1903), then promoted to Supt. in 1906. Resigned, 1912.

Took the statement of **John Arnold** and may have been sent to search Aberdeen Place for information concerning **John Sanders**, though **Frederick Abberline** excised Froest's name and replaced it with 'an officer' in his report on the search. Froest's name also appears on the indictment (along with Walter Dinnie, PS CID) against **Francis Tumblety**, though it gives his rank as PC CID. He is said (no source given) to have received a reprimand for 'an excess of zeal in pursuit of Jack the Ripper' (David McKie, *Jabez: The Rise and Fall of a Victorian Rogue*. London: Atlantic Books, 2004). Was also involved in the **Emily Dimmock** and Crippen cases.

(*See also* report of retirement in the *Penny Illustrated Paper*, 7 September 1912; obituary in *The Times*, 8 January 1930; Joe Chetcuti, 'Decades Of Distinguished Service', **The Journal Of The Whitechapel Society**, issue 23 December 2008.)

FROM CONSTABLE TO COMMISSIONER: THE STORY OF SIXTY YEARS: MOST OF THEM MISSPENT

Book by Lt-Col. Sir Henry Smith (London: Chatto & Windus, 1910). Memoirs of the man who, as assistant city police commissioner in 1888, handled much of the **Catherine Eddowes**' case in the absence on leave of Comm-Col. **James Fraser**.

Smith joined the police, aged 44, with the immediate rank of chief superintendent and the correct anticipation that retirements would ensure his rapid rise to assistant commissioner, then commissioner. The subtitle exemplifies the persistent tone of self-mocking persiflage.

The Scotland Yard library copy contains a handwritten annotation below the author's name signed 'GHE' – **George Henry Edwards**, secretary to the Metropolitan Police, 1925–7:

> A good raconteur and a good fellow, but not strictly veracious: most of the book consists of after-dinner stories outside his personal experience. In dealing with matters within his own knowledge he is often far from accurate as my own knowledge of the facts assures me.
>
> G.H.E.

The book was widely reviewed and generally well received by the critics, although few treated it as more than a collection of largely good-humoured anecdotes, 'bright and chatty' in the opinion of *Tit-Bits,* but 'naively told…[and] marked by a sort of hot-tempered positiveness and a certain amount of prejudice' according to *The Spectator* (15 October 1910), which also remarked on Smith's comments about Sir Robert Anderson that 'public recriminations between officials are greatly to be deprecated.'

For its extensive comments on Jack the Ripper, *see* **Major Henry Smith**.

FROM HELL : THE JACK THE RIPPER MYSTERY

Book by Bob Hinton (Abertillery, Gwent: Old Bakehouse Publications, 1998). Well-researched but often neglected general survey of the crimes. Concludes that **George Hutchinson** was the Ripper.

FULLER, JEAN OVERTON (1915–2009)

Daughter of Captain J.H.M. Fuller and artist Violet Overton Fuller. Educated London University (BA Eng.). A biographer and poet best known for her post-war investigation into the fate of SOE agent Noor-un-nisa Inayat Khan, GC, MBE, CdG, published as *Madeleine* (1952). She published further books about the SOE, among them *Double Webs* (1958) and *Double Agent?* (1961), before turning to mainstream biography. Her *The Magical Dilemma of Victor Neuberg* (1965) refers to **Vittoria Cremers'** story that **Robert Donston Stephenson** was Jack the Ripper, while *Sickert and the Ripper Crimes* (1990) argues on the basis of information received from **Florence Pash** that **Walter Sickert** was indeed Jack the Ripper. Overton Fuller's autobiography, *Driven To It* (Norwich: Michael Russell Publishing, 2007), refers to her research into the Ripper.

(Obituary, *Ripperologist*, no 102, May 2009)

G

GABE, DR JOHN REES (c.1853–1920)

Gynaecologist and paediatrician of 16 Mecklenburgh Square. Dr John Rees Gabe was medical officer to the London Society for the Prevention of Cruelty to Children. He became a divisional surgeon and examined the remains and assisted Spilsbury in the postmortem of the Louis Voisin murder case.

Widely reported in the press (e.g. *Daily Telegraph*, 10 November 1888) as revealing that he had seen **Mary Jane Kelly**'s body, but beyond saying that he described it as the worst mutilation he had ever seen, no paper gave further details except the *Manchester Times* (10 November 1888), which reported: 'In an interview with a London reporter he stated that the body was dreadfully mutilated; and a certain organ, he added, was missing.' A fuller report was given in the *New York Herald* (same date), which reported that:

The corpse lay, as he saw it, nearly naked on a blood-stained woollen mattress. The victim's hair was tossed upward on a pillow and matted with gore, as if the murderer had first wiped his hands. The nose and ears were sliced away. The throat was cut from left to right, so that the vertebrae alone prevented a headsmanlike severance.

Below the neck the trunk suggested a sheep's carcass in a slaughter house.

Ribs and backbone were exposed and the stomach, entrails, heart and liver had been cut out and carefully placed beside the mutilated trunk.

As in previous cases, certain portions of the body were missing. The flesh on each side of a cut on the median line was carefully folded back.

An inch or two away, from the hips to the ankles, the flesh was shredded more or less, with apparent savageness of purpose.

"It must have been the work of a full half hour," said the Doctor. "The body was just beginning to stiffen when it was discovered."'

(*See* Don Souden, 'The Murder in Cartin Court', ***Ripper Notes***, January 2005, for further discussion.)

GALLAGHER, PC JOHN, 221H (*b. c.*1853–1907)

Joined the Metropolitan Police in 1871 (warrant no. 53876). Dismissed on 10 October 1890 for idling and gossiping with a publican from whom he accepted a drink while on duty. Arrested **Charles Ludwig**, when summoned by Alexander Freinberg on 18 September 1888. Two days later was disciplined with strict caution, severe reprimand and loss of two days' pay (8s.8d.) deferred to 1 October.

GANGS IN THE EAST END

Youth gangs were a very serious problem in most English cities during the mid- to late-1800s, the most notorious being Liverpool's High Rip gang, which distinguished itself by engaging in an extraordinary degree of mindless violence. The name was adopted by or given to similar gangs around the country. It was suggested 'a sort of' High Rip gang was responsible for the murder of **Emma Smith**, the name most commonly associated being the **Old Nichol Gang**, but apart from an oblique reference to such a gang several decades later, the earliest mention of the Old Nichol Gang is in *The Identity of Jack the Ripper* (1959).

London gangs included the Hooligans and the Regent's Park gang. In the East End there was the White's Row Gang in Spitalfields and then the Monkey's Parade gang in the 1890s, which took its name from part of Bow Road. Various Jack the Ripper books also mention the so-called Hoxton High Rips, the Hoxton Market Gang and the Limehouse Forty Thieves.

GARDNER, JOHN

Labourer of 11 Chapman Street. Witness at **Elizabeth Stride**'s inquest. Saw Elizabeth and a male companion at the Bricklayers' Arms, Settles Street, on 29 September 1888. He corroborated the story of his friend, **J. Best**, in every detail. Also added (to *Evening News* reporter) that the woman he had seen had a flower pinned to her dress.

GEORGE, PRIVATE (*fl.* 1888)

Guardsman with three good conduct badges, wrongly identified by **Mary Ann Connolly** as a corporal who used her services in Angel Alley, while **Martha Tabram** went with another guards private. George was proven to have 'stayed with a woman (supposed to be his wife) at 120 Hammersmith Road' overnight on 6–7 August 1888. (**Reid** and **Arnold**'s report to assistant commissioner, CID, MEPO 3/140, ff.44–48).

GIBSON, ANDREW JOHN

Suspect who apparently used many aliases during his lifetime and died in Brisbane, in 1951, under the name of Walter Thomas Poirrott. Advanced by great-great-grandson, Steve Wilson, in Australian news magazine, *The Bulletin*, in 1997, and subsequently in *Ripperoo*. Received extensive international coverage in September 2008.

According to Wilson, Gibson was a woman-hating swindler, who was in London at the time of the murders and sailed for Australia on 9 November 1888. Personal writings – he wrote several medical books – reveal an unhealthy obsession with prostitutes and female gentitalia.

(*See also* Dusty Miller in a *Ripperoo* article entitled 'New Suspect: Walter Thomas Porriott'.)

GIBSON, PASTOR JOHN GEORGE (1859–1912)

Suspect, rumoured in 1925 to be a self-confessed murderer, and strongly advocated as the Ripper in *The Bell Tower: The Mystery of Jack the Ripper Finally Solved*.

Born in Edinburgh, Scotland. Educated at Spurgeon's College, London. From 1881–87, pastor of St Andrews Baptist Church, South Street, St Andrews, Scotland. His whereabouts are unknown from 1887–88. In December 1888, he emigrated to America. Served briefly at New Brunswick (probably New Jersey, but possibly Canada). Pastor in Red Bluff, California (1899–92). From 1892–94, pastor at Chico, California. Said to have written a book, *Outlooks from the Zenith,* at the instigation of his Oak Bluffs congregation.

In 1894, pastor of Emmanuel Baptist Church, Bartlett Street, San Francisco. There, on 13 April 1895, the mutilated body of Minnie Williams was found in the library and a further search of the church revealed the naked and mutilated body of Blanche Almont in the bell tower. Blanche's admirer, Sunday School teacher Theodore Durrant, was charged with both murders and hanged in 1898. Pastor Gibson appeared to accept Durrant's guilt and showed every disposition to shield his church from unwelcome press attention. In 1910, he resigned, offering 'want of sufficient income' as his reason. Then, in 1912, he died in Chicago.

In 1925, Edward McQuade in the *San Francisco News* reported an unverified rumour that Pastor Gibbons had confessed on his deathbed that he, and not Theodore Durrant, killed 'the women in the bell tower'. This was picked up and mentioned by crime historian, Anthony Boucher.

Robert Graysmith's *The Bell Tower* adds the following data to support his contention that Gibson was the Ripper: Gibson preferred to be called Jack, his complexion turned blotchy under stress and he had a small moustache (*cf.* the man reported by **Mary Ann Cox** as accompanying **Mary Jane Kelly**), **Emily Marsh** described a man in a clerical collar asking for **George Lusk**'s address, Gibson was unable to give the precise date of his arrival in New York and might have been in London at the time of the Ripper murders and, as a former pastor of St Andrews University, he would have been given entrée to two churches of St Andrew in the vicinity of Whitechapel. He might also have been in New Jersey at the time of **Carrie Brown**'s murder.

Reasons for dismissing the case are that there is no evidence to place Gibson in London in 1888, and Graysmith's argument that he would have been an accepted colleague at the London churches is completely mistaken as they were Anglican and Gibson was a Baptist.

GILBART-SMITH, DR THOMAS (*b. c.*1848, *d.* 1904)

Son of Irish cleric and philanthropist Revd. Joseph Denham Smith (*d.* 1889).

MB, 1869; MA, MD, 1873 – all Trinity College, Dublin; MRCS, 1871; FRC., 1873 (London). A distinguished medical man, with an address at 68 Harley Street, he was a fellow and member of several medical societies and appointed to several hospitals and other institutions. A physician at the London Hospital, Whitechapel and the Royal Hospital for Diseases of the Chest, St Marylebone General Dispensary, and the Lion Assurance Company. Gilbart-Smith contributed numerous papers to medical journals, particularly *Transactions of the Pathological Society*. Noted as an excellent raconteur and a humorous after-dinner speaker. He died from heart failure while cycling with his son in Devonshire. Obituary in *The Times*, 6 August 1904 and the *British Medical Journal*, 13 August 1904. *The Times,* 11 August 1904, carries a letter from **Robert Anderson**, which includes a tribute from **Frederick Treves**. He was a Freemason.

Prescribed Robert Anderson three months' leave at the start of the Ripper case.

Referred to by Arthur Ponsonby Moore-Anderson in his biography of his parents, *Sir Robert Anderson an Lady Agnes Anderson* (1947): 'My father was fortunate in the medical men whom he numbered amongst his friends. Dr. T. Gilbart-Smith, one of the oldest of these, wrote once: "Robert, my old friend, your friendship is one of the brightest spots in this dark London." And years later Mrs. Gilbart-Smith said: "Oh, how Gilbart loved him, I think more than any other man outside our own family."'

GILL, JOHN (1881–88)

Murdered and mutilated boy, suggested by Patricia Cornwell as a possible victim of **Walter Sickert**.

John Gill went missing from Walmer, near Bradford, on the morning of Thursday, 27 December 1888 and the following day, he was found in a manure heap. He had been tied up, his legs severed, his chest and belly opened and his heart and other organs extracted. His boots were thrust into his abdominal cavity. Ms Cornwell suggests Sickert may have committed this murder on the grounds that Bradford was accessible from London by train and one of the Ripper letters in November had threatened to kill and mutilate 'a young boy'.

GILL, DET. CON. WILLIAM HENRY (*b.* 1848)

Joined the Metropolitan Police in 1869 (previously a labourer). Warrant no. 51598. Transferred to **H Division** in 1886.

Retired on pension in 1894. Accompanied **Sgt. Don** to arrest **John Thomas Sadler** in the Phoenix public house, 14 February 1891 (MEPO 3/140 ff.13–15). It is not known whether he is the detective Gill, who shadowed **Amelia Brown**.

GILLBANK, MRS JANE (fl. 1888)

Witness who, with her daughter, averred she had seen **Martha Tabram** with a guards private on the night of 6 August 1888. But this was when Tabram was wrongly identified as a Mrs Withers, who was shown to still be alive (MEPO 3/140 ff52–59).

GILLEMAN

Supposed member of the International Workingmen's Club, who according to **Morris Eagle** (*The Times*, 2 October 1888), came into the clubroom at around 1am, on 30 September 1888, and said, 'There is a dead woman lying in the yard.' Analysis of the sources shows that Eagle was talking about **Louis Deimshutz**.

GISSING, GEORGE ROBERT (1857–1903)

Alleged suspect.

Author of naturalist novels and aesthetic *belles lettres*. Included in a list of prominent Victorians in *A Casebook of Jack the Ripper* (Whittington-Egan) who are suggested occasionally as suspects. It is believed he was in Italy throughout the period of the murders.

GLADSTONE, RT. HON. WILLIAM EWART (1809–98)

Alleged suspect.

While an undergraduate, the Victorian Prime Minister took a vow to devote his spare time to fighting the social evil of prostitution. Included in a list of prominent Victorians in *A Casebook of Jack the Ripper* (Whittington-Egan) who are suggested occasionally as suspects.

GODLEY, DETECTIVE SERGEANT GEORGE (1858–1941)

Prominent in the Ripper investigations. Born in East Grinstead, Sussex, a sawyer before joining the Metropolitan Police in 1877 (warrant no. 61230). Retired, 1908, with the rank of detective inspector.

Serving in **J Division** (Bethnal Green) CID in 1888. Observed **Mary Ann Nichols'** inquest on behalf of the CID, in company with **Abberline**, **Helson** and

Enright. On his retirement, the *Police Review* said: 'Called in each case from his bed while the bodies were still warm, Mr Godley's knowledge of this series of crimes is perhaps as complete as that of any Officer concerned.' The same article states that he was first on the scene of the Kelly murder (but see **Walter Beck**, **Walter Dew**).

Godley is today chiefly remembered as the officer who arrested the poisoner **Severin Klosowski** (**George Chapman**), after whose trial Abberline allegedly said to him, 'I see you've got Jack the Ripper at last.'

He does not feature prominently in any of the

Ripper reports, though the *Echo* (20 September 1888), misspelling his name 'Goadby', reported that he followed up a clue provided by Mary Ann Connelly; see **Buck's Row Suspect**.

GOLD, MRS ELIZA (*b.* 1846)

Catherine Eddowes' sister and witness at her inquest.

Married butcher James Gold at St Barnabas Church in King's Square, Finsbury, in January 1859. She was widowed by 1881 and living with a man named Charles Frost at 6 Thrawl Street. The couple still lived there at the time of the murder, sharing their accommodation with her son, George Gold, a woodchopper. Although unwell, she accompanied her son and a young woman named Lizzie Griffiths to identify her sister's body. She was described as 'middle-sized, with a face that retained a pleasant and agreeable appearance'.

Eliza Gold described Catherine Eddowes as being of sober habits. She said she earned her living as a hawker and had last been living at 55 Flower and Dean Street (see **Elizabeth Burns)**.

She died at the Whitechapel Infirmary on 11 January 1903. An inquest was conducted by Coroner **Wynne E. Baxter** on 16 January, various causes of death being cited, but mainly 'sudden heart disease and bronchitis accelerated by alcoholism, and want of food...'

GOLDING, POLICE SERGEANT ROBERT (*b.* 1844)

Joined the Metropolitan Police in 1865 (warrant no. 46955). Resigned, 1890.

Accompanied by PC **Thomas Costello**, found the body of **Rose Mylett** and, impressing Dr **Robert Anderson** as 'an exceptionally safe and reliable witness,' made a statement which seemed completely 'incompatible with the theory of murder'. Unfortunately, Anderson did not say what this was, but at the inquest Golding stated that on discovering the body, he examined the ground: 'The yard was not paved, but was composed of earth, and would show signs of a struggle, had one taken place' (*The Times*, 3 January 1889). The inquest jury, when returning a verdict of murder, 'commented on the conduct of Sergeant Golding in the matter' (*The Times*, 10 January 1889).

GOLDSTEIN, LEON

Passed through Berner Street shortly before the discovery of **Elizabeth** Stride's body, who may have triggered the belief in the Ripper's habit of carrying a shiny black bag.

Mrs **Fanny Mortimer** told police that the only person to pass through Berner Street in the 15 minutes or so that she stood outside her home in the street prior to **Elizabeth Stride**'s murder was a man carrying a shiny black bag. He hurried down the street, glancing up at the International Workingmen's Educational Club as he passed it.

The day after the murder, Goldstein, of 22 Christian Street, presented himself at Leman Street Police Station, and identified himself as the man seen by Mrs Mortimer. He had been going home with a bag full of empty cigarette boxes from a coffee shop in Spectacle Alley.

GORMAN, JOSEPH
See **Joseph Gorman Sickert**.

GOULSTON STREET GRAFFITO
Alleged clue some contemporaries felt was arguably left by the Ripper.

Chalked words found by PC **Alfred Long** at 2.55am, on 30 September 1888, on the black brick fascia of nos. 108–19, Wentworth Model Dwellings, Goulston Street. The writing was said to be immediately above the piece of **Catherine Eddowes**' apron discarded in the entrance. (*See* Catherine Eddowes for the importance of the location of this piece of apron.)

The precise wording is uncertain. Both the Metropolitan Police and the Home Office agreed the wording was 'The Juwes are the men That Will not be Blamed for nothing', as noted (except for the misspelling 'Juwes') by PC Long. City Police **Inspector McWilliam** used the same word order, but spelt 'Juwes' 'Jewes': 'The Jewes are the men that will not be blamed for nothing' (HO144/221/A49301C ff.162–70). DC Halse claimed it was 'The Juwes are not The men That Will be Blamed for nothing'. The further spelling 'Juews' was proposed at the inquest.

It was not decided whether the message was by the murderer, or indeed,

CLOTH MARKET, GOULSTON ST. PETTICOAT LANE.

whether it had any connection with the crimes, or if it was intended to expose, confess, create false suspicion of, or refute Jewish association with the crime, or indeed whether it meant the Jews at all. Gary Rowlands ('Jack the Ripper : The Writing on the Wall', *Criminologist,* Vol 17, No.2, Summer 1993) argued that the writing proves the murderer to be a Gentile.

Walter Dew subsequently remarked that the grafitto was one among many in the district purporting to be by the murderer and he did not believe any of them to be genuine. **Superintendent Arnold**, who immediately concluded the graffito had nothing to do with the murder, was nevertheless concerned that the writing would be seen by people coming to Petticoat Lane market and would revive the anti-Semitism provoked by the earlier **'Leather Apron'** enquiry. Arnold had had an inspector with a wet sponge in readiness when **Sir Charles Warren** saw the writing, concurred, praised Arnold for his promptitude and, despite City Police requests that the graffito be photographed, ordered the words to be erased – which they were, at approximately 5.30am. **Robert Anderson** considered the erasure, 'crass stupidity' (*Daily Chronicle,* 1 September 1908).

The location of the writing is equally uncertain. 108–119 was entered from the street, through an open archway with a jamb about a brick-and-a-half deep, which led into a hallway or recess, about 5ft deep, whence there was a staircase to the upper floors and a door to the basement stairs. The exact position of the writing is uncertain. Superintendent Arnold said the writing, 'was in such a position that it would have been rubbed by the shoulders of persons passing in and out of the building' (HO144/221/A49301C ff197–8). Sir Charles Warren said the writing was, 'On the jamb of the open archway or doorway, visible to anybody in the street, and could not be covered up without danger of the covering being torn off at once' (HO 144/221/A49301C. ff173–175). Later, Sir Charles Warren would issue a public statement that the word 'Juwes' did not mean Jews in any known language, for which he was personally thanked by the Chief Rabbi.

Donald Swanson reported PC Long as saying that he found the apron 'in the bottom of a common stairs' (HO 144/221/49301C ff.184–194). This would have been well to the back of the recess. PC Long himself said the apron was 'in the passage of the doorway' with the writing 'above it on the wall' (HO

144/221/49301C ff195–6). And at the inquest, he said the apron was, 'lying in a passage leading to the staircases' (Coroner's Inquest (L), 1888, No. 135; Catherine Eddowes Inquest, 1888; London Metropolitan Archives). DC Halse said, 'The writing was in the passage of the building itself, and was on the black dado of the wall.' A location inside the recess or hallway makes it easier to understand how Halse and Long could have missed seeing the writing with the apron below it when they previously passed the spot.

Wherever the precise location of the writing, it was chalked on the black brick dado which did not rise above 4ft off the ground, and the writing was only a brick-size in height. DC Halse said the words appeared to have been written recently. Chief Inspector Swanson, in a report to the Home Office, stated the chalk was 'blurred'.

It has been suggested the words 'Juwes' referred to the Masonic-lore figures Jubela, Jubelo and Jubelum (first suggested by researchers working on the BBC television series, Jack the Ripper (see *The Ripper File*); *see also* **Stephen Knight** and **Joseph Sickert**) and *Jack the Ripper Revealed* describes an anagram supposedly hidden in the sentence.

(See:Howard Brown 'Off the Wall', *Ripperologist* 57, January 2005, Howard Brown and Neil Bell, 'The Goulston Street Graffito Debate', *Ripperologist* 59, May 2005)

GOVAN, ANNIE
A young woman who lived in Miller's Court, who claimed to know **Mary Jane Kelly** well and attested to the affectionate relations between Kelly and **Barnett** (*Echo*, 10 November 1888).

GRAINGER, WILLIAM GRANT
See William Grant.

GRAND, See Le Grand

GRANT –
Suspect or witness associated with the investigation of **Annie Chapman**'s murder. *See* **Clippings book**.

GRANT, WILLIAM
Near-contemporaneous suspect.

Called William Grant in the 1901 Census, by **L. Forbes Winslow** and almost always by the newspapers, but William Grainger in Bansted Asylum records and in a long account in the *Pall Mall Gazette* (7 May 1895). Age variously given: 34 (*b.* 1861) in *The Times* (28 March 1895); as 26 (*b.* 1865) in Banstead Asylum records, 1891; 30 (*b.* 1865) in the *Daily News;* 41 (*b.* 1860) in the 1901 Census.

Born Cork. Widowed (Banstead Asylum Record). Allegedly trained for the medical profession. Went to sea, *c.* 1873. Joined Cork City Artillery, 1883, and trained annually with them until dismissed in 1889 as being of bad character.

During 1887–90 he repeatedly stayed in Cork Workhouse; from 1889 there were also interludes in Fulham Workhouse. In February 1891, he spent a month in Banstead Asylum suffering 'delusions of persecution and hallucinations of vision', discharged 26 March (Banstead Asylum Records London Metropolitan Archives H22/BAN/B/01/012). Returned to Cork, then to London, where he stayed in the workhouse in Fulham and St Pancras.

According to a Royal Irish Constabulary report from Cork, he had been known to associate with loose women and had frequently been stripped and robbed by them. He once claimed that he had his clothes stolen from him at Whitechapel. Twice held in police cells for drunkenness: one in Stepney in 1894, once in Spitalfields, in January 1895.

Described as a tall and gaunt-looking man (*Lloyd's Weekly Newspaper*, 24 February 1895) and 'wild, haggard-looking' (*Daily News*, 27 February 1895), he was about 5ft 10in, with grey eyes, a pale complexion, black moustache and tattoos on his arms and hands.

Met **Alice Graham** about 10pm on Saturday, 16 February 1895; visited several pubs and headed towards lodging-house in White's Row. They had an altercation in Butler Street about 2am, over what Grant considered to be her extortionate charges and Grant stabbed Graham. She had screamed loudly before collapsing from loss of blood, attracting PC Frazer 352 H to the scene. He and another constable arrested Grant. Graham was examined by Dr **George George Bagster Phillips** and then sent to Whitechapel Hospital, where her injuries were described as serious, but not life-threatening.

Similarities to the Whitechapel murders were noted and the police appear to have made strenuous efforts to establish Grant's whereabouts in 1888. The *Pall Mall Gazette* (7 May 1895) reported there is one person whom the police believe to have actually seen the Whitechapel Murderer with a woman, a few minutes before that woman's dissected body was found in the street. That person is stated to have identified Grainger as the man he saw, but obviously identification after so cursory a glance and after the lapse of so long an interval could not be reliable and the enquiries were at length pulled up in a *cul-de-sac*. (*See* **Elizabeth Long**, **Joseph Lawende**, **Israel Schwartz**.)

He appeared at the Old Bailey, where he was sentenced to 10 years' imprisonment. Curiously, the Proceedings state that 'the evidence is unfit for publication' and although the sentence was quite widely reported, no details were given. By the 1901 Census, he was serving time in Parkhurst Prison, Isle of Wight.

In 1910, following claims in **Sir Robert Anderson**'s recently published memoirs that Jack the Ripper was a Polish Jew, **George Kebbell** (1848–1911), the solicitor who had defended Grant, wrote a letter to the *Pall Mall Gazette* claiming Grant, who he believed had died in prison, was Jack the Ripper. Kebbell subsequently received information about a medical student at St Bartholomew's Hospital who had confessed to the murders to his wife, who died in 1889 from the shock. The man then abandoned his medical career and disappeared. Kebbell speculated this man was Grant. His allegations provoked a response from L. Forbes

Winslow, who claimed this could not be true because he had identified Jack the Ripper and frightened him away. There followed an exchange of correspondence (*Pall Mall Gazette*, 16, 19, 21, 25, 26 April 1910).

Winslow produced a man who he claimed was Grant, who said that he had no involvement with the Whitechapel murders, that it was Kebbell who had informed the police that he was Jack the Ripper and that Alice Graham had been killed by hooligans. Winslow took Grant to stress his innocence before R.H. Bullock-Marsham, magistrate at Bow Street, who said he could sue Kebbell. That evening, Grant encountered Kebbell in the street: 'He rushed over to him, saying, "See, I am not dead yet, but very much alive." Grant says the solicitor threw up his arms in amazement and bolted to the other side of the street.'

(*See* Nick Connell, 'George Kebbell and the Ripper Revival', *The Criminologist*, Vol. 22, No. 3, autumn 1998.)

GRAPES IN ELIZABETH STRIDE'S HAND

See **Matthew Packer**, **Dr George Bagster Phillips**, **Elizabeth Stride**, for discussion.

GRAVES, ALICE (*fl.* 1888)

Witness endorsing the testimony of **Charles Ptolemy** inasmuch as she had seen **Rose Mylett** in the company of two sailors early on the morning of her death (*Daily Chronicle,* 28 December 1888).

GRAY, ALFRED

Briefly suspected. English vagrant arrested in Tunis, January 1889, with a gang of burglars. Suspected briefly of being the Ripper when a naked woman tattooed on his arm was noticed. It was learned that he had come from Spitalfields, where he lived with an Italian woman, and he was felt to resemble descriptions of the suspect that had been published.

GREEN, MRS EMMA

Witness at **Mary Ann Nichols'** inquest. Widow, living with her daughter and two sons in New Cottage, Buck's Row – the end house of the terrace adjoining Brown's stable yard gate, where the body was found. Although Mrs Green's and her daughter's bedroom window almost overlooked the murder site and she was a light sleeper, neither heard anything unusual until the police began their investigation of the newly-discovered body. Her son washed the blood away from the gutter after the body had been removed.

GREEN, JAMES (*b.* possibly 1860)

Witness at **Annie Chapman's** inquest. A man of medium height, with short, neatly plastered-down hair, he lived at 36 Acland Street, Burdett Road, and worked for John and Thomas Bayley, packing-case manufacturers of 23a Hanbury Street. With **James Kent**, he was summoned by **John Davis** immediately on discovery of the body and after seeing it, went straight back to the workshop and did nothing, possibly in a state of shock.

GRIFFITHS, MAJOR ARTHUR GEORGE FREDERICK (1838–1908)
Crime historian.

Born 9 December 1938 at Poona, India, the second son of Lieutenant-Colonel John Griffiths. Educated at King William's College, Isle of Man. Entered the Army in 1855 and served in the Crimea; Halifax, Nova Scotia and Gibraltar, where he briefly edited the *Gibralter Chronicle*. On his return to England, he became, successively, deputy governor of Chatham Prison (1870–72), Millbank (1872–74) and Wormwood Scrubs (1874–81). Also, inspector of prisons, 1878–96. Married Harriett Reily, 18 January 1881, no issue. Briefly military correspondent for *The Times*; wrote for, and edited several journals, but particularly known to the public for stories of prison life and exciting fiction. He died at the Victoria Hotel, Beaulieu (south of France), on 24 March 1908.

Commented on the Whitechapel in *'Unsolved Mysteries of Crime'* (Cassell's Family Magazine, April 1896.)

> No real solution has been offered as of yet of the notorious Whitechapel murders, no reasonable surmise made of the identity of that most mysterious monster, "Jack the Ripper".....Various theories.....were put forward by the police in the Whitechapel affair. One was that the murderer only visited London at certain intervals, and that at all other times he was safe beyond all pursuit. Either he was at sea – a sailor, a stoker of foreign extraction, a Malay or Lascar – or that he was a man with a double personality; one so absolutely distinct from, and far superior to the other, that no possible suspicion could attach to him when he resumed the more respectable garb. It was, in fact, a real case of Dr Jeckyll and Mr Hyde. Granted also, that this individual was afflicted with periodic fits of homicidal mania, accompanied by the astuteness of this form of lunacy, it was easy to conceive of his committing the murders under such uncontrollable impulse, and his prompt disappearance by returning to his other irreproachable identity. No doubt this was a plausible theory, but theory it was, and nothing more. It was never, even inferentially, supported by fact.

Two years later he appears to have learned about the suspects named in the **Macnaghten Memoranda (see Druitt, Kosminski** and **Ostrog)** and wrote of them in *Mysteries of Police and Crime*.

Autobiography *Fifty Years in Public Service* (London: Cassell and Co., 1904); obituary in *The Times*, 26 March 1908; *Dictionary of National Biography*.

See **Alfred Aylmer**, **Littlechild Letter**, **George R. Sims**.

GRIM ALMANAC OF JACK THE RIPPER'S LONDON 1870–1900, A

Book by Neil R. Storey (Stroud, Gloucestershire: Sutton Publishing, 2004).

Although this book recites the basic facts and provides some interesting insights into social history, the Ripper is really just a hook to help sell what is a day-by-day catalogue of grim events during roughly the last third of the nineteenth century.

(*See also* **East End Murders: From Jack the Ripper to Ronnie Kray**.)

GUIVER, CHARLES (c. 1857–91)

Witness. Night watchman at lodging-house at 8 White's Row.

Saw and spoke to **Francis Coles** and **Thomas Sadler** on the night that Coles was murdered, and subsequently identified Coles in the mortuary. The sight affected him profoundly, both physically and mentally, and on Wednesday, 25 March 1891, he had a fit in bed, from which he died. An inquest was held during the afternoon of Monday, 2 March 1891, and **Dr Dukes**, who had performed an autopsy, concluded Guiver had died from apoplexy accelerated by the excitement and shock.

GULL, SIR WILLIAM WITHEY (1816–90)

Suspect.

Born at Colchester on 31 December 1816; son of John Gull (1778–1827) and Elizabeth Cooper (*b.* 1773). MD (London), 1846; FRCP, 1848; medical tutor and lecturer, Guy's Hospital, and Fullerian Professor of Physiology (1847–49). FRS, 1869. Honorary doctorates: Oxford, Cambridge and Edinburgh. Married Susan Anne Lacey, 18 April 1848; treated Albert Edward, Prince of Wales, for typhus in 1871; created baronet, 1872; physician-in-ordinary to Queen Victoria, 1887–90. Suffered a minor stroke, which left him slightly paralysed on the right side, autumn 1887; suffered three epileptiform attacks and two further strokes, dying on 29 January 1890 at his home, 74 Brook Street, Grosvenor Square, London. Buried at Thorpe-le-Soken.

First identified as a suspect by Dr **Thomas Stowell** who, discussing theories that Jack the Ripper was a surgeon, wrote that Gull was among those named and he had been seen more than once in Whitechapel on the night of a murder. There is no known independent support that Gull was a suspect or was seen in Whitechapel. Stowell also referred to the **Robert James Lees** story and said that Caroline Acland, Gull's daughter, had told him that at the time of the murders her mother had been greatly annoyed when a police officer and a medium arrived at her home one night. Sir William admitted to lapses of memory since suffering his stroke in 1887 and had once found blood on his shirt. This, Stowell explained as having got there because Jack the Ripper was a patient of Gull's. Stowell also claimed that Caroline Acland had once told him that she had seen in her father's diary an entry for November 1889, 'informed Blank that his son was dying from syphilis of the brain'. Stowell, for unstated reasons, assumed this was 'S', by which he referred to the person we now know was meant to be **Prince Albert Victor**.

Stowell's story was supposed to be supported by a diary entry of Gull's deposited in the New York Academy of Medicine (*see Prince Jack*), but Gull himself was identified as the murderer by **Joseph Gorman Sickert**, elaborated in *Jack the Ripper: The Final Solution*.

(*See also* **Michael Harrison**, **Dr Howard**, **J.K. Stephen**.)

GUMPRECHT, LOUIS (*fl.* 1864)

Photographer whose name appears on the back of the mortuary photographs of **Martha Tabram** and **Frances Coles**.

The printed notice reads:

PHOTOGRAPHS OF THE UNKNOWN DEAD.
In districts where a skilled operator CANNOT BE OBTAINED, LOUIS GUMPRECHT, of 11, CANNON STREET ROAD, E., is willing to attend on a few hours' notice, on the same terms as the Eastern Districts are served. *Wire through 'H'*

('Wire through "H"' meant communicate by telegram to **H Division**, Metropolitan Police.)

See **Joseph Martin** for the reason why Gumprecht may be believed not to have been responsible for the Ripper photographs bearing his trade advertisement. *See The First Jack the Ripper Photographs*.

GUNNER, PC WILLIAM, 426H (*b. c.* 1865)

Born in Hampshire; joined **H Division**, July 1888 (warrant no. 73744).

Joined **PC Lamb** in going to **Elizabeth Stride**'s murder site and was despatched to fetch **Dr Blackwell**.

H

H DIVISION, METROPOLITAN POLICE

From its inception, the Metropolitan Police was divided into areas or divisions for administrative purposes, and each was identified by a letter of the alphabet. H Division covered Whitechapel. The area within its jurisdiction has varied over the years, but in 1888, it included the sites of three Ripper murders: **Annie Chapman, Elizabeth Stride** and **Mary Jane Kelly**. In 1965, H Division, Whitechapel, was renamed H Division, Tower Hamlets.

HALLIDAY, ELIZABETH 'LIZZIE' (*b. c.* 1865)

Suspect, suggested in 1893.

Killed and mutilated her elderly husband, Paul, and Margaret and Sarah McQuillan at an isolated farm near the Shawangunk Mountains, New York State, in September 1893. The local sheriff speculated that she might have been Jack the Ripper after she gave confused answers to the question whether she had been in London during 1888.

HALSE, DET. CON. DANIEL (1842–94)

Witness at **Catherine Eddowes**' inquest. Joined the City of London Police (warrant no. 3429) in July 1863, having previously worked as a labourer for seven years. Retired with pension at the rank of detective constable, August 1891. Died of phthisis in West Hackney, February 1894.

Patrolling the City on the night of 29–30 September 1888, Halse was at the bottom of Houndsditch at about 1.58am with Detectives **Outram** and **Marriott**. All three responded to **George Morris**'s whistle from Mitre Square. Halse directed an immediate search of the district, and himself went via Middlesex Street to Wentworth Street, returning to Mitre Square via Goulston Street, which he passed at about 2.20; at which time he did not notice the Goulston Street graffito and the piece of Eddowes' apron.

From Mitre Square he went with Detective **Hunt** to Leman Street, and then back to the site of the Goulston Street graffito. Halse believed the chalk writing to be of recent origin, and urged that it be photographed so that **Major Smith** could have a print to examine. When Metropolitan Police objected because traders arriving for Petticoat Lane Market might see it and cause an anti-Semitic disturbance, Halse suggested only the top line containing the word 'Juwes' be erased, but he was overruled.

HALSTED, DR DENIS GRATWICKE (1865–1960)

At the London Hospital at the time of the murders, he described how suspicion fell on medical men:

> Owing the extraordinary knowledge of anatomy displayed by the murderer, no medical man, however high his character or reputation, could be entirely exempted from suspicion, and naturally those of us at the London Hospital, right in the heart of Whitechapel, were in the limelight.'

He suggested the Ripper might have been an (unidentified) North Sea fisherman.

D.G. Halsted, *Doctor in the Nineties*. London: Christopher Johnson, 1960. Also see Christopher T. George: 'D.G. Halsted and the London Hospital During the Autumn of Terror', **Ripperologist**, 22, April 1999.

HAMBLAR, EDWARD (*b. c.* 1828)

Transvestite suspected by mob.

On Saturday, 12 October 1889, Inspector **Ferrett** arrested ship's joiner Edward Hambler, who was being held by two men and threatened by a crowd of about 600, who believed him to be Jack the Ripper. Hambler was dressed in a woman's hat and veil, black jacket, print dress, two flannel petticoats and a large bustle. The magistrates said he had been very foolish and did not make a handsome woman. He was bound over for six months (*The Times,* 15 October 1889).

HAMES, or HAYES, MARGARET (*fl.* 1887)

Fellow-lodger of **Emma Smith**. Attacked in Osborne Street/Brick Lane vicinity on 8 December 1887, receiving face and chest injuries that kept her in Whitechapel Infirmary until 28 December. It is possible that a misrecollection of her assault as fatal may have lain behind press references to a murder at Christmas 1887. *See* **Fairy Fay**.

HAMMERSMITH ROAD LETTER

Letter sent to **L. Forbes Winslow** and reproduced in his memoirs *(Recollections of Forty Years*, 1910) with the date apparently altered from 1889 to 1888. It runs:

22 Hammersmith Rd
Chelsea
Oct 19th 89

Sir
I defy you to find out
who has done the Whitechapel
murder in the Summer not
the last one You had
better look out for yourself
or else Jack the R may
do you. something in your
house to before the end of
Dec mind now the 5th of Nov there
may be another murder. so
look out old mr Sir pluril fonk funk
Tell all London another \ ripper open
will take place some one told me
about the 8th or 9 of Proximo not in
Whitechapel but in London
perhaps in Clapham or the
West End. Write to the Poste
Restante Charing X. address
to PSR tonigt
[undecipherable] Oct 19th.

The 'last murder' refers to the **Pinchin Street** torso and the summer murder to **Alice McKenzie**.

Dr Martin Roberts in *Ripperana*, 43 (January 2003) reads the '[undecipherable]' as 'Lo', and 'tonigt' as 'possibly 'Luigi'.

22 Hammersmith Road (which, as Winslow observed, is not in Chelsea) and the address to 'old Sir funk' plainly links this to the Old Funk letter dated 8 November 1889 and received by the Metropolitan Police. Dr Roberts suggests the proximity of 22 Hammersmith Road to Abingdon Road, Kensington, may link this to the extraordinary accusation against a Kensington doctor sent to the police with a supposedly 'incriminating' newspaper cartoon strip showing a patient frightened by a doctor sharpening his knives (*The Complete Jack the Ripper Sourcebook*, ch. 33).

There is further discussion of the letter in *Jack the Ripper: The Final Chapter*.

HANDS, CHARLES EUSTACE (1860–1937)
Journalist.

A Fleet Street legend, he was born in Kemp Norton, Worcestershire and came to London from Birmingham in the early 1890s. In *Some Piquant People* (London:

T. Fisher Unwin, 1924), **Lincoln Springfield** says that '*The Star* [which began publication in 1888] had twinkled for the best part of a year' before Charles Hands joined the paper from Birmingham' – and was lodging in the City by the time of the (5 April) 1891 Census. He worked for the *Star* until he joined the *Daily Mail*. In *Things I Know* (1923), **William Le Queux** recalled that he, Hands and Springfield worked for the *Globe, Pall Mall Gazette* and the *Star* respectively. They were almost inseparable in the East End, covering the Ripper crimes, each coming up with theories in an effort to outdo the other. His obituary was published in *The Times*, 3 November 1937.

HANHART, THEOPHIL (*b. c.* 1864)
Son of a German minister and teaching at a school near Bath, he had suffered delusions for some time and had been brought to London to see a mental specialist, but became separated from his companions in the Strand. Seen walking up and down in a peculiar manner at 4pm, on 23 December 1888 in Dunston Road beside the Regent's Canal in Kingsland, he was questioned by PC Whitfield, 42J, who saw him. Asked if anything was the matter, Hanhart replied that he 'had a very bad mind' about the murders in Whitechapel and said that he had done them. He was brought before magistrates and sent to Shoreditch Infirmary for examination. According to *The Sunday Times,* he exactly resembled a description of the Ripper.

HARDIMAN HARRIET (*b. c.* 1839)
Witness at **Annie Chapman**'s inquest.

Sometimes called Annie (or Amma Hardiman or Hardyman) in the press. Harriet Hardiman (née Stockton) was the widow of Edward Hardiman. She was a woman of medium height with 'a curiously rounded' chin; kept a cats' meat shop in the ground-floor front room of 29 Hanbury Street, where she also slept with her 16-year-old son, William. They used the ground-floor back as a kitchen to cook the meat.

On 8 September 1888, she was woken at about 6am by the noise made by **John Davis**, **James Green** and **James Kent** in the passage. She sent her son to see what was going on, but saw and heard nothing of the murder until he returned and told her of it. Newspapers give different versions of her forename and the spelling of her surname.

HARDIMAN, JAMES (1859–91)
Suspect suggested in 2004.

Elder son of **Harriett Hardiman**, and like her, a purveyor of cats' meat; also horseflesh. At one time lived at 29 Hanbury Street, but in 1888, was living in Heneage Street. His wife, Sarah, died on 15 September 1888; their daughter Harriett had died in the June of congenital syphilis contracted from her mother.

Proposed as a suspect (Robert Hills, 'Jack a Knacker?' *True Detective,* December 2004) on the grounds that Hardiman knew the district, obviously knew the murder site at Hanbury street and most probably knew Barber's horse-slaughtering Yard, near Mary Ann Nichols' murder site. It was further suggested that Hardiman might have selected middle-aged women out of a general hatred of mothers; alternately, he might have been avenging his wife's and daughter's deaths, if he blamed prostitutes for spreading venereal disease. Two Ripper letters are cited: one that says 'I am a horse slaughterer,' the other signed 'Joe the cats meat man'. Hills added the suggestion that **George Morris** might have been Hardiman's accomplice ('Cat's Cradle' *Ripperologist*, 75, January 2007) and has identified some James, Alfred James and James Alfred Hardimans from prison and census records who might be his candidate.

HARDIMAN, WILLIAM (*b. c.* 1873)
Suspect.

Youngest son of **Harriet Hardiman**. It has been suggested proximity to the murder sites of **Annie Chapman** and **Mary Jane Kelly**, the two murders requiring a dawn escape, gave him little distance to go bloodstained through the streets; that his youth would have made prostitutes trust him and his occupation of cutting up meat gave an excuse for blood on his hands or clothes (*see* Stanley Dean Reid, 'Mister Ripper or Master Ripper?' *Ripperologist*, 62, September 2005). The 1891 Census gives his occupation as a moulder in clay cement.

HARRIS, MR
Resident of Brunswick Street (known as 'Tiger Bay', because in former years it had been notoriously dangerous), who came out of his house on hearing police whistles blowing. He was the only person **Edward Spooner** saw on the street at the time of **Elizabeth Stride**'s murder.

HARRIS, MR B (*fl.* 1888)
Secretary of the Vigilance Committee and landlord of the Crown, 74 Mile End Road, where the committee met. (NB *Eastern Argus and Borough of Hackney Times* for 15 September 1888, reporting the formation of the committee, listed a Mr H.H. Harris as a committee member and identified Mr **Joseph Aarons** as the secretary.)

HARRIS, DR GEORGE JAMES (*fl.* 1888)
Assistant to **Dr Brownfield**, the Divisional Police Surgeon.

The only doctor to examine **Rose Mylett**'s body in situ. With no prior experience of death from strangulation, he observed nothing about the body to suggest Mylett had died violently or after a struggle. He did not see any marks on her neck and concluded death was not homicidal. The following day, he assisted Dr Brownfield with the postmortem, observing the mark of what he believed to be a rope on Mylett's neck, and concluded with Dr Brownfield that she had been strangled (*Daily News*, 3 January 1889).

HARRIS, DR FRANCIS A (*fl.* 1894)

Wrote 'Death in its Medico-Legal Aspects' (A.M. Hamilton and Lawrence Godkin (ed.) *A System of Legal Medicine,* New York 1894, London, 1895), which contained important data on the state of **Mary Jane Kelly**'s cadaver, for which information Harris thanked **Dr Hebbert**.

HARRIS, HARRY

Companion of **Joseph Lawende** and **Joseph Hyam Levy**, witnesses at **Catherine Eddowes**' inquest.

Jewish furniture dealer of Castle Street, Whitechapel, he left the Imperial Club (16–17 Duke Street), with Mr Lawende and Mr Levy at approximately 1.34am, on 30 September 1888. Where Church Passage ran off Duke Street, they saw a man and a woman (Eddowes) talking. Harris paid little attention and later declared he would not be able to identify either. He was not called as a witness at inquest. He did, however, tell an *Evening News* reporter (9 October) that in his opinion, 'neither Mr Levander [sic] nor Mr Levy saw anything more than he did, and that was only the back of the man.' Lawende clearly maintained he had seen the man's face.

HARRIS, MELVIN CHARLES (1930–2004)

Theorist. Author, broadcaster.

Educated at St Julian's Grammar School, Newport, Mon.

National Service in the RAF. Commercial artist in London; lecturer and organiser for the Labour Party in Wales; joined the Trotskyist Socialist Party of Great Britain. Ran a business in Hampstead repairing oboes, acquired a large collection of recordings of early woodwind music that he donated to the University of Washington, Seattle. Married actress Maureen Gavin in 1965. Worked in radio and television: 'Strange to Relate', BBC Radio 4; researcher for *Arthur C. Clarke's Mysterious World* and *Arthur C. Clarke's World of Strange Powers*, Yorkshire Television. Specialised in exposing and debunking hoaxes and spurious stories.

Jack the Ripper: The Bloody Truth and *The Ripper File* exposed what he considered to be fraudulent Ripper stories. *The True Face of Jack the Ripper* presented his case for **Robert Donston Stephenson** being Jack the Ripper. Was an outspoken critic of the **Maybrick Diary** and submitted several papers on the subject to *Casebook: Jack the Ripper*.

His sudden, peaceful death at home came as a shock to the world of Ripper studies.

(Obituary was published in *The Times*, 3 April 2004; *Ripperana,* 48, April 2004. *See also* letter from Simon Welfare, *The Times*, 20 April 2004.)

HARRIS or HARRISON, SARAH

Resident in **Matthew Packer**'s house, but unable to give Sgt. **Stephen White** any information.

HARRISON, MICHAEL (1907–91)
Author and theorist.

Former editor, market research executive and creative director of an advertising agency, he was a prolific author of novels and biographies, and a distinguished Sherlockian.

In *London By Gaslight* (1963), he wrote, 'As a boy, I heard from my mother, my aunts, and assorted servants, exactly who Jack the Ripper was – the most slanderous identification, I remember, being that of the venereally infected son of a royal surgeon. ("They couldn't hang a man with those connections. They had to hush it up. They never brought him to trial. Locked him up in Broadmoor. He's still there, they say.")'

In *The Life of the Duke of Clarence and Avondale Clarence: Was He Jack the Ripper?*, he presented the case that the murderer was **J.K. Stephen**. In *The Listener* (17 August 1972), he said that having dismissed **Prince Albert Victor**, 'I couldn't leave the reader high and dry, so what I did was find somebody who I thought was a likely candidate.'

HARRISON, WILLIAM GREER (*d.* 1916)
Born in Donnegal, Ireland. Prominent citizen of San Francisco. Manager of the San Francisco offices of the Liverpool-based Thames and Mersey Marine Insurance Company; a poet of no great distinction (Ambrose Bierce likened his poetry to the sound of water from a pump at a horse trough), playwright, occasional author of books about physical exercise (*Making a Man – A Manual of Athletics*, San Francisco: H.S. Crocker, 1915).

In 1895, several US newspapers (*Ogden Standard*, 24 April 1895, for example), published a story attested by Harrison, who claimed a **Dr Howard**, who was visiting the Bohemian Club in San Francisco, told him that Jack the Ripper was a 'medical man of high standing', who had been committed to an asylum. The story would be published with considerable elaboration in the Chicago *Sunday Times-Herald* (28 April 1895). (*See* **Sir William Gull**, **R.J. Lees**, **Dr Benjamin Howard**.)

'HARRY THE HAWKER'
Acquaintance (possibly client) of **Annie Chapman**, mentioned at her inquest. Alleged by some witnesses (but not **Eliza Cooper**) to be the cause of the dispute and fight between Cooper and Chapman, the week before the murder.

HARSTEIN, EVA
Reported in the press as resident of 14 Berner Street, but the 1891 Census lists a Harstein family - Isaac Harstein, Kate Harstein (wife), Matilda Harstein (daughter) and Annie Harstein (daughter) - living in one of the whitewashed cottages in Dutfield's Yard, off 40 Berner street (the 1891 refers to it as 'Stable Yd.'). With her sister, **Mrs Rosenfeld**, told 'detectives' **Le Grand** and **Batchelor** that she had seen a blood-stained grapestalk and some white flower

petals in the passage entry to Dutfield's Yard, where **Elizabeth Stride**'s body was found. (*Evening News*, 4 October 1888. *See* **Matthew Packer** for significance.)

HART (OR HYDE), PC FREDERICK, 161H

Uniformed constable, first on the scene in response to PC **Ernest Thompson**'s whistle on discovering **Frances Coles**' body. Hart then went to fetch a doctor.

HART, LYDIA (*fl.* 1889)

Suspected **Pinchin Street** victim.

The Times (11 September 1891) reported that people in the area where the Pinchin Street torso was found suspected it was the remains of 'a woman named Hart, who is well known as a dissipated creature [who] has been missing for three or four days.' The *New York World*, 11 September 1889, reported the woman's full name was Lydia Hart. The identification was never confirmed (*see* **Emily Barker**, **Rosina Lydia Smith**).

HARVEY, PC JAMES, 964 City (1855–1903)

Witness at **Catherine Eddowes**' inquest.

Born Ashburnham, Sussex. Employed as a warehouseman before joining the City of London Police in 1876 (warrant no. 5045). For reasons unknown, the City of London Police had Sussex Constabulary check the authenticity of Harvey's testimonial from his previous employer when he applied to join them. The letter proved genuine – he was of good character – and Portsmouth Police reported, 'Nothing can be ascertained to his prejudice.' He was dismissed 1 July 1889, for reasons the authors have been unable to ascertain. Sgt. **Edwin Cossons** submitted a written report on Harvey's physical condition on that date – this may have been standard procedure when City Police officers left the force, as the authors are aware of other similar reports by Cossons. In 1891, he was living at Forest Gate with his wife and three children, and working as a warehouseman.

Harvey's beat took him to the Church Passage edge of Mitre Square at approximately 1.35. He saw nothing then: subsequently responded to PC **Watkins**' whistle when Catherine Eddowes' body was found.

(Neil Bell and Robert Clack, 'City Beat: P.C. Harvey', **Ripperologist**, 104, July 2009)

HARVEY, MRS MARIA

Witness at **Mary Jane Kelly**'s inquest.

A laundress living at 3 New Court, off Dorset Street, she stayed with Kelly on the Monday and Tuesday before her death. In an interview with *The Times* on 10 November, she claimed to have spent the afternoon with Kelly in New Court, then went out drinking with her, separating at about 7.30pm, with Kelly going 'in the direction' of Leman Street, which she 'was in the habit of frequenting' (i.e. soliciting in Aldgate). In this interview, she did not mention **Joseph Barnett** at all. At the inquest she said she had been with Kelly in Kelly's room during the afternoon and was in the room when Joe Barnett called (between 7.30 and 7.45pm, by his account), whereupon she left. Barnett, who had left Kelly when she allowed a prostitute named **'Julia'** to use her room and afterwards Mrs Harvey, did not say that Harvey was there when he called, only that a young woman was there (*see* **Lizzie Albrook**).

Mrs Harvey consistently stated she had left two men's shirts, a boy's shirt, a black-crêpe bonnet, a child's petticoat, a man's overcoat and a pawn ticket in Kelly's room, none of which (except the overcoat) were ever returned to her. It was reported (*Daily News*, 13 November 1888) that, 'In Maria Harvey the Court had its one amusing witness. She was the Mrs. Gamp of the day, and when she and the Coroner got at loggerheads over the question as to whether certain articles of apparel were two shirts belonging to one man or one man's two shirts, there was general laughter at Mrs. Harvey's decisive dogmatism of manner.'

It is assumed the murderer disposed of the missing items in a fire in the grate, where certainly a bonnet and some clothing had been burned. According to *The Times*, the overcoat was a pilot coat, and according to **Walter Dew**, it was hanging over the broken window, serving as a curtain – which would explain why it was not burned. *See* **Elizabeth Foster** for a further statement conflicting with Mrs Harvey's testimony.

HASLEWOOD, HENRY T, (*b.* 1853)

Wrote from his home in Tottenham to the Home Office on 14 October 1889 alleging that keeping a watch on 'Sergeant Thicke' would solve 'the great secreate [sic]'. 'CT' (presumably **Charles Troup**, a junior clerk at the time, but permanent under-secretary, 1890–1922) noted on the file, 'I think it is plainly rubbish – perhaps prompted by spite' (HO144/220/A49301, f36, ff46–47).

See **Police as Suspects**.

HASLIP, DR GEORGE ERNEST (1864–1924)

House surgeon at the London Hospital, 1888, who treated **Emma Smith** and to whom she related the events leading to her injuries.

Studied at the London Hospital and Brussels University, and qualified as MD Brux., MRCS (February 1887) and DPH. Eng. Appointed assistant divisional surgeon and attended numerous inquests. Treasurer of the British Medical Association, 1916–24. One of the first appointments to Medical Consultative Council of the Ministry of Health.

(Obituary published in *The Times*, 13 November 1924.)

HATFIELD, JAMES

Witness at **Mary Ann Nichols**' inquest. Elderly pauper inmate of Whitechapel Workhouse, assisted **Robert Mann** in stripping the body for laying out. He denied having been told not to touch the body by Sergeant Enright, and was sharply defended by Coroner Wynne Baxter when a juror pointed out that his memory was so unreliable that he had first shown the jurors Nichols' stays on the visit to the mortuary, and then denied that she had any.

HAWES, HARRY

Undertaker of 19 Hunt Street, Spitalfields, who arranged the very private interment of **Annie Chapman** at Manor Park.

HAWK, RICHARD (*fl.* 1889)

Witness. A seaman from St Ives, Cornwall. Paid off in London and then in hospital until discharged on 9 September. After visiting a public house, he walked the streets with a drinking companion he met there until 4.20am, 10 September, at which point they asked a passing policeman the time and retreated into a railway arch in Pinchin Street, where they slept. They did not see anything suspicious while in the street.

HAWKES, GEORGE CORNELIUS

Name sometimes spelt 'Hawks' in the press. Undertaker of 41A Banner Street and a vestryman of No. 4 Ward, St. Luke's. Arranged and paid for the funeral of **Catherine Eddowes** (*Morning Advertiser*, 9 October 1888), his generosity receiving much favourable comment (*Eastern Post and City Chronicle*, 12 October 1888).

HAYES, MARGARET (*b. c.* 1834)

See **Margaret Hames**.

HAYES, SUPERINTENDENT

Reported to Scotland Yard from Windsor that **Annie Chapman** had been arrested for drunkenness there, but never prosecuted.

HEBBERT, DR CHARLES ALFRED (1856–1925)

(Most often called Hibbert in the press.)

Assistant to Dr **Thomas Bond**. Examined the remains of four torsos found in various locations in London between 1887 and 1889; assisted in postmortem examination of **Mary Jane Kelly** and apparently made final copy of Dr. Bond's report; examined **Rose Mylett**'s body.

MRCS, 1880; MRCP, 1884. Sometime clinical

assistant, Bethlem Hospital and registrar, Westminster Hospital; demonstrator of anatomy, Westminster Hospital, 1889. In private practice in Nottingham, 1892. Tutor in anatomy and physiology in the Medical School, Sheffield University, 1892 (terminated some time in 1893). Lecturer in anatomy, Bishop's College, Montreal, c. 1900; at some point promoted to professor. In 1908, associate coroner, Simcoe County, Ontario; coroner (1910). Moved to Boston, Massachusetts (c. 1919) and may have lectured at Boston University. Restored to UK Register of Medical Practitioners, 1920. As ship's doctor, visited Australia at some point, and in 1922, registered with New South Wales Medical Board and settled in Armidale. Died at Tattershalls's Hotel, Armidale, in 1925.

Dr Hebbert was acknowledged and thanked by Francis A. Harris for assistance given in the writing of an essay, 'Death in its Medico-Legal Aspects', and by the editors of the book in which it appeared (*A System of Legal Medicine*, A.M. Hamilton and L. Godkin, eds, New York: E.B. Treat, 1894/5). In this essay, it is stated regarding Mary Kelly, 'that all the organs, except the heart were found scattered about the room.' Dr Bond's report indicated the heart was missing. The *Observer*, 18 November 1888, reported, 'it seems that the assassin cut the woman's heart out and carried it away', and there had otherwise been speculation in the press that one or more organs were missing. Though it was stoutly denied by the authorities that any organs were missing, it would seem from information supplied by Dr Hebbert this was not the case and that the heart was missing. (*See* Stephen Gouriet Ryan, *The Criminologist,* vol. 21, no.1, spring 1997, and *New Criminologist*, April 2006, for a full exposition of the argument.) He also published the autopsy notes on the four torso murder victims in 'Westminster Hospital Reports' under the title, 'An Exercise in Forensic Medicine', in which he argued that the cases belonged to a series of murders and dismemberment by the same hand.

HELSON, INSPECTOR JOSEPH HENRY (1845–1920)

Joined the Metropolitan Police in 1869 (warrant no. 51389); resigned, 1895.

Local inspector, CID, J Division, Bethnal Green. Prominently engaged in the investigation, especially of **Mary Ann Nichols**' murder. Testified at her inquest and made statements quoted by the press. Received news of the murder at 6.45am and went to the mortuary, where the body was being stripped. The full extent of the mutilation was shown to him. He was consulted by Inspector **Abberline** after **Annie Chapman**'s murder, and concluded she and Nichols were victims of the same hand.

Most importantly, his weekly report to Scotland Yard of 7 September described the search for 'a man named Jack Pizer, alias "Leather Apron"', thus proving **Pizer**'s name was associated with 'Leather Apron' prior to Annie Chapman's murder, and at least three days prior to his arrest. Moreover, the information came from someone who knew him intimately enough to call him 'Jack' (all other written accounts call Pizer 'John').

In 2007, the Friends of the Metropolitan Police Historical Collection purchased a stoneware tobacco jar, inscribed with Helson's name and rank, which was exhibited at the Jack the Ripper Docklands Exhibition.

HEMINGWAY, CHIEF CONSTABLE WALTER (c. 1837–89)
Chief Constable, Cardiff. Told a reporter that he had no recollection of any woman fitting **Mary Jane Kelly**'s description coming to the attention of the police.

(Account of his funeral: *Western Mail*, 8 May 1889.)

HEWITT, –
See **Sickert's unnamed veterinary student**.

HEWITT, FRANCIS
Witness at the inquest on **Martha Tabram**. Superintendent of George Yard buildings. Was sleeping 12ft from the murder spot, but heard no sound. His wife said that early in the evening, she heard a single cry of 'Murder!', which echoed through the building but did not emanate from it. 'But the district round here is rather rough and cries of murder are of frequent, if not nightly occurrence in the district,' they explained. Hewitt told *The Times* that he believed Tabram had been seen in a pub with two soldiers on the eve of her murder.

(Tom Wescott, 'The Silence of Violence: A Witness to the Martha Tabram Murder', **Journal of the Whitechapel Society**, 10, October 2006)

HEWITT, DR JOHN (1850–92)
Suggested as **Sickert's Unnamed Vetinerary Student** by Steward Hicks (1924-1993), who contacted the author Colin Wilson *c.* 1985, telling him that he was convinced he had finally solved the puzzle of the identity of Jack the Ripper.

Dr John Hewitt practised in Manchester prior to 1888. Confined to Coton Hill Asylum during that year, but was released several times during the autumn. Subsequently married a nurse from the asylum and moved to Bournemouth. Died in King's Norton of General Paralysis of the Insane. Coton Hill Asylum papers indicate Hewitt had not been at liberty on the dates of the murders.

Steward Hicks alleged that Lady Anderson (wife of Sir Robert Anderson) once remarked that the Ripper was interned in an asylum near Stone but, regrettably, Mr Hicks could not recall his source. (see **Hyam Hyams**, **Joseph Fleming**, **Oswald Puck[e]ridge**, suspects who were also sent to an asylum at Stone.) There is an oral tradition concerning a house in Stone, Gloucestershire, where 'Jack the Ripper' is said to have lived.

(Stan Russo, 'The Strange Case of Dr John Hewitt', **Ripper Notes**, 19, July 2004)

HEWITT, MRS

Resident at 25 Dorset Street. Following the murder of **Mary Jane Kelly** to a journalist for *The Star* 'She said she was up till twelve o'clock last night. She heard nothing. Her husband was up at four o'clock each morning, and he heard nothing of a disturbing character. At eleven o'clock this morning she had occasion to look out of the window which affords a view of the court; but she could see nothing. At about half past eleven she heard the shouts of a mob, and she then discovered that a horrible murder it makes me shiver to think of it, she said had been committed. She also stated that a man a drover called on her some time ago. He asked her if a summons came in the name of Lawrence to accept it. This man Lawrence, she says, she believes lived with the dead woman. He was off and on in London, sometimes being absent for five or six weeks.' (*The Star*, 9 November 1888)

HICKEY, ELLEN

Produced by PC 298H before Thames Magistrates, 7 December 1888, to answer charge of assault on N. Cohen, which was dropped because of Cohen's non-appearance. Since this was entered on the same minute of adjudication as the brothel-keeping charges brought against **Gertrude Smith** and **Mary Jones**, the likelihood is that Hickey was a prostitute who started a fight in the course of the brothel closure. The importance of the incident is that the same minute of adjudication covers **Aaron Davis Cohen**, suggesting visibly demented conduct while police were raiding Smith and Jones's brothel led to his arrest.

HIGGINGS, CHARLOTTE (b. 1874)

14-year-old maidservant, who wrote anonymous letters to her employers, Revd. Samuel and Mrs Harvey of St Marychurch, Devon, in December 1888, claiming to be 'the Whitechapel Murderer' and threatening to cut them up. The magistrates did not punish her for this, but she was sentenced to three weeks' imprisonment for stealing ribbon (*Torquay Times,* 21 December 1888).

HIGHWAYS AND BYWAYS OF JACK THE RIPPER, THE

Book by Peter Riley (P&D Riley, 2001).

Gives a brief résumé of each of the murders and illustrates geographical locations of each, plus places associated with the crimes.

HISTORY OF THE WHITECHAPEL MURDERS, THE: A FULL AND AUTHENTIC NARRATIVE OF THE ABOVE MURDERS, WITH SKETCHES

Book by Richard K. Fox (New York: Richard K. Fox, 1888; reprinted by the **Ripperological Preservation Society**).

Richard K. Fox, the famous publisher of New York's *National Police Gazette*, was in London in October 1888 to promote the bare-knuckle boxer Jack Kilrain, hoping to coax the great John L. Sullivan into a title fight. Sullivan would challenge Kilrain to fight for a purse of $20,000 and the battle was fought on 8 July 1889, with Sullivan grasping victory after 75 rounds, lasting 2hrs 16m. Fox was therefore able to experience London at the height of the Jack the Ripper terror, which may explain this special publication – one of the earliest accounts of the murders, and one to offer **Nicolai Wassili** as the prime suspect.

(also see **Mary Jane Kelly**)

HO
Prefix identifying Home Office files retained in the National Archives.

HODDEN, JANE
See Ellen **Holland**.

HOLLAND, ELLEN or EMILY ('NELLY')
Witness at **Mary Ann Nichols**' inquest. Called Ellen Holland in the Police report (HO/144/ 221/A49301, ff.129–134) and in some newspapers; Emily Holland (*East London Observer* and the *Illustrated Police News*, 8 September 1888); Jane Hodden (*Manchester Guardian*, 4 September 1888) and Jane Oram (*The Times*, 4 September 1888).

'An elderly woman with a naturally pale face' (*East London Observer*, 8 September 1888), she was described as the lodging-house keeper at 18 Thrawl Street (*Woodford Times*, 7 September 1888; *The Daily Telegraph*, 4 September 1888) and at the inquest she said that Nichols, 'has not been in my house for the last ten days' (*East London Observer*, 8 September 1888). Also a friend of Nichols, who lived with her in a room shared with four other women. After **Mary Ann Monk** suggested Nichols' body might be that of the woman she had known in Lambeth Workhouse, Ellen Holland positively identified her.

Holland was also the last person except her murderer known to see Nichols alive. She had been to see the second Fire on the Docks at Shadwell Dry Dock, and on her return (some time after 2am) met Nichols at the corner of Osborn Street and Brick Lane. Nichols told her that she had earned her doss money twice over that night, but had drunk it away in the Frying Pan pub. She was off to earn it again and refused to accompany Holland back to Thrawl Street, saying she wanted to go somewhere she could share a bed with a man (i.e. Flower and Dean Street).

An Ellen Holland appeared at the Thames Police Court on 15 October 1887, charged with being drunk and disorderly and using obscene language, being sentenced to a fine of 3 shillings or three days in prison. An Ellen Holland, aged 65, a hawker of flowers, is listed in the 1891 Census as living at 55 Flower and Dean Street. It is not known if either was the same woman.

HOLLAND, PC FREDERICK, 814 City (*b. c.* 1864)
A labourer before joining the City Police in 1885, warrant no 5802. He was ordered to resign in 1898.

Summoned by **George Morris** from the south side of Aldgate to go to the assistance of PC Edward Watkins on the discovery of Catherine Eddowes' body in Mitre Square.

HOLLAND, HENRY JOHN

Complainant about police conduct after Annie Chapman's murder.

A thin, sickly-looking youth with straw-coloured hair, living at 4 Aden Road, Mile End. Henry Holland passed along Hanbury Street en route to work at Chiswell Street, when John Davis told him about the body. He went and looked at it, and then went to fetch a policeman from Spitalfields Market. The officer was on fixed-point duty and told him that he could not leave under any circumstances. That afternoon, Holland reported his conduct at Commercial Street Police Station.

HOLT, DR WILLIAM

Amateur sleuth – 'The White-Eyed Man'. Inconclusively identified as Dr William Holt, (b. c. 1864), MRCS, 1881; Intern, St George's Hospital, 1888–89.

Frightened a woman called Humphreys on 11 November 1888 when he emerged from fog in George Yard wearing spectacles, his face blackened. She asked what he wanted, but he merely laughed and hurried away. Humphreys shouted, 'Murder!', and a crowd gathered and attacked Holt, who was rescued by the police. Taken to the police station, he established his identity and the facts that he came from Willesden and was attached to St George's Hospital. He had been going around Whitechapel in various disguises, hoping to discover the murderer. The following day, he was released.

Press reports transformed his spectacles into white rings around his eyes.

Cf. **E. Woodhall**.

HOME OFFICE FILES

A descriptive listing and transcriptions of the majority of Home Office files pertaining to the Whitechapel murders held at the National Archives, Kew, with a commentary and supporting extracts from the press, will be found in **The Ultimate Jack the Ripper Sourcebook**.

HOUCHIN, DR EDMUND KING (*b. c.*1848)

H Division Police Surgeon in 1888. Certified **Aaron Kosminski**. Attended to **Thomas Sadler**'s injuries at Arbour Square Police Station (*The Times*, 17 February 1891) and attended **Wynne Baxter**'s funeral in 1920 as acting coroner for East London.

HOWARD, SIR ANDREW CHARLES (*b. c.*1833-1909)

Served with Rattray's Sikhs, a Corps of Military Police raised in 1855 by Captain Thomas Rattray of the 64th Regiment of Bengal Infantry, during the First War of Indian Independence (Indian Mutiny), 1857–59. Received thanks of British Government for his part in the defeat of rebels and consequent arrest and conviction of Maulvi Ahmadullah, a leader of the Wahabee sect (followers of Abdel Wahab, a reformer of Mohammedanism); chief of Police Monghhyr and Patna 1864–67; succeeded Adolphus Williamson as chief constable, Metropolitan Police 1869–90; assistant commissioner, 1890–1902. Kt. 1897, C.B., 1894, K.C.B., 1902. Retired 1902 and became Magistrate for London. In 1871, he married Emily Emma Montgomery.

With Colonel Monsell, visited **Mary Jane Kelly**'s murder site in Dorset Street.

HOWARD, DR

In late April 1895, several American newspapers carried a story attributed to William Greer Harrison that a Dr Howard, described as 'a London physician of considerable prominence', who was visiting San Francisco, had told him that Jack the Ripper was 'a medical man of high standing and extensive practice' whose wife had grown so convinced he was the murderer that she sought advice from some of her husband's medical friends and they in turn consulted Scotland Yard. Together, they found evidence of the man's guilt. The physician was certified insane and committed to an asylum.

On 28 April 1895, the Chicago *Sunday Times-Herald* published a much-elaborated version of the tale, with extra details including the claim that R.J. Lees psychically guided the police to the surgeon's home, being attributed to an unnamed 'London clubman, now in Chicago, who is acquainted with Dr Howard'. Melvin Harris has argued this elaboration was the creation of a Chicago society known as the Whitechapel Club.

Later, newspapers claimed a representative of the Press Association spoke with William Greer Harrison and he confirmed that the reported story attributed to Dr Howard was as it had been told to him (*Fort Wayne Weekly Gazette*, 2 May 1895). However, other newspapers picked up a story attributed to the daily newspaper, *St Louis Star-Sayings*, which claimed it had been offered the story in late 1894 by a New York syndicate, but had doubts about its authenticity and so refused it. The newspaper was critical of the Press Association, which it described as a 'Chicago organisation', but did not suggest it was responsible for, or party to what it clearly thought was a story of dubious authenticity.

Dr Howard's identity, if he really existed, has not been established. The Chicago *Sunday Times-Herald*'s story was picked up by the British Sunday newspaper, *The People*, which identified him as Dr Benjamin Howard – who vehemently denied it.

(*See* **Sir William Gull**, **R.J. Lees**, **Unknown Medical Man of High Standing**.)

HOWARD, DR BENJAMIN (1836–1900)

MD, New York, 1858; MRCS, Eng., 1877; FRCS, Edin., 1879; corresponding member, NY Academy of Medicine; sometime resident physician, Mt Sinai Hospital, New York; sometime art. surgeon and professor of medicine, Long Island College Hospital, Brooklyn; lecturer in medicine, University of New

York; professor of medicine, University of Vermont; surgeon major and acting medical director, US Army. Author of many distinguished papers and originator of movement to start an accident ambulance service in Britain. Died in New Jersey, USA.

In 1895, several American newspapers carried a story that claimed a well-known London doctor named Dr Howard had, while visiting San Francisco, told William Greer Harrison that Jack the Ripper was a notable British physician, who had been certified insane by his peers. The story was picked up by the London Sunday, *The People*, who identified Dr Howard as Dr Benjamin Howard – who wrote privately and furiously to the editor on 26 January 1896, saying he had been absent from London and had only just seen the article. Nothing in it had 'the slightest foundation in fact,' he said. Indeed, he insinuated a threat of legal action and said he knew nothing about Jack the Ripper except what he had read in the newspapers.

(*See* **Sir William Gull**, **R.J. Lees**, **Unknown Medical Man of High Standing**.)

HOWELLS, MRS MIRIAM (*fl.* 1888)

Prankster, living in the Welsh mining village of Penrhiwceibr, who sent letters signed 'Jack the Ripper' and threatening murder to friends on 15 November 1888. She quickly told them this was a joke, but the letters had already gone to the police and Mrs Howells appeared before Aberdare Police Court, where she luckily escaped with costs against her instead of penal servitude for life.

HUGHES-HALLETT, COL. FRANCIS CHARLES MP (1842–1927)

Theorist.

Conservative MP for Rochester. Told a journalist for the *New York World* (6 October 1888) that he thought the Ripper was probably a West End gentleman, possibly a member of a club (not, as has been suggested, his own club) and driven to murder by a disease contracted from a prostitute. Hughes-Hallet claimed to have undertaken a personal detective sally in disguise to George Yard, following Martha Tabram's murder. Some doubt is thrown on his veracity by his claim that, 'the similarity of the mutilation, the identity of the district and of the woman's occupation with those of the first victim, convinced me that I had to deal with a case of homicidal mania.' There were no similarities between the assault on Emma Smith and the frenzied knife attack on Tabram.

HUNT, DET. CON. BAXTER, City Police (1845–1924)

Born Cambridgeshire. Joined the **Metropolitan Police**, 1866 (Warrant No 46894). Passed over for pay increase in May 1867. Discharged July 1867 and joined the City Police the same month (warrant no 4088). Retired, 1895, with rank of detective inspector. Died in Ambleside.

Probably the Hunt who accompanied **Halse** from Mitre Square to Leman Street Police Station. Subsequently discovered a man called Conway, who was quartermaster-sergeant with the 18th Royal Irish Regiment, and confronted him with two of **Catherine Eddowes'** sisters. They did not identify him as her husband (who had enlisted as Quinn and was pensioned before he met Eddowes – *see* **Thomas Conway**).

HURLEY, NEHEMIAH (*fl.* 1889)

Witness. A carman going to work at 6.25am, on 10 September 1889, saw a man looking like a tailor, standing at the corner of Pinchin Street. Thereafter, saw no one except the police standing beside the Pinchin Street torso in the railway arch.

HUTCHINSON, GEORGE

Informant, and discussed as a possible suspect from *c.*1999. Labourer, formerly a groom. Told police he saw Mary Jane Kelly pick up a client at 2am before she died. Hutchinson was a resident of Victoria Home, Commercial Street (sometimes described as a Peabody Building), and by 9 November 1888, he had been unemployed for some weeks.

At 6pm, 12 November, after Kelly's inquest was concluded, Hutchinson went to Commercial Street Police Station and made the following statement:

> About 2 a.m. 9th I was coming by Thrawl Street, Commercial Street, and just before I got to Flower and Dean Street, I met the murdered woman Kelly, and she said to me Hutchinson will you lend me sixpence. I said I can't I have spent all my money going down to Romford, she said good morning I must go and find some money. She went away toward Thrawl Street. A man coming in the opposite direction to Kelly, tapped her on the shoulder and said something to her they both burst out laughing. I heard her say alright to him, and the man said you will be alright, for what I have told you: he then placed his right hand around her shoulders. He also had a kind of small parcel in his left hand, with a kind of a strap round it. I stood against the lamp of the Queen's Head Public House, and watched him. They both then came past me and the man hung down his head, with his hat over his eyes. I stooped down and looked him in the face. He looked at me stern. They both went into Dorset Street. I followed them. They both stood at the corner of the court for about 3 minutes. He said something to her. She said alright my dear come along you will be comfortable. He then placed his arm on her shoulder and [she] gave him a kiss. She said she had lost her handkerchief. He then pulled his handkerchief a red one and gave it to her. They both then went up the Court together. I then went to the court to see if I could see them but I could not. I stood there for about three quarters of an hour to see if they came out. They did not so I went away.

For the description of this man furnished to the police and elaborated to newspapers, *see* **Jack the Ripper: Descriptions Of**. In newspaper interviews, Hutchinson described a red-stoned seal on the man's watch-chain and specified

the bag he carried was American cloth. Press reports also altered Hutchinson's words 'Jewish-looking' to 'foreign-looking' – possibly a police-inspired preventative against anti-Semitism.

Hutchinson also told the press that he occasionally gave Kelly a shilling and he had looked out for the man, unsuccessfully, on 13 November. Also, without being certain, he thought he had seen him in Petticoat Lane on 11 November. An American newspaper, clearly referring to Hutchinson, described him as, 'Some clever individual having invented a detailed description of the man seen walking about with Mary Kelly just before she was murdered, has been hired at five times his usual salary to walk about with the police and try to see the man again' (Wheeling Register, 19 November 1888).

Most researchers suggest he was the man seen under the archway of **Crossingham's Lodging House** by Sarah Lewis. It has been argued 'George Hutchinson' was an alias used by Joseph Fleming and that he might have been a mugger hoping to rob Kelly's client, or even the murderer waiting for his opportunity. *See also* **The Ripper and the Royals**.

HUTCHINSON, GEORGE, OF ELGIN, ILLINOIS

Alleged suspect.

Described thus in the Washington *Evening Star*, 16 November 1888:

A dispatch from Elgin, Ill., says that seven or eight years ago a man named George Hutchinson, an inmate of the asylum there, delighted to visit the hospital slaughter-house, making many peculiar toys from bones. He was an expert with the knife. After escaping from Elgin he was captured at Kankakee and placed in the insane asylum there. He escaped from that place and afterward murdered a disreputable woman in Chicago, mutilating her body in a way similar to the Whitechapel cases. He was returned to Kankakee, but afterward escaped, and has been at large three or four years. It is thought by some that he may be the Whitechapel fiend. The police here do not remember him.

The Manitoba *Daily Free Press* gave a similar report the same day, with the additional information that Hutchinson had become skilled at carving toothpicks and other articles from animal bones in the asylum slaughterhouse.

HUTT, PC GEORGE HENRY (1854–1918?)

Born in Hoxton. Served for seven years in the 88th Regiment of Foot, then one year and seven months as policeman and porter, Great Northern Railway. Joined City Police, 1879 (warrant no. 5274). PC968.

Received five bad reports during service with the City Police: not reporting information received (August 1880), absent from beat and lying (October 1880), drunk on duty (July 1883), drunk off-duty (April 1885), assaulting a prisoner while in the Dock at Moor Lane Station (September 1889). For this he was suspended, forfeited pay during his suspension, was reduced to third-class constable and removed to bottom of the list for promotion. Resigned and received permission to seek alternative appointment as constable at Central Meat and Poultry Market, Smithfield, but was refused 'parchment certificate of discharge' on order of the Commissioner, who commented severely on his 'serious offences'. Nonetheless, remained constable in Smithfield until 1906, at which time he retired with pension. In 1916, applied for post as canteen manager with British Canteens Limited, Old Broad Street.

Then, in November 1918, a George Henry Hutt of Balls Pond Road, Highbury, was found dead of syncope and pneumonia. His age was given as about 63; his occupation was lavatory attendant. He was said to have changed his name from Leather and to have served in the City Police. It is probable, but not certain, this was the same man.

On 29 September 1888, Hutt came on duty to oversee cells at Bishopsgate Police Station, 9.45pm, and so took charge of Catherine Eddowes (for light conversation and banter between them) until she was discharged at 12.55am. Hutt saw her turn left on leaving the police station and estimated it would have taken her about eight minutes to reach Mitre Square.

Neil Bell and Robert Clack, 'City Beat: PC968 George Hutt', **Ripperologist**, 103, June 2009)

HVEM VAR JACK THE RIPPER?

Book by Carl Muusmann (Copenhagen: Hermann-Petersen, 1908). Translated into English by Rikke Skipper-Pederson and reprinted by Adam Wood, 1999.

This is really an account of the investigations undertaken by a former assistant chief constable and at the time of writing, a judge named Kattrup, who wrote to the newspaper with his conclusion that Jack the Ripper was Alois Szemeredy.

HWEM AR JACK UPPSKARAREN

Book by Anon. (Kalmar, 1889). Reprinted: Ripperological Preservation Society, 2000, with an English translation.

Fifteen-page pamphlet discovered in the Royal Library of Stockholm. Gives the basic details of the crimes, especially Alice McKenzie, and describes the Ripper scare in Stockholm.

HYAMS, HYAM (1855–1913)

Suspect.

Born 8 February 1855, the son of Solomon and Fanny Hyams. Married Rachel shortly after 1881 and they had two children, William and Kate. Hyams was 5ft 7in tall, of medium build, with brown hair and a large brown moustache. He worked as a cigar salesman.

On 29 December 1888, he was arrested by PC E. Walker, 75 H, in Leman Street and charged with being a wandering lunatic (Thames Police Court, 29 December, 1888). He was taken to the Whitechapel Workhouse Infirmary suffering delirium tremens, released on 11 January 1889, but re-admitted on 15 April and transferred under restraint to Colney Hatch Asylum. Hyams was suffering from delusions that his wife was unfaithful to him and he had attacked her with a knife. Discharged on 30 August 1889 as recovered, he was re-incarcerated on 9 September, when the City of London Police sent him to Stone Asylum, Kent, (see **John Hewitt, Hyam Hyams, Joseph Fleming, Oswald Puck[e]ridge**, suspects who were also sent to an asylum at Stone.) He was sent back to Colney Hatch on 4 January 1890 and remained there until his death on 22 March 1913, from exhaustion and cardio-vascular degeneration.

Throughout his incarceration, he was violent and destructive to staff and patients, and once stabbed a medical officer with a makeshift knife. His records show that he practised self-abuse, which corresponds with one of the criteria to be Anderson's suspect. It has been noted Hyam Hyams fits several other criteria – he was male, Jewish and the date of his committal to Colney Hatch (1889) fits Melville Macnaghten's dating for Kosminski's committal. On the other hand, Hyam Hyams did not die soon after being sent to Colney Hatch, as Swanson says, but some 23 years later (which he has in common with Aaron Kosminski) and Swanson unequivocally names the Polish Jew suspect as Kosminski. There is also no evidence that he was ever suspected by the police of being Jack the Ripper.

Recent researchers have drawn some rather tenuous links between Hyam Hyams and Joseph Hyam Levy: in 1891, Fanny Hyams (Hyam Hyams' mother) lived at 24 Mitre Street, former home of the parents of Amelia Levy, Joseph Hyam Levy's wife. This suggests Levy may have recognised the man seen outside an entrance to Mitre Square with a woman later identified as Eddowes and an interesting variant of the confusion hypotheses has suggested Hyam Hyams and Aaron Kosminski were mixed up. (First noted and dismissed by Martin Fido in the first edition of *The Crimes, Detection and Death of Jack the Ripper*.)

(*See* Mark King, 'Hyam Hyams', *Ripperologist*, 35, June 2001; Scott Nelson, 'The Polish Jew Suspect', *Ripperologist*, 53, May 2004; Wolf Vanderlinden, 'Hyam Hyams: Portrait of a Suspect', *Ripper Notes*, 27, April 2007)

1

I Caught Crippen

Book by **Walter Dew** (London: Blackie & Son, 1938).

The memoirs, which were first serialised in *Thomson's Weekly News* (January to March 1935), give a first-hand account of police work on the ground. Dew prefaces the third of his book devoted to the Ripper crimes by stating that, 'it must be remembered that they took place fifty years ago, and it may be that small errors as to dates and days may have crept in.'

Dew believed that **Emma Smith** was the Ripper's first victim, although he acknowledged the assumption of the police that she had been attacked by a Whitechapel blackmailing gang. In the Nichols' murder, he wrongly believed that **Robert Paul**, (unnamed by Dew), never came forward to corroborate **Charles Cross**'s evidence. He places the Stride murder as having occurred three days after Chapman's murder in Hanbury Street.

Dew confirms that the streets of Whitechapel were exceptionally heavily patrolled by uniformed and plainclothes policemen, including some disguised as women. He suggests Stride might have accepted a client despite the scare, if he was respectably dressed, and notes that while unusually presentable pedestrians were automatically stopped and questioned, local middle-class residents, being known by sight to H Division police, came and went, unchallenged. Subsequently, however, Dew reverses his opinion, observing police patrols drafted from other divisions stopped all unusual passers-by unselectively.

His memory of **Chief Inspector Moore** as senior to **Abberline** is compatible with his status as a divisional CID constable, who was also uninformed about the controlling activities of **Swanson** and **Anderson** in Scotland Yard. He protested that the police chiefs made an unnecessary enemy of the press by withholding information from them (while recognising the need for some confidentiality), but felt that, 'the police at this time were terribly buffeted. In some cases they did not receive the support they had a right to expect.'

He remembered being sent to search an escape route from 29 Hanbury Street to Spitalfields Market: east along the street to Brick Lane, south on Brick Lane as far as Princelet Street, west along Princelet Street, back to Spitalfields Market. As the market could have been reached much more directly by going straight up Hanbury Street in the westward direction, this circuit is puzzling, though Dew does not comment on it.

It seems the only victim Dew saw in situ was **Mary Jane Kelly**, the memory of which 'remains with me – and always will remain – as the most gruesome memory of the whole of my police career.'

IDENTITY OF JACK THE RIPPER, THE

Book by **Donald McCormick** (London: Jarrold, 1959; paperback, London: Pan Books, 1962; hardback, London: John Long, 1970; paperback, London: Arrow Books, 1970).

Expands the story told by **William Le Queux** in *Things I Know* that the murders were orchestrated by the Ochrana (the Czarist Secret Police) to discredit the Metropolitan Police and were committed by a man named **Dr Alexander Pedachenko**, alias **Vassily Konovalov** and **Count Andrey Luiskovo**, and two accomplices, **Levitski** and a woman **Winberg**.

Back in Russia, Pedachenko had murdered a woman in Petrograd and been committed to an asylum, from which the Ochrana had him released to perpetrate crimes that would discredit the liberal policing which tolerated exiled revolutionaries in London. In the 1962 edition of his book, McCormick claims another alias used by Pedachenko was **Ostrog**, the authority for which was a letter from **Sir Basil Thomson**, written *c*. 1939:

> When I was in Paris recently I learned in talks with the French that they had always thought that the 'Ripper' was a Russian named Konovalov, who used the alias 'Mikhail Ostrog', under which name Scotland Yard knew him as an ex-convict and medical student. They did not, however, describe him as a surgeon, but rather as a barber's assistant.

There is no known evidence for the existence of this letter and, when writing the 1970 edition of his book with assistance from Lady Aberconway, McCormick removed the reference to Ostrog. In the revised 1987 edition of *A History of the Russian Secret Service* (London: Grafton, 1987), written under the pseudonym Richard Deacon, McCormick wrote that Ostrog, 'was named as a suspect in the Metropolitan Police archives as Mikhail Ostrog and was said to have been used as an *agent provocateur* by the Ochrana,' adding that the **Ochrana Gazette** declared as officially dead a 'man known under the names of Pedachenko, Luiskovo, Konovalov and Ostrog.' The police files do not say or even suggest Michael Ostrog was an '*agent provocateur*' and the original quote from the **Ochrana Gazette** did not include

Ostrog among the aliases of Pedachenko. In fact, Deacon quotes the alleged Ochrana entry and omits to include Ostrog among the aliases!

McCormick draws upon additional sources, chiefly **Dr Dutton**'s *Chronicles of Crime*, but with the exception of *Things I Know,* none of Mr McCormick's sources has been traced. His demonstrable tampering with the Thomson quotation and other aspects of his work have led to some severe judgements on his reliability.

See also **Hector Cairns**.

IDENTITY OF JACK THE RIPPER, THE
Pamphlet by Richard Whittington-Egan (London: Contemporary Review, 1973). Reprint of an article in *Contemporary Review.*

ILLUSTRATED GUIDE TO JACK THE RIPPER, AN
Book by Peter Fisher (Runcom, Cheshire: P&D Riley, 1996).

A collection of maps, photographs and sketches, with an outline of the murders and an A to Z of 'many of the main characters'.

IMHOFF, PC HENRY UTTO, 211H (1856–1925)
Born in Heidelberg, Germany. Worked as a butcher before joining the Metropolitan Police in 1875 (warrant no. 59797). Resigned, 1893.

Arrested **Nikaner Benelius**.

INQUESTS
Inquest papers have only survived for two of the Ripper victims: **Catherine Eddowes** and **Mary Jane Kelly** (held in the London Metropolitan Archives).

For the inquests on the Ripper victims, *see* **Wynne Baxter**, **Mr Langham** and **Roderick MacDonald**.

(see *Jack The Ripper : The Inquest Of The Final Victim   Mary Kelly)*

INQUESTS: JURISDICTIONAL DISPUTES OVER
At **Mary Jane Kelly**'s inquest a juror protested that the officiating coroner should have been **Wynne Baxter** and was firmly quashed by **Dr Roderick MacDonald**, who further asserted that he, and not Wynne Baxter, might have conducted the inquest on Annie Chapman. He stated that Chapman had died in his area, but had been taken to a mortuary in Mr Baxter's and therefore it was right that Baxter should have sat on her case. Kelly now lay in a mortuary under his jurisdiction and therefore he was the coroner hearing the case.

The dispute arose from an administrative anomaly. Spitalfields, where both Chapman and Kelly died, was administered by Whitechapel for all purposes except coroner's inquests, the newly created coroner's division of Northeastern Middlesex (under MacDonald) having acquired it. MacDonald was right to say that both murders took place under his jurisdiction.

He was also correct to say that a coroner had to hold an inquest on a body lying within his division and so Baxter had been correct to enquire into

Chapman's death once her body had been taken to Whitechapel mortuary, and he himself was right to enquire into Kelly's, once her body had been taken to Shoreditch.

The real problem would have arisen had Shoreditch vestry (justifiably) refused to meet the mortuary and burial expenses on a woman who died outside their jurisdiction. In that case, Kelly would have had to be returned to Whitechapel mortuary and Baxter would be forced to hold a second inquest on her. This happened in the case of Louisa Ellesdon, the following year.

And in December 1889, the body of a man who died in a common lodging-house in Heneage Street, Spitalfields, had to lie on the kitchen table for three days and nights while the lodgers cooked and ate around him because MacDonald would not allow it to be removed into the Whitechapel mortuary and Baxter's jurisdiction!

The question is examined in detail in Robert Linford, John Savage and David O'Flaherty, 'Ruairdh Mac-Dhômnaill', *Ripperologist*, 65, March 2006.

IN THE FOOTSTEPS OF JACK THE RIPPER: AN EXAMINATION OF THE JACK THE RIPPER MURDERS USING MODERN POLICE TECHNIQUES

Book by John F. Plimmer (Lewes, Sussex: The Book Guild Ltd, 1998. Republished as *The Whitechapel Murders Solved?* London: House of Stratus, 2004).

Author uses the Jack the Ripper case to illustrate how a modern crime scene investigation should be conducted and to compare modern deductive techniques with those available in 1888. Historical accuracy does not seem to have been considered important.

INTERNET SITES

Google registers over two million hits when you search for 'Jack the Ripper' and it's obviously impossible for us to list even a fraction of them. Below is a sample of sites active at the time of publication. If you have, or know of a site that you think merits mention, please let us know.

Casebook: Jack the Ripper
http://www.casebook.org

Jack the Ripper
Excellent German language website mirroring Casebook: Jack the Ripper, complete with active forums.
http://www.jacktheripper.de/

jtrforums.com
Discussion forum run by Howard Brown.
http://www.jtrforums.com/

Ripperologist

Being revamped at the time of writing.
http://www.ripperologist.biz

Whitechapel Society 1888

Very impressive site for former Cloak and Dagger Club and its quarterly journal.
http://www.whitechapelsociety.com/

Wikipedia

On-line encyclopedia gives the basic facts and major theories. Unfortunately, disputatious argument, vandalism and competitive efforts to suppress references to one of the Ripper journals have forced restrictions on the unsolicited contributions. http://en.wikipedia. org/wiki/Jack_the_Ripper

TruTV: Crime Library: Criminal Minds and their Methods [C]

Contains a 22-chapter narrative and reasoned examination of prominent suspects by Marilyn Bardsley, founder of the Court TV Crime Library. Narrative draws essentially from *The Complete History of Jack the Ripper*. http://www.trutv.com/library/crime/serial_killers/notorious/ripper/index_1.html

London Walks

Decent historical website with a lot of information about Jack the Ripper by Richard Jones, author of several Ripper books.
http://www.walksoflondon.co.uk/28/index.shtml

Metropolitan Police

Relatively brief illustrated account of the case on the official website of the Metropolitan Police Service (Scotland Yard), compiled by Stewart Evans, Keith Skinner and Ch. Supt. Alan Moss.
http://www.met.police.uk/history/ripper.htm

ISAACS, JOSEPH

Briefly suspected.

Polish Jew, apparently well-known to the police. On 5 or 6 November, he took accommodation at a lodging-house at 6 Little Paternoster Row, off Dorset Street, where deputy **Mary Cusins** and a lodger, Cornelius Oakes, said his behaviour was strange. He had been heard to threaten violence to all women above 17 years of age. On the night of the Mary Kelly murder, he was heard walking about his room. The next day, he disappeared from the house, behind leaving a violin bow.

On 12 November 1888, he appeared at Bamet Police Court charged with an unspecified offence of petty larceny and was sentenced to 21 days in prison with hard labour. On his release, on 5 December, he returned to 6 Paternoster Row and asked for, and was given the violin bow. When he left, Cusins followed and saw him go into Julius Levinshon's shop, where he snatched a gold watch and ran away, pawning it at a Bishopsgate pawnbrokers. The following day, he was arrested by **Detective Sergeant Record, H Division**, near Drury Lane, and taken to the Bow Street police station.

Inspector Abberline took Isaacs to Leman Street in a 'strongly escorted' cab (*Morning* Advertiser, 7 December 1888) and Abberline was reportedly overheard to say to a subordinate, 'Keep this quiet – we have got the right man at last. This is a big thing!'

It was also reported that Isaacs was wanted in connection with the attempted murder of a woman in George Street, Spitalfields (*Evening* News, 7 December 1888 – this was the attack on **Annie Farmer**, 21 November, with which he could have had nothing to do as he was in prison at the time). Eventually, he was charged and pleaded guilty to the theft of the watch, receiving a sentence of three months.

Lloyd's Weekly Newspaper (23 December 1888) reported that at the time of the murder he was in prison for stealing a coat. Since he was not in prison when Kelly was murdered, this either refers to one of the earlier murders or to the assault on Annie Farmer.

(The *Morning* Advertiser, *Northern Daily Telegraph*, 7 December 1888; *Daily News*; *Evening News*, 8 December 1888; Manchester *Evening News*, 10 December 1888; *Daily News*, 15 December 1888; County of London North, *Calendars of Convictions and Depositions 1889*, 2 January 1889, MSJ/CD.)

See also **The Fox and the Flies**, wherein author Charles Van Onselen makes a case for Joseph Isaacs being **Joseph Lis**.

ISENSCHMID, JACOB (1843–1910)

Early suspect. Name variously spelt in documents and by authors, but signed as above on his marriage certificate. Butcher of 59 Elthorne Road, Holloway, he suffered a breakdown when his business failed and spent 10 weeks in Colney Hatch Asylum during 1887.

Jacob Isenschmid was born in Switzerland (1871 Census). He married Mary Ann Joyce (*b.* Gilston or Eastwick, Essex, *d.* 1929) on 26 December 1867, and had John Richard (1869–91), Kate (*b.* 1872), Ada (*b.* 1875), Annie (*b.* 1879) and Minnie (*b.* 1880).

On 11 September 1888, Drs Cowan and Crabb of Holloway informed police that they believed Isenschmid to be the Whitechapel Murderer. Police learned that he had been lodging with a Mr Tyler at 60 Milford Road since 5 September; that he was frequently out of the house and was missing on the night of **Annie Chapman**'s murder.

By 17 September, he was confined to Fairfield Road Asylum, Bow, where **Sergeant Thick** learned that he had told a number of women in Holloway that he was **'Leather Apron'**. He had been living by collecting sheep's heads, feet and kidneys from the market, which he dressed and sold in the West End – this casual work explained absences from his lodgings. He had left his wife (of 97 Duncombe Road, Upper Holloway) following an argument.

Two days later, Abberline reported that Isenschmid was believed to be the man with a bloodstained hand seen by **Mrs Fiddymont** and that this would be confirmed as soon as the doctors thought he was fit to appear for identification. Isenschmid was not the Ripper, being safely incarcerated at the times of the later murders. He subsequently returned to Colney Hatch Asylum (MEPO 3/140 ff.242–56).

IZZARD, INSPECTOR GEORGE, (*b.* 1839)

A miller before he joined the City Police in 1859 (warrant no. 2951), he resigned on a pension in 1890. With Sergeants **Dudman** and **Phelps**, he directed the maintenance of public order around Mitre Square following **Catherine Eddowes'** murder. He also took the confession of William Bull, posing as a medical student from the London Hospital, who, while drunk, claimed to have murdered Eddowes (*The Times*, 4 October 1888).

J

J DIVISION, METROPOLITAN POLICE

Established in 1886 to cover Bethnal Green and parts of Mile End New Town, with Bethnal Green Road Police Station as its headquarters. Involved in the Ripper enquiry since Mary Ann Nichols' murder fell under the divisional jurisdiction.

(*See also* **H Division**.)

JACK L'EVENTREUR (Bourgoin)

Book by Stephane Bourgoin, with a preface by Robert Bloch (Paris: Fleuve Noir, 1992).

A sound overview (in French), taking good account of 1980s work and endorsing no controversial theories.

JACK L'EVENTREUR (Desnos)

Book by Robert Desnos (Editions Allia, 1997).

Born in Paris on 4 July 1900, Desnos worked as a literary columnist for the newspaper *Paris-Soir*, and from 1917 published poetry in various magazines and, from 1922, in book collections. An influential figure, friends with Hemingway and Picasso, he became involved in politics and during World War II was an active member of the French Resistance, being arrested by the Gestapo in February 1944 and deported successively to Auschwitz, Buchenwald, Flossenburg and finally Terezín, where he died from typhoid in 1945. He is buried at the Montparnasse cemetery in Paris.

http://www.robertdesnos.asso.fr/

JACK L'EVENTREUR (Dorsenne)

Book by Jean Dorsenne (Paris: Editions de France, 1935; trans. Molly Whittington–

Egan with an introduction by Richard Whittington-Egan, Gt Malvern: Capella Archive, 1999).

Jean Dorsenne, pseudonym of Etienne Troufleau (1892–1945), was a prolific writer of fiction and lived in Tahiti as a journalist from 1921–25, later writing 12 novels about the island. The author of historical novels and biography (*The Emotional Life of Paul Gaugan),* his books about British crime also include: *Charles Peace, Le Roi des Voleurs* (Charles Peace, King of Thieves). Active in the Resistance, he was arrested by the Gestapo on 19 February 1942.

Florid mixture of gossip and fiction, which reveals authorial fictionalising imagination and French ignorance of English police methods, but with tantalising hints of some real information: persuasive details about **Sgt. Thick** and the alleged Metropolitan police photographer **Joseph Martin** supposedly gleaned from an as-yet unidentified surviving policeman on the case 'Chief Constable G.W.H.', who at the times of the crimes was allegedly resident in Windsor and in his retirement to a Yorkshire village was visited by Dorsenne.

JACK L'EVENTREUR DEMASQUE
Book by Sophie Herfort (Paris: Tallandier, 2007).

French author tries to make a case against **Sir Melville Macnaghten** being Jack the Ripper, the primary suggested motive being to embarrass **Sir Charles Warren**.

JACK L'EVENTREUR ET LES FANTASMES VICTORIENS
Book by Roland Marx (Brussels: Editions Complexe,1987).

A professor with the Sorbonne and eminent specialist in modern British history, he was born in 1933 and died in 2000.

Uses Jack the Ripper to analyse Victorian attitudes, suggesting the fear of the murders was partially due to the morality of the time.

JACK L'EVENTREUR: LE SECRET DE MARY JANE KELLY
Book by Philippe R. Welté (Paris: Alban, 2006).

Argues without supporting evidence that **Mary Jane Kelly** murdered **Martha Tabram** in self-defence and was blackmailed by witness **Mary Ann Nichols**, whom Kelly and a French lover then murdered. Other Ripper victims follow, ending with a woman who looked like Kelly.

JACK LO SQUARTATORE
Anonymous pamphlet (Venice: 1889).

The *Pall Mall Gazette,* 11 September 1891, published a letter signed 'E.D.', in which the writer said that he saw in Venice, at Easter 1889, a paper-covered pamphlet titled, 'Jack lo Squartatore'. No copies have since been located.

JACK THE GRIM RIPPER
Book by Maurice Lipton (North Carolina: Lulu, 2006).

Engagingly written coverage of the crimes concluding with the theory that murders were committed by **Montague John Druitt** and **J.K. Stephen** to destroy evidence of homosexual activities among Apostles and **Prince Albert Victor**. Little but anagrammatic supporting evidence given (cf. *Jack the Ripper Revealed*).

JACK THE MYTH: A NEW LOOK AT THE RIPPER

Book by A.P. Wolf (pseudonym; b. 1951) (London: Robert Hale, 1993; revised edition published in digital format on Casebook, 2004).

After some strictures on the work of 'Ripperologists', the first edition propounds the theory that **Elizabeth Stride** was killed by **Michael Kidney**, essentially because the statistical probability of murder being committed by a 'significant other' and the other murders were committed by **Thomas Cutbush**. The argument is the strong case made by the *Sun* in 1894, supported by observations about Cutbush's demonstrated athletic skills and escape from incarceration, with the added suggestion that the **Macnaghten memoranda** devote so much time to Cutbush that they may well be a cover-up, seeking to remove suspicion from Superintendent Cutbush's nephew.

The revised and updated edition makes extensive comparisons with other serial killers to suggest the possible psychodynamics of Cutbush as murderer with a genetic predisposition to schizophrenia. It offers a critique of alternative theories and shows that a very attractive suspect has traditionally been discounted.

JACK THE RIPPER (Begg)

Booklet by Paul Begg (no. 29 of the part-issue series *Scandal* (London: Marshall-Cavendish, 1991).

A brief and well-illustrated overview from the unusual standpoint of examining factors that made the murders a sensation in 1888 and a continuing object of fascination thereafter.

JACK THE RIPPER (Colby-Newton)

Book by Katie Colby-Newton (San Diego, California: Greenhaven, 1990). In the *Great Mysteries: Opposing Viewpoints* series, which sets out to look at all sides of a mystery.

JACK THE RIPPER (Cook)

Book by Andrew Cook (Stroud, Gloucestershire: Amberley Books, 2009). A tie-in with a Channel 5 documentary, *Jack the Ripper: Tabloid Killer* (broadcast 24 June 2009). The premise is that **T.P. O'Connor**, editor of the *Star*, linked the murder of **Mary Ann Nichols** with that of **Martha Tabram** and recognised the circulation benefits of the idea of a lone killer. This idea was not original (*see* **The Killer Who Never Was**) and both the police and other newspapers had made the connections at an early date.

Cook went on to propose that the *Star* developed the lone killer idea by working up the **'Leather Apron'** story, which he claimed was worked up by a journalist named **Frederick Best** (*but see* **Lincoln Springfield, Harry Dam**), who he also claims wrote the **'Dear Boss' letter** when interest in the lone killer began to flag following the release of John Pizer. Very little supporting evidence is presented – a graphologist named Elaine Quigley expressed certainty that Best's handwriting matched that of the 'Dear Boss' letter, while a letter dated 7 July 1890 from the major shareholder of the *Star* referred to 'Mr Best's attempt to mislead the Central News during the Whitechapel Murders should have led to an earlier termination of his association with the newspaper.'

JACK THE RIPPER (Crowley)

1988 reprint of a 1974 *Sothis* magazine article, discussing Crowley, **Robert Donston** Stephenson and **Vittoria Cremers**. In fact, *not* written by Crowley.

JACK THE RIPPER (Farson)

Book by Daniel Farson (London: Michael Joseph, 1972; paperback London: Sphere, 1973).

A straightforward account of the murders, a general description of previous theories and then a full exposition of the case for **Montague John Druitt** as the Ripper. The book gives a full and scrupulous account of Farson's own research and its delays and setbacks. Apart from the original discovery of Druitt in the Macaghten memoranda, Farson's new work advancing on **Tom Cullen**'s *Autumn of Terror* includes the Australian evidence discussed under *The East End Murderer – I Knew Him*. Farson also suggests **Lionel Druitt**'s brief practice in The Minories might have introduced Montague to the district, noting other hearsay evidence tended to link a man called Druitt with that street. This was the first book to print the mortuary photographs of victims discovered by Francis Camps in the London Hospital.

JACK THE RIPPER (Foreman)

Book with CD by Peter Foreman (Berlin: Langenscheid Kg, 2005).

Short overview of the case as textbook for English as a Second Language students, with exercises at the end of each chapter. Excellent illustrations.

JACK THE RIPPER (Horsler)

Book by Val Horlser (London: The National Archives, 2007).

A small book in the 'Crime Archives' series, providing a brief, but intelligently written overview of the times and crimes of Jack the Ripper.

JACK THE RIPPER (McIlwain)

Book by John McIlwain (Andover, Hampshire: Jarrold, 2004).

JACK THE RIPPER (Rosinsky)

Book by Natalie M. Rosinsky (Farmington Hills, MI: Lucent Books, 2004).

In the 'Mystery Library' series for young teenagers, it provides a well-researched and amply footnoted overview of the murders and police investigation.

JACK THE RIPPER (Whitehead and Rivett)

Book by Mark Whitehead and Miriam Rivett (Harpenden, Herts: Pocket Essentials, 2001; revised and updated hardback Harpenden, Herts: Pocket Essentials, 2006).

Excellent overview of the crimes, the revised hardback being a fuller and more serious treatment of the subject.

JACK THE RIPPER A TO Z, THE

Book by Paul Begg, Martin Fido and Keith Skinner (London: Headline, 1991). Revised editions London: Headline, 1991, 1994, 1996. Re-written and revised as *The Complete Jack the Ripper A-Z*, London: John Blake, 2010.

JACK THE RIPPER AND HIS VICTIMS

Book by Neal Shelden (*b.* 1968) (pseudonym). (Hornchurch, Essex: Neal Shelden, 1999).

The standard work on the canonical victims and their backgrounds (*see also* **Annie Chapman: Jack the Ripper Victim** and **Catherine Eddowes: Jack the Ripper Victim**).

JACK THE RIPPER AND THE EAST END (Exhibition)

The first major exhibition to explore the Jack the Ripper murders and their legacy, put together by the Museum of London Docklands (with Keith Skinner and Paul Begg as consultants), which ran from 15 May to 2 November 2008. Widespread media attention was received with over 300 pieces of coverage.

Original police files and photographs were on display, as well as artefacts from 1880s London, reflecting the lives and poverty of the Whitechapel inhabitants. Programmes of talks, school history study days, films and guided walks accompanied the exhibition, which was visited by more than 56,000 people.

JACK THE RIPPER AND THE EAST END

Book edited by Alex Werner (London: Chatto and Windus, 2008).

Work to accompany the 'Jack the Ripper' exhibition at the Museum of Docklands, it contains little about the Jack the Ripper case and a lot about the East End. With an introduction by Peter Ackroyd, seven papers by academics are offered: 'The Imaginative Geography of the Whitechapel Murders' by James Marriott, 'The Immigrant Community of Whitechapel at the time of the Ripper Murders' by Anne J. Kershen, 'Law, Order and Violence' by Louise A. Jackson, 'Common Lodgings and "Furnished Rooms": Housing in 1880s Whitechapel' by Richard Dennis, '"Deeds of Heroism": Whitechapel's Ladies' by Ellen Ross, 'Mapping the East End Labyrynth' by Laura Vaughan and 'Jack the Ripper: A Legacy in Pictures' by Clive Bloom.

JACK THE RIPPER AND THE LONDON PRESS

Book by L. Perry Curtis (*b.* 1932). Emeritus Professor of History and Modern

Culture and Media, Brown University, Rhode Island (New Haven and London: Yale University Press, 2001).

Serious academic study of the ways in which a representative range of London newspapers, from the serious to the sensational, and the conservative to the radical, treated the case and shaped our view of it.

JACK THE RIPPER AND THE WHITECHAPEL MURDERS
Packet of facsimiles from the National Archives assembled by Stewart Evans and Keith Skinner (London: Public Record Office, 2002).

Records, statements, reports and Ripper letters, all in colour.

JACK THE RIPPER AND VICTORIAN LONDON
Book by Roy Gregory (King's Rippon, Hunts: ELM Publications, 1995).

Well illustrated collection of essays on the Ripper and other aspects of nineteenth-century London.

JACK THE RIPPER BY ALEISTER CROWLEY
Book by Anon (Cambridge: 1988).

Pamphlet-style booklet limited to 100 copies, discussing **Robert Donston Stephenson**, **Vittoria Cremers**, **Aleister Crowley** and the 'occult' solution to the murders.

JACK THE RIPPER CASEBOOK, THE
Pamphlet by Michael Kersting (Morrisville, North Carolina: Lulu, 2006).

A 51-page compilation of material drawn from various internet sites and largely reprinted verbatim without acknowledgement. Concludes with an original short story. Downloadable free from www.lulu.com or may be purchased in paperback.

JACK THE RIPPER IN A SEASIDE TOWN: THE WHITECHAPEL MURDERS AS SEEN IN FOLKESTONE AND ITS SURROUNDING DISTRICT
Book by Martin Easdown and Linda Sage (Hythe, Kent: Marlinova, 2002). Limited edition, 100 copies only.

Local press reports covering the case.

JACK THE RIPPER IN FACT AND FICTION
Book by Robin Odell (b. 1935) (London, Harrap, 1965; paperback London: Mayflower-Dell, 1966; new and revised edition consisting of a new introduction and a select bibliography by Wilf Gregg, Oxford: Mandrake, 2009

Odell's early scientific career was in university zoology and physiology labs, and military hospitals during military service with RAMC. Head of publications for industrial research company. Winner of F.C.Watts Memorial Prize (1957) and International Humanist and Ethical Union prize (1960).

A good and responsible account of the murders and the principal theories at the time of writing. Does not name a suspect, but suggests that a *shochet* (or ritual Jewish slaughterman) would have possessed a sufficiently respectable appearance to approach prostitutes without alarming them and the technical skill to cut throats rapidly while pushing bodies away, so that he was not bloodstained.

(*See also* **Jack the Ripper Summing-Up and Verdict**, **Ripperology**, **Writtena and Red**)

JACK THE RIPPER IN THE PROVINCES: ENGLISH PROVINCIAL REPORTING OF THE WHITECHAPEL MURDERS
Booklet by Stawell Heard (London: Stawell Heard, 2005). Limited to 100 copies.

Material from Heard's MA thesis and an unpublished article surveys the role of Ripper stories in the provincial press (mainly Midlands, Manchester and the southeast) as it developed the popular 'new journalism' pioneered by W.T. Stead.

JACK THE RIPPER LOCATION PHOTOGRAPHS, THE: DUTFIELD'S YARD AND THE WHITBY COLLECTION
Book by Philip Hutchinson (Stroud, Gloucestershire: Amberley, 2009).

Reproduces 27 images of Ripper murder scenes and related locations taken by John Gordon Whitby in 1961, and a photograph of Dutfield's Yard, where **Elizabeth Stride** was murdered, purchased from eBay and taken in 1900. The latter is accompanied by an account of the extraordinary and fascinating investigation which established the photograph's history.

JACK THE RIPPER REVEALED
Book by John Wilding (London: Constable, 1993. Revised edition published as *Jack the Ripper – Revealed and Revisited*. London: Express Newspapers, 2006).

Wilding puts forward the wholly speculative suggestion that Albert Edward, Prince of Wales, might have held orgies with **Mary Jane Kelly** in a Watling Street flat (1.5km from Miller's Court), which he is known to have shared with friends for changing his clothes when going out to watch fires. He further deduces **M.J. Druitt** and **J. K. Stephen** combined to commit the murders to hush up the scandal that might arise from Kelly's supposed pregnancy. He suggests Kelly escaped and another woman was killed in her place.

Anagrams, drawn from the Goulston Street graffito and Liverpool letter, are adduced in support.

Cypher statistical experts have said there are high odds against the relevant names in them occurring by chance. Revised edition reinforces this claim with an afterword account of a dispute with **Melvin Harris**.

JACK THE RIPPER – REVEALED AND REVISITED
See **Jack the Ripper Revealed**.

JACK THE RIPPER SUSPECTS, THE 70 PERSONS CITED BY INVESTIGATORS AND THEORISTS

Book by Stan Russo. Foreword by Christopher-Michael DiGrazia (Jefferson NC: McFarland, 2004).

Lists 71 suspects, omitting those whose drunken, eccentric or disorderly conduct led to their being momentarily suspected and taken to court without making an appearance on the police records. (*Cf.* **Jack the Ripper: Eliminating the Suspects** for many such cases).

JACK THE RIPPER WHITECHAPEL MURDERS, THE

Book by Kevin O'Donnell based on the researches of Andy and Sue Parlour (St Osyth, Essex: Ten Bells Publishing, 1997).

Advances a conspiracy theory surrounding **Sir William Gull**, embracing oral tradition in Thorpe-le-Soken that he died and was buried in 1897, not 1890 as engraved on his grave memorial. The oddity that his will was probated twice, in 1890 and 1897, is coupled with **J.K. Stephen**'s smoking habits to make Stephen the pipeman and Gull the Ripper. The book also includes data from **Mary Anne Nichols**' cousin's descendant Andy Parlour and his wife, Sue. New photographs, new family recollections and the first detailed discussion of **Catherine Eddowes**' shawl.

(Also see Andy Parlour, 'The Life and Death of William Nichols 1841-1917', *The Journal of the Whitechapel Society*, 25, April 2009)

JACK THE RIPPER: 100 YEARS OF INVESTIGATION

Book by Terence Sharkey (London: Ward Lock, 1987).

A sprightly commercial account of the murders and principal suspect theories, as known up to early 1987 and produced for the centenary of the murders. Marred by inaccuracies.

JACK THE RIPPER: 150 SUSPECTS

See **Jack the Ripper: Eliminating the Suspects**.

JACK THE RIPPER: A BIBLIOGRAPHY AND REVIEW OF THE LITERATURE

Book by Alexander Garfield Kelly (pseudonym), with an introduction by Colin Wilson (London: Association of Assistant Librarians, 1973; revised 1984; revised 1995, with David Sharp as co-author).

Sixty entries of references in contemporary press; 214 entries of information on facts and theories; 38 entries of relevant biographical material; 112 entries of related fiction and drama; 46 entries of films, music etc. A *tour de force*.

JACK THE RIPPER: A CAST OF THOUSANDS

Book by Chris Scott (Apropos Books, 2004). eBook available as a download on Casebook: Jack the Ripper www.casebook.org/ripper_media/book_reviews/non-fiction/castofthousands.toc.html or on CD.

Groundbreaking goldmine of information from one of the most respected researchers in the field about some of the bit-players in the Ripper story. Author fleshes out what are otherwise largely just names by locating them in census returns and other documents.

JACK THE RIPPER: A COLLECTOR'S GUIDE TO THE MANY BOOKS PUBLISHED
Book by Ross Strachan (Galston, Ayrshire: Strachan, 1996; revised and updated, 1997).

Comprehensive to the date published. (*See also Jack the Ripper: A Bibliography and Review of the Literature.*)

JACK THE RIPPER: A NEW THEORY
Book by **William Stewart** (London: Quality Press, 1939).

Book-length development of a suggestion that a midwife could have escaped detection as the Ripper since she would be expected to pass through the streets in a blood-stained apron.

Stewart added that she might have been an illegal abortionist (basing this on the observation made in several contemporary newspapers that **Mary Jane Kelly** was three months pregnant). Unfortunately the entire theory fell apart with the discovery of **Dr Thomas Bond**'s full medical report on Kelly, which shows that she was not pregnant.

JACK THE RIPPER: A PSYCHIC INVESTIGATION
Book by Pamela Ball (London: Arcturus, 1998; reissued as *The Search for Jack the Ripper: A Psychic Investigation.* London: Midpoint Press, 2006).

Horoscopes of the victims offer astrological character readings. 'Silent Witnesses' offers spiritualistic 'contact sessions' with, for example, **R.J. Lees** and **Mary Jane Kelly**.

JACK THE RIPPER: A REFERENCE GUIDE
Book by Scott Palmer (Lanham MD: Scarecrow Press, 1995).

Two hundred and twenty-one entries on victims, witnesses, suspects, politicians, police, coroners and doctors. Chapter seven discusses Freemasonry and its alleged role in the murders.

JACK THE RIPPER: AN AMERICAN VIEW
Book by Stephen Wright (New York: Mystery Notebook Editions, 1999).

Discusses various topics and proposes **George Hutchinson** as the Ripper.

JACK THE RIPPER: AN ENCYCLOPÆDIA
Book by John Eddleston (Santa Barbara, California: ABC Clio, 2001; paperback London: Metro, 2002).

A comprehensive collection of entries divided into sections – Victims, Police,

Witnesses, Others, Letters, Miscellaneous – rather than purely alphabetical order. Entries tend to be brief, allowing space for linear narrative, a chronological timeline and FAQ section.

JACK THE RIPPER: ANATOMIE EINER LEGENDE

Book by Thomas Schachner and Hendrik Püstow (Leipzig: Militzke, 2006).

The first part discusses the victims from **Martha Tabram** to **Mary Kelly** (embracing the torso murders between 1887 and 1889). A sensible discussion of 14 suspects follows in the second half.

JACK THE RIPPER: ANATOMY OF A MYTH

Book by William Beadle (Dagenham: Wat Tyler Books, 1995).

In this, and in *Jack the Ripper Unmasked,* makes a strong case for treating **William Bury** seriously as a suspect. Noting Bury was not by birth an East Ender and never resided in Whitechapel or Spitalfields, Beadle suggests Bury used his horse and cart to get from Bow to the murder district, pointing out that October 1888 was extremely foggy – which, he argues, meant Bury had to give up murder for that month as he would not have been able to find his way round the unfamiliar neighbourhood. He also suggests **Rose Mylett** might well have been a Ripper victim (the medical evidence that she was murdered decisively outweighing the police conviction that she was not).

He remarks that she was killed within easy walking distance of Bury's home, at a time when he had just sold his horse and cart. Moreover, she was strangled with a ligature (like Ellen Bury), whereas previous Ripper victims were manually strangled. Beadle argues Bury fitted the FBI psychological profile of the Ripper exceptionally well, and in height, age and build matched the witness identifications. By the time of his arrest in Dundee, though, he had a beard which – according to witnesses – the Ripper did not. He notes, too, that Bury always slept with a penknife under his pillow and Martha Tabram's wounds were consistent with the use of such a knife. Additionally, **Ada Wilson** was attacked in a way reminiscent of Bury's threatening Ellen. Beadle observes that the Ripper always robbed his victims of any cash or petty valuables they had on them, and compares this with Bury's constant need for money.

See also **Macnaghten memoranda**, **Caroline Maxwell**, **Martha Tabram**.

JACK THE RIPPER CLIPPINGS BOOK
See **Clippings Book**.

JACK THE RIPPER: COMPREHENSIVE A TO Z
See **The Mammoth Book of Jack the Ripper**.

JACK THE RIPPER: CRIME SCENE INVESTIGATION

Book by David J. Speare (Philadelphia: Xlibris, 2003).

Veterinary pathologist looks at the Ripper crimes from a modern Crime Scene

WITNESS, PLACE & TIME	HEIGHT	AGE	COMPLEXION & COLOURING	FACIAL HAIR	CLOTHES	GENERAL
Unnamed witness – possibly prostitute Emily Walker. Hanbury Street, 2.00am 8/9/1888		About 37		Dark beard and moustache	Short dark jacket, dark vest and trousers, black scarf black felt hat hat	Spoke with a foreign accent. Accompanied prostitute into 29 Hanbury Street
Mrs Elizabeth Darrell or Long, Hanbury Street, 5.30am, 8/9/1888	Over 5ft (Taller than Annie Chapman)	Around 40	Dark	Unknown (seen from behind)	Deerstalker hat, dark coat	Shabby genteel, foreign appearance Talking with Annie Chapman
Best, J. and John Gardner, Settles Street, 11.00pm 29/9/1888	About 5ft 5 inches		Weak sandy eyelashes	Black moustache	Morning suit and billycock (bowler) hat	Definitely English. Flirting with Elizabeth Stride
William Marshall, Berner Street, 11.45pm 29/9/1888	5ft 6 inches				Decently dressed in small black coat, dark trousers, peaked sailor-like cap	Clerk-like appearance. Mild voice: English accent. Talking to Stride.
Matthew Packer, Berner Street,					(1) long black coat, buttoned up,	(1)broad shoulders.

Witness	Height	Age	Hair	Facial	Clothes	Manner
(1) 11.00pm in a statement given to Assistant Commissioner Alexander Charmichael Bruce (2) 11.45 in press reports.	(1) None given (2) 5ft 7in	(1) None given (2) 25–30			soft felt Yankee hat (2) wide-awake hat, dark clothes	Quick in speaking rough voice. (2) stout, clerkly, with a sharply commanding manner.
PC William Smith, Berner Street, 12.30am 30/9/1888	5ft 7inches	About 28		Clean shaven	Dark clothes, dark-coloured hard felt deerstalker hat	Respectable looking. Standing with Elizabeth Stride.
James Brown, Fairclough Street (crossing Berner 12.45am, 30/9.1888	5ft 7inches				Long coat, almost reaching his heels. Self-confessedly unobservant witness did not notice headgear.	Stoutish. Talking to Street), Elizabeth Stride (?) with arm against wall as it to detain her
Israel Schwartz, 12.45 am, Berner street, 30/9/1888	5ft 5 inches	About 30	Fair, with dark hair	Small brown moustache	Dark jacket and trousers, black cap with peak	Partially intoxicated (The assailant attacking Elizabeth Stride)

Witness	Height	Age	Complexion/hair	Moustache/whiskers	Clothing	Other
Israel Schwartz, 12.45 am, Berner street, 30/9/1888	5ft 11 inches	35	Fresh, with light brown hair		Dark overcoat, old black hard felt hat with wide brim	Knife or pipe in hand. (Possible accomplice: 'the pipe man')
Joseph Lawende, Mitre Square, 1.35am, 30/9/1888	5ft 7-8 inches	About 30	Fair	Fair moustache	Pepper-and-salt coloured loose jacket, grey cloth cap with grey peak, reddish neckerchief	Shabby, with sailor-like appearance
Mrs Mary Ann Cox, Dorset Street, 11.45pm 8/11/1888	About 5ft 5 inches	About 36	Fresh, with blotches on his face	Small side whiskers and thick carroty moustache	Shabby dark clothes, dark overcoat and black felt hat	Carrying a quart can of beer, accompanied Mary Jane Kelly to her room
George Hutchinson, Commercial Street, 2.00am, 9/11/1888	5ft 6 inches	34-35	Pale, with dark hair and eyelashes	Slight moustache, curled up at the ends	Long dark coat with astrakhan collar and cuffs; dark jacket and trousers, dark felt hat 'turned down in the middle', button boots, spats with white buttons, linen collar, black tie with horseshoe pin, thick gold chain with red stone seal	Carrying small parcel wrapped in American cloth. Pulled out red handkerchief. Accompanied Mary Jane Kelly to her room where he stayed for more than 45 minutes

Investigation perspective. An overview which covers all the basics is marred by errors, the most serious of which mistakes **George Chapman** for Macnaghten's second suspect **Michael Ostrog**.

JACK THE RIPPER, DESCRIPTIONS OF
Several witnesses describing men seen with victims before their deaths have been thought to have described the murderer. *See* charts on pp. 233, 234 and 235.

JACK THE RIPPER: ELIMINATING THE SUSPECTS
Book by Christopher J. Morley (Bournemouth: C.J. Morley, 2004; revised and updated as *Jack the Ripper: 150 Suspects*, 2004).

Eliminating the Suspects was published in a limited edition of 50 signed copies and looked at 130 suspects, each receiving a brief overview and concluding with a personal, but reasonably objective assessment. The revised edition, issued later in the same year, looked at 150 suspects. It is now available on *Casebook: Jack the Ripper* *http://www.casebook.org/ripper_media/book_reviews/non-fiction/cjmorley/index.html*

JACK THE RIPPER: END OF A LEGEND
Book by Calum Reuben Knight (London: Athena Press, 2005).

Claims to show through anagrams that the Ripper murders were carried out by **Joe Barnett**, **George Hutchinson** and **Mary Jane Kelly**. Possibly a spoof fiction, in which case it is excellent. If intended as fact, however, it is unconvincing. *Cf.* **Jack l'Eventreur: Le Secret de Mary Jane Kelly**.

JACK THE RIPPER: FIRST AMERICAN SERIAL KILLER; THE LODGER
See **The Lodger**.

JACK THE RIPPER: HIS LIFE AND CRIMES IN POPULAR ENTERTAINMENT
Book by Gary Coville and Patrick Lucanio (Jefferson, N.C.: McFarland, 1999).

Self-explanatory title for a book that takes a serious look at how the Jack the Ripper murders have inspired literature, movies, radio and television.

'JACK THE RIPPER' LETTERS
See **Letters**.

JACK THE RIPPER: LETTERS FROM HELL
Book by Stewart Evans (lead author) and Keith Skinner, with a foreword by Martin Fido (Stroud, Gloucestershire: Sutton, 2001; paperback Stroud, Gloucestershire: Sutton, 2004).

Overview of alleged Ripper writings – the 'Dear Boss' letter and 'Saucy Jacky' postcard, the Goulston Street graffito, the idea that the Ripper letters were written by a journalist, the Lusk Letter, letters purporting to be from the Ripper, but by known hoaxers (*see* **Maria Coroner**, **Miriam Howells**), letters sent to the City Police, as well as examination of the Lees, story and the claims by L. Forbes Winslow.

Two chapters by Evans alone discuss Donald McCormick and Dr Dutton. Part Two is a complete listing of all the letters sent to the Metropolitan Police (*cf. Scotland Yard Investigates* for similar listing of City Police letters), with details and description. Illustrated throughout.

JACK THE RIPPER: 'LIGHT-HEARTED FRIEND'
Book by Richard Wallace (Melrose MA: Gemini, 1996).

Lays out the theory accusing Lewis Carroll and his friend and colleague, Thomas Vere Bayne, of perpetrating the Ripper murders. The evidence is largely anagrams. Wallace also puts forward the suggestion that Montague John Druitt's time at Oxford might have brought him into contact with Dodgson.

Parts of the book were published in *Harper's Magazine* (November 1996), to which Guy Jacobson and Francis Heaney riposted with an anagrammatisation of the first three sentences of Wallace's article, which undermined the whole approach (*Harper's Magazine*, February 1997).

Karoline Leach, author of the controversial life of Carroll, *In The Shadow of the Dreamchild* (London: Peter Owen, 1999), debunked Wallace's theory ('Jack Through the Looking-Glass (or Wallace in Wonderland)' *Ripper Notes*, January 2001. She argued that the anagrams are meaningless, generally too poor to be Dodgson's and completely unsupported by any external evidence.

Oddly, Wallace overlooked Carroll's one known reference to the murders. *See* Dr **G.H.R. Dabbs**.

JACK THE RIPPER: MEDIA, CULTURE, HISTORY
Book edited by Alexandra Warwick (head of English and Linguistics, University of Westminster) and Martin Willis (senior lecturer in English, University of Glamorgan) (Manchester: Manchester University Press, 2007).

A collection of academic writing on the influence of the Whitechapel murders on race, gender, the press, fiction and film.

Part One: Media
'The House That Jack Built' by Christopher Frayling, 'The Pursuit of Angles' by L. Perry Curtis, 'Casting the Spell of Terror: The Press and the Early Whitechapel Murders' by Darren Oldridge, 'Order Out of Chaos' by Gary Coville and Patrick Lucanio and 'Blood and Ink: Narrating the Whitchapel Murders' by Alexandra Warwick.

Part Two: Culture
'The Ripper Writing: A Cream of the Nightmare Dream' by Clive Bloom, 'The Whitechapel Murders and the Medical Gaze' by Andrew Smith, 'Jonathan's Great Knife': *Dracula* meets Jack the Ripper' by Nicholas Rance, 'Jack the Ripper,

Sherlock Holmes and the Narrative of Detection' by Martin Willis and 'Living in the Slashing Grounds: Jack the Ripper, Monopoly Rent and the New Heritage' by David Cunningham.

Part Three: History
'Narratives of Sexual Danger' by Judith Walkowitz, 'Jack the Ripper as the Threat of Outcast London' by Robert F. Haggard, 'Who Kills Whores?' 'I Do,' says Jack: Race and Gender in Victorian London' by Sander L. Gilman and 'Crime and Punishment' by William J. Fishman.

JACK THE RIPPER: MURDER, MYSTERY AND INTRIGUE IN LONDON'S EAST END
Book by Susan McNicoll (Canmore, Alberta: Altitude, 2005).
Well-researched, solid overview of the crimes. **Severin Klosowski** and **Francis Tumblety** offered as the most promising suspects.

JACK THE RIPPER: ONE HUNDRED YEARS OF MYSTERY
Book by Peter Underwood (London: Blandford, 1987; paperback US Sterling Publishing Company, 1978; UK paperback London: Javeline Books, 1988).
An account of the murders and the principal suspects as known early in 1987, with contributions from well-known and unknown Ripperologists; aimed at meeting the anticipated centenary market.

JACK THE RIPPER: OR THE CRIMES OF LONDON
Book by W.J. Hayne (Chicago: Utility Book and Novelty Co., 1889; republished by Thomas Schachner, 2007, in a limited edition of 50 copies with an introduction by Stephen P. Ryder).
Catalogued by the Library of Congress, but untraceable there or anywhere else. No copy was thought to exist until 2002, when an original copy was auctioned for $2,325 US and *Ripperologist* magazine (April 2002) declared this to be 'the rarest and most valuable Ripper book in the world'. Thomas Schachner's superb limited edition is a faithful reproduction of the original.

JACK THE RIPPER: OR WHEN LONDON WALKED IN TERROR
Book by Edwin T. Woodhall (London: Mellifont Press, 1937).
Pulp paperback proposing Olga Tchkersoff as the Ripper. It muddles a sentence of Melville Macnaghten's with Dr Holt's misadventure (*see* **White-Eyed Man**) and misnames Mary Jane Kelly 'Marie J. Taylor', but places Chief Inspector Swanson prominently in the enquiry at the expense of Abberline.

JACK THE RIPPER, ORIGIN OF NAME
See '**Jack the Ripper' Letters**.

JACK THE RIPPER: PERSON OR PERSONS UNKNOWN

e-book by Gary Wroe (2002) made available on Casebook: Jack the Ripper: www.casebook.org/ripper_media/book_reviews/non-fiction/garrywrote_full.html

Broad-ranging overview that draws heavily on quoted contemporary sources and discusses modern detective techniques, especially offender profiling. Without promoting a suspect, leans to George Hutchinson.

JACK THE RIPPER: QUEST FOR A KILLER

Book by M.J. Trow (Barnsley, South Yorkshire: Wharncliffe Books, 2009) to accompany the Discovery Channel documentary, *Jack the Ripper: Killer Revealed*, broadcast 11 October 2009).

Using the 1988 FBI profile as the foundation for his theory, Trow proposes Robert Mann was Jack the Ripper.

JACK THE RIPPER: SCOTLAND YARD INVESTIGATES

Book by Stewart Evans and Donald Rumbelow (Stroud, Gloucestershire: Sutton, 2007).

Gives a full account of Sir Charles Warren's career up to 1888 and provides an overview of policing Metropolitan London and internal politics when Warren succeeded to the Commissionership. There follows brief accounts of the murders and the police response, including the reaction to various pieces of correspondence (those to the City Police being listed chronologically in an appendix). Includes a convenient chronological reprinting of all the major theories and observations made by policemen, and a chapter that examines Sir Robert Anderson's assertion that the murderer's identity was known.

The book concludes with a look at some popular Ripper myths and two personal epilogues in which, notably, Donald Rumbelow advances Timothy Donovan as a suspect for three of the murders. Lavishly illustrated.

JACK THE RIPPER – SERIAL KILLER

e-book by Vickie Britton (San Antonio:Your information Center, 2005).

Originally intended to accompany an internet course, but now available online at: www.jacktheripper.yourinformationcenter.com. Designed for absolute novices interested in acquiring a basic overview of the Ripper crimes. Heavy emphasis is placed on Patricia Cornwell's *Portrait of a Killer*. Contains numerous small errors.

JACK THE RIPPER: SUMMING UP AND VERDICT

Book by Colin Wilson and Robin Odell (London: Bantam, 1987).

Survey of the known serious data timed for the centenary of the murders. A responsible and workmanlike job, but unfortunately it appeared contemporaneously with a flood of new information (for example, the Swanson marginalia), which could not be included.

JACK THE RIPPER: THE 21ST CENTURY INVESTIGATION
Book by Trevor Marriott (London: Blake, 2005; paperback, London: John Blake, 2007).

Former policeman Marriott avers that modern policing methods would have caught the Ripper. He proposes that the missing organs of Chapman and Eddowes were removed by someone with access to the bodies in the mortuary, and that the piece of apron dropped at Goulston Street was deposited by Eddowes herself, after she had used it as menstrual cloth and toilet cleanser. Marriott believes Jack the Ripper to have been a merchant seaman, unaware that the police thoroughly investigated this possibility at the time, and in the the paperback edition of his book identifies him as Carl Feigenbaum. In 'The Evil Within': The World's Worst Serial Killers (Bradford: Trevor Marriott, 2008), he develops his theory slightly, wherein he advances Emma Jackson and Harriet Buswell as early Ripper victims. See also the **De la Bott statement**.

JACK THE RIPPER. THE AMERICAN CONNECTION
Book by Shirley Harrison (London: Blake, 2003).

Retelling of the story behind the so-called diary of James Maybrick and the subsequent controversies – cf. **The Diary of Jack the Ripper** – with the addition of a case arguing that Maybrick was also responsible for the Servant Girl Annihilator rapes and murders committed in Austin, Texas, between 30 December 1884 and Christmas Eve, 1885, despite the fact that the diary itself explicitly attributes the diarist's first murders to 1888.

JACK THE RIPPER: THE BLOODY TRUTH
Book by Melvin Harris (London: Columbus Books, 1987). Also, a German edition: Jack The Ripper. Die Blutige Wahrheit, 1988).

Debunks many of the stories connected with the Ripper, notably the tale of psychic **R.J. Lees** (which Harris researched for Sorry, You've Been Duped), the Royal Conspiracy and **Sir William Gull** theories. The book is invaluable for this work. Harris also intended to debunk the **Roslyn Donston Stephenson** story, but on examining it more closely, he concluded many of the stories were true and that Stephenson had more of what he took to be the Ripper's essential qualities than any other known suspect.

Some of this material has been seriously questioned in recent years, as has his conclusion that the Dr **Benjamin Howard**/R.J. Lees story was the invention of the Whitechapel Club in Chicago. (See **The Ripper File, The True Face of Jack the Ripper**,)

JACK THE RIPPER: THE CASEBOOK
Book by Richard Jones (London: André Deutch, 2008).

Large-format illustrated book that devotes one page to a summary of the crimes and each of the primary suspects; principally distinguished for the collection of facsimile documents.

JACK THE RIPPER: THE CELEBRITY SUSPECTS

Book by Mike Holgate (Stroud, Gloucestershire: The History Press, 2008).

Not particularly useful guide to 31 not always serious suspects who achieved distinction in their day.

JACK THE RIPPER: THE COMPLETE CASEBOOK

See **The Complete Jack the Ripper**.

JACK THE RIPPER: THE DEFINITIVE HISTORY

Book by Paul Begg (London: Longman, 2002; paperback, London: Longman, 2004).

'Begg provides one of the best overarching accounts of social conditions in London's East End, as well as the history and internal politics of both the police, government and press organizations of the time. This detailed examination of *why* Whitechapel became one of the poorest districts in London goes a long way to reveal the motivation, background and history of its inhabitants. For the first time, the Ripper crimes are placed in their true social and historical context.'

'Begg's coverage of the Ripper crimes themselves comprises barely half the length of the book. Only the most salient facts of each murder (from Emma Smith to Mary Kelly) are provided.'

'...One of the most important Ripper releases of the past several years.' (© *Casebook: Jack the Ripper*.)

JACK THE RIPPER: THE FACTS

Book by Paul Begg (London: Robson, 2004; US edition New York: Barnes & Noble, 2004; paperback, London: Robson).

'Perhaps the single most comprehensive and up-to-date overview of the Ripper case currently on the market. Begg covers all aspects of the case with his usual eye for detail (and the occasional amusing tangent). Social conditions, police, government, suspects, coroners, doctors, victims, witnesses... every aspect of the case is laid out for the reader. Begg covers all victims from the mythical 'Fairy Fay' through to Frances Coles, but only the canonical five victims (and Tabram) get their own chapters. Similarly, dozens of suspects are discussed, but only the four major police suspects (Ostrog, Kosminski, Druitt and Tumblety) are explored in depth. The Royal Conspiracy theories, along with Maybrick and Sickert, are covered more briefly in the final chapter and lesser-known suspects are peppered throughout the earlier parts of the text.

'Every useful nugget that's appeared in print or online in the past decade seems to have been compiled into this book, making it essential reading for anyone interested in the case.' (© *Casebook: Jack the Ripper*.)

JACK THE RIPPER: THE FINAL CHAPTER

Book by **Paul Feldman** (London: Virgin Books, 1997; paperback, London: Virgin Books, 1998).

In the form of a memoir, it describes Feldman's involvement with the Ripper case, Ripperologists and the **Maybrick Diary** and **Maybrick Watch**, from the time when he first became interested in making a videotape about the case to when he released his video and continued research for the book, which he expected to be the final proof of his case that Maybrick really was the Ripper.

JACK THE RIPPER: THE FINAL SOLUTION

Book by **Stephen Knight** (London: Harrap, 1976; paperback, London: Granada, 1977; London: Grafton Books, 1977; London: Treasure Press, 1984; London: Chancellor Press, 2000; London: Harrap, 1976).

Presents and researches **Joseph Sickert**'s story that the Ripper was **Sir William Gull**, acting as a loyal (if demented) Freemason at the behest of **Lord Salisbury** to eliminate **Mary Jane Kelly** and her companions, who were attempting to blackmail the Government with their knowledge of the secret and illegal marriage between **Prince Albert Victor** and Sickert's grandmother, **Annie Elizabeth Crook**.

Justifiably admired for its detail, readability and contributions to knowledge of the Ripper case, but Knight's sketchy account of the murders contains important omissions and inaccuracies that are used to support his case.

In the end, there is not a single piece of solid historical evidence adduced to support the sensational and controversial elements of Sickert's story. Nonetheless, Stephen Knight's theory was widely believed between 1976 and 1988.

JACK THE RIPPER: THE INQUEST OF THE FINAL VICTIM

Book by John Smithkey III (Santa Monica: Key Publications, 1998).

The full inquest records on **Mary Jane Kelly**, with a commentary.

JACK THE RIPPER: THE MURDERS AND THE MOVIES

Book by Denis Meikle (London: Reynolds & Hearn, 2002).

An examination of the crimes and how they have been portrayed in movies and on television.

JACK THE RIPPER: THE MYSTERY SOLVED

Book by Paul Harrison (London: Robert Hale, 1991).

Harrison, a Northampton policeman who served for many years with the Ministry of Defence police, argues **Joseph Barnett** committed the murders to frighten **Mary Jane Kelly** into abandoning prostitution. The theory is a reworking of the argument more cautiously advanced by Bruce Paley ('A New Theory on the Jack the Ripper Murders', *True Crime*, April 1982, and expanded in *Jack the Ripper: The Simple Truth*). Harrison researched the wrong Joseph Barnett.

JACK THE RIPPER: THE SATANIC TEAM

Book by Karen Trenouth (Bloomington, Indiana: AuthorHouse, 2007).

Sequel to *Epiphany of the Whitechapel Murders*, heavily reliant on *The Ripper and the Royals* and research otherwise largely internet-based. *Prima facie* the theory is as improbable as it is untenable.

242

JACK THE RIPPER: THE SIMPLE TRUTH

Book by Bruce Paley (London: Headline, 1995).

An American dealer in comics, resident in London when he wrote his book. Suggests Jack the Ripper was **Joseph Barnett**, an idea he began exploring in the mid-1970s and first expounded in print (1982) – 'A New Theory on the Jack the Ripper Murders', *True Crime*, April 1982.

Paley, who was remarkably successful in tracing the movements of the obscure fish porter through the East End, from his deprived, and orphaned childhood to his peaceful retirement in Shadwell, elaborated and strengthened the arguments advanced in the magazine article, pointing out that Barnett almost exactly fits the FBI Psychological Profile; that Joseph Barnett's height, colouring and moustache, uniquely among suspects, exactly match **PC Smith**'s and **Joseph Lawende**'s descriptions of the man (or men) seen respectively with **Stride** and **Eddowes**; and that the **'Dear Boss' letter** arrived too close to the renewed murders of 30 September to be coincidental, postulating that Barnett wrote it and the **'Saucy Jacky' postcard** with the intention of frightening Mary Jane Kelly when he read the newspaper accounts of them to her.

Barnett had intimate geographical knowledge of all the murder sites and Paley argues the final spontaneous quarrel with Kelly, who had tired of him (*cf.* **Julia Vanturney**), culminating in her murder and mutilation, removed the direct need for further murders, while Barnett's long interrogation by the police probably frightened him into inactivity.

JACK THE RIPPER: THE UNCENSORED FACTS

Book by Paul Begg (London: Robson, 1988; paperback, London: Robson, 1989).

One of the top five books recommended by *Casebook: Jack the Ripper*, which describes it as 'a wonderful introduction to the case and should be on the shelf of anyone seriously pursuing the investigation'. The first fully-footnoted and detailed account of the murders. Discussion of the suspects was limited to those named in the Macnaghten memoranda. Now superseded by *Jack the Ripper: The Facts*.

JACK THE RIPPER: THE WHITECHAPEL HORRORS

Book by Tom Robinson (Daisy Book Publishing, n.d. but *c.*1920s; Andy Aliffe, 1996).

An interesting example from a period when accuracy mattered less than sensation in books about true crime.

JACK THE RIPPER: THE WHITECHAPEL MURDERS

Book by Terry Lynch (Ware, Hertfordshire: Wordsworth Editions, 2008).

A good overview of the crimes, chatty and likeable. Lynch offers three suspects: **Joseph Barnett**, **Montague John Druitt** and **John Kelly**, the partner of **Catherine Eddowes**.

JACK THE RIPPER: THROUGH THE MISTS OF TIME
Book by Peter Hodgson (Leicester: Minerva Press, 2002).

A very personal, discursive and conversational overview of the case, books, theories and fictional treatments, all casual, easy and without stridency or rancour.

JACK THE RIPPER: UNMASKED
Book by William Beadle (London: John Blake Publishing, 2009).

See also **Jack the Ripper: Anatomy of a Myth**.

JACK THE RIPPER: WHITECHAPEL MAP – 1888
Detailed referenced grid-map of the Ripper territory by Geoff Cooper and Gordon Punter (London: RipperArt, 2004).

JACK THE RIPPER'S BEDROOM
Painting by **Walter Sickert**, now in Manchester Art Gallery, identified by Sickert experts as depicting a room in no. 6 Mornington Crescent, where Sickert lodged, *c.* 1907.

Cf. **Sickert's Unnamed Veterinary Student**.

JACK THE RIPPER'S BLACK MAGIC RITUALS
Book by Ivor Edwards (originally privately published in a limited edition of 1,000 copies, Lake, Isle of Wight: Penny Publishing, 2001. Subsequently withdrawn from sale, then published London: John Blake, 2002; paperback, London: John Blake, 2003).

For 30 years, Edwards was a career criminal (though never guilty of violence or fraud), who met murderers and serial killers while in prison. He has experiences which he believes provides an insight into the workings of the criminal mind. Founder and webmaster of the now defunct jtrfotrums.co.uk.

Detailed and elaborate attempt to prove **Donston Stephenson** was the Ripper. Marked by extremely careful examination and measurement of the topography of the crimes, and application to a plan of the murder sites of the geometrical shape, Vesica Piscis (the roughly fish-shaped, point-ended oval formed by the arcs of intersecting circles of the same size). Professor Charles Henry of the Virginia Commonwealth University, an authority on the Vesica Piscis and three-dimensional geometry, noting Edwards' heavy stress on numinous and occult matter, notes remarks in his preface that Vesica Piscis, 'is perhaps the primary two-dimensional image of sacred geometry.' He commends Edwards for establishing the occult motive of the murders and, in his view, establishing the 'closest fit' suspect to be identified with Jack the Ripper.

JACK THE RIPPER'S KNIFE
A broken surgical knife, now in the possession of Donald Rumbelow (see *The Complete Jack the Ripper*), has often been exhibited or illustrated with the suggestion that it may have been the Ripper's weapon. The knife, contained in a

box lined with bloodstained velvet, was given to Miss Dorothy Stroud MBE (1910–97) in 1937 by Hugh Pollard, sporting editor of *Country Life,* who said it had belonged to Jack the Ripper. Since Pollard was the partner of gunsmith Robert Churchill, for many years Scotland Yard's ballistics expert, Rumbelow, initially sceptical, concluded that circumstantially the provenance of the knife seemed plausible. Miss Stroud burned the box and used the knife for carving and subsequently gardening.

Probably the same knife is described by **Douglas G. Browne**, who wrote in *The Rise of Scotland Yard*, 'A friend of the writer's possesses one of two surgical knives said to have been left by the Ripper beside his victims.' No such abandoned knives are known, though an initial news report claimed that a large knife stained with blood had been discovered near **Annie Chapman**'s body was later dismissed by the *Pall Mall Gazette* 8 September 1888). However, see **Thomas Coram**.

It is a 12in, double-edged amputating knife of the correct period, with a thumb-grip for ripping upwards. Made by John Weiss of Bond Street, it is now shorter than it originally was, Miss Stroud having snapped the blade when pruning a privet bush. She had the broken end ground and beveled. N.P. Warren notes in a contribution to ***The Mammoth Book of Jack the Ripper*** that 12 identical knives were purchased in 1882 and smuggled to Ireland for use in the Phoenix Park murders (the assassinations which *The Times* accused Charles Stewart Parnell of praising, leading to the Parnell Commission). Warren suggests the extreme improbability of such unusual knives being involved in two celebrated murder cases suggests Rumbelow's knife was actually one of the Phoenix Park set, and he postulates a conspiracy in which **James Monro** and the Conservative government agreed to suppress the evidence in their possession that Irish Nationalists had been involved in the Phoenix Park murders, if the Fenians would cancel their plot to dynamite Queen Victoria's Jubilee in 1887. For this reason, he suggests, the Phoenix Park knife might have been passed off as a Jack the Ripper knife.

JACK THE RIPPER'S THIRD VICTIM
See **Jack the Ripper's Tredje Offer**.

JACK THE RIPPERS TREDJE OFFER (JACK THE RIPPER'S THIRD VICTIM)
Book by Birgitta Leufstadius (Partille, Sweden: Warne Förlag, 1994; translated by Edwin R Nye. Wellington, New Zealand: First Editions, 2008).

Excellent life of **Elizabeth Stride**, slightly dated because of later research. The original hardback has interesting photographs of her Swedish locale and elsewhere, including the interior of the Frying Pan in Brick Lane when it was a pub.

Leufstadius notes (presumably from the mortuary photograph) that Stride died with a smile on her face, and suggests she may therefore have recognised her killer. She then speculates that Stride might have left Sweden for England in search of an English client, and that this client could have been **Montague John Druitt**, who is her preferred suspect as the Ripper. Ms Leufstadius has always conceded this is speculation unsupported by evidence.

JACK THE RIPPER'S VICTIMS
See **Mary Ann Nichols, Annie Chapman, Elizabeth Stride, Catherine Eddowes, Mary Jane Kelly**.

For alleged victims, *see* **Frances Coles, Alice McKenzie, Rose Mylett, Emma Elizabeth Smith, Martha Tabram**.

For additional supposed victims of certain suspects, *see* **W.H. Bury, Severin Klosowski, Walter Sickert**.

JACK THE RIPPER WALKS
See Walking Tours.

JACK UPPSKARAREN: KRIMINALFALL OCH LEGEND
Book by Glenn Lauritz Andersson (Lund, Sweden: Historiska Media, 2008).

JACK UPPSKARAREN OCH ANDRA VISOR TRYCHTA I AR
Book by Lars Forssell (Stockholm: Albert Bonniers Forlag, 1966).

JACK'S LONDON
Map and text by Daryl Sullivan and Andrew Cockell (London: Geonex Historic Maps, 1993).

Street map of Whitechapel and Spitalfields (*c.* 1870) with the five canonical Ripper murder sites identified, and a brief account of the victims and principal suspects.

JACKSON, ELIZABETH or ANNIE (1865–89)
Identified from clothing and a peculiar scar on her wrist as the woman whose dismembered remains were pulled from the Thames in mid-1889, reviving the Ripper scare. Possibly the same woman identified in **Inspector Henry Moore**'s report on **John Cleary** (MEPO 3/140 ff160–161) as **Annie Jackson**, whose thigh was found by Mr Miller of the *Star* in a garden on Thames Embankment.

Daughter of shipwright William Jackson and his wife, Hanna. She had been living with a man named John Fairclough (also known as Smith), who, a witness claimed, abused her physically and whom she had recently left. Jackson claimed he had gone in search of work and that she remained in London because she was well-advanced in pregnancy.

R. Michael Gordon (**The Thames Torso Murders**) identifies her as a victim of **Severin Klosowski** and thus a Ripper victim in his torso murders phase.

Cf. **Lizzie Fisher**.

JACKSON, Emma
Suggested victim. Advanced 2008 by Trevor Marriott in *The Evil Within: The World's Worst Serial Killers. See also* **Buswell, Harriett**.

In April 1863, 28-year-old Emma Jackson was found murdered in a room at 4 George Street, St Giles's, her throat badly cut and her bed saturated with blood. She had rented the room in the early hours of the morning, at which time she was accompanied by a man. No description of her companion could be obtained, but she was last seen in the company of a foreigner, who had appearance of a German baker or sugar-baker. Various arrests and confessions were made at the time and over successive years. Even as late 1869, it was reported that a Russian Pole was 'handed over to the police' as her murderer. A man named William Squires persistently admitted to the murder, doing so even as late as 1880 (*Daily News*, 9 August 1880).

(*See Jack the Ripper: A 21st Century Investigation*.)

JACOBS, – (Socialist)
Socialist. Member of International Workingmen's Educational Club. Seen outside by **Morris Eagle**, accompanying another man (possibly **Diemschütz**) down Berner Street toward Fairclough Street in search of police after the discovery of **Elizabeth Stride**'s body. Nothing more is known about him.

JACOBS, – (Suspect)
Butcher. Belatedly and briefly suspected. In *Lost London*, Benjamin Leeson writes that after **Frances Coles**' murder (1891),

'a story circulated that the "Ripper" was a butcher who wore blue overalls and a leather apron, and an English Jew named Jacobs, a perfectly harmless man, somehow attracted suspicion to himself. Possibly because, working in a slaughter-house, he always wore a leather apron.

People would point Jacobs out in the street as a suspected man and more than once, he had to run for it. I myself was often obliged to take him to the police station for protection. The thing so preyed on the poor fellow's mind that it finally caused him to lose his reason.'

If Leeson's memory can be relied upon here, he gives remarkable evidence of a belated revival of something very like the early '**Leather Apron**' scare.

JACOBS, ISAAC LEWIS (*b. c.* 1868)
Witness.
Russian-born Jewish boot finisher, resident in Newcastle Place in 1889, was proceeding through Old Castle Street towards Wentworth Street to buy supper from **John McCarthy**'s shop in Dorset Street, when **PC Walter Andrews** took him to see **Alice McKenzie**'s body in Old Castle Alley.

JAMES, HENRY
Bethnal Green lunatic arousing short-lived suspicion.
James was seen near the Foresters' Arms, Cambridge Heath Road, on 8 September

1888, by **Thomas Ede**. This was the height of the '**Leather Apron**' scare and James was wearing a two-peaked cap – and, Mr Ede thought, had 4in of knife blade protruding from his pocket. He also moved oddly and seemed to have a wooden arm. Ede was permitted to testify at **Mary Ann Nichols**' inquest on 17 September that he had seen this suspicious character, but returned a week later to say that he had now been shown James, a well-known harmless local lunatic, and confirmed this was the man he had seen.

'JENNY'

Prostitute interviewed at St George's-in-the-East Infirmary by a representative of Central News (see the *Star*, 10 October 1888; *Birmingham Daily Post*, 11 October 1888, for examples), who said, 'she was absolutely sure of the identity of the murderer' and that 'He frequently maltreated the women of the streets and extorted money from them under threats of "ripping them up"... She described him as a foreigner, about forty years of age. She believed he had been a doctor. He dressed fairly well, and generally carried a big heavy stick.' This appears to be a variaton on the earlier '**Leather Apron**' stories.

JESUITS

Collective suspects.

The Society of Jesus: religious order of Catholic priests established by St Ignatius Loyola in 1534. Their rigorous discipline and militant missionary activity earned them fierce hostility from some Protestants. *See* **Ernest Crawford** for the claim that they were institutionally responsible for the murders.

'JILL THE RIPPER'

Generic term for stories suggesting the murderer was a woman: a theory first proposed by the Rvd. Lord Sydney Godolphin Osborne in a letter to *The Times* (18 September 1888) stating (without specifying) that the mutilations were self-evidently carrying out the sort of threats that streetwalkers made to one another. Surgeon Lawson Tait also suggested that the killer might be a strong woman who worked as a slaughterhouse cleaner. She could, he suggested, have concealed her bloodstains by rolling up her skirt and walking through the streets covered by a heavy petticoat. And she would have known that blood must be washed off fabric with cold, rather than hot water. (Reported in the Ogden *Standard Examiner*, 16 October 1888.)

The idea is said to have been taken up by Sir Arthur Conan Doyle on the assumption that the murderer must have been heavily bloodstained when escaping through crowded streets. He proposed that a midwife in a bloodstained apron would pass unquestioned, suggesting a male murderer might have disguised himself thus as a woman.

Edwin Woodhall suggested **Olga Tchkersoff**.

William Stewart expanded Conan Doyle's suggestion to book-length, with the additional suggestion that 'Jill' was an abortionist. This theory is expanded by

Ex-**Detective Superintendent Arthur Butler**. It falls on the evidence of **Dr Bond**'s medical report showing that **Mary Jane Kelly** was not pregnant.

Donald McCormick describes **Abberline** discussing the possibility that the murderer was a woman or wore women's clothes, though this may be one of McCormick's fictional dramatisations intended to present drab speculative theory as lively narrative.

An unusual and romantic variant is 'The Secret of Ex-Convict SYF45' advanced by Richard Herd, allegedly revealed by a prisoner in Parkhurst and reported in the *Evening News* (8 September 1955). This proposed that the Ripper was a devout nurse, who was appalled when she discovered her husband, a steward on a liner, had gone with a prostitute. Borrowing his clothes and knife, she went out to avenge herself on the woman who had ruined her marriage. (A variant of this same story by Richard Herd appeared in *Weekend*, 1–7 December 1971)

Julie McCaffrey explored the possibility that **Mary Pearcey** was the killer (*Daily Mirror*, 20 May 2006).

JILL THE SAILOR
Christopher J. Morley's name for the heroine of Convict SYF45's story (*see* **Jill the Ripper**).

JIMMY KELLY'S YEAR OF RIPPER MURDERS
Booklet by the late John Morrison (London: 1988).

A photocopied collage of typescript, newspaper cuttings, handwritten comments, pages from books and an extraordinary assemblage of photographs, intended to demonstrate that **James Kelly** was the Ripper.

JOHNSON, PC JOHN, 866 City (*b.*1864)
Rescuer of **Elizabeth Burns**.

Joined City Police, April 1883 (warrant no. 5642). Over 6ft tall. On his retirement and return of uniform and accoutrements in March 1890, it was noted that he had accidentally burned his warrant card that morning and lost one legging.

On duty in The Minories during the early hours of 18 September 1888, Johnson heard a cry of 'Murder!' from Three Kings Court. There, he found **Charles Ludwig** with a one-armed prostitute, who was later identified as Elizabeth Burns. She said, 'Oh, policeman, do take me out of this!' Johnson cleared Ludwig away, and escorted Burns to the end of his beat, where she said, 'He frightened me very much when he pulled a big knife out.' She said that she had been too frightened to say so while Ludwig was present. Johnson alerted other policemen and unsuccessfully searched for Ludwig himself. (various newspapers, but see the *Evening Standard*, 26 September 1888).

JOHNSTON, EDWARD

Witness at **Elizabeth Stride**'s inquest. Assistant to Drs **Kay** and **Blackwell** at 100 Commercial Road. Informed of the murder by **PC Collins**, around 1.05am. Notified Dr Blackwell, and went to Dutfield's Yard with the policeman, where he briefly examined the body prior to Dr Blackwell's arrival, at precisely 1.16am.

JONAS, E.L.P. (fl. 1888)

Self-proclaimed witness: probably a confidence trickster.

Presented himself to Sir Augustus Paget, British ambassador in Vienna, claiming that he knew the murderer to be a former San Francisco butcher, known in America as Johann Stammer, but now a ship's cook, passing as John Kelly in London. Alleged Kelly had betrayed a secret political society to which Jonas belonged, and this society wanted him arrested, but could only act if two of its continental chiefs came to London. For this purpose, Johann requested 2,000 florins, which he would supplement and repay with society money from Paris. Dr **Robert Anderson**, **Chief Constable Williamson** and Home Office Permanent Under Secretary, **Godfrey Lushington**, were all convinced the man was a fraud, but **Sir Charles Warren** and **Henry Matthews** were unwilling to snub the ambassador and invited Paget to act on his own discretion.

Paget advanced Jonas £160, but Jonas came back, asking for a further £100. Matthews declined to pay this, and the Home Office ordered Sir Augustus be reimbursed from the Metropolitan Police funds (HO144/221/A49301D).

JONES, ELWYN (1923–82)

Co-author with John Lloyd in 1973 of the mini-series, *Jack the Ripper*, for BBC Television and the spin-off book, ***The Ripper File***.

Born in Aberdare, Wales in 1923 and educated at local elementary and secondary schools before attending the London School of Economics, which he left without taking a degree. In 1944, he joined *News Review* as a reporter and later became its features editor. When publication ceased in 1950, he became assistant to the literary critic of the *Radio Times*. Later, he moved into television drama with special responsibility for drama documentaries.

Jones was very interested in crime and police procedure, and perhaps his finest achievement was as co-creator of *Z-Cars* for BBC Television in 1962. He was head of drama series for the BBC between 1963 and 1966, when he became a freelance writer. The mini-series, *Jack the Ripper*, led to a series, *Second Verdict*, in which fictional detectives Barlow and Watt investigated other historical mysteries.

JONES, JOSEPH

Pawnbroker of 31 Church Street, Spitalflelds. According to some sources, Mr Jones issued the pawn tickets found in **Catherine Eddowes'** mustard tin. Others said the pawnbroker's name was Smith.

JONES, SERGEANT, City Police

At **Catherine Eddowes'** murder-site, Jones found three boot-buttons, a thimble and a mustard tin containing two pawn tickets beside the body.

JOURNAL OF THE WHITECHAPEL SOCIETY, THE

Journal. Edited by Adrian Morris and launched February 2005. Appears six times a year, averaging 28 pages. Reports on proceedings of the Whitechapel Society 1888; also carries news, reviews and feature articles.

JTRFORUMS.CO.UK

Now defunct website started by Ivor Edwards with Tyler Hebblewhite.

JTRFORUMS.COM

Website began by Howard Brown in 2005. While it conveys basic data on suspects, victims and witnesses, as well as forums dealing with a wide range of topics, it is notable for its attention to **Robert Donston Stephenson** and carries a facsimile of the entire 375-page manuscript by **Bernard O'Donnell**.

'JULIA'

Prostitute, who lodged temporarily with **Mary Jane Kelly**.

According to **Joseph Barnett**, he ceased living with Kelly because she brought a prostitute called Julia to live with them. And according to the *East London Advertiser*, Julia was German. She may have been **Julia Vanturney**, who was living opposite Kelly in Miller's Court by the time of the murder.

See also **Maurice Lewis**.

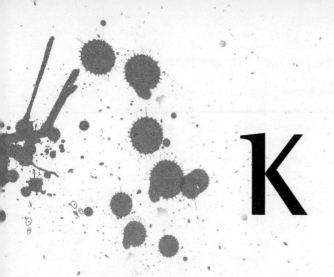

K

KAMINSKY, NATHAN (*b.* 1865)

Postulated in **The Crimes, Detection and Death of Jack the Ripper** as suspect identical with **David Cohen**.

Jewish bootmaker of 15 Black Lion Yard with one year's residence in Whitechapel parish. Diagnosed syphilitic, 24 March 1888, and treated in Ward BB, Whitechapel Workhouse Infirmary. Discharged, cured, six weeks later. No known relatives. This is all that is known of him.

Martin Fido found him to be the only person with a name approaching 'Kosminski' in his initial trawl through London infirmary and asylum records from 1888–90, and surmised he was '**Leather Apron**' (or one of the men so described) on the grounds that his race, address and occupation fit (especially) Macnaghten's alleged description of that suspect (*see also* **Philip Loftus**). He further noted Kaminsky's address, uniquely among suspects at that time, fitted the topographical indications given by the piece of **Catherine Eddowes**' apron dropped beneath the **Goulston Street graffito** and the **Metropolitan Police** Area of Search. This led him to suggest that Kaminsky was the Ripper. It will be noted the entire case is speculation based on coincidental similarities to reported conclusions drawn from the police investigation.

There being no trace of Kaminsky under that name in the death registers of England and Wales, Fido then noted his age, race and lack of known relatives are identical with those given for **Aaron Davis Cohen**, and speculated that following the hunt for 'Leather Apron', Kaminsky attempted to change his occupation and identity prior to undergoing the attack of raving mania which led to his arrest and incarceration under the incorrect name of Aaron Davis or David Cohen.

Fido postulated that some awareness of the name 'Kaminsky' in the early search for 'Leather Apron' encouraged the Metropolitan Police to believe this to be the same man as **Aaron Kosminski** when, following the discovery of the Swanson

252

marginalia, he hypothesised they might have learned something about the latter from the City Police. He suggests they had watched Kosminski without informing the Met as, conversely, the Met had incarcerated 'Cohen' without informing the City that their witness **Joseph Lawende** had thereafter identified him. Thus, he claims the Swanson marginalia combine aspects of Kosminski and aspects of Cohen under the impression that the two men were one.

KEATING, SUPT JAMES IGNATIUS (1844–1889)
In charge of **J Division** (Bethnal Green) of the Metropolitan Police overseeing 38 inspectors, 55 sergeants, and 515 constables (*Eastern Argus & Borough of Hackney Times*, 13/10/1888). Signatory to early reports by **Insp. Spratling** and **Insp. Helson**. Died in harness on 13 March 1889.

KEATING, MICHAEL
Witness
A licensed shoe black, who passed the night of 9-10 September 1889 under a railway arch in Pinchin Street. He saw and heard nothing until he woke up in the morning and lent the police his blacking sack to help in covering the body. He admitted to being too drunk to have heard much during the night.

KEATON, INSPECTOR LEWIS HENRY (1870–1970)
Informant and theorist. Joined the **Metropolitan Police**, August 1891 (warrant no. 77010). Retired, 1917.

In 1969, Keaton gave a tape recorded interview in which he recollected that beat constables during the Ripper scare had been encouraged to strap rubber to their boot soles and most policemen believed the murderer to have assaulted his victims as they presented themselves for penetration from the rear. He proposed the theory that the murderer was a doctor, collecting specimens of grossly venereally infected wombs for research purposes, in the hope of discovering an alleviation for genital burning sensations.

Unfortunately, obtrusive interviewing drowning the Inspector's words makes it difficult to detect exactly what he says at a point when he appears to identify the suspected doctor as either a 'Dr Cohn' or 'Koch', or someone else whose name he cannot recall, but who used strychnine (*cf.* **Neil Cream**).

KELLY, JAMES (1860–1929)
Proposed as suspect in 1984 by **John Morrison** in *Jimmy Kelly's Year of Ripper Murders* and considerably strengthened by **James Tully** in *Prisoner 1167: The Madman Who Was Jack the Ripper*.

5ft 7in tall, olive-dark complexion, heavy black moustache, dark eyes, a thin, pale face and spare build (in 1888), he was an independently wealthy, sometime upholsterer from Liverpool, who in 1881 moved to London and took up lodging in City Road. In early June 1883, he married Sarah Bridler, his landlady's daughter, but shortly after the marriage he became increasingly mentally unstable and suffered intense headaches with a discharge from the ears, attributed to an abscess. He had also contracted a venereal disease and seems disconnectedly to have felt guilty about this.

Furious quarrels with his wife and mother-in-law climaxed in his seizing a pocket knife and fatally stabbing Sarah in the neck. He was convicted of murder and sentenced to death, but a new Criminal Lunacy Act led to his undergoing further mental examination by specialists and they concluded he was mentally disturbed. His sentence was commuted and he was sent to Broadmoor at Her Majesty's pleasure.

In January 1888, he escaped, using a key he had made in the workshop, and climbed over two walls. Early in 1888, he was seen in East London. At the end of the year, he went to France, returning to the English Midlands at some point and going to New York in 1892. He continued to travel extensively in America, periodically returning to Britain and twice seeking return to custody, but remaining at liberty. In 1927, in a state of ill health, he turned up at the gates of Broadmoor and pleaded to be readmitted. There, he remained until his death in 1929, too old and enfeebled to succeed in his further escape attempts. His was the longest period of freedom ever achieved by an escapee from Broadmoor.

John Morrison claimed that Kelly's quarrel with his wife was over his having an affair with **Mary Jane Kelly**, and that he escaped with the intention of rejoining Kelly in London. When he discovered that she had gone on the streets and abandoned or aborted the child she had been carrying for him, he proceeded to kill her, on the way killing all the women from whom he made enquiries as to her whereabouts.

According to Morrison, the authorities determined to cover up Kelly's alarming escape from the outset and were satisfied there would be no further trouble once Mary Jane had been murdered. Only **Sir Charles Warren** persisted in wishing to notify the public and intensify the search. Therefore, his resignation was enforced.

There is not a shred of evidence to support any of this, despite Morrison's repeated claims that he had documentary proof of it.

James Tully concedes immediately that the case against Kelly is circumstantial. First and foremost, he was a known mad woman-killer on the loose at the time of the murders. He knew the East End and had associated with prostitutes. According to Tully, his background and psychopathology seems to fit that postulated by psychological profilers Robert Ressler and David Canter for sexual serial killers. Tully notes that the authorities, who had been searching feverishly for the escaped lunatic in early 1888, were mysteriously silent about him when they were actually looking for a mad perpetrator of murders. He believes the desultory search indicates a cover-up and suggests it would have been a greater scandal than Scotland Yard could tolerate, had it become known that their ignominious failure to catch the Broadmoor escapee allowed him to kill more random victims.

The case against Kelly as the Ripper is that he does not appear to have been dangerous to women other than his wife, and there is no evidence that he was actually in London at the time of the murders.

(*See* file on James Kelly in The National Archives: HO 144/10064. Berkshire Record Office have his case file.)

'KELLY, JOHN'
See **Jonas**.

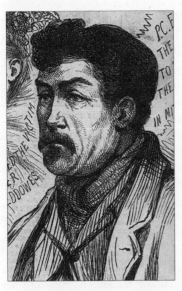

KELLY, JOHN

Witness at **Catherine Eddowes'** inquest; also her lover and advanced as a suspect in *Jack the Ripper: The Whitechapel Murderer*;

Worked several years as a jobbing market porter, frequently for a fruit salesman called Lander. Met Eddowes in a lodging-house, possibly in Flower and Dean Street in 1881. As a Catholic he may have loosely 'converted' her, since she gave that as her religion when treated for a burnt foot at Whitechapel Infirmary in 1887. He was described as 'quiet and inoffensive' with 'fine features' and 'sharp and intelligent eyes'. By the time of Catherine's murder he was a sick man, however, with a kidney complaint and a bad cough. For his movements on the day of the murder, *see* Catherine Eddowes.

Kelly presented himself to the police on reading in the newspapers of the pawn ticket in the name of **Birrell** found beside the body in Mitre Square. Prior to that, he had not suspected the Ripper's latest victim might be his common-law wife. He identified the body.

KELLY, MARY JANE or MARIE JEANETTE or MARY JANET (c. 1863–88)

Supposedly aka 'Black Mary', 'Fair Emma', 'Ginger'. Also called **Mary Jane**

Lawrence and M.J. Taylor **(When London Walked in Terror)**. Last **canonical** Ripper victim.

Kelly's early history, as related to friends in London, was thus: born in Limerick, Ireland and moved to Wales in her early childhood, where her father, John Kelly, took a job at an ironworks in Caernarvonshire or Carmarthenshire. Had six or seven brothers and one sister. Her brother Henry, nicknamed Johnto, joined the Scots Guards. Mary Jane married collier named **Davies**, *c.* 1879. He died in a pit explosion, two or three years later.

Kelly went to stay with a cousin in Cardiff and became a prostitute, but spent the best part of a year in an infirmary there. According to **Jean Overton Fuller**, **Florence Pash** said that Kelly had cleaned floors at the Infirmary. Came to London, *c.* 1884, working first in a high–class West End brothel, during which time she frequently drove in a carriage and at least once went to Paris with a gentleman, but disliked life in France and returned in a few weeks.

None of the above can be guaranteed as fact, since exhaustive research reported in books, journals and on the internet has failed to find conclusive or even generally agreed supporting evidence in birth, marriage or death registers, or the records of Cardiff Infirmary, or those of the Scots Guards. Nor did any of the friends relating it after her death claim first-hand knowledge of any part of it. Inferential support for the brother in the Scots Guards comes from the fact that **John McCarthy** observed letters from Ireland delivered for Kelly (though he thought they were from her mother), and **Joseph Barnett** correctly believed the Scots Guards to be in Ireland at the end of 1888. There is inferential support, too, for the West End brothel from **Mrs Carthy**, a lady with whom Kelly later lodged, who said that Kelly's previous landlady, from St George's Street, had accompanied Kelly to Knightsbridge, where they recovered a box of clothing from a French 'lady'.

By her account her decline to the East End seems to have been rapid. In 1988, BBC researchers for the *Timewatch* television programme Shadow of the Ripper confirmed that the nuns of **Providence Row Night Refuge and Convent** in Spitalfields had a tradition that she stayed briefly with them and was sent out into domestic service, from which she absconded to go on the streets. This was supported by the convent's solicitor, whose family had a tradition that they employed a maid sent from the convent, who absconded and became a Ripper victim.

Kelly's East End acquaintances, talking to the press, believed her to have gone to the Ratcliff Highway district on her return from France, lodging first in St George's Street (western end of today's Highway, between St George's Church and St Katharine's Dock) and, according to the *Star*, working for a **Mrs Buki**. Joseph Barnett believed she lived with a man called **Morganstone**, near Stepney gasworks. She resided with Mrs Carthy on Breezer's Hill prior to *c.* 1886, She left Mrs Carthy's to live with a man connected with the building trade, who, Mrs Carthy thought, wanted to marry Kelly. This was presumably **Joseph Fleming**, a mason or plasterer from the vicinity of Bethnal Green, with whom she had been associating prior to meeting Barnett, who used to visit her while she was with Barnett, and of whom she was apparently very fond. By April 1887, she was living at Cooley's Common Lodging House in Thrawl Street, Spitalfields (see **Cooney's Lodging House**).,

Walter Dew, who knew her well by sight, records that she was good-looking and 'paraded' around the district, usually in the company of two or three friends. She never wore a hat and she always had a spotlessly clean white apron. The author **Tom Cullen** reports she had a reputation for violence and a quick temper; also that she was nicknamed 'Black Mary'. No confirmation of this has so far been found.

Other nicknames reported are 'Fair Emma' and 'Ginger'. All may be the consequence of confusion with other women (cf. **Lizzie Fisher**). All her London acquaintances, except Joe Barnett, knew her as Mary Jane Kelly;. he used the form 'Marie Jeanette', which was also engraved on her coffin and entered on her death certificate. Suspecting this to be an affectation, we have preferred the simpler version. Several press reports citing the Central News Agency, however, suggest 'Kelly' was a name adopted from a common-law husband: some of the reports aver this to be a name used by Barnett.

Joseph Barnett told the *Star* (10 November 1888) that she had a little boy, aged 6 or 7, living with her and that she occasionally visited a fellow-prostitute in the Elephant and Castle neighbourhood. Neither contemporary nor subsequent research has traced any positive information about this child or friend. (*Cf.* **'Margaret'**.)

She met Joseph Barnett on Good Friday, 8 April, and they lodged together thereafter, always in the neighbourhood of the 'wicked quarter mile' around Dorset Street, Thrawl Street and Flower and Dean Street. Their first home was in George Street (between Thrawl Street and Flower and Dean). They moved to Little Paternoster Row, Dorset Street, until they were evicted for drunkenness and non-payment of rent. Following this, they went to Brick Lane, and finally, to 13 Miller's Court, Dorset Street, which was actually the partitioned-off, ground-floor back room of 26 Dorset Street, reached through a doorway just beyond the arched entry to Miller's Court. The rent was 4/6 [22?p] a week, and 30/- £1.50p] arrears had accumulated by the time Kelly died.

Barnett and Kelly were remembered as a friendly and pleasant couple, giving little trouble except, occasionally, when drunk. She may be the Mary Jane Kelley who was fined 2/6 [12?p] at Thames Magistrates Court for drunken disorderliness on 19 September 1888. Once she broke the window of 13 Miller's Court when drunk. This proved useful when she and Barnett lost the doorkey, as they were able to reach through the broken pane to pull back the spring-lock or bolt.

Julia Vanturney, who lived opposite, believed Kelly was also seeing another man called Joe, possibly a costermonger, who visited her and gave her money. There was some suggestion that she may have been scared of a man (or men) unknown to her East End associates. It was known to her friends that she was frightened by the Ripper murders and contemplated leaving London.

In the early evening of 30 October 1888, Barnett left Kelly. He variously described the reasons for their separation as being because she had resumed prostitution; because she had invited another woman called **'Julia'** to stay with them; because she had prostitutes to stay, 'Julia' and **Mrs Harvey** being named. He continued to be friendly with her, however, visiting and possibly giving her money.

On Wednesday, 7 November, Kelly bought a halfpenny candle at **McCarthy's** shop (adjacent to the entry from Dorset Street to Miller's Court) and was subsequently seen in Miller's Court by **Thomas Bowyer** talking to a rather smart man of 27 or 28, with a dark moustache and 'very peculiar eyes'. (*See* **Unidentified Man Seen by Thomas Bowyer**.)

On Thursday, 8 November, Kelly spent the afternoon with Maria Harvey and the early evening with **Lizzie Albrook**. Joe Barnett visited her amicably between 7.30 and 8.00. Her subsequent movements are uncertain, though she may have been drinking with **Elizabeth Foster**, and she may have been seen, intoxicated, in the Britannia at 11pm, accompanied by a young man with a moustache. She may even have been in the Horn of Plenty with Joe Barnett and 'Julia'. (*See* **Maurice Lewis**.)

At 11.45, **Mary Ann Cox** saw her return home in the company of a stout, shabby, blotchy-faced man in his thirties, with a carroty moustache and a billycock hat. He carried a quart pail of beer. Kelly was wearing a linsey frock and a red knitted crossover shawl. She was drunk and told Mrs Cox that she was going to sing. Between midnight and 1am, several witnesses heard her singing 'Only a violet I plucked from my mother's grave' in her room; **Catherine Picket** nearly went in to complain about the noise at 12.30.

At 2am, **George Hutchinson** met Kelly in Commercial Street, where she addressed him by name and asked him for sixpence. Hutchinson watched her proceed towards Aldgate and pick up a client near Thrawl Street. He examined him closely under the light on the Queen's Head at the corner of Fashion Street as the two passed him, and followed them to Dorset Street, where he watched them go into Kelly's room. Then he waited outside for 45 minutes, sheltering under the arched entry beside **Crossingham's Lodging House** before going home. Neither the client nor Kelly emerged during this time.

At Kelly's inquest, **Sarah Lewis** testified that she had gone to Miller's Court at 2.30 in the morning. In Commercial Street, she saw a man and a woman. She recognised the man as one who had frightened her and a friend in Bethnal Green Road the previous Wednesday, when he asked one of them – he did not mind which – to follow him. In Dorset Street she saw a short, stout man in a wide-awake hat standing in the entry to the lodging-house – presumably Hutchinson. She also saw a young couple walk down Dorset Street.

A woman described as **Mrs Kennedy** was reported in the press as saying she went to Miller's Court at 3 or 3.30am to stay with her parents. She saw a respectably dressed, but intoxicated young man with a dark moustache talking to an intoxicated woman in Dorset Street. He said, 'Are you coming?' and the woman turned away. A poorly dressed woman without a hat was standing by. Mrs Kennedy said the man looked like a sinister man with a bag who had frightened her in Bethnal Green Road the previous Wednesday in an encounter which seems very like that subsequently described by Sarah Lewis. The *Star* intimated doubts about the truth of Mrs Kennedy's Bethnal Green Road story and there is a strong possibility that she was the same person as Sarah Lewis (*cf.* **Mrs Darrell/Mrs Long**), giving unreliable, varied evidence.

Mrs Kennedy, Sarah Lewis and **Elizabeth Prater** all reported hearing a cry of 'Murder!' from the direction of Kelly's room shortly before 4am.

Caroline Maxwell, Maurice Lewis and an unnamed woman mentioned in *The Times* all reported seeing Kelly out of doors at times between 8 and 10am (i.e. several hours after medical and other evidence indicated she was dead). (*See* Caroline Maxwell, for discussion.)

At 10.45am, Thomas Bowyer saw the body through the window and he and McCarthy summoned the police. The lock secured the door, and in the expectation that bloodhounds might be brought, the room was not entered until 1.30pm, when **Superintendent Arnold** arrived with the information that the dogs would not be coming. On his orders, McCarthy broke open the door.

It has been suggested that Kelly's locked door, state of undress – her clothes were on a chair at the foot of the bed - and cut bedsheet indicate that she may have known her murderer and gone peacefully to sleep in his presence. All three points are capable of alternative explanation. but in any case this does not invalidate the general belief that the murderer introduced himself to his victims in the guise of a client.

For details of Kelly's extreme mutilation, *see* **Dr Thomas Bond** and **Dr Gabe**. Stephen Ryan notes that the missing heart reached at least one contemporary newspaper and postulates that pages missing from Bond's report may have

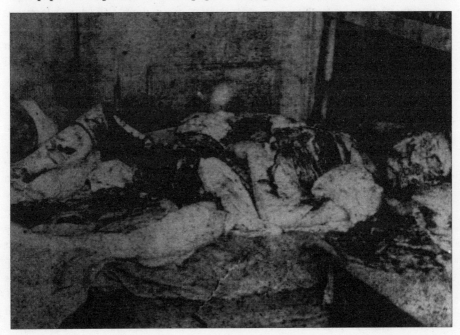

discussed the reproductive organs (*New Criminologist,* Online edition, June 2007: revision and update of article originally published in *Criminologist, 1988*). Various theorists have found the suggestion that Mary was not really the victim useful. Colin Kendell (*Criminologist,* autumn 1988) and John Wilding (**Jack the Ripper Revealed**) both suggest the body was not, in fact, Kelly's. Melvyn Fairclough (***The Ripper and the Royals***) suggests it was actually a pregnant housemaid friend of Kelly's, named Winifred May Collis. No documentary evidence for Collis's existence has been produced.

Inside the small (12 x 10ft) room were remains of a fire in the grate which contained burnt clothing, including a woman's bonnet. It had apparently burnt with sufficient heat to melt the solder at the spout and handle of a kettle in the grate. Arthur Douglas asks pertinently how it was known that the damage to the kettle occurred on that particular night. **Inspector Abberline** surmised the purpose was to illuminate the room.

An illustration in Richard K. Fox's ***The History of the Whitechapel Murders*** (1888) shows an axe leaning against the wall of a room, but it unclear whether it relates to Mary Kelly's room or the room in which Mrs Marr was murdered (the Ratcliffe Highway murders), which Fox's narrative also discusses. Another possibility stems from a report in the *Globe* (16 February 1891) which refers to a hatchet preserved in the Black Museum at Scotland Yard as having been used to hack and disfigure the victim in Dorset Street, but which is revealed by the original catalogue under item 142 to have been used by Henry Wainwright to dismember the body of Harriet Lane in 1874, a case also known as the Whitechapel murders. It is likewise identified by *Chambers Journal* (April 1885). How and why the *Globe* associated it with Dorset Street is not known. However, N.P. Warren, editor of **Ripperana** and a trauma surgeon, has detected evidence of an axe or hatchet being used in the wounds to Kelly's thighs (***Ripperana***, 18, October 1996).

For discussion of the claim that Kelly's inquest was improperly manipulated by the authorities, *see* **Inquests: Jurisdictional Disputes Over**.

She was buried at Leytonstone Roman Catholic Cemetery on 19 November. Despite widespread publicity, no member of her family was traced to attend the funeral.

As the last and most savagely mutilated victim, Kelly has featured largely in theories which propose that one particular woman was being sought by the murderer. See **Sir William Gull, James Kelly**, **'Dr Stanley'**, *Jack the Ripper Revealed*. Jean Overton Fuller (*Sickert and the Ripper Crimes*) says that she was a personal acquaintance of Florence Pash, who reported Kelly had worked as a nursemaid for **Walter Sickert**. There is no known evidential support for any of these stories.

KENNEDY, MRS

Alleged witness to activities in Dorset Street and Miller's Court on the night of **Mary Jane Kelly's** murder.

The *Star* (10 November 1888) reported Mrs Kennedy's claim to have gone to Dorset Street in the small hours of 9 November and to have seen a woman talking to a man, with another man or possibly a masculine-looking woman in the shadows. The *Star* thought her story seemed very doubtful, especially as it entailed comparison of the man she had seen with a man who had frightened her in Bethnal Green Road, the previous Wednesday, and whom she took to be the Ripper.

Nonetheless, two days later *The Times* reported that **Inspector Abberline** had interviewed her, eliciting the statement that she had gone to her parents' home in Miller's Court, and there saw a woman talking to two men.

The *East London Advertiser* (6 December 1888) printed the much fuller story (see **Mary Jane Kelly**) and other newspaper (*Illustrated Police News* (17 November 1888) reported that her companion in Bethnal Green Road was her sister, and that the encounter with the drunk man and woman took place in Commercial Street beside the Britannia or at the Commercial Street end of Dorset Street. G.R. Sims subsequently referred to the man seen by 'the Kennedy sisters'.

The similarities between her statements and the inquest testimony of Sarah Lewis create an obvious suspicion they were one and the same. It is noteworthy, though, that the *East London Advertiser* was still referring to Mrs Kennedy by that name three weeks after Sarah Lewis appeared before the press at the inquest. There are also consistent differences between their stories. Sarah Lewis said she saw a man (presumably Hutchinson) standing in the doorway of the lodging-house; Mrs Kennedy never mentioned him. Sarah Lewis said she was going to 'the **Keylers**', while Mrs Kennedy said she went to her parents. Mrs Kennedy said she saw a woman in the presence of a man and one other person. Sarah Lewis never said anything like this in public (but *see* **Sarah Lewis**).

There are differences and inconsistencies in the times given by the two. It is important, however, because *if* Mrs Kennedy was *not* Sarah Lewis, she may have seen a hatless woman (*see* **Mary Jane Kelly**) on the street after Hutchinson had stopped watching the entry to Miller's Court.

KENT, CONSTANCE (LATER, RUTH EMILIE KAYE) (1844–1944)
Suspect.

In June 1860, Constance's infant half-brother, Francis Savill, was found murdered at the family home in Road, Wiltshire. Constance, then 16, was suspected and in 1865, confessed to the crime, pled guilty on trial and was convicted. Her death sentence was commuted to life imprisonment, from which she was released in 1885. Upon her release, she spent some time at the country retreat of a religious order in Buxted, accompanying her half-brother William to Australia the following year, adopting the name of Ruth Emilie Kaye and taking up nursing. She was appointed matron of the Prince Henry Hospital and afterwards accepted a post at the Parramatta Industrial School for Girls.

E.J. Wagner (*The Science of Sherlock Holmes,* John Wiley, 2007) observed Kent had been released for three years before the Ripper murders, that her whereabouts in 1888 was uncertain and that, having committed one murder with a knife and apparently having assisted midwives in the convent, she could have committed the Ripper murders.

KENT, JAMES

Witness at **Annie Chapman**'s inquest.

Labourer at Bayleys' packing-case works, summoned with **James Green** by **John Davis**. Kent went for a brandy before fetching canvas to cover the body. The *East London Observer* found him an entertaining figure:

A youngish-looking man, with a bullet-head and closely-cropped hair, and a sandy, close-cut moustache. He wore a long overcoat that had once to be green, and into the pockets of which he persistently stuck his hands. He had a peculiar habit of lowering his neck into the blue and white spotted handkerchief which encased it when under examination and jerking it out suddenly whenever he was called upon to answer a question.

KENTORRICH, BARNETT

Resident of 38 Berner Street, where **Elizabeth Stride** was murdered. Slept until 3am, on 30 September 1888, not even disturbed by the noise accompanying the finding of the body. Expressed Orthodox Jewish hostility to the Socialist Jews of the International Workingmen's Educational Club.

KEYLER, MR AND MRS

Residents of Miller's Court, **Mary Jane Kelly**'s murder site. **Sarah Lewis** testified she went to stay the remainder of the night with them, at about 2.30am, 9 November 1888. If, however, Sarah Lewis was also the woman interviewed as **Mrs Kennedy**, then they may have been her parents, of 2 Miller's Court.

KIDNEY, MICHAEL (*b.* 1852)

Witness at the inquest on **Elizabeth Stride** and suggested as her murderer in *Jack the Myth*. Lover of Elizabeth Stride, who was seven years his senior, whom he had known for three years and lived with for most of that time, their relationship being relatively stormy and marked by several separations which totalled about five months. He had tried unsuccessfully to padlock her in their room, but she had a key (which Dr **George Bagster Phillips** found on the body). He was a water-side labourer, resident at 38 Dorset Street at the time of the inquest.

On 6 April 1887, Stride gave him in charge to PC 357H for assault, but failed to appear in court to proceed with the prosecution. Kidney was sent down for three days in July 1888 for being drunk and disorderly and using obscene language. At the time of the murder, he had not seen Stride for about five days, but was not disturbed by her absence.

On 1 October 1888 ,he turned up drunk at Leman Street Police Station, saying he would have killed himself, had he been the policeman responsible for the beat where Stride was murdered, and asking to see a detective. At the inquest he claimed to have gone because he had heard something that led him to believe he could have trapped the murderer and caught him in the act, if given command of a force of detectives with the power to position them. Pressed further, he admitted he had no information.

In June 1889 he was treated at Whitechapel Workhouse Infirmary for syphilis, and in September for lumbago and dyspepsia.

KILLEEN, DR TIMOTHY ROBERT

LRCS (Ireland), 1885; Lic.K.Q.Coll.Phys. (Ireland), 1886. Frequently spelt Keeling or Keleene in the press. Medical Directories suggest he spent less than two years at the surgery in 68 Brick Lane, from which he was called to examine Martha Tabram's body at 5.30am.

He estimated death had occurred about two hours previously. There were 39 stab wounds, including five in the left lung, two in the right, one in the heart, five in the liver, two in the spleen and six in the stomach. The breasts, belly and private parts were the principal targets. At least 38 had been inflicted by a right-handed assailant. All but one could have been caused by an ordinary penknife. The exception was a wound on the sternum, which had apparently been made with a dagger or sword-bayonet. (*East London Advertiser*, 11 August 1888). (*See* **Martha Tabram** for further discussion of bayonet wounds.)

The 1913 Medical Directory records a Timothy Robert Killeen of Ennis, Co. Clare, among deaths occurring between December 1911 and November 1912.

KILLER WHO NEVER WAS, THE

Book by Peter Turnbull (Hull: Clark, Lawrence, 1996).

A detailed account of the Ripper murders and contemporary press comment on them, followed by comparison with other cases, reaching the conclusion that more than one (unnamed) hand was responsible for the killings. *See* **Jack the Ripper (Cook)**, which advances the same idea.

KIRBY, SERGEANT HENRY (*b.* 1854)

Born in London. Joined the **Metropolitan Police** in 1874 (S Division). Warrant no. 57839. Promoted to sergeant and transferred to K Division in 1884. Transferred to newly formed **J Division**, July 1888. Reduced to constable and transferred to S Division for improperly drinking in a public house with a constable while on duty, 27 October 1888. Transferred to **H Division**, 31 October 1888.

Reinforced constables **Thain** and **Mizen** at **Mary Ann Nichols'** body. Kerby arrived on the spot while Dr Llewellyn was making his examination.

(*See* Bernard Brown, 'The Rise and Fall of Sergeant Kirby', *Ripperologist*, May 2003.)

KLOSOWSKI, SEVERIN ANTONOVICH alias GEORGE CHAPMAN (1865–1903)

Suspect, first accused 1903. (It was alleged by **Hargrave Adam** in 1930 that he had been suspected at the time of the murders.)

Born Nagornak, Poland, the son of carpenter Antonio Klosowski and Emile (née Ulatowski). Christened Severino, by which name some people referred to him throughout his life; he seems to have preferred Severin. Educated at rural public school at Krasseminsk, 1873–80. Apprentice under Senior Surgeon Moshko Rappoport in Zvolern, 1880–85. Possibly at this time learned Yiddish, which he used occasionally in later life. Student at Hospital of Praga, Warsaw, 1885–86. Qualified junior surgeon, 1887. *Feldscher* (assistant surgeon), Hospital of the Infant Jesus, Praga, 1887.

Came to England, June 1887. Worked for Abraham Radin, hairdresser of West India Dock Road; then 1888–91, self-employed in Cable Street; 1890 in basement barber shop below the White Hart (still standing) on the corner of Whitechapel High Street and George Yard (now Gunthorpe Street), first as assistant, then proprietor. July 1889, met Stanislaus Baderski at a Polish club. In August 1889, Baderski's sister Lucy co-habited with Klosowski in Cable Street; October 1889, they married or went through a form of marriage: it is alleged that a former wife of Klosowski's from Poland joined them briefly, and then disappeared.

A son, Wohystaw, was born in 1890. The couple lived variously at Cable Street, Commercial Street and Greenfield Street. In March 1891, Wohystaw died. Census records show Klosowski and Lucy resident in Whitechapel at the beginning of April. By May, they were living in Jersey City, where Klosowski again worked as a barber. In February 1892, Lucy left him and returned to England, where she gave birth to a daughter, Cecilia, in May. Klosowski returned for a short reunion in June; then left, and his movements for the next year are unknown.

From 1893–95, he worked at a hairdresser's in West Green Road, Tottenham, and cohabited with a woman named Annie Georgina Chapman. In 1894, when she left him for trying to establish a *ménage à trois*, he adopted her name and started calling himself George Chapman and claiming to be American. Then, in 1895 he took his own premises on Tottenham High Road and subsequently worked for barber William Wenzel in Leytonstone. He then worked as barber in Hastings, where he lived as man and wife with Mary Spink. In 1897, he became landlord of the Prince of Wales public house in Bartholomew Square, off the City Road, London, and there poisoned Mary Spink. In 1898, he hired Bessie Taylor as barmaid and they passed as man and wife when he moved to Bishop's Stortford as licensee, leasing the Grapes. He became landlord of the Monument, Union Street, Southwark in 1899, and there poisoned Bessie Taylor in February 1901. In August of that year, he hired Maud Marsh as barmaid, passing her off as his wife from September. He tried unsuccessfully to claim insurance on a fire fraudulently started in the Monument, then moved to the Crown in Borough High Street. Poisoned Maud Marsh, who died 22 October 1902. Arrested 25 October. Convicted after a four-day trial, March 1903, and executed in the April.

The *Daily Chronicle* (23 March 1903) reported as a result of discovering that in 1888 Klosowski had lodged in George Yard (*see* **Martha Tabram**), the police were entertaining suspicions that he might have been Jack the Ripper. The *Pall Mall Gazette* sent a reporter to get the opinion of **Inspector Abberline**, who said he had entertained a growing conviction that Klosowski was the Ripper since reading the Attorney-General's opening remarks at Klosowski's trial (*Pall Mall Gazette*, 24 and 31 March 1903). This led to exchanges with **George R. Sims** and **Inspector Reid**, both of whom rejected the idea that Klosowski was the Ripper.

Hargrave L. Adam avers that Abberline said to **George Godley**, 'I see you've caught Jack the Ripper at last,' and since Adam thanks Godley for his assistance in preparing the book, this is probably true (although it seems contrary to Abberline's own assertion that his suspicions began with the opening speech by the Attorney-General at Klosowski's trial). Adam also asserts Abberline closely questioned Lucy Baderski about Klosowski's movements at the time of the murders (although it seems almost certain the couple did not meet until 1889 (*The Trial of George Chapman*) .

Arthur Fowler Neil, who worked as a sergeant under Godley on the Klosowski case, also argued he was Jack the Ripper, writing, 'We were never able to secure definite proof that Chapman was the "Ripper", but the strong theory remains just the same. No one who had not been trained as a surgeon and a medical man could have committed the "Ripper" crimes. As we discovered, Chapman had been a surgeon in Poland and would, therefore, be the only possible fiend capable of putting such knowledge to use against humanity instead of for it. "Jack the Ripper" was a cold-blooded inhuman monster, who killed for the sake of killing.

'The same could be said of Severino Klosowski, alias George Chapman, the Borough Poisoner. Why he took to poisoning his victims on his second visit to this country can only be ascribed to his diabolical cunning, or some insane idea or urge to satisfy his inordinate vanity. In any case, it is the most fitting and sensible solution to the possible identity of the murderer in one of the world's greatest crime mysteries' (*Forty Years of Man-Hunting* (London: Jarrolds, 1932).

Both men appear to have been satisfied that a man who calculatedly poisoned, watched and possibly sadistically enjoyed the slow death of his 'wives' was compatible with his having earlier enjoyed mutilating women.

Donald McCormick, on the alleged authority of **Dr Dutton**, claims Abberline learned that Klosowski, who was working in a barber's shop below the White Hart, Whitechapel, was the double of a barber's assistant in Walworth who turned out to be **Alexander Pedachenko**, and that the two men used to exchange identities for their nocturnal perambulations. McCormick uses this story to boost his case against Dr Pedachenko, but every detail lacks independent support. It has also been demonstrated that Klosowski did not work below the White Hart until 1890 (Neal Shelden, letter to *Ripperana*, October 1993).

Philip Sugden, asserting that, 'There was no more authoritative voice on the Ripper murders than that of Abberline,' concludes Klosowski, 'fits the evidence better than any other police suspect, but that does not make him a strong suspect' (*The Complete History of Jack the Ripper*). R. Michael Gordon has stated that Klosowski definitely was the Ripper (*Alias Jack the Ripper, The American Murders of Jack the Ripper, The Thames Torso Murders of Victorian London, The Poison Murders of Jack the Ripper*).

KNAPTON, JOHN AND JOE

Two railway carmen. Witnesses at the inquest on **Frances Coles**.

The brothers testified to seeing a man and a woman standing together on the corner of Swallow Gardens and Royal Mint Street between 2 and 2.12am on the night of her murder. It was proven that their observation had nothing to do with Coles when **Thomas Fowles** and **Kate McCarthy** confirmed they were the couple in question and had recognised the Knaptons, one of whom called 'Good night' to them in passing.

KNIGHT, STEPHEN VICTOR (1952–85)

Researcher and theorist. Author of *Jack the Ripper: The Final Solution*. As a young journalist on the *East London Advertiser*, Knight was sent to interview **Joseph Gorman Sickert** when his story that the Ripper murders were carried out by **Sir William Gull** in order to protect the scandalous secret of **Prince Albert Victor**'s illegal marriage was publicised in the BBC drama-documentary, *Jack the Ripper*. Knight found Sickert persuasive, and embarked on research that convinced him his story was true.

Knight's book purveying the theory and the results of his research was a worldwide success, but one year after publication he suffered an epileptic fit and a scan revealed a cerebral infarct. Though he continued writing, the epileptic attacks increased until, by 1980, they were striking every six weeks. He learned that he had a cerebral tumour, underwent a biopsy and believed himself cured.

Following this, he joined the Bagwan Rajneesh's cult, adopting the name Swami Puja Detal and completed his last book, *The Brotherhood* (1983), an attack on

Freemasonry. In 1985, it became apparent the biopsy had not worked and the tumour had returned. An operation was unsuccessful and Knight died.

See Richard Whittington-Egan, *Ripperologist*, 41, June 2002.

KOCH, or COHN, DR

Suspect indistinctly named in 1969 taped interview by centenarian retired police officer, who joined the force three years after the Ripper murders. *See* **Inspector Keaton**.

KONOVALOV, VASSILY (died, c. 1908)

Suspect alleged by **Donald McCormick** in 1959.

Born at Torshok, Tver (today's Kalinin). A junior surgeon of medium height, slightly built, with broad shoulders, blue eyes, heavy black eyebrows, and a curled and waxed black moustache. Suspected of murdering a woman in Paris in 1887 (*see* **France, Murders in**), five women in London and a woman in Russia in 1891. He allegedly used the aliases **Alexei Pedachenko** and **Andrey Luiskovo**. Occasionally transvestite, he was wearing women's clothes when arrested in Petrograd [sic] and confined to an asylum, where he died.

The above details are cited by Donald McCormick in *The Identity of Jack the Ripper* who alleged that they were published in a lithograph copy of the *Ochrana Gazette* (see the entry, where the entire piece is quoted and the anachronistic reference to Petrograd is discussed), supposedly shown him by Prince Belloselski. McCormick quotes two other sources referring to Konovalov. The first is a letter by **Sir Basil Thomson**, which allegedly says,

'In Paris recently I learned in talks with the French that they had always thought that the "Ripper" was a Russian named Konovalov, who used the alias "Mikhail Ostrog", under which name Scotland Yard knew him as an ex-convict and medical student.'

(*See* **Michael Ostrog** for further discussion)

The second is an extract from Dr **Thomas Dutton**'s *Chronicles of Crime*:

I have learned from a French doctor of a Russian junior surgeon, or *feldscher,* who was known to him in Paris about 1885–88. He was suspected of having killed and mutilated a *grisette* in Montmartre, but he left Paris before he could be arrested. This may account for Scotland Yard's search for a Russian surgeon they believed to be in hiding. At last there appears to be a hint as to motive. This surgeon, whose name was Konovalov, was said to have a violent hatred of prostitutes, due to a relative of his having suffered cruelly from a woman of the streets. The description of Konovalov exactly fits that of Pedachenko and the final police assessment of what the 'Ripper' looked like.

The last two quotations offer interestingly suggestive parallels with information in

267

the Macnaghten memoranda and elsewhere, but fall under the caveat of unsourced material mentioned by Donald McCormick.

Searches have failed to uncover the requisite number of the *Ochrana Gazette*, but have found reference to three men named Vassilli Konovalov. Two were peasants convicted of looting and related crimes in the 1905 civil war. The third, Vasilii Vasilievitch Konovalov, from the village of Zhlobin in the Ukraine, was exiled, possibly in 1904, to the 'far North' for 28 years. He was described as stocky, of medium height, with a round, clean-shaven face. There is nothing to connect this last man with the alleged Ripper suspect, or with the long-running Russian suspect **Nicolai Wassili**, although all three came from the Ukraine.

Dr Pedachenko is known from **William Le Queux**'s *Things I Know*, and other sources cited by McCormick, none of which directly link him with Konovalov. The probability is that they were not the same person.

(See Scott Hannaford & Serge Zavyalov, 'Vassily Konovalov – Some Background Research', Ripperologist, 24, August 1999)

KOSMINSKI, AARON MORDKE (1865–1919)

Originally identified by Martin Fido (***The Crimes Detection and Death of Jack the Ripper***) as the suspect named only 'Kosminski' in the **Macnaghten memoranda** (1894); subsequently named by surname only as **Robert Anderson**'s suspect in the **Swanson marginalia** (1910; published 1987).

On-going research has identified Aaron Kosminski as Aaron Mordke Kosminski, born in Klodawa (Klodiva), in the Province of Kalish in central Poland, on 11 September 1865, the son of tailor Abram Josef Kozminski and his wife, Golda Lubnowski. He had at least three sisters and one brother. His brother Icek (Issac) appears to have emigrated from Poland, sometime between 1871–73, and he would become a prosperous tailor. Aaron may have emigrated with at least two of his sisters and their husbands, about 1880/81.

Nothing is known about Aaron's early life in Poland or England. Medical records give his occupation as hairdresser, but a witness said that he had not attempted any work for years.

In December 1889, he appeared in court arrested by PC Borer and charged with allowing a dog to be unmuzzled in Cheapside. There was some confusion, Aaron giving his surname as Kosminski, but his brother saying that whilst this was correct the family had found it more convenient to go by the name of Abrahams because Kosminski was difficult to spell. Aside from the name problem, Aaron stated the dog was not his, but belonged to a man named Jacobs. The magistrate nevertheless fined him 10s and costs, which Kosminski said he could not pay because it was the Jewish Sunday. He was given until the Monday to pay (*Lloyd's Weekly Newspaper*, 15 December 1889; *The Times*, 16 December 1889).

By July 1890, Kosminski was exhibiting mental problems which were a matter of sufficient concern for him to be admitted to Mile End Old Town workhouse. He was living at 3 Sion Square, said in the records to have been the residence of his 'brother' Wolf Kozminsky, but in fact the home of Aaron's brother-in-law,

Woolfe Abrahams (*b.* 1861, Poland), a master tailor, and his wife, Aaron's sister Betsy. Aaron was discharged three days later into the care of his brother, most probably Woolfe Abrahams, but might have been another brother.

If the Swanson marginalia are correct, he was under 24-hour surveillance by the City CID prior to February 1891, and at some point taken for identification by the Metropolitan Police, before being allowed to return to his brother's house. As Aaron was removed a short time later to the workhouse from 16 Greenfield Street (the home of another brother-in-law, Morris Lubnowski, and Aaron's sister Matilda; or possibly another house in Greenfield Street, where Aaron's brother Isaac, who at some point changed his own surname to Abrahams, lived), this surveillance was probably maintained in Greenfield Street, probably no.16.

On 4 February 1891 Aaron Kosminskiwas taken by his family from 16 Greenfield Street, to Mile End Old Town Workhouse. On this occasion Aaron Kosminski's admittance to the workhouse infirmary would result in his certification as insane and he would spend the rest of his life in asylums.

Medical Records
Mile End Old Town Workhouse
Religious Creed Register

Date of admission:	12 July 1890
Date of discharge:	15 July 1890
Christian name:	Aaron
Surname	Kosminski
Born in the year:	1865
From where admitted:	3 Sion Square
Religious creed:	Hebrew
Name of informant:	Brother
Discharged or dead to:	Brother

Colney Hatch
The Register of Patients lists him as:

Admission no.	11,190
Date of Admission	7th February 1891
Date of Continuation of reception Order 8 Jan 1893	9 Jan 1892
Christian and Surname at length	Aaron Kozminsky
Sex	*Male*
Age	26
Condition of Life and previous occupation	Hair-dresser
Previous Place of Abode	16 Greenfield St., Mile End

Union, County, or Borough to Which chargeable	Mile End
By whose Authority sent	H.C. Chambers
Dates of Medical Certificates and by whom signed	6th Feb. 1891. E.K. Houchin
Form of Mental Disorder	Mania
Supposed Cause of Insanity	
Bodily Condition and Name of Disease	
If any	Fair
Duration of existing Attacks	6 months
Age on first attack	25
Date of Discharge, Removal, or Death	19.4.94

He was under the care of the Mile End Old Town Relieving officer, although the Quarterly Returns of pauper asylum patients supported by their Boards of Guardians never includes his name. Since at his death his family took charge and erected a sandstone headstone for him, they may have retained some financial interest in contributing to his support. The headstone gives his surname as 'Kosminski', for which reason we have preferred this spelling.

The undated statement of particulars accompanying his certification and signed by Mile End Relieving Officer M. Whitfield gives his name as Koziminski, and Wolf's address as 3 rather than 8 Lion Square. Otherwise, it follows the form of the Colney Hatch Admissions Book Register, without the red ink addenda.

The Admissions Book records him thus:

(Middlesex County Lunatic Asylum, Colney Hatch Register of Admissions. Males. Vol.3, f.31)

Regd. No. of Admission	11,190
	Aaron Kozminski
Order signed by	H. Chambers Esq., J.P.
Reception order dated	6th day of February 1891
Age	26
Parish	Mile End Old Town
Civil State	Single
Previous Occupation	Hairdresser
Religious Persuasion	Hebrew
If first attack	No
Age on first attack	25
Previous Treatment	Mile End Old Town Workhouse July 1890
Duration of existing attack	6 months *[added in red]* 6 years
Supposed Cause	Unknown *[added in red]* Self-abuse

Subject to Epilepsy	No
Suicidal	No
Dangerous to Others	No
Any relative afflicted with insanity	Not known
Nearest known relative	Wolf Kosminski (brother)
	8 Lion Square
	Commercial Rd E1.

Facts indicating insanity observed by Medical Man
He declares that he is guided and his movements altogether controlled by an instinct that informs his mind, he says that he knows the movements of all mankind, he refuses food from others because he is told to do so, and he eats out of the gutter for the same reason.

2. *Other Facts Indicating Insanity Communicated by Others*
Jacob Cohen, 51 Carter Lane, St Paul's EC says that he goes about the streets and picks up bits of bread out of the gutter and eats them, he drinks water from the tap & he refuses food at the hands of others. He took up a knife and threatened the life of his sister. He is very dirty and will not be washed. He has not attempted any kind of work for years.

Signed E.M. Houchin
23 Hugh St. Stepney

[His case notes follow here]:

Form of Disorder	Mania
Observations	

Ward 9.B3.10
On admission patient is extremely deluded & morose. As mentioned in the certificate he believes that all his actions are dominated by an 'Instinct'. This is probably mental hallucination. Answers questions fairly but is inclined to be reticent and morose. Health fair.

F. Bryant

1891 Feb 10: Is rather difficult to deal with on account of the dominant character of his delusions. Refused to be bathed the other day as his 'Instinct' forbade him.

F. Bryant

April 21: Incoherent, apathetic, unoccupied; still has the same 'instinctive' objection to the weekly bath; health fair.

Wm Seward

1892 Jan 9: Incoherent; at times excited & violent – a few days ago he took up a chair, and attempted to strike the charge attendant: apathetic as a rule, and refuses to occupy himself in any way; habits cleanly. health fair.

Wm Seward

Nov 17: Quiet and well behaved. Only speaks German [?Yiddish]. Does no work.

Cecil J. Beadles

1893 Jan 18: Chronic Mania: intelligence impaired; at times noisy, excited & incoherent; unoccupied; habits cleanly; health fair.

Wm Seward

April 8:Incoherent; quiet lately, fair health.

Cecil J. Beadles

Sept 18: Indolent, but quiet and clean in habits, never employed. Answers questions concerning himself.

Cecil J. Beadles

1894 April 13: demented and incoherent, health fair.

C. Beadles

April 19th Discharged. Relieved. Leavesden.

Wm Seward
(Middlesex Asylum. Colney Hatch.
Male Patients Day Book. New Series. No. 20)

The Leavesden Case register in the London Metropolitan Archives retains sparse notes of his latter years thus:

10.9.10: Faulty in his habits, he does nothing useful & cannot answer questions of a simple nature. BH poor. AKM

29.9.11: Patient is dull & vacant. Faulty & unhealthy in habits. Does nothing useful. Nothing can be got by questions. B H weak. H.C.S.

15.4.12: Didn't test negative. FH

6.9.12: No replies can be got; dull & stupid in manner & faulty in his habits. Requires constant attention. BH weak. AKM

16.1.13: Patient is morose in manner. No sensible reply can be got by questions. He mutters incoherently. Faulty and untidy in his habits. BH weak. AKM

16.7.14: Incoherent and excitable: troublesome at times: Hallucinations of hearing. Untidy – BH fair. G.P

14.2.15: Pat merely mutters when asked questions. He has hallucinations of sight and hearing and is very excitable at times. Does not work. Clean but untidy in dress. BH fair. DNG.

2.2.16: Patient does not know his age or how long he has been here. He has hallucinations of sight and hearing & is at times very obstinate. Untidy but clean, does no work, B.H. good. JM

Register of Patients Leavesden Asylum [loose papers]
1894

Name:	Aaron Kosminski
Date of Admission:	19 April 1894
Parish:	Mile End
Religion:	Jew
Age on Admission:	29
Mental Diagnosis:	Dem Sec [Secondary Dementia]

1.4.14	Patient has hallucinations of sight and hearing, is very excitable and troublesome at times, very untidy, bodily condition fair.
1.3.15	No improvement.
1.11.15	Patient has cut over left eye caused by knock on tap in washhouse.
8.7.16	No improvement.
5.4.17	No improvement.
26.5.18	Patient put to bed passing loose motions with blood and mucous.
27.5.18	Transferred to 8a.
3.6.18	Diarrhoea ceased. Ordered up by Dr. Reese.
28.1.19	Put to bed with swollen feet.
20.2.19	Put to bed with swollen feet and feeling unwell. Temp 99°.
13.3.19	Hip broken down.
22.3.19	Taken little nourishment during day, bu very noisy.
23.3.19	Appears very low. Partaken of very little nourishment during day.
24.3.19	Died in my presence at 5.05a.m. Marks on body, sore right hip and left leg. Signed S. Bennett, night attendant.

Weight taken on 17 May 1915, 7st 8lb 10oz
On the February 1919, 6st 12lb

Note dated 25 March 1919 to Mr Friedlander, Undertaker of Duke Street, United Synagogue, London E. The body of Aaron Kosminki. Signed by H. W. Abrahams, 'The Dolphin', Whitechapel E., London, 25th March 1919. Relation to deceased: brothers.

(The signature was long-believed to be H.W. Abrahams, which caused much confusion about the relationship being given as 'brothers', but if the reading I & W by researcher Chris Philips is correct, it being the initials of Isaac and Woolf, then the relationship is explicable.)

Another document, dated 30 March 1919 from G. Friedlander, sexton and officer of the Burial Society, St James Place, Aldgate, E.C.3, to A.J. Freeman at Leavesden Asylum, acknowledges receipt of a certificate dated 28 March registering Aaron Kosminski's death.

Aaron Kosminski was buried by the Burial Society of the United Synagogue on 27 March 1919 at East Ham Cemetary at a total cost of £12. 5s. His address was given as 5 Ashcroft Road, Bow, which was the home of his brother-in-law, Morris Lubnowksi (whose family subsequently changed their name to Lubnowski-Cohen).

The inscription on the grave is no longer legible, but a transcription made by one of the authors in 1990 read: 'Aaron Kosminski who died the 24th of March 1919. Deeply missed by his brother, sisters, relatives and friends. May his dear soul rest in peace'.

H.W. Abrahams of 'The Dolphin' has not been identified. The Dolphin was a pub at 97–99 Whitechapel Road. In 1919, the licensees were Mark Abrahams (who had taken the pub over in 1917), and Edward Cecil Moore. Mark Abrahams was the son of Aaron's brother, Isaac, who was now retired and living with his son and daughter-in-law at the pub.

The first clear reference to Kosminski as Jack the Ripper was made in the Macnaghten memoranda of 1894. In the copy deposited in Scotland Yard, **Sir Melville Macnaghten** described him thus:

Kosminski, a Polish Jew, & resident in Whitechapel. This man became insane owing to many years indulgence in solitary vices. He had a great hatred of women, specially of the prostitute class, and had strong homicidal tendencies; he was removed to a lunatic asylum about March 1889. There were many circs connected with this man which made him a strong 'suspect'.

The similarity with Anderson's suspect, 'whose utterly unmentionable vices reduced him to a lower level than that of the brute' is apparent.

In the rather fuller version left with his daughter, known as the Aberconway version, Macnaghten wrote:

'the very heart of the district where the murders took place', rather than 'Whitechapel' included his belief that Kosminski was still in an asylum and concluded: 'This man in appearance strongly resembled the individual seen by the City P. C. near Mitre Square.'

Philip Loftus recalled a possible third version of the memoranda seen by him 20 years previously, in which the suspect was described as 'a Polish-Jew cobbler nicknamed "**Leather Apron**"'.

Major Arthur Griffiths, in *Mysteries of Police and Crime* (1898), wrote:

But the police, after the last murder, had brought their investigations to the point of strongly suspecting several persons, all of them known to be homicidal lunatics, and against three of these they held very plausible and reasonable grounds of suspicion. Concerning two of them the case was weak, although it was based on certain colourable facts. One was a Polish Jew, a known lunatic, who was at large in the district of Whitechapel at the time of the murder, and who, having afterwards developed homicidal tendencies, was confined in an asylum. This man was said to resemble the murderer by the one person who got a glimpse of him – the police-constable in Mitre Court [sic]

George R. Sims, clearly citing information derived from Macnaghten, but not naming the suspect, wrote in *The Referee*, 22 September 1907:

The first man was a Polish Jew of curious habits and strange disposition, disposition, who was the sole occupant of certain premises in Whitechapel after night-fall. This man was in the district during the whole period covered by the Whitechapel murders, and soon after they ceased certain facts came to light which showed that it was quite possible that he might have been the Ripper. He had at one time been employed in a hospital in Poland. He was known to be a lunatic at the time of the murders, and some-time afterwards he betrayed such undoubted signs of homicidal mania that he was sent to a lunatic asylum.

The policeman who got a glimpse of Jack in Mitre Court said, when some time afterwards he saw the Pole, that he was the height and build of the man he had seen on the night of the murder...

They [the Polish Jew and the second suspect] were both alive long after the horrors had ceased, and though both were in an asylum, there had been a considerable time after the cessation of the Ripper crimes during which they were at liberty and passing about among their fellow men.

A decisive mention of Kosminski is made in the Swanson marginalia, glossing Anderson's suspect as sketchily described in Sir Robert Anderson's memoirs, *The Lighter Side of My Official Life*.

Anderson said the suspect was a male, low-class Polish Jew, living in Whitechapel; had people (almost certainly meaning a family or co-habitees) to protect him, and who practised 'utterly unmentionable vices' (presumably masturbation, which corresponds with the 'solitary vices' of Macnaghten). Anderson said little more, but, 'I will merely add that the only person who ever had a good view of the murderer unhesitatingly identified the suspect the instant he was confronted with him; but he refused to give evidence against him.' He continued:

> because the suspect was also a Jew and also because his evidence would convict the suspect, and witness would be the means of murderer being hanged, which he did not wish to be left on his mind.
>
> And after this identification which suspect knew, no other murder of this kind took place in London after the suspect had been identified at the Seaside Home where he had been sent by us with difficulty in order to subject him to identification, and he knew he was identified. On suspect's return to his brother's house in Whitechapel, he was watched by police (City CID), by day and night. In a very short time the suspect with his hands tied behind his back, he was sent to Stepney Workhouse and then to Colney Hatch and died shortly afterwards – Kosminski was the suspect.

Some details provided by Macnaghten and Swanson do not fit what is known about Aaron Kosminski. Macnaghten says the suspect was committed to the asylum in about March 1889, which is not confirmed by the extant medical records (*cf.* **Hyam Hyams**); nor do the records suggest Aaron Kosminski had a great hatred of women, especially prostitutes, or that he was homicidal. Swanson says the suspect died soon after committal, which was not the case with Aaron Kosminski. Otherwise, however, Aaron Kosminski fits the details of the suspect 'Kosminski' given by Anderson and Swanson. In addition, no other Kosminski has been found in any asylum in England and Wales, from 1888 on.

The case for identifying Kosminski as Jack the Ripper is that Anderson was a senior and informed policeman and the only one to make a positive statement that the Ripper's identity was known. Anderson appears to have been a man of integrity and keen religious convictions which make extreme exaggeration or outright lying improbable, making him a reliable contemporary witness. Although Anderson does not name his suspect, Swanson states it was 'Kosminski'. Research has failed to unearth a viable alternative Kosminski to Aaron, and nothing in the data known about him conflicts with Anderson's description.

The case against Aaron Kosminski being Jack the Ripper is the length of time that he remained at large after the killings stopped, as George R. Sims observed, and his non-violent and non-homicidal behaviour in the asylum, which has suggested to some commentators that he was a harmless imbecile who could not have been Anderson's suspect or, indeed, ever been seriously suspected by him or anyone else of having committed the murders. Furthermore, three of the four

Scotland Yard officers who apparently knew of, and commented on Anderson's suspect did not endorse his opinion (Macnaghten, Abberline and Littlechild), while the fourth (Swanson) includes puzzling data, parts of which conflict with Anderson's description and known facts.

Some commentators have questioned Anderson's story, challenged his integrity and disbelieved the assertion by Anderson and Swanson that an eye-witness identification took place. It has been suggested that both Anderson and Swanson were victims of geriatric self-delusion (*The Complete History of Jack the Ripper*).

See Robert House, 'Aaron Kosminski Reconsidered', *Ripperologist*, 58, March 2005; Robert House, 'The Kosminski File', *Ripperologist*, 65, March 2006; Scott Nelson, '*Kosminski's Relatives*', *Ripperologist*, 39, February 2002; Chris Phillips 'Kosminski's Brother' http://forum.casebook.org/showthread.php?t=3902; Christopher Scott, *Jack the Ripper: A Cast of Thousands*.

KOSMINSKI, ISAAC (1851–1924)

Brother of **Aaron Kosminski**, with whom Aaron may have been living prior to one or more of his incidents of hospitalisation.

Born Icek Szymche Kozminska in Klodawa, in 1851. He emigrated to London in the 1870s, when for some reason he changed his surname to Abrahams, adopting his father's forename as his surname. In 1886, when his children Esther and Woolf were admitted to the Jews' Free School, the family was living at 74 Greenfield Street, where Aaron may have been living with them.

In 1917, his son Marks (anglicised to Mark) became landlord of the Dolphin, a pub at 97–99 Whitechapel Road, and would stay there until 1923, for most of that time apparently in partnership with Edward Cecil Moore. Then, in 1919, an H.W. Abrahams (see Aaron Kosminski for further information) of that address, identified as Aaron's brother, signed a receipt for his body to Mr Friedlander, undertaker of Duke Street Synagogue.

KOSMINSKI, MARTIN (*b.* 1845)

Jewish immigrant, known to **Joseph Hyam Levy**. Born Kalisch, Poland, son of a furrier. Married, 1872, at Duke's Place Synagogue. Took British naturalisation, 1877, and conducted furrier's business at various addresses until 1922, when the business continued under his son's name. His naturalisation application was supported by Joseph Hyam Levy, one of the companions of **Joseph Lawende**'s when **Catherine Eddowes** was seen outside Mitre Square with the man who was to be her murderer. While Mr Levy denied having taken in the man's appearance, one newspaper believed he knew more than he was saying, and it has been suggested he might have recognised that man with Eddowes as an associate or relative of Martin Kosminski.

Research has failed to establish any connection between Martin and Aaron Kosminski.

KOSMINSKI, WOLF

Described in Colney Hatch Asylum records as the 'nearest known relative' and brother of Aaron **Kosminski**, and resident at 3 Sion Square. Census records show that this address was the home of Kosminski's brother-in-law Wolf Abrahams, with whom 'Wolf Kosminski' is presumably to be identified.

KOZEBRODSKY, 'ISAACS' M.

Friend of **Louis Diemschütz**. Came down from International Workingmen's Educational Club with Diemschütz and **Morris Eagle** to examine the woman lying in the passage when Diemschütz, after seeing his wife in the downstairs parlour, reported the presence of **Elizabeth Stride**'s body.

Convicted with Diemschütz the following March when they fought with policemen whom they took to be reinforcements for a local mob attacking the clubhouse after an anti-rabbinical demonstration by members in support of the unemployed.

KRANZ, PHILIP (1859–1922)

Original name Jacob Rombro.

Witness at **Elizabeth Stride**'s inquest. Born in Podolia, Russia, fled the pogroms of 1881 and spent some time in Paris as a student. Came to London and changed his name on advice from Morris Winchevsky (formerly Leopold Benedikt). He became editor of *Arbeter Fraint*, published from offices behind the International Workingmen's Educational Club. In 1889, Kranz moved to America and became editor of *Arbeter Zeitung*.

From 29 to 30 September 1888, he was in the offices of *Arbeter Fraint* from 9pm until the discovery of the body at 1am. His office door and window were closed, and he heard nothing above the singing from the club. On being told of the body, he looked at it and went to find a policeman.

KUER, MRS

Laundress and landlady at 22 Batty Street (*see* **Batty Street Lodger**).

Described as a stout, middle-aged German woman, who spoke very bad English. She was the wife of a seaman (*Evening News*, 16, 18 October 1888). At the centre of confused and occasionally contradictory news reporting, when it was claimed a lodger left a bloodstained shirt with her on the morning of 30 September 1888.

KUHRT, SERGEANT TIMM NICOLAUS (b. 1845)

Born Germany 1845; joined the **Metropolitan Police** in 1874 (warrant no. 58012). Promoted to sergeant (CID) in 1884, transferred to G Division on 21 July 1888 and retired to pension, 1899.

Sgt. Kuhrt was sent by **Inspector Moore** to interview **John McCormac**, who lived with **Alice McKenzie**. He also interviewed McKenzie's landlady, **Elizabeth Ryder**. In February 1891, he submitted a report concerning the antecedents of **Frances Coles**, and in March 1891, concerning those of **Thomas Sadler**.

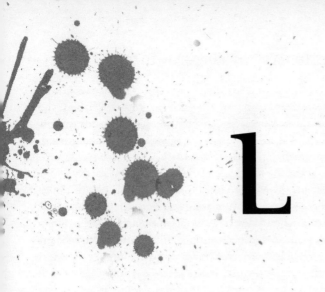

L

LABOUCHERE, HENRY DU PRÉ, MP (1831–1912)

Tentative theorist.

Radical MP, best remembered for his amendment to the Criminal Law Amendment Act of 1885, which replaced the obsolete Tudor statute imposing capital punishment for buggery with an enforceable two-year sentence for homosexual practices.

His journal, *Truth* (11 October 1888), suggested that, 'The handwriting of [the **Jack the Ripper letters**] is remarkably like that of the forgeries which *The Times* published, and which they ascribed to Mr Parnell. I do not suggest that the *The Times* forger is the Whitechapel Murderer, although this, of course, is possible; but it may be that the forger takes pride in his work, and wishes to keep his hand in' (*Cf.* **Parnell Commission.**)

LA BRUCKMAN, ARBIE aka JOHN FRANCIS (*b. c.* 1860)

Suspect, suggested in 2003 (Mike Conlon, 'A Tale of Two Frenchys'. Casebook dissertations), on the basis of an alleged trial in London in 1890, reported in the New York *World*, 30 April 1891, and the *Daily Continent* the following day.

A Moroccan (or possibly Algerian) seaman, supposedly cousin to Amir ben Ali, the Algerian convicted of **Carrie Brown**'s murder, and the suspect described as 'Frenchy no. 2' in that case, where ben Ali was 'Frenchy no. 1'.

While Ali was arrested as a suspicious resident of the hotel in which Carrie Brown was killed, the initial police statements said that his cousin La Bruckman, of similar appearance but with a lighter complexion, moustache and hair, was the prime suspect. Although New York police failed to find 'Frenchy no. 2' and turned their energies to concocting a case against 'Frenchy no. 1', he was actually arrested in New Jersey during April as 'Suspect no. 120' in the 'Old Shakespeare' case and questioned by New York police detective

McCloskey, who declared he was indeed 'Frenchy no. 2', but was not the murderer.

Allegedly La Bruckman said he had been arrested in London on suspicion of being Jack the Ripper; had been held in custody for a month before being tried and cleared, whereupon he was given £100 and a suit of clothes as compensation for his wrongful arrest. It was said that he had a savage temper, enjoyed slaughtering and dismembering injured cattle on the Meyer Goldsmith's National Line of cattle freighters, which he had worked between London and New York for 14 years, and fought fiercely with seven officers when arrested in London, injuring one.

No trace of any such trial in London has been found, and although it has been established that National Line vessels were in London on the Ripper murder nights, it has not been shown that La Bruckman was on any of them.

LACKNER, ELLEN MAY (1909–2005)

Informant. Cousin of **Joseph Gorman Sickert**, who told **Paul Feldman**, Melvyn Fairclough (*The Ripper and the Royals*) and Paul Begg in 1992 that parts of Joseph's tale concerning his mother's illegitimate parentage were circulating in the family while he was still a child. To the best of her recollection **Walter Sickert** might have been proposed as Alice Margaret (Crook) Gorman's father, and any mention of Jack the Ripper was solely intended to deter people from making close enquiries.

L'AFFAIRE JACK L'EVENTREUR

Book by Christian Coudurier (Paris: Publibook, 2004).

Forty-five page introduction to the case in French. Examines the usual suspects reasonably accurately without going into great detail.

LAMB, DAVID CRICHTON (1866–1951)

Theorist.

Salvation Army Commissioner. Made an officer of the Salvation Army in 1884, married Mary Clinton (*d.* 1939), a Salvation Army officer, in 1888. Created a CMG in 1934. A very frequent contributor of letters to *The Times* and occasional early radio broadcaster.

In his memoirs, published in *Tit-Bits*, 23 September 1939, he recalled that a visiting signwriter discussing the murders had remarked, 'I'll tell you who will be the next one to go – Carrotty Nell' (i.e. **Frances Coles**). Noting 'Carrotty Nell' was indeed killed subsequently, and recalling the man's 'visions of blood' and 'strange demeanour', Lamb concluded he was the Ripper. Lamb was subsequently misremembered by Colin Wilson for some years as **General Booth** suspecting his secretary.

(Obituary in *The Times*, 9 July 1952.)

LAMB, PC HENRY, 252H (*b.* 1851)

Witness at **Elizabeth Stride**'s inquest.

Served three years with 60th Rifles and worked at the British Museum for three years before joining the **Metropolitan Police** in 1875 (warrant no. 58824). Retired on pension, 1901.

On duty in Commercial Road early morning, 30 September 1888, he was at the corner of Grove Street when two men appeared and said, 'Come on! There's been another murder!' He accompanied them, followed by Police Constable **William Gunner**. Lamb sent one of the two men for assistance from the police station, then shut the gates to make sure no one left and searched the Club interior and yard. He remained at Berner Street until daybreak.

LANCET, THE

Professional medical journal, founded in 1823 by Thomas Wakley, with a general policy of challenging the exclusiveness and conservatism of the medical establishment. On 19 September 1888, it reported the details of **Annie Chapman**'s injuries, which coroner **Wynne Baxter** had tried to exclude from publication, and concluded, like Baxter and Dr **George Bagster Phillips**, that the killer's speed, 'pointed to the improbability of anyone but an expert performing the mutilations described in so apparently skilful a manner.' However, *cf.* **Dr Savage**.

LANE, CATHERINE

Witness at **Elizabeth Stride**'s inquest. Charwoman, married to dock labourer, Patrick Lane. Resident at 32 Flower and Dean Street since 11 February 1888, but had known Stride for six or seven years. Said Stride came to the lodging-house following a quarrel with **Michael Kidney** (denied by Kidney). Lane last saw her between 7 and 8pm on the night of her death.

LANGAN, JOHN (*fl.* 1888)

Suspect, named and cleared in 1888.

Arrested in France, in October 1888, as a vagrant without papers or means of support. He claimed to have come to France from Scotland, looking for work as a miner; finding none, he now wished to be returned to South Wales. Mr E.W. Bonham, British consul in Boulogne, thought he resembled a sketch of a suspect in the *Daily Telegraph*, refused him aid to return to Britain as he had been born in America, and persuaded the French police to detain him while he asked Scotland Yard for instructions. Within a week, Scotland Yard had established his innocence and he was released (HO144/220/A49301, f3).

LANGHAM, SAMUEL FREDERICK (1823–1908)

Coroner, conducted **Catherine Eddowes**' inquest at Golden Lane Mortuary, 4 and 11 October 1888. (HO144/221 A493018C f.167), **Inspector McWilliam**'s report on the opening of Eddowes' inquest, misreports Langham's initials as F.H.)

Educated at Holloway Academy. Articled to his father, Under-Sheriff S.F. Langham. Deputy Coroner for Westminster 1849. Coroner for London and Southwark, 1884. Secretary, then President of the Coroners' Society of England and Wales.

In June 1887, Langham received the thigh of the Rainham torso, which was found washed up at the Temple Stairs. Without consulting the police, he sent it for immediate burial and declined to hold an inquest on the grounds that a single body part was inadequate material for coronial enquiry into an unproven death.

Langham conducted Eddowes' inquest expeditiously and his notes are preserved in the London Metropolitan Archives. In an interview in *Cassell's Saturday Journal*, 30 August 1899, he said, 'It has always been my surmise that Jack the Ripper had some means of getting down the manholes leading to the sewers and thus disappearing from the scene of his exploits.'

(*See* **Robert Lindford**, **John Savage** and **David O'Flaherty**, in *Ripperologist* nos. 66 and 67 (April and May 2006.)

LARDY, JOHN

At 10.30pm, on 18 October 1888, John Lardy – who lived in Redman's Row, Mile End – and two companions saw a man enter and almost immediately leave the Grave Maurice, a pub opposite London Hospital, then cross the road and talk to two women, whom Lardy believed to be prostitutes.

Lardy and one of his companions followed the man, who eventually went into a house in King Street, a narrow road running off Royal Mint Street, emerging half an hour later, apparently having changed his clothing. They lost track of him in the very thick fog. Lardy described the man as aged between 40 and 45-years of age, and between 5ft 11in to 6ft tall. 'He wore a low hat with a square crown, but I cannot describe either his trousers or boots. He had the appearance of an American. His cheekbones were high and prominent, his face thin, cheeks sunken, and he had a moustache only, his cheeks and chin being clean shaven. The moustache was, I believe, a false one, for it was all awry, one end pointing upward, and the other towards the ground. His hair was dark, apparently black, and somewhat long.'

It was reported a man believed to be the one seen by Lardy was arrested in Bermondsey at 1am and was taken to the police station, where his conduct, demeanour and appearance aroused great suspicion, and his apprehension and general particulars were wired to the City police, who kept him under observation (*Morning Advertiser*, *Daily News*, *Daily Telegraph*, *Evening News*, 19 October 1888).

Lardy seems to have been taken seriously because he had an interview with **Inspector McWilliam** of the City Police (*Daily News*, 19 October 1888), but it was duly stated by both the Metropolitan and the City Police that no one,

American or otherwise, was arrested or was being watched in Bermondsey (*Echo*, *Evening News*, 19 October 1888).

In *The Lodger*, an effort was made to identify the man seen by Lardy with the **Batty Street lodger** and with **Frances Tumblety**, the American arrested in Bermondsey being dismissed as a look-alike, and the police denial being ascribed to an unwillingness to admit to an American being sought and the wrong one arrested.

LARKINS, EDWARD KNIGHT (*b. c.*1841– d.1895)
Contemporary theorist.

Clerk in HM Customs Statistical Department. Born in Dover, Kent. Married Isabella Learkins (*b. c.* 1836).

Atrocities committed by Portuguese peasants in the Peninsular War persuaded Larkins that the Ripper must be a Portuguese cattleman sailing regularly on the vessels, *City of London* and *City of Oporto*. He settled on **Manuel Cruz Xavier** as **Mary Ann Nichols**' murderer, and concluded **Annie Chapman**'s was a copycat killing by **Jose Laurenco** (since Xavier did not return to England). When Laurenco deserted ship in Oporto, in October 1888, Larkins suggested he had worked in partnership with **Joao de Souza Machado**, who alone murdered **Kelly**. At 41, Machado was older than the others, and Larkins commented: 'being a man of mature age, the *sang froid* displayed upon the occasion of this murder is easily accounted for. This man's coolness seems to have stood him in good stead, as in order to avoid suspicion, he continued to come over until the month of March 1889.' Since, however, he did not come over in July, when **Alice McKenzie** was murdered, Larkins ascribed this killing to Joachim de Rocha, who had sailed with Xavier at the time of Nichols' murder.

On 10, 12 and 13 November 1888, Larkins visited police stations, offering his theory to **Moore, Williamson** and **Swanson**. Visited **Samuel Montague** MP on 19 November; **Swanson** on 8 December; **C.J. Darling** MP on 12 February 1889. He wrote to various authorities on 16, 17, 22 and 26 November, 3 and 12 December 1888, and 11 January, 9 March 1889 and 7 February 1893.

The *Daily News* (20 February 1891) published the results of Larkins' 'private inquiry'. HO144/221/A4930 ff.237–8 in the National Archives outlines his thinking. The Royal London Hospital have correspondence and papers relating to the evidence collected by Edward Larkins.

Larkins' theories were investigated by the police and the British consul in Oporto, and found to be invalid. He himself was not satisfied, feeling police had failed to recognise the overwhelming evidence that the criminal must be Portuguese; he had lists of shipping movements printed and distributed to various authorities, which apparently convinced the distinguished magistrate, **Montagu Williams**. By 1893, he was accusing Dr **Robert Anderson** of conniving at the escape of the murderer, and Anderson described him in a memo to the Home Office as 'a troublesome busybody'.

(*See* **Jack the Ripper: The 21st Century Investigation**.)

LAST VICTIM OF THE BLOODY TOWER, THE

Book by Millie Heenan (Pittsburgh, Pa: Dorrance Publishing, 2003).

Twenty-eight-page monograph, which links the Ripper murders to other outrageous villainies as a product of 'cultural extravagance'. Proposes **Prince Albert Victor** as the Ripper, killing prostitutes to avenge his mother's distress at his father's promiscuity. A cover-up ensures **James Maybrick** is blamed. No evidence is adduced.

LATEST ATROCITIES OF JACK THE RIPPER, THE

Anonymous pamphlet (Stuttgart: 1889).

Pall Mall Gazette (11 April 1888) reported that Johann Kelso received 14 days' imprisonment in Stuttgart for selling a pamphlet with this title.

LAURENCO, JOSE (*b.* 1862)

Contemporaneously alleged suspect. Portuguese seaman sailing between London and Oporto on the *City of Cork*. Advanced by **E.K. Larkins** as accomplice of **Joao de Souza Machado** in killing **Annie Chapman**, **Elizabeth Stride** and **Catherine Eddowes**, 'from a spirit of devilry', and possibly to emulate **Manuel Cruz Xavier**.

According to the shipping lists, he was not actually on board the vessel when it docked on 8 November 1888, opportunely for the **Kelly** murder. Initially, the ineffable Mr Larkins believed he was on board anyway, as a stowaway. Otherwise, as he sagely remarked, he could not have murdered Kelly. Subsequently, he concluded Kelly's murder was the singlehanded work of Machado.

A further mark of Laurenco's guilt lay in the annotation 'Conduct – Good' beside his name. All other crew-members were given 'Conduct – Very Good'.

LAVE, JOSEPH

Witness at **Elizabeth Stride**'s inquest.

Passed through Dutfield's Yard shortly before her murder. A Russian-born recent immigrant from USA, Lave was living temporarily at the International Workingmen's Educational Club. He told the press that fifteen or twenty minutes before the discovery of the body he went out for fresh air and walked about for five minutes or so. The yard was so dark, he had to grope his way along the passage wall, and there was definitely no body there. 'Everything was very quiet at the time, and I noticed nothing wrong.'

According to *The Identity of Jack the Ripper*, Lave told police that a stranger who pretended to be a Polish barber from George Yard (though obviously a Russian) was in the club 'earlier' that night. The description of the man is similar to **George Hutchinson**'s suspect, with the soft hat replaced by a peaked cap. No trace of this alleged statement has been found in police files or the press.

LAWENDE, JOSEPH (1847–1925)

Informant. Witness at **Catherine Eddowes'** inquest.

Born in Warsaw. Immigrated *c.* 1871, married Englishwoman, Anne, and had 9 children. Commercial traveller in the cigarette trade, resident at 45 Norfolk Road, Dalston, with business premises in St Mary Axe. 79 Fenchurch St was also offered as one of his addresses. By 1891, he was living in Tenter Street South, close to Frances Coles' murder site. Applied for British Naturalisation in April 1889, routinely investigated by Sgt. **William Turrell** CID, whose report dated 7 May 1889 noted Lawende was 'a very respectab[le] man, and is spoken well of by his sureties who consider him worthy of the certificate he asked for'. Turrell's signature was countersigned by **Superintendent Chisolm** (HO 144/311/B6288).

In company with Harry Harris and Joseph Hyam Levy, he stayed late at the Imperial Club, 16–17 Duke's Place, on the night of 29–30 September 1888, because of rain. All three prepared to leave at 1.30am (as checked by Lawende's watch and the club clock) and left within about four minutes. Approximately fifteen yards from the club, they saw a man and a woman standing at the entry of Church Passage, which led to Mitre Square. Mr Lawende subsequently identified the woman by her clothes as Catherine Eddowes, when shown her body in the mortuary.

Lawende, walking a little apart from the other two, was the only one to take in the man's appearance. *See* **Jack the Ripper, Descriptions Of** for his description. Lawende said the woman had her hand on her companion's chest; neither appeared to be angry and there was nothing about them to draw his attention, except Mr Levy remarked that the court ought to be watched. Lawende did not think he would recognise the man if he saw him again. **Donald Swanson** reported to the Home Office that Lawende (whom he misdescribed as 'Mr Lewin') only identified Eddowes by her clothes which, he remarked, 'is a serious drawback to the description of the man' (HO144/221/A49301C, ff148–159). **Inspector McWilliam** of the City Police also noted Lawende said, 'he does not think he should know the man again and he did not see the woman's face.' McWilliam, too, misdescribed him this time as 'Mr Lewend' (HO144/221/A49301C f.168). Despite this, the City Police regarded him as a very important witness and sequestered him from the press prior to the inquest. At the inquest itself, City Solicitor **Crawford** said, 'Unless the jury wish it, I have special reason for not giving details as to the appearance of this man.' The coroner assented and Lawende described no more than the man's clothes.

Major Henry Smith's memoirs describe Lawende as 'a sort of hybrid German' and make it clear that Smith believed Lawende to have furnished a detailed description of the Ripper. He says that he regarded Lawende as the more reliable because he refused to follow leading questions, was plainly uninterested by the previous murders and honestly stated that he doubted whether he would recognise the man again after his brief glance at him.

It is frequently suggested Lawende was the witness described by Dr **Robert Anderson** as the only person ever to have had a good sight of the murderer, especially as the **Swanson marginalia** add the further gloss that this witness was Jewish.

In February 1891 he may have been called in by police to see whether he could identify **Thomas Sadler** (*Daily Telegraph*, 18 February 1891), and in 1895 he may have been called in again to try and identify **William Grant** (Grainger). This suggests he might not have been Anderson's witness.

(*See* Adam Wood and Don Souden, "The Man Who Saw: The Face of Joseph Lawende Revealed", *Ripperologist*, 87, January 2008.)

LAWLEY, DET. SGT. (*fl.* 1888)

Accompanied **Major Smith** and DCs **Halse** and **Hunt** from Mitre Square to Leman Street Police Station, and from there accompanied Halse and Hunt to Goulston Street.

LAWRENCE –

Alleged witness.

At **Catherine Eddowes'** inquest, **Inspector Collard** said, 'I failed to find anything except the witnesses to be produced named Lawrence and Levy' (*see* **Joseph Hyam Levy**). Since no witness named Lawrence was ever produced, this was probably a garbling of 'Harris' (*see* **Harry Harris**) or **Lawende** .

LAWRENCE, MARY JANE

Several American newspapers on 10 November 1888 reported that this was the name of the victim of the Dorset Street murder. The name may have been given by a neighbour **Mrs Hewitt**. (*Cf.* **Mary Jane Kelly**.)

LEACH, DET. SGT. STEPHEN (*b.* 1851)

Joined the Metropolitan Police in 1872 (warrant no. 55317). Resigned to pension, 1897.

Leach and Sgt. **Eli Caunter** took Mrs **Jane Gillbank** and her daughter to inspect the troops at the Tower, since they – (erroneously, it proved) – believed they had seen **Martha Tabram** in the company of a private. On 8 September 1888, he was assigned with **Inspector Chandler** and **Sergeant Thick** to the Annie Chapman case

(MEPO 3/140 f11) and would attend her inquest. In mid–November, he and **Sgt. White** were sent to Willesden Junction and Euston respectively to detain a man who had aroused police suspicions in Manchester and who had boarded a train for London. Sgt. White took him into custody at Euston.

LEARY, JOHN (*fl.* 1888)
Suspect, identified and immediately cleared, 1888.

Guardsman, stationed at Wellington Barracks, Tower of London, in August 1888. PC **Thomas Barrett** identified him as a guardsman he had seen in Wentworth Street on the night of **Martha Tabram**'s murder, but Barrett gave a detailed account of his movements with **Private Law**, which exactly matched Law's account. At no time had they been near Wentworth Street and **Inspector Reid** concluded Barrett had made 'a great mistake' (MEPO 3/140 ff.52–59).

'LEATHER APRON' (*fl.* 1888)
Nickname of a man supposed to have been terrorising the local East End prostitutes. From police reports and newspaper accounts it would appear that the name was first mentioned following the murder of **Mary Ann Nichols**. **Sgt Thick** soon associated it with a man named **John Pizer** who was in due course arrested, but released and exonerated when he was able to provide a cast-iron alibi. The name first appeared in the press in some American newspapers on 4 September 1888, in lurid reports which described him as 'a character halfway between Dickens' Quilp and Poe's baboon. He is short, stunted and thick set. He has small, wicked black eyes and is half crazy' (*New York Times*, 4 September 1888). In Britain, he was mentioned only by the *Star*, which merely reported, 'With regard to the man who goes by the sobriquet of "Leather Apron," he has not, it is stated, been seen in the neighbourhood much for the past few nights, but this may mean nothing, as the women street wanderers declare that he is known as well in certain quarters of the West End as he is in Whitechapel.'

The *Star*, almost alone of English newspapers, began developing the 'Leather Apron' story, providing some colourful descriptions of the man: he was short and thickset, aged between 38–40; he had black hair, a black moustache and an exceptionally thick neck. His eyes glinted, his smile was repulsive and he wore a close-fitting cap and a leather apron. He walked soundlessly, carried a sharp knife and frequently threatened, 'I'll rip you up!' A *Star* reporter claimed to have interviewed 50 women in three hours, who all gave almost identical descriptions of him. He was supposed to be a specialist slipper maker, who had done no work for years; to live in common lodging-houses, a particular one being in Brick Lane; to have a pal called '**Mickeldy Joe**', and to hang around in the shadows opposite the Princess Alice in Commercial Street.

A number of people also claimed to know 'Leather Apron', notably **Timothy Donovan**, who said he had a little while earlier kicked him out of **Crossingham's Lodging House** for threatening a woman.

The dominant feature of the story was 'Leather Apron's' Jewish appearance and considerable anti-Jewish feeling developed in the East End, especially after the murder of Annie Chapman and the finding of a leather apron (actually **John Richardson**'s) in the yard close to the body.

On 7 September, **Inspector Helson (J Division)** said in a report to Scotland Yard: 'The inquiry has revealed the fact that a man named Jack Pizer, alias "Leather Apron", has for some considerable period been in the habit of illusing [sic] prostitutes in this, and other parts of the Metropolis, and careful search has been and is continued to be made to find this man in question that his movements may be accounted for on the night in question, although at present there is no evidence whatever against him' (MEPO 3/140 ff235–8).

This was the first suggestion that the police knew 'Leather Apron's' identity.

On Sunday, 9 September, Miss Lyons believed she met 'Leather Apron'.

On 10 September, Sergeant Thick arrested John Pizer at his family home at 22 Mulberry Street, where he had been hiding since the previous weekend, apparently not so much from the police, but for fear of being torn apart by the public.

Inspector Abberline summed up the story of 'Leather Apron' in a report dated 19 September:

In the course of our inquiries amongst the numerous women of the same class as the deceased it was ascertained that a feeling of terror existed against a man known as "Leather Apron" who it appeared have for a considerable time past been levying blackmail and ill-using them if his demands were not complied with although there was no evidence to connect him with the murder. It was however thought desirable to find him and interrogate him as to his movements on the night in question, and with that view searching inquiries were made at all common lodging-houses in various parts of the Metropolis but through the publicity given in the "Star" and other newspapers the man was made acquainted with the fact that he was being sought for and it was not until the 10th Inst. that he was discovered when it was found that he had been concealed by his relatives. On his being interrogated he was able however to give such a satisfactory account of his movements as to prove conclusively that the suspicions were groundless. (MEPO 3/140 ff.242–56).

When Pizer was able to provide a cast-iron alibi for **Mary Ann Nichols**' murder night, he was dismissed from the case and the 'Leather Apron' scare died down. Whether or not John Pizer was indeed the 'Leather Apron' who ill-used prostitutes and extorted money from them is not certainly known (*see* John Pizer, for further discussion). There is, however, evidence in the press that the public still believed an unknown man nicknamed 'Leather Apron' to be the murderer. (See **'Jenny'**.)

Almost from the day when the news story broke, some newspapers speculated that 'Leather Apron' was mythical, the *Echo* on 5 September 1888 even claiming that the prostitutes had talked about 'a "wild-looking man, wearing a leather apron," who had been seen about in Whitechapel lately, and was believed to be an escaped lunatic.' The Central News reported that over the weekend of the Chapman murder, the name 'Leather Apron' was often heard in street conversations, but more often than not was accompanied by a guffaw (*Evening News*, 11 September 1888).

In later years, Lincoln Springfield, one of the most celebrated journalists of his day, wrote in *Some Piquant People* that the story of 'Leather Apron' was developed by an American journalist named Harry Dam, who did not know that there really was a man in the locality with that nickname (John Pizer, though Springfield never named him). When Pizer in due course was able to prove himself completely innocent, the *Star* faced substantial libel damages and chief sub-editor Ernest Parke had the man brought to the newspaper's offices, where he accepted a nominal amount in full settlement of any claims he might have against the paper. T.P. O'Conner, founding editor of the *Star*, referred to this incident as a 'dexterous expedient', which saved his newspaper from 'a ruinous action for libel' (T.P. O'Connor, 'A London Reign of Terror. The Mystery of Jack the Ripper', 1929).

Philip Loftus stated the version of the **Macnaghten memoranda** he had seen described as 'Leather Apron' the suspect named in the other two versions as Kosminski.

See also **Buck's Row Suspect**, **George Godley**, **Julius Lipman**, **Emily Walter**.

LEATHER APRON: OR THE HORRORS OF WHITECHAPEL, LONDON
Book by Samuel E. Hudson (Philadelphia: Town Printing House, 1888); *Ripperological Preservation Society*, 1997.

Suggests **Nicolai Vassily** was Jack the Ripper.

LEDGER, INSPECTOR CHARLES (*b.* 1854)
Joined the Metropolitan Police in 1877 (warrant no. 61795). In 1888, Inspector in G Division. Drew plans of Dorset Street for **Mary Jane Kelly**'s inquest and Pinchin Street for inquest on the torso.

Retired, 1902.

LEE, ANNIE (*fl.* 1888)
Lodger at 18 George Street, who helped deputy **Mary Russell** take **Emma Smith** to the London Hospital, following the fatal assault that she sustained on 3 April 1888.

LEES, ROBERT JAMES (1849–1931)
Medium, alleged to have psychically identified the Ripper.

Born in Birmingham, but brought up in Hinckley, Leicestershire. Supposedly evinced clairvoyant gifts aged 13. Married, 1871. For some time worked for the *Manchester Guardian*. By 1888, he lived in Peckham and was noted as a philanthropist, radical friend of socialist leader Keir Hardie and prominent Christian Spiritualist. Subsequently resided in St Ives and Ilfracombe before retirement to Leicester. He wrote several books on spiritualism and was distinguished as a medium, giving private consultations. Allegedly he came to royal notice following a séance (variously described) at which the late Prince Consort spoke through Lees' mouth. For this reason, he supposedly became known as Queen Victoria's medium. Biographers of Victoria have found no such connection.

Lees' only certainly known involvement in the Ripper story was when he offered his mediumistic services to the police and was impolitely refused, as he noted in his diaries (quoted by **Melvin Harris** in *Jack the Ripper: The Bloody Truth*):

Tuesday 2nd October. Offered services to police to follow up East End murders – called a fool and a lunatic. Got trace of man from the spot in Berner Street. Wednesday 3rd October. Went to City police again – called a madman and fool. Thursday 4th October. Went to Scotland Yard – same result but promised to write to me

A letter received by Scotland Yard on 25 July 1889 and long believed to read, 'You have not caught me yet you see, with all your cunning, with all your ["Lees"] with all your blue bottles', in fact reads 'all your 'tecs' (see *Jack the Ripper: Letters From Hell*).

In April 1895, several American newspapers carried a story that an eminent London physician named Dr Howard had claimed that a distinguished London doctor was Jack the Ripper. On 28 April 1895, the Chicago *Sunday Times-Herald* published an expansion of the story, in which it was claimed Lees had a psychic impression of the murderer, whom he later recognised on a bus and was able to lead the police to his house, the murderer being the distinguished London doctor who was committed to an asylum in Islington under the pseudonym 'Thomas Mason, 124'. He was still alive in 1895, though the public had been told that he had died and been buried in Kensal Green cemetery. The newspaper did not identify the physician, but in later years he was associated with **Sir William Gull** and Dr **Thomas E. Stowell** told a variant of what appears to be the same story, which he says he was told by Gull's daughter.

Lees did not deny the story and Cynthia Legh, who knew Lees from 1912, reported in *Light*, the Journal of the College of Psychic Studies (autumn 1970), that she had heard him tell a variant half a dozen times. In Lees' version of the story, he obtained authority from Queen Victoria to assist the police and led them to the home of a doctor, whose wife held a position at court. The doctor was removed to a place of detention and a beggar who died in Seven Dials that night was buried in his place.

The Queen asked Lees to leave London for five years, lest rumours embarrassing the doctor's wife should emerge, and he was granted a pension for this period.

Lees' daughter Eva, both before and after his death, showed her father's clients and admirers 'documentary' evidence that he received a pension for his contribution to solving the Whitechapel murders. Grateful prostitutes are also supposed to have presented Lees with a gold cross, now in the possession of his great-granddaughter. When Lees died in 1931, the *Daily Express* published an abridged version of the *Sunday Times-Herald* story with the claim that this was a 'document' left by Lees to be opened after his death. The editorial trailer the day before publication indicated the paper harboured the gravest doubts about the document's validity. Most subsequent accounts of Lees as connected with the Ripper investigation are embellishments or garblings of the *Express* story. Melvin Harris has claimed the *Express* story was the deliberately fraudulent work of its crime correspondent, Cyril Morton.

Enquiries to Scotland Yard and the Home Office by Mrs Brackenbury of the Society for Psychical Research in 1931, and D.J. West in 1948, failed to unearth anyone who had heard of Lees, or any relevant files. Mrs Brackenbury's informants included the keeper of the Criminal Record Office since 1901 and **F.P. Wensley**.

Melvin Harris argued the *Sunday-Times Herald* story was a deliberate hoax perpetrated by journalist members of the Whitechapel Club in Chicago and also argued they drew on Lees' writings to embroider their story, pointing out that Lees claimed to have had a psychic experience aboard a Marble Arch omnibus in late 1884, and wrote about it on at least two occasions: once in 1886, in which he also mentioned R. Shaw and F. Beckwith, who also featured in the Chicago newspaper article. However, it has been claimed the Whitechapel Club had disbanded in 1894 (Dr. Larry Lorenz: 'The Whitechapel Club: Defining Chicago's Newspapermen in the 1890s' *American Journalism* 15.1., winter 1998), but Harris maintains early members Wallace Rice, Edward D. Miller, and John Kelley have written that the club existed in 1895 (*see Jack the Ripper: The Bloody Truth*. Also Melvin Harris, 'The Whitechapel Club', *Ripperologist*, 31 October 2000). Whether or not the Whitechapel Club was responsible for the elaborated version of the story involving Lees, the original tale attributed to Dr Howard may have other origins.

For an account of the Society for Psychical Research's 1949 dismissal of Lees' story, *see* Stewart P. Evans, 'R.J. Lees Again', *Ripper Notes*, 21, January 2005.

(Also see Bernard Brown, 'Robert Lees' Omnibus Journey',*Ripperologist* 16, April 1998; Stephen Butt, 'Robert James Lees, The Myth And The Man', *Ripperologist* 35, June 2001; Jennifer D Pegg, 'Robert James Lees : The Facts', *Ripperologist* 96, October 2008.)

LEESON, SERGEANT BENJAMIN CHARLES (1870–1946)

Reinforcement at the discovery of **Frances Coles'** body. Joined the Metropolitan Police on 13 February 1891 (warrant no. 76483). Posted to **H Division** as PC 282. Subsequently CID, where he was closely associated with **F.P. Wensley**. Invalided out, 1911, following bullet wounds sustained in the Siege of Sidney Street.

During his first month in the service, Frances Coles was killed. Leeson says, in his autobiography (*Lost London*, London: Stanley Paul and Co, 1934), that he heard a shrill whistle blast and made for Swallow Gardens, where he found Police Constable **Ernest Thompson** and two night-watchmen, one of them a plain-clothes policeman. Leeson describes the revived '**Leather Apron**' scare, which focused on **Jacobs** (suspect) and gives what may be an account of the suspicions of ordinary police on the ground after the Ripper murders:

I am afraid I cannot throw any light on the problem of the 'Ripper's' identity, but one thing I do know, and that is that amongst the police who were most concerned in the case there was a general feeling that a certain doctor, known to me, could have thrown quite a lot of light on the subject. This particular doctor was never very far away when the crimes were committed, and it is certain that the injuries inflicted on the victims could only have been done by one skilled in the use of the knife.

(*See also* **George Cullen**.)

LE GRAND, CHARLES (*b. c.*1853)

aka Capt. Anderson, Christian Briscony (possibly his real name), French Colonel, Charles Grand, Charles Grant, Charles Colnette Grandy, Christian Nelson (possibly *b.* 1853).

Criminal posing as a private detective, who with his partner **J.W. Batchelor**, acted conjointly with the Whitechapel **Vigilance Committee**, the *Evening News* and the *Daily Telegraph*, and was responsible for the story that, when found dead, **Elizabeth Stride** had been holding grapes bought from fruiterer **Matthew Packer**. Tentatively proposed as suspect in 1998.

Danish, possibly son of a Danish diplomat or someone connected with the Danish diplomatic service. In 1877, he was convicted for a series of thefts and sentenced to eight years in prison. Then, in 1887, he wrote a letter in red and violet ink to the Commissioner of the Metropolitan Police complaining about a constable and threatening to burn down buildings. By 1888, he had reinvented himself as Le Grand and was running a business as a private enquiry agent. In June 1889, he was convicted and sentenced to

two years in prison for sending threatening letters demanding money to a Harley Street surgeon, A. Malcolm Morris. Calling himself Charles Grant in 1891, he was charged with sending letters to various wealthy women threatening to kill them, if they did not pay him substantial sums of money. Curiously, he did not need money at the time that he did this, perhaps suggesting mental illness.

Described as 'a tall man of striking appearance' (*Daily* News, 29 September 1891). It is uncertain when he and J.W. Batchelor were hired by the Whitechapel Vigilance Committee, but it was probably before the murder of Elizabeth Stride. They were responsible for organising and overseeing the Committee's nightly patrols of Whitechapel ('Amateur Detectives at Work', *East London Advertiser*, 13 October 1888). This has encouraged researcher Tom Wescott to suggest Le Grand could have been Jack the Ripper and his knowledge of the patrols might have facilitated his escape from the crime scenes.

Le Grand and Batchelor questioned Matthew Packer and learned from him that he had sold grapes to a man and a woman, that he had watched them eating the grapes for nearly half an hour and had seen them stop by the gates of the Berner Street club, as if listening to the music (*see* **Sergeant Stephen White** for conflict between White's report and Packler's testimony). The detectives also learned Miss **Eva Harstein** and her sister, Mrs **Rosenfield**, had seen a blood-caked grapestalk and some flower petals in the entry to Dutfield's Yard and they recovered a grapestalk from rubbish swept by police into the drain in the yard. The *Evening News* prominently featured this revelation, compelling the police to immediately review the routine questioning of Packer and subject his testimony to close examination at Scotland Yard, where he was taken by the two private detectives, Le Grand and Batchelor.

(*Newmarket Journal,* 17 October 1891, 24 October 1891; *The Times*, 12 July 1877, 8 June 1889, 27 June 1889, 29 September 1891, 7 October 1891, 13 October 1891. Gerry Nixon, 'Le Grand of the Strand', *Ripperologist*, 18, August 1998; Tom Wescott, 'Jack and the Grapestalk', *Ripper Notes*, 25, January 2006.)

LEOPOLD II, KING OF THE BELGIANS (1835–1909)

Suspect. Proposed by Jacquemine Charrot-Lodwidge, a researcher employed by **Daniel Farson**. Reigned 1865–1909. Best remembered for employing Henry Morton Stanley to explore Central Africa and establishing the Belgian Congo, which he exploited ruthlessly and inhumanely for personal gain.

The suspect theory is based on: the *fact* that Leopold's private life was scandalous; the *speculation* that his occasional English residence might be a house described by **R.J. Lees**'s daughter as occupied by her father's suspect who, she believed, was of far higher rank than a doctor; the *unsubstantiated suppositions* that Leopold personally visited the Congo and acquired sadistic tastes from witnessing the atrocities there, and that he made unrecorded visits to London that coincided with the Ripper murders.

LE QUEUX, WILLIAM TUFNELL (1864–1927)

Writer and theorist. Educated in London and Pagli, Genoa. Travelled widely. Journalist, appointed foreign editor of *The Globe*, 1891. Resigned, 1893, and devoted himself to freelance writing. His massive output includes novels and books of sensational gossip. An early and influential perpetrator of spy scares who played a not-insignificant part in the early history of what would become MI5. By his own account he was also a diplomat, an explorer, a flying buff and a pioneer of radio broadcasting.

In 1888, he reported the Whitechapel murders for the *Globe*, later recounting how he and Charles Hands and Lincoln Springfield, 'practically lived as a trio in Whitechapel, and as each murder was committed we wrote up picturesque and lurid details while we stood on the very spot where the tragedy had occurred. One evening Springfield would publish a theory of how the murders had been done; next night Charlie Hands would have a far better theory and then I would weigh in with another theory in the *Globe*.' Lincoln Springfield mentioned that the *Star*, which began publication in 1888, was at least a year old before Hands joined it in London.

After the October Revolution, Le Queux wrote several books on Russia. *The Rascal Monk* (1917) was a life of Rasputin. Subsequently, in *Minister of Evil* (1918), Le Queux claimed it had been based on documents found among Rasputin's effects. Later still, in *Things I Know about Kings, Celebrities and Crooks* (1923), he claimed the documents had included a manuscript on 'Great Russian Criminals', typed in French from Rasputin's dictation. This stated Dr **Alexander Pedachenko** was Jack the Ripper. In elaborating the case against him, Le Queux included information from this document, allegedly gleaned from Russians **Nideroest** and **Zverieff.**

In *Minister of Evil*, Le Queux mentions a man from Tver who escaped detection after murdering a young girl. This, too, could be a reference to Pedachenko.

It has been seriously doubted whether Le Queux received any such documents from Russia at all, and it is virtually certain Rasputin never dictated the document on 'Great Russian Criminals' ascribed to him.

Le Queux himself claimed he had not mentioned Pedachenko in earlier books on Russia, as it was only after 1918 that he acquired corroborative proof of his existence.

LETCHFORD, CHARLES

Resident of 30 Berner Street. Widely reported in the press after the murder of **Elizabeth Stride** as saying, "'I passed through the street at halfpast 12, and everything seemed to me to be going on as usual, and my sister was standing at the door at 10 minutes to one, but did not see anyone pass by. I heard the commotion when the body was found, and heard the policemen's whistles, but did not take any notice of the matter, as disturbances are very frequent at the club, and I thought it was only another row."'

LES FILS DE JACK L'EVENTREUR
Book by Norbert Spehner (Quebec, Canada: Nuit Blanche, 1995).
Reviews the Ripper literature.

LETTERS
It is generally accepted that the name 'Jack the Ripper' derives from the **'Dear Boss' letter** and **'Saucy Jacky' postcard**, posted to the Central News Agency on 27 September from London EC and 1 October from London E respectively (but see **17 September letter**).

The repeated signature nickname and references to cutting off ears suggested these came from the same source and when the Metropolitan Police published facsimiles of them, it was immediately assumed they were the work of the murderer. The Americanism 'Boss' was taken to be a clue to his nationality and 'graphologists' have attempted to describe the murderer's character from examinations of these letters.

It has long been debated that since the text of the 'Dear Boss' letter was published in the morning paper *Daily News* on 1 October 1888, the 'Saucy Jacky postcard', printed in the evening paper the *Star* the same day, might have been an imitative hoax (some details of the double murder actually appeared in the Sunday papers, 30 September). However, it was argued in **Jack the Ripper: The Final Chapter** that the postcard could not be an imitative hoax because the handwriting matched that of the 'Dear Boss' letter, a facsimile of which did not appear in print until 3 October.

There was an immediate flood of other correspondence, purporting to have been written by the murderer, sent or forwarded to the Met and City Police. One posted to the *Daily News* on 1 October was signed 'Ripper' with an inserted 'Boss', though the City Police, who ultimately received it, never made it public. Facsimiles of the 'Dear Boss' and 'Saucy Jacky' missives were published in the *Evening News* on Thursday, 4 October, and may have appeared in the final edition the previous day.

Deborah K. Dobbins ('From Who You Would Like To Know', *Ripperologist*, 78, April 2007) argues the 'Threat' letter of 6 October and the City Police's Fraser postcard are by the same hand. She uses stylistic and calligraphic points of comparison, and notes the references to **Annie Chapman** make it likely the **Fraser** postcard was the first of the group.

After 1910, **Anderson** and **Swanson** both wrote that the original 'Jack the Ripper letter' was the work of a journalist whom they could identify (*see* **Best** and **Bulling** for suggested authors). It was long held that among the more interesting of the other 'Jack the Ripper' letters was one which apparently intimated awareness that the police had heard from **R.J. Lees**. The word read as 'Lees' has now been identified as 'tecs', however, and the letter has nothing to do with Lees. **L. Forbes Winslow** in his autobiography, wrote that he received a letter from Jack the Ripper on 19 October 1888 informing him the next murder would be committed on the 9 November,(see **Hammersmith Road letter**). **Melvin Harris**, (reproducing a facsimile of the document) claimed the letter had actually been written in 1889 and the date altered to '88' by Forbes Winslow himself.

Document examiner Sue Iremonger has identified several letters on the Scotland Yard files with autographs in the same hand as the 'Dear Boss' letter, most interestingly one noted on the files by Robert Smith (*see Diary of Jack the Ripper*), posted in London NW (Threat letter), wherein the author utters misspelled threats against an unnamed police informant (facsimile reproduced in *The Diary of Jack the Ripper*). Patricia Cornwell claims a large number of the letters were written by Walter Sickert, while document examiner Anna Guetzner Robins even claimed the 'Dear Boss' letter was one of them. *See* **Sickert letters investigation** for further claims.

Jack the Ripper: Letters from Hell transcribes the Metropolitan Police letters in full. *Jack the Ripper: Scotland Yard Investigates* summarises the City Police letters.

See also **Maria Coroner, Charlotte Higgins, Miriam Howells, Liverpool Letter, Littlechild Letter, Lusk Letter, Openshaw Letter.**

LEVISOHN, WOLF

Witness at the trial of **Severin Klosowski**, who reported frequently seeing him in Whitechapel at the times of the murders. Alleged informant on **Dr Pedachenko**. Suggested as suspect or accomplice in *Alias Jack the Ripper*.

Jewish commercial traveller. In Whitechapel on business on 15 November 1888, Levisohn was abused by two prostitutes called De Grasse and Johnson when he refused their solicitations. They shouted, 'You are Jack the Ripper' and pleaded in defence that he looked like the Ripper because he carried a shiny black bag.

According to **Donald McCormick**, citing **Dr Dutton**, Levisohn assured **Inspector Abberline** that Klosowski was not the Ripper, saying that a more likely suspect was a Walworth Road barber's Russian assistant, whom he had seen in Commercial Street on 29/30 September 1888 (*cf.* **Dr Alexander Pedachenko**). The suggestion that Levisohn was Jack the Ripper rests on the suspicious frequency with which he reported meeting Klosowski in locations close to Ripper murder sites.

LEVITSKI, –

Suspect, described 1923. Alleged accomplice of **Dr Alexander Pedachenko**. In the story ascribed by **William Le Queux** to **Nicolai Zverieff**, Levitski was said to have accompanied Pedachenko to keep a look-out while he committed the

Whitechapel murders. He was also alleged to have written the '**Jack the Ripper letters**' and to have been subsequently exiled to Yakutsk, Russia.

LEVY, JACOB (1856–91)

Recently allegedSuspect.

A butcher with premises at 36 Middlesex Street, in 1886 he was spent 12 months in Essex County Asylum for insanity, his wife, Sarah, apparently running the business thereafter. He was again committed in 1890 and in the asylum the following year he died of general paralysis of the insane (tertiary syphilis).

Mark King ('Jacob Levy', *Ripperologist*, 26, December 1999 and 27, February 2000) noted that Jacob Levy's business was located about 60 yards from the butchery business of **Joseph Hyam Levy** at 1 Hutchinson Street, and argues that the two men could have been acquainted and that Jacob was the man Joseph Hyam Levy saw outside Church passage with **Catherine Eddowes**, this possibly accounting for his apparently knowing more than he was prepared to say (as reported in the *Evening News*, 9 October 1888). He suggests Levy's syphilis indicates a possible motive for his savagely butchering prostitutes and further speculates the piece of Catherine Eddowes' apron dropped in Goulston Street might deliberately have been planted by Jacob Levy to mislead the authorities into believing he was heading further east than Middlesex Street.

LEVY, JOSEPH HYAM (*b.* 1842)

Witness at **Catherine Eddowes**' inquest, 1888.

A butcher, born in Aldgate in 1842. He married Amelia Lewis in 1866, and at the times of the 1881 and 1891 Censuses was living at 1 Hutchison Street. The couple appear to have remained childless.

Accompanied Joseph Lawende and **Harry Harris** from the Imperial Club, 16–17 Duke's Place, at 1.34am, on 30 September 1888, and on seeing a couple at the entry to Church Passage, leading to Mitre Square, remarked, 'I don't like going home by myself when I see these sorts of characters about. I'm off!'

The *Evening News* of 9 October reported: 'Mr Joseph Levy is absolutely obstinate and refuses to give the slightest information. He leaves one to infer that he knows something, but that he is afraid to be called on the inquest.' At the inquest, Levy testified that he saw a woman outside Church Passage with a man about three inches taller than her, though he did not take any notice of them. Further, he thought, 'that persons standing at that time in the morning in a dark passage were not up to much good.' Pressed by City Solicitor **Crawford**, he denied thinking their appearance was 'terrible' and stated that he was, 'not exactly afraid for himself.'

His hesitations and reservations, coupled with his definite acquaintance with **Martin Kosminski** (whose application for naturalisation he supported in 1877, Levy being native-born English), led to the surmise that he might have recognised the man as a relative or connection of **Aaron Kosminski**'s and chosen to withhold the evidence. However, no connection between Martin and Aaron

Kosminski has been established, but see **Jacob Levy** for another possible explanation of his reticence.

LEWIS, (SIR) GEORGE HENRY, BT (1833–1911)
Consultant theorist.

The most famous solicitor of the late Victorian age. In 1888, he was appointed to act for Charles Stuart Parnell and the Irish nationalists before the Parnell Commission. At the same time, according to the *Philadelphia Times* (3 December 1888), he was consulted by the City Police, who believed he had an unrivalled knowledge of crime and would have reached useful conclusions about the Ripper murders.

Lewis apparently supported the City CID's conclusion that **Elizabeth Stride** and **Catherine Eddowes** were murdered by different hands, although the two killers worked in collusion. This he took to be definite. Probable, though not certain, he maintained, was the murderers' motive. They were, he thought, religious monomaniacs with a determination to stamp out prostitution and the extreme mutilations inflicted on the bodies were intended to terrify other women to leaving the streets *(Aitchison Daily Globe,* 27 October 1888 and *Philadelphia Times,* whose cutting describing Lewis's opinion is held in MEPO 3/140, f.7).
(see also **Prince Albert Victor**)

LEWIS, MAURICE (or MORRIS)
Informant. Acquaintance of **Mary Jane Kelly**. Tailor living in Dorset Street.

Told the press that he had known Kelly for about five years and said that he saw her drinking with **'Danny'** and **'Julia'** in the Horn of Plenty on the night of the murder. Numerous newspapers reported that when playing pitch and toss in Miller's Court at 8am, on 9 November he saw Kelly leave the house and return with some milk. Newspapers also reported Kelly was seen in the Britannia at about 10am and the *Illustrated Police News* (17 November 1888) attributes this sighting to Lewis, who said he was positive that he saw Mary Jane Kelly drinking with some other people there (*see* **Mrs Maxwell**).

LEWIS, SARAH
Witness at **Mary Jane Kelly**'s inquest.

Laundress of 29 Great Pearl Street. Deposed to **Inspector Abberline** that following 'words' with her husband she came to stay the rest of the night at Mrs **Keyler**'s (first floor of no. 2 Miller's Court). She testified that she arrived around 2.30am, as checked by Christ Church, Spitalfields, clock.

Abberline's notes of her deposition have her declaring that she saw 'a man standing over against the lodging-house on the opposite side of Dorset Street', and there follow the crossed-out words 'talking to a female'. In her testimony, she described him as not tall, but stout and wearing a black, wide-awake hat. She also said a young man passed along the street with a woman.

Lewis gave an account of a man in a high round hat, whom she had seen in

Bethnal Green Road when out with a friend, the previous Wednesday evening. This man had asked them to go down a passage with him, persuading them over their initial alarm by promising to treat them. In the passage, he put down a black bag he was carrying and started to open his coat and feel for something, whereupon they ran away. Mrs Lewis now declared she had seen the same man accompanied by a woman, near the Britannia, on her way to Dorset Street.

The obvious similarities between her story and that ascribed by the press to Mrs Kennedy strongly suggest they were one and the same person.

(See Mark King, 'Sarah Lewis, "Unfortunate"', *Ripperana*, 16, April 1996)

LIFE AND TIMES OF JACK THE RIPPER, THE
Book by Philip Sugden (Avonmouth, Bristol: Sienna, 1996).

Sixty-five-page mini-book that gives a very brief account of the crimes and a glance at a few suspects.

LIPMAN or LIPPMAN, JULIUS (*d.* 1900)
Alleged 'Leather Apron' (qv).

A cobbler on whose death several newspapers reported that he had been nicknamed **'Leather Apron'** and was in 1889 (*The Newcastle Weekly Courant*, 20 October 1900) or 1899 (*East London* Advertiser, 23 October 1900) suspected of being Jack the Ripper and questioned by the police. He was cleared, but could not shed the stigma and subsequently suffered a decline in business, turned to drink and died of neglect and semi-starvation. (*See also Hampshire Telegraph*, 20 October 1900; *News of the World,* 21 October 1900, among others.) No death certificate has ever been found.

LIPSKI, ISRAEL (1865–87)
Formerly Israel Lobulsk.

Murderer whose name was allegedly used in 1888 as an anti-Semitic insult. Born in Warsaw, then emigrated to England (1885) and worked as an umbrella-maker. In 1887, tried to establish his own business at lodgings in 16 Batty Street, adjacent to Berner Street. Then, in June of that year, poisoned fellow-lodger Miriam Angel with nitric acid and tried to poison himself. His conviction was highly controversial as some felt the prosecution was influenced by anti-Semitism, but he confessed the evening before his execution.

Israel Schwartz, who saw **Elizabeth Stride** assaulted in Berner Street approximately fifteen minutes before her body was discovered, told police the assailant shouted 'Lipski!' at him when he turned to watch. He was reported in the press as saying another man who stepped into the street shouted 'Lipski!' at the assailant (*see* **Pipeman**). As Schwartz spoke almost no English, this almost certainly represents a failure of interpretation and it is probable the police version is correct since Inspector **Abberline** reported that he had questioned Schwartz particularly closely about the cry, but he was unable to say with certainty *to* (not *by*) whom it was addressed.

Surviving Home Office Files contain more questions about the cry of 'Lipski!' than any other aspect of Schwartz's story because it suggests the assailant might have recognised the man stepping into the street and addressed him by name, in which case he could be traced to identify the assailant. Interested officials asked whether the word might, however, have been used as a sadistic verb: 'I am Lipskiing this woman.' Dr **Robert Anderson** replied, endorsing Abberline's opinion that 'Lipski!' was now a popular anti-Semitic insult, addressed to Schwartz on account of his strongly Semitic appearance.

Martin L. Friedman: *The Trials of Israel Lipski*. New York: Beaufort Books, 1984, is the standard study of the case.

LIS, JOSEPH
See **Joseph Silver**, *The Fox and the Flies*

LITTLECHILD, CHIEF INSPECTOR JOHN GEORGE (1847–1923)
Informant.

Born in Royston, Herts. Joined the Metropolitan Police in 1867 (warrant no. 48083). Transferred to Scotland Yard, 1871. Played a prominent part in clearing up the Turf Fraud or Mme de Goncourt scandal of 1876, in which three senior detective officers were found to be in the pay of confidence tricksters. Littlechild arrested one of the criminal masterminds. Promoted to inspector, 1878; promoted to chief inspector, 1882, and participated in investigating the Phoenix Park murders, which *The Times* wrongly accused Parnell of having praised. (*See* **Parnell Commission**.)

Head of Secret Department (subsequently Special Irish Branch), 1883–93. Resigned 1893, and as a private detective collected evidence against Oscar Wilde for the Marquess of Queensberry (1895), and investigated Harry Kendall Thaw (1906), unbalanced American playboy, who murdered architect Stanford White in America and conducted lurid sadistic orgies in Europe. These investigations apparently led Littlechild to the erroneous belief that homosexuals are generally prone to sadistic tendencies (*see* **Littlechild Letter**).

In his reminiscences (1894), he remarked of the Ripper case,

'Apart from dynamite conspiracies, and explosions, and the Whitechapel murders, perhaps no matter has been of such great importance at Scotland Yard as the discovery of the Great Turf Frauds of 1876.'

Since the last named was a massive national scandal entailing the complete reorganisation of the Detective Department into the CID, following the corruption of very senior members, Littlechild's observation indicates the immense weight officially given to the Whitechapel murders.

In 1913, he wrote the **Littlechild letter** to G.R. Sims.

(see Jan Bondeson, 'The Duke of Baker Street : An episode from the later career of Chief Inspector Littlechild', *Ripperologist*, 55, September 2004)

LITTLECHILD LETTER

A typed letter of three pages, with handwritten postscript, dated 23 September 1913, from Chief Inspector John Littlechild to G.R. Sims. Its provenance is excellent: it was purchased with other documents by Stewart Evans from antiquarian book dealer, Eric Barton.

8, The Chase,
Clapham Common. S.W.
23rd September 1913.

Dear Sir,

I was pleased to receive your letter which I shall put away in 'good company' to read again, perhaps some day when old age overtakes me and when to revive memories of the past may be a solace.

Knowing the great interest you take in all matters criminal and abnormal, I am just going to inflict one more letter on you on the 'Ripper' subject. Letters as a rule are only a nuisance when they call for a reply but this does not need one. I will try and be brief.

I never heard of a Dr D. in connection with the Whitechapel murders but amongst the suspects, and to my mind a very likely one, was a Dr T. (which sounds much like D). He was an American quack named Tumblety and was at one time a frequent visitor to London and on these occasions constantly brought under the notice of police, there being a large dossier concerning him at Scotland Yard. Although a 'Sycopathia [sic] Sexualis' subject he was not known as a 'Sadist' (which the murderer unquestionably was) but his feelings toward women were remarkable and bitter in the extreme, a fact on record. Tumblety was arrested at the time of the murders in connection with unnatural offences and charged at Marlborough Street, remanded on bail, jumped his bail, and got away to Boulogne. He shortly left Boulogne and was never heard of afterwards. It was believed he committed suicide but, certain it is that from this time the 'Ripper' murders came to an end.

With regard to the term 'Jack the Ripper' it was generally believed at the Yard that Tom Bullen [sic] of the Central News was the the [sic] originator, but it is probable Moore, who was his chief, was the inventor. It was a smart piece of journalistic work. No journalist of my time got such privileges from

ScotlandYard as Bullen. Mr James Munro [sic] when Assistant Commissioner, and afterwards Commissioner, relied on his integrity. Poor Bullen occasionally took too much to drink, and I fail to see how he could help it knocking about so many hours and seeking favours from so many people to procure copy. One night when Bullen had taken a "few too many" he got early information of the death of Prince Bismarck and instead of going to the office to report it sent a laconic telegram "Bloody Bismarck is dead'. On this I believe Mr Charles Moore fired him out.

It is very strange how those given to 'Contrary sexual instincts and degenerationes' are given to cruelty, even Wilde used to like to be punched about. It may interest you if I give you an example of this cruelty in the case of the man Harry Thaw and this is authentic as I have the boy's statement. Thaw was staying at the Canton Hotel and one day laid out a lot of sovereigns on his dressing table, then rang for a call boy on pretence of sending out a telegram. He made some excuse and went out of the room and left the boy there and watched through the chink of the door. The unfortunate boy was tempted and took a sovereign from the pile and Thaw returning to the room charged him with stealing. The boy confessed when Thaw asked whether he should send for the police or whether he should punish him himself. The boy scared to death consented to take his punishment from Thaw who then made him undress, strapped him to the foot of the bedstead, and thrashed him with a cane, drawing blood. He then made the boy get into a bath in which he placed quantity of salt. It seems incredible that such a thing could take place in any hotel but it is a fact. *This was in 1906.* [Manuscript addition]

Now pardon me – It is finished. – *Except that I knew Major Griffiths for many years. He probably got his information from Anderson who only 'thought he knew'.* [Manuscript addition]

Faithfully yours,
J. G. Littlechild
George R. Sims Esq.,
12, Clarence Terrace,
Regents Park. N.W.

(Note:The four subscript commas were added manually, as were all the superscript letters and words, the latter usually positioned by carets.)

This letter was probably part of an on-going correspondence between Littlechild and Sims about Jack the Ripper (Littlechild apologises for inflicting 'one more letter' on Sims, so had presumably written to him before), and the correspondence may have been initiated by Littlechild (he is pleased with the earlier letter from Sims, planning to keep it as a souvenir, and is apologetic for writing again, ensuring Sims that a reply isn't necessary).

Although not certain, it is likely that 'Dr D.' is a reference to **Montague John Druitt**, wrongly identified by **Sir Melville Macnaghten** as a doctor. Either Littlechild did not know about Macnaghten's error and did not recognise 'D' as Druitt, or Littlechild's ignorance shows that he was completely unaware of Druitt as a suspect.

That Tumblety was a 'very likely' suspect has been interpreted by some commentators as meaning that Littlechild thought he was very likely to have been Jack the Ripper, but alternatively meant only that Tumblety's extreme and bitter feelings toward women made him a good suspect. That Tumblety was not a sadist, which Littlechild thought the murderer 'undoubtedly was', suggests that Littlechild may in fact have discounted him as a likely Ripper. Littlechild's uncertainty about Tumblety's movements after jumping bail and erroneous belief that he committed suicide suggest that Tumblety was not a primary suspect

Because Littlechild was head of the Special Irish Branch a popular theory has emerged that Tumblety was an active Fenian and that the 'large dossier' about him at Scotland Yard concerned his Fenian activities.

Littlechild's belief that **Major Griffiths** took his information from **Sir Robert Anderson** seems mistaken since Griffiths closely follows the Macnaghten memoranda, but the emphasised quote that Anderson 'only thought he knew' may shed doubt on the certainty with which Anderson otherwise appears to have expressed himself. Whether Littlechild knew anything more about Anderson's opinion than had appeared in *The Lighter Side of My Official Life* is not known. There is no evidence that Littlechild himself played any part in the Ripper investigation: his duties with the Special Irish Branch involved no obvious overlap, and the Ripper case coincided with covert police operatives' preparations for the **Parnell Commission**.

(see *The Lodger*, *Prince of Quacks*)

LIVERPOOL LETTER

A letter (as described in text) or letters (as printed) quoted by **J. Hall Richardson** in *From City to Fleet Street* (1927). Said to have been sent to the police or press, and running as follows:

Liverpool
29th inst.

BEWARE I shall be at work on the 1st and 2nd inst. in 'Minories' at 12 midnight and I give the police a good chance but there is never a Policeman near when I am at work.
Yours, JACK THE RIPPER.
Prince William St., L'pool.
What fools the police are I even give them the name of the Street where I am living.

Various theorists have rested arguments for the Ripper's living in the Minories or Liverpool on this foundation. Few have addressed the problem that an event on 1st or 2nd inst (i.e. 'of the current month') cannot be predicted on 29th inst.

LIVRE ROUGE DE JACQUES L'ÉVENTREUR
Book by Stephane Bourgoin (Paris: Grasset, 1998).

Overview of the case, superseded by the same author's *Jack l'Éventreur*.

LLEWELLYN, DR REES RALPH (1849–1921)

Witness at **Mary Ann Nichols'** inquest. Examined her body. Matric. U. of London, 1869. Hon. Certif. in Obst., 1873. LSA, 1873; MRCS, 1874; LRCP (Lond.), 1876; Medical Officer to E and EC Districts, and City Mission. Called from his surgery, 152 Whitechapel Road, at 4am, 31 August 1888. After cursory examination of the body in Buck's Row, pronounced her dead. Noticed there was only a wine-glass and a half of blood in the gutter beside her, but had no doubt she had been killed on the spot.

Subsequently made a full examination of the body in the Old Montague Street Workhouse Infirmary Mortuary. *The Times* reported his medical testimony thus:

Five of the teeth were missing, and there was a slight laceration of the tongue. There was a bruise running along the lower part of the jaw on the right side of the face. That might have been caused by a blow from a fist or pressure from a thumb. There was a circular bruise on the left side of the face, which also might have been inflicted by the pressure of the fingers. On the left side of the neck, about 1in. below the jaw, there was an incision about 4in in length, and ran from a point immediately below the ear. On the same side, but an inch below, and commencing about 1in. in front of it, was a circular incision, which terminated at a point about 3in. below the right jaw. That incision completely severed all the tissues down to the vertebrae. The large vessels of the neck on both sides were severed. The incision was about 8in. in length. The cuts must have been caused by a long-bladed knife, moderately sharp, and used with great violence. No blood was found on the breast, either of the body or clothes. There were no injuries about the body until just about the lower part of the abdomen. Two or three inches from the left side was a wound running in a jagged manner. The wound was a very deep one, and the tissues were cut through. There were several incisions running across the abdomen. There were also three or four similar cuts running downwards, on the right side, all of which had been caused by a knife which had been used violently and downwards. The injuries were from left to right, and might have been done by a left-handed person. All the injuries had been caused by the same instrument.

LODGER, THE: THE ARREST AND ESCAPE OF JACK THE RIPPER
Book by Stewart Evans and Paul Gainey (London: Century, 1995; paperback published as *Jack the Ripper: First American Serial Killer*. London: Arrow Books, 1996); US Title *Jack the Ripper: First American Serial Killer* (hardback New York: Kodansha 1998, paperback New York: Kodansha, 1998).

The history of **Dr Tumblety** as it was known in 1995 and the authors' case that he was Jack the Ripper, combined with a full and accurate account of the murders which included previously unpublished details. It has now largely been superseded by subsequent research.

See also **J. Bulling**, **Chief Inspector John George Littlechild**, **Littlechild Letter**, **Thomas Charles Moore**, *Prince of Quacks*.

LOFTUS, PHILIP
A friend of **Melville Macnaghten**'s grandson, **Gerald Melville Donner**, Loftus recalled seeing framed on the wall of Donner's home in the early 1950s what Donner maintained was 'the original' **'Dear Boss' letter**. At the same time, Donner showed him,

'private notes, in Sir Melville's handwriting on official paper, rather untidy and in the nature of rough jottings. As I remember them, they gave three suspects: a Polish tanner or cobbler; a man who went around stabbing young girls in the bottom with nail scissors; and **M.J. Druitt**, a doctor of 41 years of age.'

In a letter to **Lady Aberconway**, dated 11 August 1972, Loftus further recalled that the Pole was 'nick-named **Leather Apron**', that the bottom-stabber was 'probably **Thomas Cutbush**' and that Druitt was named 'Michael'.

It is sometimes suggested Loftus saw Lady Aberconway's version before she had herself transcribed and typed them. This is possible, although on the two occasions when he described them (the letter to Lady Aberconway, and a statement in *The Guardian*, 7 October 1972), Loftus explicitly claimed to remember that what he had seen differed from the Aberconway notes, as described by **Tom Cullen** and **Daniel Farson**, although the name Druitt was the same.

LONDON CORRESPONDENCE: JACK THE RIPPER AND THE IRISH PRESS
Book by Alan Sharp with a foreword by Andy Aliffe (Dublin: Ashfield Press, 2005).

Excellent look at press coverage of the Ripper crimes (*cf. **Jack the Ripper and the London Press** and **News From Whitechapel**), in this case concentrating on the

Irish press, which the author shows was more overt than the London press in using the Ripper crimes to further political agendas. Irish newspapers also carried exclusive material from their own correspondents.

LONDON OF JACK THE RIPPER: THEN AND NOW, THE

Book by Robert Clack and Philip Hutchinson (Derby: Breedon Books, 2007; New and revised edition, Derby: Breedon Books, 2009).

Provides a concise account of each of the crimes from **Fanny Millwood/ Millward** to **Frances Coles**, with the emphasis on the topography. There are 210 photographs, including a small collection of never-before-seen photographs from the collection of the late John Gordon Whitby, taken in September 1961. The revised edition contains some updated information, a handful of new photographs and some necessary corrections to some image reproductions. (see *The Jack the Ripper Location Photographs*)

LONG, PC ALFRED, 254A (1855-1930)

Discovered the piece of **Catherine Eddowes**' apron and the Goulston Street graffito.

A baker, who served 12 years in the 9th Lancers; awarded Distinguished Conduct Medal in 1880. Joined the Metropolitan Police in 1884 (warrant no. 69841). Dismissed, July 1889, for being drunk on duty. Was described on his death certificate as a 'formerly builder's night watchman'.

Drafted to Whitechapel from A Division (Whitehall) among the extra patrols brought in during the Ripper scare, he discovered the bloodstained piece of apron and then noticed the graffito above it at 2.55am, on 30 September 1888, his first night on duty in that street. He had previously passed through the street at 2.20am, and believed the apron was not there at that time, but was not sure about the graffito. The implication of Long's timing is that the Ripper spent 40 minutes in the vicinity of the murder before making his escape. At the inquest he referred to his notebook entry for the wording, but had not observed the spelling: J-U-W-E-S.

He was criticised by a juror for not conducting a thorough search of the rooms in the building, but replied that he did not know of Eddowes' murder, and accepted **Mr Crawford**'s suggestion that on discovering the apron he thought the victim of a crime, and not the criminal, might be inside and so made a complete tour of the open staircases and landings.

LONG, MRS ELIZABETH

Married name of Mrs **Darrell or Durrell**, under which she testified at **Annie Chapman**'s inquest. She was, in fact, the wife of park-keeper James Long and lived at 198 Church Row, Whitechapel. It is not known why the police and some newspapers knew her by another name.

LOWENHEIM, JULIUS I. (*fl.* 1888)

Witness.

An American-German youth, resident in Dresden, in December 1888, who approached the British authorities with information against **Wirtkofsky**. In forwarding the information, however, the Dresden correspondent advised the Foreign Office that he suspected Lowenheim was principally interested in securing free passage to London (HO144/221/A49301(D) ff. 98–102).

LUBNOWSKI, MORRIS

Husband of **Aaron Kosminski**'s sister Matilda, whose addresses were given as Aaron's at the time of his hospitalisation in 1891, and on the register of his burial.

Morris and Matilda possibly came to England in 1881. He lived until December 1882 at 10 Plumbers Row. They were living at 16 Greenfield Street in February 1891, when Aaron was admitted from that address to the workhouse infirmary. Following several changes of address, in the autumn of 1910 the family moved to 5 Ashcroft Road, Bow, the address given on the registration of Aaron's burial. By that time they were using the surname Cohen or Lubnowski-Cohen.

LUCKHURST, MRS

Witness.

Former landlady of **Martha Tabram** at 4 Star Place, Commercial Road, who identified her body.

LUDWIG, CHARLES (b. 1848), ALSO CALLED WEITZEL/WETZEL

Briefly suspected.

Variously named in the press as Charles Ludwig, Charles Ludwig Wietzel or Wetzel, or as Ludwig, alias Wetzel. A German hairdresser, he came to London from Hamburg, 1887 or 1888 and found employment with Mr C.A. Partridge in The Minories, lodging with a German tailor named Johannes in Church Street, Minories, until his disorderly habits made him unwelcome and he moved to a hotel in Finsbury.

In the small hours of Tuesday, 18 September 1888, he accompanied prostitute **Elizabeth Burns** to Three Kings Court, Minories, which led to railway arches. There, he pulled a knife on her and her cries of 'Murder!' attracted City Police Constable **John Johnson** from his beat. He dismissed Ludwig, and walked Miss Burns to the end of his beat, where she said, 'Dear me, he frightened me very much when he pulled a big knife out.' She explained that she was too afraid to make the complaint in Ludwig's presence. Johnson searched unsuccessfully for Ludwig and alerted other constables to the situation.

Ludwig appeared at a coffee stall in Whitechapel High Street at 3am and aggressively asked bystander **Alexander Freinberg** what he was looking at. When Freinberg apologised, Ludwig pulled his knife on him, whereupon Freinberg threw a dish from the stall at his head and summoned Police Constable **Gallagher** 221H, who arrested Ludwig. Later in the day, he appeared at Thames Magistrates Court, charged with being drunk and disorderly, and threatening to stab.

The magistrates agreed to his being remanded in custody for a week. Police received an alarming account of him from the landlord:

He is a most extraordinary man, is always in a bad temper, and grinds his teeth in rage at any little thing which puts him out. I believe he has some knowledge of anatomy, as he was for some time an assistant to some doctors in the German army, and helped to dissect bodies. He always carried some razors and a pair of scissors with him. From what he has said to me I know he was in the habit of associating with low women. (*Echo*, 19 September 1888)

They also learned he was believed to have had blood on his hands on the day of Annie Chapman's murder. His remands continued, as he was the most promising arrested suspect hitherto. The double murder, 'committed while he was under lock and key, conclusively proved that he was not the Ripper.'

LUDWIG, PC, FRANK 273H. (*b.* 1860)
Of German origin, a baker before joining the Metropolitan Police in 1882 (warrant no. 67352). Resigned as sergeant, 1908.

Arrested a journalist dressed as a woman and prowling around Whitechapel. His masculine stride attracted the attention of PC Ludwig, who said, 'Stop! Are you not a man? I can see that you are.' The journalist said, 'Yes.' PC Ludwig then quietly asked, 'Are you one of us?' The journalist said he wasn't and admitted to being a journalist. PC Ludwig took him to Leman Street, where he was held for an hour and a half (*Daily Telegraph*, 2 October 1888).

LUSHINGTON, GODFREY (1832–1907)
Civil servant mainly responsible for Home Office attitude to the Metropolitan Police and the conduct of the Ripper case.

The fifth son of Rt Hon. S. Lushington, MP. Educated at Rugby and Balliol College. Oxford Barrister, Inner Temple, 1858; Married Beatrice Ann Shore, 1865; Counsel to Home Office, 1869; Assistant Under-Secretary of State, Home Department, 1876; Permanent Under-Secretary, Home Office, 1885–95. KCB, 1892. Served on several Royal Commissions.

Described as, 'an experienced and sagacious an advisor. One of the most capable and trustworthy members of the permanent staff of the home office' (*The Penny Illustrated Paper*, 27 August 1887), and conversely as, 'next to Sir J.A. Godley, at the India Office, the most incompetent of all the "permanent" Civil Service staff' (*The Liberty Review: Property Owners' Guardian and Free Labour Advocate*, 16 March 1895). Lushington played lawn tennis with **Robert Anderson** during the latter's early years at the Home Office and was regarded by him as a friend, but Anderson came to think of him as a dangerous individual libertarian and blamed his irritant personality for worsening relations between home secretary **Henry Matthews** and Metropolitan Police commissioner **Sir Charles Warren**, between whom it was Lushington's duty to mediate.

Lushington was also a personal friend of **Major Henry Smith**, and enjoyed annual dinner parties with him and the Rvd. William Rodgers of St Botolph's,

Aldgate, after the Police Ball. He was persuaded by **Israel Schwartz**'s testimony to the cry of '**Lipski!**' in Berner Street that the murderer was Jewish.

LUSK, GEORGE AKIN (1839–1919)

President/chairman of the **Whitechapel Vigilance Committee** and recipient of letter and human kidney allegedly from the Ripper.

Started a building and decorating business with property inherited by his wife, Susannah, née Price. Specialised in restoration of music-halls. In 1888, Susannah died, leaving him with seven children to care for. Lived at 1 Tollit St, Alderney Rd E., locality of Globe Road, Mile End. *The Times*, 29 April 1891, has under its column, 'The Bankruptcy Acts,1883 and 1890, In London. Receiving Orders. Lusk, George Akin, Alderney-road, Globe-road, Mile-end, builder and decorator.' He moved to Caxton Street, Bow. A Freemason (Doric Lodge).

On 10 September 1888, he was elected president of the newly-formed Whitechapel Vigilance Committee in the Crown public house, Mile End Road. Under this aegis, he drew attention to himself by writing to *The Times*. In October, he came to fear that his house was being watched by a sinister bearded man and asked for police protection. Then, on 16 October he received through the post the parcel containing the **Lusk kidney** and accompanying **Lusk Letter**.

LUSK KIDNEY

Allegedly **Catherine Eddowes'** left kidney.

Half a human kidney, preserved in spirits of wine, received in the post on 16 October 1888 by George Lusk. It was in a 3in square cardboard box, wrapped in brown paper, with a barely decipherable postmark: possibly London E. This was accompanied by a crudely-written letter (*see* **Lusk Letter**). Lusk assumed this was a hoax and the organ probably a dog's, but friends persuaded him to hand it over for medical examination.

Press reports said that it was examined by **Dr Openshaw**, curator of the Pathology Museum at London Hospital, who 'pronounced it to be a portion of a human kidney — a "ginny" kidney — that is to say, one that had belonged to a person who had drunk heavily. He was further of opinion that it was the organ of a woman of about forty five years of age, and that it had been taken from the body within the last three weeks' (*Daily News, Morning Advertiser, The Times*, 19 October 1888). The following day, Openshaw, 'stated that the microscopical examination of the article proved it to be the anterior of the left human kidney. It has been preserved, in his opinion, in spirit for about 10 days. The Curator further added that all other statements which had been made were entirely erroneous' (*Evening News*, 20 October 1888).

City pathologist **Dr Sedgwick Saunders** told the press, 'You may take it that there is no difference whatever between the male and female kidney. You may take it that the right kidney of the woman Eddowes was perfectly normal in its structure and healthy, and by parity of reasoning, you would not get much disease in the left. The liver was healthy, and gave no indications that the woman drank. Taking the discovery of the half of a kidney, and supposing it to be human, my opinion is that it was a student's antic. It is quite possible for any student to obtain a kidney for the purpose' (*Evening News*, 20 October 1888).

However, **Dr Gordon Brown**'s report very precisely describes signs of Bright's Disease in the kidney remaining in the body – 'The right kidney was pale and bloodless with slight congestion at the base of the pyramid'.

In his memoirs, **Major Henry Smith** wrote that he had shown the Lusk kidney to Mr Henry Sutton, senior surgeon at the London Hospital, and received from him the opinion that the kidney was not charged with fluid, as would have been the case had it been in a body handed over to a hospital for dissection; that it showed symptoms of Bright's Disease and that the length of renal artery attached was what would be expected from the length of renal artery reported as remaining in the body.

Many modern commentators have tended to dismiss Major Smith's remarks, largely because his memoirs are regarded as extremely inaccurate, but the authority on which his remarks are apparently based was **Henry Gawen Sutton**, a very distinguished physician, who with **Sir William Gull** published a revolutionary paper, 'On the pathology of the morbid state commonly called chronic Bright's disease with contracted kidney ("arterio-capillary fibrosis")' in *Medico-Chirurgical Transactions* (London, 1872; 55: 273–326), which led to Gull and Sutton giving their name to Gull-Sutton Syndrome – arteriosclerotic fibrosis of the kidney.

According to Lusk's grandson, 'My grandfather, the late George Aken [sic] Lusk, maintained in later years that the communications and parcel containing the human kidney he received were practical jokes played by hospital students' (*Sunday Express*, 17 October 1943).

According to the writer Patricia Cornwell (***Portrait Of A Killer***), who visited the London Hospital archives during her research, 'the organ was anatomically preserved at the Royal London Hospital until it became so disintegrated that the hospital disposed of it in the 1950s.'

Gunter Wolf has observed that in Hebrew tradition the kidneys are considered to be the most important internal organ and that the Bible says God judges an individual by examining the kidneys. He suggests, 'By removing the kidney from Catherine Eddowes, Jack the Ripper may have tried to take possession of the conscience, emotions and desires of one of his victims.'

(*See* Nicholas P. Warren 'A Postal Kidney', *Criminologist* 1989; Christopher-Michael DiGrazia, 'Another Look at the Lust Kidney'; ***Ripper Notes***, 4, 2000;

Thomas C Westcott, 'Lusk Kidney Revelations: A Hospital Surgeon Speaks', *Ripper Notes*, 19, July 2004; Gunter Wolf, 'A Kidney From Hell? A Nephrological View of the Whitechapel Murders in 1888', *Nephrology Dialysis Transplantation* 23, 2008; Gunter Wolf, 'Possible Mythological Meanings of Kidney Excision to Jack the Ripper', *Ripperologist*, 99, January 2009.)

LUSK LETTER
Accompanied the piece of human kidney received in the post by **George Lusk** on 16 October 1888. It read:

> From hell
> Mr Lusk
>
> Sor
> I send you half the Kidne I took from one women prasarved it for you tother piece I fried and ate it was very nise I may send you the bloody knif that took it out if you only wate a whil longer
>
> signed Catch me when
> you can
> Mishter Lusk.

The original letter was passed from the City Police to Scotland Yard and subsequently lost. Our precise knowledge of it derives from a photograph found in City Police archives, also subsequently lost. **Swanson** transcribed the letter in a report dated 6 November 1888 to the Home Office (HO 144/221/A49301C f.193.

LYONS, MISS or MRS (*fl.* 1888)
Believed she encountered '**Leather Apron**'.

On Sunday, 9 September, Miss Lyons encountered a strange man in Flower and Dean Street, Spitalfields, who persuaded her to meet him in the Queen's Head on the corner of Fashion Street and Commercial Street at 6.30pm for a drink. While they were drinking, he remarked, 'You are about the same style of woman as the one that's murdered.' On being asked what he knew about her, he replied, cryptically, 'You are beginning to smell a rat. Foxes hunt geese, but they don't always catch 'em.' Then he hurriedly left the bar. Miss Lyons followed him towards Spitalfields Church, until he realised she was behind him, at which point he rushed away down Church Street (today's Fournier Street) and she lost sight of him.

Miss Lyons claimed he looked exactly like the published descriptions of 'Leather Apron'. Excising the melodramatic details of 'glinting eyes' and a 'repulsive smile', this would mean that he was a stocky man, of medium height with a very thick neck and a black moustache, probably wearing a tight-fitting cap and a leather apron.

The *Daily Telegraph* and the *Star* (17 September 1888) called her 'Mrs Lyons', and said that she was taken to Commercial Street Police Station, where she did not identify **Edward McKenna** as the man she saw. The *Morning Advertiser* and the *Irish Times* said she was a prostitute.

McCARTHY, JOHN (1851–1935)

Mary Kelly's landlord. Suspect suggested 1988.

Probably born in Dieppe. With wife Elizabeth, had several children. Owned chandler's (i.e. grocery) shop, 27 Dorset Street, on the western side of arched entry to Miller's Court. Let rooms in Miller's Court, known locally as 'McCarthy's Rents'. Arthur Harding, a local villain of the next generation, speaking of a McCarthy in Dorset Street, claimed he began by selling old clothes and got his money 'out of swindling the poor people out of small sums'. He 'owned all the furnished rooms down there [Dorset Street]. He was an Irishman, a bully, a tough guy. Marie Lloyd used to see him, because there was a pub round the corner she used to go to. All his daughters were in show business on account of Marie Lloyd. They had plenty of money' (Raphael Samuel, *East End Underworld: Chapters in the Life of Arthur Harding*. London: Routledge and Keegan Paul, 1981). We note that although Harding may have meant 'bully' in the sense to browbeat someone, in Harding's day and earlier, this could mean a pimp.

The McCarthys certainly knew Marie Lloyd and John McCarthy's son, John Joseph McCarthy (who as a singer of comic Irish songs used the stage name Steve McCarthy). He married major music-hall star Marie Kendall and their grand-daughter was the beautiful actress Kay Kendall, who starred in the classic movie, *Genevieve* (Andy Aliffe, 'The Kendall McCarthys', ***Ripperologist***, 41, June 2002).

McCarthy and his son may well have been the 'J. McCarthy and McCarthy, jun.' who attended Inspector Abberline's retirement dinner at the Three Nuns, Aldgate, in June 1892, but it is impossible to be positive about this. It is also possible that he was the 'Jack' McCarthy who spoke eloquently and at length at a public meeting in response to a disparaging article about Dorset Street, published in the *Daily Mail* by Fred A. McKenzie (a refinement of a letter he had written to *The Times* on 3 June 1901). McKenzie was probably the author and *Daily Mail* journalist Frederick Arthur McKenzie 1869–91), however in the audience was a Mr. J. McCarthy sen. and a Mr. T. McCarthy, and it is known there were other McCarthy's in the street, so which if any of these was Kelly's landlord is uncertain (see Tom Wescott, 'The McCarthys of Dorset Street', *Ripper Notes*, 26, April 2006, for a valiant effort to sort the McCarthys out).

He sent **Thomas Bowyer** to collect Kelly's rent of 30/- (£1.50) in arrears at 10.45am, on 9 November 1888. Then, after viewing the body through the window himself, he sent Bowyer to Commercial Street Police Station. He broke open the locked door on **Superintendent Arnold**'s orders at 1.30pm, then gave press interviews evincing deep shock at the state of the body. In the press, he was reported as having lost a number of tenants, who left Miller's Court swiftly following the tragedy.

Toronto *Globe and Mail*, 30 August 1988, reports a Canadian group, including literary agent Helen Heller, whose researches led them to believe McCarthy was the Ripper. Christopher J. Morley reports the deductive case rests on the speculation that McCarthy may have allowed Kelly's arrears of rent because he was a client of hers, and the curious circumstance that as the landlord of the premises, he apparently did not own a key so the door had to be broken in.

McCARTHY, MR & MRS JOHN (*fl.* 1888)

Mary Jane Kelly's landlord and landlady subsequent to her living with **Mrs Buki**, and prior to her moving to Dorset Street. While press reports often said she lived with a **Mrs Carthy** at Pennington Street, beside the docks, it has been suggested that this must have been garbling for Mrs Mary Ann Jane McCarthy, who lived with her husband at 1 Breezer's Hill, between Pennington Street and Ratcliffe Highway. Three other residents listed in the 1891 Census were prostitutes, which has led to the suggestion that the house may have been a brothel.

(See also Paul Daniel, 'McCarthy, Kelly and Breezer's Hill,' *Ripperologist*, 8, December 1996.)

McCARTHY, SERGEANT JOHN

Involved in making enquiries concerning **Alice McKenzie** (MEPO 3/140, ff.275-78, 288) and the **Macnaghten memoranda** refers to Sergeant McCarthy C.I.D. being employed on inquiries concerning **Thomas Cutbush**, adding that he had been specially employed in Whitechapel at the time of the murders there.

First posted to G Division, he then obtained a clerkship at Scotland Yard, where he was engaged until 1885. He was than appointed to the Convict Supervision Office, and in 1888 he was appointed to be a detective sergeant. In 1892 he was prominent in the investigation of Dr **Neill Cream**. In August 1895 he was promoted to first-class sergeant. In 1896 he became an inspector and was transferred from Scotland Yard to B Division, and in 1898 to L Division at

Lambeth. On 17 March 1903 he was transferred as local inspector of the F Division at Paddington.

Towards the end of 1903 he was suspected of taking bribes and two detectives were detailed to keep him under observation. He was dismissed on 26 January 1904 when bookmaker David Curtis claimed that McCarthy had taken a bribe from him. McCarthy protested his innocence and brought a legal action against Curtis which on 23 March 1905 he lost. He was still vehemently protesting his innocence as late as 1910 (see *Penny Illustrated Paper*, 15 October 1910).

McCORMACK, JOHN aka BRYANT (*b.* 1839)

Lover of **Alice McKenzie** and witness at her inquest. Irish porter, working casually for Jewish tailors in Hanbury Street. Lived with McKenzie as his common-law wife in lodging-houses for six or seven years; on and off at Gun Street, Spitalfields, 1888–89.

On 16 July 1889, he returned from work at 4pm; he gave McKenzie 1/8d [8p] before she went out. They 'had words' as she was drunk. McCormack left her to earn their rent while he went to bed, though he claimed to be unaware she was streetwalking. He identified her body in the mortuary on 17 July.

McCORMICK, GEORGE DONALD KING (1911–98)

Theorist.

Author of *The Identity of Jack the Ripper* (1959). Prolific author of (especially) true crime, witchcraft and espionage history (often under the pseudonyms, Richard Deacon and Lichade Digen). Born Rhyl, Flintshire. Educated at Oswestry School. Freelance writer and journalist. Served in RNVR during World War II. Wounded in action, skippering landing craft in North Africa. During his naval career met Ian Fleming, who secured for him an appointment as North African correspondent with the *Sunday Times* in 1946. He went on to become commonwealth correspondent, assistant foreign manager and foreign manager successively, retiring in 1973.

McCormick was notably uncritical of his sources, inclined to accept material which made a good story, and not above embroidering material (often extravagantly), and inventing dialogue (an acceptable convention at the time he wrote). However, it is uncertain whether he invented material from the whole cloth, although by the 1980s, when *The Identity of Jack the Ripper* was coming under close scrutiny, **Melvin Harris** ('The Maybrick Hoax: Donald McCormick's Legacy' www.casebook.org/dissertations/maybrick_diary/mb-mc.html) states McCormick confessed to him that he had fabricated material, notably the rhyme 'Eight Little Whores'.

Unfortunately, Harris was threatening McCormick with exposure as a liar on national television, the elderly McCormick was in ill-health and Harris conducted the communication in such a way as to cause one to question whether McCormick really knew what he was admitting to, and whether Harris accurately interpreted him. McCormick is the source for a number of stories lacking independent substantiation, but can be shown to have discovered and made public numerous obscure stories (*see* **PC Spicer** as an example.)

(See obituary in *Ripperologist*, 16, April 1998).

See also **Hector Cairns**.

DR MACDONALD. M.D
CORONER

MACDONALD, DR RODERICK (1841–94)

Coroner at **Mary Jane Kelly**'s inquest. Born Isle of Skye, son of a crofter. Educated at Glasgow Normal School, whence returned to Skye as a teacher. Subsequently left for medical school. LRCS, LRCP (Edin.), 1867. Began practice in London, 1868. FRCS (Edin), MD (Durh.), 1883. Practised medicine in the East End and became a prominent figure in Highland Law Reform Association, working for parliamentary recognition of crofters' needs and rights. MO South District, Poplar Union. Surgeon to K Division, Metropolitan Police. MP for Ross-Shire and Cromerty as member of 'The Crofters' Party', 1885.

The 1886 coroner's election in East Middlesex consequent on the death of Sir John Humphreys was peculiarly rowdy. Eleven candidates stood, and solicitor **George Hay Young** won the show of hands in the Bethnal Green Vestry Hall on 10 December, with **Wynne Baxter** coming second. Macdonald received 'little support'. But the fighting and disorder prevented a count to determine the margin of victory and the losing candidates successfully demanded a poll. This was held three days later, and Baxter and Macdonald worked furiously to strengthen their positions in the interim. The consequence was that Baxter won the election with 1,401 votes; Macdonald came second with 1,069, while Hay Young was reduced to 696 votes.

In 1888, the coronial district was subdivided. Baxter retained the coronially lucrative South-Eastern district, where the slum areas of Whitechapel and Bethnal Green ensured many untimely deaths and much opportunity for recommending social policy. Macdonald, with the strong political support of East End radicals, including MP Sir Samuel Montagu and his party machine, easily won the election for North-East Middlesex.

MacDonald the Radical was known popularly as 'the crofter's MP'. When the Ripper murders started, he was in Scotland and pressing for land law reform. On his return, he wrote the following letter to the *Daily News* (4 October 1888):

SIR, A remarkable incident in connection with the recent murders is that in no one instance has it been found that the victim made any noise or cry while being done to death. My assistant [deputy coroner Alfred Hodgkinson] suggests that the murderer goes about with a vial of rum or brandy in his pocket drugged with an opiate – such as solution of morphia, which is almost if not quite tasteless; that he offers a swig of it to his victims (which they would all be likely to greedily accept), when he meets them; that in about ten to twenty minutes the poison begins to do its work on constitutions well soaked with alcohol, and that then they are easily dispatched without fear of making any noise or call for assistance. Having been out of town lately for my holidays I have not closely followed the evidence at the inquests, but there are two questions which would require clearing up if there is anything in this theory – 1st. Have the stomachs been ripped open to do away with the evidence of poisoning in this manner? and 2nd. Has any analysis of the contents of the stomach been made?

There is no evidence that Macdonald made any attempt to have such examination made when Mary Jane Kelly's body lay in his custody.

Her murder led both Baxter and Macdonald to visit Dorset Street, as the allocation of Spitalfields to the North-East district was illogical. In all other respects, it was a part of Whitechapel, and should have come under Baxter's domain. Baxter's attempt to claim the Kelly inquest, however, was unsuccessful, as the removal of the body to Shoreditch mortuary definitely placed it in Macdonald's jurisdiction.

He conducted Kelly's inquest (12 November 1888, at Shoreditch Town Hall) – the only Ripper victim's inquest to be completed in a single day's hearing. Early in the proceedings, it seemed that he intended to hold a long inquest. Following **Dr George Bagster Phillips**' evidence, the *Daily Telegraph* reported, 'The jury had no questions to ask at this stage, and it was understood that more detailed evidence of a future examination would be given at a future hearing.' Yet after hearing further witnesses Macdonald told the jury that a note from Dr Phillips asked whether he was required further, and immediately accepted their view that they had enough evidence on which to return a verdict, saying, 'There is other evidence which I do not propose to call, for if we at once make public every fact brought forward in connection with this terrible murder, the end of justice might be retarded.' The jury accepted the offer to conclude with alacrity.

Macdonald's change of heart, it has been suggested, arose from his perception that someone was trying to inhibit the jury from returning a verdict – a failure which would have reflected badly on him. At the beginning of the inquest, two jurors had objected that Mr Baxter was their coroner and they should not be hearing an inquest under Macdonald. He had suppressed them fiercely, threatening punitive measures, if they did not carry out their duties, but after a later short adjournment he again warned the jury against outside interference which, he said, he had learned was being attempted. A more drawn-out inquest like one of Wynne Baxter's might have allowed the jury to hear **George Hutchinson**'s late-emerging testimony.

Neither Macdonald nor the jurors' signatures appear on the inquest certificate (now in the London Metropolitan Archives) to which the witnesses statements have been appended.

In 1890, Macdonald married Frances Perceval,˙granddaughter of the Tory prime minister assassinated in 1819. Later, in 1892, he resigned from Parliament. The reason is unknown, but within a year Frances had died, and a year later he followed her.

(See Robert Linford, John Savage and David O'Flaherty, 'The Green of the Peak Part III: Ruairdh Mac Dhòmnaill' in *Ripperologist*, 65, March 2006, for a full account of his life and background.)

MacKELLAR, DR ALEXANDER OBERLIN (1845–1904)

Chief surgeon, Metropolitan Police, from 1885. His name appears variously in reports as McKenna and M'Kenna. On his death in harness, Commissioner Sir Edward Henry wrote a glowing tribute to him (*Police Orders*, 18 June 1904). A distinguished and honoured member of the medical profession, whose name was held in much esteem throughout the Metropolitan Police and among his medical colleagues at Scotland Yard (obituary, *Harrow Gazette*, 25 June 1904).

Asked to examine Alice McKenzie (MEPO 3/140, ff 294–7).

Sent by James Monro to examine the body of Rose Mylett, when Monro learned that Dr Bond was not available. MacKellar, like the overwhelming majority of the doctors who saw the body, believed she had died of strangulation caused by foul play.

McKENNA, EDWARD

Lodging-house resident of 15 Brick Lane arrested on suspicion. For uncertain reasons – (but one newspaper suggests that he threatened to stab people and Inspector **Abberline**'s report to **Chief Inspector Donald Swanson** stated that he had been seen in Heath Street and other places with a knife) – McKenna aroused suspicions in Whitechapel throughout the day of 14 September and was eventually handed over to police at Commercial Street Station. Inspector Abberline took charge of the questioning.

McKenna was 5ft 7in, slightly built, shabbily dressed, with a careworn appearance, sandyish hair, beard and moustache, and wore a skull cap. His pockets contained an assortment of rags, handkerchiefs, two women's purses, several metal and cardboard boxes, a strip of leather and a spring onion.

Particular interest was taken in him because he resembled a description of the wanted man, particularly that of the man seen by **Miss Lyons** and by the potman of the Ten Bells at about 5am, on the morning of **Annie Chapman**'s murder. But McKenna said that he was sleeping at a common lodging-house at 15 Brick Lane on the night of the murder and when investigation proved this to be true, he was released (*The Times* and *Star* 15 September 1888, and *Illustrated Police News*, 22 September 1888. MEPO 3/140 ff15–16).

McKENZIE, ALICE 'CLAY PIPE', AKA ALICE BRYANT (c. 1849–89)

Alleged Ripper victim. Said to be a native of Peterborough.

Her left thumb was distinctively injured in an industrial accident. May be the same woman, aged 37, who on 21 June 1886 failed to appear at the Thames Police Court to answer charges of being drunk. From c. 1883, cohabited on and off with **John McCormack** in East End common lodging-houses. Then, from c. April 1889 the couple were usually resident at Mr Tenpenny's lodging-house, 52 Gun Street, Spitalfields, which was managed by Mrs **Elizabeth Ryder**. McKenzie worked as a washer-woman and charwoman, principally for Jewish residents of the East End, but was also known to prostitute herself habitually. According to **Mrs Smith** of Castle Alley, she sometimes used the name Kelly. (Cf. **Mary Jane Kelly**, **Catherine Eddowes**.)

She spent the day of Tuesday, 16 July 1889 in the lodging-house while McCormack was out at work. Around 4pm, he came home slightly the worse for drink and went to bed, giving McKenzie 1s 8d (worth about £5 in today's money): 5d to pay Mrs Ryder for the rent, and a shilling to spend as she pleased. McCormack testified this was the last time he spoke to her, but since he did not dispute there was some quarrel between them that afternoon or evening, and Mrs Ryder testified that McKenzie finally left the lodging-house at about 8pm after 'having words' with McCormack, it seems likely they spoke again. Certainly, McCormack went downstairs at about 11pm and learned to his annoyance that McKenzie had failed to pay the rent!

According to a rumour reported in the *Pall Mall Gazette*, McKenzie spent the evening at the Cambridge Music Hall with a blind boy named George Discon or Dixon, also resident at Tenpenny's. Discon believed that, after seeing him home to Gun Street, McKenzie went out again to a public house to meet an unknown man she had met at the music-hall and persuaded to treat her to drinks. (Five years later, this was garbled in the *Sun* into the story that Mary Jane Kelly's murderer's voice had been heard by a blind boy in whom she took 'a passionate interest'.)

Between 11.30 and midnight, McKenzie passed along Flower and Dean Street, going towards Brick Lane, and stopped to chat to three acquaintances called Margaret Franklin, Catherine Hughes and Sarah Marney, who were sitting on the steps of a lodging-house at the Commercial Street end. All four may have gone on to a public house for a drink.

Very shortly after 12.50, Police Constable **Walter Andrews** found McKenzie's body close to a lamp-post on the western pavement of Castle Alley, her head towards the kerb, her feet towards the wall. Blood was flowing from two stabs in her throat and her skirt was pulled up, revealing blood over her thigh and abdomen. Postmortem examination showed this came from a long, but not unduly deep wound running from below the left breast to the navel, seven or eight superficial scratches from this wound towards the genitals and a shallow cut across the *mons veneris*.

Andrews heard footsteps approaching the alley and encountered local resident **Isaac Lewis Jacobs** on his way to purchase supper. Jacobs remained with the body while Andrews summoned **Sergeant Badham** and further assistance. Both Jacobs and **Inspector Reid**, who arrived some time prior to 1.10am, noticed that blood continued to flow from the throat to the gutter. But this had ceased and the blood was starting to clot when **Dr George Bagster Phillips** arrived shortly after 1.10. Jacobs also noticed (as Mrs Ryder independently confirmed) that McKenzie was wearing odd stockings. Her clay pipe and an old farthing were found under the body, leading to the belief that the murderer might have repeated the deception it was suspected had been practised on **Annie Chapman** of offering a polished farthing as a sovereign, or an old farthing as a sixpence.

In the absence of **Dr Robert Anderson** on leave, **Colonel Monsell** assisted **Commissioner Monro** in directing the investigation. Following Dr Phillips' postmortem, **Dr Thomas Bond** was sent to make a further examination of the body, and his report shows that Phillips and he differed frequently in their interpretation of marks, Phillips strongly insisting his prior observations made his conclusions preferable.

See Bond, Phillips for their differing deductions concerning the murderer, and Monro for his changing opinions.

Wynne Baxter conducted the inquest (17 and 19 July; then adjourned to 14 August), which inevitably found murder against a person or persons unknown.

MACNAGHTEN, SIR MELVILLE LESLIE (1853–1921)

Served in the Metropolitan Police, 1889–1913. Advanced as a Ripper suspect in 2007 (*see* **Jack l'Eventreur Démasqué**).

Born in 1853, the youngest of 15 children born to Elliot Macnaghten, the last chairman of the East India Company. Educated at Eton. Managed his father's estates in Bengal, India (1873–87), then in 1878 married Dora Sanderson, daughter of Canon Sanderson, headmaster of Lancing. Assistant chief constable, CID, Scotland Yard, 1889–90; chief constable, 1890–1903; asst commissioner, CID., 1902–1913. Served on Asquith's Committee to inquire into the identification of criminals, which resulted in the adoption of Sir Edward Henry's famous fingerprint system.

Knighted in 1907; CB, 1908. Also Knight Commander of the White Military

Order of Spain and a Commander of the Order of Dannebrog. In his youth an amateur actor of ability and a constant and enthusiastic theatregoer throughout his life. He loved books, especially the classics, and was a fan of boxing. In 1913, he retired following two years of ill-health and a voyage to Australia (1912), which brought no improvement. Died at Queen Anne's Mansions, Westminster, leaving three children (*see* **Christabel Aberconway**).

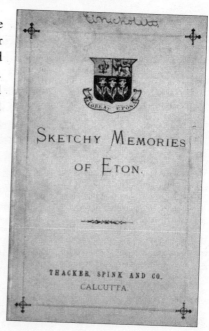

In 1881, he was attacked by Indian land rioters who, he said, 'assaulted me so badly that I was left senseless on the plain.' In consequence, he met **James Monro**, then Inspector-General of Bengal Police, who became a lifelong friend. In 1887, when he returned to England, Monro, by-then assistant commissioner in charge of CID, Scotland Yard, offered him the post of assistant chief constable, advising Commissioner **Sir Charles Warren** that, 'I saw his way of managing men when I was in India and was struck by it, for he had a most turbulent set of natives to deal with, and he dealt with them firmly and justly' (HO144/190/A46472B sub.6).

Before formalities were completed, however, Charles Warren learned that, in his words, Macnaghten was 'the one man in India who has been beaten by Hindoos.' The Home Office duly rejected Macnaghten, and Monro resigned. When Monro was appointed commissioner following Warren's resignation in 1888, he appointed Macnaghten assistant chief constable and he took up his post in June 1889. Macnaghten's memoirs explicitly refuse to rake over the 'old sore' of Monro's resignation; their persistent silence on **Anderson** and **Bradford**, however, and deprecatory mention of unnamed Warren (notably in connection with the bloodhounds' incident), suggest lifelong resentment of his mentor's treatment, especially when contrasted with his warm reminiscences of all other close colleagues.

The press welcomed the appointment of Macnaghten and most published reminiscences describe his charm and affability. **F.P. Wensley**, who said in *Detective Days* (London: Cassell, 1931) that his own career owed much to Macnaghten's encouragement, called him 'a very great gentleman'. H.L. Adam (*Police Work From Within*, London: Holden & Hardingham, 1914), noted, 'Sir Melville is somewhat reserved in manner, shrewdly preferring to listen to what you have to say to talking himself. He is most adroit at leading you away from things he does not wish to discuss.'

Major Arthur Griffiths (***Mysteries of Police and Crime,*** London: Cassell, 1898) and Adam both described his delight in attending scenes of crime, while *Vanity Fair* noted him as the first assistant commissioner to make personal arrest of a burglar. Adam recalled (*CID: Behind the Scenes at Scotland Yard,* London: Sampson Low, Marston, 1908), his 'extensive knowledge of crime and criminals, quite as extensive as that of his predecessor, Sir Robert Anderson,' adding, 'He was a familiar figure at the scene of any murder case, which had special interest to the mind of a police official.' Griffiths said he was, 'essentially a man of action,' and, 'It is Mr Macnaghten's duty, no less than his earnest desire, to be first on the scene of any such sinister catastrophe. He is therefore more intimately acquainted, perhaps, with the details of the most recent celebrated crimes than anyone else at Scotland Yard.' Both men were struck by his collection of mug-shots, and remarked that he kept the Jack the Ripper victim photos under lock and key in his office.

A cautioning note is given by Sir Robert Anderson in his memoirs, where he recalled being vexed with a senior colleague, who made a silly fuss about a threatening letter, Chief Inspector Swanson, recorded privately that this colleague was 'Macnaghten: Ch. Const'.

By 1891, matters seem to have come to a head and it was reported Macnaghten was seeking transfer to the uniform branch, but somehow they were tided over and Macnaghten continued to serve under Anderson until the latter's retirement in 1901. He then served for two years under Major Edward Henry, to whom he dedicated his book of memoirs: 'The best all-round policeman of the twentieth century'. Eventually, he stepped into the assistant commissioner's post himself.

On his retirement, the *Police Review* said: 'His tenure of office has been placid, and it is in no sense belittling his services to remark that his rule did not enhance the proficiency or reputation of the C.I. Department. He carried on the work of his office with the assistance of an experienced staff, the leading members of which are debarred from filling positions for which they act as expert advisers.' It is difficult to assess the fairness of this judgement: *Police Review* represented the rank-and-file police officers who were understandably beginning to resent the habitual appointment of chief constables and assistant commissioners from gentlemen of the professional and commissioned officer classes outside the force.

In February 1894, he wrote the **Macnaghten memoranda**, in which he named three suspects.

At the time of his retirement, Macnaghten was reported in the *Daily Mail* (2 June 1913) as saying, 'the greatest regret of his life was that he joined the force six months after "Jack the Ripper" committed suicide,' and continuing: 'Of course he was a maniac, but I have a very clear idea who he was and how he committed suicide, but that, with other secrets, will never be revealed by me. I have destroyed all my documents and there is now no record of the secret information which came into my possession at one time or another.'

In the *Days of My Years* (1914) chapter, 'Laying the Ghost of Jack the Ripper', Macnaghten discusses the crimes and gives from memory a very fair account of the scare from **Emma Smith** to **Pinchin Street** (including the last because of personal recollections from investigating that case), although he only attributes five

victims to Jack the Ripper (*see* **canonical victims**). His stated conclusions were:
Although the Whitechapel Murderer, in all probability, put an end to himself
soon after the Dorset Street affair in November 1888, certain facts, pointing
to this conclusion, were not in possession of the police till some years after I
became a detective officer.

And:

I do not think that there was anything of religious mania about the real
Simon Pure, nor do I believe that he had ever been detained in an asylum,
nor lived in lodgings. [*Cf.* **G. Wentworth Bell Smith**.] I incline to the
belief that the individual who held up London in terror resided with his
own people; that he absented himself from home at certain times, and
that he committed suicide on or about the 10th of November 1888'(*cf.*
M.J. Druitt).

The erroneous final date is a result of Macnaghten's reliance on memory.

Reynolds's News (15 May 1921) published a fanciful and inaccurate story by the
unnamed author of a book called *Crime and the Criminal*, in which the author
claimed to have heard from Macnaghten's own lips how Macnaghten returned to
England from India after the Double Event and obtained permission from Sir
Charles Warren to investigate the Ripper murders, and was even supplied with the
assistance of several uniformed men. Sir Melville had formed some opinions, we're
told, and these were confirmed when an East End woman told him about a meeting
she'd had in a pub with an elderly man, who gave her a religious tract. Macnaghten
apparently narrowed the identity to a single individual. That man committed suicide
in the Thames and Macnaghten was able to convince the authorities that he was the
Ripper, a few months later being appointed chief constable.

Inspector **Tom Divall** wrote Macnaghten received some information that the
murderer had gone to America and died in a lunatic asylum there.

For the possibility that Macnaghten believed, at some time, that the Ripper
might have been a Fenian, *see* **Balfour**.

MACNAGHTEN MEMORANDA

Report by **Sir Melville Macnaghten** refuting newspaper allegations concerning
Thomas **Cutbush** and in the process naming three men more likely than Cutbush
to have been Jack the Ripper. Two versions are known to exist, and there was
possibly a third.

The Scotland Yard Version

Contained in the Metropolitan Police files and first described publicly in *The
Complete Jack the Ripper*, this comprises seven foolscap sheets in Macnaghten's
own hand reading as follows:

Confidential

The case, referred to in the sensational story told in 'The Sun' in its issue of 13th inst, & following dates, is that of **Thomas Cutbush** who, was arraigned at the London County Sessions in April 1891, on a charge of maliciously wounding Florence Grace Johnson, and attempting to wound Isabelle Frazer Anderson in Kennington. He was found to be insane, and sentenced to be detained during Her Majesty's pleasure.

This Cutbush, who lived with his mother and aunt at 14 Albert St. Kennington, escaped from the Lambeth Infirmary, (after he had been detained there only a few hours, as a lunatic) at noon on 5th March 1891 – He was rearrested on 9th idem. A few weeks before this, several cases of stabbing, or 'jobbing' [sic] girls behind recurred in the vicinity, and a man named Colicott [*see* **Collocot**] was arrested, but subsequently discharged, owing to faulty identification. The cuts in the girls dresses made by Colicott were quite different to the cut made by Cutbush (when he wounded Miss Johnson) who was no doubt influenced by a wild desire of morbid imitation. Cutbush's antecedents were enquired into by Ch. Inspr. [now Supt.] **Chis[holm]**, by **Inspr. Race**, and by **P.S. McCarthy** C.I.D. – [The last named officer had been specially employed in Whitechapel at the time of the murders there] and it was ascertained that he was born, & had lived, in Kennington all his life. His father died when he was quite young, and he was always a 'spoilt' child. He had been employed as a clerk and traveller in the Tea trade at the Minories, & subsequently canvassed for a Directory in the East End, during which time he bore a good character. He apparently contracted syphilis about 1888, and, – since that time, – led an idle and useless life. His brain seems to have become affected, and he believed that people were trying to poison him. He wrote to Lord Grimthorpe, and others, – & also to the Treasury, – complaining of Dr Brooks, of Westminster Bridge Rd, whom he threatened to shoot for having supplied him with bad medicines. He is said to have studied medical books by day, & to have rambled about at night, returning frequently with his clothes covered with mud; but little reliance could be placed on the statements made by his mother or his aunt, who both appear to have been of a very excitable disposition. It was found impossible to ascertain his movements on the nights of the Whitechapel murders. The knife found on him was bought in Houndsditch about a week before he was detained in the Infirmary. Cutbush was a nephew of the late Supt. Executive. (*See* **Supt. Charles Henry Cutbush**.)

Now the Whitechapel Murderer had 5 victims – & 5 victims only, – his murders were
(i) 31st Aug '88. **Mary Ann Nichols**, at Buck's Row, who was found with her throat cut, & with (slight) stomach mutilation.
(ii) 8th Sept '88. **Annie Chapman** – Hanbury Street: – throat cut – stomach & private parts badly mutilated & some of the entrails placed round the neck.

(iii) 30th Sept '88. **Elizabeth Stride** – Berner's Street. throat cut, but nothing in shape of mutilation attempted, & *on same date* **Catherine Eddowes**, Mitre Square, throat cut, & very bad mutilation, both of face and stomach.

(iv) 9th November. **Mary Jane Kelly** – Miller's Court, throat cut, and the whole of the body mutilated in the most ghastly manner.

The last murder is the only one that took place in a *room*, and the murderer must have been at least 2 hours engaged. A photo was taken of the woman, as she was found lying on the bed, without seeing which it is impossible to imagine the awful mutilation.

With regard to the *double* murder which took place on 30th Sept., there is no doubt but that the man was disturbed by some Jews who drove up to a Club, (close to which the body of Elizabeth Stride was found) and that he then, 'nondum satiatus', went in search of a further victim whom he found at Mitre Square.

It will be noticed that the fury of the mutilations *increased* in each case, and, seemingly, the appetite only became sharpened by indulgence. It seems, then, highly improbable that the murderer would have suddenly stopped in November '88, and been content to recommence operations by merely prodding a girl behind some 2 years & 4 months afterwards. A much more rational theory is that the murderer's brain gave way altogether after his awful glut in Miller's Court, and that he immediately committed suicide, or, as a possible alternative, was found to be so hopelessly mad by his relations, that he was by then confined in some asylum.

No one ever saw the Whitechapel Murderer: many homicidal maniacs were suspected, but no shadow of proof could be thrown on any one. I may mention the cases of 3 men, any one of whom would have been more likely than Cutbush to have committed this series of murders:

(1) A Mr **M. J. Druitt**, said to be a doctor & of good family, who disappeared at the time of the Miller's Court murder, whose body (which was said to have been upwards of a month in the water) was found in the Thames on 31st Dec. – or about 7 weeks after that murder. He was sexually insane and from private info I have little doubt but that his own family believed him to have been the murderer.

(2) **Kosminski**, a Polish Jew, & resident in Whitechapel. This man became insane owing to many years indulgence in solitary vices. He had a great hatred of women, specially of the prostitute class, & had strong homicidal tendencies; he was removed to a lunatic asylum about March 1889. There were many circs connected with this man which made him a strong 'suspect'.

(3) **Michael Ostrog**, a Russian doctor, and a convict, who was subsequently detained in a lunatic asylum as a homicidal maniac. This man's antecedents were of the worst possible type, and his whereabouts at the time of the murders could never be ascertained.

And now with regard to a few of the inaccuracies and misleading statements made by the 'Sun'. In its issue of 14th Feb, it is stated that the writer has in his possession a facsimile of the knife with which the murders were committed. This knife (which for some unexplained reason has, for the last 3 years, been kept by Insp. Race, instead of being sent to Prisoners' Property Store) was traced, & it was found to have been purchased in Houndsditch in Feb. '91, or 2 years & 3 months *after* the Whitechapel murders ceased!

The statement, too, that Cutbush 'spent a portion of the day in making rough drawings of the bodies of women, & of their mutilations' is based solely on the fact that 2 *scribble* drawings of women in indecent postures were found torn up in Cutbush's room. The head & body of one of these had been cut from some fashion plate, & legs were added to show a woman's naked thighs & pink stockings.

In the issue of the 15th inst. it is said that a *light overcoat* was among the things found in Cutbush's house, and that a man in a *light* overcoat was seen talking to a woman in Backchurch Lane whose body with arms attached was found in Pjnchin St. This is hopelessly incorrect! On 10th Sept. '89 the naked body, with arms, of a woman was found wrapped in some sacking under a Railway arch in **Pinchin St**: the head & legs were never found nor was the woman ever identified. She had been killed at least 24 hours before the remains, (which had seemingly been brought from a distance), were discovered. The stomach was split up by a cut, and the head and legs had been severed in a manner identical with that of the woman whose remains were discovered in the Thames, in Battersea Park, & on the Chelsea Embankment on 4th June of the same year; [*Cf.* **Elizabeth Jackson**] and these murders had no connection whatever with the Whitechapel horrors. The Rainham [torso] mystery in 1887, & the Whitehall mystery [when portions of a woman's body were found under what is now New Scotland Yard] in 1888 were of a similar type to the Thames & Pinchin St crimes.

It is perfectly untrue to say that Cutbush stabbed 6 girls behind – this is confounding his case with that of **Colicott**.

The theory that the Whitechapel Murderer was lefthanded, or, at any rate, 'ambi-dexter,' had its origin in the remark made by a doctor who examined the corpse of one of the earliest victims; other doctors did not agree with him.

With regard to the 4 additional murders ascribed by the writer in the 'Sun' to the Whitechapel fiend:

(1) The body of **Martha Tabram**, a prostitute, was found on a common stair case in George Yard buildings on 7th August 1888; the body had been repeatedly *pierced*, probably with a *bayonet*. This woman had, with a fellow prostitute, been in company of 2 soldiers in the early part of the evening. These men were arrested, but the second prostitute failed, or refused to identify, and the soldiers were accordingly discharged.

(2) **Alice McKenzie** was found with her throat cut (or rather *stabbed*) in Castle Alley on 17th July 1889; no evidence was forthcoming, and no arrests were made in connection with this case. The *stab* in the throat was of the same nature as in the case of the murder of

(3) **Frances Coles**, in Swallow Gardens, on 13th February 1891 – for which Thomas Sadler, a fireman, was arrested, &, after several remands, discharged. It was ascertained at the time that Sadler had sailed for the Baltic on 19th July '89 & was in Whitechapel on the night of 17th idem. He was a man of ungovernable temper & entirely addicted to drink, & the company of the lowest prostitutes.

(4) The case of the unidentified woman whose trunk was found in Pinchin St: on 10th Sept. 1889 – which has already been dealt with.

M L Macnaghten
23rd Feb. 1894

The **Lady Aberconway** version, discovered by **Daniel Farson** in 1959, comprises seven typed and numbered quarto sheets, with two handwritten inserts, the first numbered '6A'. These are described in pencil on typed sheet 6 as 'p 6A & 6B, written in ink and attached at end'. The very brief pencilled observations on the typed sheets (e.g. 'by my Father Sir M.M.' following the typed heading, 'Memorandum on articles which appeared in the Sun re JACK THE RIPPER on 14 Feb 1894 and subsequent dates') are in the hand of Lady Aberconway, as (according to her son) are the insert sheets, despite some obvious differences in character formation and the solecism 'conjections'.

Pages 1–3, and part of 4, deal entirely with the case of Thomas Cutbush, Pages 4–5 give a brief, and not entirely accurate, summary of the murders of Nichols, Chapman, Stride, Eddowes and Kelly. The last three words on page 5 and first three paragraphs on page 6 introduce Macnaghten's personal conclusions on the identity of the Ripper, including the confidential material naming three suspects, which is on the handwritten sheets. This vital section (pages 5–6, 6A, 6B) runs thus:

A much more rational and *workable* theory, to my way of thinking, is that the 'rippers' [*sic*] brain gave way altogether after his awful glut in Miller's Court and that he then committed suicide, or, as a *less* likely alternative, was found to be so helplessly insane by his relatives, that they, suspecting the worst, had him confined in some Lunatic Asylum.

No one ever saw the Whitechapel Murderer (unless possibly it was the City P.C. who was a beat [sic] near Mitre Square) and no proof could in any way ever be brought against anyone, although very many homicidal maniacs were at one time, or another, *suspected*. I enumerate the cases of 3 men against whom Police held very [a pencilled addition in Lady Aberconway's hand reads '(here follows p 6A & 6B, written in ink and attached at end)'] reasonable suspicion. Personally, after much careful & deliberate consideration, I am inclined to exonerate the last *2*, but I have always held strong opinions regarding *no 1,* and the more I think the matter over, the stronger do these opinions become. The *truth,* however, will never be known, and did indeed, at one time lie at the bottom of the Thames, if my conjections [sic] be correct.

No. 1. Mr M.J. Druitt a doctor of about 41 years of age & of fairly good family, who disappeared at the time of the Miller's Court murder, and whose body was found floating in the Thames on 31st Dec: i.e. 7 weeks after the said murder. The body was said to have been in the water for a month, *or more* – on it was found a season ticket between Blackheath & London. From private information I have little doubt but that his own family suspected this man of being the Whitechapel Murderer; it was *alleged* that he was sexually insane.

No 2. [*Paper damaged, but no doubt should read 'Kos'*]minski, a Polish Jew, who lived in [*paper damaged, but Farson, who saw it in an earlier state, transcribes 'the very'*] heart of the district where the murders were committed. He had become insane owing to many years indulgence in solitary vices. He had a great hatred of women, with strong homicidal tendencies. He was (and I believe still is) detained in a lunatic asylum about March 1889. This man in appearance strongly resembled the individual seen by the City P.C. near Mitre Square.

No: 3. Michael Ostrog. a mad Russian doctor & a convict & unquestionably a homicidal maniac. This man was said to have been habitually cruel to women, & for a long time was known to have carried about with him surgical knives & other instruments; his antecedents were of the very,, worst & his whereabouts at the time of the Whitchapel' [sic] murders could never be satisfactorily accounted for. He is still alive.

And now with regard to the 4 additional murders aserted [sic] [*added in pencil below, 'ascribed'*] by the 'Sun' writer to the 'Ripper'. [*Added in pencil in Lady Aberconway's hand, but certainly at a different time from the inked main text,* '(here follows, on p 6.
1) The body of Martha etc:']

The remainder deals very briefly with Martha Tabram, Alice McKenzie, Frances Coles, and the Pinchin Street' murder.

Philip Loftus twice described the **Gerald Melville Donner** version of the memorandum, which he had seen in the early 1950s. The first description was in a letter to Lady Aberconway, 11 August 1972:

My recollections of the notes, which differ from those quoted in the American journalist **Tom Cullen**'s book, '**Autumn of Terror**' in 1965, were that the three suspects were (1) MICHAEL JOHN DRUITT, a DOCTOR of FORTY ONE years of age. (2) A feeble-minded man (probably Thomas Cutbush), who followed young girls and stabbed them with nail scissors. (3) a Polish Jew cobbler nick-named "Leather Apron".

Unfortunately, I didn't take advantage of Gerald's offer to take a copy of the notes, although I believe that later he let someone else do so. [Loftus' dots]

In the *Guardian* (7 October 1972) Loftus described them as private notes, in Sir Melville's handwriting on official paper, rather untidy and in the nature of rough jottings.

As I remember them, they gave three suspects: a Polish tanner or cobbler; a man who went round stabbing young girls in the bottom with nail scissors; and M. J. Druitt, a doctor of 41 years of age.

Though [*the notes quoted by Farson are*] different in some respects from what I remember of Gerald's papers, they contain the same reference to Druitt.

The Donner version has never been seen since, and its status (draft, uncorrected version, misquoted version or garbled recollection of the Macnaghten original of the Lady Aberconway version) is entirely a matter of speculation. Some Ripperologists suggest it represents memory contaminated by reading Farson's *Jack the Ripper* despite Loftus's explicit observation. Some are intrigued by Montague John Druitt's becoming Michael John. It is not known how much omitted detail Loftus represents by his dots, nor whether he correctly recollected the errors of fact (e.g. Druitt's christian name). It would be invaluable in the highest degree to recover it, if it exists, to confirm wherein Macnaghten's errors lay, whether it was Colicott who used nail scissors as a weaponand whether the Polish Jew cobbler 'Leather Apron' appears to be a description of John Pizer or some other supposed suspect.

The phrase 'sexually insane' (like the phrase 'sexual maniac' used of the Ripper in *Days of My Years*) has been much discussed. A letter of 1905 from McNaghten to **C.E. Troup** of the Home Office shows that Macnaghten believed any irrational act of cruelty to people or animals, whether perpetrated by immediate violence or slow poison, was sexually motivated; also that sexual aberrants could be physiognomically identified. He says of the Edalji case, in which a young man was wrongfully convicted of mutilating cattle and horses, 'There is no doubt that the fellow who perpetrated these outrages was a sexual maniac, and if physiognomy goes for anything, Mr Edalji has the face of such an individual.' And he says of **Neil Cream**, 'I always believed he simply poisoned so that he might have pleasurable sensations in dwelling on the sufferings of the women at the time of their death.'

The relative status of the Aberconway and Scotland Yard versions has been disputed, usually by researchers wishing to claim primacy for the version they have seen. Apart from **Stephen Knight**'s claim that the variants in the Aberconway version were introduced by Lady Aberconway herself, and represent her reflections and not her father's, such argument is unimportant. Whichever version was first drafted, there is no question both versions represent Macnaghten's beliefs and expand his references in his memoirs and elsewhere to his knowledge of the Ripper's identity and suicide.

It has been suggested that the three named suspects may have been drawn at random from a much larger list of equal status and those named were of no greater significance than that, as Macnaghten states, any one of them, 'would have been more likely than Cutbush to have committed this series of murder.' Since one of those named was believed by Macnaghten himself to have been the murderer and it is now known that another appears to have been favoured by Anderson, it seems evident those named were more significant than simply being more likely than Cutbush to have been the murderer, and this also seems to have been the opinion of commentators who knew Macnaghten and had evidently seen the memorandum, **Major Griffiths** and **G.R. Sims**.

(*See* **Jack the Myth** for A.P. Wolf's case that only Macnaghten's word dismisses Cutbush from the list of suspects. *See* **Walter Ernest Boultbee** for a suggestion of Macnaghten's possible channel of information from the Druitt family.)

McWILLIAM, INSPECTOR JAMES (1837–1916)

Head of City Police Detective Department.

A miller before joining the City of London Police in 1858 (warrant no. 2852_. Promoted to sergeant (1869), then inspector (1875), inspector of detectives (1878), superintendent of detectives (1890). Retired in 1903.

The involvement of McWilliam, whose principal expertise was in untangling financial frauds (as was common with City detectives), was welcomed by the press when **Catherine Eddowes**' murder in

Mitre Square brought in the City Police. Liaised daily with **Swanson** on the case.

His order that the **Goulston Street graffito** be photographed was misreported as ordering its erasure (*The People*, 14 October 1888) and the City Solicitor, **Mr Crawford**, wrote to the newspaper to say that the City police, 'were in no way responsible for the rubbing out' (*The People*, 21 October 1888). His long report to the Home Office (dated 29 October 1888) was considered so uninformative by an unidentified Home Office official that an appended minute sheet carries the notes, 'This report tells very little,' and 'The printed report of the Inquest contains much more information than this. They evidently want to tell us nothing.' In parenthetical notes, **Godfrey Lushington** disagreed.

MACHADO, JOAO DE SOUZA (*b.* 1847)
Alleged suspect. Portuguese cattleboat seaman advanced by **E.K. Larkins** as the accomplice of **José Laurenco** in the murders of **Chapman**, **Stride** and **Eddowes**, and single-handed murderer of **Kelly**.

MADEWELL, LIZZIE (*b.* 1879)
Traffic accident victim confused with **Alice Margaret Crook**. On 1 October 1888, Lizzie was run over by a hansom cab outside 1 New Bridge Street (opposite Anderton's Hotel in Fleet Street) and taken to St Bartholomew's Hospital, where she remained until 20 October. The accident was reported without her name being given in *Illustrated Police News*, and **Stephen Knight** wrongly identified it with **John Netley**'s alleged attempt on the life of Alice Margaret Crook.

MADURO, ALONZO
Alleged suspect.

An Argentinian born in Buenos Aires. His mother died when he was in infancy and his father lacked the discipline to raise a son properly. A 'sort of international finance mystery man', he became known through business to Griffith S. Salway, of a City brokerage firm in Gresham House, Old Broad Street, London. According to Salway, Alonzo Maduro was in his late thirties, with dark eyes and a swarthy complexion, stocky, but quick and agile and giving the impression of great physical strength. Clean shaven, he spoke with a barely discernible Spanish accent because he had spent a lot of time in the United States.

Salway would meet Maduro for dinner at the South American's hotel, near Finsbury Pavement. On one occasion he left Maduro alone with a girl named Stella and when he met her again, several days later, she almost hysterically claimed Maduro was, 'not human; he's a devil; he's a beast!' On another occasion, he met Maduro and walked with him through Spitalfields and Whitechapel, the following morning reading in the newspapers about the murder of **Martha Tabram**.

There were further murders and Maduro's behaviour became increasingly strange, until Salway met him for the last time in the Commercial Room of Anderton's Hotel in Fleet Street and discovered in the false bottom of Maduro's bag a blood-stained apron and a sharp knife.

It has been suggested (*The Mammoth Book of Jack the Ripper*) that Alonzo Maduro was the same person as **Alois Szemeredy**, *Ripperologist* contributor Eduardo Zinna having pointed out that the names could sound similar. Szemeredy's whereabouts between 1886–92 are unknown and perhaps neatly dovetail with Alonzo Maduro's appearance in London. However, there are significant differences: Maduro was in his late thirties, whereas Szemeredy was estimated to be about 47; Maduro was stocky, Szemeredy tall and thin; Maduro was clean shaven, Szemeredy possessed a thick moustache, and so on.

Nothing is known of Alonzo Maduro beyond what Salway told John Shuttleworth, editor of *True Detective*, some 60 years after the crimes.

(*See* Salway, Griffith 'I Knew Jack The Ripper', *True Detective*, March 1949; Adam Wood, 'From Buenos Aires to Brick Lane: Were Alois Szemeredy and Alonzo Maduro the Same Man?', *Ripperologist*, 25, October 1999; Eduardo Zinna, 'The Search for Jack el Destripador', *Ripperologist*, 33, February 2001.)

MAHONEY, MRS ELIZABETH (*b. c.* 1863)
Witness at Martha Tabram's inquest.

Match-girl, working 9am to 11pm in Stratford factory. Accompanied her husband Joseph, a carman, to their residence in 47 George Yard Buildings at 1.40am on 7 August 1888. Subsequently went out to buy supper at a chandler's shop, returning within five minutes. She believed there was no one at that time on the landing, where **Tabram** was subsequently found.

MALAY SEA COOK
Suspect, described by **George M. Dodge**, who said he had sailed with him on the Glen Line Steamship Company's vessel, *Glenartney*.

According to Dodge, he encountered the Malay in the Queen's Music Hall, Poplar, and learned that the cook had been robbed by a streetwalker and now declared his intention to kill and mutilate every streetwalker he encountered, unless he got his property back. Dodge told his story in New York, and the Press Association circulated it to newspapers both sides of the Atlantic. The *Chicago Tribune* (6 October 1888) gave the fullest coverage and stated that the police had visited the music hall, the East End Home for Asiatics, the Scandinavian Sailors' temperance house and Messrs Magregor's Son & Co., owners of the Glen Line. None had any record of George Dodge or the robbery, and the Glen Line vouched for the reliability of the Chinese sea cook on the *Glenartney*, adding the ship had been at sea the whole time except for the period from 14 August to 8 September, and there were no Malays in the crew. The police concluded Dodge had made up the story.

See also **Alaska**, and *cf.* **John Sanderson**.

MALCOLM, MRS MARY
Witness at **Elizabeth Stride**'s inquest.

Wife of tailor Andrew Malcolm, of 50 Eagle Street, Red Lion Square. She claimed to have been awakened at the time of the murder by an awareness of her sister Mrs. Elizabeth Watts' insubstantial presence, and feeling her kiss her. Subsequently, she feared the murdered woman was Mrs Watts, and on a second visit to St George's-in-the-East mortuary, she positively identified her from a mark on her leg caused by an adder bite in childhood. Despite warnings from coroner **Wynne Baxter** to be sure her story was accurate, she persisted in the identification, adding subsequent to being rejected for drunkenness and immorality by her husband, Mr Watts of Bath, Elizabeth had married a Poplar coffee-shop owner, who had died in a shipwreck on St Paul's Island and had thereafter lived an immoral life prostituting herself to (among others) a policeman.

She had received weekly small gifts of money from Mrs Malcolm and had once handed over a newborn baby to her. Mrs Malcolm was sure that she never used the name Stride, but believed she had been nicknamed 'Long Liz'. She did not, of course, believe her to be Swedish.

The entire identification collapsed when the former Mrs Watts, now Mrs Elizabeth Stokes, appeared at a later hearing and denied it. A good deal of her history (which included three marriages and two periods in lunatic asylums) matched Mrs Malcolm's story. Her second husband, for example, really had died after being shipwrecked on the Island of St Paul's in the St Lawrence Gulf. Mr Baxter always seemed suspicious of the story, although the British press appeared to have accepted without question that Mrs Malcolm genuinely identified Stride as the sister for whom she cared deeply.

A New Zealand journalist using the pen-name 'Elise', however, reporting from London for the *Te Aroha News* (12 December 1888), called Mrs Malcolm, 'a gin-sodden virago,' adding, 'From first to last, this woman's transparent object was to turn the catastrophe to account somehow.'

Mrs Malcolm never explained herself.

(Paul Begg, 'Mrs Malcolm's Story'. *Ripperologist*, 58, March 2005)

MAMMOTH BOOK OF JACK THE RIPPER, THE

Book edited by Maxim Jakubowski and Nathan Braund (London: Robinson Books, 1999. US Edition New York: Carroll and Graf, 1999. Republished in hardback as *Jack the Ripper: Comprehensive A–Z*, Edison, New Jersey: Castle Books, 2005.)

A chronology and summary of the case history, major witness statements with brief commentary and essays by William Beadle, Mark Daniel, Melvyn Fairclough, Martin Fido, Paul Harrison, Shirley Harrison, Bruce Paley, Sue and Andy Parlour, Gary Rowlands, M.J. Trow, **James Tully**, Peter Turnbull, Nick Warren, Simon Whitechapel, A.P. Wolf and Colin Wilson.

MAN WHO HUNTED JACK THE RIPPER, THE: EDMUND REID AND THE POLICE PERSPECTIVE

Book by Nicholas Connell and Stewart Evans (Cambridge: Rupert Books, 1999; republished as *The Man Who Hunted Jack the Ripper: Edmund Reid – Victorian Detective*. Stroud, Gloucestershire: Amberley, 2009, revised and corrected edition).

An examination of the Whitechapel murders which profiles Inspector **Edmund Reid** and includes his opinions on the case gathered from letters and articles in various newspapers.

Three chapters deal with Reid's career, before and apart from the Ripper murders, while nine handle the murders and the ongoing investigation; two look at other criminal cases handled by Reid, while eight chapters consider and assess the controversy surrounding the case and later police suggestions as to its possible solution and three chapters describe his life in retirement.

MANN, ROBERT

Pauper mortuary attendant. Advanced as suspect 2009.

Helped **James Hatfield** wash and lay out **Mary Ann Nichols**' body in Old Montague Street Workhouse Infirmary mortuary. Mann claimed he had received no instructions to do this, but coroner **Wynne Baxter** instructed the jury to disregard his evidence as he had fits and was unreliable (*See* Hatfield, Baxter, for dispute at the inquest as to whether laying-out was authorised by the police.)

Possibly the same Robert Mann (*c.* 1830–92), who is listed in the 1881 and 1891 Census returns as a resident of Whitechapel Union Infirmary and the Whitechapel Union Workhouse respectively, and was described as a labourer.

Advanced as Jack the Ripper in *Jack the Ripper: Quest For A Killer*.

MANSFIELD, RICHARD (1854–1907)

Suspect, accused 1888.

American actor. Born in Germany, son of a violin-playing wine merchant and an operetta singer. His father died when he was 4; his mother moved to Boston following a successful performance at the 1872 World's Peace Jubilee. Mansfield worked in a shop from 1875–1877, then sailed to England and after an unsuccessful attempt to establish himself as a painter, became a light comedy actor and singer with the D'Oyly Carte (Gilbert and Sullivan) provincial touring company. In 1882, he moved to New York and appeared in a succession of light comedy roles. Then, in 1886 he collaborated with a Boston friend, Thomas Russell Sullivan, to dramatise Robert Louis Stevenson's novel, *The Strange Case of Dr Jekyll and Mr Hyde*. Stevenson's approval was given, and in 1887, Mansfield first performed the dual role of Jekyll and Hyde in Boston. He used quick-change skills and dramatic lighting to produce highly successful horror and suspense effects.

After succeeding in New York and impressing Henry Irving, Mansfield took the play to London and opened at Irving's Lyceum Theatre on 4 August 1888. It closed on 29 September. It has frequently been said that the Ripper scare caused the failure of the production, and that despite making generous contributions to the Bishop of London's fund to open a laundry for the employment of reformed prostitutes, Mansfield was forced to close the production and return to America, making a loss. In fact, the play was running at a serious loss before the Ripper's activities were publicised and Mansfield had to revert to light comedies in October. He was always extravagant, both in his private life and lavish productions, and Martin A. Danahay and Alex Chisholm, in their study of Mansfield's work, *Jekyll and Hyde Dramatized* (Jefferson NC: McFarland, 2005), show that Mansfield's entire tour made a serious loss and he returned to America on bad terms with Irving, whom he owed more than £2,000. He was never to make the starring name he wanted in London, though by the time of his death he was America's leading actor and had introduced Ibsen and Shaw to the New York theatre.

His sensationally horrific performance, turning from the genteel Jekyll to the monster Hyde on stage in full view of the audience, did however lead to his being suggested as a possible Ripper. An atrociously spelt letter to the City Police, signed 'one who Prays for the murdrer to be Caught. M.P.', made the accusation, 'Now that these Horrable Murders are being Comited I think it the duty of Every one to let the Police know if they Suspect anyone... [W]hen I went to see Mr Mansfield Take the Part of Dr Jekel and Mr Hyde I felt at once that he was the Man Wanted.'

'M.P.' added Mansfield's ability at make-up and quick-change would allow him to escape easily without detection, especially if he 'carried A fine Faulse Wiskers &c in A Bag'. The City Police were unimpressed and marked the letter 'Not Acknowledged' (London Metropolitan Archives, Police Box 3:16. No.155).
(seeMartin A Danahay and Alex Chsiholm, *Jekyll and Hyde Dramatized*. Jefferson, North Carolina: McFarland, 2005, which gives a full account of the production and contains a chapter and appendix about the Ripper.)

MANY FACES OF JACK THE RIPPER, THE
Book by M.J. Trow (Chichester, West Sussex: Summersdale Publishers, 1997. Paperback: Chichester, West Sussex: Summersdale Publishers, 1998).

An attempt to provide a complete pictorial account of the crimes and application of profiling techniques.

'MARGARET'
Alleged friend of **Mary Jane Kelly**.

A Press Association report named this woman as seeing Kelly on 8 November 1888, and hearing from her that she proposed to kill herself for want of money. A further report, no longer naming the source, added Kelly had a young son living in her first-floor flat. A third version in the *New York Times* called the victim '**Lizzie Fisher**'. As Kelly is not known to have had a son (though Joe Barnett apparently believed she had), and her room was on the ground floor, it is probable the entire story describes Lizzie Fisher, mistakenly believed by 'Margaret' to be the Miller's Court murder victim.

MARKS, ELLEN

Witness. Talking with **Mary Callaghan** and cokeman **Frank Ruffle** outside 19 George Street, Spitalfields, on 21 November 1888, when a man said to have tried to cut **Annie Farmer**'s throat ran from the building, making a profane comment about an unnamed woman. She was unable to give chase as her boots were off, being rebuttoned. Marks entered the building to support Annie Farmer, held his lantern for PC256H while he searched for a knife and went to the police station to make a formal statement (*Daily Telegraph*, 21 November 1888).

MARRIOTT, DET. CON. EDWARD (*c.* 1861–1916)

Police reinforcement at **Catherine Eddowes**' murder site. Joined the City of London Police, 1885 (warrant no. 5830). Retired 1909, after injuries sustained on duty.

At 2.20am, on 30 September 1888, he was at the corner of Houndsditch, near St Botolph's Church, with detectives **Halse** and **Outram**. On hearing of the murder, all three ran to Mitre Square. Only Halse testified at the inquest.

MARSH, EMILY (*fl.* 1888)

Witness to suspicious man.

Shop assistant in her father's leather shop, 218 Jubilee street. Miss Marsh reported that a man of about 45 years old, 6ft tall, slim with a sallow complexion and dark beard and moustache came into the shop and asked in what appeared to be an Irish accent for the address of **George Lusk**, as referred to on the Vigilance Committee's poster, offering a reward. He declined to go to the Committee's headquarters at the Crown public house, so Miss Marsh gave him the address from a newspaper.

The following day, Lusk received the 'Lusk kidney' through the post. He also denied having been visited by anyone answering to the description of the man seen by Miss Marsh (*Daily Telegraph*, 20 October 1888). Theorists with suspect candidates answering or partially answering to this description (e.g. **Dr Tumblety**) sometimes suggest this might have been a sighting of the Ripper.

MARSHALL, KATE

Murderess.

On 26 November 1898 she killed her sister, Elizabeth Roberts, after a quarrel in the first-floor back room at 26 Dorset Street (the room above the one once occupied by **Mary Kelly**) in front of the deceased's husband, David Roberts, and young son. Marshall had a long history of arrests and imprisonment for violence and had only recently been released from prison, having on 10 May 1895 stabbed with intent to kill Christopher Hayes in the Britannia public house, at the corner of Dorset Street and Commercial Street. Marshall had lived with Hayes on and off, and alleged he had forced her to prostitute herself. She was tried at the Old Bailey on 20 February and sentenced to five years in prison.

The jury found her guilty of murder, but recommended mercy because the act had not been premeditated and was done in a state of drunken frenzy. Nevertheless, the judge passed sentence of death. However, Marshall's counsel maintained the verdict should be quashed because the jury clearly indicated that they thought Marshall to have been guilty of manslaughter. In due course, the sentence was commuted to life imprisonment.

Among those who investigated this case was **Stephen White**, by now an inspector (*News of the World*, 14 October 1900).

(*See* **Room Above Mary Kelly's**.)

MARSHALL, WILLIAM
Witness at **Elizabeth Stride**'s inquest.

Born in Romford, the son of William and Jane Marshall; married Mary Ann Bear in 1859 and had four children, William, Jemima, Henry and Mary. By 1881, he was a labourer in a dockside indigo wharehouse and living at 64 Berner Street.

Marshall stood outside his house for about ten minutes, around 11.45pm, on 29 September 1888. He saw a woman he later identified as Stride on the pavement opposite with a man of clerkly appearance, 5ft 6in tall, stout, decently dressed in a small black coat, dark trousers and peaked sailorly cap. His voice was mild and accent apparently English. He said to Stride, 'You would say anything but your prayers.' The pair moved away up the road (in the direction of **Matthew Packer**'s shop and Dutfield's Yard).

Marshall's description of the coat and cap suggests this may also have been the man seen by **Police Constable Smith**; less probably by **Israel Schwartz** (who followed an intoxicated assailant approaching Stride from the other end of the road). His observation was imperfect, since he denied seeing the flower that all others recollected was pinned to Stride's breast; his observation of clerkliness makes it probable this was the man who left the Bricklayers' Arms with Stride at 11pm, as witnessed by **Best** and **Gardner** and described by Matthew Packer.

MARTIN, JOSEPH (*c.* 1850–1933)
Metropolitan police photographer, who most probably took the mortuary photographs of the Ripper victims.

Son of a photographer who sent him to George Yard Ragged School, then employed him as assistant in the business from the age of 9. Ultimately, Joseph ran away from home to earn his living as an itinerant musician and, after his father had found him and brought him home, as a music-hall musician. Subsequently returned to photography as a supplementary way of earning a living and opened a shop in Cannon Street Road. In 1894, he moved the business to West India Dock Road. Then, in 1932 he retired, and in December the following year, he was knocked down crossing the road in Poplar and died of his injuries. His obituaries (e.g. *The Times*, 23 December 1933) referred to his having been the police photographer responsible for taking (among others) mortuary photographs of the Ripper victims.

A very detailed article (Adrian Phypers, ***Ripper Notes***, October 2002) traces his movements as far as possible and notes that he took over **Louis Gumprecht**'s premises in Cannon Street Road. Since Gumprecht himself disappears from the residential directories after 1887, it seems most likely Phypers' explanation for his name on the back of **Martha Tabram**'s and **Frances Coles**' mortuary photographs is correct: Joseph Martin probably received with the shop's equipment a stamp or pre-printed photographic paper giving the former proprietor's name and address.

Jean Dorsenne's *Jack l'Eventreur* gives an account of the mortuary photographer that matches known data concerning Martin. His words (ch XIV) are:

> 'No photographer! My men went everywhere without being able to lay hands on one. Do you know where we tracked one down? Don't think I'm joking: I swear I'm telling you the truth, and you can prove it if you take the trouble to look up the 1888 newspapers. The mortuary photographer only helped justice in his spare time. His real occupation was conductor at a music-hall on the Radcliff [sic] highway. The red-faced and jovial little man was busy beating time for a violin, and piano and a saxophone which struggled to accompany the gyrations of four befeathered girls whose charms were barely concealed by their frilled and gold-braided costumes'. (Trans Martin Fido)

Despite Dorsenne's confidence, modern searches have so far failed to trace reference to the photographer in the 1888 press.

(*See* **The First Jack the Ripper Victim Photographs**.)

MARY JANE KELLY AND THE RIPPER MURDERS: PROOF OF THE INVOLVEMENT OF THE HEIR TO THE CROWN

E-book downloadable from the internet by Peter Londragan (Chesterfield: eBooks-UK, 2008).

Exposition of the Royal conspiracy theory as presented in *Jack the Ripper: The Final Solution* and *The Ripper and the Royals*, but offering no new information and in some cases stretching credibility, as when the author maintains Stride's body could have been thrown unseen from a passing coach into the passage at the side of the Berner Street Club (*see* **Elizabeth Stride**). As independent corroboration of the story told by **Joseph Sickert**, the author cites the memoirs of St John Terrapin, seemingly unaware they are fiction (*The Private World of St John Terrapin: A Novel of the Cafe Royal* by Chapman Pincher).

Interesting for potted accounts of alleged unacknowledged royal marriages, children born therefrom – notably Clarence Haddon, alleged son of **Prince Albert Victor** – and retarded royals locked away from public view.

MARY JANE KELLY: LA DERNIÈRE VICTIME

Book by Didier Chauvet (Paris: Harmattan, 2002).

French account of **Mary Jane Kelly**'s life as recorded in evidence at the inquest, interspersed with poems by the author.

MARY, THEOPHIL (*b.* 1851)

Suspect, positively cleared in 1888.

German hairdresser, born Alsace, active as casual sadistic assailant, who stabbed the erogenous zones of passing women, from 1880 in Strasbourg and Bremen. Arrested in 1881 for the attempted rape of a 12-year-old girl and imprisoned in Bremen until August 1888; then transferred to Oslebshausen prison to start a 12-month sentence for the Strasbourg assaults.

Scotland Yard's missing suspect files included two reports from the Bremen police dated 27 September 1888 and 19 October 1888, describing his crimes and first imprisonment, and a report from **Abberline** dated 22 October 1888 noting Mary must be innocent. It is not known what prompted Scotland Yard to make enquiries of the German police. Since Abberline's report and the second communication from Germany use quotation marks in calling the man 'Mary', the speculation that he was transvestite or homosexual has been nursed. Jan Bondeson in *Ripperologist*, 37 (October 2001) established this is not the case: Mary was the man's surname.

MASON, THOMAS (1817–1902)

The Chicago *Sunday Times-Herald* version of the **R.J. Lees**' story describes the unnamed guilty doctor as being incarcerated in an asylum under the pseudonym 'Thomas Mason, no. 124'. **Stephen Knight** identified this man with Thomas Mason, a retired bookbinder, whose address was given as Bookbinders' Alms Houses, Balls Pond, Islington, when he died of *bronchitis senectus* in Islington Infirmary, and in turn as **Sir William Gull** pseudonymously incarcerated, misdating Mason's death as 1896. There is nothing to indicate the real Thomas Mason was in a lunacy ward. He was not on the pauper lunatic returns of the relevant years 1888–96. Indeed, he appears to have nothing to do with either Gull or the Jack the Ripper case.

MATTERS, LEONARD WARBURTON (1881–1951)

Theorist and researcher. Author of *The Mystery of Jack the Ripper*.

Born Adelaide, South Australia. One of 10 children, of John Leonard Matters and Emma Alma (née Warburton). One of his sisters, Muriel Lilah (1877–1969) became a noted suffragist in Australia and Britain, gaining notoriety in London, in October 1908 by chaining herself to a grille in the ladies' gallery of the House of Commons.

Messenger boy on the Perth *Daily News*, aged 13; chief Parliamentary correspondent, aged 20. Subsequently editor. Volunteered for the Second Boer War (1899–1902), serving in South Africa with the 5th South Australian Imperial Bushman's Contingent in the last year of the war. Thereafter, managing editor of Buenos Aires *Herald*, and travelled widely as journalist in USA, Canada, West Indies and Japan. Labour MP for Kennington, 1929–31. London representative of *Hindu*, South India's largest circulation English language newspaper.

A journalist of talent and brilliance, and a minor public figure commanding respect in widely varied areas of the world, Matters is a surprising man to become noted as the first 'Ripperologist' and more extraordinary still to be accused of deliberately purveying fiction to provide a solution. Neither his character nor his book warrants this condemnation: failure to trace his main source does not justify concluding that he invented it.

(Obituary in *The Times*, 1 November 1951.)

MATTHEWS, RT. HON. HENRY, MP, PC (1826–1913)

Home Secretary, 1886–92. First Roman Catholic minister of cabinet rank since the reign of Elizabeth. Moved to Lords as Viscount Llandaff, 1895.

Born in 1826, in Ceylon. Educated at the Universities of Paris and London. Called to the bar at Lincoln's Inn; a skilled and successful cross-examiner, who played a part in some notable trials. In 1886, he won the marginal seat of East Birmingham and was appointed Home Secretary by the Prime Minister, Lord Salisbury. Matthews, 'was so flabbergasted by the offer of a Secretaryship of State that he left Arlington House under the impression that he had declined, but, finding himself gazetted Home Secretary the next day accepted his fate' (Leslie, Shane: 'Henry Matthews Lord Llandaff', *The Dublin Review*, vol. 168, January 1921). In fact, Matthews proved unpopular with almost everyone, A.J. Balfour describing him as 'the member of the Govt. whom everyone wishes to turn out!' (R.H. William, *The Salisbury-Balfour Correspondence 1869–1892*, Hitchen: Hertfordshire Record Soc., 1988) and it has been said, 'He did more, perhaps, to render the government unpopular than any other minister' (Sir Robert Ensor: *England 1870–1914*; 'The Oxford History of England', Oxford: Oxford University Press, 1936). During the Ripper murders, **Queen Victoria** wrote to **Lord Salisbury** complaining that the Home Secretary's 'general want of sympathy with the feelings of the <u>people</u> are doing the <u>Government</u> harm'. Salisbury replied with an admission that, 'There is an innocence of the ways of the world which no one could have expected to find in a criminal lawyer of sixty.'

But Salisbury could not see how to get rid of Matthews, without risking his marginal seat in a by-election. He could not be dismissed, and quiet removal would have generated all sorts of potentially damaging and definitely unwanted speculation. However, as soon as possible he was elevated to the peerage, after which he played little part in public life. He died in 1913.

Relations between Matthews and **Sir Charles Warren** were extremely poor. **Evelyn Ruggles-Brise**, Private Secretary to four Home Secretaries, said Matthews was, 'quite incapable of dealing with men; he was a regular Gallio in his attitude to Warren's complaints. Later on he quarrelled with Bradford, and if you couldn't get on with Bradford you could get on with nobody' (Williams, Watkin Wynn: *The Life of General Sir Charles Warren: By His Grandson*. Oxford: Blackwell, 1941. p.220). **Sir Robert Anderson**, head of the CID, thought the blame lay with **Godfrey Lushington**, his Secretary, whose personality he described as an irritant 'blister' when a 'plaister' was needed (Anderson, Sir Robert: *The Lighter Side of My Official Life*. London: Hodder and Stoughton, 1910. p.126). Shane Leslie places much emphasis on how Matthews 'kept officials at a distance through his secretaries', and George Dilnot refers to 'the friction that notoriously existed between Sir Godfrey Lushington and the high officials of the police' (Dilnot, George: *The Story of Scotland Yard*. London: Geoffrey Bles, 1930. p.97).

MAXWELL, CAROLINE

Witness at **Mary Jane Kelly**'s inquest. Wife of Henry Maxwell lodging-house deputy of 14 Dorset Street (Crossingham's Lodging House, otherwise known as Commercial Street Chambers).

Had known Kelly for about four months, but had only spoken to her twice prior to 9 November 1888. Maxwell testified to seeing her standing at the corner of Miller's Court between 8 and 8.30 that morning, wearing a green bodice, dark skirt and maroon crossover shawl. She described a conversation in which Kelly said she had 'the horrors of drink' upon her, and on being urged by Mrs Maxwell to try another drink to steady herself, said she had already done so and vomited it up. Mrs Maxwell told her, 'I pity your condition.' This evidence is popular with those theorists who believe Kelly to have been pregnant, and suggest Mrs Maxwell was referring to this as her 'condition'.

About an hour later, Mrs Maxwell said she saw Kelly again, this time talking to a stout man in dark clothes and a plaid coat outside the Britannia.

Pressed by the coroner to be sure of the time and date (since medical evidence was that Kelly had been dead for several hours), Mrs Maxwell insisted she could place the date because she had been returning china her husband had borrowed from a house opposite. **Walter Dew** said she was a sane and sensible woman with an excellent reputation. Nevertheless, he disbelieved her evidence.

Mrs Maxwell's testimony is also popular with those who want the murderer to have escaped in Kelly's clothes, or somebody else to have been killed in her place. (*Cf.* **James Kelly, Konovalov,** *Jack the Ripper Revealed,* **Winifred May Collis**.)

MAY, BETTY (*fl.* 1925)

Model who claimed Aleister Crowley owned Jack the Ripper's neckties.

Widow of Raoul Loveday, a disciple of Crowley's, who entered his black magic commune, the Abbey of Thelema, on Sicily. When Loveday succumbed to acute enteritis and died, Betty May determined to expose Crowley's nauseating and unhealthy regime of drugs, malnutrition and animal blood. In articles in *World Pictorial News* (1925) and the book *Tiger Woman* (1929), she claimed that Crowley owned a number of blood-stained white dress bowties that had been Jack the Ripper's. Crowley noted in the margin of his copy of the book 'Victoria [sic] Cremers' story!!!!'

See also **Bernard O'Donnell**.

MAYBRICK, JAMES (1838–89)

Suspect identified in the **Maybrick Journal**; in the public domain since 1993.

A Liverpool cotton-broker, James Maybrick died in May 1889, apparently of arsenic poisoning. His American wife Florence was accused of his murder and convicted at an unsatisfactory trial presided over by Sir James Fitzjames Stephen (father of **J.K. Stephen**), who was on the verge of losing his mind and failed to grasp salient features of the case.

Unquestionable evidence that Maybrick had long used arsenic and other noxious poisons for stimulant and aphrodisiac purposes was not given due weight, while Mrs Maybrick's admitted adultery with another cotton merchant was allowed to create gross prejudice against her. Maybrick's own loose living was seen as giving her a motive for murder. She was reprieved, and released from prison after 15 years to die in America, in 1941. Until the emergence of the Maybrick Journal, James Maybrick was never associated with the Ripper case.

(See Jones, Chistopher. *The Maybrick A to Z.* Wirral: Countywise, 2008.)

MAYBRICK JOURNAL

Sixty-three handwritten pages in what appears to be an old scrapbook, from which the first 48 pages have been removed with a knife. Traces of gum and card show they once held pictures or photographs. The writing, signed 'Jack the Ripper', purports to be a record of the Ripper's activities from about April 1888 to May 1889. Internal evidence proves beyond doubt that the author is intended to be James Maybrick.

According to Michael Barrett (*b.* 1952), an invalid househusband attempting a new career as a contributor to (especially) puzzle books for children, he was given the journal in May 1991 by a friend named Tony Devereux (now deceased), who told him nothing beyond assurances that it was genuine. Detailed investigation since then has failed to prove or disprove this claim. Barrett identified the supposed author as Maybrick, and in April 1992 took the document to Doreen Montgomery of Rupert Crew Literary Agency. He appeared genuine, and spoke of upsets that the journal had caused in his family: an apparently unnecessary detail held by some to suggest the Barretts did not forge the diary. Ms Montgomery commissioned Shirley Harrison and her research partner Sally Evemy to undertake preliminary research with a view to writing a book.

Ms Harrison took the journal to the British Museum and Jarndyce's antiquarian book dealers, both of whom were impressed, but recommended scientific examination. In turn, manuscript and graphic art scientific analysts Dr David Baxendale and Dr Nicholas Eastaugh, psychologist Dr David Forshaw, handwriting analyst and document examiner Sue Iremonger, and several Ripper authorities (including the authors) were consulted. All expressed reservations and doubts.

Dr Baxendale wrongly believed the ink contained no iron, and that a dye called nigrosine, said to be found in the ink, was unavailable in the 1880s. However, according to forgery detector Dr Joe Nickell, it was first produced commercially in 1867. Baxendale found the ink easily soluble. Dr Eastaugh examined the ink and, while recommending further tests, found nothing inconsistent with Victorian manufacture and application. Dr Forshaw believed the psychopathology revealed by the author was consistent with that of a serial killer and suggested the journal was either genuine, or a recent hoax. Sue Iremonger concluded it was not penned by the hand that wrote Maybrick's will and signed his marriage certificate. The Ripper authorities noted factual problems, and Martin Fido observed at least 20 anachronistic, solecistic, or misspelt words and phrases, incompatible with Maybrick's time and class, and not easily explicable as slips of the pen.

In June 1992, Robert Smith secured publication rights for Smith Gryphon Limited and Paul Feldman bought the audiovisual rights. During 1993, Warner Books and The Sunday Times, bidding for the American and serial rights respectively, called in their own experts to examine the document. Kenneth W. Rendell assembled a team for Warner, comprising himself, Joe Nickell, document examiner Maureen Casey Owens, (a leader in her profession), ink research chemist Robert L. Kurantz and ion migration analyst Dr Rod McNeill.

Kurantz analysed the ink and endorsed Eastaugh's findings, but Maureen Casey Owens declared the handwriting was not that of Maybrick's will and marriage certificate, and the team observed writing inconsistent with 1880s' calligraphy, unnatural uniformity of ink flow and writing slant, and a layout indicative of a forger writing multiple entries at one time. This evidence, in their opinion, decisively showed the journal to be a fake.

Warner Books withdrew, leaving Disney subsidiary Hyperion to take the American rights and include as an appendix to their edition Rendell's report with a rebuttal by Robert Smith.

The Sunday Times published its experts' opinions on 19 September 1993. Their team comprised Dr Audrey Giles (former head of the Metropolitan Police laboratories questioned document section), Dr Kate Flint (lecturer in Victorian and modern English at Oxford University) and **Tom Cullen**. Dr Giles was suspicious of the torn-out pages, noted tampering with letter-formation and concluded Maybrick's will was not written by the diary's author. Curiously, she also noted the diary writing 'varied considerably from small and neat, to large, scrawled and apparently agitated' – characteristics not normally associated with forgery. It has also been observed that the missing front pages suggest an unsophisticated forger, whereas Dr Giles' other claims might suggest a sophisticated knowledge of Victorian calligraphy. Dr Flint cited two non-Victorian expressions, both of which were subsequently disputed. It has been suggested this is an astonishingly small number of allegedly anachronistic phrases in a supposedly poor forgery.

At this time the Maybrick watch came to light. On 27 June 1994, the Liverpool *Daily Post* reported Mike Barrett's claim to have forged the journal using a scrapbook bought from an auctioneer's and ink from the Bluecoat Art Shop. These claims have proved impossible to substantiate. Although Barrett could not name the ink, the Art Shop suggested to journalist Harold Brough that it was most likely a manuscript ink manufactured by Diamine (which, unusually for then, contained nigrosine). At the same time, Barrett claimed to have only days to live and said that he'd 'worked on the diary for five years' (i.e. since 1987).

The following day, the confession was withdrawn by his solicitors, who said that he 'was not in full control of his faculties when he made that statement which was totally inaccurate and without foundation'. From time to time, Barrett has since alternately claimed to have forged the book, then withdrawn his confessions. No final satisfactory conclusion can be reached about his conflicting stories.

The following month, Mr Barrett's recently estranged wife (they would later divorce and she would revert to her maiden name of Anne Graham) told **Paul Feldman** that she had seen the diary and its contents in 1968, though she was not more than mildly curious, being only a teenager. She had taken possession of it in the 1980s. Her father, Mr Billy Graham (now deceased), confirmed her story, saying the diary had been left to him by his grandmother shortly before World War II and that he had first seen it when he came home on leave in 1943, finally receiving it when his father died in 1950.

According to Anne Graham, the book passed into her possession in 1989, when her father moved into sheltered accommodation. She had hidden it from her husband and their daughter Caroline, but when Mike Barrett showed interest in becoming a writer, she thought the book might be inspiration for a work of fiction. Concerned that he might pester her terminally ill father, she took it 'on the spur of the moment' to Tony Devereux, asking him to give it to Mike without acknowledging its source. Apart from her father's support, no other corroborative evidence for any part of it has ever been found, and Mike Barrett denies it absolutely, claiming Anne's inconsistent accounts of the room in which she hid it from him would have led him to discover the diary when redecorating their house. (Anne Graham would later co-author with Carol Emmas, *The Last Victim,*

(London: Headline, 1999), a book about Florence Maybrick, and in the introduction touch on the story about the diary being in her family.)

Melvin Harris obtained samples of the diary ink taken for the Rendell team's tests. He submitted them to Analysis for Industry to be tested for chloroacetamide, a preservative constituent of the Diamine ink. A minute quantity was found and Harris announced, 'The tests prove that the ink used in the diaries is Diamine,' and 'there is now no doubt whatsoever that they are a recent fake. The identities of the three people involved in the forgery will soon be made known.' They were not, and the test results were quickly thrown into doubt. Melvin Harris's several papers on the Maybrick affair (which can be found at http://www.casebook.org/dissertations/) contain much useful data.

Shirley Harrison and Keith Skinner took the journal to Leeds University's Department of Dyeing and Colour Chemistry. They reported that the journal ink was not diamine and did not contain chloroacetamide or nigrosine. *Contra* Baxendale, they found it difficult to dissolve the ink in solvent.

John C. Roberts, professor of paper science at UMIST, examined both reports. He noted Analysis for Industry did not seem to have carried out a control test to see whether the chloroacetamide could be contained in the paper attached to their ink samples. (Leeds had scraped their ink away from the page.) He observed chloroacetamide was an old compound, extensively used in the 1880s, although not, as far as was known, in paper, but he concluded, 'Even if no references could be found to its use in paper in 1889, the fact that it existed well before that date would devalue the scientific evidence in support of the fact that the diaries were forged. The argument that it found its way into the ink or paper by some obscure route can never be completely discounted.'

On 30 October 1995, Alec Voller, head chemist at Diamine, saw the diary for the first time, and based on a purely visual examination declared the ink was not diamine's. He detected nigrosine (*contra* Leeds), and observed irregular fading and bronzing, both indicators of age, saying, 'The general appearance is characteristic of documents I have seen which are 90+ years old and it is certainly not out of the realms of possibility that it dates back to 1889. Certainly [the ink] did not go on the paper within recent years.'

There followed a considerable period of contention, with the diary attracting more discussion than any other topic on the Casebook: Jack the Ripper forums. Mark Angus (*Criminologist,* Spring 1995) claimed that the disparate information in the journal drawn from a variety of sources would not have been known to any one person in 1888, for which reason it could be dismissed as a forgery. Professor William Rubinstein of Aberystwyth University, writing in *History Today* in 2003, declared the diary is most probably genuine or it would have been exposed by now.

The following year, Robert Smith – who had by that time acquired ownership of the diary – sent it to Staffordshire University, requesting a conclusive scientific report on the age of the ink. The final report was the most inconclusive since Eastaugh's: Catherine Kneale and Andrew Platt applied a variety of tests and concluded there was no evidence to show whether the ink was of early or recent date.

345

With the untimely deaths of Melvin Harris in 2004 and Paul Feldman in 2005, the furore surrounding the journal died down. Professor David Canter, England's leading practitioner of geographical criminal profiling, wrote a vaguely supportive Preface to the 1998 edition of Shirley Harrison's book, and in *Mapping Murder* (2005) he argued that the Maybrick Journal was either genuine, or a work of literary genius which brilliantly captured the thought processes of a serial killer and presented them with such artifice as to seize and hold the attention.

In *Ripperana* (69, July 2009), editor Nick Warren presented his case for suggesting the Maybrick Diary had been authored by the late Jeremy Beadle, a television personality and Ripperphile who had long supported the diary as authentic. The argument advanced by Warren, who claimed that Paul Feldman had consulted Beadle soon after the diary emerged, was based on three arguments : (1) that Jeremy Beadle had an affection for Liverpool, (2) that Jeremy Beadle had a withered right hand and would therefore have found it laughable that a disproportionate number of violent criminals are left handed; the diary containing the words, 'I had to laugh, they have me down as left-handed.' (3) Claims that the phrase in the diary, 'If they are to insist that I am a Jew, then a Jew I shall be' corresponds with the title of a talk delivered by Beadle to the Cambridge University Jewish Society: 'If they are to insist that I am a Jew, then a Jew I shall be.'

The origin of the journal has never been determined.

(*See* **Ripper Diary: The Inside Story.**)

MAYBRICK TRIAL

A three-day event held in the grounds of Liverpool Cricket Club in May 2007 to mark the 200th anniversary of its founding and part of a prelude to Liverpool being the European City of Culture in 2008. Organised by Chris Jones and compèred by Jeremy Beadle (*pictured*).

Professors William Rubinstein and David Canter, authors and researchers Paul Begg, Shirley Harrison (*pictured*), Donald Rumbelow and Keith Skinner, and radio

personality Vincent Burke were featured speakers. Acting as jury, the audience returned a verdict of guilty (that James Maybrick was Jack the Ripper) by an extremely small margin.

MAYBRICK WATCH

A half-hunter gold watch made by Henry Verity of Lancaster in 1846, and purchased by Mr Albert Johnson (*d.* 2008) from Stewarts the Jewellers of Wallasey, Cheshire in July 1992 who held it for at least five years.

In June 1993, Mr Johnson reported

that he had found scratched on the inner case, behind the works, the signature 'J. Maybrick', the words 'I am Jack', and the initials of **Mary Nichols**, **Annie Chapman**, **Elizabeth Stride**, **Catherine Eddowes** and **Mary Kelly**.

In August 1993, Dr Stephen Turgoose, of the University of Manchester Institute of Science and Technology's Corrosion and Protection Centre, examined the scratchings with a scanning electron microscope and gave his opinion that they are compatible with being made in 1888–89, are unlikely to be recent and are 'likely to date back more than tens of years.'

In January 1994, Dr Robert Wild of Bristol University's Interface Analysis Centre used scanning auger microscopy and argon ion depth profiling to examine the watch, and explicitly agreed with Dr Turgoose, saying it seemed likely the scratchings were 'at least of several tens of years age,' adding that it appeared unlikely that anyone would have the skill to implant misleading microscopic aged brass particles to simulate traces of the engraving tool. Shirley Harrison, in the text of *The Diary of Jack the Ripper*, and Robert Smith, in his afterword to the Hyperon edition (USA), offer the watch as supportive evidence that James Maybrick really was the Ripper.

In 1995, the late Stanley Dangar, a horologist resident in Spain, began to take an interest in the watch, which he believed to have been faked. He was the first to observe that it was a lady's model (a claim since disputed) and he received commentaries from the Universities of Cologne and Barcelona, which allegedly declared the claims made for the Turgoose and Wild reports could not be substantiated (though neither university had actually seen the watch). Dangar also had an affidavit taken from repairer Timothy Dundas, who had serviced the watch in 1992 and was quite certain that at that time there had been no marks other than jewellers' and repairers' job numbers and dates scratched on the case.

Unfortunately, when both Mr Dundas and Robert Johnson, brother of the watch's owner, died (the latter in a motor cycle accident), Dangar came to the completely untenable conclusion that they had been assassinated at the behest of Paul Feldman. He embarked on writing a book with Melvin Harris to expose the alleged diary and watch 'conspiracy', but the two fell out in 1999 – at which time Mr Dangar revealed to Shirley Harrison that the University of Barcelona commentary had not, in fact, disputed the findings of Turgoose and Wild.

Prima facie, the watch is a far more suspicious object than the diary, emerging opportunely just months after press reportage made the supposed link between Maybrick and Jack the Ripper widely known. In the end, however, it is less easy to label the watch confidently as a fake. The concurrence of two reputable scientific laboratories, the extraordinary difficulty of engraving microscopic initials and the fact that the Johnson brothers refused an offer of £40,000 for an item which had cost Albert £250 all militate against the easy conclusion that they scratched the writings after reading about the diary.

Interest in the watch briefly resurfaced in November 2004, when a couple of national newspapers picked up the scientific findings of Manchester and Bristol and presented it as a new story.

'MERCHANT, DR' (1851–88)

Pseudonym devised by B.E. Reilly (in *City* the magazine of the City of London Police, February 1972) to conceal the identity of alleged suspect **F.R. Chapman**, identified by Reilly as a Brixton doctor whose decease shortly after the murders made him the only candidate in medical directories for Police Constable **Robert Spicer**'s suspect.

MERRICK, JOSEPH CAREY (1862–90)

Alleged suspect and the 'Elephant Man'.

Leicester-born sufferer of Proteus syndrome, which causes massive and hideous disfigurement. Thrown out by his family, the young Merrick found work exhibiting himself as a freak and eventually came under the management of entrepreneur Tom Norman, a famous operator of 'penny gaffs' throughout London. He exhibited Merrick at the back of a shop in Whitechapel Road, opposite the London Hospital, where he was seen by Frederick Treves. The shop was closed by the police because the exhibition of Merrick's deformities was deemed to be against public decency.

In 1888, another entrepreneur was displaying crude wax models of the Ripper's victims in the same shop. Merrick's management passed to others until ultimately he was abandoned on the Continent, returning with difficulty to London, where he was found by police and taken to Treves, whose card was discovered among his possessions. Treves arranged for him to live in the hospital in security and modest comfort for the remainder of his life. His deformed bones are now on exhibition in the hospital's anatomical museum, which still retains the basic layout created by Dr **Thomas Openshaw.**

The origin of the suggestion that he was Jack the Ripper is uncertain.

(Eduardo Zinna, 'Let's hear it for the Elephant Man', **Ripperologist**, 49, Septemeber 2003)

METROPOLITAN POLICE

Founded in 1829 and responsible for all of London, except the City. All Ripper murders except that of **Catherine Eddowes** fell within the Metropolitan Police's jurisdiction. As a force directly responsible to the Home Secretary, the Met was (and is) peculiarly vulnerable to political pressure.

In 1888, the Met was unpopular with the Radical press, partly because of the brutality with which it was felt the police and troops had put down the 'Bloody Sunday' demonstration by the unemployed in November 1887; partly because massed Metropolitan Police ranks turned out to control weekly demonstrations by the unemployed throughout the period and partly because in combating Fenian terrorism, senior officers in particular were inclined to tar all Irish Nationalists with the subversive brush. Indeed, an almost-obsessive desire to track down Fenians was perceived as absorbing the CID to the extent that it neglected the investigation of ordinary crimes; 'The Criminal Investigation Department under Mr Monro was so pre-occupied in tracking out the men suspected ofcommitting political crimes that the ordinary vulgar assassin has a free field in which to indulge his propensities,' said the *Pall Mall Gazette* (8 September 1888).

METROPOLITAN POLICE, AREA OF SEARCH

According to a report filed on 19 October 1888 by **Chief Inspector Swanson**, the district targeted for house-to-house interviews in the Ripper enquiry was 'bounded by the City Police boundary on the one hand, Lamb St., Commercial St., Great Eastern Railway and Buxton St., then by Albert St. [north end of today's Deal St.], Dunk St. [between today's Deal St. and Davenant St.], Chicksand St. and Great Garden St. [today's Greatorex St.] to Whitechapel Road and then to the City Boundary'.

The area includes the Thrawl Street vicinity of common lodging-houses, but excludes the immediate vicinity of two of the murder sites: Buck's Row and Berner Street. (A third, Mitre Square, fell under the jurisdiction of the City Police.)

It is not known why so much of the 'Ripper territory' was apparently eliminated from a part of the enquiry.

'MICKELDY JOE'
Friend of '**Leather Apron**'.

So-described in some press reports. The only reporter who apparently encountered him wrote for the *Star* of 5 September 1888 that 'Joe' was present in the lodging-house situated in a disreputable alley, off Brick Lane, which 'Leather Apron' was alleged to use, and thereby encouraged its hostile denizens to deny the allegation. Unfortunately, the reporter did not record any conversation with 'Mickeldy Joe', who seems to be the only known person who might have identified 'Leather Apron' with certainty.

MILES, GEORGE FRANCIS (FRANK) (1852–91)
Suspect proposed in the 1970s.

Born at Bingham, Nottinghamshire, the sixth son of Robert Henry William Miles, rector of Bingham. A partially colour-blind painter specialising in landscapes and portraits. Friend of Oscar Wilde, with whom he shared accommodation, first at 13 Salisbury Street, Strand (1879–80), and then at 44 Tite Street, Chelsea (1880–81). Won the Royal Academy's Turner Prize, 1880. Associated with some fashionable homosexuals. Claims that he preferred girls below the age of consent, to whom he allegedly exposed himself and for which police once tried to arrest him in Tite Street are rejected by Molly Whittington-Egan (*Frank Miles and Oscar Wilde: Such White Lilies*. High Wycombe: The Rivendale Press, 2008), who has traced the origin of the story to a highly questionable account by Robert Shererd, Wilde's first biographer.

Miles' friendship with Wilde ended when Miles acquiesced to demand by his father, on whom he was financially dependent, that Wilde leave Tite Street. Miles suffered a nervous breakdown and, in 1887, his mental health gave way, leading to his confinement on 27 December 1887 to a private asylum at Brislington, near

Bristol, until his death from General Paralysis of the Insane. It has been suggested (Thomas Toughill, *Ripper Code*. Stroud, Gloucestershire, Sutton Publishing, 2008) that Miles recovered sufficiently to escape temporarily from the asylum and commit the murders, but Molly Whittington-Egan dismisses such suggestion, citing sources that confirm high-security measures at Brislington.

MILL, MRS ANN

Acquaintance of **Elizabeth Stride**. Bedmaker at lodging-house, 32 Flower and Dean Street. Reported in the *Manchester Guardian* as saying of Stride, 'a better hearted, more good natured, cleaner woman never lived.'

MILLWOOD, ANNIE, or possibly FANNY (1850–88)

Possible victim of a Ripper assault, proposed in *The Complete History of Jack the Ripper*.

Widow of a soldier. Lived at 8 White's Row, a lodging-house owned by **William Crossingham**. Treated in Whitechapel Workhouse Infirmary on 25 February 1888 for stab wounds about the legs and lower part of the body inflicted by a strange man with a clasp knife. Recovered, and died of natural causes the following month.

MISSING SUSPECT FILES

The Scotland Yard files and case papers on Jack the Ripper were transferred to the National Archives, (then called the Public Record Office), under the Public Records Act 1958 and 1967 but were not available to researchers. However, members of the public could request to see these files on application to the Archives Section of the General Registry Office and a number of them were seen and transcribed, but have subsequently gone missing or been mislaid. They include material on the suspects **Theophil Mary**, **Charles Ludwig**, **Dick Austen** (or Austin), **Antoni Pricha**, **Edwin Burrows**, **Douglas Cow**, **James Connell**, **Alfred Parent**, **Joseph Denny**, **John Avery**, **John Murphy**, and **W. Van Burst** (in that order of filing). Another important file seen by several researchers before it went missing contained a long letter from **Dr Roslyn Donston Stephenson**, a statement about Stephenson taken by **Inspector Roots** from George Marsh and Roots's report on Marsh, Stephenson and Dr Davies (*The Ultimate Jack the Ripper Sourcebook* contains transcripts).

It is noteworthy that files on the suspects named in the Macnaghten memoranda are missing, as are the accompanying files that must have described the remaining 'several persons' referred to by **Major Griffiths** (*Mysteries of Police and Crime*).

MITCHELL, DET. SGT. JOHN (City Police)

Searched for **Catherine Eddowes**' husband. With **Detective Baxter Hunt**, traced a **Thomas Conway** in the 18th Royal Irish, who proved to be the wrong man.

MIZEN, PC JONAS 55H (*b.* 1848)

Sent by **Charles Cross** and **Robert Paul** to **Mary Ann Nichols**' body.

Joined the Metropolitan Police in 1873 (warrant no. 56678). Retired, 1898. Served in H Division throughout. The *Star*, 1 September 1888, and other sources (i.e., *The Star*, 3 September 1888) erroneously give his forename as George (or initial G). We take Jonas from his signature for pension.

At 4.15 am on beat duty at the junction of Baker's Row (now part of Vallance Road) and Hanbury Street, when he was approached by Charles Cross and Robert Paul. He claimed that Cross had told him he was wanted by a policeman in Buck's Row, where a woman had been found. Cross, questioned by the coroner, denied having said this, not having encountered a policeman prior to meeting Mizen, but had merely said that he there was a woman in Buck's Row, "'She looks to me to be either dead or drunk; but for my part I think she is dead." The policeman said, "All right," and then walked on." (*Daily Telegraph*, 4 September 1888) Mizen went to Buck's Row where he found **PC Neil** alone with the body of Nichols, Neil sent him to fetch an ambulance.

MONK, MARY ANN

Identified **Mary Ann Nichols**' body and testified at her inquest. A young woman 'with a haughty air and a flushed face', Monk identified the body in the mortuary after a Lambeth Workhouse laundry mark had been found on its petticoat. She had been a fellow-inmate with Nichols.

MONRO, JAMES (1838–1920)

Assistant Metropolitan Police Commissioner in charge of CID until the outbreak of Ripper murders; Home Office 'head of detective service', officially unattached to the Metropolitan Police between the murders of **Mary Ann Nichols** and **Mary Jane Kelly**; thereafter Metropolitan Police Commissioner until 1890. He is the only Metropolitan Police Commissioner not to have been given a knighthood, a point noted as early as 1910 when Irish Nationalist MP Jeremiah McVeagh wondered why **Anderson** had been knighted even though he had breached departmental guidelines by releasing confidential information damaging to Irish nationalism.

Allegedly suggested as a suspect by a twentieth-century theorist.

Educated at Edinburgh High School, and Edinburgh and Berlin Universities. Suffered infantile paralysis, which left him slightly lamed in later life and frequently needing a walking stick. Entered Indian Civil Service (legal branch) by examination, 1857. Successively assistant magistrate, collector, district judge and inspector-general of police, Bengal Presidency, then commissioner of police,

Bombay Presidency. Resigned, 1884. Assistant commissioner Metropolitan Police, 1884–88; then a two-month interval as unofficial 'head of detective service' commissioner, 1888–90, when he resigned. Founded and ran Ranaghat Christian Medical Mission, 1890–1903. He intended retirement in Darjeeling, but returned first to Scotland and thereafter to Cheltenham and other parts of England, following his son-in-law's peregrinations.

Like Dr **Robert Anderson**, a millenniarist, who looked forward to the Second Coming of Christ. A firm and decisive disciplinarian, he was nonetheless loved by practically all who served under him. Robert Anderson and **Melvin Macnaghten** left glowing accounts; **Superintendent Williamson** almost resigned from the force when Monro's resignation as assistant commissioner was accepted. Rank-and-file police long remembered his determined struggle to secure the pension conditions they demanded. **Sir Basil Thomson** and Sir John Moylan, in their respective histories of the Metropolitan Police, speak well of him. All agreed on his excellence as a detective, especially in bringing the Fenian dynamite campaigns of the 1880s under control. The rapid fall in crime figures after his appointment as commissioner was ascribed by Anderson to his influence, though others have wondered whether it might not have been Anderson's own achievement (since the trend continued throughout his decade as assistant commissioner), or merely coincidence.

Monro's equals and superiors, however, may have found him a more difficult man than published accounts and his benign features suggest. His unpublished manuscript memoirs evince an elephantine memory for a grievance and an implacable impulse to self-justification. Monro's career is studded with resignations on principle: from the assistant commissionership because he could not wrest absolute sovereignty over the CID from the commissioner; from the commissionership because he could not have his way over the Police Bill and the appointment of a chief constable.

Briefly, the disputes involving Monro were as follows: on coming to Scotland Yard, he found Edward Jenkinson at the Home Office, running an intelligence service to infiltrate the Fenian movement. Jenkinson may have been personally difficult: he expressed contemptuous views of the CID, Monro and Anderson in private (*see* **Anderson** for a more detailed account of their tangled relationships and hostilities, and for Monro's and Anderson's joint activities against terrorism). Monro complained at length to four successive home secretaries about Jenkinson, and in January 1887, Jenkinson resigned and his intelligence service was abolished. Monro was given personal charge of the entirely new Secret Department (Section D).

This gave Monro direct access to the Home Secretary. He believed the same should be true of the CID and resented Warren's insistence on exercising his authority over it, which Monro (with the support of his subordinates) believed to be deleterious. Monro was then further outraged when Warren vetoed his appointment of Macnaghten as assistant chief constable (*see* **Melville Macnaghten**). This led to his own resignation and appointment to the unauthorised post of Home Office 'head of detective service', in which the CID was encouraged to liaise with him behind Warren's back.

As commissioner, his own quarrels with the Home Secretary arose again over the appointment of a chief constable, with Monro wanting to appoint fellow Indian Civil Service veteran Andrew Howard, while Matthews was keen to have civil servant Evelyn Ruggles-Brise. The breaking point was the revised pension conditions in the new Police Bill.

In *Fenian Fire* Christy Campbell sees Monro as an unusually honest, yet naïve policeman, who was constantly outmanoeuvred by the far smarter and more devious **Anderson**. He believes that Monro not receiving a knighthood was due to Monro's inability to politic successfully within Whitehall. Campbell's point matches the query raised by Irish Nationalist MP Jeremiah McVeagh in 1910. However, it is relevant that Monro made himself unpopular with the Conservative government. Lord Salisbury, writing in the third person to Queen Victoria on 20 July 1890, noted and endorsed her wish that Henry Matthews be transferred out of the Home Office, though he believed it to be impossible and added the remarkable comment, 'His [Matthews'] unpopularity is quite phenomenal, but Lord Salisbury believes that Mr Monro's evil practices are responsible for a great portion of it.'

This background of police and Home Office infighting led many observers at the time and researchers since to conclude that Scotland Yard was pre-occupied with squabbles during the Whitechapel murders and there would have been a better chance of solving the mystery had Monro been left in charge with a free hand.

In practice, Monro was consulted by the officers on the case throughout, with Home Office encouragement. *The Times* reported that the superintendents on the case were visiting his office and not reporting to Warren. Additionally, on 22 September 1888, Matthews sent a directive to his private secretary, Evelyn Ruggles-Brise: 'Stimulate the police about the Whitechapel murders. *Absente* Anderson Monro might be willing to give a hint to the CID people if needful' (Shane Leslie, *Sir Evelyn Ruggles-Brise: A Memoir of the Founder of Borstal*. London: John Murray 1938.

In 1890, Monro told *Cassells Magazine* that he had 'decidedly' formed a theory on the case, adding, 'when I do theorise it is from a practical standpoint, and not upon visionary foundation'. He also said, however, that the police had 'Nothing positive' by way of clues, with the rider that such crimes were difficult to solve since the victims, as well as the murderer, sought secret sites.

The following year, he headed the **Alice McKenzie** murder enquiry in Anderson's absence, and reported that 'the murderer, I am inclined to believe, is identical with the notorious Jack the Ripper of last year.' According to Anderson's memoirs, he changed his mind after the investigation, having 'investigated the case on the spot and decided it was an ordinary murder, and not the work of a sexual maniac.' It is still significant, however, that his original belief indicates that he did not believe a positive identification of the murderer had been made by August 1889 (*see* **Aaron Davis Cohen**).

Monro resigned two years before the murder of **Frances Coles**, but must be assumed to have known what (especially) Anderson and **Swanson** believed up to 1890.

Monro's grandson, James, (b.1902), clearly recalled his grandfather saying 'The Ripper was never caught, but he should have been.' (Letter to Keith Skinner, 17 September 1986.) He apparently set down in a 'highly private memoranda' everything he 'knew, deduced or conjectured' and these papers passed intact to his eldest son, Charles, (b.1868), who, circa 1927, had a conversation with a younger brother, which was then told to his son, (Christopher), in India ten years later. 'The gist of this was that James Monro's theory was a very hot potato, that it had been kept secret even from his wife/widow, who survived until 1931, and that he was very doubtful whether or not to destroy the papers. He did <u>not</u> reveal the identity of the suspect(s?) to my father, who told me that he had made no attempt to ascertain them, and had just said emphatically

'Burn the stuff, Charlie, burn it and try to forget it'. (Letter from Christopher Monro to Keith Skinner, 14 November 1986.)

Monro's handwritten memoirs make no mention of the case, and are, apparently, the entirety of what he wrote or intended to write. He was stung into drafting (though not in the end, publishing) them by an article in *The Times*, 5 March 1903, which described him as 'a strong man, if not always discreet.' Printed papers in England are mentioned with reference to another case and it is possible that these included whatever he held on the Ripper. Colin Wilson and Robin Odell, in *Jack the Ripper: Summing Up and Verdict*, mention a correspondent who has devised a theory proposing Monro as a suspect.

See Anderson for Monro's later dispute over Anderson's permission to publish secret information in *The Times*; also, **Arthur Balfour** for an alleged theory which may be connected with either or both of two cases that Monro does describe in his memoirs, and which were, arguably, 'hot potatoes'.

MONSELL, COL. BOLTON JAMES ALFRED (1840–1919)

Chief Constable, Metropolitan Police, 1886–1910. Visited Buck's Row and Hanbury Street murder sites. Also, on 10 November, the interior of the Dorset Street murder site, in the company of Chief Constables Howard and Roberts. Then, in July 1891, shared responsibility with Commissioner **Monro** for directing the investigation of **Alice McKenzie**'s murder.

MONTAGU, SAMUEL (1832–1911)

Born Montague Samuel in Liverpool, 21 December 1832, the son of a wealthy watchmaker and silversmith Louis Samuel. In 1853 he founded and became head of the banking firm of Samuel Montagu and Co (sold to Midland Bank plc in January 1995 and today part of the HSBC group). Married Ellen, the daughter of Louis Cohen. MP for the Whitechapel Division of Tower Hamlets, 1885–1900. Montagu was a pillar of orthodox Judaism and a staunch Liberal. Supported many charities for the poor in general and immigrant Jews in particular. Bt, 1894. Baron Swaythling 1901.

During the Ripper scare, Montagu supported the local Vigilance Committees, forwarding several of their requests and petitions to the Home Office. He strongly favoured the offer of a reward for information leading to the killer's arrest and personally put up £100 for this purpose, trying in the first instance to offer it through the police. When his offer was leaked to the press (possibly by Montagu himself), he expressed great indignation and tried to blame the authorities for releasing the information prematurely. In November 1888, Sir Charles Warren wrote to the Home Office that Montague's real purpose in offering the reward was to show the world that Jews wanted the case to be solved and did not deserve the general suspicion that had fallen upon them (HO144/221/A49301C ff. 173–181).

(*See* Christopher T. George, 'Samuel Montagu, MP, Jack the Ripper, and the Jewish East End', ***Ripperologist***, 53, May 2004.)

MONTAGUE DRUITT: PORTRAIT OF A CONTENDER

Book by D.J. Leighton. Privately published, London: Hydrangea Publishing, 2005. Reprinted without any textual alterations as *Ripper Suspect: The Secret Lives of Montague Druitt* (Stroud, Gloucestershire: Sutton Publishing, 2006.)

Biography which suffers from the paucity of information about Montague John Druitt who, despite the author's best efforts, remains pretty much one-dimensional. His sporting career lets the author present a potpourri of late nineteenth-century cricketing characters, but there's little insight into Druitt's home life, school and university days, and his legal and teaching careers. Leighton believes Druitt might have been associated with a homosexual elite and unquestioningly accepts the Royal conspiracy theory, as set out in **The Ripper and the Royals**.

MOORE, CHARLES

See **John Moore**.

MOORE, CHIEF INSPECTOR HENRY (1848–1918)

As chief inspector, the first of the officers listed by **Walter Dew**, as sent from Scotland Yard to Whitechapel. Actually, Moore was at that time junior to **Abberline**, who was promoted before him to chief inspector.

Son of a former Metropolitan policeman. Worked as a clerk on the South Eastern and London, Chatham and Dover Railway, and subsequently in a silk warehouse. Joined the Metropolitan Police in 1869 (warrant no. 51712), serving in

W Division (Clapham). In 1878, promoted to sergeant, then transferred to Y Division (Holloway). Promoted to inspector in 1878 and transferred to P Division (Peckham). Then, in 1881, transferred to CID (P Division); transferred to Commissioner's Office, Scotland Yard, in 1888. Retired, 1899. Appointed superintendent of Great Eastern Railway Police, from which he retired, in 1913.

The Times reported on 12 November 1888 that Detective Inspectors Moore, **Reid** and **Nairn**, with Sergeants **Thick**, **Godley**, **McCarthy** and **Pearce**, had been working constantly on the case under Abberline's direction. In October, in Abberline's absence, Moore ordered **Sgt. Stephen White** to interview **Matthew Packer**. By August 1889, when Abberline was committed to investigating the Cleveland Street male brothel, Moore took charge of the detectives still working on the ground in Whitechapel and Spitalfields.

His fullest-known remarks on the case occur in the *Pall Mall Gazette* of 4 November 1889, which reproduces an interview with **R. Harding Davis** that first appeared in the Philadelphia press and in which Moore reportedly said he had seen into **Mary Jane Kelly**'s room where the murderer 'hung different parts of the body on nails and over the backs of chairs.' A 1896 memorandum of Moore's indicates that he believed the Goulston Street graffito to be the work of the murderer, and the word 'Jewes' therein to be thus spelt.

At the time of his retirement the *Police Review* carried the following:

He admits one failure, however, and that is that he did not catch Jack the Ripper. Still, there is some satisfaction to him in the thought that even if he didn't succeed in getting the fiend of Whitechapel, no one else did any better. "The police," says Moore, "were handicapped in their work. It was almost impossible to get anything like a trustworthy statement while every crank in England was sending postcards or writing on walls. The class of woman we had to deal with have told any number of stories for a shilling, and it was impossible to believe any woman, owing to the hysterical state of fear they get themselves into. If we had tried to keep under observation the persons we were told were "Jack the Ripper", we should have needed every soldier in the British Army to become a detective. We have in the East End foreigners from every corner of the earth, and when they hate, they will tell such lies as would make your hair stand on end. Of course, everyone wants to know who Jack the Ripper was. Well, so far as I could make out, he was a mad foreign sailor, who paid periodical visits to London on board ship. He committed the crimes and then went back to his ship, and remembered nothing about them. The class of victim made the work of the police exceedingly difficult. Why, once I had occasion to stand near the arch of Pinchin Street, Whitechapel [*sc.* St George's-in-the-East], and I remarked to another officer, "This is just the place for Jack the Ripper," and sure enough, some few months later a 'Ripper' body was found there in a sack. One of these days, now I have more leisure, I may go to work and before I die I might have the luck to see "Jack the Ripper" standing in the door of the Old Bailey. It's the only failure I ever had, but I'm not at all sure it is a failure yet.

11 July 1913.

MOORE, JOHN (1852–1916)
Journalist.

Manager of the Foreign Intelligence Department of the Central News Agency and later Manager of the Agency overall, Identified in the **Littlechild Letter**, wherein he is called Charles Moore, as having invented the 'Jack the Ripper' letters, although Littlechild believed Moore's underling, **T.J. Bulling**, actually penned them.

G.R. Sims' autobiography identifies Moore as regularly attending 'Corinthian' (i.e. raffish) dinner parties thrown on Monday nights by **Sir Melville Macnaghten**, who claimed to have recognised the 'stained finger' of a journalist in the Ripper letters.

MORFORD,–
Alleged suspect. Described in the *Star*, 24 September 1888, as a former surgeon who had given way to drink, and mysteriously disappeared from his lodgings in Great Ormond Street after 10 September. He was sought by the police in Great Ormond Street lodging-houses after he pawned his surgical instruments, and someone representing himself as a detective stated that the authorities had received a letter stating that Morford might be able to throw light on the Whitechapel murders.

Philip Sugden (*The Complete History of Jack the Ripper*), who first noticed the reference, suggests that he may have been the third mad medical student suspected by Scotland Yard (*cf.* **John Sanders**), adding, 'it is by no means improbable' that he was kin to John Orford, senior resident medical officer at the Royal Free Hospital, and/or Henry Orford, carter, of Rupert Street.

MORGANSTONE,– (or possibly, MORGAN STONE)
Alleged former lover of **Mary Jane Kelly**. According to Joe Barnett, she lived with Morganstone in the neighbourhood of the Stepney Gas Works when she left the West End. This would correlate her association with him to the time when **Mrs McCarthy** said she was living in St George's Street (the western end of the old Ratcliff Highway).

'MORING, MR'

Pseudonym given by R. Thurston Hopkins (*Life and Death at the Old Bailey*, 1935) to a man who fitted George Hutchinson's description of his suspect. 'Moring', known to be a friend of **Mary Jane Kelly**, was a drug-addicted poet, the son of a well-to-do East End tradesman. *See* **Ernest Dowson, Francis Thompson**.

MORLAND, NIGEL (1905–86)

Founder-editor of the *Criminologist*.

In the *Evening News* of 28 June 1976, Morland recalled a meeting with Inspector Abberline, saying that he, 'remembered distinctly [Abberline's] exact words', which were: 'You'd have to look for him [the Ripper] not at the bottom of London society, but a long way up.'

Morland also wrote an introduction for **Frank Spiering**'s *Prince Jack*, in which he recalled being told by **Sir Arthur Conan Doyle** that the Ripper was 'somewhere in the upper stratum'. He remembered learning from Edgar Wallace who the Ripper really was (**Albert Victor**, we infer from the context), and again described Abberline's words to him, this time saying, 'and I quote exactly: "I cannot reveal anything except this – *of course* we knew who [the Ripper] was, one of the highest in the land."'

In 1979, Morland published an article of his own in the *Criminologist*: 'Jack the Ripper: the Final Word', in which he argued on the basis of handwriting that there was 'no justification whatever' for the identification of Prince Albert Victor with the Ripper.

MORRIS, ANN

Martha Tabram's sister-in-law and witness at her inquest. A widow described as a very respectable woman, living in 23 Fisher Street, Mile End. Testified to seeing Martha in a pub, possibly the White Swan, Whitechapel Road, at about 11pm, on the night of her death. Police revealed that Martha had been charged three times with annoying Mrs Morris and extracting money from her, being sentenced to seven days' hard labour on the last occasion.

MORRIS, ANNIE

Alleged alias of **Elizabeth Stride**. The *Yorkshire Post*, *Daily Telegraph* and *Morning Advertiser* (1 October 1888) all carried an agency report, saying: 'A woman known as **One-Armed Liz**, living in a common lodging-house in Flower and Dean Street, told a reporter that she had accompanied Sgt. Thick to the mortuary and had identified the body as that of Annie Morris, a prostitute now living in Flower and Dean Street'.

(*Cf.* **Wally Warden, Annie Fitzgerald, Elizabeth Burns**.)

MORRIS, GEORGE JAMES (1834–1907)

witness at **Catherine Eddowes**' inquest. Suggested as accomplice suspect, 2007.

Native of Teddington. Served in the Army for four and a half years. Joined the Metropolitan Police in 1856 (warrant no. 35246); resigned, 1863. Rejoined in 1864 (warrant no. 44855). Resigned, 1882.

The watchman at Kearley and Tonge's warehouse in Mitre Square on the night of 29–30 September 1888, the *Evening News* (1 October 1888) reported that Police Constable **Watkins** called on Morris about 1.25 or 1.30 and handed him a can of tea, which he asked him to heat up. Thereafter, the warehouse door was ajar and he had not heard a sound in the square. As a rule, he heard the beat policeman's footsteps every 15 minutes, but he heard nothing until Police Constable Watkins came to the warehouse again at about 1.45am and called, 'For God's sake, mate, come to assist me!' Picking up a lamp, Morris asked what the matter was and Watkins said, 'Oh dear, here's another woman cut up to pieces.' Morris saw the body and then ran to Aldgate, where he found Police Constable **James Harvey**.

A report in the *Star* (12 September 1888) suggests that Morris's character may have been precisian, legalistic and authoritarian. He brought charges against a shoemaker for 'stealing' an empty wooden champagne case left outside Kearley and Tonge's and was priggishly disgusted when the magistrates refused to consider the appropriation of a worthless discarded piece of packaging as theft.

On 2 October 1888, a correspondent wrote to the City authorities expressing his suspicions about Morris and asking them whether they were *"quite sure of this man's character being good…"* (see **Jack The Ripper: Scotland Yard Investigates**) and Morris has more recently been suggested as an accomplice of the Ripper (Rob Hills, 'Cat's Cradle', **Ripperologist**, 75, January 2007).

MORRISON, JOHN (1926–2005)

Author of **Jimmy Kelly's Year of Ripper Murders**. In 1986, he erected a headstone over **Mary Jane Kelly**'s unmarked grave, for which he gained a good deal of publicity. Obituary in **Ripperologist**, 61, September 2005.

MORTIMER, MRS FANNY (b. 1840)

Lived at 36 Berner Street. Made important statements to the press, which were followed up by police, but did not give evidence at Stride's inquest.

Born in Roydon, Essex, the daughter of Samuel and Lydia Skipp. Married William Mortimer, a carman, on3 March 1861, and had five children: Minnie (b c.1866), Charles (b c.1867), Thomas (b c.1871), Edward (b c.1873), Rose (b c.1874), and Samuel (b c.1881). She was described as 'a clean and respectable looking woman… a strong contrast to many of those around her'.

Early reports do not name her but report that '…she heard the measured heavy tramp of a policeman passing the house on his beat. Immediately afterwards she went to the street-door with the intention of shooting the bolts, though she remained standing there for ten minutes before she did so.' After 'Locking the door, she prepared to retire to bed, in the front room on the ground floor, and so it happened that in about four minutes' time she heard the pony and cart pass the house, and remarked upon the circumstance to her husband.' She then heard the commotion following the discovery of Stride's body. (*Daily News*, 1 October 1888) However, later reports, evidently emanating from a news agency, place her outside for practically the entire half hour: '"I was standing at the door of my house nearly the whole time between halfpast twelve and one o'clock this (Sunday) morning, and did not notice anything unusual. I had just gone indoors and was preparing to go to bed when I heard a commotion outside, and immediately ran out, thinking that there was another row at the Socialists' Club close by."' She added that '"the only person whom I had seen pass through the street previously was a young man carrying a black shiny bag, who walked very fast from the direction of Commercialroad."' He looked up at the club, and then went round the corner by the Board School... If a man had come out of the yard before one o'clock I must have seen him."' (*Daily Telegraph* and numerous other newspapers, 1 October 1888) The man with the black bag was **Leon Goldstein**, but this identification was not widely known and writing in 1938 **Walter Dew** thought 'it is more than probable that a woman living in one of the cottages on the other side of the court was the only person ever to see the Ripper in the vicinity of one of his crimes. This woman was a Mrs. Mortimer.' Dew stated that she had stayed at her door for ten minutes listening to the singing from the Club and shortly before returning indoors 'observed something else, silent and sinister. A man, whom she judged to be about thirty, dressed in black, and carrying a small, shiny black bag, hurried furtively along the opposite side of the court.'(*ICaught Crippen*)

Robin Odell, in *Jack the Ripper: In Fact and Fiction*, gives an unsourced and as yet untraced reference to Mrs Mortimer's stating that while in her doorway, prior to Goldstein's passing down the street, she heard a row going on somewhere; a bump, and a stifled cry.

If the 'measured heavy tramp of a policeman' passing her house had been that of P.C. **William Smith** then Mrs Mortimer would have gone to her door just after 12.30 a.m. and it is probable that she would have seen several people going into or coming out of the Club or otherwise passing by – **Charles Letchford**, **Morris Eagle**, **Joseph Lave**, and **Israel Schwartz**. It *is* known, however, that Leon Goldstein passed through Berner Street very shortly before 1.00 a.m. On the whole, therefore, it would seem that the early reports and Walter Dew's memory were correct and that she had been standing at her door for about ten minutes before 1.00a.m.

MOULSON, PC GEORGE, 216T (*b*.1862)

Reported the discovery of **Montague John Druitt**'s body. Joined the Metropolitan Police on 9 April 1883 (warrant no. 67735). Transferred to the CID on 11 January 1890 and returned to uniformed branch as PC 420T on 17 January 1896. Retired, October 1905, by which time he was PC501 in N Division. Married in 1908.

Summoned by waterman **Winslade**, who pulled the body out of the Thames on 31 December 1888. It would appear to be Moulson's report, describing the pocket contents and wrongly estimating Druitt's age, which was in part followed in **Melville Macnaghten**'s memoranda.

MULSHAW, PATRICK

Witness at **Mary Ann Nichols**' inquest. Resident at 3 Rupert Street, Whitechapel. A night porter employed by the Whitechapel Board of Works.

On duty watching sewage works in Winthrop Street (parallel with, and converging on Buck's Row) through the night of 30–31 August 1888. Dozed during the night, but assured the inquest that he was awake from 3 to 4am, when he saw and heard no one. He was reported as saying, 'Another man then passed by, and said, "Watchman, old man, I believe somebody is murdered down the street."' Mulshaw went to see the body, joining police and **Henry Tomkins**. It is not known who the man addressing Mulshaw was, nor how he could have been 'another man', since no report has survived of Mulshaw's reporting any previous passer-by.

MUMFORD, JAMES

Saw **Mary Ann Nichols**' body. A horse slaughterman working at Barber's Yard, Winthrop Street, Mumford accompanied **Henry Tomkins** at 4.20am, on 31 August 1888, around the corner to Buck's Row, on learning of the body from Police Constable **Thain**. He and Mumford remained at the site until Police Constable **Neil** left for the mortuary.

MURDER AND MADNESS: THE SECRET LIFE OF JACK THE RIPPER

Book by Dr **David Abrahamsen** (1903–2002). (New York: Donald I. Fine, 1992; with new appendices, London: Robson Books, 1992 and New York: Avon Books, 1993.)

Dr Abrahamsen seems to have imagined there was a solid case against all the suspects and that basic psychiatric profiling techniques would reveal the most likely. He concluded the murders were committed by **J.K. Stephen** *and* **Prince Albert Victor**. The book is flawed with abundant historical errors. Scotland Yard denied its claim to be based on unpublished evidence in their possession (*Evening Standard*, 30 October 1992). The book does, however, include J.K. Stephen's full medical history.

MURDOCH, CHARLES STEWART (1838-1908)

The son of Sir Thomas William Clinton Murdoch, KCMG (1809-1891), a distinguished civil servant. Home Office 3rd class clerk 1856; **Sir Robert Anderson** recalled in *The Lighter Side of My Official Life* that Murdoch, along with **Godfrey Lushington** and Anderson himself, were among a small group of civil servants who were habitués of after-hours tennis in the inner court of the Home Office building: 'Grand games we used to have, the fastest tennis, indeed, that I ever

played, and one hour of it was ample exercise for a whole day.' Married Frances Bliss, 1880; awarded a CB in the Birthday Honours in 1892 (*The Times*, 25 May 1892); Murdoch was appointed Assistant Under-Secretary in 1896 and held that position until his retirement in 1903, during which time his name was often appended to letters in which the Home Secretary replied to petitions and appeals for the clemency in the case of people condemned to death, including that of Mary Ann Ansell, convicted and sentenced to death for the murder of her sister, Caroline, an inmate of the asylum for imbeciles at Leavesden, a minor cause celebre of the day (*Daily News*, 17 July 1899 – Ansell was hanged by Billington in St Alban's gaol on 19 July 1899). He retired in 1903, in which year he was appointed a Royal Commissioner to inquire into London Traffic (*The Times*, 7 February 1903). He died on 31 January 1908.

Charles Murdoch was a signatory on several surviving documents connected with the Ripper case, but is notably the recipient of a memo from an official 'WTB' asking if the police should be asked for information about an insane medical student from London Hospital who was the subject of 'a good deal of gossip' (HO 144/221/A49301C, ff.110–111).

MYLETT, CATHERINE (ROSE) (1859–88), aka Catherine Millett, 'Drunken Lizzie' Davis, 'Fair Alice' Downey, Fair Clar

Alleged strangled Ripper victim.

Catherine 'Rose' Mylett was born in London on 8 December 1859 to Henry Mylett, a labourer in a starch factory, and his wife Margaret (née Haley), both of whom hailed from Ireland. She was about 5ft 2in tall, had light, frizzy hair cut short and hazel eyes. By her mother's account, formerly married to an upholsterer named Davis. Bore one daughter, whom she referred to as Florrie or Flossie, who was about 6 years old and was at a school in Sutton, Surrey, when Catherine died (*Aberdeen Weekly Journal*, 25 December 1888).

The 1881 Census appears to identify Catherine as living at 40 Lincoln St, Mile End Old Town, where she is listed as Kate Davis, and stated to be married and living there with her newly-born daughter Florence Beatrice (*b.* 12 September 1880). Florence's birth certificate shows that she was born at 6 Maidman Street

(**Ada Wilson** was attacked at 19 Maidman Street), and that her father was named Thomas Davis, a commercial traveller. The 1891 Census shows Florence with the surname Mylett and resident at Kensington And Chelsea District School Or Cottage Homes, Banstead, Surrey.

Mylett lived at various addresses in the Limehouse/Poplar district and sometimes at her mother's house in Pelham Street, Baker's Row, Spitalfields. At the time of her death, she was living at 18 George Street (the same common lodging-house where **Emma Elizabeth Smith** was living when attacked by a gang earlier in the year, and next door to 19 George Street – Satchell's lodging-house – where **Martha Tabram** was living shortly before her death, and where **Annie Farmer** had been assaulted, nearly a month earlier). Mrs Mary Smith, the deputy at 18 George Street, said that Mylett had lodged with her for about three months, for much of that time with a man named Ben Goodson, but they had separated some two weeks earlier. According to Mrs Smith, Mylett was more often drunk than sober and during the time that she had lived at 18 George Street, she had been imprisoned for five days (*Daily News*, 26 December 1888, *The Times*, 3 January 1889).

She used various aliases, calling herself Rose Mylett in Bromley (Rose being a name she adopted when in Bromley Infirmary and is the name by which she had since become most commonly known, which is why we refer to her as 'Rose Mylett' throughout this book, not by her birth or married name). Elizabeth or Lizzie Davies in Whitechapel (by which name she is recorded in a Scotland Yard list of victims in the Ripper enquiry), and Alice Downey in Poplar.

She was seen by infirmary night-attendant **Charles Ptolomay** talking to two sailors at 7.55pm, on Wednesday, 19 December 1888, in Poplar High Street, near Clarke's Yard. At the time, she was sober and saying, 'No, no, no!' to one sailor, whose manner was suspicious enough to draw Ptolomay's attention. At 2.30am a young woman, **Alice Graves**, saw her with two men outside the George in Commercial Road, apparently drunk.

She was found dead in Clarke's Yard at 4.15am by Police Sergeant **Robert Golding** and PC **Thomas Costello**. Her body, still warm, was lying on the left side. The clothes were not disarranged and there was no obvious sign of injury. There were no marks of a struggle in the soft earth of the yard and she had 1/2d (6p) in her possession. Death was certified by divisional surgeon Dr **Matthew Brownfield**'s assistant, Dr **George James Harris**, the only doctor to view the body in situ. He did not suspect foul play and saw no mark on Mylett's neck. **PC Barrett**, 470 K, took the body to the mortuary and specifically looked for a mark round the neck, but did not see one (*The Times*, 10 January 1889).

Later in the morning Curtain T. Chivers, the Coroner's officer and mortuary keeper, saw the body and noticed a mark round the neck, about an eighth of an inch deep and some scratches above it. He informed Dr Harris, who said that he hadn't noticed it in Clarke's Yard, but promised to look carefully for it when he assisted the postmortem examination (*The Times*, 10 January 1889). Coroner **Wynne Baxter** thereupon sent orders for Brownfield to carry out a postmortem, which was done on Friday morning, 21 December, and the report was presented at the opening of the inquest on the same day. According to this report:

> Blood was oozing from the nostrils, and there was a slight abrasion on the right side of the face. On the neck there was a mark which had evidently been caused by cord drawn tightly round the neck, from the spine to the left ear. Such a mark would be made by a four-thread cord. There were also impressions of the thumbs and middle and index fingers of some person plainly visible on each side of the neck. There were no injuries to the arm or legs. The brain was gorged with an almost-black fluid blood. The stomach was full of meat and potatoes, which had only recently been eaten. Death was due to strangulation. Deceased could not have done it herself. Marks on her neck were probably caused by her trying to pull the cord off. He thought the murderer must have stood at the left rear of the woman, and, having the ends of the cord round his hands, thrown it round her throat, crossed his hands, and thus strangled her. If it had been done in this way, it would account for the mark not going completely round the neck.

After hearing Dr Brownfield's evidence and that of one or two other people, Wynne E. Baxter adjourned the proceedings, saying that, 'it seemed very much as if a murder had been committed and that it would be better to adjourn to give his officer and the police time to make inquiries.'

Unfortunately, Dr Brownfield, prior to giving his testimony at the inquest, did not inform the police of his conclusion that Mylett had been murdered, thereby denying them the opportunity to resolve questions arising from their own conclusion that Mylett's death had been accidental. Embarrassingly, the police had not launched an investigation.

On the morning after Dr Brownfield gave evidence, **James Monro** told **Robert Anderson** to make further enquiries on the spot and to instruct Dr **Thomas Bond** to make a second examination of the body. Anderson accordingly sent a note to Dr Bond, but he was out of town and, on learning this, Monro asked chief surgeon **Alexander MacKellar** to examine the body. Meanwhile, Dr Bond's assistant, Dr **Charles Alfred Hebbert**, had opened a note sent to Dr Bond by Anderson and had taken it upon himself to examine the body in Bond's stead. All the doctors agreed that Mylett had died from strangulation and that judging by the mark from the rope, this was homicide. The succession of doctors visiting the mortuary had been a fault of circumstance, but the police were mildly censured by Wynne Baxter during his summing up and some modern commentators have used this to charge Anderson with nefariously trying to influence medical opinion.

It is possible that it was not to the visits of MacKellar and Hebbert on that first day to which Baxter was referring; during Baxter's summing up and before the verdict, Dr Brownfield stated, 'he was called upon by an official from the Home Office, who said the Home Secretary was anxious that the doctors who had seen the bodies of the women murdered in Whitechapel should see the body of the deceased, and he took it upon himself, on behalf of the coroner, to give every facility' (*Lloyd's Weekly Newspaper*, 3 January 1889).

Meanwhile, while almost every other newspaper was reporting that the idea that Mylett had been murdered by Jack the Ripper was being ridiculed, Dr Brownfield was reported in the *Star* (24 December 1888) as having been interviewed two days earlier by a *Star* reporter. Asked if he thought Mylett had been murdered by Jack the Ripper, Brownfield – who seems to have had a curious and no doubt infuriating habit of answering a question with a question – asked whether Jack the Ripper had strangled or partially strangled his victims before cutting their throats. Brownfield voiced his personal theory that the victims had first been strangled with a cord, then had their throats cut along the line of the rope mark. Brownfield would later deny having said anything to the *Star*'s journalist other than what he had told the inquest.

The *Star* further reported that although Dr **George George Bagster Phillips** refused to talk to their reporter, they had learned via another source that Phillips thought that Mylett had been killed by the same man as had killed **Annie Chapman**.

Dr Bond examined the body on Monday, 24 December 1888, five days after Mylett's death, and concurred with the other doctors over the cause of death. Accompanied by Dr Hebbert, Dr Bond reported his conclusion to Robert Anderson. According to a report by Anderson to James Monro, 'After a long conference, in which I pressed my difficulties and objections, I referred them to you' (report dated 11 January 1889, MEPO 3/143). It is not known whether Drs Bond and Hebbert actually saw Monro, but that afternoon Dr Bond made a second examination of Mylett's body and concluded death had been accidental, not homicidal.

Dr Bond, who acknowledged that it was a difficult case and that Dr Hebbert, who was a very experienced man, did not agree with him, stated that he believed the rope mark produced when killing an able-bodied woman very quickly would not have disappeared in five days and more damage would have been done to the skin of the neck. His opinion was that the woman, in a state of drunkenness, fell down in an awkward position when the larynx was pressed against some part of the neck of the dress and that the mark around the neck was produced by the collar, either while she was dying or while she was lying dead (*Lloyd's Weekly Newspaper*, 6 January 1889). Asked by the Coroner if he had any experience of thug murders, Dr Bond replied that he had not. Dr Bond also had a tablespoon of Mylett's stomach contents analysed and found this to contain a teaspoonful of whisky (Dr Brownfield had discovered no trace of alcohol).

It is noted that at least one standard textbook of the day states, 'If the body of a person is allowed to cool, with a handkerchief, band or tightly-fitting collar round the neck, a mark resembling that of strangulation will be produced. Before any opinion is given that murder has been perpetrated, the medical proofs on which reliance is placed should be clear, distinct, conclusive and satisfactory' (Alfred Swaine Taylor, *A Manual of Medical Jurisprudence*, 8th American ed., from the 10th London ed. Philadelphia, 1880).

Researcher Debra Arif has also brought the authors' attention to the following comment in *A System of Legal Medicine* (Allan McLane Hamilton and Lawrence Godkin, New York: 1894):

Accidental suffocation may occur in people helpless from intoxication or debility, and the mouth covered over or the throat externally compressed. I am indebted to Dr. Hebbert for the report of the following cases – one a case which happened in London in 1889, and known as the Poplar mystery. A woman was found dead in an alley. The postmortem signs were those of death from asphxia. The larynx was much congested, and both aryepiglottic folds were ecchymosed. Dr. Hebbert thought that the death was due to compression of the throat and closing of the mouth, as there were bruises on both cheeks and scratches on the throat, and the larynx was so markedly ecchymosed; but Mr. Bond, the well known English expert, thought the compression was caused by the head falling forward while helplessly drunk, and being compressed by a tight collar. And though the jury brought in a verdict of murder, it did not follow that Mr. Bond's opinion was wrong.

Ms Ariif has observed that Dr Hebbert seems to have surmised from the bruises to both cheeks and scratches on the throat that the murderer put his hand over Mylett's mouth, which, if true, raises questions about whether he totally agreed with Dr Brownfield and Harris's conclusion that the murderer wound a rope round his hands and crossed them over at the back of Mylett's neck.

There was some independent support for the police view of death from natural causes, a letter from a physician and surgeon named Andrew Rowan (*Daily News*, 28 December 1888), recalling the case of a man who died from acute apoplexy after drinking ten glasses of whisky and having no food, who had on his neck what appeared to be the mark of a ligature. His landlord was charged with his murder, but Rowan had been able to prove that it had been caused by the compression of a tight collar after the man had fallen into an awkward position.

Several newspapers seem to have thought that Wynne Baxter sided with the view of Dr Bond and the police that Mylett's was an accidental death, reporting that in his summation he had stated, 'There was no evidence to show that death was the result of violence' (*Morning Advertiser*, 10 January 1889, and *Lloyd's Weekly Newspaper*, 13 January 1889). Robert Anderson seems to have thought so too, writing in a report dated 11 January 1889 that his opinion was shared, 'I think perhaps, I may add by that of the Coroner himself' (MEPO 3/143).

It seems clear from other reports of the summing up that Baxter did not hold that opinion and the dichotomy is possibly resolved by *The Times* (10 January 1889), which reported Baxter as saying, 'The usual signs of strangulation, such as protrusion of the tongue and clenching of the hands, were absent, there being nothing at all suggestive of death from violence.' However, Baxter had then gone on to explain such signs were not present if the violence was very sudden. He pointed out that the victims of thug stranglers in India often betrayed no signs of struggle and had similarly placid features; also, there was no definitive evidence that Mylett had been killed in Clarke's Yard. Baxter further countered Bond's evidence by pointing out that Bond saw the body five days after the other doctors.

Following this, the jury accepted the preponderant medical evidence and returned a verdict of 'Murder by person or persons unknown'. The *Morning Advertiser* thought, 'the jury were probably influenced by other than expert evidence', suggesting they were more influenced by the fact that Mylett was a prostitute, that the yard where her body was found was used by prostitutes and that a prostitute killer was still at large. This was echoed by Robert Anderson in his autobiography, *The Lighter Side of My Official Life* (1910), in which he wrote, 'the Poplar case of December, 1888, was death from natural causes, and but for the "Jack the Ripper" scare, no one would have thought of suggesting that it was a homicide'. Some commentators see this remark as an example of Anderson clinging obstinately to his own opinion in the teeth of the evidence.

The death certificate records thatElizabeth Myllett died as a result of 'Violent Suffocation by strangulation by a cord which has not yet been found. Murder against some person or persons unknown.'

Robert Anderson wrote in a report to James Monro that Superintendent Steed, who had attended the inquest on behalf of the police, had brought him the jury's verdict and sought instructions. Anderson wrote: 'I have thought it only fair to him and his officers to tell him plainly that neither the evidence given at the inquest, nor the verdict arrived at, affects the judgment I formed when I personally investigated the case on the 22nd ult., and that I did not intend to take any further action in the matter'. Precisely what he meant by this is uncertain.

Catherine Mylett (under the name Elizabeth Davis) was included as an 'alleged' victim in a list of the Whitechapel murders made out in very elaborate calligraphy and preserved both on the Scotland Yard files and among the papers of Chief Inspector **Swanson**, but many newspapers did not include her in the lists of the Ripper victims published (*see Lloyd's Weekly Nespaper*, 27 March 1892, for example).

(Debra Arif and Robert Clack: 'A Rose By Any Other Name: The Death of Catherine Mylett, 20 December 1888. *Ripperologist*, 108, November 2009)

MYSTERIES OF POLICE AND CRIME
Book by **Major Arthur Griffiths** (three volumes illustrated: 1898, 1901, 1902; two text-only volumes: 1899).

Important for its descriptions of senior policemen (*see* **Robert Anderson**, **Melville Macnaghten**), it refers to the three suspects, **M.J. Druitt**, **Kosminski** and **Ostrog** named in the **Macnaghten memoranda**, which Griffiths closely parallels:

The outside public may think that the identity of that later miscreant, "Jack the Ripper", was never revealed. So far as actual knowledge goes, this is undoubtedly true. But the police, after the last murder, had brought their investigations to the point of strongly suspecting several persons, all of them known to be homicidal lunatics, and against three of these they held very plausible and reasonable grounds of suspicion. Concerning two of them the case was weak, although it was based on certain colourable facts. One was a Polish Jew, a known lunatic, who was at large in the district of Whitechapel at the time of the murder, and who, having afterwards developed homicidal tendencies, was confined in an asylum. This man was said to resemble the murderer by the one person who got a glimpse of him – the police constable in Mitre Court. The second possible criminal was a Russian doctor, also insane, who had been a convict both in England and Siberia. This man was in the habit of carrying about surgical knives and instruments in his pockets; his antecedents were of the very worst, and at the time of the Whitechapel murders he was in hiding, or, at least his whereabouts were never exactly known. The third person was of the same type, but the suspicion in his case was stronger, and there was every reason to believe that his own friends entertained grave doubts about him. He also was a doctor in the prime of life, was believed to be insane or on the borderland of insanity, and he disappeared immediately after the last murder, that in Miller's Court, on the 9th of November, 1888. On the last day of that year, seven weeks later, his body was found floating in the Thames, and was said to have been in the water a month. The theory in this case was that after his last exploit, which was the most fiendish of all, his brain entirely gave way, and he became furiously insane and committed suicide. It is at least a strong presumption that "Jack the Ripper" died or was put under restraint after the Miller's Court affair, which ended this series of crimes. It would be interesting to know whether in this third case the man was left-handed or ambidextrous, both suggestions having been advanced by medical experts after viewing the victims. Certainly other doctors disagreed on this point, which may be said to add another to the many instances in which medical evidence has been conflicting, not to say confusing.

MYSTERY OF JACK THE RIPPER, THE

Book by **Leonard Matters** (London: Hutchinson, 1929; hardback, London: W.H. Allen, n.d.; London: Pinnacle Books (W.H. Allen), nd.; paperback, London: Arrow, 1964).

The first full-length English language study of the murders, rightly praised as a pioneering survey of the facts in the case and particularly valuable for its descriptions and photographs of geographical locations as they were in Matters' day. Concludes by proposing that Jack the Ripper was the pseudonymous '**Dr Stanley**', a theory Matters first proposed in an article, 'Jack the Ripper Sensation. Noted Murderer A London Doctor? Dying Confession' (The *People*, 26 December 1926), and which he claimed was based on an article he had seen in a Spanish language Argentinian journal. This reported the lengthy statement of a former pupil and brief deathbed confession of 'Dr Stanley'. No subsequent researcher has been able to trace the article and this has led to Matters being accused of deliberately purveying fiction to provide a solution – 'The "deathbed confession" bears about the same relation to the facts of criminology as the exploits of Peter Rabbit and Jerry Muskrat do to zoology' (Edmund Pearson, More Studies in Murder). Neither his character nor his book warrants this condemnation.

An account which pre-dates Matters by 25 years and may be a reference to the same suspect is given by the actor John T. Sullivan, who claimed the truth about Jack the Ripper had only recently emerged in the last three months and that he was a physician who developed a homicidal mania and had escaped from a private sanatorium in a London suburb, then fled to Buenos Ayres in Argentina (*Salt Lake Herald*, 25 August 1901).

Subsequent to the publication of Matters' article in *The People*, Matters received a statement from a former West End demi-mondaine named Mrs North, who claimed to have been regularly entertained in Monaco's, during the autumn of 1888, by a gentleman who she concluded was 'Dr Stanley'.

Colin Wilson heard from Mr A.L. Lee of Torquay that his father had met Dr Stanley, by that name, as a friend of 'Cedric Saunders', who believed him to be the Ripper (*see* **Sedgwick Saunders**). A version of this story may have been told to Michael Harrison in childhood, who writes, 'the most slanderous identification, I remember, being that of the venereally infected son of a royal surgeon'.

The earliest-known parallel story describes a 'well-known' East End medico suspecting his former assistant (*East London Observer*, 13 October 1888).

Daniel Farson's *Jack the Ripper* (1972) describes a letter from Mr Barca of Streatham, saying that between 1910 and 1920 there was a dive called 'Sally's Bar' in Buenos Aires, allegedly owned by Jack the Ripper.

N

NATHAN, Mr, CONSUL GENERAL (fl. 1888)

Interviewed informant Jonas in Vienna; it was his favourable impression of the witness that persuaded ambassador Sir Augustus Paget to press the matter in correspondence with the Home Office and the Prime Minister (HO144/221/A49301D).

NEARN, INSPECTOR JAMES WILLIAM, (1857–1926)

Recipient of Whitechapel Murder case souvenir. Joined the Metropolitan Police on 27 September 1877 (warrant no. 61557); retired, 1902, as inspector 1st class, CID. **Donald Swanson** signed his discharge certificate, describing his conduct as 'very good.'

It appears Nearn worked on the case with **Abberline** and **Moore**. He took the statement of suspect **William Wallace Brodie** and, when promoted to sergeant by 1891, the statements of witnesses **Thomas Fowles** and **Kate McCarthy** in the **Frances Coles** enquiry. He was presented with a pipe inscribed, 'Souvenir to James Nearn, Whitechapel Murders, 1888, from six brother officers'. Since October 2006, the pipe has been on display in Scotland Yard's Crime Museum as part of the Jack the Ripper exhibits.

NEATING, GEORGE (b. c. 1860)

See **George Netting**.

NEIL, SUPERINTENDENT ARTHUR FOWLER (1867–1939)

Investigating officer in the **Severin Klosowski** case, who believed him to be the Ripper. Joined the Metropolitan Police in May 1888 (warrant no. 73638). Resigned, 1927.

As detective sergeant, tracked down Klosowski's estranged wife Lucy Baderski in 1902, and brought her to confront him in prison. Argued later that Klosowski was Jack the Ripper (*Forty Years of Man-Hunting*, London: Jarrolds, 1932 – chief among those who assisted in the writing of this memoir was **Edwin T Woodhall**).

NEIL, PC JOHN, 97J (1850–1903)

Witness at **Mary Ann Nichols'** inquest; discovered her body.

Born in County Cork. Joined the Metropolitan Police in 1875 (warrant no. 59168). Posted to J Division (Bethnal Green), where he remained, apart from a brief excursus to L Division in July and August 1895, until he resigned in 1897, following injury received on duty.

Neil's beat was never further away from the murder site than Baker's Row (today's Vallance Road). He discovered Nichols' body in the gutter in Buck's Row at approximately 3.45am while walking on his beat eastwards along the Row towards Brady Street. Following this, he quietly summoned Police Constable **Thain** to his assistance by signalling with his lamp down to Brady Street, where Thain was passing. He was also joined by **Police Constable Mizen**, who had been directed to the woman lying in the gutter by the carters **Cross** and **Paul**.

P.C. NIEL
J. 97.

Neil sent Thain to fetch **Dr Llewellyn** and Mizen for the ambulance (virtually a wheeled stretcher). He remained with the body, where he was joined in succession by **Henry Tomkins**, **James Mumford**, **Charles Brittain**, **Dr Llewellyn**, **Sergeant Kerby** and **Inspector Spratling**.

At 5am Neil went with Spratling to the mortuary.

NETLEY, JOHN CHARLES (1860–1903)

Identified by BBC researchers with a man of the same name alleged by **Joseph Gorman Sickert** to have driven the carriage for **Sir William Gull** and his co-conspirators to commit the Whitechapel murders.

A carman, employed by Messrs Thompson, McKay and Co., he died in a traffic accident near the Clarence Gate of Regent's Park.

Joseph Sickert alleged that Netley was an ambitious bisexual opportunist, who prostituted himself to socially prominent homosexuals in the 1880s. He claimed that Netley drove his own cab at the time of the Ripper murders and transported **Prince Albert Victor** on his visits to **Annie Elizabeth Crook** in Cleveland Street. Sickert further claimed that Netley drove Gull and his fellow-murderer/s to the East End and that the murders took place inside the carriage, which then transported the bodies to the points where they were dumped. Sickert also alleged that Netley made two unsuccessful attempts to kill **Alice Margaret Crook** by running her down: one in the Strand or Fleet Street at the height of the Ripper scare, the other in Drury Lane in 1892, after which he fled from an enraged crowd and drowned himself off Westminster Pier.

BBC researchers working on the drama-documentary series *Jack the Ripper* (*see* **The Ripper File**) established there was a cab accident involving a little girl in Fleet Street, in October 1888 (*see* **Lizzie Madewell**) and that a man whose name was reported as 'Nickley' threw himself into the Thames, off Westminster Pier, in February 1892.

It is not known how Joseph Sickert obtained any knowledge of this obscure man, who died 20 years before his (Sickert's) birth. It is possible the John Charles Netley identified by BBC researchers was not the same John Netley described by Sickert.

NETTING, GEORGE
Suspect.

Called George Netting in a communication from the Cardiff police to Scotland Yard, following the inquest into the murder of **Mary Ann Austin** in Dorset Street, in 1901. Netting had been lodging with his wife Mable at 36 May Street, towards whom, according to the landlady Mrs Clarke, he had been extremely violent. He was believed to have served in the East End with the Metropolitan Police in 1888 and was dismissed for drunkenness. When his wife mentioned the murder of Austin, he replied, 'Shut your bloody mouth or that will be your end, if you are not careful!'

Netting was described as about 40 years of age, with very dark hair, a complexion of Jewish appearance, 5ft 10 in tall, with a cataract growing over one of his eyes. It was believed this description fitted that of the man last seen in Austin's company. Scotland Yard attempted to locate him, but it is not known whether they did so. Nor was he identified as having been a Metropolitan policeman.

The 1901 Census shows that John and Sarah Clarke lived at 36 May Street and that lodging with them were George Netting (aged 33), a blacksmith born in Plymouth, Devon; also, Mable Netting (aged 27), born in Newport, Monmouthshire, and their 11-month-old daughter, Violet.

Derek Osborne ('Line of Enquiry', *Ripperana*, 42, October 2002) notes that Neating's description fits that of the unidentified man seen by Thomas Bowyer in Dorset Street on the Wednesday before Mary Jane Kelly's murder.

(See Robert Clack, 'Murder, Death And The Lodging House: The Strange Case Of Mary Ann Austin', *Ripper Notes*, 24, October 2005.)

NEVE, PC GEORGE, 101 H (*b.* 1850)
Joined the Metropolitan Police in 1874 (warrant no. 58279). Witness at **Alice McKenzie**'s inquest. Ordered by **Sergeant Badham** to proceed from Commercial Street to Castle Alley at approximately 12.55am, on 17 July 1889, on

account of the murder. Saw the body, then searched the alley, costermongers' barrows and space behind the hoarding, but found nothing.

NEWS FROM WHITECHAPEL, THE: JACK THE RIPPER IN THE DAILY TELEGRAPH

Book by Alexander Chisholm, Christopher-Michael DiGrazia and Dave Yost (Jefferson NC: McFarland, 2002).

Annotated transcriptions of the reports on the case from what was then the largest circulation newspaper in the world.

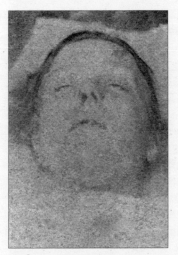

NICHOLS, MARY ANN 'POLLY' (1845–88)

First canonical Ripper victim and first in any category to be abdominally mutilated.

Daughter of locksmith, later blacksmith Edward Walker of Dean Street, Fetter Lane. In 1864, married **William Nichols**, printer of Bouverie Street, and lived with him briefly at that address; subsequently at her father's home at 131 Trafalgar Street, Walworth, and from c. 1874–80 at 6D Peabody Buildings, Stamford Street, Lambeth. During this time, bore children: Edward John (1866), Percy George (1868), Alice Esther (1870), Eliza Sarah (1877) and Henry Alfred (1879).

Considerable domestic disharmony from, at latest, 1877, at which time, apparently, William Nichols briefly eloped with a woman who had assisted at Mary Ann's accouchement with Eliza. Then, or shortly thereafter, Edward John took up residence with Edward Walker and did not speak to his father again until after his mother's death. Mary Ann, however, either from 1877 or earlier, began to drink heavily and absconded from home, five or six times. In 1880, the pair separated. Nichols retained the children (except Edward John) and paid Mary Ann 5/- [worth about £12 in today's money] per week allowance until 1882, when he learned that she was living by prostitution. She then summonsed him for maintenance, but lost the case when he proved her immoral lifestyle.

Her movements after marital breakdown are surprisingly well documented:

6 September 1880–31 May 1881	Lambeth Workhouse
31 May 1881–24 April 1882	Not known
24 April 1882–18 January 1883	Lambeth Workhouse
18 January 1883–20 January 1883	Lambeth Infirmary
20 January 1883–24 March 1883	Lambeth Workhouse
24 March 1883–21 May 1883	Lived with her father until her drinking caused friction, whereupon she left after a quarrel

21 May 1883–2 June 1883	Lambeth Workhouse
2 June 1883–25 October 1887	Lived with **Thomas Stuart Drew** at 15 York Street, Walworth. Respectably dressed, she attended her brother's funeral in June 1886.
25 October 1887	Spent one day in St Giles's Workhouse, Endell Street
26 October 1887–2 December 1887	Strand Workhouse, Edmonton
2 December 1887–19 December 1887	Probably mostly sleeping rough in Trafalgar Square. When the area was cleared and she was found destitute, she was readmitted to Lambeth Workhouse (*Morning Advertiser*, 3 September 1888). The *Daily News* (26 October 1887) reported the appearance at the Bow Street Police Court of several vagrants arrested in Trafalgar Square, one of who was a Mary Ann Nichols, aged 36, who was 'stated to be the worst woman in the square, and at the police-station was very disorderly.' It is not known if this is the same Mary Ann Nichols..
19 December 1887–29 December 1887	Lambeth Workhouse
29 December 1887–4 January 1888	No record
4 January 1888–16 April 1888	Mitcham Workhouse (Holborn) and Holborn Infirmary (Archway Hospital)
16 April 1888– 12 July 1888	Employed by Mr and Mrs Cowdry in Wandsworth until she absconded, stealing clothes.

From the Cowdrys' she wrote to her father:

I just write to say you will be glad to know that I am settled in my new place, and going all right up to now. My people went out yesterday, and have not returned, so I am left in charge. It is a grand place inside, with trees and gardens back and front. All has been newly done up. They are teetotallers, and very religious, so I ought to get on. They are very nice people, and I have not much to do. I hope you are all right and the boy has work. So goodbye now for the present. Yours truly, 'Polly' Answer soon please, and let me know how you are.

12 July 1888 – 1 August 1888	No record
1 August 1888 – 2 August 1888	Gray's Inn Temporary Workhouse
2 August 1888–24 August 1888	18 Thrawl Street, where for 4d [2p] she shared a 'surprisingly' clean room with three other women and a bed with **Ellen Holland**
24 August 1888–30 August 1888	The 'White House', 56 Flower and Dean Street: a dosshouse, which allowed men and women to sleep together.

On Thursday, 30 August she was seen walking alone in Whitechapel Road at 11.30pm. At 12.30am, she was seen leaving the Frying Pan in Brick Lane. Then, at 1.20, she went to 18 Thrawl Street, slightly tipsy. The deputy turned her away as she had not 4d, but she laughed as she went, saying, 'I'll soon get my doss money – see what a jolly bonnet I've got now!' She was wearing a bonnet that the deputy had not seen before. At 2.30am, Ellen Holland met her, drunk and staggering, at the corner of Osborn Street and Whitechapel High Street. Mary Ann told her that she had earned her doss money three times over that day, and spent it. She refused to accompany Holland back to Thrawl Street.

At approximately 3.40, **Charles Cross** and **Robert Paul** noticed her body lying in Buck's Row, with the skirt pulled up. Within five minutes, Police Constables **Neil**, **Thain** and **Mizen** were on the scene, Neil having seen by the light of his lantern that the throat had been cut. Thain and Mizen went to fetch a doctor and the ambulance (a wheeled trolley like a gurney, most frequently used for restraining and removing drunks), while Neil stayed with the body. The slaughtermen **Henry Tomkins** and **James Mumford**, from Barber's Yard in Winthrop Street, were first to join him, followed by **Charles Brittain**. They stayed until Neil left for the mortuary at dawn. Meanwhile, **Dr Llewellyn** arrived, pronounced Nichols dead and ordered the body to be taken to the Old Montague Street Workhouse Infirmary mortuary. While he was examining the body, an unknown man passed along Buck's Row, possibly the same man who told **Patrick Mulshaw** that there had been a murder.

Sergeant Kerby arrived with another officer from H Division, but Kerby and Thain had taken the body to the mortuary on the ambulance by the time **Inspector Spratling** arrived, and Mrs Green's son James was sluicing the blood from the cobblestones.

Spratling went to the mortuary and was taking down a description of the body when the skirt was lifted and the abdominal mutilations discovered. Dr Llewellyn was summoned to make further examination. By the time he arrived, the body had been stripped and washed by **Robert Mann** and **James Hatfield**, although police insisted they had been instructed not to interfere with it before the medical examination. *See* **Llewellyn** for her injuries. Not included in his postmortem, but widely reported in the press, was the claim that her finger bore the mark of a ring. It did not appear to have been forcibly removed, but *cf.* **Annie**

Chapman, the next victim, from whose fingers two brass rings had almost certainly been removed.

Ellen Holland and other occupants of the White House and 18 Thrawl Street only knew her as 'Polly'. A Lambeth Workhouse laundry mark on her petticoat led to enquiries there, and the suggestion that the whereabouts of former inmates Mrs Scorer and Polly Nichols were uncertain. James Scorer, assistant salesman of Smithfield Market, had been separated from his wife for 11 years, but knew her friend Polly Nichols by sight. He was, however, unable identify the body in the mortuary. **Mary Ann Monk** from Lambeth Workhouse eventually identified the body.

William Nichols arrived at the mortuary on the evening of 1 September 1888, respectably dressed and carrying an umbrella, to inspect the body. Outside, he met Mary Ann's father, **Edward Walker**, accompanied by Edward John Nichols, now 21 years old and an engineer. Walker said, 'Well, here is your son, you see. I have taken care of him and made a man of him.' Nichols responded, 'Well, I really did not know him, he has so grown and altered.' Inside the mortuary he made the lugubrious observation to the corpse, 'Seeing you as you are now, I forgive you for what you have done to me.' Visibly paler, he emerged to say, 'Well, there is no mistake about it. It has come to a sad end at last.'

Mary Ann Nichols was buried at Little Ilford on 6 September.

She was 5ft 2in tall, with greying hair, delicate features, high cheekbones and grey eyes. Her front teeth were missing and there was a scar on her forehead from a childhood accident. Her father and an *East London Observer* journalist both remarked that she looked a good ten years younger than her age. Ellen Holland stated that she was 'a very clean woman', while Dr Llewellyn commented on the surprising cleanliness of her thighs.

The natural tendency of the press was to blame the drunkenness and immorality of the deceased prostitutes for their marital shipwrecks, so it is worth noting that Polly Nichols' father, though himself unable to live comfortably with her drinking, clearly sympathised with her over her treatment at William Nichols' hands; that Nichols did not explicitly deny having temporarily deserted her for another woman; that her eldest son decisively took her side, and her youngest was living with her father at the time of her death, despite having been left in William Nichols' care at the time of the marital breakdown.

NIDEROEST, JOHANN (*b. c.* 1885)

Alleged link in transmission of information incriminating **Dr Alexander Pedachenko**.

German-Swiss, who peddled information to journalists. Resident in London, probably 1905–15.

In 1905, he tried to sell a bogus story of anarchists manufacturing bombs in Whitechapel. Then, in 1909 he was reprimanded for pretending to be the brother of anarchist murderer Paul Hefeld at the Prince of Wales Hospital, Tottenham, in an effort to obtain a story (*Daily* Mirror, 27 January 1909; *The Times*, 28 January 1909).

In 1910, he was alleged by A. T. Vassil'ev (*Ochrana,* 1930) to have helped Latvian anarchist Peter Straume escape from Whitechapel to Australia. Then, in June 1915, Nideroest was sentenced at Bow Street under the Defence of the Realm Act to three months' imprisonment with a recommendation for deportation (*The Times*, 17 June 1915). In 1916, in Switzerland, he claimed that with other passengers on the ferry *Sussex* he had been coerced by allied authorities to swear she had been torpedoed, whereas she actually struck a mine. The *Sussex* was in fact torpedoed by *UB-29*, a German submarine, and the *Star* claimed Nideroest had been proven 'an unscrupulous liar' (**J. Hall Richardson**, *From City To Fleet Street*, quoting the *Star*).

William Le Queux claimed Nideroest had learned from **Nicholas Zverieff** that Pedachenko was the real Jack the Ripper and passed the information to the Ochrana (Czarist Secret Police). Le Queux alleged this was documented in **Rasputin**'s manuscript, *Great Russian Criminals*, which he possessed and that Rasputin commented, 'The report of Nideroest's discovery amused our Secret Police greatly, for, as a matter of fact, they knew the whole details at the time.'

Donald McCormick deduced Nideroest was actually a Czarist counter-espionage agent. Other researchers note the very doubtful provenance of the alleged Rasputin manuscript, which supplies the only known connection between Nideroest and the Ripper case.

NORTH, MR

A resident of High Street, Poplar, possibly the landlord of The Blackneys Head at 143 Polar High Street, who complained to **Wynne Baxter** about the refusal by police at Leman Street to accept his identification of **Elizabeth Stride,** whom he claimed to have known for 15 or 16 years. He was told that his services were not required as the woman had been identified by her sister (see **Mary Malcolm**). Mr North replied that Stride did not have a sister. Mr North went on to say that Stride had kept a lodging house for foreign women at 173 High Street, had married a carpenter named Thomas Stride, who he thought was still alive and selling pencils at the docks. He said that Stride was nicknamed 'Mother Gum' because the whole of her top gum showed when she laughed. (*Illustrated Police News*, 27 October 1888)

NORTH, MRS (*b.* 1871)

Informant. Played dominoes at Cafe Monico in Shaftesbury Avenue, where, in July 1888, she met a striking and well-dressed professional man in his mid-forties. After this, she frequently saw him in the cafe and noted his attitude to women was hard and cynical. He never stayed later than 10.30pm.

During September, he spoke casually of the murders and made an appointment to meet her on Saturday, which he broke to visit the graves of his wife and son. When he met her again and apologised, he also teasingly claimed to be Jack the Ripper and told her that there would be one more murder.

In the 1920s, Mrs North contacted **Leonard Matters**. Both concluded her mysterious professional acquaintance was probably '**Dr Stanley**'. It is not known whether Matters shielded Mrs North's identity under a pseudonym, as he did 'Stanley's'.

O

OCHRANA GAZETTE

Bulletin issued by the Ochrana (Czarist Secret Police) for circulation among its European sections, one number of which allegedly identified the Ripper.

Donald McCormick says he was shown a lithograph of the *Gazette* for January 1909 by Prince Sergei Belloselski, a Russian exile in London. One entry read:

> **KONOVALOV**, Vassily, alias **PEDACHENKO**, Alexey, alias **LUISKOVO**, Andrey, formerly of Tver, is now officially declared to be dead. Any files or information concerning him from district sections should be sent to the Moscow Central District of Ochrana. Such information, photographs or identification details as may still exist might refer to KONOVALOV, PEDACHENKO or LUISKOVO either individually or collectively. If documents held by you do not contain these names, they should also be examined for any information concerning a man, answering the description of the above, who was wanted for the murder of a woman in Paris in 1886, *of the murder of five women in the East Quarter of London in 1888* [our italics] and again of the murder of a woman in Petrograd in 1891.

KONOVALOV's description is as follows:

> Born 1857 at Torshok, Tver. Height, medium. Eyes, dark blue. Profession, junior surgeon. General description: usually wore black moustache, curled and waxed at ends. Heavy, black eyebrows. Broad-shouldered, but slight build. Known to disguise himself as a woman on occasion and was arrested when in women's clothes in Petrograd before his detention in the asylum where he died.

Donald Rumbelow has argued this request for information reveals some uncertainty on the part of the Ochrana concerning the identity of the man known to have died in an asylum and his crimes.

All subsequent efforts to trace the copy of the *Ochrana Gazette* have failed. The anachronistic name 'Petrograd' for the city that was St Petersburg in 1909, subsequently Leningrad, and now again Petersburg, has encouraged researchers to look through the files for 1914–17 in addition to the date specified by McCormick.

See **France, murders in for the possible Paris victim**; also, **Konovalov** and **Pedachenko** for further details and the improbability of their being one and the same person and *The Identity of Jack the Ripper* for a caveat concerning uncorroborated material therein.

OCTOBER 6TH LETTER
See **'Threat' letter**.

ODDIE, SAMUEL INGLEBY (1869–1945)

The most famous coroner of the twentieth century. Studied medicine at Edinburgh University, qualifying in 1891 and thereafter spending some time in the Naval Medical Service. He married and set up practice in New Malden, but decided to take up law, entered the chambers of the famous criminal lawyer Sir Richard Muir and was called to the bar in 1901. He was briefed as a junior with Muir in the Crippen and Steinie Morrison trials, then became a coroner until his retirement in 1939. He died on 8 May 1945.

Oddie visit the Ripper murder sites on 19 April 1905, with a party of friends which included **John Churton Collins** and **Sir Arthur Conan Doyle. Dr Frederick Gordon Brown** was their guide and they were accompanied by three unnamed City detectives said to be familiar with the case. Oddie left an account of their tour (*Inquest*. London: Hutchinson, 1941), which in most respects agrees with that given by John Churton Collins.

Oddie attributed seven murders to the Ripper, adding Alice McKenzie and the Pinchin Street to the **canonical five**, and believed that the murderer arranged victim's possessions near the body: 'One curious feature was that on the ground in the quiet courtyards where some of these murders were committed there was sometimes found a singular collection of articles placed by the side of the body, such as farthings, a match, a comb, and other trivial things. In the case of

Catherine Eddows, Oddie said the murderer arranged 'a thimble, a comb, an empty mustard tin and a farthing on the pavement at the poor woman's feet.'

He said that in his opinion the most reasonable theory was that the murderer had some anatomical knowledge, acquired either as a butcher or a medical student, and that he obtained physical gratification from murdering and slashing the bodies of women. He thought he probably drowned himself in the Thames. This account accords reasonably well with the conclusions of Dr Brown as described by John Churton Collins, although according to Collins Brown dismissed a specific Thames suicide (**Montague Druitt**). Oddie also wrote that the murderer was never caught and was only seen on one occasion, a conclusion contradicted by John Churton Collins who said that according to Dr Brown the murderer was not seen by anyone.

Oddie concluded: 'There seems little doubt that the real explanation lies, as I have said, in some insane medical man, possibly a Russian Jew living in the East End, who was a lust murderer, a Sadist, whose insanity increased until it culminated in the wild orgy of Dorset Street and was followed by his own suicide in the Thames.' This seems contradicted by his opinion that the McKenzie and Pinchin Street might have been victims of the Ripper.

Also see **Arthur Diosy**.

(Obituary *The Times*, 12 May 1945)

O'DONNELL, BERNARD (1885–1968)

Theorist. Crime reporter and author of books on criminal cases.

In 1925, ghosted **Betty May**'s articles for the *World Pictorial News*, from which he learned of the black magician who owned the Ripper's ties. Then, in 1930 he was urged by the editor of the *Referee* to trace **Vittoria Cremers**, who knew the whole story. O'Donnell did so, and in a series of visits learned what she knew of '**Dr D'Onston**'. Although he himself was never able to find any independent records identifying D'Onston, between 1958 and 1969 O'Donnell used Vittoria Cremers' recollections, D'Onston's contributions to the *Pall Mall Gazette* and *Borderland*, and general information and gossip about black-magic practitioners to write a sensational typescript of 375 pages identifying D'Onston as the Ripper. After the manner of the period, he presented Cremers' story as a narrative which appeared to come verbatim from her lips, though it is entirely his creation based on her recollections.

O'Donnell was unable to find a publisher for his work before his death and so the manuscript remained in private hands, read by only a few researchers. Richard Whittington-Egan saw it and dismissed D'Onston as a self-aggrandising fantasist, who pretended to have been the Ripper, just as he pretended to have been a doctor and a soldier for Garibaldi. This opinion was shared and published by **Melvin Harris** in the 1970s, but when working on the hoaxers surrounding the Ripper case, Harris was able to identify the black magician Dr D'Onston as the dismissed customs clerk **Robert Donston Stephenson**, and in *The Bloody Truth* he averred his belief in Stephenson's adventures and education, and decided he was the most likely candidate to have been the Ripper. Andy Aliffe traced the O'Donnell typescript for him, and later still Aliffe and Howard Brown gained permission from O'Donnell's son Peter for the typescript to be reproduced in facsimile on jtrforums.com at www.jtrforums.com.

OLD FUNK LETTER

Four-page 'Jack the Ripper letter' in rhyming couplets, dated 8 November 1889, postmarked London S.W., and addressed to 'Superintendent of Great Scotland Yard' (MEPO 3/142 ff212–215). It opens:

30 Bangor St Novr.8/89
Dear Boss
My finest shot to justify myself I now fire,
You will see by this that I am not a liar;
Funk, stupid fool, believes me to be insane;
His next shotlog will be that 'I'm tame.
In the papers you sometimes see—
Letters written by him, but none by me

Line ten reads:

He tells the public he has my boots.

Lines 20–24 read:

At Finsbury St. Paul's hard near,
I never dost the rents are too dear,
Whitechapel High St hard near my home—
I always do my work alone,
Some months hard gone near Finsbury Sqre;

Lines 66–69 read:

The letter addressed to 22 Hammersmith Road—
Was written by some vulgar lying toad,
Old Funk, thinks me a flashaway swell
A first rate man, and in a fine house I dwell.
A fourpenny doss I have at a Common East End Doss House
And do not dine on aristocratic grouse.

The references to boots and Finsbury Square show this was written by someone who was aware of **L. Forbes Winslow**'s theory, as aired in the press in September: that 'Old Funk' is intended to be Winslow and the writer is dismissing the accusations against **Wentworth Bell Smith**.

The nickname 'Funk' and the reference to 22 Hammersmith road show that the writer was aware of the Hammersmith Road letter. The authors can find no evidence this was ever made public prior to the publication of Winslow's *Reminiscences* in 1910, which suggests the writer of this letter either penned the Hammersmith letter himself or was acquainted with its author or a police officer who had seen it.

'OLD SHAKESPEARE'
See **Carrie Brown**.

OLIVER, JAMES (*fl.* 1888)
Witness who accused '**Dick Austen**' of being the Ripper.

OLSSON, SVEN
Witness at **Elizabeth Stride**'s inquest.

As clerk to the Swedish Church at 36 Prince's Square, he had known Stride for 17 years and corrected important biographical details.

See **Elizabeth Stride**.

ON THE TRAIL OF A DEAD MAN: THE IDENTITY OF JACK THE RIPPER
Book by Chris Miles (Hove: Milestone Press, 2004).

Account of the author's personal experiences during a seven-month investigation of Ripper crimes, which concludes **George Hutchinson** was the murderer, this being chiefly based on Miles' belief that Hutchinson's description of a man seen with **Mary Jane Kelly** on the night she was murdered was too detailed and is therefore highly suspicious, and otherwise on a series of perceived connections: that Hutchinson's residence at the Victoria Home was close to Goulston Street, where the graffito was left, for example.

ON THE TRAIL OF JACK THE RIPPER
Talking book by Martin Fido, read by the author and produced by Paul Savory for LBC/Tring Long Island Records. Distributed Bookpoint, 1991 (3h, 20m).

A concise overview and up-to-date at the time of its issue.

ONE-ARMED LIZ
Informant living in Flower and Dean Street. She accompanied Sgt **Thick** to St George's mortuary, where she identified the body of **Elizabeth Stride** as that of Annie Morris, a prostitute living in a Flower and Dean Street lodging house. (see **Elizabeth Burns**).

OPENSHAW, DR THOMAS HORROCKS, MS, MB, FRCS, LRCP, LSA, CB, CMG (1856–1929)

Identified the Lusk kidney as human.

Born Bury, Lancashire, on 17 March 1856. Educated at Bristol Grammar School and Durham University; entered London Hospital Medical College, 1877. Awarded Outpatient Dresser's Prize of £15, 1879; MBBS (Durham), Member of the Royal College of Surgeons, 1883; Fellow of the Royal College of Surgeons, 1886. Other qualifications included Licentiate of the Society of Apothecaries and Master of Surgery (Durham). Appointed sssistant demonstrator of anatomy at the Medical College, 1886; curator of the pathology museum, 1888. Appointed assistant surgeon, 1890; surgeon, 1902. Served in South Africa as surgeon to the Imperial Yeomanry Field Hospital and as principal medical orderly MO No. 3 Model School Hospital, Pretoria. Awarded the Companion of the Most Distinguished Order of St Michael and St George (CMG).

Appointed consulting surgeon with the rank of colonel to the Eastern Command of the Royal Army Medical Corps (Territorial Force) during World War I. Territorial Knight of Grace of the Order of St John of Jerusalem; Colonel AMS. He was, for some time, a prisoner of war. Consulting surgeon, London Hospital; senior consulting surgeon, Queen Mary's Hospital for the Limbless, Roehampton House, SW; lecturer on Anatomy and Surgery, London Hospital; consulting surgeon, Royal National Orthopædic Hospital and surgeon, Royal Surgical Aid Society; consulting surgeon, Poplar Accident Hospital, Tilbury Dock Hospital, Sidcup Cottage Hospital, Woolwich Cottage Hospital; consulting surgeon, Eastern Command; surgeon, King Edward VII's Hospital. Fellow Royal Society of Medicine, Medical and Hunterian Societies; MS, MB, FRCS England; LRCP London; LSA London. CMG, 1900; CB, 1917. Was a recognised authority on orthopaedic surgery, helped establish the Queen Mary Convalescent Auxiliary Hospital for the Limbless at Roehampton.

Openshaw spent much of his time during the war working with amputees and developing artificial limbs. In 1917, he was awarded the Companion of the Most Honourable Order of the Bath (CB). Master of the Worshipful Company of Wheelwrights, the Worshipful Company of Barber-Surgeons and the Worshipful Company of Glovers. An active Freemason, he helped found the London Hospital Lodge, as well as lodges at his old grammar school and university. Fellow of the Old Time Cyclists Club and President of the Red Spinner Angling Society. President of the Association of Lancastrians in London and an early Master of the Lancastrian Lodge. Married a nurse, Selina Gertrude Pratt, in 1890, one son (Major Lawrence Pratt Openshaw, killed in a flying accident at an air show on 6 June 1927 – reported in *The Times*, 7, 9 June 1927) and a daughter. His wife died in 1929. Openshaw developed diabetes and died of pneumonia also in 1929 (17 November).

A short, sturdy Lancashireman, known to all his friends as 'Tommy'.

When the **Lusk kidney** was sent to him for identification, he was reported in the press as saying it was a woman's 'ginny' kidney preserved in spirits of wine. Dr Openshaw immediately wrote to *The Times* to confirm that he had said it was human and preserved in spirits of wine, but the other details were journalistic embellishments (*Cf.* **F.S. Reed**).

OPENSHAW LETTER

A Ripper letter, posted to Dr Thomas Openshaw on 29 October 1888. It read:

Old boss you was rite it was
the left kidny i wos goin to
hopperate agin close to your
ospitle just as i was goin
to dror mi nife along of
er bloomin throte them
cusses of coppers spoilt
the game but i guess i wil
be on the job soon and will
send you another bit of
innerds
Jack the ripper

O have you seen the devle
with his mikerscope and scalpul
a lookin at a kidney
with a slide cocked up.

Donald McCormick described the letter in *The Identity of Jack the Ripper* and shortly afterwards it came into the possession of author Donald Rumbelow (**The Complete Jack the Ripper**) who presented it to the National Archives in 2001.

Patricia Cornwell commissioned the Bode Technology group, which uses mitochondrial DNA testing to identify bodies recovered from combat or disasters, to test the Openshaw Letter and found mitochondrial DNA on it, which corresponded to mitochondrial DNA extracted from seven documents handled by Walter Sickert. Unfortunately, mitochondrial DNA (from outside the cell nucleus) is not a precise individual identifying 'fingerprint', but reduces the number of people from whom it might have come to one in 1,000 (i.e. in 1888, it could have been from any of 40,000 people in London alone).

Professor Ian Findlay, chief scientific officer at the Gribbles Molecular Science forensic lab of Brisbane, has vastly improved the techniques of nuclear DNA testing so that he uses far less cells than the FBI laboratories, creates a much fuller pattern of corresponding DNA segments to establish identification and estimates his results are approximately 100 times more reliable than the mitochondrial results achieved for Ms Cornwell. He examined the Openshaw Letter, but was only able to produce a partial profile, which suggested DNA on the underside of the stamp had come from a woman. On the supposition that the stamp had been licked by the letter's author and the letter might be genuine, the notion that the Ripper might have been a woman was tentatively postulated. It has to be observed that the result is very surprising indeed: the number of women in 1888 who would have known that microscopes used slides must have been extremely small.

On two occasions, articles in the *Criminologist* compared this letter with the **Lusk Letter** and concluded both were by the same hand (graphologist C.M.MacLeod in August 1968, and forensic handwriting examiner Derek Davies in the summer of 1974). Davies goes on to conclude they were written by Dr Thomas Neill Cream in disguised hands.

ORAM, JANE
See **Emily Holland**.

OSTROG, MICHAEL (*b. c.* 1833)

aka Bertrand Ashley, Dr Barker, Claude Cayton or Clayton, Max Grief Gosslar, Max Kaife Gosslar, Dr Grant, 'Grand Guidon', Stanislas Lublinski, Ashley Nabokoff, Orloff, Henry Ray, Count Sobieski, Max Sobieski and maybe 20 other aliases.

Suspect.

One of three suspects named by **Sir Melville Macnaghten** in the **Macnaghten memoranda** in 1894:

Michael Ostrog, a mad Russian doctor, and a convict, who was subsequently detained in a lunatic asylum as a homicidal maniac. This man's antecedents were of the worst possible type, and his whereabouts at the time of the murders could never be ascertained.

The **Aberconway** version gave a rather fuller account:

MICHAEL OSTROG, a mad Russian doctor and a convict and unquestionably a homicidal maniac. This man was said to have been habitually cruel to women, and for a long time was known to have carried about with him surgical knives and other instruments; his antecedent were of the very worst and his whereabouts at the time of the Whitechapel murders could never be satisfactorily accounted for. He is still alive.

It should be noted 'antecedents' is police parlance for 'criminal record'.
In *Mysteries of Police and Crime*, **Major Arthur Griffiths** follows Macnaghten very closely, without naming the three suspects, and gives a little extra detail in his account of Ostrog:

The second possible criminal was a Russian doctor, also insane, who had been a convict both in England and Siberia. This man was in the habit of carrying about surgical knives and instruments in his pockets; his antecedents were of the very worst, and at the time of the Whitechapel murders he was in hiding, or, at least his whereabouts were never exactly known.

Sir Basil Thomson obliquely referred to Ostrog in *The Story of Scotland Yard* saying that 'the belief of C.I.D. officers at the time was that [the murders] were the work of an insane Russian doctor and that the man escaped arrest by committing suicide at the end of 1888'. This appears to combine Ostrog with Montague John Druitt.

Ostrog was a confidence trickster and sneak thief whom police records variously describe as a Russian, a Russian Pole and a Polish Jew. French police recorded him as saying he was born in Warsaw in 1835. Buckinghamshire County Gaol records ascribe a superior education to him and record his dubious claim to have spent two years with the Russian army and five with the Russian navy. He also gave his religion as Greek Orthodox, although he was probably Jewish.

The earliest account of him so far traced is in 1863, when he passed himself off as a 27-year-old student named Max Grief Gosslar or Max Kaife Gosslar to perpetrate petty thefts at Oriel and New Colleges, Oxford, for which he was sentenced to ten months imprisonment (*Oxford Chronicle and Berke Gazette*, 7 March 1863, *The Times,* 7 March 1874).

In 1864 he passed himself off in Bishop's Stortford as a noble count or prince who had lived wild in the woods in Poland to escape would-be assassins. His gentle and genteel manner won him many sympathizers. He then proceeded to Cambridge as Max Sobiewski, where he was found attempting a crime in a college and was convicted as a rogue and a vagabond, and sentenced to three months. (Herts and Essex Journal, 6 February 1864)

In July 1864 he appeared in Tunbridge Wells, representing himself as Count Sobieski, exiled son of the King of Poland. He ingratiated himself with respectable people from whom he obtained money and property. On leaving Tunbridge he went to Exeter where he was sentenced in December to eight months for fraud and felony.

In January 1866 he was acquitted of a fraud charge at Gloucester Quarter Sessions. On 28 February *The Times* carried an advertisement "If Count Sobieski, who left his LUGGAGE at No. 69 Sloane Street in Nov. 1864, does not CLAIM it within 10 days from this date it will be SOLD to defray expenses." He went to Kent, where on 19 March he called at the old Archbishop's Palace in Maidstone and asked to speak to the curate, stealing a gold watch and other articles left on a table while the maid went to announce him. From Maidstone he went to Chatham where he became friendly with Thomas White, from whom he stole a gold cross on 13 April, and gave it to Esther Brenchley – apparently a barmaid at the Bull Hotel, Rochester. On 26 April he stole two books from James Burch in Chatham. In Rochester he took a suite at the Globe Hotel, accompanied by a woman. When he left without paying his bill, the landlord found a bag in his room with the books stolen from Mr Burch, and the police arrested Ostrog, who resisted desperately. Under the name of Bertrand Ashley alias Ashley Nabokoff, and described as "the great Russian swindler", his age given as twenty-two, he was tried before Mr Justice Channell at the Assizes that August. To Ostrog's manifest astonishment, Channell observed that light sentences had proved ineffective, and sentenced him to seven years penal servitude.

The 1871 census lists him under his alias Bertrand Ashley as an inmate of Dartmoor Prison. His age is given as 35 and his birthplace as Russia.

On 23 May 1873 he was released on ticket-of-leave. Later in the month he stole a valuable silver cup, a silver soap dish, a shaving pot, a glass toothbrush dish with silver top, and studs worth £5 from Captain Milner at Woolwich Barracks. He then went to Windsor, staying from July to December at the South Western Railway Hotel. During this time he introduced himself to the probably homosexual assistant master of Eton Oscar Browning and having been given the run of his library, stole two valuable books. On 15 July Etonian student Alfred Hands Cooke discovered that an inscribed trophy had been stolen from his rooms. The police traced it to Dubree's pawnshop in Charlotte Street, London, where a Dr Watkins Robert O'Connor of Osnaburgh Terrace had sold it. Dr O'Connor explained that Ostrog had introduced himself as a former acquaintance of O'Connor's former partner and claimed to have been forced to leave Russia after killing a man in a duel. He had left the cup and two books stolen from Eton College library with O'Connor asking him to sell them, which O'Connor had done, sending Ostrog the money.

There is a long piece about Michael Ostrog in Michael Davitt's *Leaves From a Prison Diary* (1885). Davitt, describing convicts who posed as aristocrats, of which there were several in Dartmoor, wrote that Ostrog was imprisoned under the name of 'Bertrand Victor A ':

He was a man of about thirty-five years of age, close upon six feet in height, and of very good address, the features presenting very slight traces of his Slavonic origin; while his manners, like those of most foreigners, were gentlemanly and agreeable, particularly when he was desirous of making a good impression. I learned that he was the son of a distinguished Russian; that he had been sent to England to complete his education; had studied for some time at Oxford University; had afterwards joined the English navy as surgeon, and had managed, somehow or other, not explained, to find himself at that period (1872) within two years of completing a sentence of seven in penal servitude. His English prison name was, of course, an assumed one, and his family were kept in complete ignorance of his being an inmate of an English convict establishment.

His command of languages was really marvellous, amply sustaining the well-known linguistic fame of his countrymen. His English was next to faultless in pronunciation, and he could converse with equal facility in French, German, and Italian, while he had also a reputed knowledge of Danish, Swedish, and Polish, with, of course, the perfect use of the Russian. In addition, he was as well read in English literature, and as well versed in the etiquette of English society, as an ordinary college-educated Englishman. He was, on the whole, about the most singular and the most accomplished individual with whom I conversed during my imprisonment in Dartmoor. In 1873 he was transferred from that prison to Chatham along with a batch of other convicts, from which place he was discharged in the beginning of the following year; his whole sentence of seven years having then expired.

Davitt went on to write that 'early in the summer of 1874 a student of E[xeter?] College engaged as foreign tutor one Count Sobriski', who entered Oxford society and met the beautiful daughter of a wealthy gentleman, and in due course Ostrog proposed and was accepted. However, the young lady became ill and a doctor prescribed two weeks' rest at Margate. The following day, when strolling along the seafront, Ostrog pleaded a sudden appointment in London and rushed off. The young lady and her father were then approached by two men, who informed them that Ostrog was a recently-released convict and most accomplished impostor.

According to Davitt, some property stolen from Eton was found in Ostrog's Margate apartment. He was traced to a West-End lodging-house, was surprised, but not captured, in the middle of the night and had to make his way over the roof in anything but full dress. He succeeded in eluding the efforts of his pursuers for some weeks after this narrow escape, but finally succumbed to a stratagem on the part of the detectives, who were at the time acquainted with the locality where he was in hiding.

Ostrog went from there to Burton-on-Trent, where he was caught and after trial sentenced to imprisonment in Chatham where, said Davitt:

Among the many old familiar faces that met my view upon attending service in the Catholic chapel in this prison the first Sunday of my arrival here in February last, was that of Bertrand Victor A, alias Count Sobriski, a convict this time in the name of von Ostrogg. I was informed by a French thief while in Dartmoor that the Russian, as he was familiarly termed, had completed

two terms of imprisonment on the continent before coming to England, one in the prison of Konigsberg, and the other in Moulins, near Paris.

Many of the details given by Davitt are supported by press accounts. Ostrog was traced to a house in London's West End by Superintendent Dunham, but escaped over the roof with a loaded eight-chambered revolver. Then he returned to Eton with an accomplice and stole some valuable cups. (By a curious coincidence, Melville Macnaghten was captaining a cricket team playing against his old school at the time.) Ostrog now wrote to a one-time friend that he was returning to Russia and could be contacted via a Mr Carl Swedenburg, Poste Restante, Berlin.

In fact, he went to Burton-on-Trent, where he was arrested at the Fox and Goose Inn by Superintendent Oswell, despite his vehement protest that he was a Swedish doctor visiting the breweries. At the police station he produced his revolver and was only prevented from firing by Superintendent Oswell's seizing his wrist and turning the muzzle back on its owner. He was taken to Slough and confronted by Superintendent Dunham.

In January 1874, he conducted his own defence, pleading guilty at Bucks Quarter Sessions, and seemed chagrined to receive a 10-year sentence on his conviction.

He was released from Pentonville Prison on ticket-of-leave in August 1883, but shortly thereafter the *Police Gazette* issued a description of him as wanted for failure to report. In addition to his height, age and colouring, this recorded flogging marks on his back. His immediate whereabouts thereafter are unknown, but he was deported from France by ministerial order in June 1886.

In July 1887, he stole a metal tankard from George Bigge at Woolwich Barracks, and was arrested after being chased across Woolwich Common by cadets. Described as well-educated and gentlemanly, he evidently looked younger than his age, which was now estimated as late thirties or early forties. He was wearing cricketing clothes and dropped a black Gladstone bag in his flight; he declared himself a visiting Belgian named Dr Bong and swallowed nux vomica on the way to the police station. While in custody, he made a further attempt to starve himself to death.

At Woolwich Police Court he claimed to have been on his way to play cricket when a fit of sunstroke gave him an irresistible impulse to run a race, which he thought he was doing when the cadets chased him. At one point, he took his overcoat from the rail, told the court he was going to France and had to be prevented from leaving. He claimed to be a medical man who would be ruined if his friends in France heard of the affair; also the last of four brothers who had all committed suicide and that his wife had been unfaithful to him. Held on remand until August, he was then confronted by Superintendent Dunham, who described him as 'one of the most desperate criminals who ever lived'. It emerged that he had attempted to throw himself under a train en route to Holloway Prison.

In September 1887, he was tried under the name of Claude Clayton at the Old Bailey and pleaded insanity, but Dr Herbert Hillier declared, 'He is only shamming,' whereupon Ostrog was sentenced to six months' hard labour. On 30 September, he was transferred from Wandsworth Prison to the Surrey Pauper Lunatic Asylum suffering from mania, cause unknown. He was discharged on 10 March 1888, on expiry of sentence, described as recovered.

In October 1888, at the height of the Ripper scare, he was again described in the *Police Gazette* as wanted for failure to report, and it was observed that, 'Special attention is called to this dangerous man.' The full description was as follows:

> Age 55, height 5ft 11ins, complexion dark, hair dark brown, eyes grey. Scars right thumb and right chin, two large moles right shoulder and one back of neck, corporal punishment marks, generally dressed in semi-clerical suit, Polish Jew.

Ostrog was arrested for the theft of a microscope by the French police in Paris on 26 July 1888 and under the name of Stanistan Sublinsky (or Lublinsky) he was sentenced on 14 November 1888 to two years' imprisonment (Ostrog's conviction record at the Archives Departmentales de Paris; see **The Complete History of Jack the Ripper**)

A year later, the British police believed him responsible for stealing gold watches and chains at Eton, as transpired when he was arrested in 1894.

In 1889, he was again listed in the *Police Gazette* and again described as dangerous. It is interesting, though maybe gratuitous, that this listing coincides with the resurgence of anxiety about the Whitechapel murders following the death of Alice McKenzie.

In the meantime, he went to the Banstead Lunatic Asylum after being apprehended for failure to report while on ticket-of leave. Then, in May 1893, **Melville Macnaghten** wrote to Banstead asking that Scotland Yard be informed if Ostrog was discharged. In fact, Ostrog had been discharged by 1893 – surviving records do not show whether Scotland Yard was informed or not. He immediately returned to Eton, where he stole two more books and a silver cup. Resisting violently, he was arrested early in 1894 and charged with the 1889 offence at Eton, plus the more recent one of stealing the Eton Fives challenge cup. Ostrog claimed to have been in an asylum in France at the time of the 1889 offence. The Home Secretary (Asquith in 1894) was told that he had been on the lunatic side of a French prison, discharged in November 1890. Bertillon measurements confirmed this and he was released with £10 compensation.

In 1898, he was charged at Woolwich with stealing books and after his release from prison in 1900, he went to a home for discharged prisoners: the St Giles's Christian Mission in Brooke Street, Holborn, whereafter no more is heard of him.

The demonstrable facts support Macnaghten's suspicion of Ostrog to the extent that we know the police were indeed looking for him in October 1888 (though not necessarily in connection with the Whitechapel murders), and there is some evidence that he could be dangerous: before arresting him in Burton-on-Trent, Supt. Oswell took the precaution of sweeping aside the table cutlery, but what is known about him does not support Macnaghten's claims that Ostrog was a homicidal maniac or habitually cruel to women and was known to have carried surgical knives about with him. However, such claims would certainly explain why he was suspected of being Jack the Ripper.

(*Cf. **The Identity of Jack the Ripper*** (1962); also D.S. Goffee, 'The Search for Michael Ostrog', **Ripperana**, Oct 1994; *The Complete History of Jack the Ripper*, especially the new introduction to the 2002 paperback; Scott Sanders, 'The Mysterious Case of MFJ Sobieski', *Ripperologist*, 55, September 2004; and **Jack the Ripper: The Facts**.)

OUTRAM, DET. SGT. ROBERT (c. 1845–1907)

Attended the scene of **Catherine Eddowes'** murder.

A groom before joining the City of London Police in 1865. Allocated to plain-clothes patrol in 1867, then in March 1876, divisional detective; in May of the same year, detective sergeant. Made detective-inspector in 1890. Most of his work (as was common for a City detective) involved financial fraud. Retired in 1895 (see 'Ex-Detective Inspector R. Outram', *The Police Review and Parade Gossip*, 22 November 1895). After retirement he became a private enquiry agent.

He achieved some notoriety in 1877 when he arrested Annie Besant and Charles Bradlaugh for their publication of *The Fruits of Philosophy, or the Private Companion of Young Married People*, a controversial book by American birth-control campaigner, Charles Knowlton. They were found guilty, but appealed and the case was eventually dropped on a legal technicality. Besant describes at some length her arrest by Sgt. Outram in her book, *Autobiographical Sketches* (London: Freethought Publishing Company, 1885).

Was talking with Detectives **Halse** and **Marriott** at southern corner of Houndsditch when they received news of the murder and immediately went to Mitre Square. Later in the day, he escorted two women and a man from a lodging-house in Spitalfields to the mortuary to identify the body, one of the women identifying her as a 'Mrs. Kelly' (an alias used by Eddowes) (*Evening Standard*, 1 October 1888).

OWEN, LOTTIE (*b. c.*1846)

In late 1891, Kathleen Blake Watkins interviewed Lottie, who lived in the room formerly occupied by **Mary Kelly**. She is listed in the 1891 Census as Lottie Owen, born in Kennington and the wife of Henry Owen (*b. c.* 1842), a dock labourer (*see* **Julia Van Turney**, who in 1888 was living with a man named Harry Owen).

OXLEY, DR FREDERICK JOHN (*d.* 1924)

Assistant to Dr Alan of 1 Dock Street. First medical man on the scene of **Frances Coles'** murder in Swallow Gardens. Also assisted with the postmortem. Expressed opinion that the murder was unconnected with the Ripper series.

P

PACKER, MATTHEW (1831–1907)

Berner Street fruiterer, whose interview at Scotland Yard of **Elizabeth Stride** was documented by Assistant Commissioner **Alexander Carmichael Bruce**, yet who was not called as a witness at the inquest.

Born in Goulston Street, Whitechapel, in 1831. In September 1867, in Bethnal Green, he married Rose Ann (or Roseann) Wallis, who was born in Maidstone, Kent. Successive censuses list him as a fishmonger of 1 Princess Street, Whitechapel (1871), costermonger of 25 Fairclough Street (1881), general dealer of 44 Berner Street (1891), fruit and sweet shop owner at 44 Berner Street (1901).

On the morning of Stride's murder, 30 September 1888, he was questioned by Sgt. **Stephen White** who, in a report to Scotland Yard (MEPO 3/140/221/A49301C, ff. 212–14), said that Packer, his wife and lodgers had not seen anyone standing about in the street nor had they seen or heard anything suspicious, and Packer had explained that heavy rain that evening had caused him to shut the shop early.

Meanwhile, two private detectives, **Le Grand** and **J.H. Batchelor**, who had been hired by the Whitechapel Vigilance Committee and by the *Evening News*, had spoken with Mrs **Rosenfeld** and her sister Miss **Eva Harstein**, who lived at 14 Berner Street. They learned that early on Sunday morning, Mrs Rosenfeld had passed the murder scene and seen on the ground a grapestalk stained with blood.

Her sister said she had also seen nearby a few small petals of a white flower. The two detectives then approached Matthew Packer and after three interviews he made a statement in writing to the effect that a woman with a white flower pinned to her dark jacket had come to his shop at 11.45pm, on 29 September, in the company of a stout, clerkly man, about 5ft 7in tall, with a wide-awake hat, dark clothes and a sharply commanding manner. The man bought half a pound of black grapes, which he and the woman ate as they stood opposite the shop in the rain for about half an hour. Packer recalled observing to his wife, 'What fools those people are to be standing in the rain like that!'

At about 12.10am, or 12.15am – Packer noted the time because the public-houses had been closed – the couple crossed the road and stood in front of the International Workingmen's Educational Club, and Packer, who had begun closing up, then lost sight of them.

On 3 October, Le Grand and Batchelor took Packer to the City mortuary in Golden Lane to test his veracity by showing him the body without revealing that it was the Mitre Square victim, not the Berner Street victim. Packer unhesitatingly said he had never seen Catherine Eddowes before, and on 4 October the *News* went to press with the major story that Packer had seen and spoken to 'the murderer'. The *News* reporter asked if any detective or policeman had enquired whether he had sold grapes to anyone that night, urging him to be careful in answering, 'for this may prove a serious business for the London police.' The paper capitalised his answer: 'NO POLICEMAN HAS EVER ASKED ME A SINGLE QUESTION NOR COME NEAR SHOP TO FIND OUT IF I KNEW ANYTHING ABOUT THE GRAPES THE MURDERED WOMAN HAD BEEN EATING BEFORE HER THROAT WAS CUT!!!'

On the afternoon of 4 October, Le Grand and Batchelor took Packer to St George's-in-the-East mortuary, where he identified Stride as the woman he had seen. On their return, they met Sergeant White, despatched to Berner Street by **Chief Inspector Moore** after he had seen the *Evening News* story to re-interview Packer and take him to identify Stride. Packer told White, 'I believe she bought some grapes at my shop about 12 o'clock on Saturday.'

At 4pm Grand and Batchelor took Packer away in a hansom cab, saying they were going to Scotland Yard to see **Sir Charles Warren**. The following details were noted by Assistant Commissioner Alexander Carmichael Bruce:

Matthew Packer
Keeps a small shop in Berner Str has a few grapes in window. black & white. On Sat night about 11 . p.m. a young man from 25–30 – about 5.7. with long black coat buttoned up – soft felt hat, kind of Yankee hat, rather broad shoulders – rather quick in speaking. rough voice. I sold him ? pound black grapes 3d. A woman came up with him from Back Church end (the lower end of street) she was dressed in black frock & jacket, fur round bottom of jacket a black crape bonnet, she was playing with a flower like a geranium white outside & red inside. I identify the woman at the St George's mortuary

as the one I saw that night. – They passed by as though they were going up Com[mercial]– Road, but instead of going up they crossed to the other side of the road to the Board School, & were there for about ? an hour till I shd. say 11.30. talking to one another. I then shut up my shutters. Before they passed over opposite to my shop, they wait[ed] near to the Club for a few minutes apparently listening to the music. I saw no more of them after I shut up my shutters.

I put the man down as a young clerk.

He had a frock coat on – no gloves.

He was about 1? inch or 2 or 3 inch – a little bit higher than she was.

ACB

4.10.88

This is the only record of Packer placing all these events between 11 and 11.30. But where he places them an hour later, as evidenced in White's report of his interview with Packer, Warren has queried this in the margins and reverted to the times given in Packer's interview at Scotland Yard.

Chief Inspector **Swanson** in his report to the Home Office, dated 19 October 1888, expressed his opinion that as Packer had unfortunately made different statements, they were rendered almost valueless as evidence.

Packer was not called as a witness at the inquest. (*Cf.* **Mrs Fanny Mortimer, Israel Schwartz**.)

On 31 October, the *Evening News* reported Packer's alarm at seeing a man, exactly like the one who had bought the grapes off him, continuously staring at him in an evil and menacing manner. Fearing for his life, he called a shoeblack's attention to him, whereupon the unknown man ran away at speed and boarded a passing tram. Packer alleged he had often seen the man prior to the murder, but not since, until that incident. In the second week of November he claimed that two men had come to his house asking for an exact description of the man to whom he had sold the grapes. One of them then revealed that he believed it was his cousin, who had been in America but returned about seven or eight months ago. He and his cousin had walked around Whitechapel, where the cousin had threatened to rip up prostitutes. Packer felt sure the men were telling the truth as both seemed concerned and unsure of what to do. Their story was investigated by the police, who later reported it had had no foundation in fact (*Illustrated Police News*, 24 November 1888).

After the murder of **Alice McKenzie**, Packer expressed the opinion that the murderer lived not far from Batty Street and a short time afterwards, when standing near his doorstep, two men rushed past him and knocked him down. He heard them say, 'Know where "Jack the Ripper" lives, do you?' Packer claimed he was sufficiently hurt to require three weeks' treatment in London Hospital (*Birmingham Daily Post*, 14 September 1889).

See Gerry Nixon, 'The Grapes of Packer', *Ripperologist*, 6, June 1996; Dave Yost 'Packer – Was He A Witness?' in *Ripperologist*, 23/24, June/August 1999; *Ripper*

Notes, 3, November 1999; Tom Wescott, 'Jack and the Grapestalk' in *Ripper Notes*, 25; January 2006; Clive Johnson, 'A Packer Of Lies?', *The Journal of the Whitechapel Society*, 13, April 2007; 'The Mystery Of The Missing Grapes', *The Journal of the Whitechapel Society*, 14, June 2007.

PAGET, SIR AUGUSTUS BERKELEY KCB, PC (1823–96)
Informant.

As Ambassador Extraordinary and Minister Plenipotentiary to the Austro-Hungarian Emperor in Vienna, and a Privy Councillor, Paget had the ear of the Prime Minister and could not be ignored when he urged attention to a most unlikely suspect (*see* **Jonas**), but the file of correspondence that ensued (HO144/221/A49301D) is fascinating in its own right and elicited **Sir Charles Warren**'s observation that he himself believed 'the last murders [i.e. those of Elizabeth Stride and Catherine Eddowes] were obviously done by someone desiring to bring discredit on the Jews and Socialists or Jewish socialists.'

MRS FARMER

PALMER, AMELIA (OFTEN DESCRIBED AS FARMER)
Witness at **Annie Chapman**'s inquest. Press reports following the murders called her Farmer; all accounts of the inquest, including the fullest press account of her, describing her husband, call her Palmer – for which reason we have preferred Palmer.

Pale-faced, dark-haired wife of ex-soldier and dock labourer Henry Palmer, she washed and cleaned for East End Jewish residents following an accident which limited her husband's ability to work. She lived at 30 Dorset Street for four years and was a friend of Annie Chapman, concerning whom she gave police some biographical evidence. She wrongly described Annie's former husband as Frederick Chapman, veterinary surgeon. (*Cf.* **John Chapman**.)

In the week before the murder, she saw Chapman several times. Early in the week, in Dorset Street, Annie complained of feeling unwell. The following day, beside Spitalfields Church, she again complained of illness, and said she had not eaten or drunk anything all day. Palmer gave her two pence, warning her not to spend it on rum. At the end of the week, the two met again in Dorset Street. This time, Chapman said she felt too ill to do anything, but added, 'It's no good my giving way. I must pull myself together and go out and get some money, or I shall have no lodgings.'

PANCHENKO, DR DIMITRI

In his book *The Medical Murderer* (1957), Rupert Furneaux writes of a St Petersburg doctor named Panchenko, who was a supplier of poisons and also suspected of being involved in several murders.

In 1911, Patrick O'Brien de Lacy, a member of the hereditary nobility of the Province of Grodno, married the daughter of General and Madame Buturlin. They were extremely wealthy, but had bequeathed the bulk of their fortune to their son. De Lacy decided to murder his brother-in-law and then his in-laws by feeding them cholera and diphtheria germs, an epidemic of both diseases at that time raging in St Petersburg. He offered Dr Panchenko 620,000 roubles to procure the germs and help in their administration. Unfortunately for de Lacy, his excited explanation of his plans to his mistress, Madame Muraviora, was overheard and reported to General Buturlin, following the death of his son. Panchenko was arrested and confessed, receiving a 15-year prison sentence. De Lacy was imprisoned for life.

More needs to be known about Dr Panchenko, but his name, his residence in St Petersburg, and his involvement in several murders, suggest that he could be the original of Dr Pedachenko.

PANNIER, MRS

See **Mrs Paumier**.

PARADOX

Book by R.A. Patterson (Presto South, Victoria, Australia: R.A. Patterson, 1998; updated 2000 and made available on the internet). Suggests that Jack the Ripper was the Catholic poet, **Frances Thompson**.

PARDONS

A pardon was offered on 10 November 1888, 'to any accomplice, not being a person who contrived or actually committed the murder', who gave information leading to the murderer's apprehension and conviction. This was expressly confined to the murder of **Mary Jane Kelly**, with Home Secretary **Henry Matthews** explaining to the House of Commons on 23 November that, 'In the case of Kelly there were certain circumstances which were wanting in earlier cases, and which made it more probable that there were other persons, who, at any rate after the crime, had assisted the murderer.'

Matthews himself had laid down the general rule on pardons: that they should only be granted, 'where more than one person appears to have been concerned in a crime with varying degrees of guilt and where all reasonable efforts have been made without success to discover the criminals.'

Home Office Permanent Secretary **Godfrey Lushington** offered cogent reasons in the October for not offering any pardon with respect to the Whitechapel murders: that it would make the public fear an accomplice, as well as a murderer, and that it would be interpreted as an admission of police failure.

It is not known what circumstances persuaded Matthews that the Kelly murder, unlike its predecessors, invited the offer of a pardon, nor what evidence for any accomplice existed, or indeed, whether this was merely a palliative to public opinion. *See* **Dr Phillips**.

PARKE, ERNEST (1860–1944)

Journalist. Educated at Stratford-on-Avon Grammar School. Worked on the *Star*, and in 1889, as editor of the *North London Press*, made the first public allusion to the possibility that **Prince Albert Victor** might be implicated in the Cleveland Street Scandal. For this *lèse majesté* he was tried and imprisoned on fabricated charges. Subsequently, he became a director of the Northern Newspaper Co., Darlington, and JP for Warwickshire.

In his autobiography, **T.P. O'Connor**, the Irish Nationalist who founded and edited the *Star*, described Parke as 'a young flossy-haired man with a keen face, an agile body, a tremendous flair for news. He might be trusted to work up any sensational news of the day, and he helped with "Jack the Ripper", to make gigantic circulations hitherto unparallelled in evening journalism.' According to **Lincoln Springfield**, Parke accepted the responsibility of paying off **John Pizer** and tempted him with a little pile of £10 in golden sovereigns, which saved the *Star* an expensive libel suit.

PARNELL COMMISSION

Public inquiry into articles in *The Times* in 1887, claiming that Charles Stewart Parnell and Irish Nationalist parliamentarians associated with Fenians and approved of terrorism. It ultimately concluded that Parnell had endorsed violence and advocated a complete breach from Great Britain when in America, but more sensationally, the proceedings revealed that *The Times* had libelled Parnell with a forged letter purporting to voice his approval of political assassination in Phoenix Park, Dublin. The forger fled the country and committed suicide after being exposed under cross-examination.

The Commission started hearings as the Ripper scare ended, and both **Anderson** and **Monro** were deeply interested as the former had assisted *The Times*, infringing departmental regulations by leaking information – a fact he was able to conceal when called as a witness. Both men also wished to limit the exposure of General Millen, an Irish-American subversive, who had been an informant for another section of the Home Office and whose reports had once been sent to Anderson.

Anderson's memoirs (1910) admitted his contributions to *The Times* and alleged that Monro had approved. This attracted far more attention than his non-political remarks on the Ripper, and Monro hotly denied having approved the pieces.

In 1888, the *Daily Telegraph* noted a Fenian rumour that **Inspector Andrews'** visit to America was connected with the Commission. The *New York Herald*, in December that year, claimed that Andrews acknowledged his purpose was to collect evidence against Parnell. Persistent rumours that the Ripper investigations turned up Irish connections need to be seen in light of the Parnell Commission as the main headline news at the time.

Cf. **Arthur James Balfour**, **Douglas G. Browne**.

PARR, ERNEST A. (*b. c.* 1872–1918)

A journalist from Newmarket. On 28 March 1908 he wrote to the Secretary of State for Scotland that in the course of gathering information about Jack the Ripper he had come across a statement in a paper claiming that **William Henry Bury** had confessed in writing to the murders and that this confession was passed to the Secretary of State for Scotland. He also stated that **James Berry**, who executed Bury, had told him explicitly that Bury was known to have been Jack the Ripper.

(See National Archives of Scotland HH/16/69.)

PASH, FLORENCE (1862–1951)

Alleged friend of **Mary Jane Kelly**. Artist.

Daughter of shoe manufacturer Daniel John Pash (1891 Census). Married (1) Albert Alexander Humphrey; (2) Major C.T. Holland. One son, Cecil. All predeceased her. Friend and close associate of **Walter Sickert**.

Florence Pash met Walter Sickert in the mid-1880s and during the 1890s she became a close friend, probable lover and patron. Sickert painted her portrait several times. Towards the end of her life she collaborated with Violet Overton Fuller (*d.* 1967) in editing a collection of letters, which she had received and preserved from Walter Sickert and which, according to Violet Overton Fuller's editor's note, she had resisted having published, feeling unequal to the task. Later, Pash changed her mind because of the increasing interest in Sickert and because, 'although she has read much about Sickert, she has not found that his unfailing kindness and gaiety of heart have been sufficiently noticed.' She added that although the letters were few in number and written in his very youthful days, Pash hoped they 'may help to bring this engaging side of his rich and varied personality before the public, and so add a little to the total acquaintance we have with Sickert the man, as well as Sickert the Artist.' It was during this time that, according to Violet Overton Fuller's daughter, Jean Overton Fuller (*b.* 1915), Florence Pash revealed piecemeal a story which the Fullers interpreted as meaning that Pash knew Walter Sickert was Jack the Ripper (*see* **Sickert and the Ripper Crimes**).

Pash claimed there were many women in Walter Sickert's life and that he had fathered an illegitimate son, Joseph. Florence had spoken of visiting an artist's studio in a bad neighbourhood, where there were prostitutes and a male brothel (*see* **Cleveland Street**). She believed that Sickert had to look after a baby girl, and that he hired as a nanny, an Irish girl named Mary Kelly, who had come to London from Wales, where for a time she had been in Cardiff Infirmary. In London, she worked as an assistant in a shoddy shop and had then been engaged by Sickert, but left his employ for unclear reasons and started blackmailing him, though for reasons unknown.

Thereafter Pash was frequently called upon to babysit and had once been out with the child when coach which mounted the pavement at the junction of Charing Cross Road and The Strand struck the child, who had to be taken to hospital, and nearly ran Florence down. Sickert believed this to be attempted murder (*see* **Alice Margaret Crook**). Florence, for unclear reasons, was of the view that the child was the illegitimate child of an heir to the throne.

Pash also told Violet Overton Fuller that Sickert had seen all the Ripper's victims' bodies in situ, had painted them and left clues in other works, especially hinting about a painting of a seagull and **Queen Victoria** (**Sir William Gull**). Violet Overton Fuller concluded from this that Sickert could only have seen all the victims in situ if he was the murderer and she also believed that Pash thought Sickert to be Jack the Ripper.

It has been observed that in the manuscript of the book that Pash worked on with Violet Overton Fuller (preserved at the Tate Archives), there is not so much as a hint that Walter Sickert was, or could have in any way been associated with Jack the Ripper.

PATRICK, PC JOHN, 91H (*b.* 1860)

Arresting officer in **Aaron Davis Cohen**'s case. Joined the Metropolitan Police in 1880 (warrant no. 65077). Served in H Division (Whitechapel) until 1891, when transferred to Division and promoted to sergeant. Retired in 1906, with the rank of sergeant and reserve standing, denoting high competence and reliability.

On 10 November 1888, he allegedly saw 23-year-old Edward Connell throwing pease pudding at some men and told him to stop. Connell then threw some pudding in PC Patrick's face, hit him and grappled him to the floor. On regaining his feet, PC Patrick hit Connell in the mouth. Connell claimed that he had been eating a saveloy and cabbage when PC Patrick knocked them from his hands, knocked him down and kicked him. Magistrate Frederick Lushington took the view that Connell was possibly drunk and disorderly, but that PC Patrick had no justification in striking him and therefore dismissed the case.

On 7 December 1888, Patrick appeared as the complainant (arresting officer) charging Cohen before Thames Magistrates with being a wandering lunatic (a person whose mental condition made him unable to look after himself and who had no apparent family or friends to care for him). When the magistrates ordered for Cohen to be sent for observation to Whitechapel Workhouse Infirmary, Patrick delivered him there at 5pm, when the patient's name was given as David Cohen.

PAUL, ROBERT

Witness at **Mary Ann Nichols**' inquest.

A carter, employed at Corbett's Court (on the corner of Hanbury Street and Commercial Street), he was on his way to work from his home, 30 Foster Street, Whitechapel, at about 3.45am when **Charles Cross** drew his attention to Nichols' body, lying in Buck's Row. Paul felt her hands and face, and said, 'I think she's breathing, but it's very little, if she is.' Together, the two went in search of a policeman, finding Police Constable **Mizen** at the corner of Hanbury Street and Baker's Row (Vallance Road). Cross was subsequently puzzled by Paul's sudden disappearance when he slipped into Corbett's Court, while Cross proceeded towards the City.

Despite Paul's instant availability for press interviews, it seems to have taken the police some time to identify and find him, and he did not appear at a hearing until the inquest reopened after a fortnight's adjournment. **Walter Dew** incorrectly recalled that, 'The police made repeated appeals for him to come forward, but he never did so.'

PAUMIER, or PANNIER, MRS
Witness who believed she saw the Ripper.

Young chestnut vendor, working on corner of Widegate Street and Sandys Row (about two minutes walk from Dorset Street) on the morning of 9 November 1888. A man of about 5ft 6in tall, dressed in a black coat, speckled trousers and black silk hat, approached from Artillery Row (Dorset Street direction). He had a black moustache and a black shiny bag, and said to her, 'I suppose you have heard about the murder in Dorset Street?' Mrs Paumier had. The man grinned and said, 'I know more about it than you do', walking away down Sandys Row. Mrs Paumier also said he had accosted three young ladies on Thursday night, saying he had something in the bag, 'the ladies don't like' (*St James's Gazette*, 10 November 1888). *Cf.* **Sarah Roney**.

Most newspapers call her Mrs Paumier, but the *Evening News* and the *Illustrated Police News* each have an instance of calling her Mrs Pannier, as does the very full report on the Kelly murder cut from the *Daily Telegraph* and held on Home Office files (10 November 1888).

PEAKALL, GEORGE
Witness.

The landlord of a lodging-house called Melbourn Chambers. **Thomas Sadler** went there at about 1.45am to ask for a bed, after being knocked down by **John Dooley** and striking his head. Peakall refused, but advised him to go to the London Hospital to have his head treated.

PEARCE, SGT. ALBERT GEORGE (*b.* 1859)
Joined the Metropolitan Police in 1881 (warrant no. 65596). Resigned on pension, 1906.

Engaged on the case under **Abberline**'s direction with Inspectors **Reid**, **Moore** and **Nairn** (Nearn), and Sgts. **Thick**, **Godley** and **McCarthy** (*The Times*, 12 November 1888), and took statements from **Margaret Franklin** and **Elizabeth Ryder** on 22 July 1889 in connection with **Alice McKenzie**'s murder (MEPO 3/140, ff.275-276).

PEARCE, PC RICHARD WILLIAM, 922 City (*b. c.* 1850)

Witness resident in Mitre Square on the night of **Catherine Eddowes'** murder.

Born in Whitechapel. Served 4 years, 5 months in the 94th Regiment of Foot and 1 year, 7 months in the Army Reserve. Labourer, 1871–73. Joined the City of London Police March in 1973 (warrant no. 4690), when living as a single man at Gloucester Street, Whitechapel. Seven disciplinary notes between 1873 and 1895 record him as: absent from his beat without explanation, spending overlong time in a urinal (and once using it for drinking on duty), bed-wetting, visiting a pub and drinking lemonade when on duty and loitering on his beat to obtain drink. Married his wife, Jane: two children, William Richard (described as an 'imbecile from birth'), May Olive (died *c.* 1889) and Alice Maud. Retired on pension in 1898.

In 1888, he was resident in Mitre Square. Lived at no. 3 (northwest side of the Square, adjacent to Kearley and Tonge's warehouse) with his wife and family. He went to bed at around 12.20am, 30 September 1888, and slept through all the disturbance until called by a policeman at 2.20am, following the discovery of Eddowes' body and arrival of doctors and police reinforcements. From his bedroom window, he could plainly see the spot where the murder had been committed.

(See Neil Bell and Robert Clack, 'City P.C. Richard Pearce', *Ripperologist*, 107, October 2009.)

PEARCEY, MRS ELEANOR (1866–90)

Suspect, proposed by **William Stewart** in 1939.

In October 1890, Mrs Pearcey murdered her lover's wife, Phoebe Hogg, and baby (also called Phoebe), and pushed the bodies for several miles around Hampstead before dumping the bodies at different places, where they were found in the morning. Mrs Pearcy was hanged at Newgate Prison on 23 December 1890.

In *Jack the Ripper: A New Theory*, William Stewart was principally concerned with reviving Sir Arthur Conan Doyle's suggestion of a midwife, but he also suggested that Mrs Pearcey's modus operandi fitted the Ripper murders as he believed some of the bodies had been dumped at the sites where they were found, having been killed elsewhere.

Letters From Hell notes a Jack the Ripper letter, dated 6th December 1890, sent to ' 'The Controller of General Savings' ,claiming responsibility for the murder of Mrs Hogg. (MEPO 3/142 ff.334-335)

'PEARLY POLL' (*b.* 1838)

See **Mary Ann Connolly**.

PEARSON, ALFRED (*fl.* 1888)

Suspect.

Surgeon, alleged in *Epiphany of the Whitechapel Murders* to have been engaged to assassinate **Mary Jane Kelly**. No evidence has been adduced to support this theory.

PEDACHENKO, DR ALEXANDER (1857?–1908?), ALIAS COUNT LUISKOVO

Suspect, first alleged by **William Le Queux** in 1928; revived by **Donald McCormick** in 1959.

Native of Tver, where he joined the staff of the Maternity Hospital. At one time, he lived in Glasgow and was a member of the Russian Secret Service, according to an article cited by Donald McCormick and attributed by him to **Hector Cairns**, though in fact the article merely cites Cairns and attributes the information to G.D.K. M'Cormick. Supposedly in 1888, when known to Ochrana (the Secret Police) as, 'the greatest and boldest of all Russian criminal lunatics', he was living with his sister in Westmoreland Road, Walworth. With Ochrana approval, he committed the Ripper murders, assisted by a friend named **Levitski** and a tailoress named **Winberg**.

The Ochrana's aim was allegedly to discredit the Metropolitan Police, who were perceived by Czarists as irresponsibly tolerant of emigrant dissidents and anarchists living in (especially) the East End. When the plot succeeded and **Sir Charles Warren** resigned in disgrace, the Ochrana smuggled Pedachenko to Moscow, destined for exile to Yakutsk. In fact, five months later he was caught red-handed, trying to murder a woman called Vogak, and sent to a lunatic asylum, where he died.

All the above, with the exception of the Cairns article, is according to William Le Queux in *Things I Know* (1928), allegedly drawing on a manuscript document dictated by **Rasputin**, which itself purportedly uses information from the Ochrana, **Nideroest** and **Zverieff**.

Donald McCormick, citing **Dr Dutton**'s *Chronicles of Crime*, adds the claims that Pedachenko was the double of **Severin Klosowski**, that he worked in Westmoreland Road, Walworth as a barber-surgeon in the employ of a hairdresser named William Delhaye; that he also assisted a Walworth doctor at St Saviour's Infirmary, which was attended by victims **Tabram**, **Chapman**, **Nichols** and **Kelly**. Also, that Wolf Levisohn advised Inspector Abberline to investigate a barber in Walworth in connection with the Ripper murders. McCormick identified the doctor at St Saviour's as John Frederick Williams.

According to a lithographed copy of the ***Ochrana Gazette*** for January 1909, allegedly shown to Mr McCormick by Prince Belloselski (but untraced by subsequent researchers), the Ochrana knew Pedachenko to be an alias of Vassily

Konovalov, the murderer of a woman in Paris, in 1886, as well as the five Ripper victims of 1888.

None of the above sources and lines of transmission, with the exception of McCormick's discovery of the existence of Delhaye and Dr Williams, and the possible exception of Hector Cairns, can be regarded as historically reliable. In fact, there is no solid evidence for the existence of Dr Pedachenko. Apart from both being described as natives of Tver, there is no similarity between Pedachenko and the alleged Ochrana description of Vassily Konovalov.

In 1995 the Jack the Ripper tour guide, John Pope De Locksley discovered in an 1887 edition of *Almanac de Gotha* (p.934) the names of 'Le major-general Levitski' and 'Le major-general Pedachenko' consecutively listed.

(See Stepan Poberowski, 'Pedachenko Revisited', ***Ripperologist***, 58, March 2005

PEMBERTON, EDWARD LEIGH, MP (1823–1910)

Civil servant with substantial input on Home Office files concerning the Ripper.

Conservative MP for East Kent, 1869–84. On leaving Parliament, became legal assistant to the Under-Secretary, Home Office (**Godfrey Lushington**) and as such, wrote many of the letters to **Sir Charles Warren**, **James Monro** and Sir Richard Pennefather, the receiver (financial manager) of the Metropolitan Police, conveying the Home Secretary's concerns about the conduct of the Ripper case.

PENNETT, PC WILLIAM, 239H (*b.* 1852)

Joined the Metropolitan Police in 1884 (warrant no. 69116). Retired, 1913. Discovered the **Pinchin Street torso**. On beat duty at 5.15am, on 10 September 1889, when he discovered the torso of a woman, lacking head and legs, under a railway arch in Pinchin Street. He summoned assistance and then assisted in the arrests of two sailors and a bootblack found sleeping under adjacent arches.

'THE PENSIONER'
See **Edward Stanley**.

PHELPS, SERGEANT (City Police)
Assisted **Inspector Izzard** and **Sergeant Dudman** with crowd control at Mitre Square after **Catherine Eddowes**' murder.

PHILLIPS, ANNIE (1863–1943)
Daughter of victim **Catherine Eddowes**. Wife of a lamp black packer, Louis Phillips; resident at 12 Dilstone Grove, Southwark Park Road, at the time of the murder.

She was described at the time of the inquest as 'a comely-looking young woman dressed in black' (*Daily News*, 12 October 1888).

At the inquest, she said that her father, **Thomas Conway**, was a teetotaller who had not got on with Eddowes and had eventually left her seven or eight years earlier because of her drinking. She had last seen her mother a little over two years earlier when Catherine attended her during her confinement, but Phillips moved home and left no forwarding address – both her own address and that of her brothers in London having purposefully been kept from Eddowes because she persistently pestered them for money. Thomas Conway lived with Annie at a former address, but they did not get on and she had not seen or heard of him for 15 or 18 months since he left suddenly, without giving a reason.

According to **John Kelly**, on the last day of her life Eddowes went to Bermondsey to solicit money from Annie. But Annie Phillips saw nothing of her that day. If Eddowes did indeed travel to Bermondsey, then she failed to find her daughter.

Annie Phillips had given birth two children, Louis (*b.* 1882) and Catherine (*b.* 1884), before marrying Louis Phillips in 1885, in which year Annie visited her mother at the lodging-house in Flower and Dean Street. It was the following year, 1886, when Eddowes attended her daughter during the birth of her third child, William. A fourth child, Ellen, was born in 1889, and a fifth, Thomas, born in 1890. It is believed that all three sons died during World War I. The youngest is known to have died in 1918, while serving with the European Expeditionary Force and to be buried at the Cairo War Memorial Cemetery, Egypt. The post-war years saw successive tragedies: her eldest daughter dying in 1919, her husband Louis in 1920 and youngest daughter Ellen in 1924, leaving Annie to raise the family. Annie Phillips died, aged 80, in 1943.

DR PHILLIPS

PHILLIPS, DR GEORGE BAGSTER (1834–97)

H Division Police Surgeon; conducted or attended postmortems on four of the five Ripper victims, and was called to the murder sites of three. MRCS, Lic. Midwif., Lic. Soc. Apoth., 1861. Police surgeon from 1865. Residence and surgery, 2 Spital Square, Spitalfields. Appointed police surgeon to H Division in the 1860s. He died from apoplexy, on 27 October 1897.

Walter Dew, in *I Caught Crippen*, wrote of him, 'He was a character. An elderly man, he was ultra-old-fashioned both in his personal appearance and his dress. He used to look for all the world as though he had stepped out of a century-old painting. His manners were charming; he was immensely popular both with the police and the public, and he was highly skilled.'

His assistant, **Dr Percy John Clark**, described him as 'a modest man who found self-advertising abhorrent. Under a brusque, quick manner engendered by his busy life, there was a warm, kind heart, and a large number of men and women of all classes are feeling that by his death they have lost a very real friend' (obituary, *The Lancet*, 13 November 1897). His obituary in the *British Medical Journal* (6 November 1897) referred to performing autopsies on the victims of Jack the Ripper, saying 'The praiseworthy manner in which he performed these duties procured in a well-merited reputation, and he has been repeatedly referred to by the magistrates at the metropolitan police courts for expert evidence. He was always courteous to and popular with his professional brethren, and his familiar presence will be sorely missed by them'.

Called to examine **Annie Chapman**'s body at 6.20am, 8 September 1888, he arrived at 29 Hanbury Street, *c.* 6.30. In addition to the body itself, he noted a piece of muslin and a comb in a paper case (presumed to be the contents of Chapman's torn pocket), placed in order at her feet. He attended the inquest on 14 September 1888 and was reported as describing the body in situ thus:

The left arm was placed across the left breast. The legs were drawn up, the feet resting on the ground, and the knees turned outwards. The face was swollen and turned on the right side. The tongue protruded between the front teeth, but not beyond the lips. The tongue was evidently much swollen. The front teeth were perfect as far as the first molar, top and bottom, and very fine teeth they were. The body was terribly mutilated.

The stiffness of the limbs was not marked, but was evidently commencing. He noticed that the throat was disseevered deeply; that the incisions through the skin were jagged, and reached right round the neck. On the wooden paling between the yard in question and the next, smears of blood, corresponding to where the head of the deceased lay, were to be seen. These were about 14in from the ground and immediately above the part where the blood lay that had flowed from the neck.

[Answering questions from the coroner]: He should say that the instrument used at the throat and abdomen was the same. It must have been a very sharp knife with a thin narrow blade, and must have been at least 6in. to 8in. in length, probably longer. He should say that the injuries could not have been inflicted by a bayonet or sword-bayonet. They could have been done by such an instrument as a medical man used for *post-mortem* purposes, but the ordinary surgical cases might not contain such an instrument. Those used by slaughtermen, well ground down, might have caused them. He thought the knives used by those in the leather trade would not be long enough in the blade. There were indications of anatomical knowledge which were only less indicated in consequence of haste. The whole of the body was not present, the absent portions being from the abdomen. The mode in which these portions were extracted showed some anatomical knowledge. He should say that the deceased had been dead at least two hours, and probably more, when he first saw her; but it was right to mention that it was a fairly cool morning, and that the body would be more apt to cool rapidly from its having lost a great quantity of blood. There was no evidence of a struggle having taken place. He was positive that the deceased entered the yard alive.

A handkerchief was round the throat of the deceased when he saw it early in the morning. He should say it was not tied on after the throat was cut.

On Saturday afternoon he made his post mortem examination at Whitechapel Workhouse Infirmary Mortuary: an inadequate and insanitary shed about which he protested, with the full support of coroner Wynne Baxter. His autopsy observations were reported thus:

He noticed the same protrusion of the tongue. There was a bruise over the right temple. On the upper eyelid there was a bruise, and there were two distinct bruises, each the size of a man's thumb, on the forepart of the top of the chest. The stiffness of the limbs was now well marked. There was a bruise over the middle part of the bone of the right hand. There was an old scar on the left of the frontal bone. The stiffness was more noticeable on the left side, especially in the fingers, which were partly closed. There was an abrasion over the ring finger, with distinct markings of a ring or rings. The throat had been severed as before described. The incisions into the skin indicated that they had been made from the left side of the neck. There were two distinct clean cuts on the left side of the spine. They were parallel with each other and separated by about half an inch. The muscular structures appeared as though an attempt had been made to separate the bones of the neck. There were various other mutilations of the body, but he was of opinion that they occurred subsequent to the death of the woman, and to the large escape of blood from the division of the neck. At this point Dr Phillips said that, as from these injuries he was satisfied as to the cause of death, he thought that he had better not go into further details of the mutilations, which could only be painful to the feelings of the jury and the public. The Coroner decided to allow that course to be adopted. Witness, continuing, said, 'The cause of death was apparent from the injuries he had described. From these appearances he was of opinion that the breathing was interfered with previous to death, and that death arose from syncope, or failure of the heart's action in consequence of loss of blood caused by severance of the throat.

[Answering questions from the Coroner]: The deceased was far advanced in disease of the lungs and membranes of the brain, but they had nothing to do with the cause of death. The stomach contained a little food, but there was not any sign of fluid. There was no appearance of the deceased having taken alcohol, but there were signs of great deprivation and he should say she had been badly fed. He was convinced she had not taken any strong alcohol for some hours before her death. The injuries were certainly not self-inflicted. The bruises on the face were evidently recent, especially about the chin and the sides of the jaw, but the bruises in front of the chest and temple were of longer standing – probably of days. He was of the opinion that the person who cut the deceased's throat took hold of her by the chin, and then commenced the incision from left to right. He thought it was highly probable that a person could call out, but with regard to an idea that she might have been gagged he could only point to the swollen face and protruding tongue, both of which were signs of suffocation.

Dr Phillips was recalled on 19 September to give the further evidence of posthumous mutilation omitted in his original testimony. He deferred to the coroner, though regretting his decision, 'in the interests of justice.' Baxter insisted the evidence must be given, 'for various reasons which he need not then enumerate,' and suggested not all medical men might agree with Phillips that the mutilations occurred after death. Both agreed the evidence was indecent, so the court was cleared of women and boys, and the daily press refrained from reporting parts of it. The following description is, therefore, a composite from *The Times* and a special report in the *Lancet*:

The abdomen had been entirely laid open: the intestines, severed from their mesenteric attachments, had been lifted out of the body and placed on the shoulder of the corpse; whilst from the pelvis, the uterus and its appendages with the upper portion of the vagina and the posterior two-thirds of the bladder, had been entirely removed. No trace of these parts could be found and the incisions were cleanly cut, avoiding the rectum, and dividing the vagina low enough to avoid injury to the *cervix uteri*. Obviously the work was that of an expert – of one, at least, who had such knowledge of anatomical or pathological examinations as to be enabled to secure the pelvic organs with one sweep of the knife, which must therefore have been at least five or six inches in length, probably more. The appearance of the cuts confirmed him in the opinion that the instrument, like the one which divided the neck, had been of a very sharp character. The mode in which the knife had been used seemed to indicate great anatomical knowledge.

[In answer to questions from the coroner]: He thought he himself could not have performed all the injuries he described, even without a struggle, under a quarter of an hour. If he had done it in a deliberate way, such as would fall to the duties of a surgeon, it probably would have taken him the best part of an hour.

This is the firmest statement made by any doctor ascribing surgical expertise to the Ripper.

From a study of the medical evidence in all Ripper cases it has been concluded that Phillips unquestionably undertook very thorough and professional autopsies and that the ascription of medical skill to the Ripper should be taken very seriously (Karyo Magellan, *Ripperologist*, 76, February 2007; see also, *By Ear and Eyes*).

At 1.20am, on 30 September 1888, Dr Phillips was summoned to Leman Street

Police Station, and directed from there to Berner Street, where he arrived around 2am. At **Elizabeth Stride**'s inquest on 3 October, he reported:

The body was lying on the near side, with the face turned toward the wall, the head up the yard and the feet toward the street. The left arm was extended and there was a packet of cachous in the left hand. The right arm was over the belly. The back of the hand and wrist had on it clotted blood. The legs were drawn up with the feet close to the wall. The body and face were warm and the hand cold. The legs were quite warm. Deceased had a silk handkerchief round her neck, and it appeared to be slightly torn. I have since ascertained it was cut. This corresponded with the right angle of the jaw. The throat was deeply gashed, and there was an abrasion of the skin about 1?in in diameter, apparently stained with blood, under her right brow. At 3pm on Monday at St George's Mortuary Dr Blackwell and I made a *post-mortem* examination. *Rigor mortis* was still thoroughly marked. There was mud on the left side of the face and it was matted in the head. The body was fairly nourished. Over both shoulders, especially the right, and under the collar-bone and in front of the chest there was a blueish discoloration, which I have watched and have seen on two occasions since. There was a clean-cut incision on the neck. It was 6in in length and commenced 2?in in a straight line below the angle of the jaw, ?in over an undivided muscle, and then becoming deeper, dividing the sheath. The cut was very clean and deviated a little downwards. The artery and other vessels contained in the sheath were all cut through. The cut through the tissues on the right side was more superficial, and tailed off to about 2in below the right angle of the jaw. The deep vessels on that side were uninjured. From this it was evident that the haemorrhage was caused through the partial severance of the left carotid artery. Decomposition had commenced in the skin. Dark brown spots were on the anterior surface of the left chin. There was a deformity in the bones of the right leg, which was not straight, but bowed forwards. There was no recent external injury save to the neck. The body being washed more thoroughly I could see some healing sores. The lobe of the left ear was torn as if from the removal or wearing through of an earring, but it was thoroughly healed. On removing the scalp there was no sign of bruising or extravasation of blood. The heart was small, the left ventricle firmly contracted, and the right slightly so. There was no clot in the pulmonary artery, but the right ventricle was full of dark clot. The left was firmly contracted so as to be absolutely empty. The stomach was large, and the mucous membrane only congested. It contained partly digested food, apparently consisting of cheese, potato and farinaceous powder. All the teeth on the left lower jaw were absent. Examining her jacket, I found that while there was a small amount on the right side, the left was well plastered with mud.

[In answer to the coroner's questions]: The cause of death is undoubtedly from the loss of blood from the left carotid artery and the division of the windpipe. The blood had run down the waterway to within a few inches of the side entrance of the club. Roughly estimating it, I should say there was an unusual flow of blood considering the stature and nourishment of the body.

Dr Phillips was recalled to the resumed inquest on 5 October, and answered further questions thus:

He had made a re-examination with regard to the missing palate, and from very careful examination of the roof of the mouth he found that there was no injury to either the hard or the soft palate. He had also carefully examined the handkerchiefs, and had come to the conclusion that the stains on the larger handkerchief were those of fruit. He was convinced that the deceased had not swallowed the skin or inside of a grape within many hours of her death. The apparent abrasion which was found on washing the flesh was not an abrasion at all, as the skin was entire underneath. He found that the deceased was seized by the shoulders, pressed on the ground, and that the perpetrator of the deed was on the left side when he inflicted the wound. He was of the opinion that the cut was made from left to right of the deceased and from that, therefore, arose the unlikelihood of such a long knife having inflicted the wound described in the neck. The knife was not sharp pointed; but round and an inch across. There was nothing in the cut to show an incision of the point of any weapon.

[H]e could not form any account of how the deceased's right hand became covered with blood. It was a mystery. He was taking it as a fact that the hand always remained in the position he found it in resting across her body. Deceased must have been alive within an hour of his seeing her. The injuries would only take a few seconds to inflict; it might have been done in two seconds. He could not say with certainty whether the sweets being found in her hand indicated that the deed had been done suddenly. There was a great dissimilarity between this case and Chapman's. In the latter, the neck was severed all round down to the vertebral column, the vertebral bone being enlarged with two sharp cuts, and there being an evident attempt to separate the bones. The murderer would not necessarily be bloodstained, for the commencement of the wound and the injury to the vessels would be away from him, and the stream of blood, for stream it would be, would be directed away from him, and towards the waterway already mentioned. He had reason to believe that the deceased was lying on the ground when the wound was inflicted.

See **Elizabeth Stride** for comments on Phillips' observations regarding the knife, grapes and Stride's teeth.

The comparison with Annie Chapman shows that Chapman's neck had been mutilated in exactly the same way as **Mary Jane Kelly**'s.

Phillips attended **Catherine Eddowes**' postmortem, and told the *Evening News,*

(1 October 1888) that the murder was not by the same hand that killed Stride. Coroner Wynne Baxter's summing-up gives an accurate précis of his evidence, so it is almost certainly from Phillips that Baxter took the point that there were 'unskilful injuries in the case in Mitre Square – possibly the work of an imitator'.

On Friday, 9 November, Dr Phillips was summoned at 11am and arrived at **Mary Jane Kelly**'s room in Miller's Court at 11.15. He later testified, 'I looked through the lower of the broken [window-]panes and satisfied myself that the mutilated corpse lying on the bed was not in need of any immediate attention from me. I also came to the conclusion that there was nobody else upon the bed or within view to whom I could render any professional assistance.'

When the door was forced open at 1.30, Phillips noted that it struck the table to the left of the bed. It was reported that cursory medical examination concluded the uterus had been taken away, but following the very thorough postmortem carried out by Phillips, in the presence of his assistant and Doctors **Bond** and **Brown**, all parts of the body were said to be accounted for. (But *cf.* the report under **Dr Thomas Bond** describing the missing heart, confirmed by Dr Hebbert's important information.) Phillips' report to the inquest was extremely brief and omitted the postmortem results:

> The mutilated remains of a female were lying two-thirds over towards the edge of the bedstead nearest the door. She had only her chemise on, or some underlinen garment. I am sure the body had been removed subsequent to the injury which caused her death from that side of the bedstead which was nearest the wooden partition, because of the large quantity of blood under the bedstead and the saturated condition of the sheet and the palliasse at the corner nearest the partition. The blood was produced by the severance of the carotid artery, which was the immediate cause of death. This injury was inflicted while deceased was lying at the right of the bedstead.

On 22 July 1889, Phillips submitted a very long report on **Alice McKenzie**, concluding:

> After careful & long deliberation I cannot satisfy myself, on purely Anatomical & professional grounds that the perpetrator of all the "Wh Ch. murders" is our man. I am on the contrary impelled to a contrary conclusion in this noting the mode of procedure & the character of the mutilations & judging of motive in connection with the latter.
>
> I do not here enter into the comparison of the cases neither do I take into account what I admit may be almost conclusive evidence in favour of the one man theory if all the surrounding circumstances and other evidence are considered, holding it as my duty to report on the P.M. appearances and express an opinion only on Professional grounds, based upon my own observation.
>
> (*Cf.* **Dr Thomas Bond**.)

411

It was very much on Phillips' urging that a Pardon for non-murdering accessories was offered, but it is not known what arguments he adduced (*The Echo*, 12 November 1888).

PHOENIX, MRS ELIZABETH

Sister-in-law of **Mrs Carthy**. Lived at 157 Bow Common Lane, Burdett Road.

On 11 November 1888, she went to Leman Street Police Station and stated that, from published description of **Mary Jane Kelly**, she believed her to be a person who lodged with Mrs Carthy, several years previously. Police action, if any, is unknown, but the press traced Mrs Carthy and recorded interviews supporting **Joe Barnett**'s story that Mary Jane had worked in the West End.

PICKETT or PICKET, CATHERINE

Witness. Flower-seller and neighbour of **Mary Jane Kelly**, annoyed by her singing on the night of her murder. David Pickett, Catherine's husband, prevented her from going to complain. The following morning, at 7.30am, she knocked on Kelly's door, hoping to borrow a shawl, and assumed her to be asleep.

A 34-year-old Catherine Pickett was sentenced at Thames Police Court on 29 September 1888 to one month's imprisonment for stealing clothing to the value of five shillings (25p).

PIGOTT, WILLIAM HENRY (1835–1901)

Briefly suspected. Son of a Gravesend insurance agent, who prospered for a time as a publican in Hoxton, but had fallen on hard times by 1888, and was apparently mentally unstable.

Pigott arrived in Gravesend at about 4pm, on Sunday, 9 September 1888, telling various people that he had walked from Whitechapel. In the Pope's Head public house, he aroused the landlady's suspicion by expressing hostility to women, and she sent for the police. Superintendent Berry noticed an injury to his hand, which Pigott explained by saying how a woman had bitten it in a back yard behind a Whitechapel lodging-house. Later, he changed the location of the incident to Brick Lane. A shirt in his bag had blood-spots on it, and the police surgeon believed his shoes showed signs of having been wiped clean of blood.

Inspector Abberline took him back to Whitechapel, where he was placed in an identity parade before **Mrs Fiddymont**, **Joseph Taylor** and **Mary Chappell**. The first two completely failed to identify him. Mary Chappell picked him out from the line, but then said she wasn't sure that he was the man that she had seen in the Prince Albert shortly after Chapman's murder.

After he had been cleared, it is uncertain whether Pigott was turned over to his friends for placement in an asylum, or sent direct to Whitechapel Workhouse Infirmary (*The Times*, 12, 13, 14, 15 September 1888).

PINCHIN STREET MURDER

Unsolved crime, briefly attributed to the Ripper, but accepted as the crime of **Severin Klosowski** or **Walter Sickert** by R. Michael Gordon and Patricia Cornwell respectively.

On 10 September 1889, **Police Constable Pennett**, on beat duty in Pinchin Street, found a woman's torso, lacking head and legs, covered by a piece of an old chemise, under a railway arch in Pinchin Street. His attention was in part attracted by the smell, as it was starting to decompose. The abdomen was mutilated, one reporter feeling that the injuries were reminiscent of the Ripper's handiwork and claiming tthe womb was missing; the arms and hands were well-formed and showed no signs of manual labour, despite which it was speculated that the woman might have been a factory worker.

One news agency speculated that it could be the body of **Lydia Hart**, an East-End prostitute, who had been missing for some days. **James Monro**'s report to the Home Office, dated 11 September, opens by noting that the estimated date of death, 8 September, is the anniversary of **Annie Chapman**'s murder. Nonetheless, he dismisses the likelihood of the killing being the Ripper's work after considering the method of operation (HO144/221/A49301K, ff1–8).

Melville Macnaghten makes several references to the case.

(See **Whitehall Mystery**.)

PINHORN, INSPECTOR CHARLES (1849–1920)

Joined the Metropolitan Police in 1868 (warrant no. 51109). On 9 July 1888, he was severely reprimanded and cautioned for an offence (unspecified) and transferred from E to H Division. Then, on 8 November 1888, Pinhorn was again severely reprimanded and cautioned. He resigned on pension in 1893. After retirement, he was active in the Temperance movement and a long-time secretary of the London United Temperance Council; he was to represent the UK as a delegate at a projected World's Prohibition Conference (*The Times*, 16 September 1908). On his death it was reported that he was 'secretary of the London United Temperance Council and a strong opponent of the granting of drink licences to theatres and music halls' (*The Times*, 17 September 1920).

With **Superintendent West**, he took charge of the on-site investigation of **Elizabeth Stride**'s murder, 30 September 1888. He was in charge of the Leman Street Police Station when **William Brodie** confessed to him of the murder of **Alice McKenzie** and personally in charge of the on-site investigation at **Pinchin Street**, on 10 September 1889.

(See Bernard Brown, 'The New Broom', *Ripperana*, 35, January 2001.)

PINNOCK, PC, JOHN 238H (*b.* 1854)

Five years' Army Service before joining the Metropolitan Police in 1878 (warrant no. 62909). Cautioned for an unknown offence, 20 September 1888. Resigned to Pension in 1902.

Various newspapers report that on finding the body of **Annie Chapman**, **John Davis** ran out of the house and called **PC Pinnock**, 238 H, who sent information about the murder to Commercial Street Police Station (*Daily News*, 10 September, 1888). Pc Pinnock is also mentioned by **Oswald Allen**.

'PIPEMAN, THE'

Descriptive name now generally used for the second man seen and described by **Israel Schwartz**, who emerged from a pub with a clay pipe in his hand and ran after Schwartz in the direction of Helen Street.

PIZER, JOHN (1850–97)

Cleared suspect, named by police as 'Leather Apron'.

John Pizer was the eldest son of Israel and Abigail Pizer. It isn't known when Israel Pizer (*b.* Poland, 1813) arrived in Britain, but he married Abigail Moss in 1842 and John Pizer (*b.* London, 1850) was seven months old at the time of the 1851 Census, when Israel (whose surname is spelt Piza) is described as a 'general dealer'. Abigail's mother, Elizabeth, was living with them at 24 Mitre Street and Israel was evidently prosperous enough to afford a servant. Pizer's mother, Abigail, died in 1853, and Israel remarried the following year, 1854. His wife, Augusta Cohen (*b.* Poland, 1851), probably hadn't been in the country for very long because she would tell a journalist that she didn't know where John Pizer was born because, 'I came here too late to know' (*Evening News*, 10 September 1888).

The family, which included Augusta's mother, Leah, moved to 32 Gower's Walk, Goodmans Fields, Whitechapel. Israel had two children by his new wife, Janet (*b.* London, 1857): Samuel Gabriel (*b.* 1860) and (Barnet (*b.* 1861). At the time of the 1861 Census, John Pizer, now aged 10, was an inmate of the German Jews' Hospital, which may confirm later claims that he suffered poor health throughout his life. By the 1871 Census, they had move to 22 Mulberry Street and the following year, 1872, Israel Pizer died. The family stayed at Mulberry Street throughout the 1880s.

John Pizer was described as 'a dark man, of slight build, with small moustache and side whiskers, and his hair is turning grey. There is no foreign accent about his talk…' (*Daily Telegraph*, 11 September). The *Echo* (12 September 1888) added that he was of medium height, with florid complexion. His family claimed that he suffered from ill-health, having some time ago been seriously injured in a vital part, a result of which was that he could not do much work.

His stepmother let slip to a journalist of the *Evening News*: 'He is unmarried, and a very simple man. He was never very bright here [touching her forehead], but he could not do such things as spoken about' (*Evening News*, 10 September), while the *Daily Telegraph* reported, 'The step-mother says he is unmarried, and not very bright in his intellect.' However, later, newspapers began to report that Pizer was an 'active politician' (*Daily Telegraph*, 11 September), a claim seemingly confirmed by the *Star*, which after Pizer's release reported that he was congratulated by, 'some East-end Liberals, to whom it now appears he is well known, and among whom he has been an active worker' (*Star*, 12 September 1888).

It was reported that he was, 'called a rather intelligent man by his associates' (*Daily Telegraph*, 12 September) and that he, 'displayed more than an ordinary amount of intelligence (*Echo*, 12 September). Certainly, quoted interviews with Pizer, if reporting anything approaching what he actually said, suggest an articulate man. The Press Association reported that several residents of Mulberry Street gave Pizer a good character and spoke of him as a harmless sort of person (*Echo*, 10 September).

It has been observed that he is the same age, has the same occupation and almost the same name as a John Pozer, with whom it is thought he might be identical. Pozer appeared at the Thames Police Court charged with attacking James Willis, another boot-finisher, at his work-place – 42 Morgan Street, St George's – in July 1887. He poked his head through the open sweatshop window and said, 'No wonder I can't get any work when you have got it all!' Willis was told to send him away, but Pozer stabbed him in the hand when he approached him. For this, Pozer was sentenced to six months' hard labour (*The Times*, 8 July 1887).

Pizer's family claimed that he had been hospitalised with a carbuncle and had then been sent to a convalescent home, from which he had been released at the end of July, or very early in August. On 4 August 1888, a John Pizer appeared before Thames Magistrates, charged with indecent assault. The case was dismissed and no further details are known at present.

On the night of 30–31 August 1888, Pizer was staying at Crossman's common lodging-house in Holloway, and at 1.30am walked down to the Seven Sisters Road, where he talked with a policeman about the glow in the sky visible from the fire at London Docks. The following day, he went to Westminster, where he stayed in a lodging-house in Peter Street.

He described a curious incident on Sunday, 2 September, however, when he claimed that two 'unknown' women in Church Street, Spitalfields, (not today's Fournier Street) asked him if he was 'the man', which he took to mean Nichols' murderer. then, contrary to his assertion that he did not leave Westminster for a week, he must have made a return to the East End. (*Cf.* **"Leather Apron"** for a more detailed discussion; **Miss Lyons**' story of a similar incident the following Sunday.)

On 4 September, the stories that the Whitechapel Murderer was an unknown local Jew, nicknamed 'Leather Apron', broke in the press. Then, on Thursday, 6 September, Pizer returned to 22 Mulberry Street, staying on and around the premises for the next four days as his brother warned him that there was 'a false suspicion' against him. On 7 September, **Inspector Helson** mentioned him in his weekly report to Scotland Yard: 'The inquiry has revealed the fact that a man named Jack Pizer, alias "Leather Apron", has for some considerable period been illusing [sic] prostitutes in this, and other parts of the Metropolis, and careful search has been and is continued to be made to find this man in order that his movements may be accounted for on the night in question, although at present there is no evidence whatever against him.'

On the morning of Monday, 10 September, **Sergeant William Thick** and another officer went to 22 Mulberry Street, where Pizer opened the door to them. Three accounts of the arrest appeared in the press. Many papers reported that Thick said, 'You're just the man I want.' The *Daily Telegraph* (11 September 1988) reported that Pizer recognised Thick, turned pale and trembled, saying to his stepmother, 'Mother, they've got me,' after which he was taken to Leman Street Police Station without further questioning. Pizer himself told a Press Association reporter (*Star*, 12 September) that Thick had said he was wanted and when Pizer asked in what connection, Thick had replied, 'You know what for. You will have to come with me.' Pizer claimed to have responded, 'Very well, sir. I'll go down to the station with you with the greatest of pleasure.' The *Globe* (10 September), which collected neighbourhood opinion hostile to Pizer, nonetheless reported (10 September) that on being accused of being 'Leather Apron', Pizer said, 'I am not, and I don't know any such man,' and walked straight over to Thick. The *Star* (11 December) reported Thick as saying 'almost positively' that Pizer was indeed 'Leather Apron'.

From Leman Street Police Station, Pizer was taken to Commercial Street Police Station where, according to the *Star*, a woman had been sitting, apparently waiting to identify him, all afternoon. This may have been **Mrs Fiddymont**, who was at some point shown Pizer and could not identify him. The *Star* believed that women from Wilmott's Lodging House, who knew 'Leather Apron', were to be brought to identify him, but this seems never to have happened. Pizer was shown to **Emmanuel Violenia**, who positively identified him as the man he had seen talking angrily with a woman outside 29 Hanbury Street in the early morning of 8 September, and said that he knew Pizer as 'Leather Apron'. Pizer expressed outraged astonishment at this identification, but Violenia was, in any event, dropped from the case as unreliable. The following day, Sergeant Thick told the *Star* that he was 'almost positive' that Pizer was 'Leather Apron'.

No other evidence was found against him, and on the Tuesday evening, Pizer was released.

On Wednesday, 11 October, he was summoned to **Annie Chapman**'s inquest to be cleared of suspicion of murder. There, in answer to the opening questions, he said that he was nicknamed 'Leather Apron'. The undoubted fact of his presence in Holloway on the night of Mary Ann Nichols' murder was brought out, and Pizer was told that he could go. He protested: 'Sergeant Thick, who arrested me, has known me for 18 years' – but was interrupted by Coroner **Wynne Baxter** with the remark, 'Well, well – I do not think it is necessary for you to say more.'

Sergeant Thick then gave the only testimony, apart from Pizer's response to Mr Baxter, ever elicited that Pizer was known as 'Leather Apron': he said that he, 'had known Pizer for many years, and when people in the neighbourhood spoke of "Leather Apron", they meant him.'

But the press was completely unable to confirm this. The *East London Advertiser* of 15 September was one of several papers reporting that Pizer's neighbours, friends and family flatly denied that he was known as 'Leather Apron', though the *Globe* (10 September) had traced a Polish cobbler, who had tried unsuccessfully to find a policeman and lay information that he believed Pizer to have murdered Annie Chapman. The *Star*, which had been the most energetic paper in writing up the 'Leather Apron' scare, described Pizer's arrest as a 'police blunder' on 12 September. They now asserted that Pizer was not 'Leather Apron' – 'at least not the "Leather Apron" who has been the terror and blackmailer of women in Whitechapel.' Pizer's somewhat self-serving interview with the Press Association averred that he had never known that he was called 'Leather Apron' until, to his surprise, Thick told him so, and also gave a very simple account of being accosted by two women in Church Street on Sunday, 2nd, with no suggestion of pursuit by a mob.

It was reported that Pizer was given handsome financial compensation by newspapers which had described him incautiously, and further reported that these sums had been exaggerated. It is possible that he received no more than £10 from **Harry Dam** for the *Star*'s 'over-enthusiastic vilification' of 'Leather Apron'. On 11 October 1888, Pizer summonsed **Emily Patswold** for calling him 'Leather Apron' and hitting him. She was fined 10/- (50p) (*Daily Telegraph*, 11, 12, 13 September; *East London Advertiser* and *East London Observer*, 15 September).

In July 1897, Pizer, whose health had always been poor (he suffered from a hernia), died of gastro-enteritis in the London Hospital, still resident at 22 Mulberry Street.

(See **Buck's Row Suspect**)

POCOCK, FREDERICK (*b.* 1892)

Informant. Told **Daniel Farson**, after publication of the first edition of Farson's *Jack the Ripper*, that his mother had known of a man called **Druitt**, who lodged in the attic of a fried fish shop, next to the railway arch in The Minories in 1888, and was reputed to burn rubbish in the cellar furnace after the murders. An alarming man who accosted Pocock's mother during the Ripper scare apparently resembled the mysterious lodger. The 1891 Census shows 69-year-old widow Eliza Pocock heading the household at 1 Peacock Court, The Minories.

PODCASTS

Audio or video broadcasts downloadable over the internet to personal computers and portable media players. *See* **Rippercast**.

POISON MURDERS OF JACK THE RIPPER, THE

Book by Richard Gordon (Jefferson, North Carolina: McFarland, 2008).

Gordon's fourth book about the Borough Poisoner **George Chapman**, otherwise **Sevein Klosowski**, this time concentrating on the murders of Mary Spink, Elizabeth Taylor and Maud Marsh, for which he was executed, with a final chapter that reviews the limited press coverage of the suggestion by **Inspector Abberline** and **Arthur Neil** that he was Jack the Ripper.

*See also **Alias Jack the Ripper**, **The Thames Torso Murders of Victorian London*** and ***The American Murders of Jack the Ripper***.

POLICE AS SUSPECTS

Home Office file HO144/220/A49301/ ff. 35-36 contains an accusation made by **H.T. Haslewood** of White Cottage, High Road, Tottenham, against Det. Sgt. **William Thick**. Haslewood's first communication, dated 10 September 1889, merely stated that he believed the murderer to be a policeman and would furnish the identity, if assured that his own name would not be mentioned. **Edward Leigh Pemberton** noted the suggestion seemed ridiculous and should perhaps not be encouraged; nevertheless he authorised junior clerk Harry Butler Simpson to give Haslewood the assurance of confidentiality that he requested.

On 14 October, Haslewood wrote, 'I believe that if Sergt T.Thicke [sic] otherwise called "Johnny Upright" is watched and his whereabouts ascertained upon other dates where certain women have met their end, also to see what deceace [sic] he is troubled with, you will find the great secreate [sic]'. **Charles Troup**, who rose to become permanent under-secretary in the twentieth century, noted, 'I think it is plainly rubbish – perhaps prompted by spite' (HO144/221/A49301, f.46).

Joseph Gorman Sickert's original story named **Sir Robert Anderson** as **Sir William Gull**'s accomplice in carrying out the murders. This was changed by **Stephen Knight** to **Walter Sickert** (Anderson's absence on sick leave precluded him from being in any way involved in the deaths of **Annie Chapman**, **Elizabeth Stride** and **Catherine Eddowes**).

POLLARD, MAJOR HUGH (1888–1966)

Important link in the provenance of **Jack the Ripper's knife**.

Sports editor of *Country Life*. An authority on ancient and modern firearms, and partner of gunsmith Robert Churchill, the well-known ballistics expert frequently consulted by Scotland Yard. Pollard gave expert evidence in more than one cause célèbre. In 1937, he gave his assistant editor, Miss Dorothy Stroud (1910–97), a late-nineteenth century surgical knife in a box lined with bloodstained velvet that had once contained a pair, telling her that it was Jack the Ripper's knife, which had been left beside a victim's body. Miss Stroud subsequently gave the knife to Donald Rumbelow.

PORRIOTT, THOMAS WALTER

See **Gibson, Andrew John**.

PORTRAIT OF A KILLER: JACK THE RIPPER CASE CLOSED (2002)

Book by Patricia Cornwell (*b.* 1956) (New York: G.P. Putnam, 2002; London: Little Brown, 2002; trade paperback, London: Time Warner, 2003; London: Time Warner, 2003; paperback, New York: Berkley, 2003).

During a trip to London in May 2001, Cornwell was invited to tour Scotland Yard in the company of John Grieve, the hugely respected then Metropolitan Police deputy assistant commissioner. Grieve offered to take her around the Ripper crime scenes in Whitechapel and, during their tour, Cornwell asked whether modern investigative and forensic techniques had ever been used to solve the crimes. Discussing suspects, Grieve suggested she look into **Walter Sickert**, who he had always wondered about. Ms Cornell became convinced that Sickert was guilty, and in due course published her efforts to prove his guilt using modern forensic science. The book received unparallelled heated criticism, some deeply personal.

Central to her theory and predicated on a remark by a collateral Sickert descendant is Cornwell's belief that as a child Sickert suffered traumatic operations for a penile fistula, which left him sexually dysfunctional and with a pathological hatred of women that led to serial killing.

A second major point in her thesis is that mitochondrial DNA comparison between the stamp on the **Openshaw Letter** and envelopes of letters from Sickert's household shows that he could have been the author of the former. Further, forensic paper examiner Peter Bower has identified a small batch of paper, which he says was used to write Ripper letters and letters by Sickert, while Sickert expert Dr Anna Gruetzner Robins has stated her belief that Sickert wrote most of the Ripper letters, including 'Dear Boss' and the 'Saucy Jacky Postcard', and that his artistic training enabled him to vary the handwriting of the letters, and that he used a variety of tricks to make them appear to come from different places at the same time. (The value of mitrochondrial DNA in this instance has been questioned, and Bower and Robins have not published their evidence, so it is difficult to assess their claims. Other experts have questioned their results.)

Cornwell, who believes that Sickert may have been responsible for more than the canonical five victims, also argues that an examination of his life and paintings exposes a psychopathic and amoral character.

Subsequent research suggests Sickert was in France when some of the murders were committed.

In an exchange of email correspondence with Keith Skinner (April 2007) Ms Cornwell remarked:- "Were I to do the JTR book again, truthfully, I would still make the same case but be more careful about absolute statements and perhaps state them as my belief and not the absolute truth, which I don't think can ever be proven, only deduced. Even a confession, if we're cold-bloodedly objective about it, really isn't enough. But I think people would have gotten angry anyway."

PORTUGUESE CATTLEMEN

Suspects proposed by **Edward Knight Larkin**.

See **Jose Lorenco**, **Joao de Souza Machado** and **Manuel Cruz Xavier**.

POZER, JOHN (b. 1850)

See **John Pizer**.

PRATER, MRS ELIZABETH

Witness at Mary Jane Kelly's inquest.

Wife of boot machinist William Prater, who had deserted her five years previously. Lived in the room above Mary Jane Kelly, but precisely where is a matter of dispute – *see* **Room Above Mary Kelly's**. Claimed to have known Kelly well for some five months and to have spoken to her on the morning before the murder – one newspaper reporting an interview in which Prater claimed that Kelly was a very pleasant girl, who seemed to be on good terms with everybody, and had expressed the hope that the weather would be fine for the Lord Mayor's Show, which she hoped to attend (*Irish Times*, 10 November 1888).

In an interview with the *Star*, she claimed that Kelly was 'tall and pretty, and as fair as a lily.' Said that she had last seen Kelly alive about 9pm on Thursday, 8 November 1888, at the entrance to Miller's Court when they had spoken for a while, 'Then I said, "Good night, old dear," and she said, "Good night, my pretty." She always called me that' (*Star*, 10 November 1888).

Prater returned home at approximately 1am, on Friday, 9 November 1888, and stood at the archway from Dorset Street to Miller's Court, beside **John McCarthy**'s shop, waiting for a man who was living with her. She spoke for a while with McCarthy. When her man did not come, she went up to bed, first barricading the door, and then quickly fell asleep. She was awakened by her black kitten Diddles (*East London Advertiser*, 17 November 1888) running over her neck; she pushed the cat off the bed and, as she turned over, she heard a cry of 'Murder!' two or three times. As such cries were common, she took no notice and went back to sleep. At 5.30am, she awoke and went to the Ten Bells for some rum, then returned to bed and slept until 11am.

Canadian journalist **Kathleen Blake Watkins** recalled visited Miller's Court in 1892, at which time a woman whom she called Eliza, presumably Elizabeth Prater, was living in the room above Kelly's with a sailor. She remembered hearing Kelly crooning to herself through the night of her murder (*Toronto Mail and Empire*, 2 October 1909).

PRESTON, CHARLES

Witness at Elizabeth Stride's inquest. A barber, resident at 32 Flower and Dean Street for 18 months, he had seen Stride in the kitchen of the lodging-house between 6 and 7pm, on 29 September 1888. He gave some biographical data about her, and mentioned a drunk and disorderly charge brought against her four or five months previously, following an incident in the Queen's Head.

PRICHA, ANTONI (*b. c.* 1858)
Suspect immediately cleared.

An artist's model employed at the Royal Academy, Pricha was about 5ft 6?in tall, with long, dark wavy hair and a long dark moustache. He was walking in Whitehall on 13 November 1889, wearing a long brown astrakhan-trimmed overcoat, when **Edward Knight Larkins** spotted him. Thinking he resembled the suspect described by **George Hutchinson**, he pointed him out to PC Thomas Maybank 61A. Pricha referred the police to Mr Osborne at the Academy, who verified his account of himself. The peculiar note on his file – 'trousers and vest in Albaman' – probably mixes the description of his dress with his actual, or postulated Albanian nationality.

PRINCE ALBERT VICTOR, DUKE OF CLARENCE
See **Albert Victor**.

PRINCE EDDY AND THE HOMOSEXUAL UNDERGROUND
Book by Theo Aronson (London: John Murray, 1994; paperback edition, London: John Murray, 1996).

Explores **Prince Albert Victor**'s involvment in the Cleveland Street Scandal and alleged links with the Jack the Ripper murders, and discusses the possibility that **Montague John Druitt** was Jack the Ripper.

PRINCE, HIS TUTOR AND THE RIPPER, THE
Book by Deborah McDonald (Jefferson: North Carolina: McFarland and Co., 2007).

Against the background of late-nineteenth century public school 'Socratic love', homosexuality and paedophilia, McDonald assesses the evidence for **Prince Albert Victor**, **James Kenneth Stephen** and **Montague John Druitt** being Jack the Ripper, concluding none seem probable. The book draws upon much new or rarely used information, including the diary belonging to J.K. Stephen's mother, which sheds interesting light on his last days. It embraces the Lipski case and the Cleveland Street Scandal, to some extent covering arguments suggested elsewhere, notably in *The Ripper Legacy*.

PRINCE JACK: THE TRUE STORY OF JACK THE RIPPER
Book by Frank Spiering (New York: Doubleday, 1978; New York: Jove Books, 1980).

An elaboration of **Dr Thomas Stowell**'s suggestion that **Prince Albert Victor** was Jack the Ripper, drawing on Michael Harrison's biography, *Clarence,* and allegedly supported by notes of **Sir William Gull**'s, which Spiering claims to have found in the New York Academy of Medicine. No trace of these notes has been found by staff of the Academy or visiting Ripperologists, though Spiering gives the correct call number for the volume of Sir Theodore Martin's essays to which he claims the notes were attached.

Spiering's written challenge to the Queen to 'open the royal family's personal files' so the world would learn the truth about Jack the Ripper was met with a polite response from a Buckingham Palace spokesman who said he was sure the letter would receive the "same consideration as all correspondence does". (*Sunday People*, 20 August, 1978)

PRINCE OF WALES (subsequently Edward VII)
See **Albert Edward**.

PRINCE RIPPER AND THE ROYAL FAMILY: AN ANALYSIS OF HOW THE MODERN MEDIA VIEWS THE ROYAL CONSPIRACY

Book by Ryan Thornsberry (St. Petersburg, Florida: The Underground Who Chapbook Press, 2005).

A short and responsible study of the royal conspiracy theory, which is not concerned with justifying or demolishing it, but focuses on the psychological and social attraction of such conspiracy theories.

PRISONER 1167: THE MADMAN WHO WAS JACK THE RIPPER

See **The Secret of Prisoner 1167: Was This Man Jack the Ripper?**

PROVIDENCE ROW NIGHT REFUGE AND CONVENT

Alleged one-time residence of **Mary Jane Kelly**. Located at 50 Crispin Street, opposite Dorset Street, and in use by the order of Sisters of Mercy throughout the twentieth century. Since then, the interior has been converted to luxury flats. The nuns had an established tradition of an association with aRipper victim (see Mary Jane Kelly). **Paul Feldman** was impressed by the coincidence that the Sisters of Mercy used small crucifixes on featuring a skull at the foot of the cross, and a similar crucifix was produced by Anne Graham, and said by her to have been in the trunk where she claimed the **Maybrick Diary** was stored when it came into her possession.

In 1860, the Revd. (later, Monsignor) Daniel Gilbert opened a night refuge for homeless women and children in former stables at Providence Row, Finsbury Square. Nuns of the Order of Sisters of Mercy ran it. When the accommodation proved too small, land once used for fairs off Crispin Street was purchased and the present home was built and opened in 1868.

According to the **Sickert/Knight** story, Mary Kelly was taken in by the nuns of Providence Row A little later, a shop-owner in Cleveland Street wanted an assistant and mentioned this to Walter Sickert, who in turn mentioned it to Edmund Bellord, a Cleveland Street estate agent, who was a member of the committee of the refuge. The nuns recommended Mary Jane Kelly, who thereupon went to Cleveland Street and became associated with Annie Elizabeth Crook.

In 1973, an elderly nun interviewed by BBC Television said that, 'in 1915, [she] had been a novice in Providence Row, directly opposite the pub where Kelly and Chapman rubbed shoulders daily.' (This was the Horn of Plenty and not, as some authors have erroneously claimed, the Britannia.) The nun also remembered being told by an old sister, who was in Crispin Street at the time of the murders, 'If it had not been for the Kelly woman, none of the murders would have happened.'

PAUL BEGG, MARTIN FIDO AND KEITH SKINNER

(See Dave Cuthbertson, 'A Chaplet Of Verses And Providence Row', *Ripperologist*, 30, August 2000; John Carey, 'Providence Row Night Refuge', *Journal of the Whitechapel Society*, 3, August 2005.)

PTOLOMAY, CHARLES
Witness at the inquest on **Rose Mylett**.

At 7.55pm, on 19 December 1888, Ptolomay saw Rose Mylett near Clarke's Yard, where her body was found the following morning. She was in the company of two men dressed like sailors, but wearing unusual headgear: one had a fur cap, the other a hard, round hat. Ptolomay was certain that he could identify the men if he saw them again.

His testimony was seen as possibly supporting that of **Alice Graves**, who saw Rose coming out of the George on Commercial Road at 11.30pm in the company of two men, who looked like seamen.

PUBLIC REACTIONS TO JACK THE RIPPER: LETTERS TO THE EDITOR: AUGUST–DECEMBER 1888
Book, compiled and edited by Stephen P. Ryder (Madison, Wisconsin: Inklings Press, 2006).

Compilation of letters to the *City Press, Daily News, Daily Telegraph, East London Observer, Echo, Evening News, Freeman's Journal and Daily Commercial Advertiser, Lancet, Lloyd's Weekly, Morning Advertiser, Pall Mall Gazette, Star* and *The Times*. Presents correspondence in chronological order, with two indexes (one by the author and the other according to topic), identifying the journals in which each entry appeared.

PUCK[E]RIDGE, OSWALD (1838–1900)
On 19 September 1888, **Sir Charles Warren** wrote to the Home Office:'A man called Puckridge was released from an asylum on 4 August. He was educated as a surgeon – he has threatened to rip people up with a long knife. He is being looked for, but cannot be found yet.'

Oswald Puckridge was born on 13 June 1838 at Burpham, near Arundel, Sussex, the fourth of five children of John Puckridge, a farmer, and his wife Philadelphia (née Holmes). He became a chemist and, on 3 October 1868, married Ellen Buddle, the daughter of a licensed victualler named Edward Buddle, at the parish church of St Paul, Deptford. They had a son – Edward Buddle Puckridge, born at Deal, *c.* 1870.

Puckridge suffered intermittent bouts of insanity and was frequently a patient in mental hospitals, often being discharged after a few days. He was a patient at Hoxton House Lunatic Asylum from January to August 1888. On 9 August 1893, he was found wandering in Queen Victoria Street, London, and admitted to Bow Infirmary, being discharged on 18 August. Puckridge was again admitted to the Infirmary on 5 February 1896 from Bridewell Police Station, being discharged on 14 February. He was then admitted to the City of London

423

Lunatic Asylum, at Stone, Buckinghamshire, being recorded in the Register of Lunatics as a 'Danger to others', but was discharged on 9 July. (see **John Hewitt**, **Hyam Hyams**, **Joseph Fleming**, suspects who were also sent to an asylum at Stone.)

On 30 September 1896, he wrote his will, at which time he was living at 11 Saint James Street, Clerkenwell Green. In 1899, he was again admitted to the asylum, this time discharged on 18 October. He was admitted to the Holborn Workhouse on 28 May 1900, at which time he was living at 34 St John's Lane, Clerkenwell, and gave his occupation as a general labourer. On 1 June, he died of 'Broncho Pneumonia', leaving effects of £300 to his son, a grocer and provision dealer.

(Philip Sugden, 'Puckridge: A Cautionary Tale,' *Ripperana*, 3, January 1993 and *The Complete History of Jack the Ripper*; Shelden, Neal: *Annie Chapman, Jack the Ripper Victim. A Short Biography*.)

PURKISS, WALTER
Witness at **Mary Ann Nichols**' inquest.

Manager of Essex Wharf (demolished 1990 – *pictured p.425*), in Buck's Row, immediately opposite the murder site, where he lived with his wife, child and a servant. He and his wife occupied the second-floor front bedroom, where they retired about 11pm, or shortly thereafter on 29 September 1888. He awoke at various times during the night, especially between 1 and 3am. His wife had a very sleepless night and believed she was pacing the bedroom at the time when the murder must have taken place (*c.* 3.30am). Neither heard anything, although the night was unusually quiet.

In 1880, a Walter Purkiss living in Bucks Row was the victim of a burglary when George Harris stole some articles of clothing, for which crime he was sentenced to eight years imprisonment (*Daily News*, 3 March 1880). According to the 1881 Census, a carpenter/joiner named Walter Boyton Purkiss (*b. c.* 1855, Braintree, Essex), was living in New Cottage, Bucks Row, with his wife, Mary Ann Purkiss (*b. c.* 1856) and their children, Lillian Ellen B (*b. c.* 1877), Sydney Walter B (*b. c.* 1878) and Florence May (*b. c.* 1881). With them, lived a mother-in-law, Sophia Ballard (*b.* 1825).

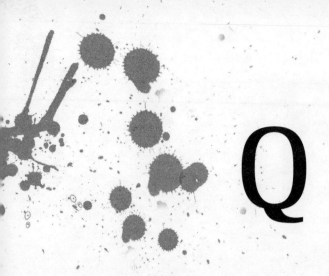

QUINN, EDWARD (*b. c.* 1853)

Suspect, charged on paltry evidence by a drinking companion.

On Saturday, 15 September 1888, Quinn, a labourer, fell in the street, cutting his face and hands badly, before going into a bar near Woolwich Arsenal. While he was there, a tall man treated him to beer and tobacco, and said, 'I mean to charge you with the Whitechapel murders,' pointing to the blood on Quinn's hands. Quinn assumed he was joking and left the bar with him, only to be turned in when they passed a police station, committed to the cells and held until the following Tuesday, when magistrates allowed him bail in his own recognisances. (Various newspapers, but see *The Daily Telegraph*, 18 September 1888)

QUINN, THOMAS

Name under which **Catherine Eddowes**' paramour, **Thomas Conway**, enlisted in the 18th Royal Irish Regiment and under which he drew his pension. This hindered the police from finding him immediately (*The Times*, 16 October 1888).

R

RACE, INSPECTOR WILLIAM NIXON (1855–1932)

Arrested **Thomas Cutbush**.

Born in Bishop Auckland, Country Durham, the second eldest of several children born to coal miner George Race and his wife Isabella; labourer in an iron works before joining the Metropolitan Police in 1880 (warrant no. 64541). Married Georgina Esther Gornall, 1875; two children, Arthur and Jane. Served on L or Lambeth Division for eight years from 1887; transferred to the Public Carriage Office, July 1895, then to H Division, December 1895. Suffered several reprimands, suspensions, transfers and attendant reductions in salary, culminating in a demotion to station sergeant; placed on the sick list suffering melancholia, December 1897, and invalided out, March 1898. He retired with his wife to 153 Clarendon Road, Notting Hill.

His illness was, no doubt, brought on by worry through the loss of his son, 21 years of age, and also through being treated indifferently in the Police Force. He had several times been recommended for promotion by his Superintendent, which his record richly deserved, but through some unknown reason he never heard anything further, a thing almost unprecedented in the service, and which worried him greatly.

(*The Police Review and Parade Gossip*, 12 August 1898)

With Chief Inspector **Chisholm** and Sgt. **McCarthy** investigated the South London stabbings, which culminated in the arrest of Thomas Cutbush. Has been identified with an unnamed police inspector who gave interviews to the *Morning Leader* (13, 15 February 1894), and was the source of information used by the *Sun* in its series of articles about Cutbush in February 1894 – *see* **Unidentified Inspector Who Believed the Ripper Had Been Caught**.

He was also engaged by the Treasury to prepare plans in the **Neil Cream** poisoning cases, being commended by the Defence and the Court were just some of the rewards and commendations he received.

See Bernard Brown, '*A Race With The Devil*', *Ripperologist*, June 2002.

RAINHAM TORSO

Suggested as possible Ripper victim (*see* **Severin Klosowski**).

The headless, legless, lower part of a woman's torso was found wrapped in canvas sacking, floating in the Thames, near the ferry at Rainham, Essex, on 11 May 1887. On 7 June, a thigh – also wrapped in canvas – was discovered in the river near Temple Stairs, and the upper part of the torso washed up in Battersea. Then, on 23 June, more body parts washed up near Battersea Park, and a week later the legs were found in the Regent's Canal, Chalk Farm. The woman was never identified. A comment on this case by Inspector **A. Hare** was attached to the file on **Rose Mylett**'s case (MEPO3/143, f K), but this was evidently to ascertain what precedents there were for the police sending doctors to examine a body without consulting the coroner.

The papers on the **Pinchin Street** torso contain various brief comments on the comparable Rainham and other Thames torso murders, culminating in **James Monro**'s final considered opinion that he was 'inclined to the belief that... [the Pinchin Street murder] is not the work of the Whitechapel Murderer, but of the hand which was concerned in the murders which are known as the Rainham mystery, the new Police buildings case [Whitehall mystery], and the recent case in which portion of a female body (afterwards identified [as **Elizabeth Jackson**]) were found in the Thames' (HO144/221/A49301K, f8).

The **Macnaghten memoranda** also compare the Pinchin Street and other torso murders with the Rainham mystery.

R. Michael Gordon (who makes a case against Klosowski in three books, *Alias Jack the Ripper: Beyond the Usual Whitechapel Suspects*, *American Murders of Jack the Ripper* and *The Thames Torso Murders of Victorian London*) notes Klosowski had come to England early in 1887 and speculates all the Thames torso murders were his handiwork, making the Rainham mystery the first 'Ripper' murder.

RASPUTIN, GRIGORI EFIMOVICH (1871–1916)

Alleged author of alleged unfinished manuscript, *Great Russian Criminals*, naming Ochrana (Czarist Secret Police) agent Dr **Alexander Pedachenko** as the Ripper. Russian monk, with increasing influence over the Tsarina from 1905 as his quasi-health healing offered the only effective treatment for her son's haemophilia. His supposed interference in state affairs was resented by the nobility, until a group of aristocrats murdered him. Subsequently, his sensational death and the assassins' over-heated defence of their actions gave him a legendary and undeserved reputation as a sinister, depraved and almost supernatural eminence grise.

William Le Queux claimed that the Kerensky government (July to November 1917) sent him two bundles of documents found among Rasputin's effects. At different times, he claimed one or the other comprised the unfinished manuscript in French, *Great Russian Criminals*. C.W. Shepherd, who ghosted three books for Le Queux, told the author Donald Rumbelow that he had once seen a large envelope 'plastered with seals and codes', which Le Queux told him contained the Russian material. This is the sole evidence for its physical existence.

Serious doubts about the Rasputin manuscript are raised by its alleged reliance on information from the Ochrana – an institution with which, according to its head, A.T. Vassil'ev, Rasputin had no connection; also, its alleged composition in French, a language apparently unknown to Rasputin (as Le Queux himself noted) and its subject, 'Great Russian Criminals', which Rasputin's daughter has assured Colin Wilson held no interest for her father. (*See also* **Hector Cairns**.)

REAL JACK THE RIPPER: THE SECRET OF PRISONER 1167, THE
See **The Secret of Prisoner 1167**.

RECORD, SGT. WILLIAM (1857–1932)
Police officer involved in investigation.

Prior to joining the Metropolitan Police in February 1877 (warrant no. 61234), he spent five years in the Navy. Was selected for 'special service' by Sir Howard Vincent, founder of the CID. Retired from the police, 1902. For the next 30 years worked as a security officer at Ascot and Goodwood race tracks. Committed suicide, following a diagnosis of cancer, in 1932.

Described in *Police Review* (24 October 1902) as 'one of five Detectives specially engaged from the outset in making enquiries in and out of London in connection with the series of Whitechapel outrages'.

He arrested **Joseph Isaacs** near Drury Lane in December 1888, was active in both the **Alice McKenzie** investigation and that into the death of **Frances Coles**.

(See *Ripperana*, 36, April 2001.)

REED, MR F.S.
Medical attendant, possibly responsible for exaggerated claims concerning the **Lusk kidney**. According to **Joseph Aarons**, members of the **Vigilance Committee** originally took the kidney to Dr **Frederick Wiles'** surgery at 56 Mile End Road, where in Wiles' absence his assistant, Reed, examined it. Reed pronounced it human and preserved it in spirits of wine, then took it on to **Dr Openshaw** at the London Hospital.

On his return, according to Aarons, Reed declared it was part of the left kidney of a woman accustomed to drinking, who had died at the time of the Mitre Square murder. Openshaw subsequently denied these details.

REEVES, JOHN SAUNDERS (b. c. 1865)

Witness at **Martha Tabram**'s inquest; discovered her body. A waterside labourer with a slight dark beard and moustache, and wearing earrings, he left his residence at 37 George Yard Buildings at 4.45am, on 7 August 1888, and found the body on the first-floor landing. He at once went to find a policeman and returned with **Police Constable Barrett**.

REFLECTIONS ON THE RIPPER: FOUR ACCOUNTS OF THE WHITECHAPEL MURDERS

Book by B.A. Rogers (self-published: B.A. Rogers, 1999). Ripper-related excerpts introduced by Rogers from *Scoundrels and Scallywags (And Some Honest Men)* (1929) by Tom Divall, *Lost London: The Memoirs of an East End Detective* (1934) by Benjamin Leeson, 'The Fiend of East London: Jack the Ripper' by F.A. Beaumont in *The Fifty Most Amazing Crimes of the Last 100 Years* (1936) and 'Can This Be Truth?' by William Boyle Hill in *A New Earth and a New Heaven* (1936). See **Echoes of the Ripper**, **Shadows of the Ripper**.

REID, INSPECTOR EDMUND JOHN JAMES (1846–1917)

Head of local CID during the Whitechapel murders. Joined the Metropolitan Police, 1872 (warrant no. 56100) after a varied career, including experience as a pastry-cook and ship's steward. Entered CID, 1874; promoted to sergeant in 1878, then detective inspector at Scotland Yard in 1884. Sent to organise J Division (Bethnal Green) CID, 1886; appointed to succeed **Frederick Abberline** as local inspector (head of CID) H Division (Whitechapel), 1888, where he remained until retirement as the longest-serving detective inspector in 1896.

He was described by the *Weekly Dispatch* (August 3 1896) as, 'one of the most remarkable men of the century,' and he reached professional standards in acting, singing and legerdemain. In the early 1880s, he made frequent balloon ascents, receiving a medal for going to a record height in 1883, and he featured as 'Detective Dier' in novels by Charles Gibbon (*See* **The Man Who Hunted Jack the Ripper**.)

He appeared at **Alice McKenzie**'s inquest to explain that he held a watching brief as coins found under the body were similar to those in **Annie Chapman**'s case. It has been noted, however, that he was on leave at the time of the Annie Chapman murder.

In 1896, he gave press interviews on his career, including references to the Ripper case. Then, on March 30 and April 6 1903, the *Morning Advertiser* published two letters from Reid following correspondence based on Abberline's suggestion that **Severin Klosowski** (**George Chapman**) was the Ripper. Reid believed there were nine Ripper murders, with **Frances Coles** being the last. He challenged the notion that the Ripper showed surgical expertise, declaring the mutilations nothing but, 'a number of slashes all over the body of the victim, even after the murderer knew his victim was dead.' Reid believed wrongly that, 'at no time was any part of the body missing.' He also believed there was evidence that the Ripper's knife was blunt and that the murderer had been dead for some years because that would be the consequence of his particular kind of mania, but he did not appear to have heard of the three suspects listed by **Major Arthur Griffiths** matching the three in the **Macnaghten memoranda**: **M.J. Druitt**, **Kosminski** and **Michael Ostrog**.

(*See* **The Man Who Hunted Jack the Ripper**.)

REVELATIONS OF THE TRUE RIPPER

Book by Vanessa A Hayes (Morrisville, North Carolina: Lulu, 2006).

Argues that Dr **Thomas Barnardo** was Jack the Ripper – he had medical training, he could move freely among police and prostitutes without arousing suspicion, he knew the East End well enough to make his escape through the warren of courts and alleys, and time spent in the US could have made him familiar with Americanisms such as 'Boss'. According to Ms Hayes, Barnardo had a 'pathological hatred of prostitutes' and a belief that any evil was acceptable if it achieved a greater good (thus the lives of a few drab prostitutes might be sacrificed, if this brought about social reforms that would save thousands of young lives).

Ms Hayes' claim that Dr Barnardo was picked up on the night of the double event is unsupported by any evidence and her claim that he had a 'pathological hatred of prostitutes' is not what his critics said at the time. In fact, he seems to have recognised prostitution as an economic and social exploitation of women rather than an embodiment of evil.

REWARDS FOR INFORMATION

Several individuals and organisations, including the Lord Mayor and Corporation of London, the Officers of the Tower Hamlets Militia, and **Samuel Montagu**, offered cash rewards for information leading to the apprehension and conviction of the Whitechapel Murderer. By October 1888 the total on offer had reached about £1,200 (say £42,000) at today's values), and Angela Burdett Coutts had promised a pension of a pound a week for life to any successful informant who secured a conviction.

The Government, however, did not offer a reward and this resulted in much opprobrium being levelled at Home Secretary **Henry Matthews** and the

Metropolitan Police Commissioner **Charles Warren**, although neither had any rigid objectionto the principle of rewards. Matthews was, on Civil Service advice, following a precedent laid down by his liberal predecessor Sir William Harcourt. Up to 1884 the Government had offered rewards in major criminal cases, usually of £100. This was discontinued following the commission of a crime and false denunciation of an individual solely for the purpose of collecting the reward money. The Government did, however, have the option of offering a reward in special cases which were, as a rule, those in which the beneficiary was not the person upon whose evidence a conviction was gained. The Whitechapel Murders were not such a case.

A rather large item of 'incidental expenditure in the apprehension and conviction of criminals' in the annual Metropolitan Police Accounts indicates that payment of small sums to professional underworld informers was, as always, a clandestine component of efficient detective work.

(see **Pardons**)

RICHARDSON, MRS AMELIA (*b.* 1822)

Mentioned in the press as 'Emilia' and in the 1891 Census as 'Ann', which also gives her grandson's name as James.

Witness at **Annie Chapman**'s inquest.

Widow of Thomas Richardson, whose business as a packing case manufacturer she continued to run from the cellar and rear yard of 29 Hanbury Street with the help of her son **John Richardson** and a man named Frances or John Tyler (press accounts differ). She also cared for her 14-year-old grandson, Thomas. A short woman, with a pale face and dark hair streaked with grey, she had rented the house for about 15 years, sub-letting all the rooms except the downstairs rear and the first-floor front room, which she occupied herself, and an attic room in which she charitably allowed an elderly woman to live rent-free. She was religious and accustomed to holding weekly prayer meetings in the downstairs rear room.

Her son, John Richardson, discovered the body of Annie Chapman on 8 September 1888, but she herself knew nothing of the murder until she heard a disturbance at about 6am and sent her grandson to investigate: 'I sent him down to see what was the matter as there was so much noise in the passage. He came back and said, "Oh, grandmother, there is a woman murdered!" I went down immediately and saw the body of the deceased lying in the yard. There was no one there at the time, but there were people in the passage. Soon afterwards a constable came and took possession of the place. As far as I know, the officer was the first to enter the yard.'

JOHN RICHARDSON

RICHARDSON, JOHN

Witness at **Annie Chapman**'s inquest, briefly suspected of the murders.

Described as a tall, stout man with dark brown hair, brown moustache and a very pale face, aged about 35. Son of Amelia Richardson, he lived at 2 John Street, Spitalfields, and worked in his mother's packing-case business and as a porter at Spitalfields Market.

About 4.45am, on 8 September 1888, he called in at 29 Hanbury Street on his way to work to check the cellar-door padlock. The cellar was broken into some months earlier and two saws and two hammers had been stolen, since which time he had taken to visiting the house on market mornings.

Richardson also occasionally checked the building to make sure prostitutes and their clients were not using it, having once found a man and a woman on the stairs. He saw nobody on the premises, or in the yard, where he sat on the second step and tried to trim a piece of loose leather off his boot with an old table knife. It was not quite light, he said, but claimed that he would have seen the body, had it been there.

He was not more than three minutes in the house and only learned of the murder when told of it at the market.

The inquest insisted on seeing his knife when it transpired that he had carried one and it proved impossible that it should have been used for the murder. A temporary sensation was caused by the discovery of his leather apron under the tap in the backyard as the '**Leather Apron**' scare was at its height and Richardson briefly came under suspicion.

Police tried to reconcile Richardson's testimony with **Dr George Bagster Phillips**' estimate that Annie Chapman must have been dead for at least two hours when he inspected the body (about 6.30am), claiming the back-door opening to the left obscured the body from Richardson's view as he sat on the steps. Contemporary photographs and drawings of the yard make this deduction unconvincing. The virtual certainty is that George Bagster Phillips' estimate was wrong.

RICHARDSON, JOSEPH HALL (c. 1857–1945)

Informant.

The son of a manufacturer and merchant named John Richardson, he was educated at Saint-Germain from 1870–73 and then worked in the Stock Exchange from 1873–80. He embarked on a career in journalism, briefly edited a publication in Surrey, and in 1881, joined the staff of the *Daily Telegraph*. In 1882, he married Harriet Eliza Bussey. Then, in 1906, he was appointed assistant editor of the *Daily Telegraph* and from 1923–28 was general manager of the *Daily Express*. He died at Orpington, Kent, in March 1945.

In *From the City to Fleet Street*, he wrote of the murder period: 'To me, personally, it was a time of great nightmares, as one never knew when there would be a repetition of the tragedies. It involved the most unpleasant work, long hours of vigil in the streets of the East End, contact with repulsive people, constantly "up against" the inventions and fictitious stories of competitors in journalism'.

Richardson was scathing of **Sir Charles Warren**'s erasure of the **Goulston Street graffiti**, quoted what he believed was a 'semi-official' dismisal by the police of **William Le Queux**'s theory on the grounds that it came from an 'unscrupulous liar' named **Johan Nideroest**, and published the **Liverpool Letter** and referred to a kind of photo-fit picture dummied up from his 'collection of criminal portraits', which he showed to a dairyman who had supposedly seen Jack the Ripper. To his astonishment, the dairyman declared that it resembled the man he had seen. The police dismissed this as having any resemblance and for the first time published an official description of the possible murderer, which Richardson claimed to be a tangible result of his effort.

Richardson claimed that over the years he got to know all the police involved

in the Ripper inquiry – in one or two cases actually writing their reminiscences, but never hearing any suggestion that the police knew who the murderer was; adding that **James Monro** was a great personal friend, who he was sure would have indicated, had the police known: 'I, therefore, remain of the conviction that the police never knew and are never likely to know who actually was the Whitechapel Murderer.'

(See also *Police!* co-authored with Charles Tempest Clarkson. London: Field and Tuer, 1889.)

RINGER, MATILDA (*b.* 1844)

Widow of Walter Ringer. Four children: Arthur (*b.* 1868), Harry (*b.* 1868), Edith (*b.* 1875) and Ada (*b.* 1877). Landlady of the Britannia public house on the corner of Dorset Street and Commercial Street, locally known as 'The Ringers' or 'Mrs Ringer's'. According to the *Penny Illustrated Paper* (17 November 1888), Mrs Ringer was known as 'Mother Ringer' and was, 'said to do a great deal of good in the neighbourhood.'

RIPPED FROM THE HEADLINES: BEING THE STORY OF JACK THE RIPPER AS REPORTED IN THE LONDON TIMES AND THE NEW YORK TIMES, 1888–1895

Book by Anon (Shreveort LA: Ramble House, 2005).

Tongue-in-cheek introduction is followed by consecutive newspaper reports from major publications on either side of the Atlantic, enabling quick and easy comparison or reportage. The reports appear to be lifted from the **Casebook: Jack the Ripper** website.

RIPPER AND THE ROYALS, THE

Book by Melvyn Fairclough (London: Duckworth, 1991; revised paperback edition, London: Duckworth, 1992; reissued London: Duckworth, 2002).

Retelling of **Joseph Sickert**'s claim that the murders were committed as part of a cover-up of his grandmother's alleged clandestine marriage to **Prince Albert Victor** (*cf. Jack the Ripper: The Final Solution*), but diaries allegedly written by Inspector **Abberline** provide the foundation for new claims implicating **Lord Randolph Churchill**, who allegedly employed **John Netley** and **Frederico Alberici** as the principal conspirators. Also, further allegations that Prince Albert Victor lived as a secret prisoner in Glamis Castle until the 1930s, a photograph purporting to be of the Prince, taken in 1910, being among the illustrations.

The diaries – three leatherbound volumes, two black with ruled pages, one maroon manufactured by Charles Letts & Co. as Diary for 1896 – were first mentioned in public in the *Evening Standard*, 21 April 1988. Claims they were available to, but unused by Stephen Knight lack substantiation and, prima facie, they are forgeries. Details about the victims appear to derive from and reproduce minor errors made in a magazine article ('Victims of Jack the Ripper', *True Detective*, January 1989) and Abberline's forename initials are reversed in a supposed signature.

The revised paperback includes photographs of Reg Hutchinson and his father, George, who is alleged to be the witness George Hutchinson. Document examiner Sue Iremonger expressed her opinion to Martin Fido (telephone conversation, 22 September 1993) that the signature of Reg Hutchinson's father was not in the same hand as the signature on witness **George Hutchinson**'s statement, although she did note the ten year gap between signatures and observed that they could change markedly.

RIPPERCAST

Podcast devoted to the discussion of all aspects of the Ripper case (http://www.casebook.org/podcast). Conceived and hosted by Jonathan Menges and launched in 2008, each podcast runs for at least an hour and features various authorities in a round table discussion, often with a guest.

RIPPER CODE, THE

Book by Thomas Toughill (Stroud, Gloucestershire: Sutton, 2008).

Toughill revealed his theory that the Ripper was **Frank Miles** in correspondence with Colin Wilson in the 1970s, while Wilson, in turn, made passing reference to Miles in his introduction to Donald Rumbelow's *The Complete Jack the Ripper* and discusses him at greater length in *Jack the Ripper: Summing Up and Verdict*. Toughill theorises that Miles was driven to commit the murders through a combination of the break-up of his relationship with Oscar Wilde, the decline of his popularity as an artist, and his syphilitic insanity. According to Toughill, Wilde knew that Miles was guilty of the murders and left clues to his guilt in his novel, *The Picture of Dorian Gray* (*see* **Jack the Ripper: Light Hearted Friend** for the theory that Lewis Carroll left literary clues that he was the Ripper).

A problem for the theory is that Miles was detained in Brislington Asylum, near Bristol, in December 1887, and was there throughout the whole period of the murders until his death in 1891. Toughill suggests Miles escaped, but provides no supportive evidence.

RIPPER DIARY: THE INSIDE STORY
Book by Seth Linder, Caroline Morrison and Keith Skinner (Stroud, Gloucestershire: Sutton, 2003).

Presents an account of the emergence and subsequent heated controversy surrounding the so-called **Maybrick Diary** that, in certain quarters, dominated Ripperian debate for about 10 years. It also includes a full account of the alleged **Maybrick watch**. Wherever possible, using documented sources and interviews, the authors chart the long and complicated saga in what *Casebook: Jack the Ripper* describes as, 'a near-perfect chronological summation of events.'

RIPPER FILE, THE
Book by **Elwyn Jones** and John Lloyd (London: Arthur Barker, 1975; paperback, London: Sphere, 1975).

Book accompanying still-to-be-bettered BBC TV drama-documentary, *Jack the Ripper*. Written by Elwyn Jones and fellow Welshman John Lloyd, a television scriptwriter for many successful series, including *Braden's Week, Comedy Playhouse* and *That's Life,* fictional police detectives Barlow and Watt investigate the crimes from the supposed standpoint of modern policemen. Interlinking speculations of Barlow and Watt present an uncritical dismissal of the police of 1888 as incompetent and lean heavily towards a mysterious and unproven wish to suggest Freemasons' involvement in the crimes. In general, however, the BBC research behind the scenes (by Paul Bonner, Leonard Lewis, Karen de Groot, Ian Sharp and Wendy Sturgess) was outstanding and the bulk of the book can be recommended as an excellent collection of abridged factual reports and statements pertaining to the case.

RIPPER FILE, THE
Book by Melvin Harris (London: W.H. Allen, 1989).

Not to be confused with the work of the same title by **Elwyn Jones** and John Lloyd (above), Melvin Harris's second contribution to the subject is largely a reconstruction of the Ripper crimes through extracts from the contemporary press.

RIPPER IN RAMSGATE, THE: THE WHITECHAPEL MURDERER AND A SEASIDE TOWN
Booklet by Christopher Scott (Ramsgate: Michaels Bookshop, 2008).

Considers some of the links between 'Jack the Ripper' and Ramsgate, touching on the lodger story, **Joseph Fleming** (Aaron Kosminski's brother who ran a boarding house for orthodox Jews) and **Walter Sickert**.

RIPPER LEGACY, THE
Book by Martin Howells (lead author) and Keith Skinner (London: Sidgwick and Jackson, 1987; paperback, London: Sphere Books, 1988).

Assuming **Montague John Druitt** to be homosexual, the authors postulate a complicated and largely speculative motive for the murders and suggest he may have been assassinated by high-placed Oxbridge associates to protect the establishment from the discovery that the Ripper was one of their number. Immensely readable, notably advancing an explanation of the alleged Australian document: *The East End Murderer – I Knew Him*.

RIPPER LETTERS
See **Jack the Ripper Letters**.

RIPPER M.D.
Book by Charles Cameron (Glendale, California: Exotica Fine Books, 1993; reprinted in the *Journal of the Whitechapel Society*, 5, December 2005).

100 copies were distributed at the launch party of Exotica Fine Books. The work reviews a Jack the Ripper novel and otherwise overviews the Royal Conspiracy and **William Gull** theories.

RIPPER NOTES
Journal.

Founded 1999. Edited successively by Christopher T. George (1999–2002), Christopher-Michael DiGrazia (2002–04), and Dan Norder (2004–). Handsome book-like 9.25 x 6in format, averaging 106–130 pages and distinguished for its generally high-quality content. Published quarterly until 2006, but sporadic since then.

RIPPER SUSPECT: THE SECRET LIVES OF MONTAGUE DRUITT
See **Montague Druitt: Portrait of a Contender**.

RIPPERANA: THE QUARTERLY JOURNAL OF RIPPEROLOGY

Founded in 1992 and edited by N.P. Warren, this was the first of the specialised Ripper journals. In recent years, the Ripper content has diminished and *Ripperana* is more or less a useful digest of true crime reports culled from various newspapers.

RIPPERATURE

Term for writing concerning Jack the Ripper. Coined by Richard Whittington-Egan in *Antiquarian Book Monthly*, May 1995.

RIPPEROLOGICAL PRESERVATION SOCIETY

Formed in 1997 under the aegis of **Casebook: Jack the Ripper**, the Society has discovered and published reprints of rare Ripper books, some of which have been made available online.

RIPPEROLOGIST

Journal.

Founded in December 1994 as the newsletter of the Cloak and Dagger Club, from which it separated in 2005. Edited successively by Mark Galloway, Paul Daniel, Paul Begg, Eduardo Zinna and Don Souden, with design and layout by Adam Wood, and by Jane Coram (since 2007). Originally published quarterly, it became a monthly e-journal in 2006.

RIPPEROLOGY: A STUDY OF THE WORLD'S FIRST SERIAL KILLER AND A LITERARY PHENOMENON (2006)

Book by Robin Odell, with an introduction by Donald Rumbelow (Kent, Ohio: Kent State University Press, 2006).

A critical and descriptive study of English-language Ripperature from 1888 (John Paul Bocock's reporting in, inter alia, the *Atlanta Gazette*) to 2004 (Chris Miles' *On the Trail of a Dead Man*). Odell describes seven phases: 1) 1888–1900, being the initial wave of journalism that followed the crimes; 2) 1900–25, when those involved in the investigations, be they policemen, journalists or other contemporaries, wrote of the crimes; 3) 1925–49, when sensational and factually shaky book-length 'solutions' were proposed; 4) 1950–75, the dawn of more responsible study; 5) 1975–90, when better documented studies began to appear; 6) 1990s, when Odell perceives an explosion of Ripper theories, and 7) the current theories. Odell provides a sober assessment of the key theories offered during these phases, lingering a little over the Macnaghten suspects.

RIPPEROLOGY AND RIPPEROLOGISTS

Terms coined by Colin Wilson in 1972 to describe expertise and experts on Jack the Ripper, which once had derogatory connotations.

RIPPEROLOGY: THE BEST OF RIPPEROLOGIST MAGAZINE

Book edited by Paul Begg (New York: Barnes and Noble, 2006 (hardback); London: Magpie Books, 2007 (paperback), 2007) .

Twenty-seven articles from the first 12 years of the magazine's existence. Contributions from Andy Aliffe, James A. Bailey, Paul Begg, Neil Bell, Jeffrey Bloomfield, Michael Conlon, Carmen Cumming, Perry Curtis Jnr., Martin Fido, Christopher T. George, Deborah McDonald, Karyo Magellan, Madeleine Muphy, Gerry Nixon, Robin Odell, Jon Ogan, Daniel Olsson, Andy and Sue Parlour, Ann Perry, Stepan Poberowski and Eduardo Zinna.

RIPPEROO

Journal.

Now defunct and wittily titled Australian journal, founded in 2002.

RISE OF SCOTLAND YARD, THE

Book by Douglas G. Browne (London: Harrap, 1956).

Claims that, '**Sir Melville Macnaghten** appears to identify the Ripper with the leader of a plot to assassinate Mr Balfour at the Irish Office' (*see* **Arthur Balfour** for discussion).

When the original author Ralph Strauss died, the book was completed by Douglas G. Browne, who acknowledges in his introduction, 'the generous help of the authorities at New Scotland Yard.' In five passages, the book uses words drawn directly from the Home Office and Scotland Yard Files, and not known to occur anywhere else. It follows that Browne, Strauss (or both) had access to the files prior to 1956, 20 years before any other researcher, and presumably found evidence for this statement in folios known to have gone missing before the National Archives put them on microfilm.

See also **Jack the Ripper's Knife**.

ROBERTS, CHIEF CONSTABLE WILLIAM ARTHUR (1840–1906)

Joined the Metropolitan Police in 1886. District superintendent, 1886; chief constable, 1887. Permitted to resign after his appearance in the Court of Bankruptcy in 1895.

Accompanied Chief Constables Howard and Monsell to inspect the interior of the Dorset Street murder site on 9 November (*Daily Telegraph,* 10 November 1888).

ROBINSON, HANNAH (1866–91)

Proposed as Ripper (**Severin Klosowski**) victim.

A well-dressed, well-behaved housemaid noted for thriftily saving her earnings, she worked for the minister of Trinity Church and his wife in Hewlette, Long Island. On Saturday, 2 August, she took her week's wages, saying she was going to visit her sister in New York and do some shopping. Her strangled body was later found on a building site near Glendale, Long Island.

Robinson's employer believed that she had been going to visit her ex-fiancé.

Since the only thing known about this man was his forename, Martin, the police never found him. R. Michael Gordon in *The American Murders of Jack the Ripper* compares her death by strangulation with that of **Rose Mylett** and speculates that her habitual state of comfortable solvency may mean that, despite her good reputation with her employers and being a former Sunday School teacher, she may have practised prostitution on the side. She had earlier had an illegitimate baby.

ROBINSON, DET. SGT. JOHN (1848–1928)

Detective (G Division), disguised in woman's dress as part of the Ripper investigation. Joined the Metropolitan Police in 1868 (warrant no. 50767). Retired, 1899.

On 9 October 1888, Sgt. Robinson, disguised in woman's clothing, and Det. Sgt. Mather, in ordinary dress, were summoned to the Gunmaker's Arms in Eyre Street, Clerkenwell. A number of local Italian residents believed they saw a man who looked like published descriptions of the Whitechapel Murderer behaving suspiciously with a woman. Accompanied by civilian Henry Doncaster and a number of Italians, Robinson and Mather followed the suspect to Phoenix Place.

There, Robinson was accosted by cab-washer William Jarvis, who asked him, 'What are you messing about here for?' Robinson took off his hat and declared that he was a police officer, whereupon Jarvis said, 'Oh, you are cats and frogs, are you?' and struck him violently, then proceeded to pull a knife and stab him in the face. Robinson hit Jarvis over the head with his truncheon, while James Phillips, another cab washer, came forward and kicked Robinson after stabbing Doncaster. All four men appeared with their faces bandaged when the Clerkenwell stipendiary magistrates remanded Jarvis and Phillips for trial (*Morning Advertiser*, 10 October 1888).

On Robinson's retirement, 11 years later, it was reported that he had seen Jack the Ripper approaching a woman one night. He saw him again the following night, this time wearing a false beard and, donning his woman's hat and cloak, followed the suspect and his prey, only to be stabbed by a man that he was convinced was Jack the Ripper.

It is often reported that detectives were disguised as women in the Ripper enquiry and this is the one recorded occasion known to the authors.

ROBINSON, PC LOUIS FREDERICK, 931 City (1865–1916)

Arrested **Catherine Eddowes**. First name sometimes given as 'Lewis'. Born Therfield, Hertfordshire, the son of gardener Edward Robinson and his wife, Ellen.

He was 5ft 9in tall, with hazel eyes, dark brown hair and birthmarks on his back and hip. Worked as a coachman for mail-order company, Messrs Copestake, Hughes, Crampton & Co., before joining the City of London Police on 9 December 1886 (warrant no. 5921). Twice reprimanded for drinking alcohol while on duty, once in January 1888 and again in August 1899. Married Edith Mary Taperell on 4 October 1910. Resigned (as PC3O3C Bishopsgate) on 1 February 1912. Died on 30 December 1916.

On duty in Aldgate High Street at 8.30pm, he saw a crowd gathered around a woman (Eddowes), who was drunk on the pavement outside no. 29. He stood her up and leaned her against the house shutters, but she slipped sideways. Asked her name, she made the reply, 'Nothing.' No one in particular appeared to be in her company when she was picked up, according to Robinson. With the assistance of Police Constable **George Simmons**, he took her to Bishopsgate Police Station.

(See Neil Bell and Robert Clack, 'City Beat: PC 931 Louis Robinson', *Ripperologist*, 102, May 2009.)

ROBINSON, PIERCE JOHN (*b.* 1854)
Suspect, cleared after investigation.

Tall, dark-bearded Robinson came under suspicion on 14 January 1889 when his business partner Richard Wingate, a baker of Church Street, Edgware Road, conveyed his misgivings to Scotland Yard C.I.D when Robinson wanted to sell his share of the business and go to America. He said that Robinson fell suspiciously quiet when conversation turned to the Whitechapel murders. Suspicions were further aroused when a letter posted to his mistress in Portslade, Miss Peters, was found to express a fear that he would be 'caught today'.

Since he had once lived in Mile End, had received some medical training, was known as a religious fanatic and had served a short prison sentence for bigamy, he fitted the profile tentatively ascribed to the Ripper by some investigators. He was decisively cleared when it was learned that he had been in Portslade with Miss Peters on the night of **Mary Jane Kelly**'s murder. (*See The Ultimate Jack the Ripper Sourcebook*.)

(The 1881 Census lists a Pearce [sic] J Robinson (29), described as a Baptist Missionary living with his family in Bethnal Green. The Thames Police Court Registers for 25 February 1888 records a Pearce [sic] John Robinson (38) committed for bigamy.)

ROCHA, JOACHIM DE (*b.* 1865)
Alleged suspect. Portuguese cattleman, advanced by **E.K. Larkins**.

ROMERO, TOMAS
Would-be witness. Wrote to **Lord Salisbury** saying that a man known to him had boasted of extracting organs from recently-dead people for anatomical studies. Further claimed to have killed a prostitute who annoyed him in 1880 or 1881. Romero

claimed to have saved prostitute Nelis Cherinton from his clutches and offered to show the man's London haunts to police (HO144/221/ A49301D, ff 83–96).

RONAN, KITTY (1860–1909)

Prostitute found murdered in the room formerly occupied by **Elizabeth Prater**.

Daughter of Andrew Ronan. Known locally as 'Little Kitty', she supplemented her income as an ironer in a local lodging-house and as a flower-seller by casual prostitution. Lived in a room at 12 Miller's Court – 'the first-floor front room' measuring 12 by 12ft 2in (testimony of PC Harry Woodley at the Old Bailey trial). It is claimed to have been the room formerly occupied by Elizabeth Prater.

Had for the previous five weeks lived in the room with Henry Bensted, who on 2 July 1909, discovered her on the bed, fully clothed, with her throat cut. Bensted went first to **John McCarthy**'s shop, where he met Jeremiah O'Callighan, the occupier of 13 Miller's Court, the room formerly occupied by **Mary Kelly**. He then reported the murder to the police and was accompanied back to the room by Inspector Thomas Travis and, in due course, by Detective Inspector **Wensley** and Divisional Surgeon **Percy John Clarke**, who thought Ronan had been first strangled and then had her throat cut.

On 19 July, Harold Hall confessed to police in Bristol that he had committed the murder after finding Kitty rifling through his pockets. The police accepted his confession and at Hall's trial, at the Old Bailey in September ,Wensley stated that he had provided details unreported in the press, such as there being no gas in the room and the location of the fireplace in relation to the bed. Ronan also had a penny in her hand, which was not reported – which Wensley thought corroborated Hall's claim that he had become enraged when he found her going through his pockets.

Hall, however, changed his plea to one of not guilty, claiming that his confession was bogus. Inspector Travis, noting there was no sign of a struggle, stated that he did not accept Hall's claim to have flown into a rage. Hall did not appear to know that Ronan had first been strangled for the position of her body looked as if she was preparing for casual intercourse (the implication being that she was improbably rifling Hall's pockets before sex had taken place and been paid for). Meanwhile, the market porter, Alfred Wilkins, who had previously identified Hall as a man he had seen with Ronan, retracted the identification, saying that he had been suffering from a severe hangover at the time and couldn't now be sure that Hall was the man he had seen.

Nevertheless, Hall was sentenced to death, but the death sentence does not appear to have been carried out and his fate is currently unknown.

(Andy Aliffe, 'Kit, Kitty, Kitten', *Ripperologist*, 21, February 1999)

RONEY, SARAH (*b. c.* 1868)

Believed she was accosted by the Ripper. Friend of **Mrs Paumier**.

Walking with two friends through Brushfield Street (Spitalfields Market) on Wednesday, 6 November, Sarah Roney was approached by a man who wanted one of the women – he didn't mind which – to come with him alone. They refused, and asked him what he had in the bag that he was carrying. 'Something the ladies don't like,' was his reply. They believed him to be the Ripper, and Mrs Paumier thought him to be the the man that she saw in Artillery Row on 8 November (*Manchester Guardian*, 10 November 1888).

The similarity of this tale to that told by **Sarah Lewis** and **Mrs Kennedy** marks the suspicion that fell on men who accosted young women incautiously during the Ripper scare.

ROOM ABOVE MARY KELLY'S

It is widely stated that **Elizabeth Prater** occupied the room above **Mary Kelly**'s, but whether or not she did so remains uncertain.

According to the *Daily Telegraph* (10 November 1888), 26 Dorset Street was a three-storey house with seven rooms, Elizabeth Prater occupying 'the first-floor front room...' and 'the couple in the room overhead [having] slept soundly without being awakened by scuffling in the room beneath them.' In its account of Kelly's inquest (13 November 1888), the same newspaper reported Prater as saying, 'I live at 20 Room, in Miller's-court, above the shed,' the shed being a reference to the downstairs front room, used for storing costermonger's barrows.

A description of the upstairs of 26 Dorset Street was given during the trial of Kate Marshall, who murdered her sister in the first-floor back room (directly above what had been Mary Kelly's room), which was separated from the first-floor front by a passage and a room (at the time of the murder used at night for lodgers with children), occupying a space of approximately 9ft.

See **Kitty Ronan**.

ROOTS, INSPECTOR THOMAS (1849–90)

A gunsmith and afterwards a baker before joining the Metropolitan Police in 1869 (warrant no. 51651).

Enjoyed a very distinguished career – was, 'a master in unravelling intricate frauds and was the terror of long-firm thieves.' With **Inspector Littlechild**, he had arrested famous conman William Kerr, who was involved in the scandal of bribing several senior detectives (*Pall Mall Gazette*, 4 November 1890). Died in service. His son, Reginald, who was born on 4 October 1888, was admitted to the Metropolitan and City Police Orphanage on his thirteenth birthday in 1901.

Sent to Durham in September in the company of Dr **George George Bagster Phillips** to investigate reports that the nature of **Jane Beadmore**'s murder suggested the Ripper had travelled to Tyneside. Also author of a report dated 26 December 1888, addressed to **Inspector Abberline** and giving details on **Robert Donston Stephenson**, whom he said he had known for 20 years.

ROSENFELD, MRS

Witness, who said she saw the bloodstained grapestalk near **Elizabeth Stride**'s hand. Sister of **Eva Harstein**.

'ROSY' (*fl.* 1888)

Spitalfields prostitute. Found sitting on a brick dustbin at the back of a yard, off Heneage Street, by Police Constable **Robert Spicer** on the night of 29–30 September 1888. She was accompanied by a 'Brixton Doctor', whom Spicer strongly suspected of being Jack the Ripper. (*Cf.* **'Dr Merchant'**.) Her receipt of a florin (10p) was exceptional, the usual fee being 4d–6d (2–2?p).

ROYAL RIPPER, THE

Book by Godfrey Kwok (privately published in 1972).

Apparently limited to 50 copies, the work was unknown until rediscovered by author Stewart Evans and it appears to be the first book published about **Dr Stowell** and the Royal Conspiracy theory.

RUFFLE, FRANK

Witness. Talking with **Mary Callaghan** and **Ellen Marks** in George Street, Spitalfields, on 21 November 1888, when the man accused of trying to cut **Annie Farmer**'s throat ran out of the building. Joined by the lodger Sullivan, Ruffle chased the man in the direction of Thrawl Street, but lost him near the Frying Pan public house, on the corner with Brick Lane (*Daily Telegraph*, 22 November 1888).

RUGGLES-BRISE, EVELYN JOHN (1857–1935)

Son of Colonel Sir Samuel Ruggles-Brise, MP. Educated at Eton and Oxford. Private secretary to four successive home secretaries, including **Henry Matthews**. Prisons commission chairman, 1895–1921; introduced the Borstal system. KCB, 1902.

As a civil servant and son of a civil servant, Ruggles-Brise was fully conversant with the mandarin view of tension between police and Home Office, which makes his sympathetic assessment of **Sir Charles Warren** all the more valuable. He was well informed on the Ripper case, seeing and annotating many of the documents sent to the Home Office.

(Obituary in *The Times*, 20 August, 1935. See also Shane Leslie, *Sir Evelyn Ruggles-Brise: A Memoir of the Founder of Borstal*. London: John Murray 1938.)

RUSSELL, POLICE SGT. ALFRED (*b.* 1861)

Joined the Metropolitan Police in 1881 (warrant no. 65198). Resigned to pension, 1906.

In an article in the *West Herts and Watford Observer* (18 January 1936), the retired officer recounts some of the incidents of his career, including 'being on duty in the East End of London many weeks during the Jack the Ripper crimes and at the funeral of one of the victims.'

The Times (2 December 1941) reported, 'Mr and Mrs Alfred Russell, of Watford, celebrated their diamond wedding yesterday. Mr Russell was in the Metropolitan Police and was on duty in the East End of London during the "Jack the Ripper" crimes.'

RUSSELL, FRANCIS CHARLES HASTINGS, 9TH DUKE OF BEDFORD (1819–91)

Alleged suspect mentioned by Philippe Jullian (1962).

Jullian's passing reference in his *Edouard VII* is unsupported by any evidence and has never been corroborated.

RUSSELL, GEORGE WILLIAM FRANCIS SACKVILLE, MARQUIS OF TAVISTOCK, SUBSEQUENTLY 10TH DUKE OF BEDFORD

Suggested as possible suspect, 2004.

In *The Jack the Ripper Suspects*, Stan Russo notes that Phillippe Jullian, in asserting that 'the Duke of Bedford' was a suspect, does not specify which particular Duke. The 9th Duke was 69 in 1888, while his son and heir, the Marquis of Tavistock, was 36 – which, Russo suggests, makes him in some ways a more plausible candidate.

RUSSEL, HERBRAND ARTHUR, 11th Duke of Bedford (1858–1940)

Grenadier Guardsman, became Colonel in 3rd Battalion, Bedfordshire Regiment, and held several positions, including Lord Lieutenant of Middlesex (1898–1926), President of the Zoological Society (1899) and Mayor of Holborn (1900). Described by his grandson, 13th Duke of Bedford (*A Silver-Plated Spoon*, World Books, 1959) as, 'a selfish, forbidding man, with a highly developed sense of public duty and ducal responsibility, he lived a cold, aloof existence, isolated from the outside world by a mass of servants, sycophants and an eleven-mile wall.'

Brief reference by Phillipe Jullian (*Edouard VII*, 1962) that some commentators had 'attributed the crimes committed in Whitechapel to the Duke of Bedford', however there is otherwise no known connection between the Duke and the crimes until he was advanced as co-conspirator in *Epiphany of the Whitechapel Murders*.

RUSSELL, MARY (*fl.* 1888)

Witness. Deputy of George Street lodging-house, who helped **Emma Elizabeth Smith** get to the London Hospital following the lethal assault on her. Also testified at her inquest (*The Times* 9 April 1888).

RYDER, ELIZABETH

Witness at **Alice McKenzie**'s inquest, who identified her body. Wife of cooper Richard John Ryder and deputy of the lodging-house at Gun Street, where McKenzie lived, she gave evidence on McKenzie's movements on the night of her death.

RYGATE, DR BROUGHAM ROBERT (*b. c.* 1853)

Succeeded his father, Dr J.J. Rygate, as medical officer of health and public analyst for St. George's-in-the East.

Attended the postmortem on **Elizabeth Stride** carried out by Drs **Blackwell** (dissecting) and **Baxter Phillips** (directing and keeping notes) – (*The Times*, 4 October 1888).

S

SADLER IN THE DOCK
AT THE THAMES POLICE COURT

2

S, MR

Theorist, cited by **Ernest Crawford** as suspecting the Jesuits of instigating the murders.

SADLER, JAMES THOMAS (*b.* 1838)

Suspected by police of the murder of **Frances Coles**. Briefly, a Ripper suspect.

Born to James Meal Sadler, a head clerk in a solicitor's practice in Lincoln's Inn Fields, and his wife, Mary. His father died from consumption in 1841 (interview with his mother, *Daily Telegraph*, 20 February 1891). Lived for a while in Jubilee Street, in the East End, and was educated at Primrose School. After a brief period of employment as a clerk in the London Docks, he went to sea. Married Sarah Maria Chapman at St John's Church, Clapham, in 1876. They already had a daughter, Ruth (*b.* 1873) and would have two further children: Daisy (*b.* 1880) and Primrose (*b.* 1884).

Worked as hackney carriage driver, Elephant and Castle, until *c.* 1878, when he moved to Poplar and worked as an omnibus conductor. At this time threatened wife Sarah with a pocket-knife and, according to landlady Rose Moriarty, with a dagger-shaped knife. Subsequently moved to Kennington, where he opened a greengrocer's shop that failed. A four-month residence in Bethnal

Green is known, but at present we have no further information until December 1887, when he started work at Torr's Tea Warehouse, Houndsditch, and apparently lived, or had been living in South London.

Mrs Sadler later said that because he disliked crossing London Bridge, they moved to Buck's Row, Whitechapel (she also gave detailed descriptions of their fellow-residents). The police could not confirm this: they found that Sadler had rented a room in Commercial Road in 1887, where his wife joined him, and from which they ultimately went to nearby Johnson Street, where the marriage collapsed on 2 August 1888 and Mrs Sadler went to live with her mother in Chatham. From 1889, he visited her occasionally in Chatham, and in 1891, she made complaints to the police that he was threatening her.

Between 1888 and 1891, he found employment as a merchant seaman and produced 36 discharge papers when he was arrested in 1891, showing that he had been of good conduct when at sea. On 11 February 1891, he was paid off as a fireman on the *Fez* at London Docks.

He picked up Frances Coles in the Princess Alice in Commercial Street that night and spent the night with her. The following afternoon, Sadler paid for Frances to buy herself a secondhand crêpe bonnet at a shop in Baker's Row. She kept her old bonnet, pinned under her dress. The two continued drinking in various pubs until Sadler was mugged by a woman in a red shawl, and some men who came and kicked him, when she had knocked him down in Thrawl Street between 5 and 6pm. To his disgust, Frances did nothing to help him and so they parted.

He turned up at her lodging-house, 8 White's Row, at 11.30pm and asked if she had the money for a bed. When she said that she hadn't, he asked Sarah Fleming, the landlady, if he could stay overnight on the strength of wages coming to him the next day, but she refused. Samuel Harris witnessed his appearance in and departure from the lodging-house.

Shortly after 1am, he turned up at the Victoria Lodging House in Upper Smithfield and asked the deputy, John Johnson, whether he might have a bed, although he had no money. Johnson refused, and Sadler cursed him and went on his way.

At 1.15am, **PC Bogan** found him lying in the entrance gate to London Dock. Sadler asked to be admitted to the dock to return to his ship, but Bogan told him that he was too drunk. When two dockworkers (John Dooley and – Harvey) came out of the dock, Sadler abused them and started hitting them. Dooley said he would, 'give him something; if the policeman were not present,' whereupon Bogan moved away from the dock gates and left. Dooley and Harvey then knocked Sadler down, hitting his head against a gate as he fell. At 1.45am, Sadler staggered away and went to a lodging-house called Melbourne Chambers, where he saw the landlord, George Peakall, in the kitchen and asked him for a bed. Peakall refused, but advised him to take the nasty cut on his head to the London Hospital.

Just before 2am, Sadler approached **Police Sergeant Wesley Edwards** on the Mint Pavement and complained about the assault made on him at the dock gates. They were joined by PC Edward Hyde as the Tower clock chimed 2am, and shortly thereafter PC Bogan also joined them. Frederick Smith observed most of this meeting.

Fifteen minutes later, Frances Coles' body was found by **PC Ernest Thompson** in Swallow Gardens. Sadler's precise whereabouts at that time are unknown, but he had been only a few hundred yards from the murder site when seen by Edwards, Hyde, Bogan and Smith.

At 3am, he appeared at the White's Row lodging-house again, where Sarah Fleming refused to admit him. He called her a hard-hearted woman and failed to mention this incident in his subsequent statement to the police.

Then, at about 3.30am, he was halfway along the Whitechapel Road, staggering towards the London Hospital, when he was stopped and questioned by a young policeman, PC Arthur Sharp, 522 J. Sadler claimed to have been attacked with a knife and the policeman searched him, but found that he himself was not carrying one. Sadler claimed his shipmates, Matt Curley and Frederick Bowen, would testify that he never carried one.

Thereafter, Sadler promised to visit the hospital, but either he didn't immediately go there, or PC Sharp's times were wrong because Joseph Richards, manager of a coffee shop at 19 Whitechapel Road, said that Sadler turned up at his establishment at about 4.05am and asked for a cup of coffee, which he had no money to pay for. Richards turned him out of the shop at about 4.15.

Following this, Sadler went to the London Hospital, where night porter Wiliam Fewell tended his scalp and a small cut over the eye. Sadler claimed to have been robbed of 7s. or 8s. and a watch, and Fewell let him sleep on a sofa for an hour and a half, and gave him a penny when he went off-duty. This incident cannot be precisely timed, as it was suggested that he arrived at the hospital at about 5am, which would mean that he left about 7.30. But around 6am, he was back at the Victoria Lodging House, begging for ha'pence and/or apologising to John Johnson for his conduct during the night. Then, at 6.30, he was in a coffee house at 73 Whitechapel Road, where waiter Charles Littlewood gave him a cup of cocoa, noticed blood on his wrist and that he smelt as if he had just received medical attention, and refused him a second cup, believing him to be drunk. At 7.30, the manager, Stephen Longhurst, saw him reading a paper in the shop and exchanged a few words. Sadler left at 8.30am.

Two different accounts were given of his actions at 10.30. According to an elderly sailor named **Duncan Campbell**, Sadler came to the Sailors' Home in Well Street and sold him a clasp knife for a shilling and a bit of tobacco: an incident witnessed by seaman Thomas Johnson. Campbell later pawned the knife for 6d at Thomas Robinson's Marine store in Dock Street, and that evening went to Leman Street Police Station and described the incident. The police took him to a gas-lit cellar where, despite his bad eyesight and the poor lighting, he picked out Sadler from a semi-circle of about 15 men, saying he would recognise him anywhere by the cut over his eye. Subsequently, Johnson also identified Sadler by the cut and his beard, and the police optimistically called in Mrs Moriarty, the Poplar landlady, to see whether the clasp knife was the one with which Sadler had threatened his wife 10 years earlier. She was unable to identify it.

Sadler vigorously denied ever having possessed such a knife, let alone sold it to Campbell, and Edward Gerard Delaforce (or Edward Delaforce Gray, sources vary), the Deputy Superintendent of Tower Hill Shipping Office, stated that in fact Sadler came to the office at 10.30 to receive wages of £4.15s.1d that he was owed. Delaforce noticed blood on the document that Sadler produced to prove his claim and he explained that he had been knocked about by 'some hags in Thrawl Street' and robbed of a watch worth £2.10s.

After this, Sadler went back to the Victoria Lodging House (also known as Dann's), and stayed there for the remainder of the day, going out only to visit the Phoenix, 12 doors away, and to return an empty whisky bottle to the Swan in Whitechapel.

The following day, Samuel Harris – who had seen Sadler speak to Coles in a lodging-house in Thrawl Street – went to the police when he heard about the murder and identified Coles' body in the mortuary. Acting on Harris's information, **Detective Sergeant John Don** and **Detective Constable Gill** searched dockland pubs and lodging-houses, and found Sadler in the Phoenix. He told them: 'I expected this,' and subsequently, as they took him to Leman Street Police Station: 'I am a married man and this will part me and my wife. You know what sailors are: I used her for my purpose, for I have known Frances for some years. I admit I was with her, but I have a clean bill of health and can account for my time. I have not disguised myself in any way, and if you could not find me, the detectives in London are no good. I bought the hat she was wearing and she pinned the old one under her dress. I had a row with her because she saw me knocked about and I think it was through her.' At Leman Street, **Chief Inspector Swanson** questioned him, assuring him, however, that he was not charged with the murder.

Nevertheless, on Sunday, 15 September, **Inspector Henry Moore** charged Sadler with the murder of Frances Coles and searched him, finding a purse with £2.17s.4d, some lottery tickets, 36 seaman's discharges, a wages account, some loose tobacco and a postal order for £2. Sadler remarked, 'The old man has made a mistake about the knife. He never saw me before.'

It is also seems that the police suspected him of having committed all the Jack the Ripper murders; it is generally accepted that the police confronted Sadler with **Joseph Lawende,** although the latter is not named (*Daily Telegraph*, 18 February 1891).

Sadler managed to pull himself together and at the inquest was represented by H.W. Lawless, appointed by solicitors Messrs Wilson and Wallace, who had been engaged by the Stokers' Union, of which Sadler was a member. Witnesses were presented, who as far as was possible confirmed Sadler's account of his movements on the night of 12–13 February. On Saturday, 28 February 1891, Coroner Wynne Baxter concluded the inquest into the death of Frances Coles and gave a very full and able summing up. The jury returned a verdict of murder by person or persons unknown and Sadler was exonerated.

On Monday, 2 March, the Director of Public Prosecutions wrote to Sadler's solicitors informing them that it was not intended to proceed with the prosecution and, on Tuesday, 3 March at the Thames Police Court Treasury Counsel, stated that after careful consideration of 'the evidence given in the course of the inquiry before the coroner, as well as the most able summing up to the jury impanelled before him, and having regard to the verdict returned by that jury, after a patient and exhaustive inquiry, I do not propose, on the materials at present in our possession, to proceed further with this prosecution.' Amid cheers from the crowd outside, Sadler left the court in a cab, accompanied by his solicitor and a representative of the *Star* newspaper.

Sadler's health broke down soon after his release, which Sadler attributed to his poor treatment at the hands of the police, who he felt had tried to fit him up, even alleging that Duncan Campbell had been in their pay. Sadler also said that his solicitors, Messrs. Wilson and Wallace, were taking proceedings against about halfadozen newspapers which had published a 'villainous, lying, and scandalous socalled interview with my wife', starting with the *Daily Telegraph*, the action apparently being financed by *The Star* (*East London Observer*, 28 March 1891) According to James Moffatt, a retired pensioner who lodged with the Sadlers in Streatham from mid-May, Sadler received money from a number of newspapers. Sadler used this money to stock a chandler's (grocer's) shop in Lower Streatham, into which he and Sarah moved in May.

Perhaps celebrating his good fortune, Sadler was arrested for drunkenness in Maidenhead and sentenced to seven days with hard labour (Hull *Daily Mail*, May 1891). The shop apparently did a good trade – in January 1892, Sergeant Boswell reported that their takings averaged £2.10s a day. Nonetheless, relations between Sadler and his wife were not good. Boswell was investigating complaints made by Sarah against James in December 1891. Moffatt said Sadler's language to her was worse than any he had heard when at sea; that Sadler threatened to kill Sarah and the only reason he could discern was that Sadler accused Sarah of not helping him in the shop.

In March, the accusations of marital violence were renewed, with the further charge that Sadler had forced his wife to stay in the house, taking particular exception to the idea of her going to church or chapel. Then, in May, he was bound over in his own recognisances at Lambeth Magistrates Court. In January 1893, he left the marital home and took up lodgings in Camberwell.

Nothing further is known of him.

SAGAR, DET. CON. ROBERT (1852–1924)

Reported as describing the watch on a suspect in his apparently unpublished memoirs.

Born Simonstone, Lincolnshire, son of Robert and Sarah Sagar of Old Hall Farm. Educated at Whalley Grammar School and practised as assistant to Dr Badeley of Whalley. Medical training at St Bartholomew's Hospital (1871–78). He shared lodgings in Bartholomew Close with a 'celebrated City detective' called Potts and developed an interest in criminology. This led to his giving evidence for the prosecution at the City Police Courts and the Old Bailey so frequently that Sir

James Fraser suggested he should accept a handsome cheque for services rendered or join the police.

In fact, Sagar joined the City Police in 1880. Apparently, he never walked the beat or wore a uniform, although he was only gazetted detective constable in 1884. In 1888, he became sergeant, then detective sergeant (1889) and detective inspector (1890). Retired to Brighton, 1905, and lived there for 15 years before a fall in the street broke down his health. **Major Henry Smith** wrote, 'a better or more intelligent officer than Robert Sagar I never had under my command.'

City Press (7 January 1905) reported on his retirement:

His professional association with the terrible atrocities which were perpetuated some years ago in the East End by the so-styled 'Jack the Ripper' was a very close one. Indeed, M. Sagar knows as much about those crimes, which terrified the Metropolis, as any detective in London. He was deputed to represent the City police force in conference with the detective heads of the Metropolitan force nightly at Leman Street Police Station during the period covered by those ghastly murders. Much has been said and written – and even more conjectured – upon the subject of the 'Jack-the-Ripper' murders. It has been asserted that the murderer fled to the Continent, where he perpetrated similar hideous crimes, but that is not the case. The police realised, as also did the public, that the crimes were those of a madman and suspicion fell upon a man who, without a doubt, was the murderer. Identification being impossible, he could not be charged. He was, however, placed in a lunatic asylum and the series of atrocities came to an end.

Burnley News, 17 December 1924, wrote:

It is stated that it was his theory of the notorious Jack the Ripper crimes that led to the cessation of these outrages.

In *Reynolds News*, 15 September 1946, Justin Atholl wrote:

Inspector Robert Sagar, who died in 1924, played a leading part in the Ripper Investigations. In his memoirs he said: 'We had good reason to suspect a man who worked in Butchers' Row, Aldgate. We watched him carefully. There was no doubt that this man was insane – and after a time his friends thought it advisable to have him removed to a private asylum. After he was removed, there were no more Ripper atrocities.'

Sagar's obituary in the *Brighton and Hove Herald*, 6 December 1924, ascribed the same opinion to him, without mentioning memoirs. To date, the authors have not succeeded in tracing these memoirs. (*See* **David Cohen**, **Aaron Kosminski**, **Swanson marginalia**.)

SALISBURY, MARQUIS OF, RT. HON. ROBERT CECIL (1830–1903)
Prime minister, 1886–92.

Not directly involved in Ripper investigation, though his determination to retain his only Catholic cabinet minister and avoid a risky by-election forced **Henry Matthews** to remain home secretary, and gave political urgency to the enquiry. He came in for fairly severe criticism in the press for retaining Matthews. Over time, even **Queen Victoria** expressed her dissatisfaction with Matthews and Salisbury wrote to her, on 20 July 1890, that he 'entirely shares your Majesty's wish to transfer Mr. Matthews to another sphere of usefulness.'

Salisbury was accused by **Joseph Sickert** and **Stephen Knight** of promoting Freemasons' conspiracy to murder **Mary Jane Kelly**. In fact, he was not a Freemason.

Knight and **Jean Overton Fuller** both claim Salisbury visited Walter Sickert's studio and silently paid him £500 for an inferior painting – which, they say, was a bribe to enforce his silence over the conspiracy. However, in *Noble Essences* (London: MacMillan, 1950), Osbert Sitwell describes Sickert as telling the story about Antoine de Vallon and not himself. The painting was a commissioned family portrait and Salisbury's silent payment was evidence of his disgust at the quality of the finished work, not of any form of bribery.

SANDERS, JOHN WILLIAM SMITH (1862–1901)
Suspect. Son of an Indian Army surgeon (*d.* 1867). Entered the London Hospital as student, 1879. Out-patient dresser, 1880–1. At this time he was living with his mother, Laura Tucker Sanders, at 20 Abercorn Place, Maida Vale.

Early in 1881, hospital records note: 'Became ill and was placed in an Asylum. Away with Dr Swete [?].' The hospital examination book records that Sanders, 'Retired because of ill-health'. If the name 'Swete' is correctly transcribed, this would appear to be Dr Edward Horatio Walter Swete of Worcester: the only Dr Swete in the Medical Directories of the time. Medical certificates issued in February 1887 show that Sanders' condition had worsened to the point that he was subject to attacks of violence; he also made unprovoked assaults on friends and tyrannised his household, although he had previously been of a shy and retiring nature.

He was placed in an asylum in West Malling, Kent, in 1887, and then in Holloway Asylum, Virginia Waters, where he is identified by the initials 'JWSS' in the 1891 Census. His occupation is stated as medical student, but his age is given as 29 and his birthplace as Glasgow. An oral tradition recorded in 1990 named a room in the basement 'Jack the Ripper's room' (N.P. Warren, 'The Asylum at Ascot', *Ripperana*, July 1992.) In 1899, Sanders was transferred to Heavitree Asylum, Exeter, where he remained until his death. His death certificate inexplicably describes him as 'Medical Student of Barnsley'.

On 19 October 1888, **Chief Inspector Swanson** supplied reports on the murders for transmission to the Home Office. The report on **Annie Chapman** included the remark, 'Enquiries were also made to trace three insane medical students who had attended London Hospital. Result, two traced, one gone abroad' (*Cf.* **Major Henry Smith**). An undated Home Office memo of about 27 October 1888 runs: 'Please see Mr Wortley's memo on **Sir Charles Warren**'s letter. Shall the police be asked at the same time for report as to what has become of the 3rd insane Medical Student from the London Hospital about whom (under the name of Dr –) there is a good deal of gossip in circulation' [Dash in original].

Two days later, the Home Office made the request, writing to Warren: 'Reference is made to three insane medical students, and it is stated that two have been traced and that one has gone abroad. Mr Matthews would be glad to be informed of the date when the third student went abroad and whether any further enquiry has been made about him.'

Warren's reply quoted a report sent in by **Inspector Abberline**: 'I have to state that searching enquiries were made by an officer in Aberdeen Place [sic], St John's Wood, the last known address of the insane medical student named "John Sanders", but the only information that could be obtained was that a lady named Sanders did reside with her son at no. 20, but left that address to go abroad some two years ago.'

Since Laura Tucker Sanders continued to be listed as the occupant of 20 Abercorn Place (evidently the address mistranscribed by Abberline) and John was in an asylum in England, presumably the neighbours were underinformed about the family's misfortunes.

The 'good deal of gossip in circulation' about Sanders is not known to have percolated to the press. Some garbling of Sanders may lie behind the frequent suggestions that Scotland Yard believed the Ripper to be a medical student (*see* **Ostrog, Sergeant Stephen White**), apparently sometimes confusing him with **M.J. Druitt** in the suggestion that he drowned in the Thames.

SANDERS, DR JOHN WILLIAM (1859–89)

Tentatively proposed suspect.

MB, 1880; FRCS, 1884; Dip. Pub. Health, 1887. Member of the British Gynaecological Society; Surgeon to St John's Ambulance Brigade. Medical Superintendent at Croydon Fever Hospital, the Bethnal Green Infirmary and, at the time of his death, St George's-in-the-East Infirmary. Died under anaesthetic in January 1889 of heart failure. *The East London Advertiser* (23 February 1889) reported 'The sudden death of the late Dr. Saunders, *[sic]* the medical officer of the St.George's East Infirmary, was hushed up for some unknown reason, and his place filled by the quiet appointment of Dr.Harris.'

It has been suggested that noting his surgical and gynecological skill, and time of death, might have led police to confuse him with John William Smith Sanders (Jon Ogan, *Ripperana,* summer 1993).

SANDERSON, JOHN
Suspect, described by sea cook John Long as reported in the *Galveston Daily News,* 6 December 1897.

According to Long, Sanderson was on the crew of the bark *Annie Laurie,* sailing from Shields, England to Iquique, Chile, some years prior to 1897. Early in the voyage, Sanderson was taken ill and, on becoming delirious and violent, was put ashore at Iquique and sent to hospital. Soon afterwards, Long became ill and was hospitalised in the bunk next to Sanderson, who then confessed to him and a priest that he was the Ripper. He said he was the son of a surgeon and knew how to handle a knife. One night in Whitechapel he met a woman, then killed and mutilated her in a dark alley. Developing a taste for such murders, he acquired a confederate and the two wore butchers' smocks so their blood stains seemed natural. Subsequently, he worked on a farm in the country, before returning to the sea and signing on the *Annie Laurie.*

The reporter who took down the story doubted Long's veracity when he begged for money.

(*Cf.* the comparable case of **John Anderson**; also, the **Malay Sea Cook**.)

SAUCY JACK: THE ELUSIVE RIPPER
Book by Paul Woods and Gavin Baddeley. Hersham, Surrey: Ian Allen, 2010.

'SAUCY JACKY' POSTCARD
The 'Saucy Jacky' postcard, apparently in a cruder and more rushed form of the same handwriting as the 'Dear Boss' letter read:

> I was not codding dear old Boss when I gave you the tip youll hear about saucy Jackys work tomorrow double event this time number one squealed a bit couldnt finish straight off. had not time to get ears for police thanks for keeping last letter back till I got to work again.
> Jack the Ripper

It was posted to the Central News Agency on 1 October, and like the 'Dear Boss' letter, was forwarded to the police. The repetition of the word 'boss' and the reference to the promise in the letter to cut off the next victim's ears suggested that they came from the same source and that it had been posted before news of the double murders.

Its present whereabouts, if it has survived, is unknown and its appearance is known to us from facsimiles made at the time.

See **Letters** for Further Discussion.

SAUNDERS, DR WILLIAM SEDGWICK (1824-1901)

Witness at **Catherine Eddowes**' inquest. Medical Officer of Health and Public Analyst, City of London.

Born in 1824, at Compton Gifford, near Tavistock. MRCS (St Thomas's Hospital), 1846; MD, Castleton Medical College (USA). In 1849, he joined the Army as assistant-surgeon in the Royal Fusilliers, serving in the West Indies and North America. On his return to the UK, he was appointed medical officer at the military prison at Fort Clarence, Rochester. Thereafter resigned his commission and began private practice. Succeeded Dr Lethaby as medical officer for the City in 1874. Author of numerous papers. His obituary was published in *The Times*, 19 January 1901.

At Eddowes' inquest, Saunders said that he had found no trace of poison in his analysis of the contents of the stomach. He attended the postmortem at Golden Lane Mortuary and agreed with Dr **Sequeira** and **Dr Gordon Brown** that the murderer did not possess any anatomical skill, nor, in his opinion, had he any designs on a particular organ. His stated concurrence with Dr Brown is curious since Brown, though declining to accept the coroner's invitation to ascribe 'skill' to the murderer, consistently asserted that he thought the murderer displayed 'anatomical knowledge' and apparently thought this had been employed to locate the missing kidney.

Following the publicity given to the **Lusk kidney**, with the misinformation that it was a woman's 'ginny' kidney, reported in the press as emanating from **Dr Openshaw** (*cf.* **F. Reed**), Saunders told the *Evening News*: 'It is a pity that some people have not the courage to say they don't know. You may take it that there is no difference between the male and female kidney. You may take it that the right kidney of the woman Eddowes was perfectly normal in its structure and healthy, and by parity of reasoning you would not get much disease in the left. The liver was healthy and gave no indication that the woman drank. Taking the discovery of half a kidney and supposing it to be human, my opinion is that it was a student's antic. It is quite possible for any student to obtain a kidney for this purpose.'

(However, *see also* **Dr Gordon Brown** for signs of Bright's Disease in the right kidney.)

In 1972, Mr A.L. Lee of Torquay wrote to Colin Wilson that his father had worked in the Golden Lane Mortuary under Saunders' direction. (He had misheard or misremembered his forename as 'Cedric'.) A **Dr Stanley** had been a close friend of Saunders, and frequently visited him at the mortuary, until one day he remarked in Mr Lee senior's hearing, 'The cows have got my son! I'll get even with them.' Shortly afterwards, the murders started and subsequently, Saunders told Mr Lee senior, 'Yes, he was Jack the Ripper.'

Prima facie, this is confirmation of the existence of 'Dr Stanley', though puzzling that Leonard Matters should have indicated the made up the name to conceal the identity of the suspect. Noting the possibility that Stanley was the doctor's forename, however, we must also observe that Mr A.L. Lee further recalled having read an article in the *People* in the 1920s naming Dr Stanley – probably the piece Matters had written, and which elicited his second witness to the doctor's existence (Mrs North).

SAVAGE, DR (*fl.* 1888)

Theorist, who proposed in *Fortnightly Review* that it was 'going too far' to suggest that the murderer was a medical man (as seemed to be implied by **Dr George Bagster Phillips**, coroner **Wynne Baxter** and the *Lancet*). Savage's article, 'Homicidal Mania', suggested he might have been a butcher. (Cited in the *Star*, 29 September 1888.)

SCHWARTZ, ISRAEL

Witness (possibly **Anderson**'s witness) to an assault on **Elizabeth Stride**. Immigrant of Hungarian, probably Jewish, extraction. Resident of 22 Ellen Street (which crosses Berner Street). In appearance, Semitic and thespian. Possibly Israel Schwartz, married with two children, of 22 Samuel Street, in the 1891 Census. On 30 September 1888, he gave information to the Metropolitan Police that was recorded on file by **Chief Inspector Swanson**:

> 12.45 a.m. 30th Israel Schwartz of 22 Helen Street [*sc.* Ellen Street], Backchurch Lane, stated that at this hour, on turning into Berner Street from Commercial Street [*sc.* Road] and having got as far as the gateway where the murder was committed, he saw a man stop and speak to a woman, who was standing in the gateway. The man tried to pull the woman into the street, but he turned her round and threw her down on the footway and the woman screamed three times, but not very loudly. On crossing to the opposite side of the street, he saw a second man standing lighting his pipe. The man who threw the woman down called out, apparently to the man on the opposite side of the road, 'Lipski', and then Schwartz walked away, but finding that he was followed by the second man, he ran so far as the railway arch, but the man did not follow so far.
>
> Schwartz cannot say whether the two men were together or known to each other. Upon being taken to the Mortuary Schwartz identified the body as that of the woman he had seen. He thus describes the first man, who threw the woman down: age, about 30; ht, 5ft 5in[s]; comp., fair; hair, dark; small brown moustache, full face, broad shouldered; dress, dark jacket and trousers, black cap with peak, and nothing in his hands.
>
> Second man: age, 35; ht., 5ft 11 in[s]; comp., fresh; hair, light brown; dress, dark overcoat, old black hard felt hat, wide brim; had a clay pipe in his hand.

Swanson's report goes on to observe:

> If Schwartz is to be believed, and the police report of his statement casts no doubt on it, it follows – if they [Schwartz and Police Constable **William Smith**] are describing different men that the man Schwartz saw and described is the more probable of the two to be the murderer.

He points out, however, that 15 minutes separated the incident witnessed by Schwartz and the finding of the body – ample time for Stride to have escaped and accosted, or been accosted, by her murderer.

Schwartz was barely noticed in the press: the *Manchester Guardian* of 2 October, for example, saying, 'During the day all sorts of stories were brought to the police. Another story was to the effect that a man of light complexion had been struggling with the woman Stride in Berner Street and that he threw her down, but it being thought that it was a man and wife quarrelling nobody interfered with them.'

On 1 October, the *Star* published an interview with Schwartz – the only detailed account of his story known outside the Home Office Files:

Information which may be important was given to the Leman Street police yesterday by an Hungarian concerning this murder. The foreigner was well dressed, and had the appearance of being in the theatrical line. He could not speak a word of English, but came to the police station accompanied by a friend, who acted as interpreter. He gave his name and address, but the police have not disclosed them. A *Star* man, however, got wind of his call, and ran him to earth in Backchurch Lane. The reporter's Hungarian was quite as imperfect as the foreigner's English, but an interpreter was at hand, and the man's story was retold just as he had given it to the police. It is, in fact, to the effect that he saw the whole thing.

It seems that he had gone out for the day and his wife had expected to move, during his absence, from their lodgings in Berner Street to others in Backchurch Lane. When he first came homewards about a quarter before one he walked down Berner Street to see if his wife had moved. As he turned the corner from Commercial Road he noticed some distance in front of him a man walking as if partially intoxicated. He walked on behind him and presently he noticed a woman standing in the entrance to the alleyway where the body was found. The half-tipsy man halted and spoke to her. The Hungarian saw him put his hand on her shoulder and push her back into the passage, but feeling rather timid of getting mixed up in quarrels, he crossed to the other side of the street. Before he had gone many yards, however, he heard the sound of a quarrel, and turned back to learn what was the matter, but just as he stepped from the kerb a second man came out of the doorway of a public house a few doors off, and shouting out some sort of warning to the man who was with the woman, rushed forward as if to attack the intruder. The Hungarian states positively that he saw a knife in the second man's hand, but he waited to see no more. He fled incontinently to his new lodgings.

He described the man with the woman as about 30 years of age, rather stoutly built, and wearing a brown moustache. He was dressed respectably in dark clothes and felt hat. The man who came at him with a knife he also describes, but not in detail. He says he was taller than the other but not so stout, and that his moustaches were red. Both men seemed to belong to the same grade of society. The police have arrested one man answering the description the Hungarian furnishes. The prisoner has not been charged, but is held for inquiries to be made. The truth of the man's statement is not wholly accepted.

On the same day, apparently unaware of the interview on a separate page, the *Star* also remarked that, 'the story of a man who is said to have seen the Berner-street tragedy, and declares that one man butchered and another man watched is, we think, *a priori* incredible.'

The following day the *Star* commented further, 'In the matter of the Hungarian who said he saw a struggle between a man and a woman in the passage where the Stride body was afterwards found, the Leman-street police have reason to doubt the truth of the story. They arrested one man on the description thus obtained, and a second on that furnished from another source, but they are not likely to act further on the same information without additional facts.'

The *Star* was unduly sceptical. There is every sign in the files that his story *was* 'wholly accepted' by the police both on 30 September when it was taken, and in November, when an exchange of memos discussed the cry of 'Lipski!' (*qv.* for discussion of Abberline's probable greater accuracy than the *Star* reporter's).

Other differences between the *Star* account and police files are the suggestion that Stride was pulled into Dutfield's Yard, not thrown on the pavement of Berner Street; that the man leaving the pub carried a knife and not a pipe, and that he shouted the warning to the assailant and apparently chased Schwartz. Those differences are probably owing to interpretation difficulties and the immediacy of the police report makes it more likely to be accurate.

The most puzzling feature of the Schwartz incident is that there is no report in the press of his being called to testify at Stride's inquest and no report of any closed session when he might have testified *in camera*. As Schwartz's evidence was in the highest degree material, it would have been a serious offence for the police to have withheld his testimony from the coroner, and Wynne Baxter was not a coroner who would let any such defalsification of duty pass by lightly. Two other witnesses did not testify either (Mrs **Fanny Mortimer** and **Matthew Packer**).

Israel Schwartz has been suggested as the witness who, according to Sir Robert Anderson in *The Lighter Side of My Official Life*, positively identified a Polish Jew suspect, whom Anderson appears to have believed was Jack the Ripper. The other possible witness was **Joseph Lawende**..

SCOTLAND YARD FILES

The files have been available to all researchers in the National Archives (formerly the Public Record Office) at Kew since 1976, and had been used by certain individuals (notably **Douglas Browne**, **Stephen Knight**, BBC researchers and Donald Rumbelow; also, apparently, **Leonard Matters**) prior to being opened generally. (*See* **Files** for discussion of their supposed closure in 1892.)

The version of the **Macnaghten memoranda** deposited among them gives a clear and important pointer to Scotland Yard's principal suspects. (*See* Douglas Browne for the suggestion of another clue that the files may once have held.)

The purloining of papers as souvenirs goes back to at least the second decade of the twentieth century, when a person stole Ripper- and Crippen-related documents, which were only returned to Scotland Yard in 1987. About 100 papers from the 'Suspects' file went missing some time in the late 1970s or eighties. A full account, including transcriptions of these missing files made independently by Donald Rumbelow, Paul Bonner and the late Stephen Knight, comprises Chapter 38 of *The Ultimate Jack the Ripper Sourcebook*. The documents in these files are not in date order, but prior to microfilming in 1988, were provided with an index which lists the contents in chronological order. *Sourcebook* reproduces most of them fully with a detailed commentary.

SCOTT, PC RALPH HENRY, 355H (*b.* 1858)
Second officer on the scene of **Frances Coles**' murder: the first to respond to PC **Ernest Thompson**'s whistle.

Born in Durham. Employed as a butcher before joining the Metropolitan Police in 1880 (warrant no. 65032). Resigned to pension, 1905, after serving his entire police career in H Division.

PC Scott stated that he found Coles' pulse to be beating faintly, which supported Thompson's suggestion that she was still alive when he found her (*The Times*, 14 February 1891).

SEARLE, PERCY KNIGHT (1880–88)
Murdered boy.

On 26 November 1888, 8-year-old Percy Knight Searle was found murdered in Havant, Hampshire, his throat cut in four places. A bloodstained pocket-knife was found nearby. Playmate, Robert Husband, aged 11 years, who had earlier played with a knife and told a companion, 'I am Jack the Ripper. I do not mean any harm,' was charged with the crime, but subsequently acquitted.

The Times (27 November 1888) had given a frisson of interest by reporting the the receipt magistrate at Thames Police Court the on 21 November of a letter bearing a Portsmouth postmark and signed 'Yours, Jack the Ripper'. Portsmouth is near Havant, 'The general opinion was at the outset that this was the work of "Jack the Ripper," a letter read a few days since and some writing on the shutter in Hanover-street, Portsmouth, giving some colour to this supposition."

A letter dated November 14 1888, signed *Jack the Witechapel* [sic] *Ripper,* was found in Plumstead where the writer warned of his intention to murder *"2 girls and a boy about 7 years old."* (Mepo 3/142 ff.306-307)

See also:- Did Jack the Ripper kill a Hampshire schoolboy? *Independent On Sunday, 31* January 1999.

SEASIDE HOME, THE

Alleged site of identification of **Anderson**'s suspect.

The **Swanson marginalia** say that the suspect was, 'identified at the Seaside Home where he had been sent by us with difficulty in order to subject him to identification.' By 1910, when Swanson was writing, 'the Seaside Home' was said to have been normal police vernacular for the Convalescent Police Seaside Home.

The first Convalescent Police Seaside Home opened at 51 Clarendon Villas, West Brighton, in March 1890, though ad hoc boarding houses had been used since 1887. In 1893, a purpose-built police Seaside Home was opened, and subsequently the establishment moved to other addresses. Thus, if Swanson was correct, and unless he intended a reference to one of the ad hoc boarding houses, the identification took place at least 18 months after the original sighting, and 16 months after the last murder.

Stewart Evans and Donald Rumbelow, in *Jack the Ripper: Scotland Yard Investigates,* offer a tentative explanation of the Seaside Home reference by suggesting that, 'it is easy to see how the failed attempt to identify **Sadler** as Jack the Ripper could have evolved into Anderson's identification.' This is because a witness who had *not* seen Jack the Ripper (**Duncan Campbell**) identified Sadler as a man who sold him a clasp knife in a Sailors' Home, while a witness who *had* seen Jack the Ripper (**Joseph Lawende**) was also called in to identify Sadler, but failed to do so.

SECRET OF PRISONER 1167, THE: WAS THIS MAN JACK THE RIPPER?

Book by James Tully (London: Constable and Robinson, 1997). Published in US as *Prisoner 1167: The Madman Who Was Jack the Ripper* (paperback, London: Robinson, 1998 – uses US edition, inside title being the US title; reprinted as *The Real Jack the Ripper: The Secret of Prisoner 1167* (London: Magpie Books, 2005).

The work makes a good circumstantial case for suspecting James Kelly. Comprises an excellent account of Kelly's life, with fascinating detail about nineteenth-century Broadmoor. A sober and responsible account of the murders.

SENIOR, ELIZABETH (c. 1819–92)

Suggested as victim of **Severin Klosowski** by R. Michael Gordon (*The American Murders of Jack the Ripper*, 2001).

Wife of watch-repairer and taxidermist Joseph Senior, who also worked as nighwatchman at Fouratt's hat shop. During his absence on the night of 30–31 January 1892, an intruder entered the Seniors' house at Milburn, New Jersey, and stabbed Elizabeth 11 times in the breast, leaving many defence wounds on her arms before he succeeded in cutting her throat. He then ransacked the house and stole $45.

The police arrested a dissolute engineer named August Lyntz, who had been fired from Fouratt's for drinking. They remained convinced that he was the murderer, although an inquest jury, dissatisfied with the circumstantial evidence, brought in a verdict of murder by a person or persons unknown.

R. Michael Gordon notes that Klosowski was in the general area at the time and was running low on funds.

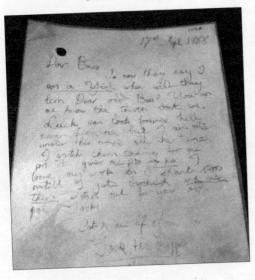

SEPTEMBER 17th 1888 LETTER

'Jack the Ripper' letter found in the National Archives (then Public Record Office), file (HO144/221/A49301C), in 1988 by Peter McClelland. It was, he said, contained in a card folder which appeared not to have been opened, and was next to correspondence from **Godfrey Lushington** of the Home Office discussing a letter opened in error, which was to be returned to the Post Office. Contrary to McClelland's initial belief, this did not refer to the newly discovered letter, which read:

17th Sept. 1888

Dear Boss
So now thay say I
am a Yid when will thay
lern Dear old Boss? You an
me know the truth dont we.
Lusk can look forever hell
never find me but I am rite
under his nose all the time.
I watch them looking for me
an it gives me fits ha ha. I
love my work an I shant stop
untill I get buckled and even
then watch out for your old
pal Jacky

Catch me if you can

Jack the Ripper
Sorry about the blood still
messy from the last one. What
a pretty necklace I gave her

The writing is round and appears to artificially imitate a semi-literate hand. Like only two other letters in the Ripper collection, the ink is clear blue. The language consistently uses phrases found in known Ripper letters (**'Dear Boss' letter**, **'Saucy Jacky' postcard**, **Lusk Letter** and a rhyme 'I'm not a butcher/I'm not a Yid' quoted in **Macnaghten**'s memoirs). These details lead the majority of commentators to believe it to be a modern forgery planted in the files.

Correspondence in the authors' possession shows that McClelland spent two years trying to gain permission from the Home Office to have the letter scientifically tested and only gave up when he ceased to get replies to his letters.

(*See* John Bennett, 'The 17th September Letter: A Closer View', *Ripper Notes*, 26, 2006 for a general discussion and facsimile reproduction.)

SEQUEIRA, DR GEORGE WILLIAM (1858–1926)

First doctor to examine **Catherine Eddowes**' body.

MRCS, LSA (London Hospital), 1886. With a surgery at 34 Jewry Street, Dr Sequeira was quickly called to the scene in Mitre Square, where he pronounced the body dead, but made no detailed examination while **Dr Gordon Brown**'s arrival was awaited. At the inquest, he stated that he agreed with Dr Brown's evidence, but in answer to questions from the coroner, said that he believed the murderer showed no skill and had not been seeking any particular organ in extracting the kidney and the uterus. (Brown had said that he showed anatomical knowledge, apparently because he thought the kidney had been specifically sought.)

SHADOWS OF THE RIPPER

Book, ed. B.A. Rogers (privately published: B.A. Rogers, 2000).

Compilation of Ripper-related extracts from *Round London: Down East and Up West* (1892) by Montagu Williams, QC; *Canon Barnett: His Life, Work and Friends, By His Wife Vol II (1918)* by Henrietta Octavia Weston Barnett; 'George Chapman' by H.L. Adam from *The Black Maria* (1935), ed. Harry Hodge; and *From Constable to Commissioner* (1910) by Lieut.-Col. Sir Henry Smith. *See also* **Echoes of the Ripper**, **Reflections of the Ripper**.

SHAW, GEORGE BERNARD (1856–1950)

Commentator. The great dramatist submitted letters on the murders to the *Star*, the most famous of which, 'Blood Money to Whitechapel' (24 September 1888), included his ironic comment, 'Whilst we conventional Social Democrats were wasting our time on education, agitation and organisation, some independent genius has taken the matter in hand, and by simply murdering and disembowelling four women, converted the proprietary press to an inept sort of communism.' This encouraged **William Stewart** to suggest that Shaw, 'professed, with true Irish unaccountability, to hold the view that the reason for the murders was to focus attention on the appalling conditions of the poor in the East End,' and **Tom Cullen** to propose that social reform might seriously have been a part of **Montague John Druitt**'s motive.

Shaw was disgusted by such literal-mindedness, and wrote 'Utter nonsense' in the margin of the proof copy of *Jack the Ripper – A New Theory* that Stewart sent him. And on the title page he objected to the revival of the subject on the grounds that it might stimulate an imitator.

(See Andy Aliffe, 'Pictures, Paint and Prosceniums', *Ripperologist*, 14, December 1997.)

SHAW, JAMES (*fl.* 1888)

Rumoured to be the Ripper while under arrest in New York.

Shaw, a Yorkshireman whose real name was Heddington, travelled steerage on the *SS Wyoming* to America and was arrested when the ship docked on 23 November 1888. The British Consul asked New York Police to hold him as he was believed to be James Pennock, aka Shaw, wanted for the murder of his wife in Yorkshire. The rumour circulated that the police had the Riper in custody, as Shaw fitted his description and had an illustrated account of the Whitechapel murders in his possession. The rumour was untrue, and Shaw bore no resemblance to the description of Pennock (*Frederick Times*, 26 November 1888; *New York Times*, 28 November 1888.)

SHORE, SUPERINTENDENT JOHN (*b.* 1839)

Born at Farmborough, near Bath. A police officer in Bristol before joining the Metropolitan Police on 10 January 1859 (warrant no. 37737). Promoted to sergeant-temporary on 9 April 1862, then detective sergeant (17 September 1854), inspector (16 July 1869), chief inspector (3 December 1877) and superintendent CID (19 November 1887). Retired, 1 May 1896. The American master-criminal Adam Worth and detective William Pinkerton both commented adversely on Shore's character and competence.

His involvement in the Ripper case investigation appears to have been marginal, but his name is appended to various documents in the official files, including the memorandum of 15 September 1888, appointing **Swanson** to take overall charge of the Whitechapel murder case. The *New York Herald* (23 December 1888) reported **Inspector Andrews** stating that British detectives were working undercover in American and Canadian Irish Nationalist organisations, who were commanded by Fred Jarvis and Chief Inspector Shore, whom Andrews met at 'Niagra'.

(Personal file at the National Archives, MEPO 3/2883)

SICKERT AND THE RIPPER CRIMES

Book by **Jean Overton Fuller** (Oxford: Mandrake, 1990; paperback, Oxford: Mandrake, 2001; revised paperback, Mandrake: Oxford, 2002). Proposes that **Walter Sickert** was Jack the Ripper.

Jean Overton Fuller was the daughter of Captain J.H.M. Fuller and artist Violet Overton Fuller. Educated at the London University (BA Eng.). A poet and author whose work frequently touches tangentially on modern occultists. *The Magical Dilemma of Victor Neuberg* (1965) refers to **Vittoria Cremers'** story that **Robert Donston Stephenson** was Jack the Ripper. Her autobiography, *Driven To It* (Norwich: Michael Russell Publishing, 2007), refers to her research into the Ripper.

The conclusion that Walter Sickert was Jack the Ripper is based almost wholly on a claim, attributed to Sickert's friend **Florence Pash**, that he had seen the bodies of all the victims and the assumption by Ms Fuller's mother that this must have been at the murder sites.

Ms Fuller attributes to Florence Pash prima facie corroboration of Joseph Sickert's claim that Walter was his father, and the catalyst of the Ripper crimes was the relationship between his maternal grandmother, **Annie Elizabeth Crook**, and **Prince Albert Victor**.

It is relevant to note that Florence Pash told Violet Overton Fuller several stories which also appear in *Jack the Ripper: The Final Solution*, notably the tale of a £500 bribe paid to Sickert by Lord Salisbury. This is a variant of a story known to have been told by Walter Sickert about the artist Vallon, the £500 being the fee for the painting, not a bribe.

SICKERT, JOSEPH WILLIAM CHARLES GORMAN (1925–2003)

Artist and picture restorer. Born Joseph William Charles Gorman, son of fish curer/professional boxer William Gorman and the illegitimate **Alice Margaret Crook**, whose true paternity has never been established. Claimed to be the illegitimate son of Walter Sickert; also that his mother was the offspring of an illicit union between his grandmother, **Annie Elizabeth Crook**, and **Prince Albert Victor**.

Name legally changed by Deed Poll to Gorman-Sickert on 8 July 1970, under which surname his death was registered.

According to Henry Lessore (brother of John), in November 1969 Joseph Gorman-Sickert visited the Beaux Art Galleries, run by Helen Lessore (sister-in-law of Sickert's third wife), claiming to be Sickert's grandson. This was also what Joseph Gorman-Sickert's cousin, **Ellen May Lackner**, recalled in 1992, when interviewed by Paul Begg, Melvyn Fairclough and **Paul Feldman**, saying that parts of Joseph's story had been current in the family at least as early as Joseph's infancy and recalling in particular that Walter Sickert was supposed to be the putative father of Alice Margaret Crook (Joseph's mother) rather than of Joseph himself. She remembered there was some sort of mysterious association with a royal personage and a mysterious and frightening connection with Jack the Ripper.

Joseph Gorman-Sickert's story was first publicised in August 1973, as part of the six-part BBC TV drama-documentary, *Jack the Ripper*. In a five-minute insert (episode 6), he said that he was the son of Walter Sickert and that in his teens, Walter had told him a story which he didn't really believe to the effect that his mother, Alice Margaret Crook, was the issue of a liason between his grandmother, Annie Elizabeth Crook, and Prince Albert Victor, the future Duke of Clarence. According to Walter Sickert, he had looked after Alice, helped by various local friends and an Irish servant girl called **Mary Jane Kelly**, but when the authorities learned of an alleged marriage in 1888 between Annie Elizabeth and the Prince, they separated the couple.

At the same time, Mary Kelly (known to the nuns of a convent in Harewood Place) also disappeared into the sister convent in the East End. The Government and the Royal Household became concerned about the news getting out and decided to silence Kelly, the operation being carried out by **Sir William Gull** and **John Netley**: 'To conceal the motive behind Mary Kelly's death, she was killed as the last of five women in a way that made it look like the random work of a madman.'

This story was subsequently followed up by **Stephen Knight** (*East London Advertiser*, 7 December 1973), and then enlarged by him in ***Jack the Ripper: The Final Solution*** and Melvyn Fairclough in ***The Ripper and the Royals***. Some slight independent corroboration was provided in ***Sickert and the Ripper Crimes***, which attributed to Walter Sickert's friend **Florence Pash**'s confirmation that Joseph was Walter's son, but alleged Sickert was Jack the Ripper.

In 1978, while continuing to claim descent from Walter Sickert and Prince Albert Victor, Joseph Sickert confessed to *The Sunday Times* that the story of the Masonic conspiracy was, 'a hoax; I made it all up.' It would be all too easy to conclude that he made up the whole story himself, but the tale of the Prince's marrying a prostitute, whence the murders, was reported by **Freda Thomson** as something she heard in 1915.

After Knight's death, Joseph Sickert retracted his earlier confession, saying that he only made it to save the reputation of Walter Sickert. He also produced diaries purportedly written by **Inspector Abberline**, which were in a revised version of the story in *The Ripper and the Royals*.

Sickert alleged that Prince Albert Victor had been kept alive in captivity in Glamis Castle until the 1930s (for which service the Bowes-Lyonses were repaid by having the Duke of York, later George VI, marry Elizabeth Bowes-Lyon, later Queen and then Queen Mother.

No part of Joseph Gorman-Sickert's story, as allegedly told him by Walter Sickert, has ever been substantiated by concrete evidence and many details of Stephen Knight's representation of the story have been conclusively disproved.

(Obituary, ***Ripperologist***, March 2003.)

SICKERT LETTERS' INVESTIGATION

Forensic paper historian and paper analyst Peter Bower has made the intriguing discovery that **Walter Sickert** possibly wrote two of the Ripper letters.

Bower is a past Fellow of the Royal Society of Arts (RSA), Member of the Committee of the British Association of Paper Historians, Visiting Research Fellow at London University School of Advanced studies, editor of *The Quarterly: The Journal of the British Association of Paper Historians*, editor of *Studies in British Paper History*, registered as an expert witness on the UK Register. With major work on Michelangelo drawings, Constable's use of paper and Turner, and forensic examinations of $200 million dollars' worth of forged US Treasury Bonds and the 'Black Diaries' of Sir Roger Casement, he is one of the most internationally respected paper examiners.

Examining Ripper letters and Sickert papers found by Patricia Cornwell to be watermarked products of the same paper-making companies, Bower found some that came from the same batches (i.e. large rolls of newly manufactured paper) and some that did not, which Ms Cornwell interpreted in the first edition of *Portrait of a Killer* as meaning that Sickert might have written some of the Ripper letters.

However, Dr Anna Gruetzner Robins, reader in art history at Reading University, who believes doodles in a Cornish hotel guestbook and maybe as many as 200 Ripper letters are all in Sickert's hand, subsequently discovered a cache of Sickert letters watermarked Gurney Ivory Laid. Leppard and Smith, the manufacturers, guillotine-cut this paper in small batches of 24 sheets, and Peter Bower was able to establish by microscopic examination that two Ripper letters and three pieces of Sickert's correspondence came from the same batch of 24 sheets of paper. This makes it almost certain that Walter Sickert's known interest in the Ripper went so far as to include writing hoax Ripper letters.

Unfortunately, Bower has not yet been able to publish his work. Ms Cornwell does not identify the relevant Ripper letters, and in the 2003 Berkley Mass

Market paperback edition refers to them as *two* Ripper letters on p.173 and *one* Corporation of London Records Office (i.e. City Police) letter on p.174. We take the correct number of letters from Bower's statements at the November 2003 Tate Britain symposium on 'The Art of Murder: Representation and Crime in Late Victorian Britain' at which Paul Begg and Anna Gruetzner Robins were also panelists.

SICKERT, WALTER RICHARD (1860–1942)

Suspect, proposed by **Stephen Knight** in 1976; also by **Jean Overton Fuller** in *Sickert and the Ripper Crimes* and then by Patricia Cornwell in *Portrait of a Killer*. In addition, since 1993 suggested as responsible for one or more of the Jack the Ripper Letters.

Major British painter, born in Munich; the eldest of four sons and one daughter of Danish–German painter Oswald Adalbert Sickert and his English wife. The family moved to England in 1868 to avoid the boys becoming liable for conscription into the German army. Educated at King's College School, Wimbledon, and the Slade School of Fine Art. Worked briefly under the name 'Mr Nemo' (1877–81), an actor in Henry Irving's company prior to Slade. Left the Slade School prematurely in 1882 to work as assistant to **James McNeill Whistler**, and then in Paris under Edgar Degas, who influenced him to produce striking studies of music halls, with artistes and audience members shown in unusual positions suggesting important activity outside the picture frame. Critics, however, attacked the vulgarity of the subject matter.

In 1885, married Ellen, daughter of radical politician Richard Cobden. They honeymooned in Dieppe, a town where Ellen had been brought up, and to which Sickert returned repeatedly in later life. By the 1890s, his constant infidelities were destroying the marriage. In 1896, the Sickerts separated and Ellen divorced him in 1899.

From then until 1905, Sickert lived in Dieppe, with three long intervals in Venice where, in 1903, he painted a series of prostitutes in shabby rooms, foreshadowing his future work. On his return to London he championed avant-garde painting and himself concentrated on painting petit-bourgeois couples and individuals in drab interiors. He took rooms in 6 Mornington Crescent, Camden, where his landlord and landlady told him that they believed Jack the Ripper had previously boarded. (See **Jack the Ripper's Bedroom**, **Sickert's unnamed veterinary student**.)

In 1911 he married Christine Drummond Angus, with whom he returned to Dieppe after World War I. Christine died there in 1920, and Sickert was devastated for a time, returning to London in 1922. In 1926, he married Thérèse Lessore, a painter and former member of his Fitzroy Square and London Groups, who had helped him through the desolation he felt after Christine's death. RA, 1934; resigned, 1935. From the mid-1930s, he painted controversial portraits and scenes based on newspaper photographs. This subject matter enabled him to leave London and live first at Thanet, Kent, and then at Bathampton, Wiltshire, where he died in 1942.

Patricia Cornwell's reason for suspecting Walter Sickert to be the Ripper was the remark made by Metropolitan Police Service deputy assistant commissioner John Grieve that he thought Sickert worth investigating. Cornwell considered this, noting, 'most people have always found the notion laughable,' but in examining Sickert's art, she found in the work, 'morbidity, violence and a hatred of women.' Thereafter, she intentionally eschewed any communication with Ripper authorities. Instead, she pursued expensive forensic scientific examinations of Sickertiana for comparison with Ripper letters, and found that DNA analysis showed that DNA she assumed (without positive proof) to be Walter Sickert's was identical with mitochondrial DNA, shared by only 1% of the population, that was found on the stamp used to mail the **Openshaw Letter**. (This would amount to 40,000 people in London alone.) In 2006, Professor Ian Findley, apparently using a more sophisticated technique, established that the DNA on the stamp was probably female.

Ms Cornwell also believed that Sickert's personality and medical history pointed to his guilt. Hostile critical reactions to Sickert's supposedly vulgar subject matter in the music-hall period, morbid subject-matter in the Camden period, and imitative work in the final period provide a fertile source of contemporary adverse comment. When asking Sickert's wife's nephew (John Lessore) about Sickert's fistula, she was told by Lessore that it was a 'hole in [Sickert's] penis' (the extremely rare condition of a hole in the penis penetrating the urethra). Cornwell established that he underwent two unsuccessful surgeries for fistula as a child in Munich, and a third in London, in 1865.

Sickert himself, according to Ms Cornwell's research, used to joke that he came to London to be 'circumcised'. However, the London surgeon who operated on him was a proctologist, specialising in treating the far more common anal fistula (a tear in the inner wall of the anus) and neither he nor staff at St Mark's Hospital (where Sickert was taken) are known to have ever operated on penile fistula.

Ms Cornwell also builds on Sickert's known eccentricities: his habit of changing his appearance by shaving his head or growing different types of beard; his adoption of varying clothes, even wearing check suits and slippers to occasions demanding formal dress (*see also* **Willie Clarkson**). She believes that these things point to a personality capable of murdering women and mocking the police with Ripper letters.

Cornwell may, however, have found the genuine possibility that Sickert could have written two of the 300 or more Jack the Ripper Letters (*see* **Sickert Letters' Investigation**).

Graphologist Marie Bernard was reported in *Daily* Express, 31 December

1993, as having compared Walter Sickert's handwriting with that of the 'Dear Boss' letter and being 'absolutely convinced' that he was, 'the man behind the Jack the Ripper letter.' She expected to publish her findings in a book in 1994, but it has never appeared.

Both theories accusing Sickert of the Ripper crimes allege that he left painted clues in some of his pictures. In the opinion of Sickert authorities Wendy Barron and Matthew Sturgis these claims cannot be sustained.

The two theories conflict over Sickert's capacity for fatherhood: Ms Cornwell's belief that he was incapable of engendering children and Joseph Gorman's claim that he was Walter Sickert's illegitimate child. His three marriages were all childless, but he had many mistresses and it has often been alleged that the son of one of them was Sickert's child. Matthew Sturgis, in his recent exhaustive life of Sickert, believes that he has identified a daughter born to one of Sickert's mistresses on the continent without the artist ever realising that he had fathered this child.

Sturgis's book, *Walter Sickert: A Life* (2006), includes a postscript refuting the claim that Sickert was the Ripper. At its heart lies the fact that he was in Normandy at the time of most of the Ripper murders.

SICKERT'S UNNAMED VETERINARY STUDENT
Alleged suspect.

Sir Osbert Sitwell, in *A Free House* (1947) and *Noble Essences* (1950), stated that **Walter Sickert**'s conversation persistently returned to murder cases and Jack the Ripper, the latter because, 'he thought he knew the identity of the murderer.'

Some years after the murders Sickert took a room in 'a London suburb' (believed by Sacheverell Sitwell to refer to his lodgings at 6 Mornington Crescent). The elderly couple who owned the house told him that the previous occupant of his room was the Ripper. He was a consumptive and delicate-looking veterinary student, who would sometimes stay out all night and then rush to buy the first edition of the morning newspaper. Sometimes he burned the clothes that he had been wearing. When his health began to fail, his widowed mother took him home with her to Bournemouth, where he died, three months later. Sickert noted the man's name in the margin of a copy of Casanova's *Memoirs*, which he subsequently gave to Albert Rutherston, who did not decipher Sickert's marginal scrawls, and lost the book in the Blitz.

Donald McCormick claimed to have been told the story by, 'a London doctor who knew Sickert and whose father had been at Oxford with **Montague John Druitt**.' McCormick claimed his informant said the student's name was something like Druitt. He also suggested to McCormick that Sickert had repeated this story to **Sir Melville Macnaghten** at the Garrick Club, this being the 'private information' which convinced Macnaghten of Druitt's guilt.

It has been established by **Ripperana**'s editor Nick Warren, that the only appropriately named veterinary student at the Royal Veterinary College (itself the only veterinary college outside Scotland in 1888) was **George Ailwyn Hewitt**, aged 17 to 18 in 1888. He lived at Aldershot and died in 1908. Of 131 Royal

Veterinary College students who cut short their studies before the end of 1888, only one came from Bournemouth: Joseph Ride, who was 27 in 1888.

An Egyptian-born medical student named Waller is recorded in the 1891 census as lodging at 6 Mornington Crescent.

SICKINGS, LAURA

Child who thought she found bloodstains left by the Ripper. Reported in the press, 12 September 1888, as having discovered a stain or sprinkle of blood on the fence of no. 25 Hanbury Street, which, coupled with bloodstained paper found in the Bayleys' Yard, suggested the murderer had escaped after killing **Annie Chapman** by crossing two yard fences to the west, then leaving through the house passage of no. 25. In the evening papers the same day, **Inspector Chandler** confirmed that the stain was urine.

SILVER, JOSEPH (1868–1917)

Most commonly used alias of internationally active pimp and racketeer, who was born Joseph Lis in Poland. He emigrated in 1887, passing through England on his way to America, and thereafter had a varied career in the USA, South America, Europe and South Africa. South African historian Charles van Onselen, intrigued by the frequency with which South African and German Southwest African authorities were distracted from other priorities by the need to control this man's activities, researched his life. He found it peculiarly difficult to trace Silver's movements through England in 1887–88, but established reasons for believing that he spent time in Whitechapel, fathered a daughter there and somehow caused the death of one of the first prostitutes he managed in London.

It appeared both Silver and his daughter tried to obscure the fact that he had been in Whitechapel during the latter half of 1888 and when Mr van Onseler realised this was the period of the Ripper murders, and the man he was studying was a cruel and sadistic pimp, who might well have contrived the death of a prostitute he controlled at that time, he considered the identification of Silver as the Ripper was being forced upon him.

(*See **The Fox and the Flies**.*)

SIMM, CLARENCE (*d.* 1951)

Suspect, named in 1989. His widow, Betty Simm, was reported in the *Weekly World News,* 20 June 1989, as saying that he had made a deathbed confession to having killed 14 prostitutes as a teenager, 'to free them from a life of sin.' She herself had met him in London, in 1905. Polygraph operator Gerald Mevel, who tested Mrs Simm, said: 'There is less than one half of 1 per cent chance she is lying.'

SIMMONS, PC GEORGE (959 City) (*b. c.* 1839–1905)

Joined the City of London Police in 1861 (warrant no. 3224). Resigned, 1890.

Assisted Police Constable **Louis Robinson** in taking **Catherine Eddowes** to Bishopsgate Police Station on 29 September 1888 and made a preliminary tentative identification of her body in the mortuary (*The Times*, 3 October 1888). Died in 1905, aged 67, when he fell from a cart (*Police Review*, 27 October 1905). Inquest reported in the *West Sussex Gazette* (12 October 1905).

SIMONDS, MARY ELIZABETH

Witness at **Annie Chapman**'s inquest. Nurse at Whitechapel Infirmary who, with **Frances Wright**, stripped and washed Chapman's body on the orders of the Clerk to the Parish Guardians, and not the police.

SIMPSON, PC AMOS (1846–1917)

Original holder of Catherine Eddowes' shawl.

Born in Acton, near Sudbury, Suffolk. Joined the Metropolitan Police in 1868 (Warrant No: 49611), posted to Y Division (Kentish Town). Promoted to acting sergeant, 1881, and transferred to N Division (Islington) in 1886. Moved to Cheshunt, Hertfordshire Constabulary (*c.* 1893). Resigned, 1893, and retired to Acton in 1905.

According to Simpson's niece Elsie Hayes (*b. c.* 1902) and great-great nephew David Melville Hayes, family tradition is that Simpson was the first policeman to find the body in Mitre Square and he picked up the shawl that night. There are obvious problems with this story. Inquest testimony and newspaper reports are quite clear that City PC **Edward Watkins** found the body and there is no apparent reason for Metropolitan PC Simpson to have been in the Square. Nevertheless, both Mrs Hayes' recollections and Simpson's obituary (*Suffolk and Essex Free Press*, 18 April 1917) give him an excellent character.

SIMS, GEORGE ROBERT (1847–1922)

Journalist, author and playwright with good police contacts; a discriminating interest in criminology, frequently reporting Ripper stories. Also, self-alleged casual contemporaneous suspect.

The eldest of six children of businessman George Sims and his wife Louisa (née Stephenson). Educated at preparatory school in Eastbourne, at Hanwell Military College and Bonn. After briefly working in his father's office, turned to journalism and in 1877, joined the newly founded newspaper, the *Referee*, where he began writing the 'Mustard and Cress column' under the pen–name of Dagonet. Sims also wrote a weekly column for the *Weekly Dispatch*. Of radical political persuasion he often wrote poems on social issues, which became known as the 'Dagonet Ballads', the most famous being 'Workhouse: Christmas Day'.

Wrote two books exposing the extreme poverty and related conditions in which some people lived: *How the Poor Live* (1889) and *Horrible London* (1889). Achieved great success as a playwright. Thrice married, he died in 1922. His 'crime relics' were auctioned in April 1923, but the prices obtained were reportedly poor – some books and a collection of newspaper clippings fetched just £18.

From 1889, he made frequent reference to an incident of 1888, when a coffee-stallholder in Whitechapel remarked that Sims' portrait, advertising his latest book, was the perfect likeness of a suspicious man with bloodstained cuffs who had come to his stall shortly after the double murders and announced that the stallholder would hear of two more murders the following day (*Referee*, 6 October 1889 onwards). From at least 1899, he began describing the Ripper as a man known to the police as having drowned in the Thames at the end of 1888 (*Referee*, 22 January 1899), having learned this either from **Major Arthur Griffiths'** *Mysteries of Police and Crime* (1898), or from **Melville Macnaghten** (*see* **M.J. Druitt**). Newspaper reports suggesting **George Chapman** was Jack the Ripper (*Daily Chronicle*, 23 March 1903) led to **Inspector Abberline** publicising his suspicions (*Pall Mall Gazette*, 24, 31 March 1903) and a response by Sims (*Referee*, 29 March 1903) and by **Inspector Reid**.

See **Mrs Kennedy, Littlechild Letter**.

Autobiography: *My Life: Sixty Years' Recollections of Bohemian London* (London: Evleigh Nash and Grayson, 1917); obituary in *The Times* and *New York Times*, 6 September 1922.

SKIPPER, PRIVATE (*fl.* 1888)

Guardsman stationed at Wellington Barracks, wrongly identified by **Mary Ann Connelly** as the client who accompanied **Martha Tabram** to George Yard at 11.45pm, on the night of her murder. Skipper's presence in barracks from 10.05pm that night was recorded in a book kept by the regiment.

SMITH, ELIZABETH

A woman who lived in Miller's Court, who said, 'I have known her [Mary Kelly] a long time. She and Barnett were as happy as possible until she gave way to drink' (*Echo*, 10 November 1888).

SMITH, EMMA ELIZABETH (1843–88)

Possible victim of a violent gang mugging, but believed by some (**Walter Dew**) to be an early victim of Jack the Ripper.

Described at her inquest as the widow of a soldier, possibly the John Smith who appears in the 1881 Census as living at 118 Central Street, St. Luke's, with his wife Emma Smith, whose age was given as 37, which would correspond very well with her estimated age of 45 in 1888. The Census gave Emma Smith's place of birth as Margate, Kent, and husband John was said to be a pensioner of the 35th (Royal Sussex) Regiment. The couple had two children.

Emma Smith was 5ft 2in tall, with light brown hair and a scar on her right temple.

According to Walter Dew, she was something of a mystery. Her past was a closed book, even to her most intimate friends. All that she had ever told anyone about herself was that she was a widow, who more than 10 years before had left her husband and broken away from all her early associations.

There was something about Emma Smith that suggested there had been a time when the comforts of life had not been denied her. In her speech there was a touch of culture that was unusual in her class.

Once, when Emma was asked why she had broken away so completely from her old life, she replied, a little wistfully: 'They would not understand now any more than they understood then. I must live somehow.'

Mary Russell, deputy keeper of the lodging-house at 18 George Street where Smith had been living for the previous 18 months at the time of her death, said Smith was often drunk and that when she was drunk, she acted like a madwoman. Often, she came home bruised or black-eyed after an altercation with a man and on one occasion claimed she had been thrown out of a window. It is possible that she was the Elizabeth Smith whose frequent appearances at Thames Magistrates Court on drunk and disorderly charges ceased abruptly after 14 December 1887.

On 2 April, Bank Holiday Monday, she was seen in Bethnal Green by **Margaret Hayes**, talking to a man dressed in dark clothes and a white scarf. Hayes, who only minutes' earlier had been struck in the mouth by one of two men who stopped her in the street, said, 'there had been some rough work' going on that night, but it isn't clear what she meant.

About 1.30am, Emma Smith was making her way down Whitechapel Road when she saw three men, one a youth aged about 19, and crossed the road to avoid them. She turned into Osborne Street, and when opposite no. 10 Brick Lane, near Taylor Bros Mustard and Cocoa Mill on the corner of Brick Lane and Wentworth Street, she was robbed and raped, a blunt instrument being forced into her vagina and tearing the perineum.

Smith was 300 yards from 18 George Street, but she did not reach there until some time between 4 and 5am (more than two hours after the assault). Mary Russell and a fellow lodger named **Annie Lee** took her to the London Hospital. Russell said that Smith didn't say what had alarmed her about the youths, didn't describe them and seemed unwilling to go into any details. Nor did she or her companions inform a policeman. Inspector **Edmund Reid** noted in his report that, 'She would have passed a number of PCs en route, but none was informed of the incident or asked to render assistance.'

At the London Hospital she was questioned a little by the doctor who attended her and received treatment, but she subsequently passed into a coma and died of peritonitis on 5 April.

The police concluded Emma Smith was attacked by one of the gangs in the area (*see* **Gangs, East End**), but the perpetrators were never arrested. In September, the press began describing her as a Ripper victim and Walter Dew was of the opinion that Smith was the first victim of Jack the Ripper: 'The silence, the suddenness, the complete elimination of clues, the baffling disappearance all go to support the view which I have always held that Emma Smith was the first to meet her death at the hands of Jack the Ripper.'

(See Walter Dew, *I Caught Crippen*, London: Blackie and Son, 1938.)

SMITH, FOUNTAIN (*b.* 1861)

Annie Chapman's brother and witness at her inquest. A tall man, with dark hair and a heavy brown moustache. He said that he had seen his sister shortly before the murder and given her 2/- (10p).

SMITH, G. WENTWORTH BELL

Alleged suspect. Described as agent of the Toronto Trust Society (NB: the authors suspect mistranscription of the Truss Society, which had office in Finsbury Square and solicited donations). Came on business to Britain for a period of months or a year, 1888–89. Established office in Godliman Street, St Paul's. In August 1888, moved to rooms at 27 Sun Street, Finsbury Square, advertised as vacant in the *Daily Telegraph* by Mr and Mrs E. Callaghan.

Mr Callaghan noticed that he wrote 50 to 60 foolscap sheets of religious outpourings at a time. He had religious delusions about women and claimed to have performed 'some wonderful operations'; also seemed obsessed with prostitutes, saying that many walked through St Paul's Cathedral during services and they (and especially East End prostitutes) should be drowned. He wore a different suit every day, stayed out very late at night, coming and going silently in rubber-soled felt-topped galoshes. On his return, he often threw himself down on the sofa and 'foamed'. He kept three loaded revolvers hidden in his chest of drawers, talked to himself and once received a postcard reading: 'We can't get through it. Can you give me any help? Dodger.'

On the night of **Martha Tabram**'s murder, he arrived home at 4am, falsely claiming that his watch had been stolen in Bishopsgate. Two or three days later, he left the Callaghans', declaring he must return to Canada, but he was still in England the following month. The Callaghans believed him to be a lunatic, and Mr Callaghan concluded, 'Without doubt this man is the perpetrator of these crimes.' He then claimed to have gone to the police and advised them of Bell Smith's suspicious behaviour; also to have been visited independently by police enquiring for Smith, following reports from a lady south of the Thames. (Subsequently, **Abberline** and **Swanson** could find no record of these contacts.)

The following year, a female acquaintance told Mr Callaghan that she had been accosted by a man that she had seen washing himself at a standpipe at 4am after one of the Whitechapel murders. Mr Callaghan decided this must be Smith. He informed Dr **L. Forbes Winslow**, and stories promptly began to appear in the press that Winslow knew who the Ripper was. Chief Inspector Swanson interviewed Winslow on 23 September 1889, who maintained the press had misinterpreted his claims. He showed Swanson Callaghan's written statements and Swanson observed that somebody had changed the date of Smith's late homecoming at 4am from 9 August to 7 August, thus making possible the suggestion that it related to Martha Tabram's murder.

SMITH, GERTRUDE (*b*. 1831)

Procuress, with **Mary Jones** charged by **Inspector Ferrett** with brothel-keeping, 7 December 1888. Fined £10 with 5 guineas costs the following day. Entered on same minute of adjudication at Thames Magistrates Court as **Aaron Davis Cohen**, suggesting his arrest was part-and-parcel of the activity surrounding the brothel raid.

SMITH, Dr THOMAS GILBART

See **Gilbart-Smith, Dr Thomas**.

SMITH, H.

Undertaker of Hanbury Street, who supplied the hearse for **Annie Chapman**.

SMITH, MAJOR HENRY (1835–1921)

Subsequently, Lieutenant Colonel Sir Henry, KCB. Acting commissioner, City of London Police, September 1888. Educated at Edinburgh Academy and University. Worked as a bookkeeper in Glasgow until the death of his father. In 1869, commissioned in Suffolk Artillery Militia, taking care of his mother; first as man-about-town in London, thereafter as a sporting country gentleman in Northumberland, where he remained after her death. In 1879, he began casting about for employment, preferably in the senior ranks of the police. He failed to gain appointments in Scotland, Newcastle and Liverpool. In 1885, six years after his original application, he was appointed chief superintendent, City of London Police. Commissioner, 1890–1901; KCB, 1910.

Popular and worldly, he was good at public relations and was given a favourable press (especially compared with Scotland Yard) at the time of the Whitechapel murders. Sir James

Fraser, the Commissioner, was on leave at the time of the Mitre Square murder within the City Police boundaries, so Major Smith took immediate charge of the investigation. The press felt that the City Police, under his direction, were frank and helpful, whereas the Metropolitan Police were viewed as obstructive and secretive. However, *see also* **James McWilliam** for the Home Office view that the City was more secretive than the Met.

The publication in 1910 of Major Smith's memoirs, *From Constable To Commissioner: The Story of Sixty Years Most of Them Misspent*, was generally well-received as a good collection of fine anecdotes, though it garnered criticism from some reviewers, who commented on Smith's heavy criticism of the Metropolitan Police. The *Manchester Guardian* observed that Smith's tone became 'a little incoherent' when he wrote, 'of the blunders of the heads of the Metropolitan Police, especially Sir Robert Anderson...' The *Yorkshire Post* commented on the book's sub-title, pointing out that Smith never served a day in the ranks and that his position and subsequent promotions were achieved by favour.

Smith wrote: 'There is no man living who knows as much of those murders as I do.' He claimed that he was, 'within five minutes of the perpetrator one night, and with a very fair description of him besides' – apparently a reference to his story of finding a public sink, where the Ripper had just washed his bloodstained hands, shortly after the Mitre Square murder. Yet the Major's documented movements that night make it impossible for him to have been five minutes behind the Ripper, and a few pages later he placed the same incident shortly after the Miller's Court murder.

Other important stories told by the Major include his tracing of an insane (but innocent) suspected medical student with a reputation for passing off polished farthings as half-sovereigns when the Metropolitan Police requested his help in searching for him (*cf.* **John Sanders**, **Inspector Reid**); his giving orders to his constabulary to frequent pubs, smoke sociable pipes and collect gossip when on duty during the scare and his receipt of an unsigned letter from Hoxton, promising information if the Major would keep an assignation with the writer – an assignation which produced no acknowledged recognition of him, only a subsequent letter promising definite information (which never materialised) in the future.

Smith accepted the **Lusk kidney** as unquestionably genuine, though his account of how it came into the hands of the City Police is most inaccurate. It is important to note, however, that his expert adviser on the state of the kidney, **Henry Gawen Sutton**, was in fact an extremely distinguished physician and his opinion should not be lightly dismissed. Smith expressed lasting indignation towards **Sir Charles Warren** for erasing the Goulston Street graffito before it had been photographed, as Smith claimed that he had ordered that it should be.

Smith fiercely attacked **Sir Robert Anderson**'s claim to know the identity of the Ripper, accusing him of irresponsible anti-Semitism and designating his investigation 'fruitless'. The clear implication is that the Ripper's identity was completely unknown, but see below. An amusing satirical spoof letter from **Sir Robert Anderson** was published in the *Penny Illustrated Paper*:

TO SIR HENRY SMITH, EX-COMMISSIONER OF POLICE, FROM SIR ROBERT ANDERSON, K.C.B., LATE HEAD OF CRIMINAL INVESTIGATION DEPARTMENT.

Dear Smith,

Your volume of reminiscences is very interesting, especially where you explain how the police didn't capture Jack the Ripper.

But take warning, We Scotland Yard men have given some hard knocks in our time, and the people we dealt with have still a little kick in them.

Keep to Ripper stories, and the worse you will do will be to make **Dr. Forbes Winslow** rush into print. Don't tell your other doings, as you may get into a mess like I did when I told the secret history of the Parnell Commission. – Yours truly,

R. Anderson.

Without naming Smith, **Sir Melville Macnaghten** challenged his memory when he wrote:

Only two or three years ago I saw a book of police reminiscences (not by a Metropolitan officer) in which the author stated that he knew more of the 'Ripper murders' than any man living, and then went on to say that during the whole of August 1888, he was on the tiptoe of expectation. That writer had indeed a prophetic soul, looking to the fact that the first murder of the Whitechapel miscreant was on 31st August of that year of grace.

A copy of Major Smith's book in the Scotland Yard library was received from the collection of George Edwards and contains a handwritten note on the title page, expressing the opinion that Smith's veracity was not always to be trusted.

H.L. Adam, in the preface to *The Trial of George Chapman*, names Major Smith as one of the senior policeman who had confidentially told him that the Ripper's identity was definitely known (it is quite clear they were not referring to **Chapman** alias **Severin Klosowski**). It is worth noting, therefore, that Smith's personal profession of ignorance is rather restrictively worded: 'I must admit that [the Ripper] completely beat me and every police officer in London; and I have no more idea now *where he lived* than I had twenty years ago' [our italics]. There is no clue in the Major's writing as to who his suspect might have been (*cf.* **Sagar**), nor do his generalised diatribes against Anderson indicate whether or not he knew who Anderson's suspect was.

The curious wording above draws our attention to the fact that while the tone implies Anderson's claim was completely false, the Major's words are restricted to saying that Anderson's investigation was fruitless and his comments an outrageous affront to the law-abiding Jewish community since he asserted that the Ripper's 'people' shielded him from the law.

SMITH, MRS of CASTLE ALLEY (*fl.* 1888)

Witness. Superintendent of Castle Alley washhouses, who told the police that **Alice McKenzie** occasionally washed clothing there, using the name 'Kelly'.

SMITH, NEWLAND FRANCIS FORESTER (c. 1863–98)

Suspect.

Educated at London University (1881–87) and Lincoln's Inn (1887–90). Called to the bar, June 1890, but certified insane and transferred to Holloway Asylum and Sanatorium, Virginia Water (*cf.* **John Sanders**) in October. Discharged October 1891, but immediately re-admitted on an urgency order, his case notes recording that he believed himself, 'Accused of being Jack the Ripper'. Transferred to Cane Hill Asylum, 1894, where he died in 1898.

The grounds for his accusation are unknown, but as an unruly and depressive patient with organic brain disease, he might have incurred suspicion. Until the twentieth century, the legend that his room in Virginia Water was 'Jack the Ripper's room' lived on.

(See John Carey, '"Jack The Ripper's Room" and Newland Francis Forester Smith', *Ripperana*, 24, April 1998.)

SMITH, ROSINA LYDIA

According to her mother, Rosina Smith went missing from her home in Jesmond or Jessamine Street, off the Old Kent Road, shortly before the discovery of the **Pinchin Street** torso. The mother thought that she resembled the description of the torso, in particular the mark of an old injury on her index finger (*Reynolds's Newspaper*, 24 November, 1889), but she was aged only 16, considerably younger than the victim. (*See* **Emily Barker, Lydia Hart**.)

SMITH, PC WILLIAM, 452 H (1862–1951)

Witness describing a man accompanying **Elizabeth Stride**.

Joined the Metropolitan Police in 1883 (warrant no. 67565), transferring into H Division, 1886. Retired, 1910.

His beat on 29–30 September 1888 was around Commercial Road, Gower

Street, Christian Street and Fairclough Street, including such interior streets as Berner Street. It took 25 to 30 minutes to walk. About 12.30am, on 30 September, he saw a woman whom he later identified as Elizabeth Stride standing in Berner Street with a man, opposite Dutfield's Yard. The man was about 5ft 7in, clean-shaven, aged about 28 and respectable-looking. He was wearing dark clothes and a dark-coloured hard felt deerstalker. Stride had a flower in her jacket.

At about 1am, when he returned to Berner Street, he saw a crowd gathered around Dutfield's Yard, and on investigation, found Police Constables 12H and 232H present. He saw Stride's body and went to the police station for an ambulance, with **Edward Johnston** arriving as he left.

According to the family, he was very disillusioned and bitter over the way he was treated in the Ripper case. On his retirement in 1910, he moved to Canada with his family and would not be drawn to talk about the case, but eventually opened up and his son formed the impression that there had been a royal connection and some kind of cover-up, which had left a bad taste in his father's mouth.

(See Gavin Bromley, 'Smith's Beat', *Ripperologist*, no. 70, August 2006.)

SOLOMON, LOUIS (*fl.* 1888)

Suspected by officers of Woking Prison, where he was presumably an inmate.

On 15 November 1888, the letter suggesting Solomon might be the Whitechapel Murderer was received in the Home Office, where it was destroyed after its receipt had been recorded, with a note that Solomon's was, 'an ordinary criminal case' (HO144/221/A49301C).

SOMERSET, HENRY ARTHUR GEORGE 'PODGE' (1851–1926)

Alleged co-conspirator named in *The Ripper and the Royals* and *Epiphany of the Whitechapel Murders*.

Son of the 8th Duke of Beaufort, major in the Royal Horse Guards and equerry to Albert Edward, Prince of Wales. Identified as a patron of the male brothel at 18 Cleveland Street and fled to France to avoid prosecution. He never returned to Britain.

There is no corroborative evidence for **Joseph Sickert**'s claim that he was involved in the alleged conspiracy supposedly headed by **Lord Randolph Churchill**.

SPENCER, MARTHA (*fl.* 1889)

Witness who suspected James Connell for no reason other than his conversing about Jack the Ripper when she strolled with him in Hyde Park, after meeting him for the first time near Marble Arch (*The Ultimate Jack the Ripper Sourcebook*, Chapter 38).

SPICER, PC ROBERT, 101H (1866–1947)

Self-alleged captor of Jack the Ripper.

Joined the Metropolitan Police, 1887 (warrant no. 72541). Discharged, April 1889, for being drunk on duty, unnecessarily interfering with two private persons and considered unfit for the Police Force. Thereafter, school groundsman and resident in Saville Row, Woodford Green.

He wrote to the *Daily Express* that one night after the Ripper had committed two murders:

> I had worked my beat backwards, and had come to Henage [sic] Street, off Brick Lane. About fifty yards on the right down Henage Street is Henage Court. At the bottom of the court was a brick-built dustbin. Both Jack and a woman (Rosy) were sitting on this. She had 2s (10p) in her hand, and she followed me when I took Jack on suspicion. He turned out to be a highly respected doctor and gave a Brixton address. His shirt cuffs still had blood on them. Jack had the proverbial bag with him (a brown one). This was not opened and he was allowed to go.
>
> I saw him several times after this at Liverpool Street Station, accosting women, and I would remark to him, 'Hello, Jack! Still after them?' He would immediately bolt.
>
> He was always dressed the same – high hat, black suit with silk facings, and a gold watch and chain. He was about 5 feet 8 or 9 inches and about 12 stone, fair moustache, high forehead, and rosy cheeks.
> (See *Daily Express*, 16 March 1931.)

Interviewed by an *Express* reporter, Spicer said that eight or nine inspectors all working on the case were at the station, and Spicer, to his amazement, got into trouble for arresting a respectable doctor. The CID allowed him no further part in investigating the man's story, and Spicer said that he was so disappointed that his heart was no longer in police work. He did not, however, as some writers have assumed, make the specifically false claim to have resigned over the issue.

An oral tradition, deriving from Spicer's family, is that the suspect was not a qualified doctor, but a medical student at the London Hospital. PC Spicer's granddaughter said that 'Rosy' wrote to her grandfather after the event, thanking him for saving her from murder and thereafter always sent him Christmas cards (Shirley Harrison, *The Diary of Jack the Ripper*. London: Blake, 1998, pg.157–158.)

See also **F.R. Chapman, Rosy, B. Reilly, 'Dr Merchant'**.

SPIERING, FRANK (b c.1941–d. 1996)

Author of *Prince Jack*. A one-time private investigator in New York, Spiering turned to writing. His first book, *The Man Who Got Capone*, was the tale of Treasury agent Frank Wilson, who found the evidence to put Al Capone away on tax evasion charges. He followed this with *Prince Jack*, a reworking of the Royal conspiracy theory, and after a brief flirtation with fiction, returned to true crime, with a look at the Lizzie Borden murder case. Spiering then set up his own publishing business, Monteray Press, which he launched with a title of his own, *Who Killed Polly?*, but he died soon after publication.

(See **Ripperologist**, August 2000, for his obituary.)

SPITZKA, DR EDWARD C.

A noted 'alienist' involved in the examination of Charles Guiteau, who murdered US President James A. Garfield. The *Anaconda Standard*, 5 May 1901, reported that Jack the Ripper, 'was safely locked up in an English insane asylum some time ago, and, if he is not dead, he is undoubtedly there yet...' It went on to tell how at the time of the murders, a lunatic had called upon Dr Spitzka, seeking treatment, and how the doctor, 'became convinced beyond any reasonable doubt that his patient was an insane physician and none other than the famous criminal...' Other alienists and the police authorities agreed. Another version of the **Sir William Gull/R.J. Lees** story? (Coincidentally, Guiteau is alleged to have stayed at the same hotel as Dr Tumblety.)

SPOONER, EDWARD

Witness at **Elizabeth Stride**'s inquest. A horse-keeper, resident at 26 Fairclough Street. Between 12.30 and 1am, he stood outside the Bee Hive public house with a young woman. At 1am, he saw **Louis Diemschütz** and another man running towards him, shouting, 'Murder!' and 'Police!' Thereafter, he accompanied them back to Berner Street, where he saw blood flowing from Stride's throat. He mentioned the flower on her jacket and cachous in her hand, but not the grapestalk.

SPRATLING, INSPECTOR JOHN (1845–1938)

Policeman. Witness at **Mary Ann Nichols**' inquest.

A clerk prior to joining the Metropolitan Police in 1870 (warrant no. 53457). After a fairly rapid series of promotions, he became divisional inspector, J Division (possibly succeeding **Inspector Reid** in 1887). Retired, 1897, and died in Beccles, Suffolk, on 22 November 1938. He is said to have boasted that he smoked blacker tobacco and drank blacker tea than anyone else in the Met, and that he lived so long that he drew more from the Met in pension than pay.

Described as 'a keen-eyed man with iron-grey hair and beard' (*Star*, 3 September 1888), he was called to Buck's Row at 4.30am, on 31 August 1888, as Nichols' blood was being washed away.

He went to the mortuary to take a description of the body, but did not discover the abdominal wounds until he subsequently lifted the skirts to take a description of the undergarments. Following this, he sent for **Dr Llewellyn**. The flesh, he said, was turned over from left to right, the intestines exposed.

Spratling did not feel very well at the time and the sight 'turned him up' so that he did not make a very precise examination (*Daily News*, 3 September 1888). He and **Sergeant Godley** searched the murder area, especially the East London and District Railway embankments and lines, and the Great Eastern Railway Yard. They found nothing to excite interest.

SPRINGFIELD, LINCOLN (c. 1866–1950)

Prominent and popular journalist. Worked for the *Pall Mall Gazette*, then joined the *Star* as chief reporter, and the *Daily Mail* as news editor and acting editor. In 1909, he formed a company and acquired *London Opinion*, which he edited until 1924. He was a member of the Savage Club and an enthusiastic player of contract bridge. In 1950, he died in Salisbury, Southern Rhodesia.

In *Some Piquant People* (1924), he claims that **Harry Dam** fled to England following tenure as private secretary to the Governor of California, during which time he amassed thousands of dollars through the illicit sale of pardons to convicted criminals. Also claims that Dam was responsible for the '**Leather Apron**' story, which very nearly resulted in a libel case against the *Star*. **William Le Queux** says that he, Springfield and Charles Hands all tried to outdo each other with Ripper theories for their respective newspapers. Springfield does not mention Le Queux in his autobiography.

'SQUIBBY'
See **George Cullen**.

STAMMER, JOHANN
See **Jonas**.

'STANLEY, DR' (d. c. 1918)
Alleged suspect. Proposed by **Leonard Matters** in *The People* (26 December 1926) and thereafter in ***The Mystery of Jack the Ripper***. Matters' source was an article in a Buenos Aires Spanish-language journal, allegedly written by an anonymous former student of the doctor, who claimed to have been summoned to a Buenos Aires hospital with information that a man he would know as 'Dr Stanley' was a patient there, whereupon he heard the dying man's confession.

A brilliant London doctor at 'X' Hospital (Charing Cross?) with a large and aristocratic practice. Resided in Portman Square. Devoted his life to the study of cancer. Once acted as anaesthetist for Joseph Lister at a Berkeley Street Sanatorium. Had a son named (possibly by Matters) 'Herbert' or 'Bertie', in whom he placed great hopes. Herbert contracted syphilis from **Mary Jane Kelly** on Boat Race night, 1886, and subsequently died. 'Stanley' set out to avenge his son by killing Kelly and her friends. His mission complete, he travelled the world, settling in Buenos Aires in 1908.

(*See* **John T. Sullivan** for an account which might refer to 'Dr Stanley' and predates Matters by 25 years.)

STANLEY, TED 'THE PENSIONER'

Witness at **Annie Chapman**'s inquest. A bricklayer, resident at 1 Osborn Place, Brick Lane, known to associates as an ex-soldier drawing a pension from the Essex Regiment. Sometimes paid for Chapman's bed at Crossingham's Lodging House at weekends, as well as for **Eliza Cooper**'s. (*See* **Annie Chapman** for the allegation that the fight between the two women concerned soap borrowed for his use.) Members of the coroner's jury knew the other man in Chapman's life, 'Harry the Hawker', but wanted the less-familiar Stanley summoned in case the Sussex Regiment envelope found near her body was connected with him.

Stanley admitted that he had never been in, nor drawn a pension from any regiment (though he was in the Hampshire militia). He had known Chapman for about two years, since she had lived at Windsor. Between 6 August and 1 September 1888, he had been in Gosport and had last seen Chapman when he met her at the corner of Brushfield Street on 1 September.

STAPLES, WILLIAM FRASER MACKENZIE (*b. c.* 1847–91)

Chief clerk in the Metropolitan Police Commissioner's office from 1884 until his death in harness, in 1891. His signature on many letters in the files is evidence that he copied them: he should not be mistaken for their composer. Staples got a brief mention in the press when he was apparently the first person to visit **James Monro** after he assumed the Commissionership. Also, **Dr MacKellar** addressed a letter to Staples, in which he forwarded a brief response by **Dr Brownfield** to police queries.

STEAD, WILLIAM THOMAS (1849–1912)

Publicist of crimes and alleged informant. Journalist.

Worked for the *Northern Echo*, 1871–80. Assistant editor, *Pall Mall Gazette*, 1880–83; editor, 1883–90. Started *Review of Reviews*, 1890. Took up psychical research. Drowned on the *Titanic*.

As editor of the radical and, by the standards of the times, sensational *Pall Mall Gazette*, Stead gave heavy coverage to the Whitechapel murders, using them as part of the radical campaign (more vehemently conducted in the *Star*) that attacked the Metropolitan Police.

He accepted articles on the case from **Robert Donston Stephenson**, who, according to **Melvin Harris**, he once thought might have been the Ripper. Stephenson claimed that Stead told him medical evidence showed that **Mary Jane Kelly** had been sodomised by her killer.

STEMLER, LEWIS (b. c. 1884)

Belated and extraordinary suspect.

In May 1915, Stemler, an unemployed Austrian waiter, was found in a hallway in 17th Street, New York, by the father of some 5- and 6-year-old boys that he had been chasing down 1st Avenue. Since a child had recently been murdered on 1st Avenue and his mother had received a letter boasting the killer would soon strike again, feelings ran high and Stemler was suggested as possibly having been Jack the Ripper *(Indiana Evening Standard*, 8 May 1915). Since he would have been 4 years old in 1888, he may be the most improbable suspect ever postulated.

STEPHEN, JAMES KENNETH (1859–92)

Suspect proposed by Michael Harrison in 1972. Educated at King's College, Cambridge. BA, 1882; tutor to **Prince Albert Victor** during his formal residence at Cambridge, 1883; MA, 1885; Fellow, 1885. Suffered serious blow to the head in 1886, which ultimately caused brain damage and death. Published and edited the *Reflector*, 1888; contributed to the *Pall Mall Gazette*. Clerk of Assize, South Wales circuit, 1888–90. Returned to residence in Cambridge, 1890, publishing a pamphlet in defence of compulsory Greek. In 1891, he was committed to St Andrew's Hospital, Northampton, where he died.

Stephen was a scintillating political speaker and president of the Cambridge Union, 1880. He contributed to *Granta* and other university journals; also published three volumes of undistinguished verse. Some friends felt that the *Reflector* showed marks of mental instability, and his shifting career – don, journalist, lawyer, and again don – is quite unlike the steady Victorian legal progress of his brothers. He furiously resisted the notion that his mind had given way at the end of his life and his untimely death provoked a good deal of undistinguished obituary verse in Cambridge University journals.

Stephen was proposed as a suspect in Michael Harrison's *Clarence* (1972). Harrison's motive was unusual: in an interview on BBC Television (reported in the *Listener*, 17 August 1972), he remarked that he had to deal with **Dr Thomas Stowell**'s suggestion that Clarence (i.e. Albert Victor) was the Ripper. 'I didn't agree,' said Harrison. 'But I couldn't leave the reader high and dry, so what I did was find somebody I thought was a likely candidate.'

He based his argument on the speculation that Clarence and Stephen had become homosexual lovers during, or after Clarence's time in Cambridge. He thought that some of Stephen's verse indicated misogyny and some showed sadistic tendencies; he suggested the affair was necessarily broken off, and Stephen then killed prostitutes on dates which would seem significant to his former lover – birthdays of members of the Royal Family, or pre-Christian religious festivals. Harrison suggested two rugby songs, 'Kafoozelum' and 'They Called the Bastard Stephen', influenced the pattern of the murders: the former because he erroneously believed there to have been 10 victims (which apparently parallels a version of 'Kafoozelum' known to Harrison).

The only known external support for the Stephen theory comes from a letter written by Mrs Marny Hallam of Newbury to *The Sunday Times* (16 February 1975), in which she states that her great-grandfather, a barrister, had long ago told his daughter that the authorities knew Stephen to be the Ripper.

Stephen is named in the forged **Abberline** diaries, in **David Abrahamsen**'s *Murder and Madness* and in John Wilding's *Jack the Ripper Revealed*. See also, *The Prince, His Tutor and the Ripper: The Evidence Linking James Kenneth Stephen to the Whitechapel Murders*.

STEPHENSON, ROBERT DONSTON (1841–1916)

Self-styled Dr Roslyn D'Onston. Contemporary theorist, supposedly suspected of being the Ripper at one time by W.T. Stead. Inferentially suggested as the Ripper by **Betty May** in 1925 on evidence apparently deriving from Baroness **Vittoria Cremers**, which was eventually recounted to Bernard O'Donnell by the Baroness in the 1930s. **Melvin Harris** concluded Stephenson was the Ripper after creating a list of attributes that he believed the Ripper needed, and which he believed Stephenson uniquely satisfied, including: demonstrable presence in Whitechapel in 1888, sufficient strength to commit the crimes and a genteel appearance to lull prostitutes' suspicions.

He claimed the murders stopped when Stephenson's health broke down due to excessive use of chloral hydrate. Much greater emphasis is placed on the black-magic motivation in *Jack the Ripper Black Magic Rituals*.

Born 20 April 1841, in Sculcoates, Hull, the son of Richard Stephenson, a seed-oil mill owner, and his wife Isabella (née Dawber).

By his own account, he studied chemistry in Munich and Geissen, and medicine in Paris. Signed on as a volunteer with Garibaldi in 1859, falsifying his age as 22 (muster roll, Holyoake Collection, Bishopsgate Institute), but Garibaldi's expedition was postponed for a year and Stephenson does not appear on the list of excursionists who departed with him. Melvin Harris says Stephenson stayed with an unnamed old school friend in Islington, in 1860, and did in fact serve with Garibaldi (no source given). Stephenson himself claimed that he served as a medical officer with Garibaldi in the campaign of 1860, amputating the limbs of large numbers of injured soldiers, and on one occasion using magical lore learned from Sir Edward Bulwer Lytton to treat a woman cursed by the Evil Eye (but see below).

He is listed on the census taken in April 1861 as living with his parents in Hull, with no medical degree or employment given. The following year, 1862, by his own very precise and circumstantial dating, he met in Paris the diplomat Edward Robert Lytton, the son of occultist Sir Edward Bulwer Lytton (later first Baron Lytton). Edward Robert Lytton, however, was at that time based in Copenhagen. Stephenson claimed Edward Robert Lytton introduced him to Bulwer Lytton the following year and that Bulwer Lytton trained him in occult knowledge. The date of the meeting may be wrong as Stephenson's claim to have used occult lore against the Evil Eye in Italy, in 1860, would suggest that if the meeting ever took place, it must have been in 1859.

According to articles written in the 1890s, in the 1860s Stephenson visited Africa, learning about West African black magic and encountering a fearful Obeah woman in the Cameroons, who was very like the dreadful sorceress in H. Rider Haggard's *She*. The stories are manifest lies, postulating that Stephenson visited the Cameroons 15 years before the first European explorers reached them, and displaying complete ignorance of West African geography.

What is known is that in 1863, Stephenson bowed to family pressure and took a post as a clerk with the Customs in Hull. He claimed that his family attempted to engineer his marriage to an heiress and that he was obliged to end an affair with a prostitute, which he did on a bridge over a canal in August 1867, agreeing to meet her there on the bridge on the annual anniversary of their parting. Prior to the second anniversary, Stephenson was accidentally wounded and went to the bridge in a wheelchair. He heard and saw his lover, then heard heavy footsteps following her. She disappeared and he later learned that she had died three months previously (article in the *Review of Reviews,* 1892).

Stephenson's dating of the incident does not correspond with the known facts. The accidental wounding took place in 1868 on a wildfowl-shooting boating excursion off Flamborough, when Stephenson claimed he was accidentally shot in the thigh by the boat's skipper, Thomas Piles, who was a smuggler. Newspaper reports suggest Stephenson was shot by a crewmember or by a friend (*Bridlington Free Press*, 11 July 1868; *Eastern Morning News and Hull Advertiser*, 13 July 1868; *Bridlington Quay Observer*, 14 July 1868; *Hull Packet*, 17 July 1868; *Hull and North Lincolnshire Times*, 18 July 1868).

It is claimed that about this time Stephenson was suffering from a venereal disease and that his employment with the Customs Office was terminated because of his association with prostitutes. However, Custom House records,

1863–68, indicate that he was suffering from 'brain fever' (meningitis) and say only that he had been living an immoral life, which does not necessarily mean cavorting with prostitutes.

Stephenson would later claim that he participated in a California gold rush, during which a companion of his casually shot a Chinese prospector. Stephenson himself killed a man who had seduced a girl loved by his cousin, and dipped the girl's handkerchief in his blood for the cousin to return to her. These incidents would have occurred during the second (1869) gold rush. Other records suggest Stephenson was living in London in 1869, working as a freelance journalist.

In 1871, he was living at 2 Acorn Court, Strand, London, lodging with a compositor named John Murray and his wife Martha. The census for that year lists him as Roslyn D. Stevenson and gives his occupation as a lieutenant in the Coast Guard.

On 14 February 1876, he married Anne Deary in St James's Church, Holloway, and claimed that in 1878 he visited India, where the younger Lytton was now viceroy. Stephenson said he witnessed amazing black magic feats performed by the celebrated Simla gem dealer and occultist Alex Jacob (Ali Yacoub) – who was portrayed as 'Lurgan, the healer of sick pearls' in Rudyard Kipling's *Kim*; also as the eponymous hero of H. Marion-Crawford's *Mr Isaacs*.

The Indian experience was questioned in correspondence with W.T. Stead's journal *Borderland*, in which it was described in 1896, but surprisingly a correspondent who knew Jacob personally wrote in 1897 that the man was still alive and remembered the occurrence, even explaining two of the conjuring tricks which had completely deceived Stephenson.

In 1881, the census lists him as living with Annie at 10 Hollingsworth Street, North. He was described as a non-practising MD and scientific writer for the London press. In 1886, he applied unsuccessfully for the secretaryship of the Metropolitan and City Police Orphanage. Melvin Harris and Ivor Edwards speculate that Stephenson murdered his wife and suggest the Rainham torso may have been Annie, but researcher Nina Brown discovered a report of the death by poisoning from a gas leak of a cook named Ann Stephenson in Hampstead (*Daily News*, 28 April 1896). As her age fitted Annie's, and her occupation was comparable with Annie's prior to her marriage, it has been speculated that this was Stephenson's wife.

In 1888, he was staying at the Cricketers Arms in Brighton, and Ivor Edwards speculates he might have murdered Edward Gurney, an investigator for the Society for Psychical Research, who was examining claims that Mme Helena Blavatsky (among others) was fraudulently claiming supernatural powers. Gurney died of chloroform poisoning in his Brighton hotel, the inquest concluding this was accidental death following his attempt to use the drug as a sleeping aid. Edwards suggests Stephenson's supposedly close links with Mme Blavatsky could have led him to act murderously on her behalf, but there is no evidence Stephenson knew, or had even met Blavatsky until 1890, when he wrote an article, 'African Magic', for Blavatsky's *Lucifer* magazine.

In July 1888, he left Brighton and entered the London Hospital as a private patient suffering from neurasthenia, a complaint characterised by nervous excitement and best treated by rest, freedom from stress and fresh air. Melvin Harris has said it was irrational for Stephenson to leave Brighton for London with such a complaint and suggested the illness might be feigned. Howard Brown, webmaster of **JTRForums.com**, has argued that neurasthenia cannot easily be feigned, it is diagnosed by a doctor, and suggests Stephenson was actually being treated for alcoholism.

During his time in the London Hospital the Whitechapel murders occurred and Harris and Edwards both maintain Stephenson perpetrated them by slipping out from the hospital at night into the adjacent East End. However, Stephenson was in the Currie Ward until at least 16 October 1888, and in 2007 Jonathan Evans, curator of the London Hospital Museum, told researcher Mike Covell that Currie Ward patients were prevented from leaving the ward at night.

From the hospital and using the name Major R.D'O Stephenson, he wrote to the City Police in October suggesting the **Goulston Street graffito** might use the word '*juives*' (French for Jewish females) and at the beginning of December he contributed a piece to the *Pall Mall Gazette* making the same suggestion (London Metropolitan Archives, Police Box 3.23 no. 300 and 1.12.1888 respectively).

In November, he shared a private ward with a Dr Evans, who was nightly visited by **Dr Morgan Davies**. On one of these visits, he saw Dr Davies perform such a graphic and over-excited re-enactment of the Ripper's supposed modus operandi that it convinced him that Davies was the Ripper, a view confirmed when he allegedly learned from W.T. Stead that the Ripper sodomised Mary Jane Kelly, as Davies's mime indicated.

On 7 December, he left the hospital and moved into lodgings off St Martin's Lane. In the Prince Albert public house he met **George Marsh**, an ironmongery salesman, who had been out of work for a couple of months. The two agreed to act together as private detectives following up the Dr Davies' theory. On Christmas Eve, Marsh went to Scotland Yard and told **Inspector Roots** about Stephenson, who was using the alias 'Sudden Death'. Then, on Boxing Day, Stephenson went to Scotland Yard to give his own contemptuous account of the meeting with Marsh.

Roots recognised Stephenson as a man that he had known for 20 years and whom he understood to be, 'a travelled man of education and ability, a doctor with diplomas of medicine upon diplomas of Paris and New York', and to have been a major in the Italian Army. He added, 'He has led a Bohemian life, drinks heavily, and always carries drugs to sober him and stave off delirium tremens' (see *The Complete Jack the Ripper Sourcebook*, Chapter 39).

In May 1889, Stephenson was back in the London Hospital, this time for 10 or more weeks, being treated for the adverse effects of over-using the sleep-inducing drug chloral hydrate.

By 1890, he was living in Southsea with the novelist **Mabel Collins**, who was at that time editing *Lucifer*, the journal of the Theosophical Society, to which he contributed, under the name 'Tau-Triadelta', an article: 'African Magic'. They were visited by Baroness **Vittoria Cremers**, rumoured to be a lover of Collins, and the three went into business, forming Pompadour Cosmetics. During this period, Collins and Cremers became convinced that Stephenson was Jack the Ripper, especially when Cremers found in Stephenson's room a small, black-enamelled deed box containing bloodstained made-up ties. Eventually, the commercial partnership broke up when Stephenson sued Collins for the return of some letters.

Stephenson abandoned theosophy and the occult to work on his edition of the gospels in translation – *The Patristic Gospels* (1904) – an eccentric variant of the Revised Version, preferring readings from church fathers to the earliest codices.

His subsequent history is uncertain.

See **Melvin Harris**, *The True Face of Jack the Ripper*; Ivor Edwards, *Jack the Ripper: the Black Magic Rituals*. There is extensive coverage on JTRForums.com. Also, *Crowley's Ripper: The Collected Works of Roslyn D'Onston* (ed. Jarett Kobek), *http://kobek.com/crowleyripper.pdf*; Kim Farnell, *Mystical Vampire* (Oxford: Mandrake, 2005). (*A Life of Mabel Collins* offers the erroneous information that Stephenson adopted a boy named Harman Wheas after his conversion. This apparently confuses him with another Robert Stephenson of Hull.) Tom Wescott, 'Have You Seen The Devil: D'Onston and the Ripper Letters', *Ripperologist*, 56, November 2004; Howard Brown, 'The Cremers Memoirs: Another Crumbled Pillar', *Ripperologist*, 98, December 2008; Mike Covell, 'D'Onston Stephenson: From Robert to Roslyn', *Ripperologist*, 98, December 2008.

See also **Bernard O'Donnell**.

STEVENS, FREDERICK

Fellow-lodger of Annie Chapman's at Crossingham's. Told the *Star*, on 8 September 1888, that he had drunk a pint of beer with her at 12.30am and she did not finally leave the lodging-house until 1am.

STEVENS, WILLIAM

Witness at **Annie Chapman**'s inquest. A printer who lodged at **Crossingham**'s, he saw Chapman in the lodging-house kitchen at 12.12am, where she picked up a piece of an envelope beside the fireplace, transferred some pills from a broken pill-box into it and left the kitchen. (*Cf.* **Inspector Chandler**.)

STEWART, WILLIAM DOUGLAS (1883–1965)

Theorist and researcher. Author of *Jack the Ripper – A New Theory*.

Born in Greenwich in July 1883, the son of the playwright and author Douglas Stewart.

Became Advertising Director of the London Press Exchange in 1903 commissioning pen-and-ink drawings for Fleet Street newspapers. Contributed drawings to *Punch* and weekly short stories to the *Evening Standard*. During WWI he was official war artist for the *Illustrated London News*. At the end of the War he became a scenic designer for the Oswald Stoll theatre group (which became Moss Empires), and was a member of the British Water Colour Society and RBA. Worked closely with actor Tod Slaughter, notably producing sets for Slaughter's Christmas pantomimes. Returned to advertising as production manager for British Commercial Gas Association. Developed an interest in the East End and Jack the Ripper and spent much time photographing East End scenes and the Ripper sites. In 1938 a photograph of 29 Hanbury Street when developed showed a woman dressed in Victorian working-class clothes in a front window. It was sent to the Society for Psychical Research, but as far as is known the mystery was never resolved. He researched the Ripper case and spoke with several policemen involved in the investigation. His **Jack the Ripper – A New Theory** was published in March 1939. He also wrote *Characters of Bygone London* (1960)

Andy Aliffe, *Pictures, Paint and Prosceniums'*, **Ripperologist**, 14, December 1997

STOCKLEY, CHIEF INSPECTOR JAMES (1863–1954)

Warrant no. 70995. Perhaps the longest-living policeman engaged on the Ripper case.

Joined the Metropolitan Police in 1885, at Leman Street Station, H Division. Chief inspector by the time of his retirement in 1911. Set up as a private detective and included among his clients Miss Florence Pratt, the Singer sewing machine heiress. On her death in 1934, she left him her fortune of £1,000,000. The will was contested, but Stockley enjoyed a very comfortable old age in a Devon cottage on £5,000 a year interest from the bequest. His part in the Ripper enquiry was small, but it was reported that he used various disguises – as loafer, costermonger, chimney sweep and itinerant musician.

STOKES, MRS ELIZABETH

Witness at **Elizabeth Stride**'s inquest. Sister of witness, Mrs **Mary Malcolm**, according to whom she was the murder victim.

Mrs Stokes and Mrs Malcolm were two of the four daughters and four sons of a publican named Perrin from Colerne, near Chippenham, Wilts.

Elizabeth married a Bath wine merchant called Watts. She claimed his family disapproved of her and persuaded him to go to America, after which they had her two children put into someone else's care, and placed Elizabeth in Fisherton House Insane Asylum, near Salisbury.

Some time after Watts' death, Elizabeth was found to be sane and released. She went to Walmer for domestic service and met her second husband, a man named Sneller who (as Mrs Malcolm correctly stated) was stranded on St Paul's Island, near New Zealand, where he died. Left destitute, Elizabeth broke down and was committed to Peckham Lunatic Asylum. Pronounced sane by the Lunacy Commissioners, she was subsequently released and married Mr Stokes in 1884.

Mrs Malcolm's story, which she described as a pack of lies, had greatly embarrassed her: partly because it claimed untruly that she had been caught in flagrante delecto by Mr Watts and proceeded to a life of mendicancy and prostitution, partly because acquaintances of Mr Stokes accused her of bigamy.

Apart from a few parallels between her life story and Elizabeth Stride's, Mrs Stokes resembled the dead woman in her limp – caused by an adder bite in childhood. (*See* **Dr Phillips** for the medical report on Stride, including her deformed leg.)

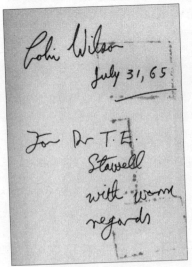

Colin Wilson
July 31, 65

For Dr T. E.
Stowell
with warm
regards

STOWELL, DR THOMAS EDWARD ALEXANDER (1885–1970)

Theorist.

Educated at St Thomas's Hospital. MRCS, LRCP, 1910; FRCS, 1912. Worked at hospitals in Leeds, Liverpool, Newcastle, Vienna, Harvard and Manchester. Specialised in industrial medicine, becoming chief medical officer to ICI and organising the ninth International Congress on Industrial Medicine. Honorary Dip. Indust. Disease, Buenos Aires, 1949. Honorary Dip. Indust. Health, Society of Apothecaries, 1953. Published on the etiology of Dupuytren's contracture.

In August 1960, following publication of a series of articles about the Ripper by Colin Wilson in the *Evening Standard* (8–12 August), Stowell invited Wilson to lunch at the Athenaeum and expounded his theory that the Ripper was **Prince Albert Victor**, mistakenly believing that Wilson also suspected him. Wilson has recounted the meeting several times (for example, in *Jack the Ripper: Summing Up and Verdict*), but his memory or Stowell's account contained several factual errors.

Stowell eventually published his theory ('Jack the Ripper – A Solution?', *Criminologist,* November 1970), calling his suspect 'S', apparently at the suggestion of his editor **Nigel Morland** (see Morland's introduction to *Prince Jack*, but giving sufficient clues for him to be identified as Prince Albert Victor). Stowell further claimed that **Sir William Gull** had been suspected at the time, having often been seen in Whitechapel when the murders were committed. He further suggested it was to Gull's house that **Robert James Lees** had brought the police and claimed that Caroline Acland, Gull's daughter, had told him about a visit to her parent's home by a psychic and the police.

Stowell later denied in a letter to *The Times* (9 November 1970) that he meant Prince Albert Victor. Sadly, Dr Stowell died the day before his letter was published. (Nick Warren, 'The Stowell Papers and the Duke of Clarence or Otherwise', ***Ripperana,*** 2, October 1992)

STRIDE, ELIZABETH (1843-88)

Third canonical Ripper victim (but see below). Also known as 'Long Liz', 'Epileptic Annie', 'Hippy Lip Annie', 'Mother Gum', Annie Fitzgerald.

Born on 27 November 1843, the second daughter of farmer Gustaf Ericsson and his wife, Beata Carlsdotter, in Stora Tumlehed, Hisingen Island, Torslanda, near Gothenburg, Sweden. She had an elder sister named Anna Christina and would have two brothers, Carl-Bernhard (*b.* 1848) and Svante (*b.* 1851). Swedish police records describe her as having blue eyes, brown hair, a straight nose, oval face and to be of slight build.

On 25 October 1860, she was granted a certificate of altered residence and moved to Gothenburg. Her whereabouts are unknown between that time and February 1861, when she found employment as a domestic servant to Lars Frederick Olofsson (*b.* 1825) and his wife Johanna (*b.* 1828) and their children. She worked for them until 2 February 1864, when she left their employment, apparently suddenly and for unknown reasons. By March 1865, she was registered by the police of Gothenburg as a professional prostitute.

On 4 April 1865, she was admitted to Kurhuset, the hospital for the treatment of venereal disease in the red-light district near Gottenburg harbour, to be treated for venereal warts. While there, on 21 April she gave birth to a stillborn daughter. She was discharged as healthy on 13 May 1865, but readmitted on 30 August to be treated for a venereal ulcer and discharged on 23 September. The same ailment caused her to be sent to the hospital for a third time on 17 October until 1 November.

On 14 November, she was struck off the police register of prostitutes. Apparently the only way this could happen would be if the prostitute got married or found employment, neither being easy to achieve. Elizabeth found employment with a woman named Maria Wejsner, who in a letter accepted responsibility for her good behaviour:

13 November 1865
The maid Elisabeth Gustafson has entered my service on 10 November and answers to me for her good behavior for as long as she remains in my custody.
Gothenburg, 13 November 1865
Mrs Maria Wiesner
Husargatan House No. 42

Author Birgita Leufstadius (***Jack the Rippers Tredje Offer***) suggested that Maria Wejsner may have been an influential brothel keeper, but this is without foundation. She was the wife of Carl Wenzel Wejsner, a musician with the band of the West Götha Artillery Regiment and an immigrant from Bohemia, now part of the Czech Republic. Originally Wiesner, he appears to have changed his name to the more Swedish-sounding Wejsner and he lived with his family at 27 Husargatan Street, Haga Parish, Gothenburg. It has been suggested that the Wejsners were Jewish and that it was during the short time that she was with them that Elizabeth learnt to speak Yiddish, as claimed by her future lover, **Michael Kidney.**

Elizabeth's mother had died on 25 August 1864 and in December 1865, or January 1866, she received a substantial inheritance of 65 Swedish Crowns. She applied to move to London, the application being granted on 2 February 1866. On 7 February, she sailed to London. She would later claim that she came to London in the service of a gentleman (according to **Charles Preston**), or in a situation with a family (according to **Michael Kidney**, although initially he said that she had told him that she first came as a tourist, a claim he doubted). Kidney also added that she had lived as a servant to a gentleman somewhere near Hyde Park (see *Daily Telegraph*, 4 October 1888). On 10 July 1866, she registered with the Swedish Church, Princess Square, St. George's-in-the-East.

On 7 March 1869, she married **John Thomas Stride** at St Giles's in the Fields, giving her maiden name as Gustifson and address as 67 Gower Street. John and Elizabeth Stride opened a coffee shop at Upper North Street, Poplar, and a year or two later, they moved their establishment to 178 Poplar High Street. They did not live on the premises, but a few doors away at 172.

On 21 March 1877, she was taken by the police from the Thames Magistrates Court to the Poplar Workhouse. We do not know why. The following year, 1878, the steamer *Princess Alice* sank in a collision off Woolwich with considerable loss of life, among whom Stride would later claim were her husband and two children. This claim has since proved untrue.

In January 1879, Stride appealed to the Swedish Church for financial aid because of her husband's illness.

By 1881, the couple were living at 69 Usher Road, Old Ford Road, Bow, but the marriage was troubled and appears to have broken down that year. On 28 December 1881, when Elizabeth Stride was suffering from bronchitis and spent some time in the Whitechapel Workhouse Infirmary, she gave as her address a lodging-house in Brick Lane. After leaving the workhouse in January 1882, she moved into a common lodging-house at 32 Flower and Dean Street.

John Stride was admitted to Poplar Workhouse in August 1884 and would die in Stepney Sick Asylum of heart disease on 24 October. On 13 November, Elizabeth was sentenced to seven days' hard labour for being drunk, disorderly and soliciting.

By 1885, she was living with Michael Kidney at 38 Dorset Street, deserting him from time to time for the remainder of her life. In 1886, she made two claims for financial aid on the Swedish Church, giving her address as Devonshire Street, Commercial Road. During 1887–88, Stride amassed eight convictions for drunkenness at Thames Magistrates Court under her own name; possibly one other under the false name Fitzgerald. In April 1887, she charged Michael Kidney with assault, but failed to appear to prosecute. The relationship with Kidney broke down and in September 1888, Stride returned to 32 Flower and Dean Street, where she had not stayed for the previous three months. She was allegedly seen there some days before her death by **Dr Barnardo** when he visited common lodging-houses and urged prostitutes to place their children under his care.

On 29 September 1888, she cleaned rooms at 32 Flower and Dean Street, for which Mrs **Elizabeth Tanner** paid her 6d. At 6.30pm, she went to the Queen's Head public house. Then, at 7pm, she returned to the lodging-house, where she borrowed a clothes brush from Charles Preston and gave **Catherine Lane** a piece of velvet to look after until she came back. She left looking cheerful.

At 11pm, **J. Best** and **John Gardner** saw her leave the Bricklayers' Arms in Settles Street in company with a young Englishman of clerkly appearance and go in the direction of Commercial Road and Berner Street. At 11.45pm, **William Marshall** saw her with an Englishman in Berner Street, the two moving away in the direction of Dutfield's Yard and **Matthew Packer**'s greengrocer's shop.

Packer claimed to have sold half a pound of black grapes to a man accompanying Stride, at a time variously fixed as 11pm, 11.45pm and around midnight. He then watched the pair cross the road and stand in the rain for almost half an hour facing Dutfield's Yard. Police Constable **William Smith** saw Stride standing there with a man at 12.30am. **James Brown** saw a woman that he was 'almost certain' was Stride at 12.45am, standing with a man in Fairclough Street. But at the same time, **Israel Schwartz** saw Stride assaulted and thrown to the pavement outside Dutfield's Yard (or pushed into the Yard itself) by a young, intoxicated man that he had been following down Berner Street from Commercial Road. Schwartz ran away, pursued, or so he thought, by another man ('the pipe man'), who came out of the pub (or pub doorway) at the same time and, Schwartz thought, ran after him.

About 1am, **Louis Diemschütz** drove his horse and cart into Dutfield's Yard and found the body. It was his impression that death had been so recent that the murderer must have been hiding in the yard and escaped while he went into the International Workingmen's Educational Club to report and investigate what he believed to be a drunk woman lying behind the gates.

For Stride's injuries, see **Dr Phillips**, who reported to the inquest that she had definitely not eaten grape skins or pips for several hours before her death, though he confirmed that stains on her handkerchief were fruit juice. This apparently conflicts with Packer's testimony to having sold grapes to her companion and the reports in the press that some of the witnesses saw a grapestalk clutched in her left hand or dropped in the Yard after her body had been removed. (See **Louis Diemschütz, Eva Harstein**.) **Walter Dew** may offer an explanation in his recollection that detectives searching the Yard found several spat-out grape skins and seeds.

Her inquest was inevitably protracted – satisfactory evidence as to her identity was delayed by the need to investigate her own extraordinary lies about her past and Mrs Mary Malcolm's erroneous identification of her with Mrs Elizabeth Stokes.

Three witnesses do not appear to have been called to the inquest: Mrs Fanny Mortimer (whose negative evidence of seeing and hearing nothing suspicious while she stood outside her house in Berner Street might have helped fix the time of death), Matthew Packer and Israel Schwartz (see above).

Phillips also testified that all the teeth from Stride's lower left jaw were missing.

Stride's funeral was sparsely attendedand she was buried in pauper's grave, no. 15509, in East London Cemetery at the expense of the parish by undertaker **Hawkes**.

Walter Dew remarked that, 'traces of prettiness remained in her face, and there must have been a time when she was exceedingly proud of her curly black hair.' Discovery of Stride's mortuary photograph in 1988 confirmed that she had indeed attractive facial bone structure.

Newspapers at the time and senior police then and subsequently (**Abberline**, **Anderson**, **Macnaghten**, **Smith**, **Swanson**) accepted without question that Stride was a Ripper victim, assuming the murderer was alarmed by Diemschütz's approaching vehicle and either hid or made his escape, thereupon proceeding to Mitre Square to murder **Catherine Eddowes** and satisfy his frustrated lust. But **Walter Dew** remarked that he had always suspected Stride might not have been a Ripper victim and **Edwin Woodhall** simply asserted that she was not. The following details distinguish Stride's murder from the other victims:

(i) No abdominal mutilations.

(ii) No extravasation of blood in neck and head region, which would indicate asphyxiation before throat-cutting.

(iii) Injuries caused by a short, broad and possibly blunt knife with a bevelled end, unlike the long, narrow-bladed knife sharpened to a point used in other cases.

(iv) Position of body that indicated falling on its left side, rather than on its back, as in other cases.

See also *Jack the Myth* for the suggestion that Michael Kidney killed her; *Elizabeth Stride and Jack the Ripper*, Daniel Olsson; 'Elizabeth's Story', *Ripperologist*, 52. March 2004; *Mrs Wenzel*, published in *Ripperologist*, 52, March 2004; 'The Executioner, the Musician, his Wife and her Friend', published in *Ripperologist*, 61, September 2005; 'Elizabeth Stride: The Yiddish Connection', *Ripperologist*, 96, October 2008.

STRIDE, JOHN THOMAS (1821–84)

Husband of **Elizabeth Stride**. Son of a shipwright, he himself was originally a ship's carpenter. Resident at Munster Street, Hampstead Road, and working as a carpenter when he married Stride at St Giles's in the Fields, 1869. Entered in trade directories as proprietor of coffee house at Upper North Street, Poplar, 1870–72; then at 178 Poplar High Street, 1872–74. His movements for the last

10 years of his life are unknown, though his marriage seems to have broken down by 1882. Died of heart failure in Bromley Sick Asylum, his address given as Poplar Workhouse.

STRIDE, PC WALTER FREDERICK (1858–1913)

Witness at **Elizabeth Stride**'s inquest and nephew of her deceased husband. Joined the Metropolitan Police in 1878 (warrant no. 62349). Retired, 1902. Testified that he recognised in the mortuary photographs a woman who had married his uncle.

SULLIVAN, – (fl. 1888)

Witness. Waterside labourer and lodger at 19 George Street, Spitalfields, on the morning when **Annie Farmer** was found with her throat lightly cut. Said he had gone out in search of work, and being unsuccessful, came home at 9.20, left his waterman's hook in the kitchen and stood in the front doorway, at which time the alleged assailant must already have left, since he did not pass Sullivan. After Annie Farmer screamed, Sullivan went outside and followed **Frank Ruffle** in the unsuccessful pursuit of the assailant towards Thrawl Street.

SULLIVAN, JOHN TAYLOR (d. 1904)

Actor and theatrical manager. Briefly and tempestuously married to famous actress Rose Coghlan (divorced, 1904). He appeared in **Richard Mansfield**'s production of *Dr Jekyll and Mr Hyde* on Broadway and in London in the role of Gabriel Utterson.

Recalled in an article called 'Hunting "Jack the Ripper": Thrilling Experiences of a Man Who Posed in Woman's Garb' in the *Salt Lake Herald*, 25 August 1901 (originally published in the *Denver Post*), that while appearing at London's Lyceum Theatre in 1888, it was suggested that he dress as a woman and go armed into Whitechapel, followed at a discreet distance by two companions.

Sir Charles Warren apparently gave his blessing to the scheme and Sullivan took to the streets on 2 October 1888. He claimed that 12 nights later in Dorset Street he encountered a man, aged about 45 years, with a stubbly, reddish beard and wearing a leather apron, who looked about to attack him but ran noiselessly away when Sullivan seemed ready to defend himself. The man was apprehended and Sullivan claims the newspapers were full of the arrest, although he turned out to be an eccentric, but harmless employee in a harness shop in Fleet Street.

Sullivan concluded his account by saying that the murderer:

…was a physician, a reputable man in London – a perfect Jekyll and Hyde. He had developed a homicidal mania and had been confined in a private sanatorium in a suburb of London. How he escaped was a mystery, but Scotland Yard knows that man today. He is an exile from his country. He lives at Buenos Ayres, in the Argentine Republic, and there being no law of extradition between that nation and England, he is entirely safe there. I have this on the best authority, although this is the first time the facts have been given to the public.

"Jack the Ripper" has not been in evidence since Dr. E left England. I need hardly say that he is under close surveillance in the Argentine capital, so that there will no repetition of his offense.

Sullivan's death was reported in *The New York Times*, 21 June 1904.

See **Dr Stanley**.

SUTTON, DR HENRY GAWAN (1836–91)

Reported to **Major Henry Smith** on the Lusk kidney.

Senior Surgeon and lecturer in physical anatomy, London Hospital, 1888. Co-author with **Sir William Gull** of a revolutionary paper, 'On the pathology of the morbid state commonly called chronic Bright's disease with contracted kidney' (arteriosclerotic fibrosis of the kidney was thereafter known as Gull-Sutton syndrome). Smith, therefore, was not exaggerating in calling him, 'one of the greatest authorities living on the kidney and its diseases.' Smith said Sutton affirmed that he would, 'pledge his reputation that [the Lusk kidney] had been put in spirits within a few hours of its removal from the body.' This meant that it could not have come from a dissecting room, where the body would have had to be held intact for a day or more to await the inquest.

SWANSON, CHIEF INSPECTOR DONALD SUTHERLAND (1848–1924)

In charge of the Whitechapel murders investigation, 1 September to *c.* 6 October 1888. Thereafter, desk officer in charge under **Dr Robert Anderson**'s command until the end of the case.

Born in Geise, near Thurso, on the north coast of Scotland, in 1848; the son of John Swanson, a brewer. Attended the Miller Institution, Thurso, where he was a brilliant pupil. Afterwards, he taught there and at Castletown. Briefly moved to London, where he worked as a clerk in the City's Seething Lane before joining the Metropolitan Police in 1868 (Warrant No. 50282) He was described as 5ft 8in, with dark brown hair, hazel eyes and a dark complexion. Served in A Division from 27 April 1868, until transferred to Y Division on 9 September 1870, K Division on 12 December 1871, A Division on 15 September 1876 and Central Office on 19 November 1887. Swanson's contemporary, John Sweeney, called him, 'One of the best class of officers…' (*At Scotland Yard*, 1903). **Sir Melville Macnaghten** described him as, 'a very capable officer with a synthetical turn of mind.' The *Police Review* reported that he had, 'for years been regarded as the first gentleman of the services by all his confreres' (15 May 1896). He reportedly viewed 'his work as decidedly a secret service' and was 'opposed to public "reminiscences"'.

He married Julie Ann Nevill, the daughter of James Nevill, on 23 May 1878 at West Ham Church. The couple had three sons and two daughters. Retired, 1903. His grandson, James Swanson (1912–2001), recalled, 'I stayed with my grandparents frequently. There was nothing old about him – he had a mind like a rapier.' Died on 25 November 1924 at 3 Presburg Road, New Malden, Surrey, from: '(1) Arterio Sclerosis (2) Heart Failure Asthemia'.

Swanson was a close associate of Sir Robert Anderson, whose will he witnessed after they had both retired. He continued to send affectionate Christmas letters to his 'old master' (in his words) until Anderson's death. Papers and notebooks preserved by his grandson indicate that the cases in which Swanson took most pride were the recovery of the Countess of Dysart's jewels, recovery of Gainsborough's painting of the Duchess of Devonshire (stolen by the master-criminal Adam Worth), the tracking and arrest of a now-forgotten confidence trickster and a crackdown on 'rent boys' (blackmailing homosexual prostitutes) in 1897. Contemporary newspapers, however, were more impressed by Swanson's part in arresting railway murderer Percy LeFroy Mapleton, suppressing Fenian terrorists and preventing the Jameson Raid in South Africa from sparking war with the Afrikaaners earlier than 1899.

Today, he is best known for his prominence in the Ripper investigation, although this has only been widely recognised since the publication of the **Swanson marginalia** in 1987. Reports in February 1891 (*Bristol Times* and *Daily Mirror*) refer to a prominent and experienced police officer as believing the Ripper had worn women's clothes to perpetrate his murders, and thinking the two hats found with **Frances Coles** appeared to corroborate this. The *San Francisco Chronicle* (14 February 1891) ascribes this belief to Swanson. The *Pall Mall Gazette* (7 May 1895) reported, 'The theory entitled to most respect, because it was presumably based upon the best knowledge, was that of Chief Inspector Swanson, the officer who was associated with the investigation of all the murders, and Mr Swanson believed the crimes to have been the work of a man who is now dead.' (Personal file at National Archives: MEPO 3/2890)

SWANSON MARGINALIA, THE

Pencil notes written in the margins and on the endpapers of **Chief Inspector Donald Swanson**'s personal copy of **Sir Robert Anderson**'s memoirs, *The Lighter Side of My Official Life* (1910), which bears the writing on the inside of the front cover: 'Donald S Swanson 3 Presburg Rd New Malden'. The book is part of a small cache of others, some containing marginal notes, papers and official documents inherited by the Swanson family. Gummed inside the front of the book is a handwritten letter from Anderson to Swanson, dated '25.12.05' [sic] referring to some enclosed papers and at the same time asking Swanson's 'acceptance of an accompanying book' (evidently not the copy of *The Lighter Side...* which in 1905 was unpublished). Underneath this letter is the inscription, 'To Donald with every good wish from Fred'.

Anderson's suspect is neither named nor clearly defined in his printed text, beyond the observations that he was a poor Polish Jew from Whitechapel whose people would not hand him over to justice, and that 'the only person who ever saw the murderer unhesitatingly identified the suspect the instant he was confronted with him; but he refused to give evidence against him'. Swanson continues, under the text:

'because the suspect was *also a Jew* and also because his evidence would convict the suspect, and witness would be the means of murderer being hanged, which he did not wish to be left on his mind. D.S.S.'

In the margin he continues, 'And after this identification which suspect knew, no other murder of this kind took place in London.'

On the endpaper appears: 'After the suspect had been identified at the Seaside Home where he had been sent by us with difficulty in order to subject him to identification and he knew he was identified.

'On suspect's return to his brother's house in White-chapel he was watched by police (City CID) by day and night. In a very short time the suspect with his hands tied behind his back he was sent to Stepney Workhouse and then to Colney Hatch and died shortly afterwards – Kosminski was the suspect – D.S.S.'

On the death of Donald Swanson in 1924, the book passed to Swanson's unmarried daughter, Alice Julia, and when she in turn died in 1981, it went to her nephew, James Swanson (1912–2001), according to whom, 'Though my grandfather had made these notes circa 1910, no one, not even his family, knew of their existence. It was not until his library, inter alia, came into my possession in 1981, when my aunt, his last surviving child, died that they were discovered.' The marginalia was discovered by James Swanson's brother, Donald Swanson (information supplied in a letter from Jim Swanson to the authors).

He reported having tried unsuccessfully to have the marginalia published in the *News of the World*, receiving a nominal fee for the rights, but the newspaper never used the material and the rights were returned. An article mentioning Kosminski – 'Jack: The Gripping Tale' by Charles Nevin, *Daily Telegraph*, 3 October 1987 – led him to contact that newspaper, which in due course made the marginalia public: 'Has This Man Revealed the Real Jack the Ripper?' by Charles Nevin, 19 October 1987.

The provenance, insofar as it could be established, met the usual standard

My Official Life

people of that class in the East End will not give up one of their number to Gentile justice.

And the result proved that our diagnosis was right on every point. For I may say at once that "undiscovered murders" are rare in London, and the "Jack-the-Ripper" crimes are not within that category. And if the Police here had powers such as the French Police possess, the murderer would have been brought to justice. Scotland Yard can boast that not even the subordinate officers of the department will tell tales out of school, and it would ill become me to violate the unwritten rule of the service. So I will only add here that the " Jack-the-Ripper" letter which is preserved in the Police Museum at New Scotland Yard is the creation of an enterprising London journalist.

Having regard to the interest attaching to this case, I am almost tempted to disclose the identity of the murderer and of the pressman who wrote the letter above referred to. But no public benefit would result from such a course, and the traditions of my old department would suffer. I will merely add that the only person who had ever had a good view of the murderer unhesitatingly identified the suspect the instant he was confronted with him ; but he refused to give evidence against him.

138

requirements: the book was in the possession of a descendant of Donald Swanson, the line of transmission was straightforward and it was part of a small cache of books, papers and official documents, some of the books also containing marginal notes, which insofar as they could be verified, were accurate. Nothing about the marginal notes, except the story they told, raised suspicions and there was otherwise no reason to suspect the notes were other than what they purported to be. The authors nevertheless provided photocopies (photocopies were less than ideal, but they did not at that time have access to original documents) to Mr. R.N. Totty, assistant director of the Home Office Forensic Science Laboratory. Mr Totty confirmed in a letter dated 5 October 1988 that the handwriting, 'matches that in the pencilled footnotes in the copy of Anderson's memoirs...' which he had seen. He expressed the wish to see further examples of the marginalia. This report has since been superseded (see Dr Christopher Davies below).

In July 2000, the author Stewart Evans examined the marginalia and observed that two pencils had been used; also slight differences in the handwriting between the marginal and endpaper notes. These had not been hitherto observed. On **Casebook Jack the Ripper**, 16 January 2006, he wrote:

501

I was very surprised at how faint the penciled notes were, images I had seen of them previously showed them to be much darker. This isn't meant to imply that something had been done to them, they were just much fainter than I expected them to be. However, the biggest surprise was that the marginalia inside the book on page 138 was written with a grey pencil but with a distinct purplish tinge to it and the writing was indented into the page as if hard pressure had been applied when writing. However, on turning to the notes on the rear free endpaper beginning "continuing from page 138..." it was clear that they were written with a different pencil of a pale grey hue and not indented into the page. There was a slightly different appearance to the writing that could easily be accounted for by the fact that there was much more room to write whereas the writing in the text, of necessity, had to be cramped.

The authors note that the 'distinct purplish tinge' – not observed by them when they examined the document in 1987/88 – suggests the use of indelible pencil.

In July 2006, following a suggestion by Keith Skinner, the Swanson family handed the book to the Metropolitan Police to be placed on permanent loan in the Crime Museum. The press treated it as a completely new discovery, quite unaware that its identification of Kosminski as Anderson's suspect had been in the public domain for 18 years. It was submitted to document examiner Dr Christopher Davies, MA, D. Phil (Oxford) of the Forensic Science Service London Laboratory, who produced a 10-page report dated 3 November 2006:

I have noted that these two sets of entries, although both written in pencil, appear to have been written with different pencils. I have further noted that the underline of the words "also a Jew" in the Set 1 entry appears to be in a similar pencil to that used for the Set 2 entries. These observations cause me to conclude that these two sets of entries were written at different times and that the Set 1 entry was written first.

The writing of these annotations is of reasonable quality although the writing of the Set 1 entry is of slightly better line quality than is the writing of the Set 2 entries. In particular the Set 2 entries show evidence of occasional tremor which is similar to that sometimes found in the writing of individuals with certain neurological conditions, such as Parkinsonism. This may mean that the Set 2 entries were written some time after the Set 1 entry but I am unable to determine any more precisely what the time interval between these entries may have been.

The report concludes:

I have not found any differences between the known and questioned writings in features that I consider are clearly fundamental structural features of the writing. However, in certain circumstances my findings might occur if

Swanson were not the writer of the questioned writing. Consequently, my findings do not show unequivocally that Swanson is the writer of the questioned writing but they do support this proposition.

I have therefore concluded that there is strong evidence to support the proposition that Swanson wrote the questioned annotations in the book *The Lighter Side of My Official Life*.

If I were able to examine known writings by Swanson that were more nearly contemporary with the questioned writing then I might wish to alter this conclusion. Such writings would enable me to determine whether or not the differences that I have attributed to the passage of time between the production of the known and questioned writings are truly caused by this.

The authors note that the marginalia poses the following historical problems:

(1) The assertion that Kosminski was dead, when he was still alive.
(2) The claim that he was released into his brother's custody after being positively identified.
(3) The claim that the City CID kept him under observation on Metropolitan Police territory.
(4) The claim that the suspect was taken by the Metropolitan Police 'with difficulty' for identification.
(5) The claim that this identification took place in 'the Seaside Home'.
(6) The claim that he was taken to the workhouse infirmary with his hands tied behind his back, when this is unrecorded.
(7) The identification of the Workhouse as Stepney, when Kosminski was actually taken to Mile End Old Town Workhouse.

For an attempt to reconcile some of these problems with known historical facts, *see* **Confusion Theory** and **Aaron Davis Cohen**.

Less-important marginalia in the volume identify 'Macnaghten. ch: constable' as the senior colleague who vexed Anderson by making undue fuss over a threatening letter and assert that all '*head* officers of CID' at Scotland Yard knew the identity of the journalist who perpetrated the 'Jack the Ripper' Letter.

SWINBURNE, ALGERNON CHARLES (1837–1909)
Alleged suspect.

Poet and critic whose sexual preference was for masochistic encounters with up-market prostitutes in St John's Wood. Included in a list of prominent Victorians in *A Casebook of Jack the Ripper* (Whittington-Egan) who are suggested occasionally as suspects.

SZEMEREDY, ALOIS (1840–92)
Alleged Austrian police suspect.

Born in Budapest.

Joined the Austro-Hungarian Army, but deserted on 7 July 1863. Joined the Argentine Army in October 1865. Declared insane, May 1866, but escaped from Hospicio de las Mercedes in the same year. From 1867–73, worked as a barber in various parts of Argentina and had two short prison terms for theft. Was arrested for the attempted murder of an Italian named Guido Benonati. In 1873, joined the Uruguay Army as a doctor, was captured at the Battle of Talita at the end of the year, but escaped from transportation to military prison. In 1874, offered free passage to Europe by the Austro-Hungarian consulate in Buenos Aires, but jumped ship at Rio de Janeiro.

On a subsequent attempt to gain free passage to Europe he was discovered to have kidnapped a young woman for sale into prostitution and was deported to Buenos Aires, but jumped ship. From early 1875, passed himself off as a doctor in various places in Argentina and perpetrated numerous thefts; in May, travelled to Milan, where he rejoined the Austrian Army, but soon deserted and returned to South America.

Met pimp Baptiste Castagnet and was introduced to prostitute Carolina Metz in Buenos Aires brothel. On 26 July 1876, Castagnet left Szemeredy with Metz in her room, where Castagnet later found her with her throat cut. Szemeredy was arrested in Buenos Aires and was sentenced to an indeterminate term in prison in 1880. The following year, he was released when his legal counsel demonstrated the weaknesses in the case against him.

Szemeredy returned to Europe. Arrested for desertion and confined in a military prison in 1882, he was declared insane in 1885. He was first committed to a military asylum and then afterwards to a state asylum, near Pest. Released into the custody of his family, he is known to have made a living as a sausage salesman; also to have tried to sell his memoirs to a newspaper called *Egystertes*, a sub-editor describing him as, 'a tall, thin man, about 44, with a bronzed complexion, brown smooth hair, a peculiar bushy moustache, unsteady small eyes, and large muscular hands.'

In 1886, he was interviewed in Budapest by Dr Gotthelf-Meyer, a specialist on South American law. He went to Vienna in 1889, and from 1890 lived in Budapest with a widow, Julianne Karlovicz, for whom he worked in her pork butcher's shop. On 1 October 1892, he left partial confessions to charges of murder and robbery, for which he had been arrested in Vienna, then committed suicide. An article about Szemeredy was written by Mayor Kattrup of the Danish town of Sorrel and published in a Danish newspaper on 4 October 1892. Kattrup was in due course interviewed by **Carl Muusmann**, who wrote a book, *Hvem Var Jack The Ripper?*, in 1908.

See also **Alonzo Maduro** and **Griffith Salway**.

(Adam Wood, 'From Buenos Aires to Brick Lane: Were Alois Szemeredy and Alonzo Maduro the Same Man?', *Ripperologist*, 25, October 1999; Eduardo Zinna, 'The Search for Jack el Destripador', *Ripperologist*, 33, February 2001; Jose Luis Scarsi, 'Jack el Destripador: una pista en la Argentina'. 'Buenos Aires, Argentina: Historias de la Ciudad', Año 4, 31, June 2005 (trans. Eduardo Zinna); 'On the Trail of Jack the Ripper: Szemeredy in Argentina', *Ripperologist*, 63, January 2006.

T

TABRAM, HENRY SAMUEL

Husband of **Martha Tabram**. Very occasionally called 'John Tabram' in the press (i.e. *Bradford Observer*, 24 August 1988). Separated from Martha, *c.* 1875, because of her drinking. By 1888, was a foreman furniture packer living at 6 Riverside Terrace, East Greenwich. Described as short, well-dressed, with iron-grey hair, moustache and imperial. He learned of Martha's death from the newspapers and identified the body on 14 August 1888.

Probably identical with Henry Samuel Tabram, who was born in 1836, the youngest of five children of John (*b.* 1791) and Hannah Tabram (*b.* 1796). Married Matilda (1839–69) and had one child, Henry (*b.* 1861). Married Martha White, 25 December 1869. The couple had two children: Frederick John (*b. c.* 1871) and Charles Henry (*b. c.* 1872). Died on 17 May 1890 in Charing Cross Hospital from shock following the amputation of his arm necessitated by injuries received while collecting machinery in the pumping room at the New Wandsworth Workhouse.

TABRAM, MARTHA, AKA MARTHA OR EMMA TURNER (1849–88)

Possible Ripper victim.

Born Martha White, 10 May 1849, at 17 Marshall Street, London Road, Southwark, the daughter of warehouseman Charles Samuel White (*d.* 1865) and Elisabeth (née Dowsett). She had two brothers: Henry (*b. c.* 1837) and Stephen (*b. c.* 1841), and two sisters: Esther (*b. c.* 1839) and Mary Ann (*b. c.* 1846). Married foreman furniture packer **Henry Samuel Tabram** at Trinity Church in St. Mary's Parish,

Newington, 25 December 1869. Two children: Frederick John (*b.* 1871) and Charles Henry (*b.* 1872).

Martha and Henry separated in 1875, with Henry blaming Martha's heavy drinking. He paid her 12/- (60p) a week maintenance at first, reducing it to 2/6d (12?p) because, 'he had found out how she was going on.' At one point she took out a warrant against him and had him locked up. Around 1879, he discovered that she was living with another man, William Turner, and thereafter refused to support her. Tabram lived on and off with Turner, though he, too, found her drinking a disincentive to cohabitation. The pair had most recently lodged with Mrs **Mary Bousfield** at Star Place, Commercial Road, but decamped owing two weeks' rent. Subsequently, Martha lodged at 19 George Street, Spitalfields. On Saturday, 4 August 1888, Martha met Turner in Leadenhall Street and he gave her 1/6d (7?p). He never saw her again.

On Bank Holiday Monday, 6 August 1888, Martha went out in the evening accompanied by 'Pearly Poll' (*see* **Mary Ann Connelly**). Various witnesses thought they saw Martha in pubs from time to time with a soldier (or soldiers). 'Pearly Poll's' story seems most likely: that she and Martha picked up two guardsmen – a corporal and a private – and drank with them in various public houses, including the White Swan on Whitechapel High Street. Around 11.45pm, the party split up. 'Pearly Poll' and the corporal went into Angel Alley for intercourse leaning against the wall; Martha and the private went into George Yard (today's Gunthorpe Street) for a similar purpose.

At approximately 2am, **Police Constable Barrett** on beat duty saw a young Grenadier Guardsman in Wentworth Street (at the north end of George Yard), who told him that he was waiting for a 'chum who had gone off with a girl'. At 3.30am, licensed cab driver **Alfred Crow** returned home to George Yard Building, a tenement converted from an old weaving factory, at the northeast of George Yard. He noticed what he took to be a tramp sleeping on the first-floor landing. At 4.50am, **John Saunders Reeves**, another tenant of George Yard Building, came downstairs and found Martha's body in a pool of blood on the first-floor landing. For the injuries, *see* **Dr Killeen**. A correspondent suggests Killeen might not have been aware that the old triangular bayonet had been withdrawn from infantry issue the previous year and the new bayonet might have made wounds similar to Tabram's. *See* **Mary Ann Connelly** for 'Pearly Poll's' unhelpfulness, which probably contributed to the insoluble nature of the crime.

The **Macnaghten memoranda** gives a clear and reasonably accurate account of 'Pearly Poll' and the enquiry's failure to reach a satisfactory conclusion beyond the likelihood that Martha's soldier client had killed her. For several years after the discovery of the memoranda, most researchers accepted Macnaghten's five as the canonical Ripper victims and dismissed Martha Tabram from consideration. Today, it is noted that Martha Tabram was endorsed as a Ripper victim by **Inspector Abberline** and Dr **Robert Anderson**.

Jon Ogan, 'Martha Tabram – The Forgotten Ripper Victim?', *Journal of Police History Society,* 5, 1990. Bill Beadle, 'Martha Tabram – A Case of Linkage Blindness?'

Journal of the Whitechapel Society, 12, February 2007; Martha Tabram...First Ripper Victim? *Journal of the Whitechapel Society,* 24, February 2009

TAKE IT FOR A FACT
Book by Ada Reeve (London: Heinemann, 1954).

Memoirs of actress who was a child performer in East End music-halls. It includes information on her father's activities as a member of the **Whitechapel Vigilance Committee**. He may well be the 'Mr Reeves' cited in various newspapers (*Daily Telegraph*, 19 October 1888) as accompanying the party taking the **Lusk kidney** for medical examination.

TANNER, ELIZABETH
Witness at **Elizabeth Stride**'s inquest. Deputy of the common lodging-house at 32 Flower and Dean Street where, she said, Stride had lodged on and off for about six years. She gave familiar and generally erroneous biographical information about Stride as bereaved in the *Princess Alice* disaster.

On Saturday, 29 September 1888, Stride – who normally did cleaning work for local Jewish residents – had cleaned rooms in the lodging-house, for which Mrs Tanner paid her 6d (2?p). At about 6.30pm, she was in the Queen's Head public house and then, at 7pm, she briefly returned to the lodging-house kitchen.

TAPPER, ANNIE B. (*b* c.1880-*d*.1964)
Informant. Told **Tom Cullen** that it was she who sold a pound of green Almira grapes to Jack the Ripper on 29 September 1888, while minding the shop in Berner Street for Mr and Mrs **Packer**. He was, she said, a dark bearded stranger and, 'looked just like he was dressed for a wedding.'

Though Cullen did not doubt this was her honest recollection and belief, but he did wonder how closely her memory corresponded with the events of that night. (*Autumn of Terror*, Chapter 9).

TAYLOR – (*d.* some time prior to 1929)
Suspect, described in 1929.

In an interview given to *John Blunt's Monthly*, 16 December 1929, a recently discharged Broadmoor (criminal lunatic asylum) patient alleged that a former inmate had been known to warders and patients alike as Jack the Ripper. A mild-mannered, studious man, with apparent skill at medical diagnosis, he was said to have been caught after one of the murders, but was immediately pronounced insane, so he could never be charged. He died after an unsuccessful escape attempt, which led to him falling off the asylum wall onto a glass frame. The article called him 'Mr Taylor', but averred this was a pseudonym.

TAYLOR, JOSEPH (fl. 1888)

Witness who followed the man suspected by **Mrs Fiddymont** along Brushfield Street and into Bishopsgate, as far as Dirty Dick's (the Jerusalem Tavern). He described him as having, 'eyes as wild as a hawk's,' and said that he was between 40 and 50, about 5ft 8in tall, with a ginger moustache and short, sandy hair. Also, that he was shabby-genteel, with ill-fitting pepper-and-salt trousers and a dark coat, which he had to hold together.

TCHKERSOFF, OLGA

Suspect proposed in 1935 by **E. T. Woodhall**, who claimed Olga revealed her story to two elderly Russian immigrants, who subsequently went to live with their son in the USA, where their story was written up by a journalist. Much of Woodhall's *Jack the Ripper: or When London Walked in Terror* rests on genuine source material, so it is just possible that there is some such journalistic account somewhere in the American press which has evaded subsequent researchers. This is not the same thing as saying Olga Tchkersoff ever existed, or the story is probable.

Supposed immigrant from Russia, settled in England with her parents and younger sister, Vera. Vera became a prostitute and died of sepsis after an illegal abortion. Olga's father died of pneumonia in the spring of 1888, while her mother took to drink and died from a fall. Olga, blaming Vera's seduction from the path of virtue for the entire chapter of misfortunes, set out to murder **Mary Jane Kelly**, who had persuaded Vera to join her in prostitution.

TEENAGE SUSPECT

See **Dundee-born Teenage Suspect**.

THAIN, PC JOHN, 96J (b. 1852)

Witness at **Mary Ann Nichols**' inquest.

Joined the Metropolitan Police in 1875, transferred to the newly-formed J Division in 1886; resigned, 1899. Warrant no. 58753.

Passed the end of Buck's Row, along Brady Street, every 30 minutes on his beat. At 3.45 am, on 31 August 1888, he was signalled by Police Constable **Neil**, flashing his lamp. Thain responded with his lamp, and went and found Neil standing beside **Mary Ann Nichols**' body. Thain then fetched **Dr Llewellyn** and returned with him to Buck's Row. He found that Neil had been joined by two workmen (**Tomkins** and **Mumford**).

Thain helped put the body on the ambulance, finding the back of the dress covered in blood, which got on his hands. The body was removed to the mortuary by Sergeants **Kerby**, **Neil** and an officer from H Division. Thain waited under orders at the site until Inspector **Spratling**'s arrival and watched Mrs Green's son wash away the blood. On the spot where the deceased had lain there was congealed blood (about 6in in diameter) and some had run towards the gutter.

Thain's cape had been left with the horse-slaughterers at Barber's Yard in Winthrop Street, but he denied having visited them, saying that he sent it there by a brother officer, but *see* **Tomkins**; also, **PC Cartwright**.

THICK, SERGEANT WILLIAM (1845–1930)

After **Abberline**, the best-known H Division detective involved in the case. Also named as a suspect in 1889 (*see* **H.T. Haslewood**). His name frequently spelled 'Thicke' in both press and official documents. We take the spelling from his signature.

Joined the Metropolitan Police in 1868 (warrant no. 49889). Posted to H Division. After brief service with B Division (Chelsea) and P Division (Camberwell), he returned to H Division and spent the remainder of his career there.

Described as a stout-built, keen but pleasant-faced man, with a thick, drooping, yellowish moustache. Nicknamed 'Johnny Upright' – according to American author Jack London, the nickname had been bestowed by a convicted villain in the dock. A report of Thick's retirement (*Lloyd's Weekly Newspaper*, 30 April 1893) confirms the nickname was bestowed by a prisoner in the dock, who declared that Thick was the only 'upright witness' and the judge, Mr Justice Kerr, was overheard to refer to Thick as 'Upright John'.

An earlier report (*Pall Mall Gazette*, 29 October 1891) reported Thick was proud of the soubriquet because it indicated, 'a generous appreciation of the fair and square dealing which has been his motto all through his long years of detective work'. **Walter Dew** claimed the nickname was, 'because he was very upright, both in his walk and in his methods.' Arthur Harding, a Bethnal Green villain of the next generation, suggested that the intention was sarcastic.

Thick retired in 1893 and went to live in the former Dempsey Street, between Jubilee Street and Jamaica Street, Stepney. Chapter 2 of Jack London's *People of the Abyss* describes him meeting Thick, his wife and daughters at Dempsey Street. Following his wife's death, Thick moved to live with his daughter and her family in Clapham. His granddaughter later recalled her mother saying that Thick had once been knocked up in the middle of the night with the cry, 'Come on, there's been another Jack the Ripper murder!'

F.P. Wensley called Thick one of the finest policemen he had known. Walter Dew said he was, 'a holy terror to the local law-breakers.' Superintendent Arnold, at the time of his retirement, said that H Division, 'has some of the smartest men attached to its criminal investigation department. I need only mention the names of Detectives Thicke and **Read** [sic] as an instance of that.'

Newspaper reports in 1888 were impressed by his knowledge of the district; also by his striking checked suits and blond moustache.

Thick's most prominent action during the Ripper investigation was the arrest of **John Pizer** and the evidence he gave at **Annie Chapman**'s inquest that Pizer was locally known as '**Leather Apron**'.

Jean Dorsenne's curious semi-fictional account in *Jack l'Éventreur* has Inspector GWH say, 'It was my colleague Sergeant Thicke who first told me about "Leather Apron". I was told he was a sort of legendary figure who terrorized the East End. He walked the streets with a leather apron flapping against his knees, brandishing a huge knife.' GWH also claims that 'Mrs' **Lyons** and her neighbour told Thick about her encounter with him and that GWH took it upon himself to arrest Pizer because the evidence against him was so slender.

Constant references to Thick show that he was heavily, though not exclusively, engaged in working on the case throughout. Police Printed Orders for Friday, 9 November 1888 show an award of 7/- (35p) to him, apparently on loan to J Division at the time. He took '**One-Armed Liz**' to view the body of **Stride** and spent most of the time after the murder of **Kelly**, 'writing down the names, statements, and full particulars of persons staying at the various lodging-houses in Dorset-street. That this was no easy task will be imagined when it is known that in one house alone there are upwards of 260 persons, and that several houses accommodate over 200' (*The Times*, 12 November 1888). Along with Detectives **New** and **M'Guire**, he was also ordered by Superintendent **Arnold** to look for the man described by **Annie Farmer**.

(See Frogg Moody, 'Sergeant William Thick', *Journal of the Whitechapel Society*, February 2006.)

THOMAS, DR WILLIAM EVAN[S] (1856–89)

Alleged suspect. Born Anglesey. Lic. Apoth. Hall, Dublin, 1880; Lic. R. Coll. Phys., Edinburgh, 1881. Middle name given as 'Evans' on death certificate: 'Evan' in medical directories, which he presumably approved.

From at least 1884, Dr Thomas practised at 190 Green Street, Victoria Park, about three-quarters of a mile away from Buck's Row. Local oral tradition in Anglesey exaggerated the location to Spitalfields (though one account suggests that he only visited Spitalfields during the relevant 10 weeks of 1888), and added that he had returned home unexpectedly to stay with his father in Aberffraw after each murder. Following 'the last' killing, he suffered a breakdown and after he had been fetched back to Anglesey, then poisoned himself.

Since Thomas died on 21 June 1889, his death preceded the murder of **Alice McKenzie** and fell seven months later than the murder of **Mary Jane Kelly**. It is not known whether the tradition (made public in 1993), also exaggerated the relation to Ripper murders of his earlier visits home. North Wales' villagers give him the Welsh name 'Jacripa'.

P.C. THOMPSON 240 H.
"found the body in the archway.

THOMPSON, PC ERNEST WILLIAM, 240H (1864–1900)

Discovered the body of **Frances Coles**.

Born in Norfolk. Joined the Metropolitan Police, 1890 (warrant no. 76476). Previously, a railway porter.

On beat duty for the first time, 13 February 1891, at 2.20am, as he passed along Chamber Street towards Swallow Gardens he heard footsteps retreating from Swallow Gardens to Royal Mint Street. In Swallow Gardens (an alley under a railway arch, leading to Royal Mint Street), he discovered a woman lying in the darkest part of the archway. Turning his lantern on her, he saw that she was bleeding profusely from her savagely-cut throat, but her eyes were open and she was still alive.

At that moment Thompson followed precisely the revised and strict Standing Orders on procedure in the case of discovering a body: he remained with the body. He was, however, criticised for not having given chase along Royal Mint Street and, according to **F.P. Wensley**, reproached himself for the rest of his life for not having raced away to arrest 'Jack the Ripper'. **Benjamin Leeson** called him 'my pal' and claimed to have joined him just after he discovered Coles' body.

In December 1900, he was murdered by **Barnett Abrahams**, who stabbed him when Thompson went to arrest him for causing a disturbance at a coffee-stall.

THOMPSON, FRANCIS (1859–1907)

Suspect proposed in **Paradox**.

Educated at Ushaw College (Seminary), Durham and Owen's College, Manchester.

Prescribed laudanum in 1879 for a serious lung infection, became an opium addict and, following unsuccessful attempts to hold down a job in London, became a vagrant addict in East End docklands, later claiming that at that time he had fallen in love with a prostitute. Rehabilitated under the care of Wilfred Meynell and his wife Alice, the former being editor of the journal *Merry England*, who recognised merit in Thompson's poetry.

At this time, Thompson wrote some of his best work, including 'The Hound of Heaven', the long lyrical outpouring of a soul pursued by Christ's love, for which he is best known. His health had been seriously undermined, however, and he died at the age of 48.

The case for Thompson being the Ripper rests on him being in the East End docklands at the time of the murders, that he was allegedly associating with prostitutes, allegedly carried a surgeon's scalpel and allegedly owned a leather apron; that a few of his poems deal with (medieval) men who mutilated women; that the various saints' days on which the murders took place might have had some morbid significance for Catholic Thompson and that his physical appearance was not unlike that of the man seen by **George Hutchinson**. Patterson has also received the opinion of a mathematical authority on chance that his correlations are too many and too concrete to be dismissed as mere coincidence.

It has also been suggested that, as a drug-addicted poet with a rich father, he might have been **Mr Moring**, but *see* **Ernest Dowson**.

THOMPSON, ROBERT (*fl.* 1888)

Resident of 29 Hanbury Street (**Annie Chapman**'s murder site). A carman employed by Goodson's of Brick Lane, he lived in the second-floor front room with his wife and adopted daughter. Thompson rose and went to work at 3.30am on 8 September 1888, without going into the yard. He saw nothing untoward.

THOMSON, SIR BASIL HOME (1861–1939)

Informant. Assistant commissioner of the Metropolitan Police, 1913–19; director of Special Branch, 1919–21.

Son of the Archbishop of York. Educated at Eton and New College, Oxford. Called to the bar, 1886. Varied career with Colonial Office (including prime ministership of Tonga) and Prison Service (respectively, governor of Cardiff, Dartmoor and Wormwood Scrubs prisons; also inspector of prisons and secretary to the prison commissioners). Appointed successor to **Sir Melville Macnaghten** as head of CID, 1913.

Gave himself the title 'director of intelligence' in 1919, with specific responsibility to deal with Bolsheviks. Resigned in 1921, following the absorption of his Intelligence section by what would become MI5. After his resignation from the police in 1921, he had some hopes of being recalled as commissioner, but was completely discredited when arrested in flagrante with prostitute Thelma de Lava in Hyde Park. He attempted to evade proceedings by offering to use his influence to further the careers of the arresting officers and giving his name as Hugh Thomson. When he finally reached the magistrates' court, armed with defending lawyer and a complete denial, his case was hopeless – Miss de Lava had gone before him and pleaded guilty.

Books include: *Queer People* (1922), *The Criminal* (1925), *The Story of Scotland Yard* (1935) and *The Scene Changes* (1939).

In *The Story of Scotland Yard* he wrote:

The belief of CID officers at the time was that [the Whitechapel murders] were the work of an insane Russian doctor and that the man escaped arrest by committing suicide at the end of 1888.

Eleven years earlier, he gave a similar opinion to *Radio Times* (3 October 1924), designating the doctor a student and the suicide as drowning in the Thames. This appears to confuse **Michael Ostrog** (the insane Russian doctor) with **M.J. Druitt** (the suicide recovered from the Thames on 31 December 1888), both named in the Macnaghten memoranda.

See also Ostrog for **Donald McCormick**'s varying account of a letter, allegedly written by Thomson towards the end of his lif, and identifying **Konovalov** as the French police suspect for Jack the Ripper; in one of McCormick's accounts further asserting Konovalov was known to the British as Mikhail Ostrog.

Cf. **Ochrana Gazette**, **William Le Queux**.

THORNTON, DR LEONARD BOOKER (1859–1935)
Suspect, investigated by police in 1888; made public, 2006.

Born in Bethnal Green, the son of a linen-draper. In 1867, employed to transport sick horses from a blacksmith's to the knacker's yard. Used savings for education at the London Hospital; qualified chemist and druggist, 1884. Married Hannah O'Sullivan in 1885.

By 1888, there were sexual and religious tensions in the marriage between Catholic Hannah and atheist Leonard. Hannah noticed that during the Ripper scare, when sexual relations were impossible because of her second pregnancy, Leonard frequently arrived home late with his clothes bloodstained. This, he said, was because of his work at the hospital. After **Mary Jane Kelly**'s murder, he was briefly arrested and questioned, then followed by plain clothes officers.

Subsequently became a respected analytical pharmacist and assisted Sir Bernard Spilsbury in the Crippen murder case. Became depressed following the death of Hannah in 1932 and was extremely upset when one of his granddaughters became a static nude at the Windmill Theatre. He was preoccupied by the plight of fallen women and on his deathbed, told another granddaughter, 'If you knew what I have done, you would not even come near me.' That granddaughter became convinced he had been Jack the Ripper and her half-brother Michael Thornton published the details of his grandfather's career and the family suspicions in the *Daily Mail*, 26 December 2006.

(*See also* **Aberconway, Christabel, Lady**.)

'THREAT' LETTER OF 6 OCTOBER 1888
MEPO3/142 ff.139-140.

Letter posted to Scotland Yard from London NW and received on 8 October. Identified by document examiner Sue Iremonger as being in the same hand as the **'Dear Boss' letter** and **'Saucy Jacky' postcard**. It reads:

6 Oct 1888
You though your-self very clever I reckon
when you informed the police But you
made a mistake, if you though I dident

see you Now I know you know me and
I see your little game, and I mean
to finish you and send your ears to
your wife if you show this to the police
or help them if you do I will finish
you. It no use your trying to get out
of my way Because I have you when
you don't expect it and I keep my
word as you soon see and rip you
up
Yours truly
Jack the Ripper

Down the left side is written, 'You see I know your address'.

Deborah K. Dobbins, in *Ripperologist* 78, April 2007, surmises, (without having had sight of the original document), that the letter was written slowly, tensely and with heavy pressure on a firm surface. She detects shakiness and poor formations of some of the letters and suggests that the author was aggravated by some sort of medical condition causing nervous twitches or tremors.

In *Jack the Ripper: The Final Chapter*, **Paul Feldman** speculated that the phrase, 'You see I know your address', suggested the letter was sent to **Matthew Packer**.

A facsimile is reproduced in *The Diary of Jack the Ripper*.

See also **Fraser Postcard**, **Letters**.

THREE LETTERS FROM HELL: LETTERS REPUTEDLY IN THE HAND OF THE WHITECHAPEL MURDERER (1988)

Limited collectors' edition: 6-page leaflet with handsomely presented transcriptions of the 'Dear Boss' and 'Lusk' letters; also, the 'Saucy Jacky' postcard.

THYNE, DR THOMAS (*b.* 1840)

Employed Lionel Druitt in 1879. MD (Edin.), MRCS (England). Residence and surgery, 140 The Minories.

Dr Joseph Ogilvie Taylor, Dr Thyne's junior partner of the previous 10 years, suffered congestion of the lungs in 1879 and treated himself with morphine. In the November, he died of an accidental overdose. Lionel Druitt is listed in Medical Directories as practising at 140 The Minories in 1879, evidently assisting Dr Thyne during Taylor's indisposition, prior to Thyne's appointment of Dr John Cotman as his permanent junior partner. Census returns show that Thyne's assistants were resident at the practice.

Daniel Farson's discovery of this listing led him to speculate that **Montague John Druitt**, a cousin close to Lionel in age, might have visited him while he was in The Minories and thus established an acquaintance with the East End.

TOMKINS, HENRY

Witness at **Mary Ann Nichols**' inquest. Horse-slaughterer employed at Barber's Knacker's Yard, Winthrop Street. Resident at Coventry Street, Bethnal Green. Described as 'a rough-looking man', testified that around 4am, on 31 August 1888, he was told of the murder by **Police Constable Thain** and went in company with **James Mumford** and **Charles Brittain** to view the body.

This evidence appears to conflict with that of Thain, who claimed the workmen were present at the murder site when he returned with **Dr Llewellyn**. It is possible that the inquest rightly detected an inclination on Thain's part to slope off from his beat for a chat with the slaughtermen, although he denied this.

TOTTERMAN, EMIL, AKA CARL NIELSON (*b. c.*1868 or *c.* 1862)

Belated suspect. Finnish seaman who murdered and mutilated prostitute Sarah Martin in Kelly's, Hotel, New York, on 20 December, 1903, very close to the hotel where **Carrie Brown** was killed. This led to speculation that he had been Carrie's killer, possibly even the Ripper. The West Virginia *Bluefield Daily Telegraph* of 22 December called him 'Calor', but this paper was very inaccurate, reporting on 18 April 1904 his execution by electrocution, when in fact Totterman was reprieved in recognition of his heroic naval services during the Spanish-American war. He was released and returned to Finland in 1929.

TRIAL OF JACK THE RIPPER: THE CASE OF WILLIAM BURY (1859–1889), THE

Book by Euan Macpherson (Edinburgh: Mainstream Publishing, 2005).

Account of the life and trial of **William H. Bury**. The story of Bury, the murder, and his subsequent trial is excellent and exhaustively researched from the local press and files in the Scottish Public Records Office. Macpherson's case against Bury is essentially that he moved to London and the murders were committed a year later; that Bury left London for Dundee, where he killed his wife in a Ripper-like manner; that the message chalked on the wall was a confession and that the man who hanged Bury – **James Berry** – believed him to be Jack the Ripper.

TROUP, CHARLES EDWARD (1857–1941)

At the time of the Ripper murders, Home Office junior clerk, who drafted long memoranda on the conditions under which rewards for information might (or might not) be appropriate (HO144/220/A49301B ff.110–219) and a follow-up letter to fellow-clerk **Charles Murdoch**, detailing a further case that he had forgotten (ibid., f.220).

Subsequently, Home Office permanent under-secretary and recipient of correspondence from **James Monro** in 1910 concerning **Sir Robert Anderson**'s contributions to *The Times* series investigated by the Parnell Commission.

TRUE FACE OF JACK THE RIPPER, THE
Book by **Melvin Harris** (London: Michael O'Mara, 1994; paperback, London: Michael O'Mara, 1995. London: Brockhampton Press, 1999).

Account of the life of **Robert Donston Stephenson**, much of it drawn from the rediscovered memoirs of his one-time business partner, **Vittoria Cremers**.

Framed in a recapitulation of Harris's belief that Stephenson was the murderer. The appendices include a facsimile of **James Maybrick**'s will.

TULLY, JAMES CHARLES H. (1930–2001)
Author.

While working as a banker, he contributed to Peter Underwood's *One Hundred Years of Mystery* and, after retirement to live in Spain, wrote *The Secret of Prisoner 1167*, which proposed that Broadmoor escapee James Kelly could have been Jack the Ripper. He followed this up with a controversial novel, *The Crimes of Charlotte Brontë*, in which he presented his seriously-held theory that Charlotte Brontë and her husband poisoned Branwell and Emily Brontë, Charlotte in turn poisoning her husband. Tully made infrequent trips to London, but it was on one of these that he was taken ill and died.

(see obituary in *Ripperologist*, 39, February 2002)

TUMBLETY, DR FRANCIS (1833–1903)
Suspect. By his own admission arrested on suspicion of being Jack the Ripper; was charged with indecent assault, released on bail and fled Britain.

Born in Ireland to James and Margaret Tumblety, the youngest of 11 children: Patrick, Lawrence, Jane and Bridget (twins), Alice, Margaret, Ann, Julia, Elizabeth and Mary. Moved with his family to Rochester, New York.

He was said to have learned something about medicines from a Dr Lispenard, described as a 'celebrated special practitioner' (*Brooklyn Daily Eagle*, 10 May 1865), but later as carrying on a 'medical business of a disreputable kind' (Interview with Edward Hayward, *Rochester Democrat and Republican*, 3 December 1888). Lispenard was an alias of Ezra J. Reynolds, who specialised in the treatment of venereal and related diseases, and who often advertised himself as if he was in partnership with Lispenard. In 1873, he pleaded guilty to sending through the mail certain circulars, books, articles and things, 'of an obscene character and for immoral use.' He was fined $750 (*Buffalo Daily Courier*, 17 September 1873). Hostile newspaper reports in the late 1880s, which recalled Tumblety as dirty and uneducated, averred that in adolescence he had sold pornographic literature to travellers on canal boats.

Tumblety also worked with an 'Indian herb doctor' named H.J. Lyons or R.J. Lyons, who had an office over the Post Office in Rochester. Later, he is supposed to have opened an office of his own in Smith's Block, Rochester, practising under the name of Philip Sternberg (*Rochester Daily Union and Advertiser*, 9 May 1865). He left Rochester around 1850, possibly accompanying a group of strolling players to Toronto, but some reports say he went to Detroit, others New York.

According to a newspaperman named Fred Hart, in 1856 Tumblety was practising as a doctor in New York and was arrested there for offences which included 'selling obscene and suggestive circulars and pamphlets' and for circulating scurrilous rhymes about a man named Giles, the owner of a drugstore. He was imprisoned for a year in the Tombs (*Daily Examiner*, 23 November 1888). There is currently no evidence to suggest that Tumblety was imprisoned and the reliability of Fred Hart is open to question: described as a 'joyous, happy, bright, honourable man' and 'all-around most useful newspaperman' in the 1870s, his character changed and 'he became a terror to his friends'. He was declining mentally when he spoke about Tumblety (*Salt Lake Semi-Weekly* Tribune, 7 September 1897).

From at least January 1857, Tumblety was in Toronto and apparently a very successful herbalist. Although often described as a 'quack', he wasn't a tub-thumping peddler of noxious remedies of his own concoction like the snake-oil salesmen: 'Tumblety's rhetoric, his approach to medicine and his way of life link him to Thomsonianism, the most influential movement of herbalists in Canada, the United States and Britain' (Michael McCulloch, 'Dr. Tumblety, the Indian Herb Doctor: Politics, Professionalism and Abortion in Mid-Nineteenth-Century Montreal', *Canadian Bulletin of Medical History/Bulletin Canadien d'Histoire de la Médecine*, 10 (1) 1993). Herbal medicine was almost as reputable as the orthodox drug-dispensing 'allopathic' medicine in the 1850s, when both schools used little but laxatives and purgatives to bring down fever and the orthodox school's mercurial and arsenical drugs were often dangerous.

In the summer of 1857, he was in Niagara Falls, New York, where his advertisement appeared in the local newspaper offering to cure all manner of diseases, even by letter, and specialising in 'diseases peculiar to females and children' and saying that, 'The poor will be liberally considered' (*Niagara Falls Gazette*, 22 July 1857). However, on 22 September 1857, he was arrested on the charge of attempting to induce a miscarriage, it being alleged that he had sold pills and a bottle of liquid for that purpose to a 17-year-old prostitute named Philomene Dumas. Tumblety had been set up by the police and the case was thrown out of court (*Montreal Pilot*, 23–30 September 1857; the story even made the British press: *Liverpool Mercury*, 12 October 1857; *Le Courier du Canada*, 4, 6 November 1857). Tumblety stayed on in Montreal, a prominent and controversial individual, who it was claimed was asked to represent the Irish of the city in the 1857 provincial election (McCulloch).

By March 1858, he had moved back to Rochester, New York (*Rochester Daily Union and Advertiser*, 11 March 1858). He then went back to Canada, where in November he was in Ontario (*Perth Courier*, 26 November 1888). At some point he was also in Boston, where he was remembered as having an office in the Horticultural Buildings, Tremont Street, and for his liking for the slums (*Chicago Tribune*, 22 November 1888).

In 1859, Tumblety was in Buffalo, New York.

In July 1860, the Society of St Vincent of Paul held a picnic for the poor on Anatolian Island, a J.H. Tumblety being listed as one of the members from whom tickets could be obtained (*The Constitution*, 13 July 1860). Tumblety appears to have moved from Washington to St John, New Brunswick, in 1860, where he was fined £20 and costs for assuming the title of MD, 'contrary to the provisions of the Medical Act'. The conviction was subsequently overturned (*Morning Freeman*, 11–27 August 1860).

Almost immediately, he was charged with causing the death of a patient named James Portmore, a verdict of manslaughter being brought against him (*Morning Freeman*, 29 September, 16 October 1860). It is likely, however, that Tumblety was the victim of orthodox medicine's increasing determination to eliminate 'alternative' competition and that Portmore's death was caused by aggressive mercury-based drugs administered by his physician before and after the short time that he transferred to Tumblety's care. Nevertheless, Tumblety fled Canada to Eastport, Maine, then to Boston, and finally, New York.

In 1861, he advertised himself as having an office on 933 Broadway, New York City (*New York Herald*, 21 March 1861). *The Herald* later recalled that he opened an office in Washington Street, New York, and lodged with a Mrs Foster at 95 Fulton Street (*New York Herald*, 20 November 1888). He was involved in a curious action against the Chemical Bank in New York, claiming that two cheques that the bank said he had signed were forgeries. The bank claimed they possessed information that Tumblety's real name was Sullivan, that he had been a servant of Dr Tumblety and had assumed his identity when Tumblety died. They threatened to reveal the man's colourful background (*St. John's Dispatch*, 28 March 1861).

This incident seems to have begun when a young man named Charles Whelpley, who appears to have been working for Tumblety, filled out a cheque for $100, which Tumblety signed. A little later, he presented the bank with another cheque for $400 and although the bank honoured the cheque, suspicions were aroused. On 21 February, Whelpley was brought before Justice Osborn and charged with having forged the cheque. He protested his innocence (*New York Daily Tribune*, 22 February 1861).

By the middle of 1861, Tumblety was in Washington, his offices located at 11 Washington Buildings on Pennsylvannia Avenue (*Daily National Intelligence*, 22 March 1862 and other Washington newspapers through to June 1862), where it was rumoured he had been appointed surgeon general on the staff of General McClellan, it even being reported that he had treated the son of Abraham Lincoln, met Mr and Mrs Lincoln and gained the appointment through their intercedence. However, later inquiries showed that the story was untrue (*Newark Advocate*, 29 November 1861; *The Headquarters*, 12 February 1862). Nevertheless, he was sufficient of a Washington celebrity to be named in the city's vaudeville: the great entertainer Tony Pastor (1837–1908) included a verse about him in one of his comic songs.

In September, at Canterbury Hall in Washington the programme of entertainment included an item called 'Tumblety Undone' (*Evening Star*, 4 December 1861 – possibly the 'laughable burlesque'; 'Dr Tumblety Outdone', *New York Herald*, 6 October 1861). In 1862, it staged a farce called 'Dr Tumblety's First Patient'. Tumblety sued for libel. He was described as 'a very handsome man, is rather eccentric and odd in his manners, appearing at times on the streets dressed as an English sportsman, with tremendous spurs fastened to his boots, and accompanied by a pair of greyhounds lashed together, and at other times in full highland costume. His skill as a physician, however, is undoubted, his practice in Washington being very extensive and among the higher classes of society' (*Rochester Union and Advertiser*, 14 March 1862, quoting *The Washington Republican*). Later, a Colonel C.A. Dunham would claim that the character of Tumblety was played by Tumblety himself, the whole thing being a piece of ingenious self-advertisement. This may or may not be true. Unfortunately, 'Dunham' was one of the aliases of the unscrupulous and mendacious Sanford Conover, whose chequered career (including a conviction for perjury) and sensational lies about all and sundry makes it unlikely any of his description of Tumblety is true. Tumblety did not complete his lawsuit, but may have planted a stooge in the audience to shout protesting praise of the good doctor, at which point the actor hurried off stage and left the city with the planted plaudits as his last word.

It was at this time, according to later reports, that he first evinced extreme misogyny although the source again is Dunham, who claimed that Tumblety gave an all-male dinner party followed by a game of poker. Asked why there were no ladies present, he responded, 'No, Colonel, I don't know any such cattle, and if I did I would, as your friend, sooner give you a dose of quick poison than take you into such danger.' Dunham also claimed Tumblety's office contained a collection of preserved uteri and that the doctor claimed that as a young man he had married a woman whom he later discovered to be an active prostitute (*Williamsport Sunday Grit*, 9 December 1888).

William Pinkerton later stated that Tumblety, 'was scattering broadcast his advertisements of a cure for a certain class of complaints. A little inquiry soon showed that he had flooded the army with his handbills and with objectionable books, so much so that General McLellan issued strict orders that the circulation of these books in the army should be suppressed, on the grounds that many of the books were calculated to debase the soldiers, their contents being of an immoral character and their illustrations still more so.' His actions being placed under closer scrutiny, it at last, 'became known that he was in the habit of indulging in certain vices that finally resulted in his being driven from the city' (*The Daily Inter-Ocean*, Chicago, 20 November 1888).

He went from Washington to Baltimore, where he advertised himself as having an office at 220 West Baltimore Street (*Sun*, 25 September 1861).

In 1864, Tumblety had returned to New York, where his huge moustache was the subject of comment and he was otherwise described as wearing a 'butternut-colored suit, the unusual width of his pantaloons being counterbalanced by the brevity of his coat tails. A pork-pie cap and a stout yellow cane complete the outfit of this singular personage. He is generally accompanied by a large yellow dog, long and lean, which looks so much like his master that one is supposed to know nearly as much as the other. The Doctor has been seen on horseback, but generally travels on foot, accompanied by his faithful poodle.'

He managed to get into the newspapers again when he allegedly kicked a patient named Fenton Scully out of his office, but the case was dismissed when it reached court, Tumblety producing witnesses who asserted Scully's claim was false (*Brooklyn Daily Eagle*, 6, 10 May 1864).

In December 1864, Tumblety sailed on the steamer *George Cornwell* from New York to New Orleans (*New York Times*, 4 December 1864).

Tumblety opened an office in St. Louis in 1865, first above Hart's Oyster Saloon on Olive Street. He hired a newsboy, whose face he painted red (and who wore feathers on his head), to stand at the foot of the stairs to his office, handing out fliers. Later, he moved to 52 North Third Street. He was briefly under arrest for wearing military clothing. At this time it was claimed (*Rochester Union and Democrat*, 13 May 1865) that Tumblety had once used the name J.H. Blackburn, but he was confused with Luke Prior Blackburn, a Confederate who, it was alleged, had devised a plot to import clothing infected with yellow fever from Bermuda into the Northern states.

It was also said that John Wilkes Booth was a frequent patient of Tumblety's and that a co-conspirator to assassinate President Lincoln, David Herold (1842 – hanged at Washington Penitentiary, 7 July1865), had been his assistant (*Daily Cleveland Herald*, 8 May 1865). Tumblety was arrested at his Third Street office on 6 May 1865 and taken to Washington, where he was imprisoned in the Old Capitol Prison. A Washington correspondent for the *New York Tribune* described him as, 'just as vain, gaudy, dirty and disgusting as ever' (*Rochester Daily Union and Advertiser*, 12 May 1865).

On 26 May 1965, when no evidence was forthcoming, he was released. He wrote a letter to the *New York Times* refuting all the charges and produced a pamphlet doing the same thing: *A Few Passages in the Life of Dr. Francis Tumblety, the Indian Herb Doctor*. Some newspapers speculated the whole incident was a 'smart advertising dodge' by Tumblety himself (*Hamilton Evening Times*, 29 May 1865; *Evening Star*, 2 June 1865; *The New York Times*, 10 June 1865).

Around 1868, he was in Pittsburg, calling himself, 'the Great American Herb Doctor' – 'In his manner he was most genial and made many friends, only to lose them when they got an insight into his character. He had among his patients some of the city's first families, who, towards the end, found that he was a charlatan and dispensed with his services' (*New York World*, 2 December 1888).

Tumblety was recalled taking a suite of six rooms at the Northern Hotel, Cortlandt Street, in New York, around 1871. According to Clement R. Bennett, a stenographer at the Circuit Court, Tumblety, 'cordially invited any young men whom he fancied, wherever he met them, in the parks, squares or stores, to call upon him at this hotel, where he was wont to say he would show them "an easy road to fortune." By his suavity he was successful beyond comprehension in enlisting and securing the attendance, at certain hours of the day and evening, of good-looking young men and boys, greenhorns, to "walk into my parlor." He pretended to be a "specialist" and to have a cure for some of the ills which flesh is heir to' (*San Francisco Chronicle*, 20 November 1888).

Tumblety may also have gone to San Francisco. A Dr. C.C. O'Donnell recalled him arriving there in 1871 and that he took an office on Washington Street and, 'paraded the streets, as he did in New York, with a negro behind him, who led a greyhound.' O'Donnell recalled that Tumblety had come from Australia and that he was compelled to leave when it was shown that he had no medical diploma. It may be that Tumblety was being confused with other people, or that he took an alternative name. Chief Cowley of the San Francisco Police claimed that he was being mixed up with a Dr Stanley, a one-time surgeon in the British Army, who had come to San Francisco from Australia and taken offices with a Dr Sharkey, on Washington Street. Stanley, he said, dressed peculiarly and was always followed by two greyhounds. He too fell foul of the law and fled town (*Daily Evening Bulletin*, 23 November 1888).

In 1872 Tumblety was allegedly the subject of an exposé in *Frank Leslie's Weekly* (no such piece has as yet been found) and he confronted the editor, a man named Ralston, in the barroom of the Fifth Avenue Hotel. There was a fight and Tumblety was arrested for assault, but Ralston refused to press charges (*New York Herald*, 19 November 1888).

In 1872, he wrote another self-aggrandising autobiographical book, *Narrative of Dr. Tumblety*, in which he claimed: that he had been given medals and military rank by the Kaiser and the Emperor Louis-Napoleon; had treated Charles Dickens, enabling him to complete the novel he was writing; had commanded an American travelling ambulance at the Siege of Paris. He published a photograph of himself in a theatrical costumier's outfit, which he pretended was his Prussian hussar's uniform.

Tumblety came to England in 1873, and in or about October, in London, he met an 18-year-old youth: a carpenter named Henry Carr, who lived at 20 Chichester Road, Paddington. He hired him as his secretary and induced him against his parents' wishes to go away with him to Liverpool. At some point he gave the boy a gold chain to take care of and it was still in his possession when Carr, not liking Tumblety's manner, left him and returned to London.

In December he attempted to use the chain as a pledge with a pawnbroker, but unable to satisfactorily account for it being in his possession, he was charged with having stolen it. The magistrate dismissed the charge, but the police retained the chain (*The Times,* 1 December 1873). William Pinkerton recalled the incident, saying that Tumblety had reported the chain (and an accompanying watch) missing. The police, he said, traced the chain and arrested the boy, who confessed to the theft, but, made a statement to the police, which caused a warrant to be issued for the Doctor's arrest. **Superintendent Shore** apparently sought Pinkerton's advice and he confirmed that the boy's story tallied with what was known about Tumblety. Tumblety, he said, had fled to Paris. (*Daily Picayune*, 20 November 1888).

In 1874, he set up business at 177 Duke Street, Liverpool. He called himself the Great American Doctor (*Liverpool Mercury*, 2 September 1874), and throughout the last quarter of 1874, his advertisements appeared in local newspapers, but in January 1875, Edward Hanratty died after taking medicines given to him by Tumblety. Vexatious charges were brought against Tumblety, it being quite clear that Hanratty had died of natural causes (*Liverpool Mercury*, 19 February 1875). No sooner had the case completed than Tumblety was charged in the County Court with falsely inserting in one of his advertisements a testimonial from William Carroll. The case was settled out of court (*Liverpool Mercury*, 24 February 1875). It was during his time in Liverpool, in the 1870s, that Tumblety met and seduced Thomas Hall Caine (1853–1931),who would, in due course, become a very famous writer.

Tumblety moved from Liverpool to Birmingham (*Birmingham Daily Post,* 14 August 1875).

He returned to New York via Havre aboard the steamship *Greece*, arriving on 17 September (*New York Daily Tribune*, 18 September 1875), and in October was reportedly in Montreal, Canada (Irish Canadian, 12 October 1875).

In 1878, according to a lawyer named William P. Burr, Tumblety met a young man called Lyons, who was looking for work and hired him as an amanuensis, it being claimed that Tumblety was almost illiterate. He gave him power of attorney concerning $100,000 in bonds while he was abroad. On 23 April 1878, Tumblety sailed for Liverpool on the Guion line steamer *Montanta*. When he returned to America, Tumblety found that some of the bonds had been sold, but as Lyons had disappeared Tumblety brought charges against his elderly mother, Mary Lyons (*Syracuse Daily Standard,* 2 July 1880), but the case fell apart and Mrs Lyons was released. Tumblety then brought a case against William P. O'Connor, a broker, for disposing of the bonds, but this did not come to anything either. According to Burr, Tumblety, 'had a seeming mania for the company of young men and grown-up youths. He never failed to warn in his correspondence against lewd women, and in doing it used the most shocking language' (*Rochester Democrat and Republican*, 3 December 1888).

Tumblety was apparently in Toronto in 1880 and was arrested for 'a serious offense which, however, was reduced to a common assault' (*Rochester Daily Union and Advertiser*, 4 April 1881).

In March 1881, he was arrested in New Orleans on a charge of having picked the pocket of Henry Govan, an employee of the US District Attorney. Apparently, Tumblety had approached Govan on the street, engaged him in conversation and then taken him to a local bar. They had met again the following day and conversed, and after that meeting Govan found that his wallet was missing. He engaged the services of a private detective, D.C. O'Malley, who duly arrested Tumblety who, O'Malley claimed, admitted to the theft and in whose lodgings he saw burglar's tools.

His landlady said that Tumblety, 'received a great many visits, principally from young men between the ages of 16 and 20 years, with whom he appeared very intimate, some of them remaining with him all night.' Tumblety claimed Govan's charges were an attempt to blackmail him and that O'Malley's testimony was bogus. Govan's accusation collapsed under questioning and O'Malley's claim that Tumblety confessed, used the argot of the underworld and possessed burglarious, utterly lacked substantiation. The judge discharged Tumblety, who for some reason had apparently been defended in court, 'by the English Consul, A de Grenier de Fonblanque' (*Daily Picayune*, New Orleans, 23, 25, 26, 30 March 1881).

Then, on 7 November 1888, he was arrested in London on suspicion of being connected with the Jack the Ripper murders. According to Tumblety:

'My arrest came about this way: I had been going over to England for a long time – ever since 1869, indeed – and I used to go about the city a great deal until every part of it became familiar to me.

'I happened to be there when these Whitechapel murders attracted the attention of the whole world, and in the company with thousands of other people, I went down to the Whitechapel district. I was not dressed in a way to attract attention, I thought, though it afterwards turned out that I did. I was interested by the excitement and the crowds, and the queer scenes and sights, and did not know that all the time I was being followed by English detectives.

'My guilt was very plain to the English mind. Someone had said that Jack the Ripper was an American, and everybody believed that statement. Then it is the universal belief among the lower classes that all Americans wear slouch hats; therefore, Jack the Ripper must wear a slouch hat. Now, I happened to have on a slouch hat, and this, together with the fact that I was an American, was enough for the police. It established my guilt beyond any question.'

The doctor produced from an inside pocket two magnificent diamonds, one thirteen carats and the other nine carats, both of the purest quality, and a superb cluster ring set in diamonds. He said that in his opinion his arrest was due, in a measure, to the police desiring his diamonds and thinking they could force him to give them up. He was held in prison for two or three days, but, 'I don't care to talk about it. When I think of the way I was treated in London, it makes me lose all control of myself. It was shameful, horrible.

'I think their conduct in this Whitechapel affair [the London police] is enough to show what they are. Why, they stuff themselves all day with potpies and beef, and drink gallons of stale beer, keeping it up until they go to bed late at night, and then wake up the next morning heavy as lead. Why, all the English police have dyspepsia. They can't help it; their heads are as thick as the London fogs. You can't drive an idea through their thick skulls with a hammer – I never saw such a stupid set. Look at their treatment of me. There was absolutely not one single scintilla of evidence against me. I had simply been guilty of wearing a slouch hat, and for that I was charged with a series of the most horrible crimes ever recorded (*New York World*, 25 January 1889).

Although Tumblety claimed to have been charged with committing the Ripper murders, the police were unable to make the charges stick and, on 16 November 1888, he was instead charged with eight counts of gross indecency, and indecent assault with force and arms against four men on 27 July, 31 August, 14 October and 2 November respectively. He was granted bail and two men who had only recently met him stood surety for him and so he was released.

On 19 November, the Chief of Police in San Francisco, Patrick Crowley, sent a message to Scotland Yard, offering examples of Tumblety's handwriting (*Daily Evening Bulletin*, 23 November 1888) and on 22 November, **Robert Anderson** replied: 'Thanks. Send writing and all details you can in relation to him. ANDERSON' (*Daily Evening Bulletin*, 23 November 1888).

Due to appear at the Old Bailey on 20 November, Tumblety learned that his trial was postponed to 10 December and, on 24 November, seized the opportunity to flee to France, where he boarded the *La Bretagne* under the assumed name of Frank Townsend and sailed for New York, arriving on 3 December. Two detectives at the quayside followed him to Mrs MacNamara's boarding house on East 10th Street and kept him under surveillance (*Evening Star Sayings*, 3 December 1888). At the Old Bailey, on 10 December, the two men who had stood bail for him lost their money (*New York World*, 2 December 1888).

When a journalist asked William Pinkerton if he thought Tumblety might have been Jack the Ripper, Pinkerton replied, 'People familiar with the history of the man always talked of him as a brute, and as brutal in his actions. He was known as a thorough woman-hater and as a man who never associated or mixed with women of any kind. It is claimed that he was educated as a surgeon in Canada and was quite an expert in surgical operations.' Pinkerton went on to say that he thought Jack the Ripper would be a woman-hater and guilty of the same practices as Tumblety (*Daily Picayune*, 20 November 1888).

Police interest in Tumblety may have been because of suspicions that he was associated with the Irish Nationalists, with one newspaper in 1890 reporting, 'He was last heard of a couple of years ago in New York, where for a time he was under suspicion on account of his supposed connection with the advanced branch of the Irish national party' (*Brooklyn Daily Eagle*, 27 April 1890).

In 1889, Tumblety again skipped bail. This time, he had been indicted in New York for assaulting a man named George Davis with a cane on 4 June. He skipped town, while his banker, Henry Clews, settled the bond (*Richfield Springs Mercury*, 27 July 1889). In due course the case was thrown out of court by Judge Goldersleeve, following assertions by the District Attorney, Colonel Fellows, that, 'Dr Tumblety was a gentleman of the very highest standing and moral character [and] that the complainant was a confirmed liar' (*Brooklyn Daily Eagle*, 2 August 1889).

In 1890, in Washington D.C., a detective named Ned Horne observed Tumblety loitering in some shadows and arrested him on a charge of being a suspicious character. When searched at the police station, he was found to have several thousand dollars worth of valuables on him, a pamphlet of testimonials and an article replying to the charges brought against him in London. He was described as, 'an enormous man, over six feet in height, with broad shoulders. His hair is black, tinged with gray, and his skin is red and coarse. His moustache is a rather large affair, evidently dyed black, and extends around the corners of his mouth. His eyes are steely blue, and he gazed steadily at nothing, as he spoke in a weak, effeminate voice. He was dressed in a big black overcoat and wore a German cap, and had on rubber boots' (*Washington Post*, 18 November 1890).

He appeared in court, but the judge was, for unspecified reasons, compelled to dismiss the case 'with reluctance and commented strongly upon the reputation borne by the notorious doctor' (*Washington Post*, 19 November 1890). This arrest was the subject of a rare news report about Tumblety in the British press, the *Western Mail* reporting, 'Dr Francis Tumbety, who was at one time suspected of being "Jack the Ripper", has been committed to gaol as a suspicious character.'

Tumblety was in Hot Springs, Arkansas, in 1891, and staying at the Plateau Hotel, when it was robbed by hotel thieves. He lost $2,000 in cash and diamonds worth between $5–7,000 (*Arkansas Gazette*, 19 April 1891).

From 1893, he lived with his sister in Rochester, although he travelled – one report mentioned a visit to Richfield Springs, between Albany and Syracuse, where he stayed at the Union and presumably took the water from the town's famous sulphur springs. The report said that for the last few years, Tumblety had, 'been engaged in literary work to some extent' (*Richfield Springs Mercury*, 6 July 1893).

In 1903, under the assumed name of Dr Townsend, Tumblety died in St. John's hospital, St Louis, leaving an estate worth at least $150,000. On 16 May, 12 days before he died, he had made out a will, in which he left $10,000 each to various relatives, $5,000 to his coachman, Mark A. Blackburn, and $10,000 each to Cardinal James Gibbons and Archbishop John Ireland for charitable purposes. On the day after Tumblety died, the will was offered and probated without any notice to heirs or next of kin, which was contrary to the law. Tumblety was revealed to have $138,000 deposited with the bankers Henry Clews in New York and a demand was made for that money, but the bank refused to surrender pending an investigation, which in turn led to numerous relatives across America and as far away as Ireland being contacted and efforts being made to overturn the will in favour of an earlier one.

On 23 September 1913 **Chief Inspector Littlechild** wrote to the journalist **George R. Sims**, who in an earlier letter appears to have referred to a 'Dr. D' in connection with the Ripper Crimes. Littlechild replied, 'I never heard of a Dr. D. in connection with the Whitechapel murders but amongst the suspects, and to my mind a very likely one, was a Dr. T. (which sounds much like D.) He was an American quack named Tumblety…' (*see* **Littlechild Letter**).

The Littlechild Letter was purchased by Stewart Evans from an antiquarian bookseller and formed the basis of a book, written with Paul Gainey, *The Lodger*, in which they attempted to build a case for Tumblety being Jack the Ripper. Timothy B Riordan attempted to dismantle many of their arguments as well as question the reliability of many contemporary newspaper sources in **Prince of Quacks**.

Also see Wolf Vanderlinden, 'On The Trail of Tumblety', **Ripper Notes**, 23, July 2005, 24, October, 2005; Carman Cumming, 'The American Connection: Sandford Conover aka Charles A Dunham and Dr Francis Tumblety', **Ripperologist**, 63, January 2006; Joe Chetcuti, *Ripperologist*, 64 (February 2006); R.J. Palmer, 'Tumblety Talks', *Ripperologist*, 79, May 2007; Timothy B. Riordan, 'The Nine Lives of Dr Tumblety', *Ripperologist*, 92, June 2008 (contains the only known photograph of Tumblety),

TURNER, MARTHA or EMMA
Alternative name used by **Martha Tabram**.

TURNER, WILLIAM (or HENRY)
Witness at **Martha Tabram**'s inquest. A carpenter by trade, but in 1888 he had, for several years, lived as a street hawker. Described as a short, dirty, slovenly dressed young man, with a pale face, light moustache and imperial. Resident at the time of the inquest at the Victoria Working Men's Home, Commercial Street.

Turner lived with Tabram, on and off, for 10 years. He left her from time to time because of her drunkenness, reporting: 'If I gave her money, she generally spent it on drink. In fact, it was always drink. When she took to drink, however, I usually left her to her own resources, and I can't answer for her conduct then.'

He had left her about three weeks before her death and last saw her in Leadenhall Street, near Aldgate pump, on Saturday, 4 August 1888, when he gave her 1/6d (7?p).

TURRELL, DETECTIVE SERGEANT WILLIAM (b. 1856)
Born Ingatestone, Essex, the son of James W. Turrell, an agricultural labourer. Married Ellen Jacobs, 1889; three children. Joined the Metropolitan Police in 1876 (warrant number 60987). Rose to inspector and resigned to pension, 1905.

In March 1888, in company with Detective Everett, arrested **Michael Ostrog** for failing to report to the police following his release from prison (*Daily News*, 18 April 1891).

In May 1889, he routinely investigated **Joseph Lawende** following his application for naturalisation.

He was among those present at a dinner at the Three Nuns Hotel to celebrate **Inspector Abberline**'s retirement in June 1892.

U

ULTIMATE JACK THE RIPPER COMPANION: AN ILLUSTRATED ENCYCLOPEDIA, THE
See **The Ultimate Jack the Ripper Sourcebook**.

ULTIMATE JACK THE RIPPER SOURCEBOOK: AN ILLUSTRATED ENCYCLOPEDIA, THE
Book by Stewart Evans (lead author) and Keith Skinner (London: Robinson, 2000). Published in the US as *The Ultimate Jack the Ripper Companion*, New York: Caroll and Graf, 2000; paperback, (London: Robinson, 2001.)

Transcriptions by Stewart Evans of all the major Home Office and MEPO files on the case, with a representative selection of newspaper reports, together with an explanatory commentary, and appendices offering a timeline of the major incidents from 1888 to 1896, with brief biographical notes on the principal police officers and civil servants involved. An invaluable resource for anyone wishing to explore the crimes in detail.

UNCLE JACK: THE TRUE IDENTITY OF BRITAIN'S MOST NOTORIOUS MURDERER – JACK THE RIPPER – REVEALED AT LAST
Book by Tony Williams and Humphrey Price (London: Orion, 2005; paperback, London: Orion, 2006).

Makes the case against **Dr John Williams**.

UNCOVERING JACK THE RIPPER'S LONDON
Book by Richard Jones (London: New Holland, 2007).

Beautifully illustrated overview of the Ripper crimes with an illustrative emphasis on the topography by one of London's leading walking-tour guides. *See also* **Jack the Ripper: The Casebook**.

UNFORTUNATES
Self-published book by Shannon Christopher (Booksurge Imprints, 2003).

A basic outline of the murders, with a reliable statement of the familiar case for **Joe Barnett** as the Ripper.

UNKNOWN MEDICAL MAN OF HIGH STANDING
Suspect.

William Greer Harrison claimed that in late 1894 he was told by a visiting English doctor, **Dr Howard**, that Jack the Ripper was, 'a medical man of high standing and extensive practice', who from time to time would undergo a change of personality and take pleasure in inflicting pain, and whose wife in due course told medical friends of her suspicions that he had committed the Jack the Ripper murders. Proofs were forthcoming and the doctor was committed to an insane asylum, within months losing all semblance of sanity and becoming the most intractable and dangerous lunatic confined in the institution.

The story was told with considerable elaboration in the Chicago *Sunday Times-Herald* (28 April 1895) – *see* **R.J. Lees** for the full story – and **Thomas Stowell** suggested the medical man was **Sir William Gull**, recalling that Gull's daughter, Caroline Acland, had told him a story recounted to her by her mother of a visit from the police which corresponds with elements of the Lees' tale. Stowell did not believe Gull was the murderer, but felt that Gull was used as a scapegoat to divert attention away from **Prince Albert Victor**.

Although popularly believed to be Sir William Gull, the identity of the medical man of high standing and the identity of Dr Howard (*see* **Dr Benjamin Howard**) remains unknown.

UNIDENTIFIED INSPECTOR WHO BELIEVED THE RIPPER WAS IN DARTMOOR
An unidentified inspector of the Metropolitan Police gave two interviews to the *Morning Leader* (13, 15 February 1894), in which he claimed a man that he thought very likely to have been Jack the Ripper was incarcerated in the Dartmoor Prison Asylum [sic], 'since the last Ripper murder' – there is no indication whether he meant **Mary Kelly** or **Frances Coles**. The newspaper said of the inspector that, 'the amount of interest that he has evinced in the "Jack the Ripper" case has made him conspicuous amongst the members of the force.' By his own account, his interest in the case had begun when he was stationed in the vicinity of Whitechapel and he, 'secured the evidence, in my judgement ample to lay before the Scotland Yard authorities.' This evidence included a breakdown of the suspect's movements at the time when the murders were committed and a knife of Chinese manufacture, with which he believed the Whitechapel crimes were committed.

In the follow-up story on 15 February, an unnamed head official at Scotland Yard dismissively stated that the story was about three years old. The unnamed inspector also backtracked a little, explaining that his evidence was circumstantial and capable of an alternative construction.

However, the story gained some currency in newspapers in the US, notably the *Daily Nevada State Journal* (9 March 1894), *Fresno Weekly Republican* (9 March 1894), *Marion Daily Star* (10 March 1894) and the Iowa *New Era* (14 March 1894).

The inspector's story appeared at the same time as the *Sun* ran a series about a patient and Jack the Ripper suspect in Broadmoor (*see* **Thomas Cutbush**) and the two stories were confused by some newspapers (see *Western Mail*, 17 February 1894). Modern commentators have made the same connection (see Bernard Brown, 'A Race With The Devil', *Ripperologist*, 41, June 2002, and Nicholas Connell and Stewart Evans in the revised (2009) edition of *The Man Who Hunted Jack the Ripper*).

UNIDENTIFIED MAN SEEN BY THOMAS BOWYER

Thomas Bowyer stated that he last saw **Mary Jane Kelly** alive on the Wednesday previous to her death. She was in Miller's Court, talking to a man of 27 or 28, with a dark moustache and 'very peculiar eyes'. His appearance was, 'very smart and attention was drawn to him by his showing very white cuffs and a rather long white collar, the ends of which came down in front over his coat'. The white collar and cuffs have been noted as items of dress associated with **Prince Albert Victor** and **Montague John Druitt**; the peculiar eyes suggest **George Netting**.

UNIDENTIFIED MAN SEEN IN BUCKS ROW

At **Mary Ann Nichols**' inquest, **Inspector Abberline** said police were, 'unable to find the man who passed down Buck's Row while the doctor was examining the body.' Nothing more is known of this man, unless he was the man mentioned by Patrick Mulshaw as telling him in Winthrop Street of the murder.

UNIDENTIFIED POLICE CONSTABLE IN VICINITY OF MITRE SQUARE

In the '**Aberconway**' version of the **Macnaghten memoranda**, **Sir Melville Macnaghten** wrote of the suspect **Kosminski**: 'This man in appearance strongly resembled the individual seen by the City PC near Mitre Square'. No City police constable is known to have seen anyone suspicious in the vicinity of Mitre Square on the night of Eddowes' murder. It has been surmised that Macnaghten confused the City policeman with Metropolitan **Police Constable Smith** (who saw Stride in Berner Street) or that Macnaghten misdescribed **Lawende**, the City Police witness, but it is also possible that **Eddowes** was seen in the company of a man by an unknown City constable after her release from Bishopsgate cells. Unfortunately, the City Police files were destroyed during the Blitz.

UNIDENTIFIED WITNESS AT MITRE SQUARE

According to the *Daily Telegraph* (12 November 1888): 'About ten minutes before the body of **Catherine Eddowes** was found in Mitre Square, a man about thirty years of age, of fair complexion, and with a fair moustache, was said to have been seen talking to her in the covered passage leading to the square. [This description] was given by two persons who were in the Orange Market and closely observed the man. The City police have been making inquiries for this man for weeks past, but without success...'

The Orange Market was a popular name for St. James's Place and a covered passage led from there into Mitre Square.

It is known that at 1.34am, **Joseph Lawende, Joseph Hyam Levy** and **Harry Harris** saw a woman, later identified from her clothing as Eddowes, talking to a man at the Duke Street entrance to Church Passage, which also led into Mitre Square, but this would have been invisible from St. James's Place. Had the two persons in the Orange Market spotted the same man as seen by Lawende, Levy and Harris, then they must have observed either the initiation or a continuation of Eddowes' discussion with the man. If, however, the two men in St. James's Place saw a different couple then it remains to be seen whether they saw Eddowes or Lawende and company saw her.

There was a night fire station in the Orange Market, manned by two firemen, who told **Superintendent Foster** that they had seen nothing unusual nor anyone come out of Mitre Square (*Evening News*, 1 October 1888) and **Inspector McWilliam**, in a report to the Home Office dated 27 October, wrote that nobody had seen Eddowes between her departure from Bishopsgate Police Station and the sighting by Lawende, Levy and Harris, so the possibility remains that the *Daily Telegraph* mislocated the sighting by Lawende, Levy and Harris, and for some reason reduced the number of men from three to two. The witnesses in the Orange Market were not called to the inquest, nor were the two firemen.

UNMASKING JACK THE RIPPER: A HISTORICAL AND ASTROLOGICAL ATTEMPT (1996)
Book by J.H. Tyson (Annville, PA: TVC Press, 1996).

After a standard account of the murders draws horoscopes for **James Maybrick** and **George Chapman** (**Severin Klosowski**), concluding the latter was more likely to have been the Ripper.

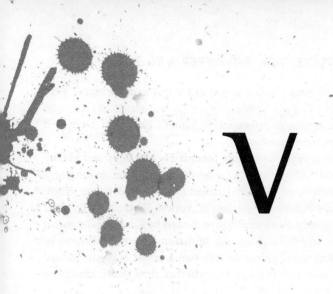

V

VALENTINE, GEORGE (1842–1912)

Headmaster of 9 Eliot Place and employer of **Montague John Druitt**.

Born in Bombay, the eldest son of Revd. George Meaker Valentine, headmaster of the Church Missionary School in Bombay and his wife, Louisa (*b.* Nevis, West Indies). His father died in a cholera epidemic in 1842 and the family returned to England. Attended Lincoln College, Oxford, in 1860, graduating in 1865. He ran a small school until 1873, when he took over 9 Eliot Place from Revd. Thomas Nunns. In 1893, he sold the school and retired, unmarried, holding a retirement party at the Criterion. He died of coronary artery disease on 26 May 1912.

Employed Montague John Druitt as a teacher, dismissing him at the end of 1888 for an unspecified 'serious offence'. Druitt was subsequently found drowned in the Thames and several newspapers reported that he, 'left a letter, addressed to Mr Valentine, of the school, in which he alluded to suicide' (*Southern Guardian*, 1 January 1889).

(See Stawell Heard, 'Mr Valentine's School', *Ripperologist*, 32, December 2000 and 'George Valentine Revisited', *Ripperologist,* July 2003.)

VAN TURNEY OR VAN TEURNEY, VANTURNEY, VENTENEY OR VENTURNEY, JULIA (*b.* 1841)

Witness at **Mary Jane Kelly**'s inquest.

Daughter of a Kensington carpenter named John Cook. Married and had two children, Rosina Antonet and Charlotte (or Charlotta) Ann. The surname is variously spelt on birth certificates and census records. In 1871, was living with her father and daughters in Fulham, her occupation recorded as 'professional'. By 1881, her father lived in Bayham Street (Camden Town) and her residence has not been traced.

At Kelly's inquest, she said that she was a widowed laundress, resident at 1

Miller's Court (opposite Mary Jane Kelly's room) and living with a man called Harry Owen. She testified that **Joseph Barnett** and Kelly lived together without quarrelling; that he was kind to Kelly and gave her money. She stated Kelly had broken the window a few weeks previously when she was drunk – something Mrs Van Turney said occurred frequently; also revealed that Kelly had another admirer called Joe, a costermonger who ill-used her for living with Barnett, and that Kelly said she was fond of him and could not bear Barnett. Van Turney had slept through the night of 8–9 November 1888, and did not hear the cry of 'Murder!' described by **Mrs Prater** and **Sarah Lewis**, or the singing recalled by **Mrs Cox**, which she insisted she would have heard, had it happened. She did, however, report hearing a door make a strange sound, which was unlike Kelly's usual way of closing her door.

It was once proposed that Mrs Van Turney's name and the *East London Advertiser*'s erroneous report that she was German (17 November 1888) suggested she might have been the '**Julia**' whose residence in 13 Miller's Court provoked Barnett's withdrawal. The discovery of further details about her background makes this unlikely. There is no evidence that she was ever a prostitute.

VASSILI, VASSILY or VASSILYEFF, NICOLAI (*b.* 1842)
See **Nicholas Wassili**.

VELLENSWORTH, POLICE SERGEANT JOHN (*b. c.* 1854)
Officer serving with Kent Constabulary, who was sent to investigate **W.H. Pigott** at the Pope's Head, Gravesend. The matter was then taken out of his hands by Superintendent Berry and **Inspector Abberline**.

VENTURNEY, MRS JULIA
See **Julia Van Turney**.

VICTORIA, QUEEN (1819–1901)
The Queen's interest in the Ripper case has been noted by several writers. It is also suggested by some historians (e.g. Stanley Weintraub, *Victoria: An Intimate Biography*, 1987) that she was either aware of, or protected from suspicions surrounding her grandson, **Prince Albert Victor**. There is, however, no record of Prince Albert Victor being linked in any way to the crimes prior to the article by **Dr Thomas Stowell**.

According to the *Complete History of Jack the Ripper*, her immediate reaction to the first murder (presumably **Martha Tabram** or **Mary Ann Nichols**) was to telephone the Home Secretary. **Stephen Knight** made much of a 'memorandum dated 9 November' 1888 (actually, a cypher telegram to the Prime Minister from Balmoral dated 10 November). It reads:

> This new most ghastly murder shows the absolute necessity for some very decided action.
> All these courts must be lit, & our detectives improved. They are not what they shld be.
> You promised, when the 1st murders took place to consult with your colleagues about it. (Royal Archives RA VIC/A67/19/)

In response, Lord Salisbury politely pointed out:

> This horrid murder was committed in a room. No additional lighting could have prevented it. (RA VIC/A67/20)

The brief Ripper-related correspondence was stimulated by the press criticism of Home Secretary **Henry Matthews** following **Sir Charles Warren**'s resignation. The Queen's final letter on the subject (sent in the hand of her private secretary, Sir Henry Ponsonby) listed her recommendations for action:

> The Queen fears that this resignation will have a bad effect in encouraging the lawbreaker to defy the police, who under Sir Charles Warren have always done their duty admirably.
> At the same time the Queen fears that the Detective department is not so efficient as it might be. No doubt the recent murders in Whitechapel were committed in circumstances which made Detection very difficult.
> Still The Queen thinks that in the small area where these horrible crimes have been perpetrated a great number of detectives might be employed and that every possible suggestion might be carefully examined and if practicable followed.
> Have the cattle boats & passenger boats been examined?
> Has any investigation been made as to the number of single men occupying rooms to themselves?
> The murderer's clothes must be saturated with blood and must be kept somewhere.
> Is there sufficient surveillance at night?
> These are some of the questions that occur to The Queen on reading the accounts of this horrible crime.

Ponsonby's view of this royal advice on policing was cynical: in a footnote at the end, he suggested, 'Perhaps these details might be omitted'! (RA VIC/B40/82)

VIGILANCE COMMITTEES

These were not vigilantes in the sense that they formed armed bands to pursue criminals and take the law into their own hands. They were groups of respectable citizens, who organised street patrols to supplement the police, agitated for the offer of rewards for information, petitioned for improved street lighting and hired private detectives. It is not certain how many existed.

The first committee formed appears to have resulted from a meeting in August, after **Martha Tabram**'s murder, at which about 70 citizens appointed 12 men to act as watchers. This was the St Jude's Vigilance Committee, described as, 'a large Vigilance and Patrol committee' (*Star* of 10 September).

The most important of the Vigilance Committees connected with the murders was that formed at a meeting of ratepayers on 10 September 1888 in the Crown public house, Mile End Road. Sixteen of them, including a cigar-maker, a tailor, a picture frame maker and an actor, constituted themselves a committee, with Mr **George Lusk** as president, Mr B. Harris as secretary and Mr **Joseph Aarons** as treasurer. They announced in the press that members would be available every morning in the Crown to receive information or suggestions from the public and Mr Harris wrote to Scotland Yard from time to time, urging the offer of a reward. This discreet gathering of respectable burghers, urging policies **Sir Charles Warren** tended to favour, was probably very much in his mind when he applauded the Vigilance Committees' work in his article in *Murray's Magazine*.

Following the murder of **Catherine Eddowes**, a meeting was held at Leadenhall House, Leadenhall Street, where a City Vigilance Committee was formed, an account being opened with Lloyd Bosanquet and Co., of Lombard street and it being proposed to ask **Samuel Montagu** to act as chairman.

Another Vigilance Committee appears to have been created in early October 1888, following a meeting of delegates from the labour organisations of East and Southeast London at the Three Nuns Hotel, Aldgate. Mr F. Wedgington, general secretary of the Watermen's Society, took the chair and said that working men were forming a Workmen's Vigilance Committee and that Mr. L.H. Phillips, representing the district in the Corporation of the City, had promised to become chairman of that committee (*Daily News*, 4 October 1888).

The Jewish population too apparently formed a Jewish Vigilance Committee and intended to offer a reward (*Reynolds's Newspaper*, 16 September 1888).

Newspapers in October reported, 'upwards of a score of citizen detectives went out on duty at twelve o'clock last night', that Whitechapel was divided into beats, that the 'detectives' met regularly at pre-arranged times to report to the police, that many wore noiseless boots (*Star*, 4 October 1888), and that they stayed on duty until dawn: 'The local Vigilance Committees have charge of this movement, and they hope to arrange matters so that no man shall be required to give more than one night per week to the work' (*Evening News*, 5 October 1888).

The creation of these Vigilance Committees was not greeted with warmth in all quarters, however, and *The Irish Times* (17 September 1888), which may have been working to its own agenda, reported the observations of, 'a police officer

534

with a long experience of street work in the East End of London.' He said of the Vigilance Committees:

It won't last a month. They'll get little help – at least no more help than anyone else – from our chaps: and if they get interfering with respectable people our men will "run them in" as a caution for future behaviour. With regard to the roughs, well, all I can say is "they will have a high old time of it" and to the benefit of our men. They can, to use their own words, "smell a fly copper" – i.e. plain clothes man; and when they get hold of an "amateur" or two, God help the amateurs! Kicking a regular policeman is a pleasure at any time not lightly to be spoken of, but the chances of "booting" the head or ribs of an amateur "slop" will afford a new and indescribable pleasure, and one to be indulged in on every possible occasion. These "vigilants" will be looked upon as "copper's noses" or "copper's narks" – i.e. police informers – and to use the roughs own words, "a copper" is bad enough, but his "nark!" – well, kill him, and that is about what he will get, or something very near it. They have forgotten one thing in their outfit, and that is an "ambulance" – that will be wanted oftener than truncheons. At least I think so.

Nevertheless, the Committees themselves felt that they had gathered some important information and come up with a few theories of their own, with the *Daily Telegraph* (3 October 1888) reporting, 'A member of the Vigilance Committee informed our representative last night that a great deal of information about the state of the streets, and suspicious men who frequent them, had been collected by them, and they believed that at least some of it might turn out of value.'

A year later, when the scare had died down, however, the original committee members allowed the organisation to fall into the hands of **Albert Bachert** and the young agitator turned it into a noisy gadfly that was far less appealing to the authorities.

The Spitalfields Vigilance Committee (president J. or A. Cohen; secretary Mr Ivan Gelder) was another body which restricted itself to writing courteous letters to the authorities in which they urged improvements in street lighting and rewards for information. Declining interest as the scare receded can be seen in Mr Gelder's plaintive report that more funds were needed in January 1889. At the end of that year, presentation portraits of the leading vigilance men were given to Mr Gelder, Mr George Evans and Mr M. Martin at the Paul's Head in Crispin Street (former landlord Abraham Cohen), Mr Evans being described as the Vigilance Committee's sergeant.

VIOLENIA, EMANUEL DELBAST
Discredited witness.

Half-Spaniard, half-Bulgarian, of mulatto appearance. Said he had walked from Manchester to London with his wife and two children, hoping to emigrate to Australia (*The Times* and *Pall Mall Gazette*, 12 September 1888). It is possible that his real name was Emmanuel Delbart Violina, who appears in the marriage records for the third quarter of 1888 as a resident of Altrincham in Cheshire. If so, the children were from a previous marriage or they were his new wife's.

He lodged in Hanbury Street and claimed that in the early morning of Saturday, 8 September 1888, he saw a woman quarrelling with a man (or two men, according to some press reports), one of whom threatened to knife her. Later, he attended an identity parade at Leman Street Police Station and unhesitatingly picked out **John Pizer** as one of the men he had seen, adding that he knew Pizer as '**Leather Apron**'. Pizer expressed immediate astonishment at Violenia's claim to know him.

Under further questioning, however, police came to mistrust Violenia when he was apparently unable to identify **Annie Chapman**'s body. They came to the conclusion that he had pushed himself forward with false or irrelevant information in the morbid hope of seeing the body and dismissed him with a severe reprimand. Pizer subsequently told the press, 'One of the authorities asked me if I had any objection to go out to see if I could be identified. I at once went into the station yard. There were several men there. One of them I know to be a boot finisher. He is a stout, stalwart man, of negro caste. He came towards me, and without saying a word he deliberately placed his hand on my shoulder. I promptly replied, "I don't know you; you are mistaken"' (*Star*, 12 September 1888). The authors note the apparent conflict in Pizer's story in that he claimed that he did not know Violenia, yet said that he knew him to be a boot finisher.

W

WADDLE, WILLIAM (1866–88)

Murderer who said he was inspired by the Ripper, and whose crime was briefly suspected of being the Ripper's handiwork.

Between 1886 and 1888, Waddle – a Gateshead slag-breaker – was the lover of **Jane Beadmore**. In that year, however, she declared that she had 'found someone nicer' and broke off with him. On 22 September 1888, Beadmore went out in the evening to visit friends in her home village of Birtley. At the second house she visited, Waddle arrived drunk, and he left soon after her at 8pm. The following morning, Beadmore's body was found in a ditch, her intestines protruding through several knife wounds. This feature led to the suggestion that the Ripper had travelled to Tyneside.

Scotland Yard took the rumours seriously enough to send **Inspector Roots** and Dr **George Bagster Phillips** up to Gateshead, but it was quickly apparent that Waddle was guilty, and he confessed. He claimed that reading about the Whitechapel murders must have deranged his mind, and his friends confirmed that he had been obsessively interested in them and had discussed how he might kill someone.

William Waddle was hanged on 18 December 1888.

WALKER, ALFRED J.

Feeble-minded, but inoffensive resident of 29 Hanbury Street (**Annie Chapman**'s murder site), who occupied the first-floor back room with his father, described by Amelia Richardson as an 'old gentleman'. Mr Walker sr. made some sort of equipment for tennis, variously described as 'shoes' or 'rings' (*The Times* 10 September 1888).

WALKER, EDWARD

Father of **Mary Ann Nichols**. Locksmith, subsequently blacksmith. Grey-haired and bearded at the time of her death. Residence variously described in the press as 15 Maidwell Street, Albany Road, Camberwell, 16 Maidswood Road and 16 Maidwood Street. The first, 15 Maidwell Street, was most definitely wrong as the resident, Mr Edward Tasker, wrote to the papers to complain.

Mr Walker identified the body in the mortuary by its general appearance, the loss of some front teeth and a small mark on her forehead caused by an accident when she was a child.

Mary Ann had lived with him between March and May 1883, but her drinking caused friction and she left after an argument. He last saw her in June 1886, at her brother's funeral and last heard from her when she wrote to him in the summer of 1888 from **Mr and Mrs Cowdry**'s. His answer to her letter received no reply, and until the murder, he did not realise that she had left them.

WALKING TOURS

Nightly, guided tours in the East End, visiting some of the Ripper sites, with an account of the murders. Guides include several authors of books about Jack the Ripper, notably Donald Rumbelow (*The Complete Jack the Ripper*), Richard Jones (*Uncovering Jack the Ripper's London* and *Jack the Ripper: The Casebook*) and Philip Hutchinson (co-author of *The London of Jack the Ripper Then and Now*).

WALTER or WALTON, EMILY (*fl.* 1888)

Informant. Told the *Star* (10 September 1888) that a man asked her to go with him into 29 Hanbury Street in the small hours of Saturday, 8 September. She did not confess to having gone, but other papers (including the *Daily News*, 11 September) stated that she did so and that he gave her two polished brass medals which she mistook for half-sovereigns, and that he seized her by the throat. There was some disagreement as to whether her description of him was accepted by the police and published as that of a man they wished to interview, or whether it was discounted because it differed from the descriptions of '**Leather Apron**'.

WARD, WILLIAM HUMBLE, 2nd EARL OF DUDLEY, (1867–1932)

Suggested as a co-conspirator in the Jack the Ripper murders in *Epiphany of the Whitechapel Murders*.

Inherited the Earldom in 1885, was Secretary to the Board of Trade (1895–1902), Lord Lieutenant of Ireland (1902–05) and Governor-General of Australia (1908–11), achieving little beyond generating criticism. He held no further public office and, apart from military commands during World War I, retired to his private estates. His first wife died in 1920. In 1924, he married former actress Gertie Millar (she had abandoned the stage in 1918).

WARDEN, WALLY

Alleged alias of **Elizabeth Stride**, by which '**One-Armed Liz**' first identified her body.

WARREN, SIR CHARLES (1840–1927)

Metropolitan Police Commissioner, 1886–88.

Born at Bangor, the second son of Major-General Sir Charles Warren and his second wife, Mary (née Hughes). Educated at Cheltenham College, Sandhurst and Woolwich. Joined the Royal Engineers in 1857. Employed on the Gibralter Survey 1859–65 (assistant instructor in surveying at Chatham, 1865–67). Served in Palestine for the Palestine Exploration Fund and undertook archaeological excavations, which he recounted in three books, 1865–70. Ill-health forced his return to Britain, where he served at Dover, 1871–72, and then Shoeburyness, 1872–76. Posted to Africa as special commissioner for the Colonial Office, for which he received the CMG, 1876–77; commanded Diamond Fields Horse in the Kaffir War, where he was severely wounded, and at the conclusion of which he was promoted to lieutenant-colonel, 1877–78.

Appointed special commissioner to investigate native questions in Bechuanaland (now Botswana), 1878, and administrator and commander-in-chief of Griqualand West in central South Africa (now Northern Cape Province), 1879. Chief instructor, School of Military Engineering, Chatham, 1880, but was detached in 1882 to lead a search in Egypt for the missing expedition of Professor Edward Palmer, whose murderers, for which he was awarded KCMG in 1884. Participated in second expedition to relieve his intimate friend General Gordon at Khartoum, then sent to restore order in Bechuanaland, for which he was awarded the GCMG. Commanded troops at Suakim, before recall to England to succeed Sir Edward Henderson as commissioner of the Metropolitan Police. Resigned following a stormy two years, then returned to an army career. Played a controversial role in the Battle of Spion Kop during the Boer War. For the latter part of his life, he threw his energies into the Boy Scout Movement and researching Freemasonry.

Appointed Metropolitan Police Commissioner following the resignation of Sir Edmund Henderson over his mishandling of the Trafalgar Square Riots on 8 February 1886. Took up his duties on 30 March and was generally welcomed, with *The Times* saying that he was, 'precisely the man whom sensible Londoners would have chosen to preside over the police of the Metropolis.' The *Pall Mall Gazette*, while expressing its delight at the appointment, prophetically warned that

Gladstone's home secretary, Hugh Childers, should 'allow his chief commissioner a free hand, and back him up like a man…' (13 March 1886). Childers did so, but when Gladstone's government fell in June 1886, his successor, the vacillating Conservative **Henry Matthews**, did not.

Warren's popularity quickly began to decline with his perceived mishandling of public events which got out of hand and resulted in rioting, particularly a mass demonstration of the unemployed in Trafalgar Square on 13 November 1888, what became known as Bloody Sunday, when he called in the troops and there was extraordinary violence in the course of which two men died. He was also criticised for his tactless handling of the Cass case, in which a case was brought against P.C. Bowden Endacott for wrongful arrest when he charged Elizabeth Cass with soliciting in Regent Street.

Warren's relations with Matthews became strained and he came into conflict with **James Monro**, whose personal fiefdom of the Secret Department reported directly to the Home Office and who tried to manoeuvre similar independence in the CID, and also with Richard Pennefather, the Receiver of Police (**Evelyn Ruggles–Brise**, who regarded Warren as 'the finest man we had in Whitehall', described him as, 'a very able man, but disagreeable to deal with; he rubbed everybody up the wrong way'). **Sir Robert Anderson** also commented on personality clashes with **Godfrey Lushington**.

Warren, accused of introducing mindless militarism to police and of demoralising the CID, came in for particular criticism as the Whitechapel murders' scare grew. The Radical press, headed by the *Star*, called for his resignation and the Conservative press ultimately followed suit. When his resignation was accepted and announced on 9 November – the day that **Mary Jane Kelly**'s body was found – it was widely assumed that this climactic murder had forced Warren out. 'Whitechapel has avenged us for Trafalgar Square,' crowed the *Star* (12 November 1888). This belief has been widely repeated ever since.

The real reason for the resignation is believed to have been the culmination of Warren's difficulties in the Commissionership, which concluded in an article, 'The Police of the Metropolis' in *Murray's Magazine*, in which Warren responded to press attacks on his force. In writing the article without permission from the Home Office, Warren breached approved procedure and Matthews sent a reprimanding memorandum, to which Warren immediately offered his resignation, stating that he would never have taken up the post of commissioner, had he been told the Home Office rule applied to him.

As far as is known, Sir Charles Warren left no expressed opinion about the identity of Jack the Ripper. Asked about the Whitechapel murders in an interview, Warren replied:

We are following up slight clews all the time. We received about fourteen hundred letters. Every single idea was investigated. For example, we were asked to drag a canal at a certain spot. We did so, but there was nothing to be found. People talk as if nothing had been done.

As for the Malay story it cannot hold. We have had the water police on the alert from the first. Then we have followed up the idea of the murderous cook, and every slaughter house is under watch for a murderous butcher. In fact, every clew has been closely followed up, and there are some clews and ideas which still occupy our attention, but which it would be impolitic to foreshadow to the public.

(New York Herald, 13 November 1888)

Tom Cullen in **Autumn of Terror** quotes from a letter that he received from Watkin Wynn Williams, who wrote a biography, *The Life of General Sir Charles Warren: By His Grandson* (Oxford: Blackwell, 1941), who said, 'I cannot recall that my grandfather, General Sir Charles Warren, ever stated in writing his personal views on the identity of Jack the Ripper. It was a subject about which he very seldom spoke. My impression is that he believed the murderer to be a sex maniac who committed suicide after the Miller's Court murder – possibly the young doctor whose body was found in the Thames on December 31st, 1888' (*cf.* **Montague John Druitt**).

Jack the Ripper: the Final Solution and *The Ripper and the Royals* both allege that Warren, a Freemason, used his position and influence to cover up the Freemasonic conspiracy headed by **Sir Wiliam Gull** or **Lord Randolph Churchill**.

(For a critical reassessment and re-evaluation of Warren's life see *The Crimes, Detection & Death of Jack The Ripper*. Jeffrey Bloomfield, 'The Making of The Commissioner: 1886', *Ripperologist*, 47, July 2003.)

WASSILI, NICOLAI (1847–)

Also transcribed Nicolas Vassili, Vassily or Vasilyeff. Alleged suspect.

Born Tiraspol, Province of Kherson, Ukraine. Educated at Tiraspol and the University of Odessa. Inherited sufficient income to live without work. Joined the fanatical Shorn sect, an off-shoot of the self-castrating Skoptsy. In 1872, following the Russian Orthodox Church's vigorous attempts to suppress the sect, Wassili went into self-imposed exile in Paris, where he tried, largely unsuccessfully, to convert and reform prostitutes.

When his religious convictions brought to an end a relationship with a young woman named Madeleine, Wassili suffered a breakdown and began murdering women, including Madeleine. After five murders in the space of two weeks he was caught by the police and committed to an asylum in Bayonne, afterwards being deported to Tiraspol and in January 1888 going to London, disappearing after the first Whitechapel murder.

International newspapers in late 1888 reported the story of Wassili and it was also widely published in the British press, but no part of the tale has been substantiated. No records of Wassili have been found at the University of Odessa, no reports of such murders as he was alleged to have committed have been discovered in French newspapers. It was reported that M. Gustave Macé, head of the Sûreté, averred, 'no such person committed murders in Paris in 1872' (*Star*, 17 November 1888).

See Stepan Poberowski, 'Nikolay Vasiliev: The Ripper from Russia', ***Ripperologist***, 50, November 2003.

WATKINS, PC EDWARD (881 City) (b c1845–d.1913)

A carpenter before joining the Metropolitan Police Officer in October 1870 until May 1871, when he joined the City of London Police (warrant no. 4420). Retired, 1896.

Watkins' beat along Duke Street (today's Duke's Place), Creechurch Lane, Leadenhall Street, Mitre Street, Mitre Square and St James's Place took him 12 to 14 minutes to traverse. On 30 September 1888, he passed through Mitre Square at 1.30am and found it empty. Returning at approximately 1.44am, he discovered the body of **Catherine Eddowes** in the southwest corner, thereupon he ran into Kearley and Tonge's warehouse opposite and sought the assistance of **George James Morris**. Morris went into Aldgate for assistance and Watkins remained with the body until the arrival of **Police Constable Holland.** An anonymous letter posted to **Sir Charles Warren** from Trowbridge, Wiltshire, on 13 October 1888, suggested Watkins might be the murderer.

WATKINS, KATHLEEN BLAKE (1856–1915)

Also known as Kathleen Blake Coleman. Born Catherine Ferguson, at Castleblakeney, Ireland, the daughter of Patrick Ferguson and Mary Burke. Educated in Ireland and Belgium. Married wealthy Irish merchant, Thomas Willis, in 1876. After the death of her husband and a brief sojourn in London as a governess, emigrated to Canada in 1884. Married Edward J. Watkins, two children. He was a heavy drinker, philanderer and possibly a bigamist, and their relationship did not last. Turned to journalism, writing for several journals, and in 1889, joined the Toronto *Daily Mail* (*Mail and Empire* after 1895). Writing as 'Kit', she published a weekly column ('Woman's Kingdom)until 1911. It was one of the most widely-read columns in the country, and thereafter a syndicated column.

From 1892, she became a travel writer and, in 1898, distinguished herself as a war correspondent during the Spanish-American War where, according to **Charles E. Hands**, she, 'knew everybody worth knowing in about a quarter of an hour.' Married Theobald Coleman that same year. Helped establish and in 1904 became first president of the Canadian Women's Press Club.

In late 1891, she was sent to London and ventured into Whitechapel to visit the Ripper sites, leaving a grim account of her experiences there. At Miller's Court she met '**Lottie**', the current occupant of **Mary Jane Kelly**'s still-bloodstained room. Lottie spoke with difficulty because her nose was broken and battered after receiving a kick from her husband, but claimed to have been a friend of Kelly's: 'I was her friend and two nights before the murder, she came to my rooms. I was living farther up the court then and "Lottie," says she, "I'm afraid to go alone tonight because of a dream I had that a man was murdering me. Maybe I'd be the next." She said it with such a laugh, ma'am, that it just made me creep – "they say Jack's busy again down this quarter," and sure enough, ma'am, she was the next. I heard her through the night, singing – she had a nice voice – but that was all we 'urd – "The violets that grow on mother's grave"' (Toronto *Daily Mail*, 27 February 1892).

Watkins mentioned Whitechapel several times in subsequent pieces, but in the longest she recalled that in a room above Kelly's, which she identified as the one where **Kitty Ronan** had recently been murdered, a woman named Eliza lived with a sailor. She recalled hearing Kelly crooning to herself through the night and was found murdered the following morning. This was presumably a reference to **Elizabeth Prater** (Toronto *Mail and Empire*, 2 October 1909).

See 'Kit', Kathleen Blake Coleman: Pioneer Canadian newspaperwoman: An Appreciation from the Hamilton Branch of the Canadian Womens Press Club (1934); Barbara M. Freeman, *Kit's Kingdom: The Journalism of Kathleen Blake Coleman*, Ottowa, (Canada: Carleton University Press, 1989).

WATTS, MRS ELIZABETH
See **Elizabeth Stokes**.

WEBB, INSPECTOR RICHARD, J Division (*b.* 1851)

Worked for Great Western Railway and served for five years in the Coldstream Guards, achieving the rank of sergeant, before purchasing his discharge and joining the Metropolitan Police in 1873 (warrant number 57292). By 1887, he was divisional inspector and posted to Bethnal Green, where he remained until his retirement in 1899. The *Police Review* (9 February 1900) records that, 'In conjunction with other officers he took a very active part in the endeavour to trace the perpetrator of the "Ripper" murders in the East End.'

WENSLEY, FREDERICK PORTER (1865–1949)

Informant.

Joined the Metropolitan Police in January 1888 (warrant no. 73224). Served for many years in H Division CID. He retired in 1929, and published his memoirs, *Detective Days* (London: Cassell, 1931).

Porter comments in his autobiography that, 'Officially, only five (with a possible sixth) murders were attributed to Jack the Ripper.' He also mentions the murder of **Frances Coles** and describes the murder of Police Constable **Ernest Thompson**. In 1901, he was present when **Inspector Divall** charged **Barnett Abrahams** with murdering Thompson and heard Abrahams' confession. Then, in 1909, he arrested Harold Hall in Bristol for having murdered **Kitty Ronan** in **Elizabeth Prater**'s former room in Miller's court.

WEST,

Resident of Crossingham's Lodging House. He confirmed knowing '**Leather Apron**' by sight, and having seen him hanging around Crossingham's in the weeks prior to the murders.

WEST, CHIEF INSPECTOR JOHN, ACTING SUPERINTENDENT (*b.* 1842)

Officer responsible for combining the enquiry into the Whitechapel murders under **Abberline**.

Joined the Metropolitan Police in 1865 (warrant no. 45737). Promoted to chief inspector and transferred to H Division, 1884. Resigned to pension, 1891. Acting superintendent in charge of H Division at the time of the murder of **Mary Ann Nichols** and **Annie Chapman**. The former fell within the province of J Division, despite Police Constable **Mizen**'s early arrival at the scene and the removal of the body to a mortuary on H Division's territory.

The latter was entirely an H Division case, but in the absence on leave of Inspector **Reid**, head of the local CID, West reported to Scotland Yard: 'I would respectfully suggest that Inspector Abberline, Central, who is well acquainted with H Division, be deputed to take up this enquiry as I believe he is already engaged in the case of the Buck's Row murder which would appear to have been committed by the same person as the one in Hanbury Street.'

On 10 September, **Samuel Montagu** MP visited him at Leman Street Police station with the offer of a reward. West promised to pass the information on to Scotland Yard, and the following day visited Montagu with the information that the offer had gone before the Home Secretary who, West thought, would receive it favourably. That afternoon, however, the news of Montagu's offer was leaked to the *Star*.

By the time of **Elizabeth Stride**'s murder, **Arnold** was back in charge of H Division and West had reverted to his substantive rank of chief inspector.

WEST, WILLIAM (REAL NAME WOOLF WESS), 1861–1946

Anarchist leader. Witness at **Elizabeth Stride**'s inquest.

Born in Vilkomar (or Ukmerge), near Kovno, Lithuania in 1861 to a Hasidic master baker. Emigrated to England in 1881 to avoid military service. Became secretary of the International Workingmen's Educational Club in Berner Street. Active in the Hackney branch of the Socialist League, typesetter for the newspaper *Freedom* and editor of *Arbeiter Fraint* (1895). Also active in the labour movement, founded and was secretary of the Federation of East London Workers' Unions and served with Rudolf Rocker on the strike committee of tailors.

About 12.30am, on 30 September 1888, he left the side entrance of the Club in Dutfield's Yard and went into the printing office  to return some literature, before returning again to the Club. He then called his brother and a man called Louis Stanley, and together they left the Club by the front door (in Berner Street) and walked towards Fairclough Street. While returning from the printing office to the Club, he looked towards the gates and the point where the body was later found, seeing nothing unusual. He admitted, though, to being shortsighted and did not know whether he would have seen the body, had it been there.

WESTCOTT, DR WILLIAM WYNN (1848–1925)

Suspect, proposed in the late 1980s and early 1990s in numerous newspaper articles, mainly of West Country origin, reporting theories and opinions of Ron Maber, Christopher Smith (*d.* 1997) and Andrew Holloway.

Educated at University College, London. Practised as a doctor in Martock, near Yeovil, 1871–79. In 1887, took up residence in Camden and became Coroner for Central London. Retired from public life, 1918, and in 1921, went to live in Durban, South Africa, where he died.

Westcott revelled in societies which purported to initiate members in mysterious or occult lore. In 1887–88, he joined with MacGregor Mathers and Dr William Robert Woodman to found the Order of the Golden Dawn, a pseudo-Masonic society with Rosicrucian rituals and liturgy. The only reason for suspecting Westcott of being the Ripper appears to be the belief that Golden Dawn members committed the murders as occult sacrifices.

(See Christopher Smith, 'Jack the Ripper: The Alembic Connection', *Criminologist*, winter 1992 to autumn 1993.)

WHEN LONDON WALKED IN TERROR
See **Autumn of Terror**.

'WHEN THE PEOPLE WERE IN TERROR'
Eight-part newspaper serial by Norman Hastings, in *Thomson's Weekly News* (Dundee), September to November, 1929. Reprinted with an introduction by Nicholas Connell in **Ripper Notes**, 21, January 2005.

An overview of the case, paying serious attention to **William Henry Bury**.

WHISTLER, JAMES ABBOTT McNEIL (1834–1903)
Artist born in Lowell, Massachusetts, the son of Major George Washington Whistler and his second wife, Anna Matilda McNeill. Moved to France, then England (1859), where he became famous for his wit, lavish lifestyle and love of notoriety. In 1872, painted 'Arrangement in Grey and Black, No. 1: Portrait of the Artist's Mother', better known simply as 'Whistler's Mother'. Sued the art critic John Ruskin for libel in 1877 and won the case, but was awarded only a farthing damages, the expense responsible for his bankruptcy in 1879. He recovered, married in 1888, and during the late 1880s and 1890s, his stature as an artist grew.

'Artist Whistler, the eccentric American who is one of London's celebrities, is painting a horrible picture of one of the Whitechapel victims as her mutilated body appeared when it was discovered' (*Atlanta Constitution*, 1 December 1888). 'It is said that Whistler, the celebrated artist, is at work on a picture representing one of the victims of the Whitechapel murder as she was found mutilated and bleeding. "Realism in art" is what such indecencies are called, but the term is frequently synonymous with the apotheosis of disgusting naked filth' (*Frederick News*, 6 December 1888).

It is not known on what authority this story was based or indeed, whether it had any foundation in truth.

WHITE, SERGEANT STEPHEN (1854–1919)
Interviewed **Matthew Packer**. Reported as the only officer in the investigation to come face to face with the Ripper.

Born Oare, near Faversham in Kent. Married, April 1875: two children (Percy and Edith). Joined the Metropolitan Police in October (warrant no. 59442). Posted to L Division Kennington, and lived in Kennington and Lambeth until 1881. Transferred to H Division (Whitechapel) August 1881, promoted to sergeant, and was living in Mile End with his wife and daughter when his son was born in 1882. Promoted to sergeant, 2nd class, 1886; transferred to S Division (Hampstead) and promoted to sergeant, 1st class, 1891. Transferred back to H Division (1893) and promoted to local inspector, 1895. Retired, 1900.

On his retirement, White gave a lecture in Dunkirk, Kent, on life and crime in the East End, which was profusely illustrated with his own sketches and photographs. Regarded as one of the ablest and most experienced detectives in the force, he died of prostate cancer in 1919. His son, Percy, went into the Railway Police.

When Matthew Packer's story of selling grapes to the man accompanying **Elizabeth Stride** shortly before her death broke in the *Evening News*, **Chief Inspector Moore** confirmed that White had interviewed Packer and all members of his household on 30 September 1888 and received assurances that they had seen and heard nothing unusual the previous night. White then returned to Berner Street with instructions to re-interview Packer and take him to identify the body in the mortuary. He found Packer returning from having identified the body positively in the company of private detectives **Le Grand** and **Batchelor**. White extracted little useful information from Packer before the fruiterer was taken by Grand and Batchelor in a hansom cab to see **Sir Charles Warren**.

Shortly after White's death, an article, 'By a Scotland Yard Man', appeared in the *People's Journal* (27 September 1919). It asserted that White was one of the many policemen sent out in disguise to patrol the streets, and then presented a long passage, allegedly from 'One of White's reports on his nightly vigil':

"STEVE" White as we knew our deceased colleague, Mr Stephen White, believed to be the only man engaged in the hunt who met "Jack the Ripper," was a detective of the old school who worked without the finger-print system and other devices favoured at the "Yard" to-day.

Anarchists were unusually active in London in the "eighties" and it was the duty of White to visit their dens and to be able to lay hands on some of the most desperate men in Europe. In addition, there were the ordinary criminal classes to be watched, and on top of that the activities of the miscreant known as "Jack the Ripper" engaged the attention of the East End police during the decade under review.

White was one of the officers forced to spend weary nights in different disguises, loitering about the narrow courts and evil-smelling alleys of the Whitechapel area on the offchance of detecting the murderer at his practice of decoying women to death and subsequently horrible mutilation.

One of White's reports on his nightly vigils contains the following passages:

The Alley's Grim Secret
For five nights we had been watching a certain alley just behind the Whitechapel Road. It could only be entered from where we had two men posted in hiding, and persons entering the alley were under observation by the two men. It was a bitter cold night when I arrived at the scene to take the report of the two men in hiding. I was turning away when I saw a man coming out of the alley. He was walking quickly but noiselessly, apparently

wearing rubber shoes, which were rather rare in those days. I stood aside to let the man pass, and as he came under the wall lamp I got a good look at him.

He was about five feet ten inches in height, and was dressed rather shabbily, though it was obvious that the material of his clothes was good. Evidently a man who had seen better days, I thought, but men who had seen better days are common enough down East, and that of itself was not sufficient to justify me in stopping him. His face was long and thin, nostrils rather delicate, and his hair was jet black. His complexion was inclined to be sallow, and altogether the man was foreign. The most striking thing about him, however, was the extraordinary brilliance of his eyes. They looked like two luminous glow worms coming through the darkness. The man was slightly bent at the shoulders, though he was obviously quite young – about 33, at the most – and gave one the idea of having been a student or professional man. His hands were snow white, and fingers long and tapering.

Man With Musical Voice

As the man passed me at the lamp I had an uneasy feeling that there was something more than usually sinister about him, and I was strongly moved to find some pretext for detaining him; but the more I thought it over, the more was I forced to the conclusion that it was not in keeping with British police methods that I should do so. My only excuse for interfering with the passage of this man would have been his association with the man we were looking for, and I had no real grounds for connecting him with the murder. It is true I had a sort of intuition that the man was not quite right. Still, if one acted on intuition in the police force, there would be more frequent outcries about interference with the liberty of subject, and at that time the police were criticised enough to make it undesirable to take risks.

The man stumbled a few feet away from me, and I made that an excuse for engaging him in conversation. He turned sharply at the sound of my voice, and scowled at me in a surly fashion, but he said "Good-night" and agreed with me that it was cold.

His voice was a surprise to me. It was soft and musical, with just a tinge of melancholy in it, and it was a voice of a man of culture – a voice altogether out of keeping with the squalid surroundings of the East End.

As he turned away, one of the police officers came out of the house he had been in, and walked a few paces into the darkness of the alley. "Hello! what is this?" he cried, and then he called in startled tones to me to come along.

In the East End we are used to shocking sights, but the sight I saw made the blood in my veins turn to ice. At the end of the cul-de-sac, huddled against the wall, there was the body of a woman, and a pool of blood was streaming along the gutter from her body. It was clearly another of those terrible murders. I remembered the man I had seen, and I started after him as fast as I could run, but he was lost to sight in the dark labyrinth of East End mean streets.

White's description of the suspected murderer was widely circulated and used by the police at the time, but the man was never seen. It was this description that gave the late **Sir Robert Anderson** his conviction that the murderer was a Jewish medical student, who had taken this method of avenging himself on women of the class to which his victims belonged.

The mystery, however, that baffled police more than anything was how the murderer and the victim managed to get into the alley under the eyes of the watching police. It was clear that the couple had not been in any of the houses, and they were not known to any of the residents. Therefore, they must have passed into the alley from the Whitechapel Road, and the two police officers were positive that, in the four hours of their vigil, not a soul had entered the alley. White had his own suspicions regarding the truth of this declaration and they were shared by Sir Robert Anderson – who afterwards, in comparing notes with White, expressed the opinion that the murderer and his victim had entered the close during the temporary absence of the two watching policeman. The men later admitted that they had gone away for not more than a minute. It was a very short absence undoubtedly, but long enough to give the murderer time to walk into the alley with his victim.

A version of the story that appeared in the *East London Advertiser* (27 September 1919) explicitly states that White did *not* see the murderer and gives quite a different account of his movements:

'His experience of murders was perhaps unique. He was engaged on the whole of the Jack the Ripper crimes which caused such a grim sensation among East Enders. One night he was on what appeared to be a certain clue to the mysterious murderer of women in the Whitechapel region. He kept watch in an East End street, but the murderer's movements were not in accordance with anticipation. For about ten minutes only he left the street, and to his amazement he found on his return that a woman had been stabbed. He saw no man anywhere, and the mystery became even more baffling. As is well known, Jack the Ripper was never discovered.'

WHITECHAPEL ATROCITIES, ARREST OF A NEWSPAPER REPORTER
Sixteen-page booklet, published by Woodford Fawcett & Co, a nineteenth-century publishing house (Dorset Works), based in Salisbury Square, London, and reprinted by Andy Aliffe. There is an original copy in the Bodleian Law Library at Oxford.

WHITECHAPEL JOURNAL
Bi-annual newsletter on Ripper-related matter produced by Stephen Wright between 1997 and 2000.

WHITECHAPEL MURDERS, THE (1976)

Booklet (27pp) by Susan Mylechreest. Outlines the case and royal theories, concluding that Michael Harrison's **J.K. Stephen** proposal is the most likely.

WHITECHAPEL MURDERS OF 1888, THE: A SUBJECTIVE LOOK INTO THE MYSTERY AND MANIPULATION OF A VICTORIAN TRAGEDY (2005)

Book by John Malcolm. Privately published in 2005 in a limited edition of 50 copies.

A personal commentary on the case, giving Malcolm's evaluations of various theories (favouring **Sir Robert Anderson**'s conclusion that the murderer's identity had been ascertained) and the many books in his own collection.

WHITECHAPEL MURDERS OR THE MYSTERIES OF THE EAST END

Book by G. Purkess (London: G. Purkess, 1888).

Contemporary account of the murders.

WHITECHAPEL MURDERS SOLVED? THE

See **In the Footsteps of Jack the Ripper**.

WHITECHAPEL 1888 SOCIETY

Formerly the Cloak and Dagger Club founded by Mark Galloway in 1994. Informal body, promoting the study of the Whitechapel murders and their social impact, and also the study of Victorian-Edwardian life and culture in the East End of London. Meetings are held six times a year, to which guest-speakers are invited. The Club produces a bi-monthly publication, *The Journal of the Whitechapel Society*.

'WHITE-EYED MAN, THE'

Alleged suspect advanced by **E.T. Woodhall**.

Woodhall claims that among several practical jokers who sprang out at women during the scare, one particularly alarming character painted his face black with white rings around his eyes. One day he was arrested and taken to Scotland Yard, where he seized a heavy ebony ruler, assaulted two very senior officials (whose rank **Sir Melville Macnaghten** makes clear) and escaped. Three weeks later, his body was found in the Thames, trapped beneath a paddle-boat. The constable in Buck's Row – 'the only living person who ever saw and spoke to [the murderer]' – believed the 'White-Eyed Man' to be the same person. The constable himself was later murdered by a man named **Abrahams**.

This concoction is apparently drawn from several sources: the 'White-Eyed Man' is an exaggeration of Dr Holt, whose spectacles have become white painted eyes, while the escape after assaulting two officials appears to be a misunderstanding of Melville Macnaghten's remark, 'he committed suicide on or about the 10th of November 1888, after he had knocked out a Commissioner of Police and very nearly settled the hash of one of Her Majesty's principal Secretaries of State' (i.e. damaging the careers of **Warren** and **Matthews**).

The police constable murdered by Abrahams was **Ernest Thompson**, who heard footsteps which were probably those of **Frances Coles'** murderer – but not, of course, in Buck's Row: near Swallow Gardens.

WHITEHALL MYSTERY, THE

Unsolved crime, briefly associated by the sensational press with the Ripper. On 2 October 1888 it was found that during the night someone had executed a difficult climb over the palings protecting the building site on the Embankment, where New Scotland Yard was going up, and deposited the limbless, headless torso of a woman in a remote vault of the new cellarage. The lady's arms were separately deposited in the Thames. However, the police never imagined there was any connection with the Whitechapel murders, despite press speculation. There might have been some connection with the similar **Pinchin Street** and **Elizabeth Jackson** murders of the following year, though.

R. Michael Gordon and Patricia Cornwell, however, postulate that this was a torso of a Ripper victim, since they propose that their preferred candidates, **Severin Klosowski** and **Walter Sickert** respectively, perpetrated many more murders than those recognised by other writers.

WHO WAS JACK THE RIPPER?

Magazine by Winston Forbes-Jones (London: Pipeline Promotions Limited, 1988).

Produced to accompany Thames Television's 1988 two-part mini-series, *Jack the Ripper*.

WHO WAS JACK THE RIPPER? (Dearden)

Chapter by Harold Dearden in A.J. Alan (ed.) *Great Unsolved* Crimes (London: Hutchinson, 1935). Reprinted in a limited edition, 1999.

WHO WAS JACK THE RIPPER? (Wolff)

Edited by Camille Wolff (London: Grey House Books, 1995).

Fifty-four brief contributions from Ripper writers, readers and researchers, with photographs of all but one of them, and a limited edition signed by most contributors.

WILKINSON, FREDERICK WILLIAM (b. c.1856)

Witness at **Catherine Eddowes'** inquest.

Born in Manchester. Listed in 1891 Census as married and living with his wife Mary Ann at **Cooney's Lodging House**, 55 Flower and Dean Street, where he is described as Lodging House Manager.

WILL THE REAL JACK THE RIPPER?

Book by Arthur Douglas (Chorley, Lancashire: Countryside Publications, 1979). Also available on cassette and read by William Maxwell (distributed by Speak Eezee Voice Print).

Though brief, this survey of the known material at the time it was written is accurate, responsible and perspicacious.

WILL THE REAL MARY KELLY...?
Book by Chris Scott (London: Publish and Be Damned, 2005).

Identifies many of the **Mary Kelly**s whose birth certificates, census records and movements have been traced, without any of them having been conclusively shown to be the Ripper's victim.

WILLIAMS, DR (LATER, SIR) JOHN, BT, KCVO (1840–1926)
Suspect, proposed by Tony Williams (his nephew) and Humphrey Price in 2005.

Born in Carmarthenshire, son of a Congregationalist minister and farmer, who died in 1842. Educated at Swansea Normal School, Glasgow University and University College Hospital, London. Practised as a GP in Swansea, where he married in 1872; moved to London as assistant obstetric physician, UCH. In 1886, accoucheur at the birth of Princess Beatrice. From 1887–93, Professor of Obstetric Medicine, then from 1887–88, President of the Obstetrical Society of London. 1894, baronet; 1902, KCVO. Retired, 1903, and returned to Wales, where he was a major benefactor and founder of the National Library, donating his priceless collection of rare books and manuscripts. From 1913–26, president of University College, Aberystwyth. *The Dictionary of National Biography* describes him as, 'quiet, friendly, entertaining, possessing the perfect "bedside manner."'

Uncle Jack includes the following incriminating observations: a six-inch scalpel with a broken point was found among Dr Williams' effects. On 8 September 1888, Dr Williams wrote to a correspondent addressed as 'Morgan' apologising for being unable to meet him as he would be attending a clinic in Whitechapel. It is speculated that the addressee would have been **Dr Morgan Davies** and observed that this placed Williams in Whitechapel on the day of **Annie Chapman**'s murder. An 1888 diary he kept has many pages missing, while a notebook had the following entries on one page:

Abortion – Chamberlain 1879 p 454
Jane Johnson. 1884 – vol 1 p.280
McCausland 1885 p 630 Elborne 1885 p 632
Barrett 1885 p 641 Johnson 1885 p 709
Mary Anne Nichols 1885 p 710

This was interpreted as meaning that Dr Williams had operated on Ripper victim Mary Anne Nichols in 1885 and so knew her by sight. However, the arguments advanced in *Uncle Jack* did not stand up to scrutiny and the case against Sir John Williams collapsed completely when an examination of a facsimile of the original notebook naming Mary Ann Nichols supplied by the National Library of Wales showed that it differed from the one published in *Uncle Jack*. It was also apparent that the published version had been tampered with, before or after Williams and

Price received it. Tony Williams vehemently denied tampering with the document.

(See Jennifer Pegg, 'Uncle Jack Under the Microscope', **Ripper Notes**, no 24, October 2005 and '"Shocked and Dismayed" – An Update on Uncle Jack', Ripper Notes, 25, January 2006.)

WILLIAMS, DR JOHN FREDERICK (fl. 1888)

Alleged informant. Physician employed at St Saviour's Infirmary who, according to **Donald McCormick**, told **Dr Dutton** that Russian barber-surgeon **Alexander Pedachenko** worked for him as an unpaid assistant at the same time as he worked part-time for Walworth hairdresser William Delhaye in Westmoreland Road.

Usually, this story has been regarded as fabricated, though it is not known whether McCormick or Dutton would be held responsible, but R. Michael Gordon notes that Williams and Delhaye can be shown from directories to have existed and suggests that it would be highly plausible for Severino Klosowski to have adopted yet another identity and masqueraded as Pedachenko.

WILLIAMSON, CHIEF CONSTABLE ADOLPHUS FREDERICK (1830–89)

Senior professional policeman in the Metropolitan CID at the time of the Ripper murders.

A clerk before joining the Metropolitan Police in 1850 (Warrant No 27623). Promoted to sergeant in the CID, 1852; inspector, 1863, then chief inspector, 1867, thus becoming the effective head of the serving detective officers in the Detective Branch. Superintendent, 1870. Chief constable, CID, 1886. Died in harness.

The Dear Boss letter was marked for his attention and his name is on the document appointing Swanson to take overall charge of the enquiry.

Williamson had worked closely with both **Robert Anderson** and (especially) **James Monro** in combating the Fenians. Nevertheless, when **Sir Charles Warren** devised the rank of chief constable as an intermediary between the 'gentlemen' commissioners and 'other ranks' up to superintendent, it was Monro's wish to bring in **Melville Macnaghten** over Williamson's head. He greeted Macnaghten, when he joined the force as deputy chief constable in 1889, with the cynical observation that in the police he would be blamed if he didn't do his job – and similarly blamed if he did so.

He is peripheral in the Ripper investigation, the *Dear Boss* **letter** was marked for his attention and his name is on the document appointing **Swanson** to take overall charge of the enquiry.

WILSON, ADA

Postulated by Martin Fido (1987) as possible attempted victim. Young sempstress of 19 Maidman Street, Mile End. On 28 March 1888, when she was alone in the house, Ada answered a knock at the door and was confronted by a man aged about 30, 5ft 6in tall, with a sunburnt face and fair moustache. The stranger demanded money and when she refused, he stabbed her twice in the throat and ran away, leaving her for dead. He was nearly apprehended by neighbours.

It has been suggested this might have been an early and unsuccessful assault by the Ripper on the grounds that the description of the assailant is similar to that of men seen with several Ripper victims. To this it has been objected that a clear motive of robbery is stated.

WILTON, HENRY (1820–1907)

Verger and clerk to St. Leonard's Church, Shoreditch, and keeper of the Shoreditch mortuary, where the body of **Mary Jane Kelly** lay prior to burial.

Born in Frome, Somerset, on 4 July 1820, the son of a builder. He went to London in 1834 and for a while lived with his sister, who was married to an undertaker. In 1835, he took lodgings with Mrs Francis, sextoness of Shoreditch Church, who died in 1849. Wilton succeeded her. Wilton held the office until his death, receiving an illustrated address in 1899 in honour of his length of service. He was the grandfather of a child actress known as Baby Wilton.

Paid for the funeral of Mary Kelly, it being reported that, 'he provided the funeral as a mark of sincere sympathy with the poor people of the neighbourhood, in whose welfare he is deeply interested' (*East London Observer*, 24 November 1888). Apparently he hoped that he would be reimbursed in whole or part by a public subscription, but it is not reported funds were forthcoming. The *Daily Telegraph* (14 November 1888) reported that Wilton's action averted the need for a second inquest, which would have been required, had the body been moved into the Whitechapel district for burial.

Wilton once received a visit from an elderly woman, the friend of a blind spiritualist, who felt that she could identify the murderer if she was provided with a lock of Kelly's hair. Wilton refused to supply one (*Walthamstow and Leyton Guardian*, 24 November 1888; *Hackney and Kingsland Gazette*, 2 October 1901; *Shoreditch Observer, Hackney Express and Bethnal Green Chronicle*, 9 March 1907, 4 May 1907).

WINBERG, MISS

Supposed accomplice of **Dr Pedachenko**. A young tailoress, who allegedly held victims in conversation to allay their suspicions until Pedachenko struck. Meanwhile, another accomplice (**Levitski**) kept a lookout. Miss Winberg was said to have been exiled to Yerkutsk with Levitski.

WINSLADE, HENRY (b. 1860)

Waterman who pulled **M.J. Druitt**'s body from the Thames.

Son of James Winslade, a waterman, and his wife Mary. Living at 4 Parkstone Cottages, Short Street, Paxton Road, Chiswick. (the *Acton, Chiswick and Turnham Green Gazette*, 5 January 1889, says 4 Shore Street). Some newspapers give his name incorrectly as Winslow.

WINSLOW, LYTTLETON STEWART FORBES (1844–1913)

Contemporary theorist, allegedly very briefly suspected. Educated at Rugby and Downing College, Cambridge. LLB, 1866; LLM, 1870; MB, 1870; MRCP (Lond.), 1871; DCL Oxon., 1873; LLD (Cantab.).

Good and humane asylum physician, who carried on his distinguished father's campaign for necessary reforms of the lunacy laws. Suffered extreme stress in 1888 as his grasping and dishonest brother-in-law successfully appealed to the law to

oust Winslow from the asylums that he had lovingly maintained as his father's legacy. He was also the central villain and victim of Mrs Georgina Weldon's successful law suits protesting against her improper certification and incarceration.

Frequent commentator on the Whitechapel murders during 1888 and, from 1889, became convinced Jack the Ripper was **G. Wentworth Bell Smith** and that he had been frightened into abandoning murder and leaving the country. He was interviewed on the subject by **Chief Inspector Swanson** on 23 September. Alterations have been noted to written evidence of Mr E. Callaghan produced for Swanson and to the date of the Hammersmith Road Letter (reproduced in *Recollections of Forty Years*, 1910). By 1893, was reportedly claiming his suspect was a medical student and had been committed to an asylum for the insane (Marion *Daily Star*).

In 1903, Winslow rejected **Abberline**'s identification of **George Chapman** as the Ripper because Chapman was not the man that he had identified (*Daily Chronicle,* 8 March 1903). Then, in 1910, he rejected the identification of **William Grant** (Grainger) as the Ripper (*Pall Mall Gazette*, 19 April 1910).

Donald McCormick alleged that the police briefly suspected Winslow of being Jack the Ripper, but Molly Whittington (*Doctor Forbes Winslow: Defender of the Insane*, Great Malvern: Capella Archive, 2001) found no support for McCormick's claim.

WIRTKOFSKY, JULIUS (*fl.* 1888)
Suspect.

A Polish Jew staying in 'a "Christian home" in Finsbury Square' told **Julius I. Lowenheim** that he intended to kill the woman who had passed on a venereal disease to him, 'and the rest of her class' (HO144/221/A49301D/6 f97).

WITNESS IN WHITECHURCH LANE
The *Star* (1 October 1888) reported: 'From two different sources we have the story that a man when passing through Church Lane at about half-past one saw a man sitting on a door-step and wiping his hands. As every one is on the look out for the murderer the man looked at the stranger with a certain amount of suspicion, whereupon he tried to conceal his face. He is described as a man who wore a short jacket and a sailor's hat'.

WOODHALL, EDWIN THOMAS (1885–1941)
Theorist.

Former policeman, who wrote accounts of police work – among them, his *Jack the Ripper: or When London Walked in Terror* (*see* **Olga Tchkersoff**, 'The White-Eyed Man'). Joined the Metropolitan Police in 1907 (warrant no. 94985). CID (Special Branch), 1910. Resigned, 1919.

(Andy Aliffe, 'Guardian of the Great', *Ripperologist*, 11, June 1997.)

WRIGHT, FRANCES
See **Mary Elizabeth Simonds**.

WRIGHT, STEPHEN (1922–2000)
Theorist and editor.

Best-known as an apologist for gay matters and author of *Different: An Anthology of Homosexual Short Stories* and the *Brief Encyclopedia of Homosexualty*. His interest in True Crime surfaced in 1984, when he started the quarterly newsletter, *Stephen Wright's Mystery Notebook*. In 1997, he began the ***Whitechapel Journal***, which appeared every six months until his death in 2000. Then, in 1999, he published *Jack the Ripper: An American View*. Like most of his work, it was self-published.

Obituary, ***Ripperologist***, 37, October 2001

WRITING ON THE WALL, THE
See **Goulston Street Graffito**.

FINES
5¢ PER DAY
FOR
OVERDUE BOOKS

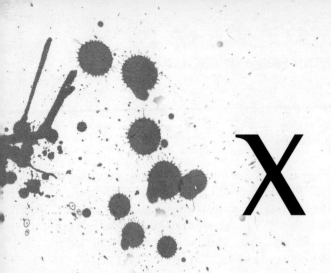

X

XAVIER, MANUEL CRUZ (*b.* 1851)

Alleged suspect. Portuguese cattleman advanced as **Mary Jane Kelly**'s murderer by **E.K. Larkins**.

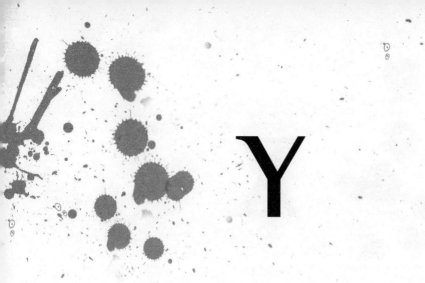

Y

YOUNG, GEORGE HAY (1857–1936)

Admitted as a solicitor in 1879, he joined his father's practice and appeared mainly at the Thames Police Court, where he was affectionately known by East Enders as 'the Attorney-General'.

In 1886, he contested the coroner's election for East Middlesex, coming third after **Wynne E. Baxter** and **Roderick Macdonald**. 1887, he defended Isaac Angell (husband of Miriam Angell, murdered by **Israel Lipski**), who was charged with assaulting Leah Lipski, landlady of the house in which the murder was committed (*The Times*, 26 August 1887). In 1890, he prosecuted William Whitwell, described as 'one of the most desperate characters in the East End', who led a gang called the Bowery Boys and had threatened to 'Jack the Ripper' a pub landlady (*The Times*, 13 September 1890).

According to the *News of the World* (5 July 1936), one night in a dense fog a tall, sinister-looking man approached Young and asked for directions to Stepney. An hour or two later, the mutilated body of a woman was found in an alley and Young was so convinced that the man he had seen was Jack the Ripper that he gave a description to the police.

Retirement notice, *The Times*, 5 January 1934.

Z

ZVERIEFF, NICHOLAS
Alleged informant.

According to **William Le Queux**, Zverieff was an elderly member of the Jubilee Street Club, an East End anarchist centre which opened in 1906, who told **Johann Nideroest** that Jack the Ripper was **Dr Pedachenko**. No evidence for his existence is known outside the pages of Le Queux. *Cf.* **Rasputin**, **Konovalov**.

LIST OF ILLUSTRATIONS

INDEX

Burrows, Edwin, **77**
Bury, Ellen, **77**
Bury, William Henry, 53, **78–9**, 232, 399, 514, 545
Buswell, Harriet, **79–80**, 240
Butler, Detective Chief Superintendent Arthur Henry, **80**, 170, 248
Byfield, Sergeant James George, **80**
Byrnes, Chief Inspector Thomas, 69, **81**

C

Cadoche, Cadosch or Cadosh, Albert, **82**, 89
Cairns, Hector, **82**
Callaghan, Mary, **83**
'Calor', **83**, 514
Cameron, Professor James Malcolm, **83**
Campbell, Duncan, **83**, 449, 461
Camps, Francis, **83–4**
Canonical Five, **84**, 241, 379, 419
Carroll, Lewis, 50, **84**, 126, 237
Carthy or Carty, Mrs, **84–5**, 256, 314, 412
Cartwright, PC, **85**
Casebook: Jack The Ripper (www.casebook.org), 79, **85**, 219, 230, 236, 238, 243, 345
Casebook on Jack The Ripper, A, **85**
Catch Me When You Can, **86**
Catherine Eddowes: Jack The Ripper Victim, **86**
Caunter, Sergeant Eli, **86**, 105, 286
Causby, Inspector William, **84**
Chandler, Inspector Joseph Lunniss, **86**, 89, 470
Chapman, Annie, **87–90**, 90, 203, 490
  Allen, Elizabeth, and, 18
  in books, 32
  inquest of, 49–50, 57, 218–19, 406–8, 472
  inquest of, witnesses, 106–7, 130, 262, 306, 396, 475
    Crossingham's Lodging House, 141, 160, 483
    Hanbury Street, 82, 131–2, 190, 197, 432, 433
  and Macnaghten memoranda, 324
  murder of, and after, 19, 41, 43, 86
  murder suspects, 104, 198, 284, 318, 416
Chapman, Frederick Richard, **90**
Chapman, George, 5, 6, 9, **90**
  alias Severin Klosowski, 264–6
Chapman, John, **90**
Chappell, Mary, **91**, 168, 412
Charlie The Ripper, **91**
Charrington, Frederick Nicholas, **91**
Cheeks, Margaret 'Mog', **91**
'Cherinton, Nelis', **91**

Chisholm, Superintendant Colin, **91–2**
Chronicle of Crime, The, **92**
Churchill, George Charles Spencer, Marquis of Blandford, **92**
Churchill, Lord Lord Randolph Henry Spencer, **92**
City of Dreadful Delight: Narratives of Sexual Danger in Late Victorian London, **92–3**
City of London Police, **93**
City Police suspect, **93–4**
Clapp, George Thomas, **94**
Clarence, Duke of see Albert Victor Christian Edward, Prince
Clarence: The Life of HRH The Duke of Clarence and Avondale, **94**
Clark, Dr Percy John, **94–5**
Clarke, George, **96**
Clarkson, Willy, **96**
Cleary, John, **96**
Cleary, John or Stephen, aka John Arnold, *32*
Cleveland Street scandal, *17*, **96**, *398, 421*
Clippings book, **96–7**
Cloak and Dagger Club, 220, 438, 550
Cohen, Aaron Davis aka David Cohen, **97–9**, *206, 252, 400*
Cohen, Jacob, **99**, *271*
Cohen, Morris, 274, 307
Cohen, N., **100**, *168, 206*
Cohn (or Koch), Dr, **100**, *253, 267*
Coins and Rings, pile of, *19, 89 see Chapman, Annie*
Coles, Frances, 80, **100–1**, *280, 327, 392, 460, 551*
  body of, and inquest, 50, 266, 460
  and Sadler, James Thomas, 447–50
  seen by, 39, 175, 177, 192
Collard, Inspector Edward, **101**, 155, 286
Collier, George, **101**
Collins, John Churton, 74, **101–2**, 379, 380
Collins, Reserve PC Albert, 12HR, **101**
Colocott, John Edwin, **102–3**, 120
Colonial farmer (Unnamed), **103**
Colwell, Mrs Sarah, **103**
Complete History of Jack The Ripper, The, 10, 56, **103**, 266, 350; 532
Complete Jack The Ripper, The, 10, 83, **104**, 141, 323
Conder, Col. Claude Regnier, **104**
Conferences, **104**
Connell, James, **105**
Connelly or Connolly, Mary Ann, 76, **105–6**, 473, 505
From Constable to Commissioner: The Story of

Dodgson, Revd. Charles Lutwidge, 50, 84, 237

Dolden, PC Charles (CID), **140**

Don, Police Sergeant John Carmichael, **140**, 450

Donner, Gerald Melville, **140**, 305, 329

Donner, Mrs Julia, 12, **140**

Donovan, Timothy, 88, 90, 115, **141–2**, 160, 239, 287

D'Onston, Dr Roslyn, 111, 380, 486–90

Doughty, John, **142**

Dowson, Ernest Christopher, **142**

Doyle, Sir Arthur Conan, 74, 102, **142–3**, 248, 358, 379

Drage, PC Joseph William, 282H, 107, **143**

Drew, Thomas Stuart, **143**, 374

Druitt, Ann, **143–4**

Druitt, Dr Lionel, 144, 150, 514

Druitt, Montague John, 64, **144–6**, 166, 305, 531

  in books, 35, 225, 229, 241, 243, 245, 355, 367, 421, 437

  and Farson, Daniel, 150–1, 164, 226, 417

  and Littlechild letter, 302–3

  and Macnaghten Memoranda, 325, 328, 329

Druitt, William Harvey, **147**

Dudman, Sergeant Amos, **147**

Dukes, Dr William Profit, **147**, 192

Dundee-born teenage suspect, **148**

Durrell, Mrs, 130, 233, 306

Dutton, Dr Thomas, 92, **148–9**, 266, 296, 553

E

Eagle, Morris, 137, **150**, 184, 247, 278

By Ear and Eyes: The Whitechapel Murders, Jack The Ripper and the Murder of Mary Jane Kelly, 80

East End Murderer - I Knew Him, The, **150–1**

East End Murders from Jack The Ripper to Ronnie Kray, 151

Echoes of the Ripper, **151**

Eckert, Dr William Gamm, **151–2**

Eddowes, Catherine, 80, 93, **152–7**, 213, 441

  in books, 86

  family of, 106, 171, 185, 404–5, 426

  identified by, 55, 255, 285–6, 529

  inquest witnesses, 94, 101, 175, 194, 201, 297, 359, 551

  modern speculation on murder of, 83, 83–4

  post mortem and inquest, 69–73, 110–11, 281–2, 456, 463

Eddowes' Shawl, **157–8**, 230

Ede, Thomas, **158**, 247–8

Edwards, Frank, **158**

Edwards, George Henry, **158**, 178

Elizabeth Stride and Jack The Ripper: The Life And Death of the Reputed Third Victim, **158–9**

Elliott, PC George, **159**

Ellisdon, Inspector Ernest, **159**

Enright, Setective sergeant Patrick, **159**

Epiphany of the Whitechapel Murders, 96, **159–60**, 403, 538

Euston, Earl of, 171–2

Evans, John, 88, **160**

Eye to the Future, An, **160**

F

'Fairy Fay', 103, **161–2**, 241

Famous Crimes Past and Present, **162**

Farmer, Amelia, 396

Farmer, Annie, 130, **162–3**, 336, 497

Farquharson, Henry Richard, **163**

Farrow, PC James 106M, **163–4**

Farson, Daniel Negley, **164**, 226, 328

  loss of files, 36, 150–1

  on TV, 94, 146

Father of G.W.B., **164**

FBI Psychological Profile of the Ripper, **164–5**, 232

Feigenbaum, Karl aka Karl Zahn, **165–6**, 240

Feldman, Paul Howard, **166–7**, 241–2, 343, 346, 422, 514

Fenians and Fenianism, 20, 41, 42, **167**, 245

Fenwick, Collingwood Hilton, **167–8**

Ferrett, Inspector Arthur, **168**, 195, 476

Fiddymont, Mrs, 91, **168**, 412

Files, **169**

'Fingers Freddy', 14, 80, **170**

First Fifty Years of Jack The Ripper Vols. I and II, The, **170**

First Jack The Ripper Photographs, The, **170**

Fisher, Albert, **171**

Fisher, Elizabeth, 106, 153, 156, **171**

Fisher, L. E., **171**

Fisher, Lizzie, **171**, 335

'Fitzgerald, Annie', **171**, 493

Fitzroy, Henry James, Earl of Euston, **171–2**

Fleming, Joseph, **172–3**, 212, 256

Fogelma, –, **173**

In the Footsteps of Jack The Ripper: An examination of the Jack The Ripper murders using modern police techniques, 219

Foster, Detective Superintendent Alfred Lawrence, **173–4**

Foster, Elizabeth, **174–5**, 258